100 DECISIVE BATTLES
FROM ANCIENT TIMES TO THE PRESENT

100 DECISIVE BATTLES

FROM ANCIENT TIMES TO THE PRESENT

PAUL K. DAVIS

OXFORD
UNIVERSITY PRESS

OXFORD
UNIVERSITY PRESS

Oxford   New York
Athens Auckland Bangkok Bogotá Buenos Aires Calcutta
Cape Town Chennai Dar es Salaam Delhi Florence Hong Kong Istanbul
Karachi Kuala Lumpur Madrid Melbourne Mexico City Mumbai
Nairobi Paris São Paulo Shanghai Singapore Taipei Tokyo Toronto Warsaw

and associated companies in
Berlin   Ibadan

First published by ABC-CLIO, Inc., 1999
130 Cremona Drive, P. O. Box 1911, Santa Barbara, CA 93116-1911

First issued as an Oxford University Press paperback, 2001
198 Madison Avenue, New York, New York 10016

Library of Congress Cataloging-in-Publication Data
Davis, Paul K., 1952–
100 decisive battles: from ancient times to the present / Paul K. Davis.
p. cm.
Originally published: Santa Barbara: ABC-CLIO, 1999.
Includes bibliographical references and index.
ISBN 0-19-514366-3 (Pbk.)
1. Battles. 2. Military history. I. Title: One hundred decisive battles. II. Title.

D25.D37 2001
904'.7--dc21   00-049183

3 5 7 9 10 8 6 4 2
Printed in the United States of America
on acid-free paper

Anyone who clings to the historically untrue—and thoroughly immoral—doctrine that violence never settles anything I would advise to conjure up the ghosts of Napoleon Bonaparte and the Duke of Wellington and let them debate it. The ghost of Hitler would referee. Violence, naked force, has settled more issues in history than has any other factor, and the contrary opinion is wishful thinking at its worst. Breeds that forgot this basic truth have always paid for it with their lives and their freedoms.

—*Robert Heinlein*

For Jerri and trips to Europe

CONTENTS

Preface, xi

100 Decisive Battles

PREFACE

This work has been undertaken to fulfill a niche in military history that has been somewhat overlooked: that of a detailed survey of the 100 most decisive battles in history. Here, the criteria for including a battle as "decisive" are defined as including any or all of the following:

1. The outcome of the battle brought about a major political or social change. For example, the Battle of Hastings (or Senlac Hill) in 1066 would fit in this category. The Norman invasion of England completely altered the future of the British Isles, determining the heritage of its people and the nature of its political and social systems. The resulting society then proceeded to have major impacts on events in Europe and, ultimately, the world.

2. Had the outcome of the battle been reversed, major political or social changes would have ensued. Under this category, a battle such as Trenton in the American Revolution appears. Had Washington lost this battle in December 1776, the defeat almost certainly would have spelled the end of the revolutionary army and therefore the revolution itself, leaving Britain in control of the North American colonies for an indeterminate period in the future, perhaps as a dependent dominion like Canada. Because of battles such as Trenton, multiple battles sometimes appear in the course of a single war; if Trenton had been a British/ Hessian victory, the Saratoga and Yorktown battles, also included in this work, would not have been fought.

3. The battle marks the introduction of a major change in warfare. Adrianople in 378 was such a battle. Before that battle, the infantry in general and Roman infantry in particular had dominated warfare; in this battle, the Goths' victory introduced cavalry as the dominant weapon for the succeeding thousand years.

The battles that have been selected for this work are in the main my choices, but I want to thank the members of H-WAR, an Internet newsgroup of military historians worldwide, who offered a myriad of suggestions for deletions and inclusions. The debate engendered by the offering of my original list to that newsgroup became at times rather heated, and I have no doubt that historians who look at the list that is presented here will have their own opinions about other battles that should have been included. Although I recognize H-WAR's input, the final decision to include or reject anyone's suggestions in the course of that discussion was mine alone.

The format of this work is chronological, which should help those readers who find in the course of an article reference to another; it should appear soon thereafter or immediately before. To meet space constraints, I targeted each article at a length of 2,000 to 2,500 words. A few are longer or shorter, but most fall within that range. Thus, details of the background, events, or results of chosen battles have usually been condensed to maintain the target length. Knowing that most of these battles have entire books devoted to them naturally makes many of the articles entirely too short to do justice to the event, but such are the constraints of publishing.

Another aspect of the format also needs to be addressed. Decisive changes came sometimes in the course not of a single battle but of a campaign. Poland fell in 1939 as a result of a series of battles within a month's span, no one of which was key to the entire campaign. In cases such as this, I am entitling the center section of the article "The Campaign" rather than "The Battle." This is perhaps stretching a point, given the book's title, but key events brought about by warfare are the thrust of this book's intent, and so occasionally single battles are not available. Yet, can one deny that Israel's existence, brought forth in battle in 1948, is not important to today's world even if a single battle did not determine its fate?

The niche this book is intended to fill, as indicated earlier, is defined by both length and breadth. On the market today, the majority of books chronicling the major battles of history tend to be in the format of a dictionary, giving descriptions in the space of a paragraph or two to cover as much information as possible. In *100 Decisive Battles*, I hope to provide much more depth of coverage for a more limited topics list. Other books that do go into deeper detail tend to be limited in their scope of topics. J. F. C. Fuller's *A Military History of the Western World*, the classic upon which I have drawn heavily for topics, ignores decisive battles that have been fought in the nonwestern world.

Also, its publication date of 1954–1956 limits its coverage to the time up to World War II. Edward Creasy's *Fifteen Decisive Battles of the World* was also a source of topics, but a mere fifteen overlooks too many, and that work stops at Waterloo in 1815. Thus, I provide more depth than do the dictionary-style works prevalent today, while covering a much more worldwide set of topics than Fuller or Creasy. Although the choice of 100 as a number may seem arbitrary, any fewer makes the choice for decisiveness even more difficult. Although some topics chosen may have produced results that were decisive regionally rather than internationally, to overlook battles simply because they occurred outside the purview of western experience makes them no less important for millions of people.

MEGIDDO

15 May 1479 B.C.

FORCES ENGAGED
Egyptian: Unknown (probably
approximately 10,000 men).
Commander: Pharaoh Thutmose III.
Kadesh alliance: Unknown.
Commander: King of Kadesh.

IMPORTANCE
By reestablishing Egyptian dominance in Palestine,
Thutmose began a reign in which Egypt reached
its greatest expanse as an empire.

Historical Setting

In the early years of the eighteenth century B.C., the power of Egypt's Middle Kingdom was waning. That coincided with the immigration of the Hyksos, a Semitic population probably from the region of Palestine, that used superior weaponry to topple the faltering Thirteenth dynasty. The Hyksos dynasty began ruling Egypt in 1786 B.C. and lasted until 1575 B.C. By then the Hyksos had become sufficiently complacent and content to lose their edge, and the Egyptian population reasserted control over their own nation. The new pharaoh, who began the New Kingdom era, was Ahmose (ruled 1575–1550 B.C.). Ahmose was not content with merely regaining his country, but wanted to extend Egypt's northeastern frontier to establish a strong buffer zone. He also wanted to extend Egypt's power because exposure to foreign peoples had given the Egyptians a taste for things that could come only from outside their country. Hence, conquest and trade as well as security motivated Ahmose's war making.

Following in Ahmose's footsteps, later pharaohs extended Egyptian authority into the region along the eastern Mediterranean as well as southward into Nubia, modern Sudan. Under the direction of Thutmose I, Ahmose's grandson, Egypt established hegemony in Palestine and Syria. Upon his death in 1510, however,

Egyptian expansion was temporarily halted because of the attitude of the new pharaoh, Hatshepsut. Hatshepsut was daughter of Thutmose I and stepsister and wife to Thutmose II. When Thutmose II died in 1490, Hatshepsut at first ruled as regent for their young son Thutmose III, but soon threw off all pretense at regency and ruled openly as pharaoh, the only woman ever to do so. Her rule (1490–1468 B.C.) was marked by more than 20 years of peace, during which time Egypt embarked on a serious building program of constructing temples and monuments.

Hatshepsut's passive foreign policy, however, encouraged subject kings in the Middle East to ponder the idea of independence. Under the direction of the King of Kadesh, supported by the powerful Mitanni population east of the Euphrates, the states of Palestine and Syria broke free of Egypt's rule about the time of Hatshepsut's death.

Early rumblings of discontent had not been punished by Egyptian forces, so the King of Kadesh, who probably exercised suzerainty over most of Syria and Palestine, demanded and received affirmations of loyalty from his subject kings. Some small kingdoms in southern Palestine hesitated, perhaps remembering the days of Ahmose and the penalty for disloyalty. Kadesh sent troops to compel them to cooperate, and it seems that the kingdom of Mitanni gave Kadesh covert support. They were an up-and-coming power themselves, currently competing with the nascent power of early Assyria. If Kadesh could hurt Egypt, then the Mitanni certainly hoped to benefit.

The cause of Hatshepsut's death has never been positively determined; it may have been assassination at Thutmose III's direction. Whatever the reason, Thutmose III was eager to take the throne and restore Egyptian power. After directing that Hatshepsut's name be obliterated from all public buildings, he set about rebuilding an army that had been idle for more than two decades. His southern flank was secure because the Nubians had become increasingly

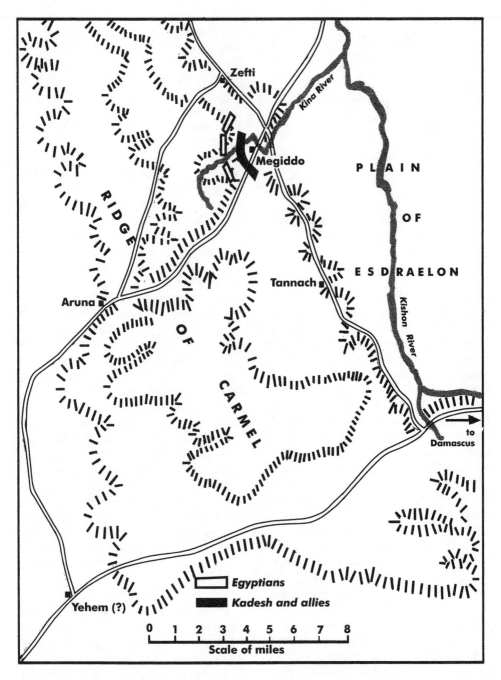

Egyptians

Kadesh and allies

0 1 2 3 4 5 6 7 8
Scale of miles

Egyptianized. He could therefore focus on the rebellious kings to the northeast without having to worry about threats to the rear of his army.

How many men Thutmose enrolled has never been determined. Most historians believe that no Egyptian expeditionary force ever numbered more than 25,000 to 30,000, and the first army to take the field after such a long hiatus would almost certainly not be that large. The Egyptian army was comprised primarily of infantry, carrying shields and side arms— either axes or sicklelike swords. The aristocracy fought from chariots and probably as archers. Weapons at this time were bronze. The forces that Egypt faced were equipped in much the same fashion.

In his second year as pharaoh, Thutmose III took his army into action. He appears to have been skilled as an organizer because the rapid progress his army made implies a well-laid-out logistical system. He was also the first pharaoh who, apparently, took his own chroniclers on campaign with him because the details of the march and the battle are contemporary with the campaign. Megiddo was the first battle in history for which that can be said. Thutmose departed the Nile delta at Tharu on 19 April 1479 and just 9 days later was at Gaza, some 160 miles up the coast. He arrived there on the anniversary of his coronation, but spent no time in celebration; his troops were on the march the next morning.

The Battle

Twelve days from Gaza, the Egyptians encamped at Yehem, about 80 to 90 miles from Gaza and probably about 16 miles southwest of Megiddo. That walled city was the target because Thutmose's intelligence corps had reported that the King of Kadesh and all his vassal kings were there. At this point, Thutmose had three possible routes to Megiddo. The road north to Aruna, along the ridge of Mount Carmel, turned northeast at that town and ran through a narrow pass directly to Megiddo. His second alternative branched north-northeast just past Aruna and intersected the Tannach road north of Megiddo. The third possibility was to take the road toward Damascus. This road ran eastward from Yehem and then hit a junction, which led north-northwest through Tannach. This route would enable him to approach Megiddo from the south. Thutmose's advisors counseled either of the latter alternatives, as the pass was too narrow, inviting an ambush. Thutmose brushed their cautions aside, determined to take the direct route. He told them they could go by any route they pleased, but he was going through the pass. "For they, the enemy, abominated of Ra, consider thus, 'Has His Majesty gone on another road? Then he fears us,' thus do they consider" (Petrie, *A History of Egypt,* vol. II, p. 105). His subordinates reluctantly agreed to go with him.

Whether through accurate supposition or by good intelligence, Thutmose was correct in his choice. Apparently, the King of Kadesh never thought that Thutmose would be stupid enough to commit his force to a narrow defile, so he concentrated the bulk of his army on the road near Tannach. Thutmose led his men out of Yehem toward Aruna on 13 May. As they approached the pass, he took the point position in his chariot, certainly a decision designed to inspire his troops and assure them of the correctness of his decision. As they debouched from the pass, they encountered only a small covering force, which they quickly drove away. Here Thutmose heeded his subordinates. Instead of launching a pursuit, he agreed to deploy his force in a defensive posture to allow the entire column to come up. Hearing of the arrival of the Egyptian army, the King of Kadesh withdrew his forces back to Megiddo.

Thutmose, either that afternoon or during the evening, decided not to attack the forces of Kadesh but instead to take up a position to the west of the city. He deployed his men in an arc athwart the small river Kina, with his flanks resting on high ground. This gave him a good route of retreat, if necessary. On the night of 14 May, the two armies camped, facing each other. At dawn, Thutmose spread his forces in three groups. He commanded in the center, and his left flank extended to the northwest of Megiddo, to be in a position to block any enemy retreat on the road that led northwest from the city. The details of the battle are too sketchy to determine how it was conducted. All the contemporary chroniclers state is that the enemy fled before the pharaoh's forces: "His Majesty went forth in his chariot of electrum adorned with his weapons of war, like Horus armed with talons, the Lord of might, like Mentu of Thebes, his father Amen-Ra strengthening his arms" (Petrie, *A History of Egypt,* vol. II, p. 107).

Whatever the missing details, the Egyptians gained the upper hand, and the enemy fled in haste for the protection of the city walls, abandoning their camp and much of their materiel. That was what saved the Egyptians, at least temporarily. The Egyptian troops, lured by the prospect of loot, abandoned the chase and turned themselves over to pillage. That allowed the enemy to escape, although just barely. The residents of the city closed the gates rather too quickly, and the fleeing troops had to be hauled over the walls with ropes made of clothing. Thutmose was not happy, and chastened his men. "Had ye afterwards captured this city, behold I would have given [a rich offering to] Ra this day; because every chief of every country that has revolted is within it" (Breasted, *A History of Egypt,* p. 290).

Having failed to capture the city in a rush, Thutmose settled down for a siege. He ordered a wall of circumvallation built of wood from the surrounding forests; the rampart was called "Thutmose, encloser of the Asiatics." In the wall, one gate was built, through which those inside the city that wished to surrender could exit. The details of the siege were recorded on a roll of leather stored in the temple of Amon, but only the reference to that scroll survives. The countryside was sufficiently lush to allow the Egyptians to eat well out of the fields and off the cattle and sheep herds. The length of the siege is debatable, sources listing it as anywhere from 3 weeks to 7 months, although it was probably shorter rather than longer. However long it took, the besieged finally ran out of food and surrendered.

Results

Although a number of kings were taken captive, surrendering either during the siege or at the city's fall, the King of Kadesh managed to escape, probably in the immediate wake of the battle. Thutmose took little retribution on the captive kings or the city, although he did remove back to Egypt much of the city's wealth. Thutmose, however, had captured on the battlefield the king's son, who he took back to Egypt as a hostage, along with others of the king's family as well as the sons of the other rebellious but now humbled kings. The description of the spoils of war is long and impressive, including 924 chariots, 2,238 horses, 200 suits of armor, and the tent belonging to the King of Kadesh along with all his furniture and household goods. Added to the spoils of later victories on this campaign, 426 pounds of gold and silver were acquired.

With Megiddo now firmly in hand, Thutmose marched his men northward toward Lebanon, taking possession of the cities of Yenoam, Nuges, and Hernkeru. It is not known if these cities had sent their submission to him during the siege of Megiddo or if Thutmose had to capture them upon his arrival; either way, they came under his control quickly. He ordered a fortress built in the area in order to keep back any threat the escaped King of Kadesh might mount and then proceeded to reestablish Egyptian hegemony by either accepting the vassalage of the local kings or replacing them with successors who would swear loyalty. Just as he had done with the son of the King of Kadesh, Thutmose took the sons of those rulers back to Egypt. This not only ensured cooperation, but it allowed the Egyptians to raise the hostages in a manner that would immerse them in Egyptian culture and power, making them more amenable to control when the hostages were in a position to succeed their fathers.

Thutmose was back in his capital city of Thebes in early October and master of a new

MEGIDDO IN HISTORY

Although historians know of battles before Thutmose III and the King of Kadesh fighting in 1479 B.C., this battle was the first to be recorded by eyewitnesses, making it the first recorded battle in history. Because of disputes over dating, however, just when the battle took place is a matter of some debate. James Breasted in 1905 gave a detailed account of the battle, and his dating has been used in the Megiddo entry as the most specific, giving day and month as well as year. William Petrie's translation of the Annals of Thutmose III gives contemporary dates, not in years B.C. but by years of the pharaoh's rule. Hence, we learn that Thutmose began his campaign toward Megiddo when he left the town of Tharu on the Nile delta on the twenty-fifth day of the month Pharmuthi in the twenty-second year of Thutmose's reign. That also creates some problems because he dated his reign not from the previous year when he succeeded Hatshepsut, but from the death of his father and the year he should have begun his rule. The battle at Megiddo is placed variously in 1458, 1467, 1469, etc.

Megiddo remained an important location in the ancient world, on the crossroads between the Hittites in the north and the Egyptians in the south, as well as those of the trade routes from the Mediterranean eastward to the empires of Assyria, Babylon, and Persia. The Book of Judges describes an eleventh-century B.C. battle along the River Kishon, flowing along the Plain of Esdraelon, which Megiddo overlooked. In that battle, Israelite forces under Deborah and Barak defeated the Canaanite forces of King Jabin. In 609 B.C., King Josiah of Judah was defeated and killed at Megiddo by the Egyptian Pharaoh Necho.

Even more unspecific about the date of the first battle at Megiddo is the date of the last one. The Hebrew word for Megiddo is Armageddon, described in the biblical Book of Revelation as the site of the final battle between the forces of good and evil. The foundation for one of the great ironies of history is thus foretold: the beginning and the end of military history occur at the same site.

---

and more stable Egyptian Empire. It would not always be happy; he conducted another fifteen campaigns in the northeast to either subdue rebellions or beat back foreign threats. During his eighth such campaign, he fought and defeated the Mitanni on the other side of the upper Euphrates, taking Egypt to the limits of its empire. This completely transformed Egypt as a nation. The wealth that came into Egypt in the form of annual tribute was so massive that it allowed for the construction of temples and public buildings for which Egypt is best known today, barring only the Pyramids and Sphinx.

Through both the Old and Middle Kingdoms Egypt had striven to remain isolated; after the expulsion of the Hyksos and the wars of the New Kingdom, commerce with foreign powers was too profitable to ever go back to the old days. The administration of an empire required the establishment of an expanded bureaucracy as well as a large standing army, both of which are expensive propositions. The wealth was the gift of the gods, so the priesthood also expanded, gaining in both wealth and power. Their temples demanded the best in craftsmanship, and the artistic life of Egypt benefited. Two hundred years after Thutmose III, Rameses II fought to maintain the borders of the empire. No pharaoh fought as often as he, but by the thirteenth century B.C. the power of Egypt had reached its height. From then onward, the Sea Peoples, the Hittites, the Assyrians, the Persians, the Greeks, and finally the Romans all either weakened Egypt or exercised dominion over Egypt.

References: Benson, Douglas. *Ancient Egypt's Warfare.* Ashland, OH: Book Masters, 1995; Breasted, James Henry. *A History of Egypt.* London: Hodder & Stoughton, 1905; Gabriel,

Richard, and Donald Boose. *The Great Battles of Antiquity.* Westport, CT: Greenwood Press, 1994; Petrie, William. *A History of Egypt,* vol. II. Freeport, NY: Books for Libraries Press, 1972 [1904]; Steindorff, George, and Keith Seele. *When Egypt Ruled the East.* Chicago: University of Chicago Press, 1957.

THYMBRA

546 B.C.

FORCES ENGAGED

Persian: Possibly 50,000.
Commander: Cyrus II, the Great.
Lydian: Unknown, but probably more than those of Persia. Commander: Croesus.

IMPORTANCE

Cyrus's victory gave him control of the vast wealth of Lydia and denied Babylon a strong ally. From this victory, Cyrus challenged and won the Neo-Babylonian throne, establishing the Persian Empire.

Historical Setting

In 612 B.C., the Assyrian Empire, which had dominated and terrorized the land from the Persian Gulf to the Mediterranean since the middle of the eighth century, was overthrown. In that year, two subservient populations, the Babylonians and the Medes, joined forces and captured the Assyrian capital of Nineveh. In the wake of that victory, the empire was divided between the victors: Nabopolassar of Babylon ruled the southern half, and Cyaxeres of Media ruled the northern. Media was originally the region that today encompasses northwestern Iran along the southern bank of the Caspian Sea into Armenia. Under Cyaxeres, Median power was stretched westward to the frontiers of Asia Minor and eastward almost to Afghanistan. Cyaxeres died in 585 B.C., the year that he and the kingdom of Lydia in Asia Minor agreed that the border between their territories would be the Halys

River. Cyaxeres was succeeded by Astyages, who apparently was quite a tyrant and who alienated the Median aristocracy by depending on religious advisors for his policy formulation.

In 580 B.C., Astyages's daughter gave birth to a son, named Cyrus. Legend has it that Astyages dreamed that this grandson would overthrow him, and Astyages ordered his death, but Cyrus was saved in a fashion virtually identical to that of Moses in Egypt. Whatever the exact details, Cyrus lived in the region called Persis (Persia), which today would lie in southwestern Iran near the Persian Gulf coast. The Greek historian Herodotus claimed that in 553 Cyrus was approached by Harpagos, sometime commander of the Median army, asking that Cyrus begin a rebellion against Astyages; if he would do so, the Median aristocracy would support it. The length of the rebellion is difficult to determine because sources from the time (and soon thereafter) vary considerably. Probably it went on for 4 years until the battle at Pasargadai (the capital of Persis), when Harpagos defected to Cyrus. Allying himself with the Scythians and Hyrcanians (from the southern Caucasus), Cyrus captured the Median capital of Ecbatana during 550–549.

Cyrus immediately gained the confidence of not only the Median aristocracy but almost all of Astyages's former subjects because Cyrus went to great lengths to show himself a just and merciful conqueror. Many of the Median military leaders received high command positions in the Persian army. While Cyrus consolidated his throne, trouble was brewing on his western frontier. The King of Lydia, Croesus, was the son of Alyattes, who had established with Cyaxeres the Halys River as the border between Lydia and Media. Croesus apparently had had good relations with Astyages and viewed Cyrus with alarm. Croesus began developing alliances with Egypt, Babylon, and Sparta. Lydia was well known for its superior cavalry, and with all those extra troops it could prove a serious threat to Cyrus's new realm. While visiting Gubaru, future satrap of Susa in

Elam, Cyrus learned that Croesus had led troops across the Halys into the province of Cappadocia and was pillaging the countryside. Cyrus gathered his forces and marched west in the spring of 547. His army marched along the Median-Babylonian frontier, crossed the Tigris River at Arbela (site of a later victory by Alexander the Great), picked up some reinforcements from Armenia and Kurdistan, and descended into the Cappadocian plain late in 547.

The Battle

The two armies met near the town of Pteria and fought a hard but inconclusive battle at the beginning of winter. No details are available, other than there was no clear winner. As the Cappadocian plain had been stripped of resources during the Lydian occupation, Croesus decided it was best to withdraw to his capital at Sardis. After wintering there, he would regather his forces, supplemented by those of his allies, and resume the war in the spring. When he reached Sardis, Croesus dismissed his Greek mercenary troops and sent messages to his allies, detailing his military needs for the next season's campaign.

Cyrus met with his advisors after the battle and received much the same counsel: go home for the winter and start up again next spring. Here, however, Cyrus showed his first flashes of genius. Sure that Croesus would not want to keep his mercenaries on the payroll during the winter, and that Lydia's allies could not possibly dispatch reinforcements for a few months, Cyrus decided to follow Croesus to Sardis. After waiting sufficient time for Croesus to get home and dismiss his forces, Cyrus launched a forced march through Anatolia. Croesus heard a rumor of Cyrus's approach but put no stock in it. Indeed, not until the Persian forces appeared at the city gates did Croesus believe what was happening.

In spite of what Cyrus had supposed, Croesus was able to call up a large army. How large is unknown, but it almost certainly was significantly more than the Persians. Xenophon gives Cyrus's strength as 200,000, but it was probably somewhere between 20,000 and 50,000. The two forces met just outside Sardis on the Plain of Thymbra early in 546. Cyrus placed his army in square, with flanking cavalry and chariot units set back. The Lydians deployed in the traditional formation of long parallel lines. The battle opened with the Lydian cavalry attempting to envelop the square. As they advanced, the enveloping units moved ahead of the center, leaving gaps in the Lydian line. Here Cyrus deployed his secret weapon. At Pteria, one of his generals had noticed the way in which Lydian horses had shied at the presence of Persian camels used for transport. Cyrus formed his pack animals into the first camel corps in history and sent them forward. Catching the smell of the camels, the Lydian horses panicked.

The cavalry dismounted and attempted to fight on foot, but their lances proved too unwieldy to be effective. Inside Cyrus's square formation, his archers launched volley after volley of arrows into the Lydian ranks, further disorganizing them. Cyrus's infantry and chariots on the flanks charged into the dismounted Lydian cavalry, and then, with the gaps on either side of the Lydian center wide open, Cyrus sent his cavalry through them. The result was a rout, as Lydian survivors ran for the walls of Sardis. Persian forces immediately surrounded the city and besieged it for 14 days. Learning of a possible weak point in the defenses—where the city's walls met and melted into a cliff—Cyrus sent a small force up the hill and onto the walls, which at that point overlooked the citadel; his troops quickly captured it and Croesus. The city opened its gates to Cyrus the following morning. From this point, Lydia ceased to exist as an independent kingdom.

Results

Although Cyrus's victory over Croesus came in 546 B.C., 7 years before his conquest of

Babylon, the victory at Thymbra marked the turning point in Cyrus's campaign to establish a Persian Empire. Babylon, as co-inheritor of the Assyrian Empire, was a natural rival, in spite of the fact that they had done little to provoke Cyrus.

The Babylonian King Nabonidus was in the midst of his own internal crisis. Although intent on maintaining strong trade routes between the Persian Gulf and the Mediterranean, which would of course continue to enrich the wealthiest of ancient cities, Nabonidus provoked his population over religious matters. He had come to power from his position as a general, rather than through birth. Thus, he distrusted the Babylonian establishment. He preferred the worship of Sin, the moon goddess, over Marduk, the Babylonian national deity. He established temples to Sin in Babylon, a direct affront to the people. In response to a dream, Nabonidus marched the army to the city of Harran to reestablish the Temple of Sin there. He then spent 7 years campaigning in Arabia, capturing territory as far as Yathrib (Medina). He colonized a string of oases through Arabia, although it is unclear if this was for military or trade purposes. This expedition also alienated the Babylonians because the king was supposed to be in attendance at the New Year's festivals, and Nabonidus missed seven in a row. His son and regent, Balshazzar, oversaw the business of government. When, after extending his power far to the east in campaigns up to Bactria (modern Afghanistan), Cyrus turned toward Babylon, Nabonidus finally tried to appease his subjects and defend his land. He sent for all the idols of Marduk to be collected in Babylon to strengthen its spiritual defenses. But apparently it was too late. Cyrus seems to have been in contact with the religious leaders in Babylon, assuring them of his religious tolerance, and thus fomenting a resistance movement in Nabonidus's backyard.

There are two completely different accounts of the fall of Babylon to Cyrus. In September 539 B.C., Cyrus and his army defeated the Babylonians at Opis, the former capital of Akkadia, which city he proceeded to destroy. On 10 October, the town of Sippar surrendered without a struggle. Hearing this, Nabonidus fled Babylon. One of his former governors, now in Cyrus's camp, was Ugbaru, governor of Gutium (a region somewhere east of the Tigris), who entered Babylon against no opposition. Cyrus then entered to a massive welcome on 29 October; the people proclaimed him the agent of the god Marduk, delivering the city from the heretic Nabonidus.

The other version speaks of a two-year siege, 539–538 B.C. According to this version, put forth by Herodotus, Cyrus was on the verge of giving up the siege because the inhabitants of Babylon had amassed a huge hoard of supplies. Instead, he decided (or was advised) to divert the channel of the Euphrates River, which flowed through Babylon. By diverting the river into a marshland, the water level fell to a point where Persian troops could wade the river and enter Babylon through the floodgates. "The Babylonians themselves say that owing to the great size of the city the outskirts were captured without the people in the center knowing anything about it; there was a festival going on, and they continued to dance and enjoy themselves, until they learned the news the hard way" (Herodotus, *The Histories*, p. 118).

The capture of Babylon marked the reunion of the old Assyrian Empire, now expanded by Cyrus to include Asia Minor and the Persian Gulf coast almost to India. After founding the Persian Empire, Cyrus went on campaigning and was finally killed in combat in his seventieth year against Scythian forces near the Jaxartes River. It was the campaign against Lydia, however, which deprived Babylon of a powerful ally and secured Cyrus's western flank, that put Cyrus in a position to become an emperor; "when once Lydia had been overthrown the balance of power and the interests of Babylonia and Iran [Persia] were in conflict." A showdown was probably inevitable, and Nabonidus was no match for Cyrus.

The Persian Empire proved to be the first "world" empire in history. Before this, there had been large-scale conquest, such as that the Assyrians had accomplished, resulting in what was an empire in size but not in administration. That is what Cyrus initiated, an imperial administration. By offering religious tolerance, peace, and improved roadways to facilitate trade, the Persians continued to build on Cyrus's foundation and expand the empire even farther, into Egypt and parts of southeastern Europe, although they met their match in the Greeks at Marathon and Salamis in the early fifth century B.C. Cyrus was virtually worshiped by his subjects, not because he demanded it like a pharaoh, but because he earned it. His release of the captive Jews, who had been in Babylonian captivity for decades, reestablished a Jewish homeland that lasted until the Romans dispersed the Jews again in the first century A.D. Although viewed by the Jews as an instrument of God to deliver them (just as the Babylonians viewed him), Cyrus's return of the Jews to the east coast of the Mediterranean certainly had strategic overtones, for they provided a friendly population to act as a buffer zone against an expansive Egypt. To all, he was a welcomed change from the brutality of the Assyrians, the last major conquerors in the region. By extending an understanding demeanor, Cyrus readily gained support where the Assyrians had gained only discontent and hatred. Unlike the Assyrian Empire, which was overthrown by rebellion, the Persian Empire's life of more than two centuries came to an end only with the arrival of Alexander the Great.

References: Cook, J. M. The Persian Empire. New York: Schocken Books, 1983; Gershevitch, Ilya. The Cambridge History of Iran, vol. 2. Cambridge, UK: Cambridge University Press, 1985; Herodotus. The Histories. Translated by Aubrey de Selincourt. Baltimore: Penguin, 1954; Lamb, Harold. Cyrus the Great. Garden City, NY: Doubleday, 1960; Xenophon. Cyropaedia. Translated by Walter Miller. Cambridge, MA: Harvard University Press, 1979–1986.

MARATHON
c. 21 September 490 B.C.

FORCES ENGAGED
Greek: 10,000 Athenians and 1,000 Plataeans. Commanders: Callimachus and Miltiades. Persian: Possibly 20,000. Commander: Datis.

IMPORTANCE
Persian defeat stopped a major invasion of Europe and established the Greek military as a force to be reckoned with. This event set up the later Persian invasion that was defeated at Salamis and Plataea.

Historical Setting

At the beginning of the fifth century B.C., Persia owned an empire that stretched from India to the Mediterranean. Begun two generations earlier by Cyrus the Great, the Persian Empire at this point was under the control of Darius. Darius had been the architect of the campaigns that stretched the empire to its current limits, and he seemed constantly to be hungry for more land. The Persian Empire acquired lands by conquest and then incorporated the captured nations into the established Persian administration. Thus, the army that the empire fielded was made up of a wide range of races with a variety of military talents. At its core, the Persian military depended on the original populations of the empire, the Medes and the Persians. These were the best trained and equipped troops, as well as the most highly motivated. These two populations also provided the officers that commanded the other troops brought in via conquest. By the start of the fifth century, they were a seemingly unbeatable force, for no enemy had been able to withstand their might.

In the first decade of that century, however, problems arose that ultimately led to Darius dispatching an expedition to Greece. The Persian Empire exercised hegemony over the western coast of Asia Minor, then called

Ionia, which was inhabited by Greek colonists. The Ionian Greeks swore fealty to the Persian Empire and provided troops, but were not overly enthusiastic about Persian rule. When Darius campaigned up the Danube valley in 512 B.C., he left an Ionian Greek contingent guarding a bridge along his line of supply. When the Scythians, upon whom Darius was making war, prevailed over Darius, the Persians withdrew toward that bridge. The Greek commander, Miltiades, proposed destroying it and letting the Scythians destroy the Persians, but he was overruled by other Ionian leaders. Darius escaped, but swore vengeance on Miltiades, who abandoned his homeland of the Chersonese (the modern Gallipoli peninsula) and fled to Athens, the city of his birth. There he entered into Athenian politics.

Athens had recently overthrown the tyrant Hippias, who fled to Persia and entered Darius's court. The city, under the leadership of Cleis-

thenes, established a republic in 510. This provoked some of the city's aristocrats to appeal to the military state of Sparta to remove Cleisthenes, which they did temporarily, but Cleisthenes (with the support of most of the population) expelled the Spartans. Afraid of Spartan retribution, Cleisthenes toyed with the idea of courting Persian support. Although Athens ultimately conceded to Sparta political preeminence in Greece, a faction of the Athenians covertly leaned toward Persia.

In 499, the Ionian city-states began a rebellion against Persia, and they appealed to the Greek city-states for aid. Sparta and most of the others declined, but Athens provided twenty warships and the city-state of Eritria provided another five. The major Persian city of Sardis in Asia Minor was burned by the Greeks in 498. When Darius suppressed the Ionian revolt, he swore revenge on Athens, who had dared to aid the Ionian rebels. That fact,

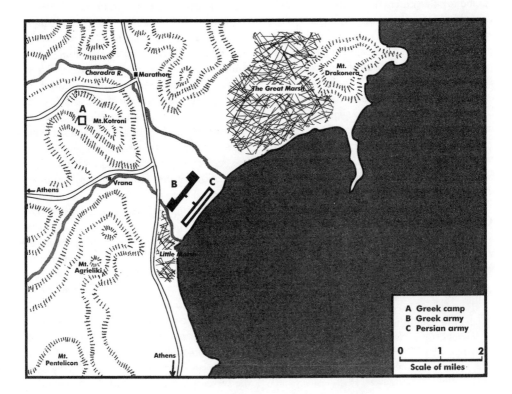

coupled with the fact that his enemy Miltiades was active in Athenian politics, gave Darius a double reason for invasion. In 492, Darius sent an army to subdue Thrace, and in the process forced the kingdom of Macedonia to swear fealty. This put the Persians in position to invade Greece from the north, but a storm wrecked the Persian fleet, which necessitated a second attempt. This Darius mounted in 490 (some sources argue 491 B.C.), sending 600 ships full of infantry and cavalry to subdue Athens and establish Persian might in Greece. Before the campaign started, however, he sent heralds throughout Greece demanding the surrender of all the city-states. When the expedition sailed, under the command of Darius's general, Datis, the deposed Athenian tyrant Hippias was with it. He was to agitate among the disaffected Athenians and provoke a rebellion, in return for which he would become governor of Greece within the Persian Empire. As mentioned earlier, a pro-Persian faction existed in Athens to respond to this call for action.

As the Persian forces sailed for Greece, the Greeks were in disarray, with political infighting taking place in Athens, as well as the latent Athenian hostility to Sparta. Troops of the largest empire the world had known up to that time descended on a small set of city-states without a proven military record. All the odds were in the Persians' favor.

The Battle

The nature of the Athenian military system was that each of the ten tribes of the city-state had a commander leading its forces, with a *polemarch* in overall command. As the Persians approached, the serving polemarch was Callimachus; among the tribal commanders was Miltiades. When the Persian fleet sailed across the Aegean and attacked the city-state of Eritria, the Athenians correctly surmised the Persian strategy. Datis, commander of the Persian fleet, hoped to draw the Athenian military out of the city to march to the aid of Eritria; this would give the Persians the opportunity to either destroy the Greek army in the open or bypass it and sail directly for Athens, attacking the city while the army was away. The Athenians sent for Spartan assistance on 9 September 490, but were disappointed to learn it would be delayed because of religious reasons; a festival had to be observed and the army could not march until the full moon, on the night of 20–21 September. Thus, Athens was on its own for a while.

The size of the Persian force is unknown, but probably was approximately 25,000 infantry and 1,000 cavalry. Datis placed some of these forces under Artaphernes and sailed with the remainder to the Bay of Marathon, about 25 miles from Athens. Datis landed his troops, probably about 12,000 to 15,000 strong, on the Plain of Marathon. The Athenians arrived with about 10,000 men and occupied the high ground on the west side of the plain. They were soon reinforced by 1,000 troops from Plataea, a city-state long allied to Athens. For 8 days, the two armies faced each other: the Greeks unwilling to abandon the safety of their position and the Persians unwilling to attack it. Within the command council, the Athenians argued the merits of action or inaction. On the ninth day, word arrived that Eritria had fallen, meaning that Persian reinforcements would not be long in coming. Half the commanders were in favor of waiting for the Spartans to arrive, they being the best troops Greece had to offer. Miltiades, however, argued against waiting. Knowing that a faction within Athens favored peace at any price (which meant giving the Persians everything and accepting Hippias back as tyrant), he argued that the sooner action was taken and victory achieved, the less likely they would be stabbed in the back politically. The deciding vote fell to Callimachus, who agreed with Miltiades.

On 21 September (probably), Miltiades formed up the Athenian army. The Plain of Marathon was flanked by marshes and bisected by a stream, the Charadra. The Persian cavalry, for which the Greeks had no corresponding forces of their own, were not present, having been taken to the northern marsh to water. With the cavalry being more than a mile away and on the other side of the fast-flowing Charadra, the Greeks hoped to force a decisive action quickly on the southern half of the plain. The Greek forces were stretched over a front almost a mile wide, as was the Persian infantry. Miltiades thinned the center ranks to extend the front and strengthen the flanks. The standard Greek military formation, the phalanx, was made up of spearmen in a unit usually eight ranks deep. On this day, the center was but four ranks deep, with the flanks being eight (some sources say twelve) ranks deep.

As the two forces were relatively equal in number, the Greeks depended on the speed of their attack to neutralize the most effective part of the Persian army, its archers. As the Greek line descended from its high ground and approached the Persian line parallel and backed up against the ocean, they approached steadily at first. When, however, they came within about 200 yards of the Persians, the range at which the archers could effectively fire, the Greeks broke into a run to both throw off the aim of the archers as well as to minimize the time they were exposed to their fire.

Whether by design or by plan, the Greek flanks reached the Persian line first, thus bending their line in the center. The Persian counterattack took advantage of this and the weakened Greek center broke and the troops began to withdraw. This coincided with the success of the attacking Greek flanks, which doubled the Persian army back on itself. Thus, the Persian flanks retreated back and toward the middle of their position, while the Persian center left its position to pursue the Greeks in front of them. The Athenian center withdrew off the plain to the high ground and then regrouped and counterattacked. This sent the Persian center retreating into the confused mass of the collapsing Persian flanks, and the entire Persian force began disintegrating. The cavalry was never able to form up and assist the infantry; by the time they were alerted to the danger and ready for battle, it was too late. The Persian troops that survived the slaughter fled for their ships, but they left behind, according to the Greek historian Herodotus (*The Histories*, p. 430), 6,400 men killed as well as seven ships destroyed. The Greeks lost 192 killed.

Results

Although the battle was a total victory for the Athenians, they could not spare the time to celebrate. Artaphernes was sailing from Eritria, and Datis still had a number of men and ships under his command. Thus, the Athenians quickly left Marathon and marched through the night back to Athens. The Persians indeed had joined forces and sailed for the city, but when they approached the next day and saw the Athenian army drawn up awaiting them, they decided against landing and sailed home.

Too late, the Spartans arrived. Learning of what had transpired, they marched to Marathon to view the Persian dead. Seeing the results of the battle, the Spartans praised the Athenians and then marched home. The Athenians took their 192 dead and buried them in a common grave, the mound of which was one of the major landmarks of the Marathon plain from that day forward.

Legend has it that Pheilippides, an Athenian courier, ran from the battlefield to Athens, announced the victory, and collapsed in death. He was in fact the one who was sent to alert the Spartans earlier in the month and covered the 150 miles in 2 days, but the run to Athens after the battle probably did not happen. This, however, is the basis of the modern marathon race, supposedly the distance he ran to announce the battle's outcome.

Miltiades, the Younger. Athenian mercenary commander in the army of the Persian emperor Darius I. (Archive Photos)

The Greek victory at Marathon was not conclusive, in that it did not keep the Persians away; they returned 10 years later to be defeated at the even more decisive battle of Salamis. However, Marathon does mark a significant turning point. The limits of the Persian Empire were reached. Darius, who had stretched the empire to such distant lands, did not live to see it go farther. Darius died in 486, so his successor Xerxes led the second invasion of Greece. It also marks a change in momentum. Although the Persians had suffered a defeat at the hands of the Scythians (mentioned earlier), the Scythians did not follow up. The Greeks, however, used their victory here as the springboard for their future world power. The Greeks, never before tested against serious military opposition, established themselves at Marathon as an army of note. More importantly, it gave them a psychological boost for future conflicts, for in the second round of fighting, a decade later, they did not stand in awe of an invincible Persian military. As J. F. C. Fuller writes, the victory "endowed the victors with a faith in their destiny which was to endure for three centuries, during which western culture was born. Marathon was the birth cry of Europe" (Fuller, *A Military History of the Western World*, vol. 1, p. 25).

References: Burn, A. R. *Persia and the Greeks: The Defence of the West, c. 546–478 BC.* Stanford, CA: Stanford University Press, 1984 [1963]; Creasy, Edward S. *Fifteen Decisive Battles of the World.* New York: Harper, 1851; Fuller, J. F. C. *A Military History of the Western World*, vol. 1. New York: Funk & Wagnalls, 1954; Hansen, Victor, ed. *Hoplites: The Classical Greek Battle Experience.* London: Routledge, 1991; Herodotus. *The Histories.* Translated by Aubrey de Selincourt. Baltimore: Penguin, 1954.

SALAMIS

23 September 480 B.C.

FORCES ENGAGED

Greek: 370 galleys. Commander: Themistocles.
Persian: Approximately 1,000 galleys.
Commander: Xerxes.

IMPORTANCE

The Persian naval defeat, followed by the military defeat at Plataea, ended the attempt to expand the Persian Empire into Europe and made the Greeks the dominant population in the Mediterranean region and Europe.

Historical Setting

Although Darius's attempt to invade Greece in 490 B.C. failed, he was not about to allow the Greeks to go unpunished for their earlier aid to rebellious provinces in Ionia. He would have immediately mounted another invasion, but first had to deal with a rebellion in Egypt. Before subduing that revolt, Darius died in 486 B.C., to be succeeded by his son Xerxes. Xerxes finished the job in Egypt and then set about mounting the punitive expedition to Greece. It is impossible to know for sure just how large an expedition it was because contemporary writers are notorious for exaggerating numbers, whether to make their own victory look better or because the Persian juggernaut seemed so immense it had to be the 2.6 million people Herodotus claimed. Then again, if one assumes that this number includes not only soldiers but also all the various support personnel (cooks, clerks, launderers, etc.), then perhaps it is not too outrageous. Herodotus, however, claims that with the support personnel the total number on campaign with Xerxes was more than 5 million. More modern writers (Maurice, *Journal of Hellenic Studies,* and Munro, *The Cambridge Ancient History*) place the fighting forces at between 150,000 and 180,000, drawn from all the Persian Empire.

Since their stunning victory in 490 over the Persians at Marathon, the Greeks had not been as focused as the Persians on the upcoming war. Athens, Sparta, and most other poleis (city-states) had returned to their contentious ways and fallen out among themselves. When hearing the news of Xerxes's oncoming forces in the winter of 481, they finally sublimated their differences by meeting in a pan-Hellenic conference under Spartan leadership at the Isthmus of Corinth. Many of the northern poleis did not send representatives, however. The major point of discussion was where to make their defensive stand. Sparta argued that, because the Peloponnese, the peninsula upon which they lived, was the heart of Greek independence, the stand should be made at the Corinthian isthmus. This, however, would abandon all of northern and central Greece to Persia without a fight, and such a decision might lead to the poleis north of the isthmus defecting to Xerxes in order to save their lands from destruction. If the defense was mounted farther forward, narrow passages at Thermopylae or the Vale of Tempe could be held by a small military force, while the straits between mainland Greece and the island of Euboea offered a narrow body of water where the Persian numeric naval superiority meant little.

When an expedition to the north found too many passes to hold, the force returned to the south, giving the northerners the impression that they were about to be abandoned. To make bad matters worse, when the Greeks consulted the famous Oracle at Delphi for advice, the response was extremely negative: it implied that Athens would be destroyed, but the other poleis would not if they held themselves aloof. A second attempt at consultation was more positive, but also somewhat puzzling. The Athenians were told to defend themselves behind "wooden walls," which could mean either their city walls or the bulkheads of the ships of the Athenian navy. The second interpretation was the most widely accepted, and an appeal went to the Greek colony of Syracuse for its powerful navy. They could not respond, however, because they were about to be attacked by the Carthaginians of North Africa, possibly under the direction of Xerxes, for he held sway over the Phoenicians who had established the city of Carthage. The Greeks finally decided to mount a northern defense, the Spartans too afraid of having to fight alone at the Isthmus of Corinth.

Meanwhile, Xerxes in the spring of 480 began moving his massive force around the perimeter of the Aegean. He did so by crossing the Hellespont (the straits near modern Istanbul) on two bridges of boats in one of the most massive engineering feats of its day. As Darius had done before him, Xerxes sent heralds into Greece to demand tokens of submission; they received positive responses only in the northernmost city-states. Having passed his force out of Asia Minor and into Europe, the Persian army marched along the coast, with the navy carrying their supplies. They moved around the Aegean rim toward the Greeks awaiting them at Thermopylae and the narrow Euboean Channel.

The Battle

A force of 7,000 to 8,000 led by King Leonidas of Sparta stood at the pass of Thermopylae, a stretch of beach along the Gulf of Malis. Three hundred thirty-three ships blocked the channel through which the Persian ships would have to travel if they were going to continue supplying the army. The Greeks were hoping for the naval battle to be decisive, with the army delayed only as an excuse to force the Persian navy into the narrow waters. The Greeks were fortunate that the Persian fleet ran into a storm and lost 400 warships. Themistocles, commanding the Athenian ships in the fleet, counseled an immediate attack to take advantage of the Persian disaster. The two navies fought two battles, but both were draws. The Greeks retreated, however, upon hearing that the Greeks at Thermopylae had been betrayed and overrun following a gallant last stand by King Leonidas and his bodyguard of 300.

With the Persian army on the march, the citizens of Athens decided to abandon the city, leaving only a defensive post on the Acropolis:

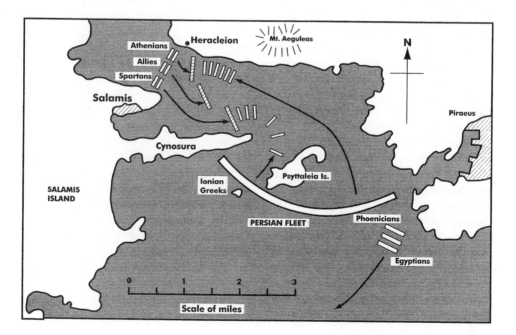

they were putting their faith in the wooden walls of the Greek navy. Themistocles led the navy to the narrow waters between the coastline below Athens and the island of Salamis. If the Persians sent ships to sail both directions around Salamis, the Greeks would be bottled up in a very small area, but Themistocles placed his fleet in that dangerous position to tempt the Persians to attack rather than bypass the fleet and march directly for the Spartan defensive position at the Corinthian isthmus. Meanwhile, Xerxes's army overwhelmed the Acropolis and burned Athens. As the Persian navy approached, dissension among the Greek naval commanders welled up. Eurybiades, the Spartan, was in command even though the Spartan naval contingent was small. Because Sparta commanded the entire defense of Greece, however, a Spartan commanded the fleet. Many ship captains did not want to put themselves into the dangerous position Themistocles counseled, but he prevailed when he threatened to take his Athenian ships (which were the bulk of the entire Greek navy) and leave the rest to their fate. When on the morning of 22 September 480 another challenge to this strategy was mounted, Themistocles gambled even more heavily. He sent a secret message to Xerxes offering to turn traitor in the midst of the battle if the Persian ships would attack. He had no intention of doing this, but it forced Xerxes's hand as well as forcing the rest of the captains to fight when the Persian fleet came rowing toward them on the morning of 23 September.

Xerxes sent a contingent of 200 Egyptian ships to enter round the west coast of Salamis, blocking a Greek retreat, while the remainder of his ships entered the narrow waters from the east, rowing right into Themistocles's trap. The Persian fleet of about 1,000 ships had to divide itself to round the island of Psyttaleia to enter the Salamis channel and then they had to round a long peninsula to enter the channel proper, which was way too narrow for their huge numbers to maneuver. The Persian fleet depended on speed and maneuverability,

neither of which they now had. The 370 larger and heavier Greek galleys needed only to row forward into the confused Persian fleet, ramming anything and everything in their path. For 7 to 8 hours the sound of shattering wood and the shouts of battle and death rose up to Xerxes, who sat on a throne watching what was supposed to be his naval coup de main. Instead he saw more than half his fleet destroyed while the Greeks suffered the loss of only forty ships.

Results

Although Xerxes stayed in Athens for a few more days and gave the impression that he was going to renew the battle, he was actually making plans for his retreat. Fearful that the Greek navy might chase his remaining ships all the way back to Asia Minor and then destroy his boat bridge, he made plans to withdraw his army from Europe back into his own lands. He left a force of possibly 180,000 under his general Mardonius to finish off the Greek armies. This he did on the advice of Artemesia of Halicarnassus, a queen who not only had provided ships for the Persian invasion but had distinguished herself in battle at both Euboea and Salamis. She told Xerxes that this was the best solution, for if Mardonius was victorious, Xerxes could claim the credit for leaving him in command, but if Mardonius lost, then Xerxes could disavow any fault for the defeat because he had not been personally in command. Indeed, Mardonius did lose the following August at Plataea after attempting to take advantage of the Greeks who were soon squabbling again. He did have some Greek allies with him at the battle, but the 80,000 Greeks under the command of the Spartan general Pausanias proved too disciplined a force for the polyglot Persian army to stand against.

The battles of Salamis and Plataea ended this round of the Greco-Persian wars; for the next 150 years, Greece and Persia fought intermittently, mainly in Ionia, the east coast of

Asia Minor populated originally by Greek colonists. From naval, military, and political points of view, the world changed after these battles.

The Persian navy had dominated the eastern Mediterranean for half a century, with the Phoenicians making up the bulk of the navy and the Ionian cities providing both ships and bases. Further, the Phoenician colony of Carthage, as stated earlier, by acting in concert with Persia, extended Persian sway across almost the entire Mediterranean Sea. This was reversed after Salamis. As long as the Persian Empire existed, and it lasted until its defeat by Alexander the Great in 331 B.C., it maintained a navy to be reckoned with, but the Athenian navy was the primary power for decades after the Salamis victory. When the Peloponnesian War broke out between Athens and Sparta in the second half of the fifth century B.C., Sparta dealt with the Persians in order to use their fleet against Athens. Still, the Persian navy was never the same power it had been. Athens came to dominate trade in the eastern Mediterranean, and the Ionian cities were encouraged by the Greek victory and began making trouble for their Persian masters. Maintaining order in Asia Minor became an ongoing problem for the Persians from this time forward.

Militarily, the Greek army had become the best in the world. The heavily armed hoplite, the Greek infantryman with spear, armor, and discipline, became the standard by which other soldiers were measured. The phalanx in which he fought was the formation that dominated the battlefield until the Roman Empire adapted and modified it into the cohort. Indeed, from this point forward, Greek soldiers and formations were used by the Persians, who hired Greek mercenaries in large numbers to fight their wars in Asia. With the hoplites, Philip of Macedon controlled Greece, and his son Alexander built an empire that reached India.

The greatest change came politically and socially. Many commentators point to Salamis and Plataea as the turning point in all of European history, the point at which Europe became a culture based on Greek civilization and not a vassal of Eastern emperors. Fuller (*A Military History of the Western World*, vol. 1, p. 52) states that these two battles "stand like the pillars of the temple of the ages supporting the architecture of western history." Durant (*The Life of Greece,* p. 242) describes the Greek victory as the most momentous "in European history, for it made Europe possible. It won for western civilization the opportunity to develop its own . . . political institutions, free from the dictation of Oriental kings. It won for Greece a clear road for the first great experiment in liberty; it preserved the Greek mind for three centuries from the enervating mysticism of the East, and secured for Greek enterprise full freedom of the sea." Thus, the basis of western political institutions, philosophies, and sciences comes from Greece; little is done today, or even conceived of, that the Greeks did not ponder upon more than two millennia past.

Had the Persians prevailed, they might well have spread their empire deep into Europe. If they had been able to maintain some sort of order in Greece itself (a tall order to be sure) and drawn on Greek soldiers to supplement the already massive and talented Persian army, little in Europe stood in their way. No European population had the organization to mass against them; even the previously successful Scythians may have failed against a reinforced Persian military. A Persian navy carrying the empire's soldiers across the Mediterranean may even have quelled the nascent power of Rome. The world, indeed, could have been completely different but for Themistocles's gamble at Salamis.

References: Burn, A. R. *Persia and the Greeks: The Defence of the West, c. 546–478 BC.* Stanford, CA: Stanford University Press, 1984 [1963]; Durant, Will. *The Life of Greece.* New York: Simon & Schuster, 1939; Fuller, J. F. C. *A Military History of the Western World,* vol. 1. New York: Funk & Wagnalls, 1954; Herodotus. *The Histories.* Translated by Aubrey de Selincourt. Baltimore: Penguin, 1954; Hignet, Charles.

Xerxes' Invasion of Greece. Oxford, UK: Clarendon Press, 1963; Maurice, Frederick. "The Size of the Army of Xerxes," *Journal of Hellenic Studies* 50, 1930; Munro, J. A. R., in *The Cambridge Ancient History,* vol. 4, J. B. Bury, S. A. Cook, and F. E. Adcock, eds. New York: Macmillan, 1928.

SYRACUSE

415–413 B.C.

FORCES ENGAGED

Syracusan: Unknown, although probably roughly equal to Athenians; included 4,400 Spartans. Commander: Gylippus.
Athenian: Approximately 200 galleys and 45,000 to 50,000 men. Commander: Nicias and then Demosthenes.

IMPORTANCE

Athenian defeat broke the naval dominance of the eastern Mediterranean by the Athenians, led to their downfall as the dominant Greek polis, and kept them from possibly establishing their authority throughout the Mediterranean world, including Carthage and Rome.

Historical Setting

The first Peloponnesian War pitted Sparta and its allies in the Peloponnesian League against Athens and its allies in the Delian League. Since the defeat of the Persian invaders at Salamis and Plataea in 480 and 479 B.C., Athens had risen to the top in Greek politics. As the leading naval power, Athens had made itself the strongest member of the Delian League, a grouping of Greek poleis (city-states) dedicated to stopping Persian expansion and carrying the war to Persian possessions in Asia Minor. No polis could challenge Athenian dominance, and Athens reached the point where it could demand virtually any dues to the League from the member poleis and did not have to account for the money sent to the League treasury. Rather than

focus on defense spending, the Athenians spent much of that money turning their city into a cultural and architectural showplace. Not surprisingly, this did not please the poleis contributing the money.

Athens entered into a shifting set of alliances, some voluntary and some that it forced on weaker neighbors. Between 460 and 445, Athens challenged the armies of Sparta and its allies in a number of battles, at the same time trying to aid Egyptian rebels against Persia. With no clear outcome to the fighting, Sparta and Athens agreed on a truce in 445, but their political rivalry continued. It is difficult, anywhere in history, to find a set of circumstances as convoluted as the ones that started the second Peloponnesian War. Continued Athenian domination over the northern Greek poleis kept them resentful, while yet more diplomatic maneuvering and alliance making resulted in Athens seemingly being poised to establish a Greek Empire. The Athenian navy continued to enforce as well as to expand Athenian dominion over as much of the Mediterranean as possible. Finally fed up with the cavalier attitude of the Athens, most Greek poleis turned to Sparta for leadership. When Athens attempted to meddle in the political affairs of the southern Greek Peloponnese peninsula, long Sparta's sphere of influence, fighting resumed in 431.

The war often has been described as the classic struggle between the elephant and the whale. Sparta had the finest army of the day and Athens possessed the finest navy, but neither could come to grips with the other. Sparta and its allies laid siege to Athens after capturing the countryside around it, but they were unable to capture the port of Piraeus, so Athens kept a constant supply of food and other necessaries brought in by its shipping. The Athenian navy also conducted raids on the coastline of Sparta, liberating the helots who toiled under harsh Spartan rule. Both powers could hurt the other, but not finish the other off. Fighting was fairly constant for 10 years, but another peace was finally negotiated in 421.

Manuscript illumination showing the Byzantine attack on Syracuse, from the collection of the Biblioteca Nacional, Madrid. (Corbis/Archivo Iconographica, S.A.)

The two main adversaries were glad of the break, but some of their allies were unhappy without a peace treaty that restored lands that they had lost in the war. Although Sparta and Athens had a treaty, their client states argued and fought among themselves and, when pressed, called on the two powers for aid. Peace was kept between the two for 6 years, but much of the blame for the renewal of war between them in 414 can be laid at the feet of Alcibiades, a rabble-rousing general in Athens.

Alcibiades convinced the citizenry of Athens to go to war against the city-state of Syracuse on the island of Sicily. Syracuse was providing valuable foodstuffs to Sparta, he claimed, and if Athens could establish itself in Sicily (Syracusans were originally Greek colonists), then it would be in a commanding position. Not only could Athens cut off the needed food to Sparta, weakening it to the point of subjection, but possession of Syracuse would give Athens the key to dominating the western Mediterranean as well. Defeating the nascent power of Carthage and Rome, Athens would be able to draw on the people of Italy, North Africa, and Iberia (homeland of most of Carthage's mercenary army) to defeat Sparta and make Athens the ruler of the known western world. Alcibiades's speaking ability won over

the citizens in support of his plan over the more cautious suggestions of his political rivals. Athens voted to mount the attack. Better still, the Sicilian city of Segesta offered to pay for the expedition; it was currently being threatened by Syracuse. Alcibiades was sent to Sicily, with Nicias and Lamachus as co-commanders.

The Battle

The Athenian invasion force, totaling about 27,000 troops and departing in June 415, included 134 triremes and 130 transports, the latter carrying about 5,000 hoplites (heavy infantry), 1,300 archers, various javelin throwers and slingers, and 30 horses. Another 130 supply ships sailed with them as well. For the most part, the Syracusans ignored rumors of a Greek invasion until the enemy arrived in sight. The only thing that saved them was the well-known Greek inability to agree on anything. Nicias wanted to go home once it was learned that the city of Segesta could not pay for the mission. Lamachus wanted to launch an immediate attack on Syracuse, taking advantage of its lack of preparation and their low morale. The oratory of Alcibiades again won the day; he argued that the Athenians should travel across the island, amassing support from the

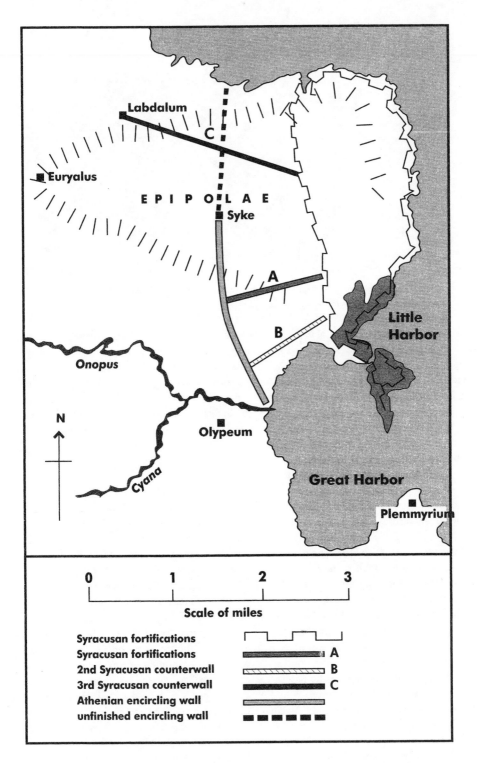

Labdalum

C

Euryalus

E P I P O L A E

Syke

A

B

Onopus

Little
Harbor

N

Olypeum

Cyana

Great Harbor

Plemmyrium

| 0 | 1 | 2 | 3 |

Scale of miles

Syracusan fortifications

Syracusan fortifications ———————— A

2nd Syracusan counterwall ///////// B

3rd Syracusan counterwall ———————— C

Athenian encircling wall

unfinished encircling wall ▬ ▬ ▬ ▬ ▬

local cities that disliked Syracuse. That, however, gave the Syracusans time to begin training their troops and repairing their defenses. Alcibiades's plan was a failure because no Sicilian city voluntarily joined them.

Word soon arrived from Athens that Alcibiades had been tried in his absence for blasphemy and must return for judgment. He was taken away, but managed to escape his jailors when the ship stopped in Italy. He fled to Sparta, which he had spent most of his life trying to provoke. There he revealed Athens' plan for empire and the detrimental effect the loss of Syracuse would have on Sparta's supplies. At first, Sparta refused, still observing their latest truce with Athens, but altered their stand somewhat when emissaries from Syracuse arrived. The Spartans promised to send a general to command the Syracusan army; further, a fleet from Corinth, Sparta's ally, was dispatched.

With Alcibiades gone, the Athenians began to attack Syracuse. They defeated a poorly prepared Syracusan force, but failed to win a complete victory because of their lack of cavalry; even worse, Lamachus was killed in the fighting, leaving Nicias in sole command. He was not a decisive leader. As winter approached, they settled into siege warfare, building a wall parallel to the defensive wall protecting Syracuse. This would cut the city off from any help from the land, while the superior Athenian fleet was supposed to keep the seaward side of the city covered. Both strategies failed. The Syracusans raided the Athenians just often enough and successfully enough to keep their wall from being finished. Still, morale in the city was slipping. A town meeting was called to discuss opening surrender negotiations, but the Corinthians arrived and stopped them. The Spartan general, Gylippus, landed up the coast and roused some support for a force of some 2,000 men to fight with him against the Athenians. He marched them onto the high plateau just to the west of Syracuse, so surprising Nicias that the Athenians were unable to stop Gylippus from reaching the city. Gylippus oversaw the construction of a counterwall to stop the Athenian effort; it split the plain and gave Syracuse control of the northern half, which gave it access to the rest of the island.

In the summer of 414, Nicias sent a message to Athens, counseling abandonment of the invasion or the dispatch of a second force equal to the first. Athens reinforced, but Sparta broke the truce and attacked to delay or cancel the second force. The summer of 414 in Sicily was spent in wall building, and Gylippus gained the advantage. When the spring of 413 arrived, he was ready to begin his attacks on the Athenians. This he did with a two-pronged assault. His navy attacked Nicias's base at Plemmyrium on the southern end of Syracuse's harbor. When the soldiers left their positions defending the town in order to watch the sea battle, then Gylippus attacked and captured the town. The Athenian fleet badly hurt the attacking Corinthians, but lost its base. They were obliged to move to another mooring deeper in the harbor, which would severely limit the navy's superiority in maneuverability. This was the beginning of the end for the Athenian military effort in Sicily.

A few weeks later, Gylippus heard of the dispatch of the second Athenian force, and he determined to win if possible before they arrived. He launched another attack at the Athenians, this time using his army first to distract the Athenian sailors. In this he succeeded; when his ships entered the harbor bent on close-quarters action with the Athenians, they found a disorganized navy scrambling to operate its ships and engage. The engagement lasted intermittently for 3 days, but this time the combined fleet of Corinth and Syracuse gained the upper hand. At close quarters, they were able to rain arrows down on the Athenian ships, killing large numbers of sailors. It was a major defeat, but still not decisive. When the second Athenian force under Demosthenes arrived in July 413, hope for a successful invasion reappeared.

Demosthenes received command of the entire Athenian force from an ailing Nicias, and immediately went on the offensive to regain control of the plateau overlooking the city in order to restart the siege. He sent a force secretly up the steep slope of the western end of the plateau, and it captured a surprised Syracusan force at the town of Euryalus. However, Gylippus ordered a counterattack, and, in the confusion of the night fighting, the Athenians lost their momentum and lost the battle. Unable to reestablish a position on the plain, Demosthenes decided to abandon the entire mission. The Athenian force loaded onto ships for the return home and then stopped at the last minute because of a full lunar eclipse on 27 August 413. The superstitious Nicias decided to wait a month before sailing, and that gave Gylippus his last chance to win. He parked his fleet across the mouth of the harbor and chained the ships together. Again the small space the harbor provided kept the Athenians from using their superior maneuverability and they lost fifty ships to the Syracusans' twenty-six. At that point, the Athenian crews refused to fight and demanded a retreat by land. On open ground, Gylippus was able to separate the Athenians into two groups and defeat each individually.

Results

Of the 45,000 to 50,000 men that Athens had sent to gain control of Syracuse and Sicily, only 7,000 survived the final battles. They were all sold into slavery, although Nicias and Demosthenes were killed, against Gylippus's orders. The Syracusans, poorly prepared for this war and on the verge of surrender, survived thanks to the organizational and fighting ability of Gylippus. This kept the city free and a major power in the western Mediterranean for another couple of centuries, until finally crushed in the conflict between Rome and Carthage in the third century B.C.

Athens' fortunes took a definite turn for the worse. The ships and crews lost in Sicily were not irreplaceable, but it severely damaged Athenian naval power and, more importantly, their prestige. Members of the Delian League seized the opportunity to break away, Persian forces opened an offensive to regain their lost territory in Asia Minor, and Sparta began exploring the possibility of sea power, both with their own ships and with others provided by Persia, which was eager to wreak vengeance on Athens. That refocused Athenian attention on its eastern possessions, and, when its lost ships were replaced, that was where Athens sent them. The replacement crews, however, did not match the quality of those lost in Sicily. In spite of the occasional victory, Athens was destroyed as a naval power at Aegospotami in 405. There, in the Hellespont connecting the Aegean and the Black Seas, a Spartan fleet commanded by Lysander attacked the last Athenian fleet as it was drawn up on the beach and its crews were ashore gathering provisions. Lysander captured intact 170 ships and their crews, almost all of which were slaughtered by sailors who either were or knew victims of previous Athenian depredations. Without their fleet, the city of Athens could not resist the siege that Sparta was then conducting. The city held out through the winter of 405–404, but surrendered in the spring.

Athens' defeat at Syracuse made all of that possible. Had they followed Lymachus's advice and attacked as soon as they landed, Syracuse certainly would have fallen easily. A strong Athenian force stationed there could soon have gained the loyalty (albeit grudgingly) of the Sicilian population, and a major power center could have been established. Carthage and Rome were at that point mere shadows of the power that they became two centuries later, and it would have been little problem for Athenian ships and troops to control them as well. With the supplies and forces available from these acquisitions, no one would have been able to match Athenian power, and the empire of which Alcibiades dreamed could have existed. Rome either without power or with delayed power may never have built their empire, and Europe, at least, would never have been the same. As it was, the defeat ended Athens' reign as the dominant polis. Sparta for a time tried to rule Greece, but its militaristic society was not meant for other cities and it too failed to establish hegemony. No one dominated Greece after this time until Philip of Macedon arrived in the 340s to unite the poleis under one ruler; his son Alexander took that unity and built an eastern empire instead of the western one Athens would have built. Thus, the fate of Asia changed as well.

References: Creasy, Edward S. *Fifteen Decisive Battles of the World.* New York: Harper, 1851; Fuller, J. F. C. *A Military History of the Western World,* vol. 1. New York: Funk & Wagnalls, 1954; Kagan, Donald. *On the Origins of War.* New York: Doubleday, 1995; Thucydides. *The Peloponnesian Wars.* Translated by Benjamin Jowett. New York: Twayne Publishers, 1963.

LEUCTRA
July 371 B.C.

FORCES ENGAGED
Theban: 6,000 hoplites and 1,500 cavalry. Commander: King Epaminondas.
Spartan: 10,000 hoplites and 1,000 cavalry. Commander: King Cleombrotus.

IMPORTANCE
Theban victory broke the power of Sparta, which had dominated the Greek peninsula since the Peloponnesian War. Theban supremacy in Greece was temporary, and hostile relations led to Macedonian invasion and control.

Historical Setting

After Athens' defeat in the Peloponnesian Wars in 404 B.C., Sparta assumed the dominant role among the Greek poleis, or city-states. Although that may have been a good thing from

a military point of view—Sparta had long fielded the finest army in Greece—it was not a good thing politically or socially. The discipline practiced in Spartan society did not translate to other regions, and the other poleis began chafing under Spartan domination. When Sparta, as defender of the Greeks, began experiencing some setbacks in a conflict in Asia Minor against their former ally Persia, city-states such as Athens and Thebes saw an opportunity to strengthen their positions.

In 394 B.C., Sparta's naval power was broken after a defeat off Cnidus. The victorious Persian fleet was actually commanded by an Athenian, Conon, and many of the ships were run by Athenian crews. Islands under the Spartan thumb began to cede from their alliances; in the meantime, a Persian agent traveled the Greek countryside spreading money and sowing dissension. At Lechaion in 390, Athenian light troops, backed by their heavy hoplite phalanx, defeated the Spartan phalanx, marking the first signs of a decline in Spartan military might. Peace was temporarily restored by the Persians, who in 387 imposed the Peace of Analcidas. This recognized Athens' return to prominence, if still not Sparta's equal, and threatened Persian hostility to any party that violated the truce. Sparta retained its preeminence and reestablished its suzerainty over smaller communities that had shown signs of independent action. The reinforced Peloponnesian League was expected to provide taxes to Sparta and personnel in case of emergency. Troop shortfalls would be supplemented by the hiring of mercenaries. Spartan rule became overly arbitrary, and the members of the League hoped for deliverance from some outside source.

That source proved to be Thebes. Leading member of the Boeotian League, Thebes had for a time alternated as rival and ally with neighboring Athens. As allies, they expelled Spartan forces from central Greece and then defeated the Spartans in a naval battle in 376. However, when they began arguing between themselves, Sparta regained some ground. Sparta sponsored a peace conference in 371, but Thebes refused to step back from its growing influence as head of the Boeotian League. Faced with Spartan intransigence on the matter, Theban representatives, led by King Epaminondas, left the conference. Not wanting to allow Thebes time to build up a strong defense force, Sparta's King Cleombrotus decided on quick invasion.

The Battle

Cleombrotus gathered together a mixed force of Spartan and allied troops numbering some 10,000 infantry and 1,000 cavalry. The infantry were the standard hoplite heavy infantry of the time, wearing armored breastplate and greaves, carrying a heavy shield, and armed with a long spear. The standard method of fighting was for the troops to form in a square, usually ten ranks deep and wide, with their spears leveled in the direction of the enemy. Combat consisted of two phalanxes marching into each other; whichever proved the stronger or more durable prevailed, while the other broke and ran. In this type of warfare, the Spartan discipline had long been the key to victory. With 10,000 hoplites, Cleombrotus outnumbered the Theban force. The cavalry was used by the Spartans more as a scouting force and was not effective in combat.

The Thebans too fought in the phalanx, although their cavalry was more combat ready than that of Sparta. Thebes's problem was one of numbers. The Boeotian League was smaller than the Peloponnesian League, and King Epaminondas could muster only 6,000 infantry and 1,500 cavalry. In the shoving match that was phalanx warfare, a two-to-one disadvantage was a recipe for disaster. Epaminondas realized that something had to be done to tip the balance in his favor. He thus developed a strategy seen in military history for the first time. He decided to place the bulk of his forces on one flank while weakening the other; both

would be covered by his superior cavalry. Having decided upon this formation, he then placed the heavier, left flank in a forward position with his weaker right flank in echelon to the rear; this is called in modern terminology "refusing one's flank." His plan was for the strengthened flank to use its local superiority of force to overpower the Spartan flank, while his weaker right flank acted as no more than a holding force. To further enhance his chances, he placed the elite 300 troops of the Sacred Band in the center of the strengthened flank.

Epaminondas was prepared for the Spartans. He established a fortified camp near the village of Leuctra, some 8 miles to the southwest of Thebes, in the path of the oncoming Spartan army. Cleombrotus thus found himself lacking the element of surprise, so he encamped his force just over 1 mile away with an open plain separating the two. Thus, Epaminondas had the advantage of having chosen his battlefield.

The exact date of the battle is unknown, but it took place sometime in July 371. Epaminondas opened the battle by deploying his men before his camp. Cleombrotus responded by arraying his men in standard formation, in ranks twelve men deep. He placed his allied troops on his left wing, opposite the Theban refused flank, and placed his cavalry in front of his right flank. Although both armies at his point seemed ready for battle, in reality there were some differences. The Theban army is reported to have been suffering low morale and that possibly is why the weaker right flank was stationed farther to the rear, where the more dispirited troops would be under less threat of attack and therefore less likely to break. Most sources report that the Spartans began drinking early in the day and by noon were well in their cups, thus making them slightly more aggressive. Other sources mention that the day Epaminondas chose was a religious holiday for the Spartans and that they would therefore rather wait for combat. Knowing that, Epaminondas began withdrawing some of his men,

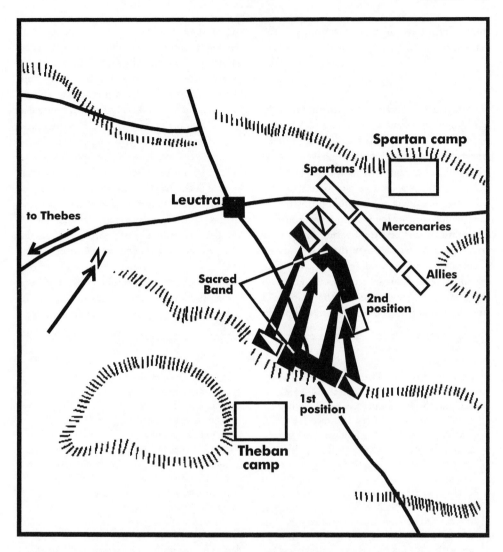

appearing to send them back to camp. Seeing this, the Spartan force also began to break up. When some of the Spartans had withdrawn toward their own camp, the Thebans quickly reformed ranks and charged. The Theban king had thus reduced the Spartan superiority in numbers.

The battle opened with the Theban cavalry on their army's left charging their Spartan counterparts and easily driving them from the field. In their retreat, they either fled too far to the flanks to further influence the battle, or withdrew into the infantry lines, creating confusion. The time was ripe, and Epaminondas ordered his infantry forward. The stronger Theban flank, led by the elite Sacred Band, soon began overpowering the weakened Spartan force. Breaks in the Spartan ranks soon formed and Theban infantry penetrated. The troops of the Peloponnesian League tried to encircle the Thebans, but the refused flank was too far away and the reinforced right wing was too strong to break, so they fell back as well. The Spartans at this point could do nothing but retreat to their camp, leaving behind perhaps 2,000 casualties.

Results

Although the Thebans had lost only a negligible number of men, the battle had proven exhausting. The Spartans still outnumbered them and to attack a fortified camp would prove too costly. Thus, they were receptive when King Cleombrotus proposed to negotiate. He realized that this single battle would probably not be the only one of the war, so risking further losses would not be wise. Spartan forces were granted permission to withdraw, and the Thebans were soon standing at the Corinthian isthmus with Spartan troops cleared from northern and central Greece. The prestige of the Spartan army had been broken, and politi-

cal power was not long in collapsing either. Fearing a dominant Thebes, however, Athens entered into an alliance with its former enemy Sparta. The poleis struggled with each other through 362, when Epaminondas was killed at the battle of Mantinea. His death prevented an overwhelming Theban victory, resulting in no polis exercising overwhelming power. The resulting weakness laid Greece open to outside threat, which Philip of Macedon took advantage of at the battle of Chaeronea in 338.

Sparta had long viewed itself as the defender of Greece from outside threat because it had the premier military force. After Leuctra, that preeminence did not exist, and Greece suffered for it. Thebes, although temporarily strong, neither unified Greece nor had sufficient forces in the Boeotian League to control the peninsula. Greece, long the leader of "civilization,"

SACRED BAND OF THEBES

The Sacred Band of Thebes was founded in ancient Greece by the Theban leader Gorgidas. It was probably first formed as a guard for the city-state's citadel. It contained 300 men for whom Thebes provided training facilities and barracks. At first the Sacred Band did not distinguish itself in combat, possibly because Gorgidas placed its soldiers in the front ranks of the central Theban phalanx, where it was integrated with other soldiers. This did not allow the special training of the Band to be demonstrated because other less talented soldiers diluted the Band's strength. The army therefore did not benefit from the striking power that the Band was supposed to provide.

The Sacred Band derived its reputation for outstanding fighting ability not only from its training, but from the makeup of the unit. The 300 soldiers were 150 homosexual couples. Homosexuality was not uncommon in ancient Greece and attracted no negative comment. The theory within this organization was that the desire to protect and impress one's lover would bring out the best fighting spirit in each soldier. No one would dishonor himself or his partner by fleeing battle and bringing shame upon them both. Therefore, the unit would remain close-

knit, as each soldier acted not only for himself but also his partner, as well as for the unit and army as a whole.

The Band remained the elite of the Theban army until both unit and army were defeated in 338 B.C. Thebes and Athens that year formed an alliance against the rising power of Macedon under Philip II. They marched to meet the Macedonians at Chaeronea, but could not withstand the power of the Macedonian army and the brilliance of its leader. The Macedonian victory brought Philip to power in Greece while destroying the power of the city-states. After the battle, Philip walked the field. When he came to the area where the Sacred Band had fought and died to the last man, he is reported to have commented, "Perish any man who suspects that these men did or suffered anything that was base."

The Sacred Band achieved its reputation by defeating the premiere army of ancient Greece, the Spartans, but they could not match the new organization and tactics introduced by Philip, whose army, under his son Alexander, would conquer most of the known world. The Sacred Band existed for only a few decades and was never revived after its annihilation at Chaeronea.

after Leuctra and certainly after Chaeronea could only claim philosophical preeminence, not military or political.

The battle at Leuctra has great military significance because it introduced a new view of warfare. Some sources even say that this is the first battle in which tactics played a part, rather than mere strength or luck. Epaminondas was the first leader to effectively use his cavalry. This is not surprising because Thebes was regarded as the center of horse breeding in ancient Greece. Depending on hoplites, neither Sparta nor Athens had employed cavalry to any great extent. Indeed, as is seen in the Middle Ages, a rank of pikes is invulnerable to a cavalry charge, so a frontal assault on a phalanx would have been suicide. Even in this battle, cavalry did not play as significant a role as it would soon afterward, when the Macedonians employed it as an arm almost equal in importance to infantry. Still, the disorder in the Spartan army that the Theban cavalry caused was important to the battle's outcome, and the discipline that the Theban army displayed kept it organized and functioning as a unit, rather than a collection of individual horsemen. The future of warfare was now a mixing of types of units, rather than dependence on a single type of force.

The decision to unbalance his line was also unknown before this time, and the stronger flank forward became a widely used tactic. Indeed, Epaminondas in Thebes' victory at Mantinea executed an almost exact repeat of Leuctra. What is somewhat surprising in looking at Leuctra is the negligible role played by light troops. At Lechaion, the Athenians had prevailed by using *peltasts*, lightly armored troops armed with javelins that caused heavy casualties among the tightly packed Spartan phalanx. The extremely conservative nature of the Greek military showed in the slow uptake on that development, although the Macedonians learned from it. All of these facets of military action, the unbalanced line, the refused flank, and the combination of force types, were employed by Alexander the Great in his conquests. Although the Macedonian use of cav-alry was far superior to that of the Greeks, both Philip and Alexander learned from the tactics of the Greeks and used those tactics to over-power them.

References: Buckler, John. *The Theban Hegemony, 371–362.* Cambridge, MA: Harvard University Press, 1980; Ferrill, Arther. *The Origins of War.* London: Thames & Hudson, 1985; Markov, Walter. *Battles of World History.* New York: Hippocrene Books, 1979; Plutarch. *The Lives of Noble Grecians and Romans.* Translated by John Dryden, revised by Arthur Hugh Clough. New York: Modern Library, 1979; Xenophon. *A History of My Times.* Translated by Rex Warner. Baltimore: Penguin, 1966.

CHAERONEA
2 August 338 B.C.

FORCES ENGAGED
Macedonian: 30,000 infantry and 2,000 cavalry. Commander: King Philip II.
Allied: 36,000 infantry and 2,000 cavalry. Commanders: Stratocles, Lysicles, and Chares for the Athenians; Theagenes for Thebes.

IMPORTANCE
Philip's victory ended Greek independence for decades and laid the groundwork for Alexander the Great's championship of Hellenism in his conquests.

Historical Setting

In 359 B.C., Philip of Macedon became king of his country. For some time, he had to suppress rival contenders to the throne, but he managed to solidify his claim and began turning Macedon from a second-rate power into the base of a world empire. He did this through the development of the Macedonian army into the finest fighting machine of the age. Spending time in Thebes in his early twenties, Philip became an admirer of things Greek and fashioned his political skills after the best minds of Greece at the time. The timing of his rise to power is key, for the Greek city-states were more divided than usual. Philip was able to play power politics in Greece by cajoling, complimenting, threatening, or bribing various factions into cooperating with him.

Philip's nemesis was the Athenian orator Demosthenes. He seemed to be one of the few men in Athens who saw Philip for what he was, a man with overwhelming ambition against which Greece could stand only through unification. Demosthenes spent his adult life opposing Philip in word and deed and was the major reason that Athens, chief among all the Greek city-states, stood firm against Macedonian expansionism. Between 352 and 338 B.C., Athens and Philip sparred, each gaining or losing allies against each other. Athens was in a most precarious position during this time because its main government expenditure was the *theoric* fund: money spent on the populace to attend meetings, be jurors, partake in festivals, etc. This meant a corresponding lack of money spent on defense. In turn, this meant that Athenian contributions to Greek defense were often insufficient to either rescue its allies or motivate major expenditures on the part of other city-states.

In 346, Philip conquered the Greek province of Phocis and, by doing so, was able to assume its seat on the Amphictyonic Council, a sort of United Nations organization dealing with religious life in Greece. A conflict between Athens and the people of Amphissa, of the province of Locris, over supposed sacrilegious acts that they had both committed was the flash point that set up the final battle between Macedon and Athens. Amphissa was one of the cities that looked favorably on Philip; many in Greece saw him as a leader who could unite Greece against what many considered their true enemy, Persia. Athenian representatives in the Amphictyonic Council convinced the body that the Locrians had committed a greater sacrilege than had the Athenians, and the Council considered direct military action against them. Athens opposed that, however, because it would certainly bring in Philip to champion Amphissa.

More directly, Amphissa was also friendly to Thebes, long a rival to Athens. Thebes had been obliged to accept a Macedonian garrison in Boeotia, its province, but had ejected it as an infringement of their sovereignty. Demosthenes saw that Thebes was wavering in its relations with Macedon and was therefore a potential ally that it was not wise to anger. Demosthenes hoped that Athens and Thebes could bury their differences and together resist Philip's aggression. Thus, it was not in Athens' best interests to pursue a punitive expedition against Amphissa. A meeting of the Amphictyonic Council in early 339 ordered such an expedition, however, since Athenian representatives did not attend. When that expedition failed to call the Locrians to account, the Council appealed to Philip to serve up the punishment.

Both Philip and Demosthenes realized that a showdown was inevitable. It has been argued since 339 B.C. whether Philip was bribing key persons in this debate or if Demosthenes was taking bribes from Amphissa. No matter what the backstage maneuvers, Macedonian troops were going to march into Greece, either to enforce the Amphictyonic Council's charge against Amphissa or to support Amphissa and the Locrians against such an attack led by Athens. When Philip marched his troops into central Greece in September 339, Thebes had to decide whether Macedon or Athens was the more acceptable bedfellow. Responding to a powerful oration from Demosthenes, the Theban council voted to join Athens against the invader. Demosthenes promised the full commitment of the Athenian navy, Theban command of the joint land forces, and payment of two-thirds of the cost of the war.

The Battle

Philip's army marched toward Amphissa as if they were going to enforce the Amphictyonic Council's mandate, but, after occupying Cytinium (some 15 miles), they turned east to occupy the town of Elateia. From there, they could threaten Thebes without actually entering its province of Boeotia, thereby perhaps convincing Thebes to join Macedon or at least stay neutral. Control of those two towns also gave Philip control of the lines of communication back to Macedon. Philip then halted to await developments.

Demosthenes had hurried home to Athens to raise money and an army. He convinced the Athenian Assembly to dip into the theoric funds to pay for the military expansion. He also steeled the population's resolve as bad omens and prophecies spread through the city. Athenian troops soon marched to Boeotia and quartered themselves in Theban homes and then marched into the field. Troops were stationed at every pass in the mountain chain, which runs east-west parallel to the Cytinium-Elateia road; they also stationed a garrison north of Amphissa in the Gravia Pass. All of these deployments served to block Macedonian access to the Gulf of Corinth and any possible support from allies on the Peloponnesian peninsula. The key pass, however, was at Parapotamii, just south of Elateia, through which runs the Cephissus River and the main road to Thebes.

Throughout the winter of 339–338, the Greeks successfully defended these passes from any Macedonian probes. This raised the morale of both Thebes and Athens and made Demosthenes a major hero, but it failed to threaten the Macedonians because all these battles were defensive stands. Standing there would probably have ultimately forced Philip to withdraw because of lack of supplies and forage, but the longer the Greeks stood in camp, the more restless they grew; an army of Thebans, Athenians, allies, and mercenaries would have had a difficult time maintaining amicable relations. Thus, a waiting game favored the Greeks, but such was not their temperament.

Philip, a master at psychological warfare, set his disinformation campaign to work. He apparently spread rumors that he was about to withdraw and then allowed a fake letter to that effect to fall into enemy hands. To further this ruse, he withdrew his troops from Cytinium, at the northern end of the Gravia Pass. Both these actions resulted in the mercenary force stationed at Amphissa, at the southern end of the pass, to lower its guard. Philip then forced a night march through the pass, wiped out the defenders, and occupied Amphissa. Another quick thrust took troops to Naupactus, which was west of Amphissa on the Gulf of Corinth and which he occupied and turned over to his allies, the Aetolians. Now he had access to the gulf, by which he could obtain assistance from friends in the Peloponnese, and he was in a position to threaten the allied forces at Parapotamii. While he returned to Elateia, a detachment pillaged the countryside east of Amphissa.

Philip offered peace at this point, but Demosthenes's influence remained high, and he convinced both the Thebans and Athenians to remain steadfast. The allied troops holding the pass at Parapotamii pulled back to the plain before Chaeronea, robbing Philip of a chance to catch them in a pincer. Philip in turn withdrew the harassing force to join him at Elateia, and his reconstituted force marched through the pass to confront the allies. The Greeks deployed in a line perhaps a mile wide, anchoring their left flank on Mt. Petrachos, upon which the town of Chaeronea was situated, and their right flank on Mt. Acontion and the Cephissus River. Two small streams, the Haemon and Marius, flowed along their front and rear, respectively. The right half of the line was occupied by the Theban soldiers, numbering 800 cavalry and 12,000 infantry. The key element was the 300 members of the Sacred Band, 150 pairs of homosexual lovers who had been the elite of the Theban army for decades. The Athenians occupied the left of the line with 10,000 infantry and 600 cavalry. Troops of smaller provinces and mercenary soldiers filled out both contingents, the total number of allied troops numbering some 36,000 infantry and 2,000 cavalry.

Philip's army arrayed itself directly opposite the Greeks. His force numbered about

30,000 infantry and 2,000 cavalry and was much more highly trained and experienced than their foes. On the Macedonian left, command went to Alexander, Philip's 18-year-old son. Philip commanded the forces on the right flank, opposite the Athenians.

The most hotly contested arena was the northeastern Theban flank, where Alexander, in charge of the elite cavalry corps, the Companions, led the Macedonians against the Thebans led by the Sacred Band. The Macedonians slowly forced the Theban flank back. At the same time, the Athenians were pushing Philip's flank back. Whether this was from superior weight or skill, or through a ruse on Philip's part, is unknown. Either way, the advancing Athenians expended more energy than did the Macedonians. When word came that the Theban flank was buckling, Philip ordered his men to charge. Behind the original Athenian position had been the pass through which ran the road to Coroneia. This had been a potential route of retreat where Macedonian cavalry would be unable to operate. The Athenian advance, however, put at their back not the pass but Mt. Petrachos. Feeling the weight of the Macedonian attack, and realizing that their escape route was no longer available, Athenian morale broke. As the force collapsed, Alexander's wing was in a position to completely encircle the allied force. The battle ended in a rout, with some 1,000 Athenians killed and another 2,000 taken prisoner; the Theban army was virtually wiped out.

Results

In the wake of a hard-fought battle, Philip showed himself to be remarkably generous. He freed his prisoners and then sent Alexander to Athens to discuss terms. All Philip asked was to be named commander of Greek forces against Persia. Expecting the worst, the Athenians jumped at the chance to get off so easily. Philip assumed more than just a military position, however. He oversaw the creation of a league of Greek states, the Corinthian League, with which war against Persia could be conducted. All the members pledged men, money, and materiel for the campaign. Philip immediately began making plans for the war he had spent his life preparing to fight.

This league proved to be the most lasting Greek political body yet. Over the previous two centuries, Athens, Sparta, and Thebes had all tried and failed to lead a successful Greek national entity. Now, a foreign king succeeded in doing just that. Knowing that the Greeks were a notoriously independent-minded lot, however, Philip (and later Alexander) kept a representative in Greece to make sure no city-state began to reassert dominance. This both kept the peace and maintained Macedonian preeminence. Peace was a great boon to trade, and Philip and Alexander both saw the resources of Greece and its well-established trade routes as the foundation of their drive for empire. Peace was also good for culture, and Alexander in his conquests made sure that Greek philosophy and science was spread as far as his military could take it. This established a social fabric, Hellenism, that stretched from Greece to the borders of India, and became the foundation for the bulk of Roman culture as well.

Athens, Sparta, and Thebes had all struggled for local dominance; Athens came the closest with what it called an empire, but by and large it consisted of colonies designed to benefit the home country. Philip and Alexander, by unifying Greece under their control, took the Greeks much further than any Greek city-state could ever have done on its own. On the other hand, the Greek city-states never again exercised any real political power. They had since the early fifth century B.C. been the economic determinant in the Mediterranean; from 338 forward, they were under the thumb of someone else, Macedonian or Roman, for almost a thousand years.

References: Borza, Eugene. *In the Shadow of Olympus: The Emergence of Macedon.* Princeton, NJ: Princeton University Press, 1990; Ellis, John. *Philip II and Macedonian Imperialism.* London:

Thames & Hudson, 1976; Hammond, N. G. L. *Philip of Macedon.* Baltimore: Johns Hopkins University Press, 1994; Pickard-Cambridge, A. W. *Demosthenes.* New York: Putnam, 1914; Plutarch. *The Lives of the Noble Grecians and Romans.* Translated by John Dryden, revised by Arthur Hugh Clough. New York: Modern Library, 1979.

GAUGAMELA (ARBELA)

1 October 331 B.C.

FORCES ENGAGED

Greek: 47,000. Commander: Alexander.
Persian: Approximately 200,000.
Commander: Darius III.

IMPORTANCE

Alexander's victory ended the Persian Empire and opened territory all the way to India for Greek invasion and conquest.

Historical Setting

In the 350s B.C., Philip I assumed the throne of Macedon, a relatively poor province north of Greece. He developed a first-class army and, taking advantage of the temporary weakness of Athens (Greece's dominant city-state) after the Social War (358–355), began conquering Athenian-dominated provinces on the Greco-Macedonian frontier. While the Greek poleis continued their almost constant squabbling, Philip extended Macedonian control over areas to Macedon's north, and then he attacked Greece itself. In 338 B.C., Philip's army defeated an Athenian-Theban alliance at Chaeronea, giving him mastery of the Greek peninsula. He established the Hellenic League the following year, uniting almost all the Greek poleis into an alliance aimed at defeating the Persian Empire. As the forces of the Hellenic League prepared to cross the Hellespont into Asia Minor in 336, Philip was assassinated and succeeded by his son Alexander.

In spite of the fact that Alexander was only 20 years old, his tutelage at his father's side and his valor at the battle of Chaeronea earned him the immediate loyalty of his father's Macedonian army. The rest of the League was not as true, however. While putting down rebellions in the north, Alexander learned that Athens, thinking him dead, had left the League. He returned to Athens very much alive and reinforced his authority, and then he turned to continue his father's plan of invading Persia. Educated by Aristotle, Alexander was both a brilliant scholar and a Greek nationalist; he aimed not only to defeat Persia and revenge the destruction that they had inflicted on Greece in the invasion of Xerxes (480–479 B.C.) but to spread Greek culture and knowledge wherever he went.

Alexander quickly established a reputation as a courageous and innovative general, defeating armies sent against him by local Persian governors or by the Persian Emperor Darius III. His army established Greek control over Asia Minor, defeated Darius at Issus (333), and then secured the eastern Mediterranean coast. This gave Alexander control over all the harbors, thus denying Darius the use of his navy. Through the years 332–331, he extended his dominion to Egypt, where he was named pharaoh. This title made him officially the son of the highest god in the Egyptian pantheon, Amon-ra; that fact, coupled with the insistence of Alexander's mother, Olympias, that he was actually fathered not by Philip but by Zeus, greatly affected the Macedonian king. After his visit to the holy shrine at Siwa in Egypt, Alexander encouraged those who would deify him. Whether this was through megalomania or as a calculated attempt to play on the religious/political views of the Orient is a question debated for 2,300 years. It does seem that at this time, however, Alexander's intention not just to defeat Persia but to build a homogeneous world empire solidified.

After wintering in Egypt and establishing the city of Alexandria, Alexander marched his army in pursuit of Darius in 331. Darius had been busy since his defeat at Issus, building another army and preparing his strategy for luring Alexander into a decisive battle where Persian numerical superiority would come into full play. Darius placed his army on the left bank of the Tigris River on a large open plain 70 miles west of the town of Arbela and then waited for Alexander to discover this and come to him. Alexander obliged. He marched his army with little opposition across the Euphrates and Tigris Rivers, arriving at the village of Gaugamela at the end of September 331.

The main source for Alexander's campaign was written by the Roman historian Arrian several centuries after the battle. Arrian claimed, however, to have the journals of two of Alexander's generals as his source material, and his work is generally regarded as being as accurate as possible. However, his claim that Darius fielded an army of at least a million men is hotly disputed. Given the description of the units that Darius deployed at Gaugamela, modern sources estimate a Persian army of probably about

200,000 infantry and perhaps 45,000 cavalry. Darius placed much of his faith in victory in his 200 scythe-chariots and his fifteen elephants, the first time these war animals were used outside India. Alexander, whose army had received reinforcements from Macedonia, probably commanded 40,000 infantry and 7,000 cavalry. Thus, even the more conservative modern estimates of Persian strength still give Darius a five-to-one advantage in troop strength, and his choice of the plain around Gaugamela was based on giving his army room to move without being restricted by terrain features. Indeed, while awaiting Alexander's army, Darius had ordered the ground leveled even more, so his chariots would have no trouble attacking.

The Battle

Alexander arrived on high ground overlooking the plain at the end of September. He resisted the urging of some of his generals for an immediate attack, instead spending a day recon-

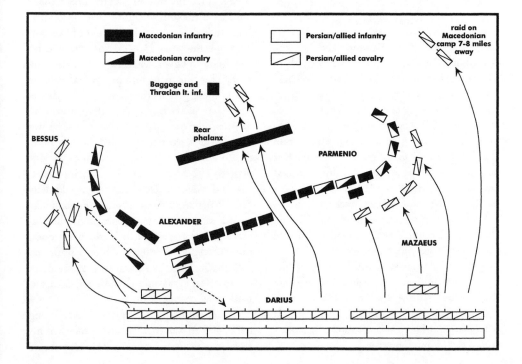

noitering the battlefield. This apparently gave Darius the impression that a night attack was in the offing, so he kept his troops awake all night for an attack, which did not come. Therefore, the next morning Alexander's men were rested and ready, whereas the Persian army was exhausted.

Darius deployed his army in traditional style: primarily infantry in the center and cavalry on the flanks, with the chariots spread out along the front and the elephants front and center. It was an army made up of troops from all parts of the Persian Empire, including some surviving Greek mercenaries, which had remained with him after the defeat at Issus. Knowing their discipline and familiarity with Greek tactics, Darius depended on the mercenaries to stabilize the forces surrounding them on the left side of the Persian line. Alexander's deployment was in much the same fashion, although his entire army when deployed was only as wide as Darius's center. Fearing a possible encirclement on either or both flanks, Alexander put cavalry forces at an angle on either flank to be prepared for such an eventuality and also created a second line of infantry in two bodies. These were to support the cavalry if a Persian flanking movement occurred or to act as a reserve for the main body to exploit any opportunity that might arise. The two sides faced each other on the morning of 1 October 331.

Alexander, commanding the cavalry on the Greek right flank, opened the battle. He moved his men forward in echelon: cavalry leading, lighter armed infantry just behind and to the left, and the heavy phalanx of infantry behind and to the left of them. They struck at the infantry units on the left of the Persian center. Seeing this group well ahead of the main Greek body, the Persian chariots moved forward to try and sweep the phalanx with their scythed wheels, but the light infantry used their speed and missile weapons to inflict casualties on the soldiers in the chariots or the horses pulling them, negating their effectiveness. The chariot attack was followed by some of the cavalry from the center of the Persian line. They broke through the gap between Alexander's right wing and the force in the Greek center, but rather than turning either left or right to envelop one or the other of the units, they instead kept riding forward to attack and loot the Greek base camp. By attacking, they had opened a gap in the Persian line that Alexander was quick to exploit. He drove his men into the gap and attacked straight at Darius, who rallied his troops for a while and then fled to save himself. His flight broke the morale of the Persian center and left flank, which soon followed him.

In the meantime, the Persian right wing had moved forward and engaged the Greek left, which was commanded by Parmenio, one of Alexander's most trusted subordinates. He had his hands full just maintaining his position against overwhelming numbers, but the second line that Alexander had placed in reserve came to his aid. That almost was not enough, and the Greek left wing was on the verge of collapse when Alexander, alerted to the peril, wheeled his wing about and struck the flank of the Persian right wing. That attack, coupled with the news that they just received of Darius's retreat, caused the Persian attack to disintegrate.

Accurate casualty counts are as impossible to determine as the total number of troops engaged. Arrian claims a mere 100 Greek deaths as opposed to 300,000 Persian; other Roman-era historians, Curtius and Diodorus, put the Persian losses at 40,000 and 90,000 while numbering the Greek casualties as 300 and 500, respectively. Modern estimates are no better than surmises, but it is clear that the Persians lost a significantly higher number of men than did Alexander's army.

Results

To officially claim the Persian Empire as his own, Alexander needed Darius in his custody. The need to go to Parmenio's aid, however, delayed that pursuit, and Darius got a comfortable head start. Alexander, therefore, decided to pursue him later and to seize the key Persian cities of Babylon, Susa, and Persepolis. Capture of these cities placed the wealth of the Persian Empire in Alexander's hands in addition to the political power he claimed. With the seat of the Persian government and treasury in his possession, Alexander then marched north toward Ecbatana (modern Hamadan, Iran) in search of Darius. Just as he was closing in on Darius, however, the deposed emperor was assassinated by Bessus, one of his own governors.

As Darius had been dealing with a disintegrating empire before the Greek invasion, Alexander realized that he could not stop conquering now. He had to impose his will on all the Persian possessions if he was to be recognized as emperor. He thus marched toward the Caspian Sea, conquering all who opposed him in Afghanistan, the Caucasus, and all the way into northwest India. Only the stubbornness of his troops stopped him from driving all the way through India toward the ocean; they had had enough fighting by 326, when they prevailed on their king to return to Persia and rule. The last stretch of the march went through the desert between India and modern Iraq, where thousands of Alexander's men died.

When he arrived in Susa in 324, Alexander gave up fighting and concentrated on administration. Still styling himself as semidivine, he fulfilled the Oriental view of such a monarch. By adopting that attitude, and by also adopting some Persian modes of dress and behavior, he impressed his newly conquered subjects while distressing his own men. The strain of mollifying the troops that had conquered for him, while trying to assimilate all the subject races and ethnic groups into a cohesive empire, proved too much for him. Alexander, always prodigious in his appetites, drank himself to death. At age 33 he died of a fever, which his alcoholism would not allow his body to resist.

Creating the largest empire ever known up until that time was significant enough as a result of Gaugamela and the battles that followed,

but more important was Alexander's mission. In possession of untold wealth and power, Alexander was more interested in unifying the world into a cooperative society. Although his tutor Aristotle had taught him that any non-Greek was merely a barbarian, Alexander came to believe that anyone who thought and acted in a positive fashion could be called civilized, whether Greek or Persian or any other group. Thus, people who acted badly were the barbarians, no matter their origin. The concept of one people, led by Greek intellect and vision, was just beginning to coalesce when Alexander died. Leaving behind no heir of ruling age, his generals soon destroyed his empire and much of his dream, but the spread of Greek culture into the Middle East continue in spite of the struggles of Alexander's successors. Philosophy, language, art, all the aspects of "civilization" in the lands from the Mediterranean to India, for centuries afterward were the legacy of the victory that Alexander accomplished at Gaugamela.

References: Arrian. *The Campaigns of Alexander.* Translated by Aubrey de Selincourt. Baltimore: Penguin, 1958; Creasy, Edward S. *Fifteen Decisive Battles of the World.* New York: Harper, 1851; Fuller, J. F. C. *A Military History of the Western World,* vol. 1. New York: Funk & Wagnalls, 1954; Keegan, John. *The Mask of Command.* New York: Little, Brown, 1982; Tarn, W. W. *Alexander the Great.* Cambridge, UK: Cambridge University Press, 1948.

IPSUS
Spring 310 B.C.

FORCES ENGAGED

Allied: 64,000 infantry, 15,000 mostly light cavalry, and 400 elephants. Commanders: Lysimachus and Seleucus.
Antigonid: 70,000 infantry, 10,000 mostly heavy cavalry, and 75 elephants. Commanders: Antigonus and Demetrius.

IMPORTANCE

Ipsus was the high point of the struggle among Alexander the Great's successors to create an international Hellenistic empire, which Antigonus failed to do.

Historical Setting

Legend has it that, when Alexander the Great lay dying in June 323 B.C., one of his subordinates asked who was to inherit his empire. The response was: "the strongest." The largest empire the world had yet known, stretching from Greece to the borders of India, could in reality only be held together by a man of Alexander's vision, and few men in history rise anywhere near that level. Alexander's only natural heir was an infant who, along with his mother Roxanne, was soon killed. Thus began the struggle to determine which of Alexander's subordinates could prove himself strongest.

Fairly quickly four men rose to serious contention. In Egypt, Ptolemy was Alexander's governor. He had the immense wealth of Egypt upon which to draw (vital for hiring Macedonian troops, the core of any successful army). He also had Alexander's body, which he acquired through some trickery in order to bury it at the shrine of Amon where Alexander was supposedly named a god. Unfortunately for him, Ptolemy lacked the bold temperament necessary to gamble for really high stakes. In Macedon itself was Antipater, left behind to maintain control over the homeland and Greece during Alexander's campaigns. Antipater soon died, however, and was succeeded by his son Cassander. Cassander was well placed to influence Alexander IV, nephew of the great conqueror, who was also a child, but the manpower and wealth of Macedon were both significantly diminished by Alexander's campaigns. In the east was Seleucus, who in time rose to governor in Babylon and thus could also draw upon a mass of wealth inherited (looted) from the Persian Empire. He was the last of the rivals to reach a significantly powerful position to challenge for the top spot and had the largest amount of land to try to maintain to have a stable base of operations.

The last of the rivals was Antigonus, the One-Eyed. A general serving for a time directly under Alexander, he possessed territory in the middle of the others, for his home base was Asia Minor. After Alexander established his authority in Asia Minor, he left Antigonus there as governor while he marched on to his victories in Egypt and Persia. Of all the men trying to succeed Alexander, Antigonus had the necessary military skill, wealth, troops, and ambition. His central position was both a blessing and a curse because he could defeat each of his enemies in detail if he was sufficiently skillful and lucky, or he could be surrounded if the other three could manage to bury their differences and cooperate. Of all the rivals, known as the Diodachi (Successors), he was the one to beat. The war to do so lasted for 15 years.

To trace the course of events leading to the battle of Ipsus in a brief account is virtually impossible. Suffice it to say that after 316 B.C., Antigonus found himself facing an almost constant alliance mounted by his three rivals. In the spring of 316, Antigonus had won the battle of Gabiene, near Susa in modern southwest Iran. That victory over Eumenes, chancellor of Macedon's government, gave Antigonus the largest number of Macedonian veterans, the removal of the man who controlled the upper part of Asia Minor, and access to the treasury that Eumenes controlled. With that, Antigonus had a large and well-trained army, a large territorial power base, and enough money to spend on troops and equipment. Antigonus's threatening manner toward Seleucus drove him to Ptolemy for aid, which began the coalition against Antigonus. Learning of Anitgonus's aggressive intent, Ptolemy sent word to Cassander in Macedon and Lysimachus, governor of Thrace (immediately west of Byzantium). In 315, Antigonus demanded an armistice on the basis of the status quo (which at that time would have isolated his rivals in Egypt and Macedon/Greece while he controlled everything else); they replied with a demand for an equitable distribution of land and wealth from Alexander's empire. Thus was born the alliance when Antigonus made himself a threat to all the others.

For the following 14 years, the fortunes of all these men waxed and waned. All made limited gains at each other's expense, for even the allies occasionally fought among themselves over the limits of power. None, however, could deliver a killing blow. Most of the fighting took place in the west, along the eastern Mediterranean shore, through Asia Minor, into Greece, and through the Aegean and eastern Mediterranean islands. It was a naval as well as military conflict that none could completely dominate. Throughout this give and take, Antigonus was served by one of his sons, Demetrius. He proved to be a commander of uncommon courage but of irregular quality. At times, he was brilliant in his dash and audacity; other times, he seemed too focused on a particular aspect of a campaign to sufficiently grasp the big picture. He was both the greatest asset and worst liability of Antigonus's campaigns.

In 306, Demetrius scored a major victory over Ptolemy's fleet off the city of Salamis in Cyprus. That secured for Antigonus his hold over the eastern Mediterranean islands and seaboard. In the wake of that victory, Antigonus named himself king and called on the others to recognize him as such. This would have conferred upon him the succession of Alexander's sovereignty. In response, Ptolemy named himself King of Egypt and urged Cassander in Macedon, Lysimachus in Greece, and Seleucus in Babylon to each name themselves king of their realms. By doing that, each was affirming that Alexander's empire no longer existed. With each of the rivals following Ptolemy's lead, the only way Alexander's empire could survive was through Antigonus.

Antigonus at that point should have launched a decisive campaign against each of his rivals in turn. He tried to do so in an invasion of Egypt, but bad weather and massive bribes from Ptolemy to the invading troops spelled defeat. Instead of renewing the invasion or turning toward one of his other rivals, Antigonus instead sent Demetrius to invade the island of Rhodes. Possession of that island would strengthen his naval power, but Demetrius overplayed his hand by demanding too much of the Rhodians, who, instead of cooperating, prepared for a siege. The resulting investment of the island took a year (305–304) and accomplished little in the end, while it gave Antigonus's rivals time to coordinate actions against him. Antigonus sent Demetrius to reestablish authority in Greece, and Demetrius did indeed deal Cassander's forces a severe blow, so much so that Cassander sued for peace with Antigonus. Instead of following up on that opening, Antigonus decided on a killing blow, which forced Cassander to appeal for direct assistance from Ptolemy and Seleucus. Finally, in 302, the allies began a coordinated effort against Antigonus; prior to this time, all their efforts had been basically chipping away at the edges.

The Battle

In 302, Lysimachus of Thrace, whose forces were supplemented by contingents from Cassander, invaded Asia Minor and began capturing cities loyal to Antigonus. Antigonus sent for Demetrius, who was in Greece and had Cassander in a death grip. Instead of finishing him off, Demetrius responded to his father's call, signed a truce, and sailed for Ionia. Cassander immediately sent even more troops to Lysimachus. Demetrius proceeded to campaign along the Ionian coast, reestablishing his father's authority. Antigonus, who was in the process of establishing a new capital city (Antigoneia, on the Orontes River in Syria), hastened with his own troops to meet the threat. While Demetrius marched up the coastline toward Byzantium, Antigonus cornered Lysimachus at the town of Dorylaeum. Lysimachus was in a strong defensive position that Antigonus was forced to try and reduce by siege;

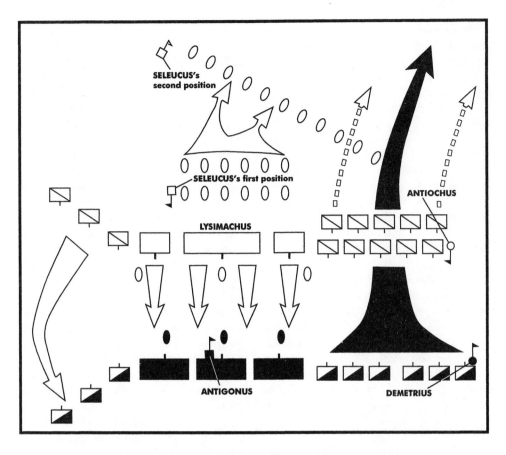

after several weeks, Lysimachus effected an extrication and established another strong position several miles to the north. As autumn was drawing to a close, he retreated again to northern Asia Minor into winter quarters. Antigonus returned to Dorylaeum for the winter, while Demetrius settled in to the northwest near the Hellespont. As winter arrived, so did Seleucus from Babylon, who encamped his forces east of Ankara. Ptolemy began marching northward from Egypt, but returned home upon hearing a false report that Antigonus had won a great victory.

In the spring of 302, the forces combined, Demetrius marching to Dorylaeum to join his father, while Lysimachus and Seleucus met somewhere near Ankara. Where the north-south road between Dorylaeum and Synnada

intersected the old Persian Royal Road lies flat terrain near the town of Ipsus, modern Sipsin. Antigonus was able to field an army of 70,000 infantry, 10,000 heavy Macedonian cavalry, and about 75 elephants. His opponents possessed 64,000 infantry and probably about 15,000 cavalry. This was the lighter Persian-type cavalry, used more for archery harassment than for massed charges. Seleucus had acquired 500 elephants from the Indian King Chandragupta in return for not invading India; by the time of the battle, he still had about 400.

There are no contemporary accounts of the battle at Ipsus. Plutarch's *Lives* has a chapter on Demetrius, and this is the main source of information. The dispositions seem to have been thus: both armies stationed their infantry in phalanx formation in the center of their lines. Antigonus placed Demetrius in command of his heavy cavalry on one wing with the light cavalry held back on the other. Opposite Demetrius was the bulk of the Seleucid cavalry, with a smaller contingent on the opposite flank. Antigonus lined his elephants in a screen along his front, while Lysimachus commanded about 100 elephants in a screen before his army. Seleucus commanded the remaining 300 elephants somewhere in the rear. Apparently Antigonus's plan was to have Demetrius and the heavy cavalry break the Seleucid cavalry on the enemy flank and then wheel into the infantry rear. His advancing infantry would then play the anvil to Demetrius's hammer.

The battle started well enough for Antigonus. Demetrius's attack did indeed force the allied cavalry from the field. It has been argued whether this was an actual or a feigned retreat; whichever, it accomplished the allies' purpose. Demetrius, caught up in the moment, pursued the retreating cavalry completely off the field and took himself out of the battle. Seleucus then deployed his reserve elephants in a screen behind his infantry, so that if Demetrius returned he could not engage.

The smaller light cavalry unit then advanced against Antigonus's phalanx flank and rear, showering arrows down into the mass of bodies. There was apparently a heated encounter between the two elephant screens, of which Lysimachus seems to have gained the upper hand. The archery fire, coupled with the advance of Lysimachus's infantry, broke the spirit of Antigonus's troops. Many surrendered immediately, while most of the rest fled. Antigonus, convinced that his son would return, stood his ground as his army began melting away. He was at this time 81 years old and had decided before the battle that he would win or die. He therefore died fighting, for Demetrius did not return. Instead, after learning the outcome of the battle, he led 4,000 cavalry and 5,000 surviving infantry back to Ephesus.

Results

"The battle of Ipsos was a turning point in history. A decisive victory for Antigonos and Demetrios would have enabled Antigonos to recover control over such of the upper satrapies [Persian provinces] as he wished, and Kassandros —a great part of whose army fought at Ipsos— would not have had sufficient strength to withstand a new assault on Macedon. Only Ptolemy would have been left of Antigonos's enemies, and he could have been dealt with at leisure" (Billows, *Antigonos the One-Eyed and the Creation of the Hellenistic State,* p. 183). That is true enough, but such a scenario would have depended on Antigonus remaining alive, which, at 81, would have been only for a limited time. Demetrius would have been his successor, and it has been shown that he did not have the consistency necessary to succeed his father. Still, with the land and wealth of Asia Minor, the Levant, and Persia to draw upon, neither Cassander nor Ptolemy really was in a position to challenge either Antigonus or Demetrius. Thus, a revived Alexandrian empire could have been a strong probability. Instead, the result of the battle at Ipsus was that the multiple monarchies proclaimed in 305 B.C. accomplished what Ptolemy had intended, the de facto breakup of the empire.

Antigonus, by losing his final battle and failing to accomplish his dream, has been regarded by history as little more than a failure. In reality, his tenure in command of Asia Minor and the Levant established a bureaucracy that survived him by centuries. Had he won, Antigonus would have centered his empire not in Persia, as Alexander did, but in Syria. That central location would have been much more able to control events than an administration far to the east. Antigonus also began a campaign of colonization that resulted in the founding of many of the major cities of western Asia. By claiming kingship (although of humble birth), he established a theory of monarchy that lasted for centuries. He was elevated to divine status by the people of Greece, which only Alexander had accomplished before him. The concept of "divine right of kings" thus gained its foundation, influencing monarchs for the next two millennia.

As Rome was beginning its long rise to power in the near future, a strong power in the eastern Mediterranean could have presented a serious threat to Roman expansion. Instead, Seleucus established a short-lived empire based on Persia that soon fell to the Parthians. He failed to establish himself in Macedon after defeating Lysimachus in 283 because he was assassinated by Ptolemy's son, Ptolemy Keraunos, in 280. Thus, the eastern Mediterranean and Persia broke into rival monarchies that could not stand before the power of Rome.

References: Bar-Lochva, Bezalel. *The Seleucid Army.* New York: Cambridge University Press, 1976; Billows, Richard A. *Antigonos the One-Eyed and the Creation of the Hellenistic State.* Berkeley: University of California Press, 1990; Cary, M. *The History of the Greek World, from 323 to 146 B.C.* London: Methuen & Co., 1932; Diodorus. *Diodorus of Sicily.* Translated by C. H. Oldfather. Cambridge, MA: Harvard University Press, 1933–1952; Plutarch. *The Lives of Noble Grecians and Romans.* Translated by John Dryden, revised by Arthur Hugh Clough. New York: Modern Library, 1979.

METAURUS RIVER
207 B.C.

FORCES ENGAGED
Roman: 50,000. Commander: Caius Claudius Nero.
Carthaginian: 50,000. Commander: Hasdrubal Barca.

IMPORTANCE
Carthaginian defeat ended the attempt to reinforce Hannibal, dooming his effort in Italy, and Rome was able to establish dominance over Spain.

Historical Setting

Carthage, near the site of modern Tunis, started as a colony of Phoenicia. As the Phoenician cities of Tyre and Sidon waned because of invasions, many of their wealthy citizens emigrated to Carthage. Soon, it was the dominant city in northern Africa, controlling western Mediterranean trade and the grain production of the region. Carthage's wealthy merchant class fielded armies of mercenaries recruited primarily from Spain. With these, they subdued local tribes and enforced their trading monopoly. Economic rivalry with the Greek colony of Massilia (Marseilles) led to raids on the city and its shipping, but Massilia's ties to Rome led to war.

Rome and Carthage had maintained fairly amicable relations for decades; treaties recognized spheres of influence for both. In 265 B.C., Roman forces finished conquering all of Italy for Rome. Because Rome was gradually expanding into Gaul (France) as well, and therefore into the region of Massilia, Carthage's aggression was worrisome. It was not Massilia, however, but Sicily that provided the spark for war between the two regional powers.

A group of Italian adventurers calling themselves Mamertines ("Sons of Mars") began conquering towns in Sicily. They appealed to Rome and Carthage for aid when King Hiero of Syracuse went to war against them, and both responded, probably in hopes of gaining dominance over the island themselves. The Carthaginians relieved the Mamertines first, but, fearing their proximity, the Romans entered into an alliance with Hiero against them. Thus began the First Punic War. It lasted from 264 to 241 B.C., with both sides fighting themselves to exhaustion. As the war progressed, Rome began construction of a battle fleet, the first navy they had ever built. Neither side could really impose its will on the other, but, after the Roman naval victory at the Aegates Islands in 241, they were able to dictate the terms of peace. Carthage was forced to abandon any

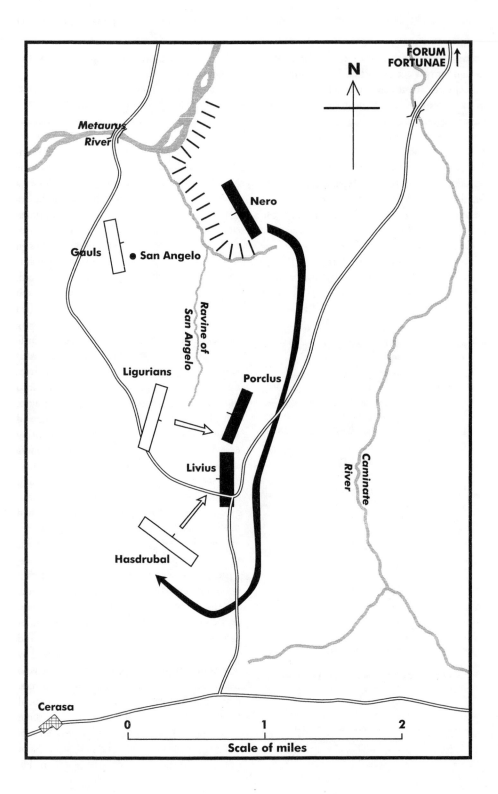

FORUM
FORTUNAE

N

Metaurus
River

Nero

Gauls

● San Angelo

Ravine of
San Angelo

Ligurians

Porclus

Livius

Caminate
River

Hasdrubal

Cerasa

0   1   2

Scale of miles

claims to Sicily, which Rome then claimed as its own, except for Syracuse at the western end of the island. Carthage was also forced to pay a hefty amount in reparations.

Relations between the two powers remained tense for the next two decades. In 238 B.C., Rome seized Sardinia, after Carthaginian mercenaries occupying the island rebelled against their masters. From 225 to 222 B.C., the Romans had their hands full beating back an invasion from Gaul, and then they went to war against Illyria on the eastern Adriatic coast, defeating them and establishing Roman preeminence in 219. That same year, war clouds began to loom with Carthage again. The treaty that ended the First Punic War divided Spain into spheres of influence as well, with Rome dominant above the Ebro River and the Carthaginians in control below it. The point of conflict was the town of Saguntum, well south of the Ebro on the Mediterranean coast, but with a government favorable to Rome. When Hannibal of Carthage besieged the city, the elders of Saguntum appealed to Rome for aid. It has long been argued whether this was a deliberate attempt on Hannibal's part to provoke a war with Rome, but that was the outcome. When Hannibal refused to lift the siege in 219 B.C., Rome declared war. Hannibal captured the city after 8 months and then initiated plans for an invasion of Italy. In the spring of 218, he began an overland march with 90,000 men through the Pyrenees, southern Gaul, and through the Alps into northern Italy by October. He had remaining only 20,000 infantry, 6,000 cavalry, and a few of his original eighty elephants. This invasion surprised the Roman government, who had to cancel their own operations to deal with Hannibal. They did poorly. For the next 17 years, Hannibal was able to march at will through the Italian peninsula, defeating virtually every force the Romans fielded against him. The constant fighting, however, forced him to recruit local soldiers of dubious quality and loyalty. Needing reinforcements, he called for his brother Hasdrubal to come to his aid.

The Battle

While Hannibal campaigned in Italy (never able to capture Rome, however), the Romans committed troops to Spain in hopes of severing the lines of communication that Hannibal had back to Carthage. The Romans controlled the sea lanes, but the Carthaginians were able to transport men and materiel across the Straits of Gibraltar through Spain. Roman fortunes in Spain varied, but brightened with the appointment of Publius Cornelius Scipio to command. His predecessors had lost Roman territory north of the Ebro, but he regained it and marched south of the river with the intent of engaging Hasdrubal's army. After an inconclusive battle in 108 B.C. near modern Cordova, Hasdrubal responded to his brother's call for reinforcements, realizing that to march his army into Italy could mean abandoning Spain to Scipio. Hasdrubal marched into southern Gaul and wintered there, recruiting troops. In the spring of 207, he crossed the Alps with 50,000 men, about half of them Gauls. He proceeded to lay siege to Placentia, but abandoned that and moved southward to Fanum Fortunae (Fano) on the Adriatic. There he encountered Roman forces under M. Livius Salinator.

Hannibal, knowing his brother was on his way but ignorant of his progress or whereabouts, remained in winter quarters in the south of Italy. When he learned of the investment of Placentia, he began moving north but taking his time, knowing a siege could be lengthy. He established a camp at Canusium (Canosa) and awaited word. His movement was shadowed by Roman forces under Caius Claudius Nero, who remained between the two Carthaginian forces. Luckily for Nero, his men captured two of Hasdrubal's couriers and learned from them Hasdrubal's intention to march south and join his brother in the province of Umbria. Nero gambled that there were no other couriers. He

*Hannibal recognizes the head of his brother,
Hasdrubal. Eighteenth-century painting.
(Corbis/Francis G. Mayer)*

left a covering force watching Hannibal but led a contingent of 6,000 of his best infantry and 1,000 cavalry to join with Livius. He sent word for the farmers along his line of march to have provisions ready for his men, and by traveling light he was able to reach Fanum Fortunae in 7 days and then secretly entered Livius's camp in darkness.

Nero convinced Livius and his officers to give battle as quickly as possible, before Hasdrubal could learn of his arrival, but Hasdrubal had deduced the fact already and was not going to fight. He withdrew under cover of darkness with the intent of retreating up the Via Flaminia, but his guides deserted him and he was therefore delayed in reaching that road. Nero was soon in pursuit and caught up to Hasdrubal near the Metaurus River, probably along the modern Ravine of San Angelo.

Hasdrubal hastily deployed his men in three sections: Gauls on his left (northern) flank behind a ravine, Ligurian troops in the center fronted by war elephants, and Spanish troops on the left, which he commanded. The Romans drew up in mirror image, with Nero commanding a body on the Roman right flank opposite the Gauls across the ravine, the praetor Porcius in the center, and the consul Livius on the Roman left flank. In neither of the armies were the three sections deployed closely alongside each other. The Spaniards attacked first while the Ligurians, soldiers from northern Italy described by Livy as "a hardy race of warriors," closed with Porcius. With the deep ravine separating them, Nero could not come to grips with the Gauls. He soon realized that they could not come to grips with him either, so, leaving a small contingent to watch them, he abandoned his position and marched his men southward behind the battle and then swung right onto the rear of the Spaniards. In spite of Hasdrubal's brilliant leadership, the troops buckled under the weight of the pincer. The Carthaginian commander intentionally rode directly at the Romans in order to die fighting, which he did. The elephants, which had at first caused serious disarray in the Roman center, became uncontrollable and had to be killed by their riders. The Carthaginian effort fell apart.

Results

The number of Carthaginian dead was around 10,000, with the Roman dead numbering some 2,000. Nero did not pause to savor his victory, but instead initiated another forced march south. He returned to his force covering Hannibal after only 6 days. News of the victory caused riotous celebration in Rome, for it was the first major victory the Romans had scored over the Carthaginians in Italy. Legend has it that Hannibal learned of the outcome of the battle when a Roman rider approached his camp and threw a weighted sack into his lines. When it was taken to Hannibal and opened, Hasdrubal's head was found inside. Whatever the mode of discovery, Hannibal retired southward in the toe of Italy to the port of Bruttium, the port where he received what supplies Carthaginian ships could deliver to him.

For 11 years Hannibal had had his own way in Italy, defeating every force the Romans could send against him. Still, the constant warfare and inability to recruit quality troops locally meant that he had to have reinforcements if he was going to capture Rome itself and dictate terms. Hasdrubal's defeat near the Metaurus River meant that would not happen. Hannibal remained in Italy for another 6 years, but his dwindling force was increasingly unable to implement his brilliant command. The Romans for years had followed the advice of Q. Fabius Cunctator, which was to implement a strategy of attrition, introducing so-called Fabian warfare. After the Metaurus victory, however, the morale boost meant that Rome could continue to not only get recruits for their army, but that the Italian towns and tribes that Hannibal had so desperately tried to convince to abandon Rome would also be heartened and remain loyal. Had Hasdrubal joined with his brother, the resulting force could well have captured Rome and changed the fortunes of the Mediterranean basin.

By marching the bulk of Carthaginian forces through Gaul into Italy, Hasdrubal abandoned Spain to Rome's successful general Scipio, who proceeded to defeat any and all Carthaginian generals sent against him. In 206 B.C. at the battle of Ilipa, Scipio defeated a 70,000-man Carthaginian army with only 48,000 Romans. This expelled Carthage from its long dominance of Iberia and placed Rome in control for another 600 years. Not until the

Visigoths arrived in the early fifth century A.D. would Rome surrender Spain. Roman rule increased Spain's productivity and wealth far beyond what the Carthaginians had already begun, and the introduction of Roman administration methods became the basis of Spanish government even after the barbarians arrived. With Spain under its control, Rome drew on the manpower that Carthage had been tapping for centuries for its mercenary armies, and, because the Carthaginian people themselves rarely fought, their ability to keep the war going was severely hampered. Rome in 207 B.C. took a major step toward establishing itself as an imperial power.

References: Creasy, Edward S. *Fifteen Decisive Battles of the World.* New York: Harper, 1851; Dorey, T. A., and D. R. Dudley. *Rome against Carthage.* Garden City, NY: Doubleday, 1972; Fuller, J. F. C. *A Military History of the Western World,* vol. 1. New York: Funk & Wagnalls, 1954; Lazenby, J. F. *Hannibal's War: A Military History of the Second Punic War.* Warminster, UK: Aris & Phillips, 1978; Livy. *The War with Hannibal.* Translated by Aubrey de Selincourt. Baltimore: Penguin, 1965.

KAI-HSIA
203 B.C.

FORCES ENGAGED

Han: 300,000 men. Commander: Liu Pang, also known as Kao-ti.

Ch'u: 100,000 men. Commander: Hsiang Yu.

IMPORTANCE

Liu Pang's victory removed his last rival for power in China and allowed him to establish the Han dynasty.

Historical Setting

Established in the eleventh century B.C., the Chou dynasty had been seriously weakened after the loss of its capital city in 771. The dynasty reestablished itself to the east in Loyang in the central Chinese plains. It flourished for a time, but by the fourth century B.C. a number of rulers began to claim independence for their regions. Eight kingdoms emerged, and, although the Chou dynasty officially still existed, each of the kings strove to establish his own ruling line. The eight fought each other for a century and a half (401–256 B.C.) in what has come to be called the Era of the Warring States. In 256, a new ruler came to the throne of the westernmost state, Ch'in. As ruler, his title was Ch'in Shi Huang-ti. Between 230 and 221 B.C., Shi Huang-ti conquered his seven rivals and unified China into an empire. His reign was relatively brief, and he left behind no strong successor after his death in 210, so rebellions quickly began breaking out across the new empire.

Two men fought their way into contention to replace the falling dynasty. One was Hsiang Yu, a professional soldier described as a huge, uncultured man, but an outstanding military leader. His homeland was Ch'u, in modern east-central China, and had been the largest of the warring states. His main rival was Liu Pang, born a commoner but rising to hold a minor bureaucratic position in the administration of Shi Huang-ti.

Hsiang Yu established his reputation while leading Ch'u forces against those of the dying Ch'in Empire. That recognition brought support from other regions in rebellion, which were willing to follow him. He, along with his uncle, had started an uprising in the province of Ch'u in 209, and he soon led a growing army northwestward toward the capital city of Hsien-yang. Liu Pang, who had been raising forces in the north in modern Hubei province, marched to join Hsiang Yu in the fourth month of 208. Together they named a new king of Ch'u as a rival to the Ch'ins and then marched to relieve a Ch'in siege of Chu-lu; there Hsiang Yu scored a major victory that vaulted him to preeminent command of all the provinces arrayed against the Ch'in.

While Hsiang Yu was engaged at Chu-lu, the king of Ch'u had dispatched Liu Pang to attack the territory around the Ch'in capital at Hsien-yang. In that area, Liu Pang scored a number of victories, culminating with a battle at Lan-t'ien in the tenth month of 206. After that battle, the final Ch'in king fell into his hands, and that allowed Liu Pang to occupy the capital. The records indicate that Liu Pang was a wise and tolerant victor, and he began reforming some of the harsher Ch'in legal practices under which much of the population had suffered. All was peaceful in Hsien-yang until Hsiang Yu arrived 2 months later. He ordered the Ch'in king executed and then allowed his men to pillage the city after he had looted the treasury for himself and his officers. Such actions alienated Liu Pang, who for a time remained passive.

Hsiang Yu began reorganizing China, not along the Ch'in lines of centralized rule but by decreeing the creation of nineteen minor kingdoms, which were to operate within a confederacy, which he would lead. He was able to assume that position by killing the king he had recently enthroned in Ch'u. Liu Pang was awarded with one of the three kingdoms carved out of the original Ch'in territory, his being located in the southern part of the region, that is, the most remote. Probably Hsiang Yu was looking to distance himself from a leader who was a strong potential rival. That territory had been the region of Han, and Liu Pang named himself the king of Han. The reward of such a poor area in return for his services, as well as rumors that the advisors of Hsiang Yu were recommending that he have Liu Pang assassinated, motivated the new king of Han to challenge his former ally.

The Battle

Liu Pang went on campaign in the fifth month of 206, beginning by conquering the other kingdoms of the west that had made up the old Ch'in homeland. As he advanced toward

Loyang, word came that Hsiang Yu had murdered the king of Ch'u. That inspired Liu Pang to call for a general rising of the provinces to aid him in punishing a regicide. A quick strike at Hsiang Yu's capital city of P'eng-ch'eng was a disaster, however, and Liu Pang found himself defeated by his enemy's army. Only a timely storm covered his escape along with only a few dozen cavalry. Things looked grim; not only were the provincial kings beginning to join Hsiang Yu but also he had captured some of Liu Pang's family, including his father. The only positive in this entire situation was the work of Liu Pang's loyal generals, who continued to raise troops for him and seize provinces away from the main theater of battle.

Liu Pang's luck did not improve. In a strike at Hsing-yang on the Yellow River, he once again found himself besieged and escaped with only a few men. Hsiang Yu was unable to take advantage of this because Liu Pang's subordinate, General Han Hsin, was conquering provinces in the east. At one point, the enemy armies encamped for several months on either side of the Yellow River at Guangwu. Hsiang Yu threatened to execute Liu Pang's father, but to no avail. Failing that, Hsiang Yu challenged his foe to determine everything in single combat, but Liu Pang knew that he was no physical match for Hsiang Yu. From a distance, however, Hsiang Yu was able to hit Liu Pang with a crossbow bolt that wounded but did not kill him. Liu Pang withdrew from the river to the nearby city of Chenggao, where Hsiang Yu once again besieged him.

Liu Pang's subordinates were so successful in liberating provinces that Hsiang Yu had conquered and harassing his supply lines, that Hsiang Yu was forced at one point to take a part of his army to recover some of his losses. While Hsiang Yu was gone, Liu Pang's army provoked a battle with the remaining besiegers and defeated them. Hearing of that, Hsiang Yu marched his men back, but Liu Pang refused to give battle, retreating into the mountains. Hsiang Yu at this point (203 B.C.) offered Liu

Pang a deal: divide China between them, with Liu Pang being lord of the west and Hsiang Yu being lord of the east. Liu Pang agreed and received his hostage relatives in return. The agreement was short-lived. Liu Pang's subordinates convinced him that the tide had turned and that many of the provincial leaders now supported him. That, plus the fact that the Ch'u forces were exhausted from their continued marching and were short on supplies, convinced Liu Pang to return to the east for a final battle.

The confrontation took place at Kai-hsia, in modern Anhui province. For the first time, some of Liu Pang's subordinates hesitated to join him, but with assurances that they would be rewarded with provinces of their own after the war, they marched. At Kai-hsia, Hsiang Yu built himself a walled camp, which Liu Pang's forces surrounded in the twelfth month of 202. The only relatively contemporary account describes Liu Pang in command of 300,000 men and Hsiang Yu in charge of 100,000. The battle started with General Han Hsin attacking the Ch'u center, but failing to break through. He withdrew, and Generals Kong and Bi attacked from the flanks. As the Ch'u army began to falter, Han Hsin renewed his attack in the center, and the enemy retreated to its camp.

After a night of drinking and tears with his wife, Hsiang Yu gathered 800 cavalry and broke out of his surrounded camp in the early morning darkness. The following morning, when Liu Pang learned what had happened, he dispatched 5,000 cavalry in pursuit. Hsiang Yu crossed the Huai River at the head of only 100 horsemen. Lost, he stopped and asked a farmer for directions. He was tricked and rode into a swamp, where the Han cavalry cornered him. Surrounded, Hsiang Yu was defiant. He swore to his men that Heaven was against him and that nothing he had ever done in battle had warranted such a fate. To prove his worthiness, he told his men, "For your sake I shall break through the enemy's encirclements, cut down their leaders, and sever their banners, that you may know it is Heaven which has destroyed me and no fault of mine in arms" (Sima Qian, *Records of the Grand Historian: Han Dynasty I*, pp. 45–46).

Promising to kill an enemy general, he divided his remaining men into four squadrons, each to ride down from their encircled hilltop in a different direction, and then reassemble on the east side. His charge scattered the Han cavalry, and he did kill a general and then rejoined his men. They formed into three groups this time, and the returning Han horsemen did not know which group Hsiang Yu was in, so they divided into three groups as well and again surrounded them. Another charge resulted in Hsiang Yu killing a colonel and a reported 50 to 100 men. Again regrouping, he found that his force had lost only 2 men. This running battle drifted southward toward the Yangtze River. There a boatman offered to aid his escape, but Hsiang Yu would not delay Heaven's judgment. He gave the man his horse, which he had ridden in 5 years of combat, and then led his men dismounted back to face the Han. After a fierce fight and being wounded numerous times, Hsiang Yu was surrounded. Knowing a price was on his head as a reward, he removed it with his own sword.

Results

After Hsiang Yu's death, all of his domain of Ch'u surrendered, except for the city of Lu. Liu Pang set out with his entire army to capture the city, which refused to submit. Moved by their courage, Liu rode up to the city walls with Hsiang Yu's head. Upon seeing that, they surrendered and were treated with honor. He also buried the dismembered body of Hsiang Yu with full honors and refused to execute any of his family.

After the battle, Liu Pang's subordinates urged him to take the title *huang-ti*, emperor. He accepted the title, and thus he began the Han dynasty, taking the throne name Kao-ti. He was regarded as a good emperor, reigning until 195. After a few years of struggle, he had inherited the united empire formed by Ch'in Shih Huang-ti, and he and his successors improved and expanded it.

Although at first anti-intellectual, Kao-ti realized over time the benefits of wise men, and he overturned the ban on books that Shih Huang-ti had implemented. Kao-ti embraced the teachings of Confucianism; he saw in it the means to rule well. Confucius taught that a good leader would inspire his people, and so Confucian scholars in a bureaucracy, leading the administration, should be the path to a secure and prosperous country. The bureaucracy that administered China until the twentieth century began here and survived through multiple successive dynasties. Kao-ti attempted to retain the administrative organization of the Ch'in emperor, keeping the country divided into provinces overseen by appointed imperial governors. He had to keep his promise, however, to reward his generals. He did so, but over time transferred them around until they became more governors than lords.

The most successful of the Han emperors was Wu Ti (147–81), who extended Han borders well to the west. He was successful in defeating the Hsiung-nu, driving them westward across Asia's steppes until they arrived a few hundred years later in western Europe as the Huns. The Han dynasty also revived and expanded the trade with the west along the famous Silk Road. Securing that trade route, as well as mounting military and exploratory expeditions, Han envoys reportedly traveled as far as Parthia (modern Iran), where the Roman Empire occasionally fought. The dynasty that Liu Pang established in the wake of his victory at Kai-hsia consolidated the beginnings of the empire that Shih Huang-ti instituted, handing down to later dynasties a unified population, which to this day call themselves the "people of Han."

References: Grousset, René. *The Rise and Splendour of the Chinese Empire.* Translated by Anthony Watson-Gandy and Terence Gordon. Berkeley: University of California Press, 1953;

Sima Qian. *Records of the Grand Historian: Han Dynasty I.* Translated by Burton Watson. New York: Columbia University Press, 1993; Twitchett, Denis, and Michael Loewe. *The Cambridge History of China,* vol. 1. New York: Cambridge University Press, 1986.

ZAMA
202 B.C.

FORCES ENGAGED
Roman: 34,000 infantry and 9,000 cavalry. Commander: Publius Cornelius Scipio.
Carthaginian: 45,000 infantry and 3,000 cavalry. Commander: Hannibal Barca.

IMPORTANCE
Roman victory brought an end to the Second Punic War and made Rome the dominant power in the western Mediterranean while severely weakening Carthage.

Historical Setting

In 218 B.C., the Second Punic War had just gotten under way. Hannibal Barca, Carthaginian commander in Spain, had challenged Roman power in 219 B.C. by laying siege to the city of Saguntum. According to the treaty concluded at the end of the First Punic War, the city lay within a region recognized as under Carthage's suzerainty, but the fact that Saguntum had a pro-Roman government brought a Roman declaration of war. Hannibal responded by capturing the city and then staging a brilliant forced march through the Pyrenees, southern Gaul (France), and through the Alps into northern Italy.

Hannibal's arrival in the Po River valley forced the Roman government to cancel its original plan to land forces in Spain. Consul Publius Cornelius Scipio sailed to Massilia (Marseilles), but failed to catch Hannibal in time, so then marched down the coast into Italy to fight the invader. Meanwhile, his brother,

Gnaeus Cornelius Scipio, sailed to Spain, landed in nominally Roman territory north of the Ebro River, and secured the region by defeating Hanno, one of Hannibal's brothers. Having little luck against Hannibal in Italy, Publius Scipio was later transferred to Spain to aid his brother. They campaigned in central Spain but were defeated and killed in 211 by another of Hannibal's brothers, Hasdrubal. The Roman Senate, desperate for a general who could score some victories, in 210 B.C. named Publius Cornelius Scipio to command in Spain. This was the son of the Publius killed the previous year. Although only 25 years old, he commanded instant respect and launched a military career that never knew defeat.

In 209, Scipio went into action north of the Ebro, securing again for Spain the land between that river and the Pyrenees. Then, in a bold move bordering on rashness, he sailed down the east coast of Spain with more than 27,000 men and attacked and captured the Carthaginian capital of Spain, New Carthage (Cartagena). This placed him in a position to threaten the lines of communication of Carthage's army in Spain, and Hasdrubal marched to face the danger. At Baecula in 208, the two armies fought an inconclusive battle; Hasdrubal withdrew north and crossed into Italy along the same route his brother had taken 10 years earlier. Scipio did not pursue, instead searching out the remaining Carthaginian forces in Spain under Mago and Hasdrubal Gisco. He defeated them in 206 at the battle of Ilipa, where his army of 48,000 crushed an enemy force of 70,000.

Scipio was at this point master of Spain and, with Hasdrubal Barca's defeat at the Metauraus River, Hannibal was isolated in Italy. Planning to use Spain as his base to invade North Africa, Scipio secretly traveled to Numidia (Tunisia) to deal with the two primary Numidian leaders, Syphax and Massinissa. Scipio entered into an alliance with the latter, whereas the former sided with Carthage. Scipio was invited by the Senate to return to Rome to receive his honors for his victories and to retire, but he was intent on taking the war to Carthage. Older senators and military leaders, jealous of his youth and success, instead granted him command of Sicily. Rome had dominated the bulk of the island since the end of the First Punic War, except for the kingdom of Syracuse. When Syracuse allied with Carthage in the Second Punic War in 213 B.C., the Roman general Marcellus laid siege for 2 years before finally overcoming the city's defenses. Placing Scipio in charge was more an exile than a reward because the troops occupying the island were veterans of Roman defeats at Hannibal's hands. Undaunted, Scipio began retraining the beaten troops while recruiting new soldiers, and in 204 he was prepared to sail for Africa whether the Senate liked it or not.

The Battle

Because Rome had command of the sea, Scipio in 204 B.C. easily was able to transport 30,000 men across the Mediterranean to North Africa and lay siege to the city of Utica (in modern Tunisia). He had to abandon the siege, however, at the approach of a Carthaginian force under Hasdrubal Gisco and the Numidian leader Syphax. Near the coast, Scipio established a fortified camp, which seemed too isolated to hold for long. Hasdrubal therefore offered Scipio peace terms, which the Roman seemed eager to negotiate. In fact, he was lulling his enemies into a false sense of security; as he was talking with them, he was planning a surprise attack on their camps. In the darkness, Scipio attacked Hasdrubal's camp while his Numidian ally Massinissa attacked Syphax's camp. The results were devastating for the Carthaginians. The encampments were set afire and reportedly 40,000 men were killed by the flames or while escaping them, with another 5,000 men taken prisoner. The Carthaginian commanders escaped, but left behind virtually their entire army. Scipio proceeded to reinvest Utica.

The government of Carthage was so shocked by this development that they ordered Hannibal, after 16 years of campaigning in Italy, to return home. This accomplished the first of Scipio's goals: to take the war out of his homeland. Hannibal complied with his orders and embarked his 15,000 to 20,000 men for the voyage home on 23 June 203 B.C. With their most successful commander at hand, the Carthaginians gained heart and rejected Scipio's rather generous peace terms. Outraged at this response, Scipio marched up the coast toward Carthage, burning every village along the way. At that, the rulers of Carthage urged Hannibal into action. He did not want to fight because his soldiers were either veterans exhausted from their long Italian campaign or raw recruits with little training or ability. Knowing also that Scipio's force far outclassed his in cavalry, Hannibal marched out of Carthage, but contacted Scipio about negotiating. The two met at Zama, about 5 miles southwest of Carthage, and Hannibal offered Rome everything outside of Africa, but Scipio refused; after all, he reasoned, how could he trust Carthaginian promises?

Hannibal returned to his camp and prepared for battle. He deployed his men in three parallel lines: in front were the Gauls, both from southern France and from Liguria in northern Italy; in the second line he placed his weakest troops, the newly recruited Carthaginians and others from area tribes; in the rear he placed his most trusted veterans. Carthaginian cavalry was deployed on his right flank, with Numidian cavalry under Syphax on his left. Across his entire front he ranged his elephants. In total, he had approximately 45,000 infantry and 3,000 cavalry.

Scipio faced him with his 34,000 infantry in three lines as well, but out of the usual Roman formation. The Roman army was organized into maniples, or companies, numbering between 120 and 180 men. They normally deployed in a checkerboard fashion, but Scipio

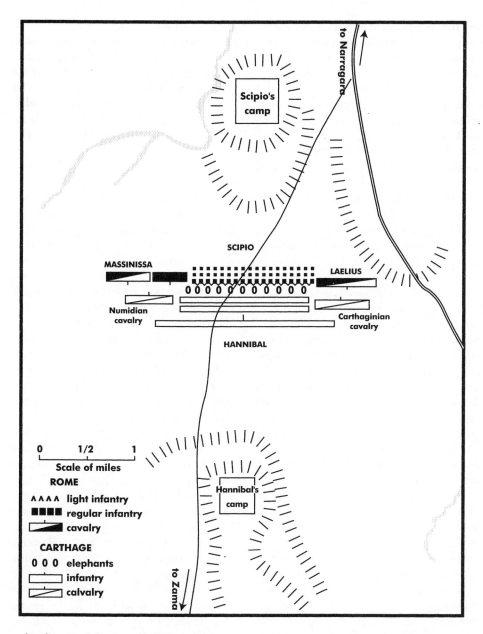

on this day paced them in columns. In front he placed his *hastati*, the youngest veterans. In the line of maniples behind them, he placed his *principes*, veterans about 30 years old with more combat experience. In the rear line he placed his *triarii*, the oldest and most steady of the veterans. In the spaces between the columns of maniples he placed his *velites*, the youngest soldiers armed as light infantry. Scipio range d his maniples in columns to allow paths for the charging elephants to pass through. Like Hannibal, he flanked his army with cavalry, of which he had about 9,000: Massinissa led his Numidian cavalry on the Roman right flank opposite Hannibal's Numidians, while Laelius commanded the Roman cavalry on the left.

Hannibal opened the battle by sending his elephants forward. Those on the left wing panicked at the sounds of Roman trumpets, however, and turned back into the Numidian cavalry, which threw a fright into their horses and disorganized them. Massinissa did not hesitate, but threw his cavalry into the melee and pursued the Numidian cavalry off the battlefield. Laelius quickly followed suit, charging into the untrained Carthaginian cavalry; they too broke, and the Roman cavalry was in hot pursuit on their end of the battlefield.

The infantry of both armies, which had stood fast during all this confusion, now began to advance toward each other. Hannibal's superior numbers should have won in the battle, which soon degenerated into a series of single combats, but his first line fought it out alone because the second line refused for some reason to advance in support. Believing themselves abandoned, the Carthaginians turned and fled toward the rear, but the second line refused to let them pass. The result was a fight among Carthaginians as the young *hastati* veterans pressed down on them. When the *principes* moved forward to support their first line, both the Carthaginian lines then broke into retreat into the third line, which also refused to let them through. All of this resulted in a massive number of dead and wounded as well as incredible confusion on the Carthaginian side. With the oldest veteran *triarii* advancing and joining the assault, the relatively well organized Romans were able to launch a coordinated attack on their foe. The solid Carthaginian third line stood and fought well, but they were badly outnumbered by this time.

Still, the battle seemed in doubt as Hannibal's infantry matched the quality of fighting of the Romans. The death blow, however, came from behind. Having given up their respective pursuits, both the Roman and Numidian cavalries returned to the battle and struck the Carthaginian rear. This proved too much, and the Romans began a slaughter. For a loss of 1,500 men killed and probably about 4,000 wounded, the Romans killed 20,000 Carthaginians and captured another 15,000. Hannibal, accompanied by a handful of retainers, fled.

Results

Scipio decided against laying Carthage under siege. It was a massive and well-situated city on the end of a strongly fortified peninsula. He lacked the siege engines he would need and the necessary supplies. Further, fearing he would be recalled to Rome before the siege was finished, Scipio decided against allowing anyone else to take the credit for capturing the city. He also felt that it was the Roman way to offer generous terms. He demanded (1) that Carthage hand over all but ten of its warships and all the elephants; (2) that Carthage fight no war against anyone without Roman approval; (3) recognition of Massinissa as king of Numidia; and (4) an indemnity of 10,000 silver talents (approximately 500,000 pounds). This was fairly lenient, considering that Rome could have annexed all of Carthage's merchant fleet and, with it, access to its markets.

Hannibal, in spite of his defeat at Zama, was elected to lead the new Carthaginian government. Under his wise leadership, Carthage paid off its indemnity early and rebounded strongly from the very long war. He provoked Roman jealousy, however, and he spent the rest of his life after 196 B.C. in the courts of various kings as military advisor before finally committing suicide rather than fall into Roman hands. Hannibal's campaign in Italy has long been recognized as one of the genuine masterpieces of military history, but in the end he was a victim of his own success. Scipio, on the other hand, was ultimately surnamed Africanus for his victory over Hannibal. The meeting of these two generals marked one of those rare occasions in warfare when the best military minds of an era face each other. Probably not until Wellington faced Napoleon at Waterloo was there another such monumental encounter.

Peace between the two powers lasted 50 years, but, when Massinissa demanded too much territory at Carthage's expense, he provoked an invasion in 151 B.C. Because this was undertaken without Rome's consent, the Roman government went to war. The Carthaginians immediately announced their willingness to stop fighting, but would not abandon their capital city. After a 3-year siege, Carthage finally fell to Roman forces in 146 B.C. The city was razed, and Utica became the provincial capital of the survivors, who came under the direct rule of Rome. Roman control over this region guaranteed grain supplies for the empire for centuries to come.

The Roman victory at Zama catapulted the victors from a regional to an international power. Already enlarged by the acquisition of Spain, Roman control over Sicily, northern Italy (Cisalpine Gaul), Corsica, and Sardinia meant that the entire western Mediterranean was under its direct or indirect control. Although this was an empire in fact, not until Caesar Augustus came to rule in Rome in 31 B.C. was it formally recognized as such. This political and economic dominance was further solidified in 168 B.C. with the Roman victory over Macedonia at Pydna. That victory placed virtually the entire Mediterranean under Rome's sway. All that the Roman Empire became was launched at Zama. Had Hannibal won the day, Carthage would probably have continued the war. Although the Carthaginian government was always niggardly in its support of Hannibal during his time in Italy, had he returned to Italy with a victorious army, the capture of the city of Rome was not beyond the realm of possibility. Whether a Carthaginian Empire in Europe would have resulted is problematic, but it certainly would have made sure that Spain was returned to its

control. That may have set up an interesting rivalry over Gaul, and the future of western Europe may have had Phoenician roots from Carthage rather than Latin and Greek influence from Rome.

References: Fuller, J. F. C. *A Military History of the Western World*, vol. 1. New York: Funk & Wagnalls, 1954; Liddell Hart, Basil. *A Greater Than Napoleon: Scipio Africanus.* New York: Biblo & Tannen, 1971 [1927]; Livy. *The War with Hannibal.* Translated by Aubrey de Selincourt. Baltimore: Penguin, 1965; Morris, William. *Hannibal: Soldier, Statesman, Patriot.* New York: Knickerbocker Press, 1978; Polybius. *The Histories.* Translated by W. R. Paton. New York: Putnam, 1922–1927.

PYDNA
22 June 168 B.C.

FORCES ENGAGED
Roman: 25,000 infantry. Commander: Lucius Aemilius Paulus.
Macedonian: 40,000 infantry and 4,000 cavalry. Commander: King Perseus.

IMPORTANCE
Pydna marked the final destruction of Alexander's empire and introduced Roman authority over the Near East.

Historical Setting

Rome first got involved in Greece in 215 B.C., when the Carthaginian leader Hannibal concluded an alliance with Philip V of Macedon. This proved a serious diversion from Rome's focus on its ongoing war with Carthage, but enough Greek states joined with Rome to keep Philip from overrunning the peninsula. The 10-year war was inconclusive, but Philip remained dedicated to establishing Macedonian control over Greece. In 200 B.C., Philip entered into an alliance with Antiochus III, king of the Seleucid Empire based in Syria, one of the divisions of Alexander the Great's empire. When Philip again made aggressive moves toward Greece, Rome declared war.

The major battle of the Second Macedonian War was at Cynoscephalae in 197. Rome won the battle primarily because of the nature of its army, which was based on the maniple formation. Although fighting in squares as the Greek phalanx did, the maniple was much more flexible and, because the primary Roman weapon was the *gladius,* a short double-edged sword, the maniple was able to maneuver much more easily than the phalanx, which depended on the *sarissa,* the long spear that protruded in front of the phalanx. That meant that the Greeks could fight in only one direction and were in trouble if they were attacked from the flank or rear, as the Roman units did in this battle. After losing 13,000 men, Philip abandoned his designs on Greece, Rome declared the peninsula independent, and Roman troops went home in 194. Thus, Rome fought against aggression in order to maintain stability in a region on its frontier, rather than fighting for national territorial gain.

Rome was soon at war with Antiochus, defeating his forces in Asia Minor at the battle of Magnesia in 190. The battle there was directed, on the Roman side, by Scipio Africanus, victor over Hannibal and Carthage in the Second Punic War. Again, Rome acquired no territory for itself and brought its troops home after the fighting. In this war, Philip V of Macedon aided the Romans, but was upset with the lack of recognition he received for his assistance. When he died in 179, his son Perseus succeeded him on the Macedonian throne; he hoped to revive his father's dream of conquering Greece.

As a result of these wars, the big winner was Pergamum, whose king, Eumenes, took advantage of his neighbors after Rome defeated them. Pergamum, which sat astride the Dardanelles, began to acquire territory in both Asia

Minor and the Balkans. Eumenes's growing power worried both Rome and Macedon. Perseus showed his underhanded nature by attempting an assassination; when it failed, the two countries went to war in 172. The Senate in Rome decided that Perseus and Macedon were the greater threat, so they declared war and went to aid Eumenes. The Roman effort was dismal. Roman troops landed in Illyria on the east coast of the Adriatic and marched toward Macedon. Perseus defeated them in three separate campaigns during 171–170 B.C. Had he followed up on any of his victories, he could have crushed any Roman force in southeastern Europe and imposed his will on Greece. Instead, he wrongly decided on a defensive strategy, apparently fearing the Romans too much or exhibiting his innate cowardice. While the Roman government fumbled, Perseus missed another chance to strengthen his hand. He possessed immense wealth, supplies, and manpower, but failed to wisely use any of them. He attempted to bribe both Eumenes and Rome's ally Rhodes, but refused to meet anyone's price when they showed interest. He also entered into negotiations with Gauls living north of Macedon, whose cavalry would have proven almost invincible, but again he tried and failed to get them cheaply.

Finally, the Roman government got serious. Realizing that the previous commanders they had dispatched against Macedon had been more worried about enriching themselves than fighting a successful war, the Senate finally nominated Lucius Aemilius Paulus to command. After dispatching an investigation commission to determine just what troops and supplies were needed, and exactly where enemy forces were located, Paulus launched his campaign in 168. Before leaving Rome, he spoke to the public, commenting that plenty of people seemed to know exactly what to do in this war and were loud in their opinions. He invited them all to come with him and fight or to stay home and shut up.

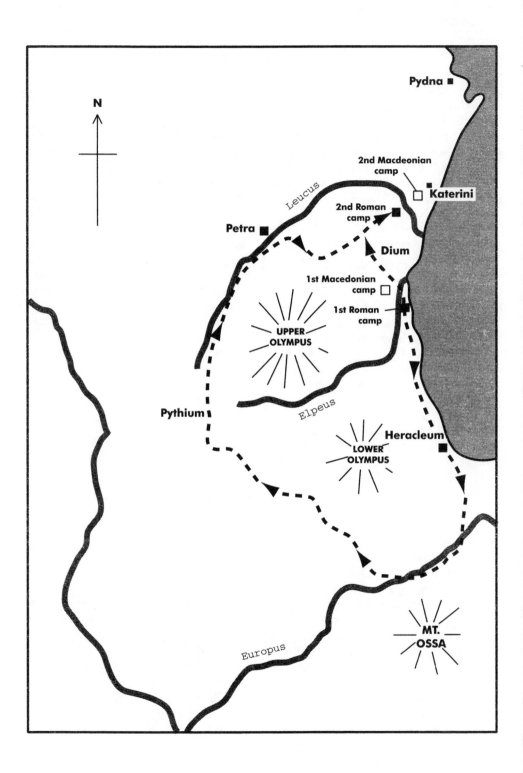

The Battle

Paulus hurried to war, reaching the Macedonian position on the Elpeus River, which flows into the Gulf of Thessalonika. Once taking charge from the previous commander, he began retraining the army. It had been lying dormant too long and needed direction and discipline. He decided on a surprise attack on Perseus's rear. With a fleet based in the Gulf, Paulus prepared to mount a holding attack on Perseus's camp while feinting with the ships toward the Macedonian line of supply. As he did this, he sent a force along paths at the base of Mount Olympus to strike Perseus from the northwest—a classic hammer and anvil operation.

Paulus launched this operation in early June 168 B.C., using some local merchants as guides to lead his forces though the mountains. Perseus learned of the flanking march, however, and withdrew his force before it could be completed, extricating his entire army. Paulus followed, joining with the flanking force at Dium; they then marched in pursuit of Perseus and caught up to him as he was establishing a new camp near Pydna at the Leucus River, in a peninsula formed by that river and a tributary, the Aeson. Paulus placed his forces in the foothills of Mount Olocrus to the west, overlooking the Macedonian camp.

On the night of 21–22 June 168, a lunar eclipse took place. A Roman officer correctly predicted it and explained exactly what was going to happen. When it occurred as he had said, the Roman soldiers were impressed with his foresight, assuming the gods must favor him. At the same time, the Macedonians were extremely upset by the eclipse, spending much of the night shouting at the moon in order to encourage it to reappear. Thus, the Romans viewed the eclipse as a good omen; the Macedonians, as an evil one.

On the afternoon of 22 June, both Macedonians and Romans were observing a truce to allow both sides to draw water from the Leucus River. A misunderstanding over a bolting horse led both sides to grab their weapons. Perseus rallied his men first and crossed the Leucus in formation: probably two phalanxes in the center flanked by mercenaries on his left and cavalry on his right. In total, Perseus commanded 40,000 foot and 4,000 horse. Paulus formed his men on the plain at the base of the hills: probably he had two legions in the center with allies from Latium (central Italy) on his right and some cavalry on his left. Paulus also had some war elephants to the rear on his right.

The Macedonians enjoyed early success as the phalanxes drove the partially deployed Romans backward. On the Roman right flank, a force of Pelignians, a Latin tribe, attempted a counterattack. They were driven back by the mercenary contingent, and the pursuing Macedonian left flank surged ahead of the rest of the line. The phalanxes were slowing in their rush as they moved from the level plain (the only ground on which they can operate successfully) onto the broken ground of the foothills, thus creating a gap between units. Paulus was quick to exploit it. The phalanxes began to lose their cohesion as Paulus ordered his legions, in their maniple formation, into their flanks. At this point, the elephants came up on the mercenaries and, with the regrouped Latin troops, isolated them. Seeing his troops losing their formations, Perseus fled with his cavalry.

Results

The Romans proceeded to slaughter the tightly packed phalanxes. The Macedonians lost as many as 20,000 dead and 6,000 prisoners on the field, with another 5,000 captured in pursuit. The Roman losses were reportedly light, just over 100 killed and another 400 wounded. Perseus was later captured and taken to Italy, where he died in captivity.

The Roman victory at Pydna ended the Third Macedonian War, but the Romans changed their standard operating procedure from the previous two wars. No longer content to allow the squabbling Greeks to provoke each other into constant wars, the Senate in Rome decided this time to occupy Greece and Macedon. The population was forced to disarm, and anyone who had been involved in aiding Perseus was sent to Italy or killed on the spot. Even leaders who had supported Rome found themselves prisoners, held without charge in Italy for 17 years. Similar treatment was imposed on Illyria. Roman dominance there gave Rome total control over the Adriatic. Eumenes of Pergamum, whom the Romans had originally gone to war to assist, was also accused of a number of crimes and, although not killed, became nothing more than a vassal of Rome. The island of Rhodes was stripped of its naval power, which was transferred to Roman control.

Thus ended the last remaining vestige of Greek-Macedonian power. Since the defeat of the Persians in 480 B.C., the Greeks had dominated the eastern Mediterranean and influenced much of the western. They had seen their culture spread through most of the Middle East with Alexander's conquering armies. Greek was the language of trade and intellectual discourse in the civilized world. The influence of its culture remained for some time to come, but the ability of either Greece or Macedon to spread that influence by force ended at Pydna. The empire that Alexander established, weakened considerably after his death, came to an end. Antiochus IV of Syria bowed to Roman pressure, abandoning any claims to Asia Minor and withdrawing from Egypt.

All of this meant that Rome supplanted Greece and Macedon as the only major power in the Near East. The Seleucid Empire was waning, pressed by Rome from the west and Parthia from the east. Egypt remained out of the Roman sphere for more than another century, but it was not a threat. Rome, fresh off its victory over Carthage in the Punic Wars, now dominated the Mediterranean basin. "And thus," writes Polybius, 'within a period of not quite fifty-three years [219–167 B.C.] ... almost the whole inhabited world was conquered and brought under the dominion of the single city of Rome.' A period in which, he says, world history passed from a series of 'disconnected transactions' into 'a connected whole'" (Fuller, *A Military History of the Western World*, vol. 1, p. 167). Although the Romans came to political power after this war, it was the Hellenistic culture of Greece that continued to spread, however. Roman generals, and then merchants, began to steal or buy the cultural treasures of Greece to decorate their mansions in Rome. Greek scholars were hired to tutor Roman children. Greek scientific discoveries were introduced to Rome, where Roman engineers adapted them for public use. Greece benefited from the stability that Roman law enforced, but the Romans benefited from Greek knowledge more than they could ever know. Almost every engineering advance that marked Roman civilization around Europe was adapted from Greek ideas; it has been said that Greece had the brains and Rome had the drains. The dominance of Greek thought, established by Greece's victory over Persia three and a half centuries earlier, continued in Europe, thanks to the Roman Empire.

References: Adcock, Frank. *The Roman Art of War under the Republic.* Cambridge, MA: Harvard University Press, 1940; Fuller, J. F. C. *A Military History of the Western World,* vol. 1. New York: Funk & Wagnalls, 1954; Gabba, Emilio. *Republican Rome, the Army, and the Allies.* Translated by B. J. Cuff. Berkeley: University of California Press, 1976; Keppie, L. J. F. *The Making of the Roman Army.* London: B. T. Batsford, 1984.

ALESIA
July–October 52 B.C.

FORCES ENGAGED
Roman: 50,000 to 55,000 men. Commander: Julius Caesar.

Gallic/Celtic: 333,000 men.
Commander: Vercingetorix.

IMPORTANCE

Caesar's defeat of the combined Gallic forces
established Roman dominance in Gaul for the
next 500 years. Caesar's victory also created a
rivalry with the Roman government, leading to his
invasion of the Italian peninsula.

Historical Setting

In 60 B.C., Julius Caesar entered into the Triumvirate, a political alliance with the two most
powerful men in Rome, Crassus and Pompey.
All three worked together to wield power in
the Roman Empire, while each at the same time
worked to maneuver himself into a dominant
position within the government. To do this, it
was necessary for each man to have not only
wealth and political influence, but military experience and support as well. Crassus already
was an experienced general, making himself
famous by putting down the slave uprising led
by Spartacus. That was insufficient for his ambition, however, and he had himself appointed
governor of Syria so he could win more laurels
and wealth in a war against the Parthians. He
died in the attempt, however. Caesar, meanwhile, took the position as governor of Gaul,
both Cisalpine and Transalpine (northern Italy
and southern France). In Gaul, Caesar hoped
to gain the military and financial power that
he needed to improve his political position.

He wasted no time getting into combat,
fighting between 58 and 53 B.C. against tribes
of Gauls (the Roman term for the population
of northwestern Europe/France; they called
themselves Celts) throughout modern France
and across the Rhine into Germany. He was almost universally successful, gaining necessary
leadership experience while enriching himself
with untold pillage. He also launched two invasions of Britain at this time. During 54–53,
tribal uprisings in Gaul attracted his attention
away from Britain. He quickly defeated the
Nervii and Belgae tribes by the spring of 53,
establishing a strong Roman presence in the

region of modern Belgium. Caesar himself left
for north Italy to reinforce his political contacts.

Even those major victories did not awe many
Gauls. They began to realize, however, that as long
as they practiced their traditional internecine
warfare, they would never stand against Rome's
power, so in 53 B.C. the tribes finally rallied around
a single leader, Vercingetorix, chieftain of the
Arverni. Getting the tribes to unite behind one
leader was a virtually impossible feat, and it is a
tribute to the personality and leadership characteristics of Vercingetorix that dozens of tribes
and literally hundreds of thousands of people
swore allegiance to him. Many tribes that Caesar had thought securely loyal changed sides.
Vercingetorix organized and trained the Gallic
warriors such as they had never been trained
before, and he launched his opening attack
against Cenabum (Orléans) in late 53 B.C. Upon
capturing the town, he killed the entire Roman
population and took control of the major Roman grain cache in Gaul. Caesar realized that the
entire Roman position northwest of the Alps
was in danger. In January 52, he returned from
Italy to his headquarters in Provence.

From Provence, Caesar marched his troops
north to join with his legions in Belgica and
then led them in an attack on Cenabum on the
Loire River. He captured that city, which was
the source of the current rebellion, and then
marched southward while dispatching a sizable
force under Labienus to secure northern Gaul.
All of this marching and fighting took place in
the late winter months, a factor Vercingetorix
used to his advantage. He commanded that
every bit of food and forage that was available
along Caesar's assumed line of march, out to a
distance of a day's march, should be removed
or destroyed. This denial of supplies to the Roman army was a brilliant strategy, and Caesar
soon felt its effects. To compound his problem,
Caesar's primary ally in Gaul, the Aedui, upon
whom he had depended for food, began wavering in their loyalty. Some leaders convinced
the tribe that the Romans had been ravaging
the countryside and killing Aedui hostages.

Caesar intercepted a column of 10,000 men, which had set out originally to reinforce the Romans before being persuaded by some of the discontented leaders to join Vercingetorix. When Caesar produced the hostages that had supposedly been killed, the rabble-rousers fled, and he absorbed the remainder of the force.

Caesar next invested the town of Avaricum (Bourges) in March. He captured the town before Vercingetorix could arrive to relieve it, and that put some food in Roman supply wagons. He next attacked and captured Gergovia, capital of Vercingetorix's tribe. Through April and May, Caesar laid siege, but the countryside surrounding the town had been stripped of supplies, which had been stockpiled inside the fortress. Desperate to take the town before Gallic reinforcements could arrive to relieve the siege, Caesar ordered it assaulted. It was a mistake that cost him more than 700 casualties, including almost fifty centurions. The defeat, compounded by lack of supplies, forced him to retreat. He marched north to join with Labienus, who had just captured Lutetia (Paris), and then together they aimed toward Provence. Vercingetorix was determined that they not reach it.

The Battle

Accurately predicting Caesar's intent, Vercingetorix placed his army of 80,000 infantry and 15,000 cavalry in the fortress town of Alesia (Alise-Ste. Reine), near the source of the Seine River. As he was assembling his troops, he sent a cavalry force north to harass and delay the Romans. The cavalry fought Caesar's cavalry, made up of German auxiliaries, at Vingeanne, and the Gauls had the worst of it. Some 3,000 men were lost, but it gave Vercingetorix time to herd all the region's cattle into Alesia. The town of Alesia sat atop a mesalike hill, Mount Auxois. The flat top of the oval-shaped hill fell off on steep sides, which were virtually impossible to climb. The city walls had been built almost as an extension of the mountainside. Running east-west above and below the town are the Ose and Oserain Rivers. Vercingetorix ordered a trench to be dug on either side of the hill, running north-south between the rivers. This made approach to the city almost as difficult as assaulting it. With some 90,000 troops, Vercingetorix was sure Caesar could not possibly harm him.

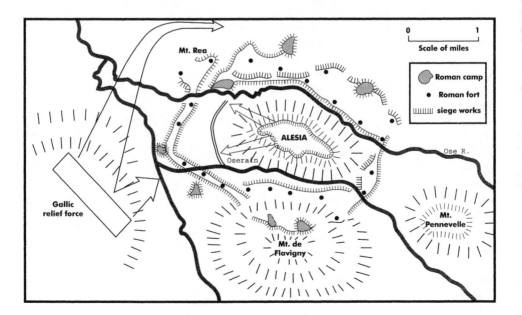

Caesar's army consisted of some 55,000 men; 40,000 of these were Roman legionnaires, about 5,000 were Germanic cavalry, and the remainder were auxiliary troops of one type or another. Rather than assault the town, he laid siege sometime in July 52. Caesar ordered the digging of a trench completely surrounding the hill. When finished, the trench stretched 10 miles in circumference. The Roman soldier was used to digging because he had done so every evening on campaign while he had been in the army: it was standard procedure to dig a trench and set up a palisade around camp every evening. This, however, was much more elaborate. The trench was 15 to 20 feet wide, and the excavated dirt was used to build a 12-foot-high wall with observation towers every 130 feet. To discourage any Gallic sortie against their lines, the Romans crossed the rivers to dig more trenches, in which they lodged sharpened stakes. These were interspersed with foot-long wooden blocks with iron rods protruding, designed to slow attackers during the day and completely disrupt any night foray.

Unfortunately for Caesar, Vercingetorix had dispatched riders just prior to the investment, ordering them to rally as many men as possible to come to his aid. Thus, if the siege went on too long, the Romans could easily find themselves fighting back Gallic relief attacks while attempting to maintain their siege. Caesar therefore ordered the preparation of a line of circumvallation, a second set of trenches and walls, which stretched for 14 miles outside the first set. This would be used as a defensive line against the relieving force. Although giving the maximum defensive strength, it had the negative aspect of potentially having his besieging army becoming besieged themselves.

In October, the relieving force arrived, numbering perhaps 240,000 infantry and 8,000 cavalry. (Although ancient sources often exaggerate enemy strength, modern historians accept these numbers as fairly accurate.) Caesar had made sure that whatever food was within foraging distance had been gathered into his

lines, so he continued with his siege. The relieving force attacked twice, using ladders and sandbags for overcoming the outer trenches, while Vercingetorix led sorties out of Alesia in support. The Romans with difficulty managed to beat back all assaults. The third and final attack almost succeeded. The Gauls had discovered what they thought to be the weakest point of the Roman position, on the northwest corner of the outer line. They approached the position at night and then screened themselves behind a hill all morning. When a diversionary attack had gained Roman attention to the south, the northern attack was launched. Wave after wave of Gauls pressed the assault, gaining ground and then turning the attack over to the next, fresher line of men. The Romans were pressed to the point of breaking, when the German cavalry attacked the Gallic rear. This broke the assault and the Gauls retreated in disorder. When the fighting was at its height, Caesar, wearing a bright red cloak so his men knew he was with them, led the last reserve into the fight.

Food supplies in Alesia were almost gone. Vercingetorix had taken the desperate measure of expelling all the civilians and wounded, but Caesar denied them access to his lines. They lay at the base of the hill, starving. Vercingetorix finally admitted defeat, asking his subordinates to do with him what they would: kill him or turn him over to the Romans. The entire force surrendered.

Results

Although the besieged garrison was taken prisoner, most of the relieving force scattered and fled to their homes. The casualty figures in the fighting are unknown, but there were sufficient prisoners taken for each Roman soldier to be awarded one as a slave; each officer received several. Vercingetorix was taken in chains to Rome, where he languished in a cell for 6 years after being a showpiece in Caesar's triumphal parade. He was finally executed.

After Alesia, there were no more serious uprisings against Roman rule in Gaul. Caesar had spent 6 years in the province trying to establish Roman power, and he had finally succeeded. The acquisition of Gaul proved to be one of the most profitable for the Roman Empire. It also stretched the limits of Roman civilization well past the Italian peninsula. Will Durant wrote, "The siege of Alesia decided the fate of Gaul and the character of French civilization. It added to the Roman Empire a country twice the size of Italy and opened the purses and markets of 5,000,000 people to Roman trade. It saved Italy and the Mediterranean world for four centuries from barbarian invasion; and it lifted Caesar from the verge of ruin to a new height of reputation, wealth, and power" (Durant, *Caesar and Christ*, p. 177). This may overstate the threat to Italy because the Gauls, who for the time had organized behind Vercingetorix, probably would not have maintained a united effort had they won at Alesia. There were too many tribal feuds for that to happen. Still, it could well have stretched Celtic society into northern Italy, where it had resided less than a century earlier. A Celtic invasion, even a disorganized one, could have wrought immense havoc through the Italian peninsula. With the Roman government in a state of flux, no telling what may have happened. The great Roman general Marius had built his own army and turned back a Celtic invasion in 102 B.C.; perhaps another such leader would have risen to the occasion. It probably would not have been Julius Caesar, and the course of Roman history could have been radically altered.

As it was, Caesar was victorious, and the notoriety he received for his conquest of Gaul provoked jealousy in the other remaining member of the Triumvirate, Pompey. He was illegally appointed to be the sole consul (there were normally two), and then he demanded Caesar return to Rome without his army or be declared a traitor to the Roman Republic. Undaunted, Caesar marched his legions into Italy, crossing the Rubicon River 11 January 49 B.C. That action spelled the end of the republic and laid the groundwork for the empire.

References: Caesar, Julius. *War Commentaries of Caesar.* Translated by Rex Warner. New York: New American Library, 1960; Dodge, Theodore A. *Caesar: A History of the Art of War among the Romans.* Boston: Houghton Mifflin, 1892; Durant, Will. *Caesar and Christ.* New York: Simon & Schuster, 1944; Meier, Christian. *Caesar.* Translated by David McLintock. New York: HarperCollins, 1995 [1982]; O'Reilly, Donald. "Besiegers Besieged," *Military History* 9(6), February 1993.

PHARSALUS
9 August 48 B.C.

FORCES ENGAGED
Roman: 22,000 infantry and 1,000 cavalry. Commander: Gaius Julius Caesar.

Roman: 45,000 infantry and 7,000 cavalry. Commander: Gnaeus Pompeius (Pompey the Great).

IMPORTANCE
Caesar's victory took him to the pinnacle of power in Rome, effectively ending the republic.

Historical Setting

In the wake of the Punic Wars, Rome underwent significant changes. Politically, the Senate, which had long ruled the city of Rome and immediate areas, found itself unable to deal with foreign possessions, as if in the United States a city council found itself governing all of America. This coincided with a shift in the economy of Rome as well because the huge influx of slaves in the wake of the wars against Carthage transformed a nation of freehold farmers into a nation of estate owners, working slaves instead of peasants. The country folk, without employment, moved to the cities and caused a severe drain on public resources while the rich got richer with the newly expanded overseas trade. As the foundation of the army of Republican Rome had always been the yeoman farmer, the traditional soldier dedicated to serving his country so he could get back to his farm ceased to exist. Thus, both the government and the population needed leadership, and this led to the rise of dictators.

The first to rise to power was Gaius Marius who, as a tribune for the lower plebeian class, opened the army to volunteers from the cities and even from foreign tribes and lands. The army became loyal primarily to its recruiting general and only secondarily to Rome. Marius led his army to victory over the Gauls in 102 and 101 B.C. and then suppressed a revolt of Italian tribes jealous of Rome's wealth and self-ishness. He exercised great influence in Rome, but was surpassed by Lucius Cornelius Sulla, who made himself dictator in 82 B.C. in name as well as fact after winning martial glory in defeating the Parthians, as well as public fear in defeating a combined army of Republicans and the Italian Samnite tribe. In spite of his excesses, he reformed the government and made it more democratic in his 3 years as dictator. His government lasted almost two decades, but was ultimately brought down by the internal squabbling of the Triumvirate.

After the third major war against Parthia (in modern Iran/Iraq), the most powerful general was Gnaeus Pompeius, better known as Pompey. Like Marius and Sulla, he hoped to turn his military reputation to political advantage. In 60 B.C., he allied himself with Licinius Crassus and Gaius Julius Caesar in a partnership designated the Triumvirate, designed to break the resistance of powerful senators led by Porcius Cato. Caesar, newly returned from a tour of duty in Spain, ran for the consulship with the support of his partners: Marius wanted government grants to his veterans; Crassus wanted favorable tax laws for his businesses. Once Caesar won the consulship in 59, these goals were achieved. Then, Caesar led armies into Gaul (France) to suppress revolts against Roman rule. In 56 B.C., Caesar was richer than before he entered Gaul in wealth and military experience and possessed an army loyal to himself. Pompey commanded forces in Spain, whereas Crassus, also needing military experience and support, led an expedition against Parthia. He died in the process, leaving Caesar and Pompey the two most powerful men in the Roman Republic. Both were intensely ambitious and knew that to become sole ruler of Rome the other had to be eliminated. Pompey moved first, because Caesar was busy with his military efforts in Gaul. In 52 B.C., Pompey arranged to have himself elected the sole consul in a government that had always had two. He acted like a dictator and began a propaganda campaign against Caesar, whose term as consul for Gaul came to an end in 49. If he wanted to run for that position again, Caesar had to surrender command of his army, as the Senate demanded. When Pompey would not do the same, Caesar decided that military action was his sole option.

Caesar was in Cisalpine Gaul (northern Italy) when he was informed of the Senate's order. He commanded a legion of 5,000 infantry and 300 cavalry at Ravenna, with another eight legions under his command, but stationed in Transalpine Gaul on the other side of the Alps. Pompey commanded two legions hastily assembled in Rome, but could draw on seven in Spain, with perhaps another eight being recruited in Italy and another ten scattered at various points throughout Rome's many possessions. Outnumbered, Caesar realized that his only hope lay in boldness, of which he had no shortage. Announcing "the die is cast," he marched his troops out of Ravenna across the Rubicon River, the northern boundary of Roman Italy.

Pompey and the Senate were not prepared for this action, and they quickly fled Rome for the southern Adriatic port of Brundisium (Brindisi). Caesar overcame a Pompeyan garrison at Corfinium, due east of Rome, and then arrived at Brundisium in time to see Pompey and many of the senators sailing away. Instead of following, he established control over Corsica and Sardinia and then sailed to Spain. There he surrounded one army at Ilerda and forced its surrender (2 August 49), after which the second army in Spain, at Gades (Cadiz), gave up as well. He also captured Massilia (Marseilles), securing southern Gaul. Upon returning to Rome, he had the Senate name him dictator.

The Battle

Finally in January 48 B.C., Caesar had gathered sufficient shipping to transport half his army across the Adriatic to Dyrrachium (Durrës), where Pompey was building an army of his own. Caesar laid siege, but Pompey's ability to supply himself by sea made the investment almost impossible. After Caesar's chief subordinate, Marcus Antonius, arrived with reinforcements in March, Pompey sallied out of the besieged city and drove Caesar away, but failed to pursue. Leaving a strong garrison in Dyrrachium, Pompey cautiously trailed Caesar eastward into the Greek province of Thessaly. An army loyal

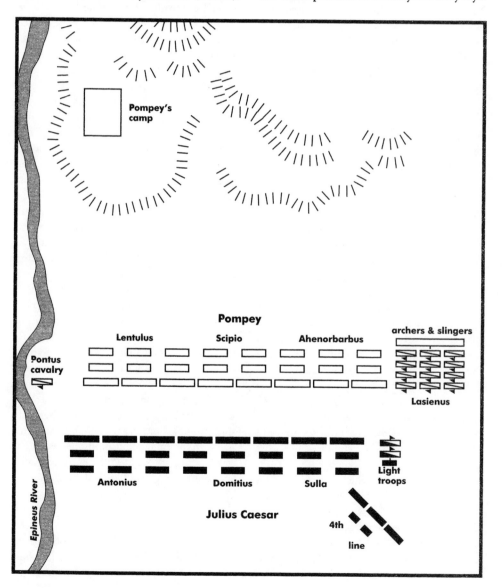

to Pompey, commanded by Metellus Scipio, occupied Macedon. Caesar hoped that by threatening that force he could draw Pompey into battle. Pompey's intent was to finish off Caesar before returning to Rome, unwilling to leave such a dangerous adversary in the field.

The two armies approached each other on the Plain of Pharsalus, near Cynoscephalae, site of a major Roman victory over Macedon in 197 B.C. The exact site of the battle has been disputed for ages, as contemporary writers disagree; it was probably near Palaepharsalus (modern Farsala). Caesar established a camp on the northern bank of the Epineus River, while Pompey established his a few miles to the northwest. Each day, the two armies deployed and then returned to camp. Each day, Caesar placed his troops closer to Pompey, hoping to entice him into an attack. As Pompey's camp was on the slopes of Mount Dogandzis, he was unwilling to leave his superior defensive position. As his grain supply dwindled, Caesar decided to march northeast in search of new stocks, but, as his army broke camp on 9 August 48 B.C., they saw that Pompey had indeed come down from his mountain. Caesar countermanded his march order and deployed his men forward.

Pompey's army of eleven legions, or approximately 45,000 men and 9,000 cavalry, was far superior to Caesar's in number. Caesar fielded a force of eight legions, or 22,000 men, plus two cohorts of 1,200 men left behind to guard the camp. The primary difference, however, was not one of numbers but of command. Pompey, for all his previous victories, was past his prime and burdened with meddlesome senators. Caesar was the sole leader and commanded troops personally loyal to him and confident of his and their abilities.

Pompey deployed his forces with 600 cavalry on the right flank, which was anchored on the Epineus River. Then his infantry stretched out in line three cohorts deep. (At this time, the cohort was the basic Roman unit, numbering 600 men.) On his left flank, he placed archers and slingers fronted by the remainder of his cavalry, with the intent of turning Caesar's flank and driving his force into the river. Caesar also arranged his force in lines three cohorts deep and with his small cavalry force on his right flank, away from the river and facing Pompey's. Correctly guessing Pompey's plan, Caesar also placed behind the cavalry a reserve infantry contingent, facing obliquely outward and hidden by the forward units, to oppose the cavalry charge he knew was coming. Caesar opened the battle by launching his front two lines of infantry forward, but stopping them halfway across the field. Pompey had ordered his men to stand fast so that Caesar's troops would tire, so Caesar's troops caught their breath by stopping midfield. They then pressed forward, and Pompey's troops marched to engage. As the two forces clashed, Pompey launched his cavalry at Caesar's flank. There they met the staunch defense of Caesar's infantry, which drove Pompey's cavalry from the field and back into the hills. The archers and slingers, unprotected from the assault of the heavy cohorts, fled or died. This left Pompey's flank open, and Caesar's reserve cohorts turned it.

Pompey at this point panicked and fled, leaving his army leaderless and collapsing. Caesar's men drove their opponents all the way back to their camp, which they proceeded to overrun and loot. Pompey mounted the nearest horse and rode away, with Caesar in hot pursuit. Driving Pompey's army through the camp and on to a hilltop, Caesar's men surrounded them; the encircled force was without food or water and surrendered the next morning. Caesar drove on toward the town of Larissa, where Pompey was hiding. Pompey hopped a ship and sailed to Egypt, where he sought refuge with the ruling pharaoh, Ptolemy XII. Instead, he found death; Ptolemy feared Caesar and sent him a gift of Pompey's head.

Results

Caesar's legions inflicted about 6,000 casualties on Pompey's army for the loss of about

1,200 men themselves. Although this established Caesar as the leader of Rome, it was not the final conflict he fought. He spent the next 3 years suppressing various rebellions in Spain and northern Africa, while also expanding Rome's reach in campaigns in Egypt and Asia Minor. He was assassinated in March 44 B.C. after having ruled Rome for 5 years, most of which time was spent on campaign rather than in the capital. He ended his days with a well-deserved reputation for energy and vision.

As ruler of Rome, he was king in all but name, for ages-old Roman tradition disallowed the title. He had himself appointed dictator for life, in addition to holding the titles of tribune and *pontifex maximus,* virtual leader of Rome's religious life. He was killed within a month of the dictator-for-life declaration because powerful forces within the Senate feared that he might vault from that position to deified king, much as did Alexander the Great before him and Augustus after him.

As dictator, Caesar had the vision of empire that the Senate had never possessed. He therefore proceeded to expand the Senate with his appointees in order to have a more responsive body. He appointed men from the equestrian order (just below the patrician) as well as men from Italian regions outside Rome itself as he extended the honor and privilege of Roman citizenship to more of the peninsula. He realized that loyalty was necessary to hold the ground that Rome now owned, and the rights of the Roman citizen were sufficiently attractive to buy loyalty. By sending out colonists to Rome's provinces and at the same time removing governors dedicated to enriching themselves, he began the serious spread of Roman culture throughout Europe. He also implemented reforms within Roman society even if they opposed tradition; most notable was the introduction of the Julian calendar. He was a champion of the people much more than a friend of the aristocracy, and that too was one of the reasons for his death.

With Caesar's assassination, the Roman Republic was dead, although not officially declared so. The era of one-person rule with a virtual rubber-stamp Senate began with Julius Caesar and was solidified by his adopted son and successor Octavian, who became Caesar Augustus. Had Caesar lost the battle at Pharsalus, Pompey would probably have attempted to do the exact same things Caesar did, but, being older and less energetic, he probably would have failed. Dictatorial rule would probably have remained the norm, but the line of Julius Caesar's descendants, for better or worse, would not have ruled. "Though in his short reign he could do no more than sow the seed of the autocratic empire, much of which was trampled into the mire by his successors, he changed Rome from a municipality into a world-kingdom, and extended it in idea until the hub was swallowed by the circumference" (Fuller, *A Military History of the Western World,* vol. 1, pp. 200–201).

References: Caesar, Julius. *War Commentaries of Caesar.* Translated by Rex Warner. New York: New American Library, 1960; Fuller, J. F. C. *A Military History of the Western World,* vol. 1. New York: Funk & Wagnalls, 1954; Grant, Michael. *Julius Caesar.* New York: M. Evans & Co., 1992 [1969]; Starr, Chester. *A History of the Ancient World.* New York: Oxford University Press, 1965; Suetonius. *The Twelve Caesars.* Translated by Robert Graves. London: Penguin, 1957.

ACTIUM
2 September 31 B.C.

FORCES ENGAGED
Roman Republic: Approximately 400 ships. Commander: Gaius Julius Caesar Octavianus. Roman/Egyptian: Approximately 500 ships. Commander: Marcus Antonius.

IMPORTANCE
Victory by Octavianus gave him complete power in Roman government, ending the Roman Republic and establishing the Roman Empire.

Historical Setting

After the assassination of Julius Caesar on 15 March 44 B.C., two men positioned themselves to assume the mantle of government in Rome. The first was Marcus Antonius, or Mark Antony, a successful general and protégé of Caesar. Antonius was popular with the army and had the support of a number of senators. The other was Gaius Julius Caesar Octavianus, who had been adopted by Julius Caesar and named in his will as heir.

Octavianus, who had been in the eastern provinces controlled by Rome, hurried back to the capital to claim his legacy. There he found that Antonius had already spent much of it. Still, with Caesar's name to bank on, Octavianus began marshaling support in both the political and military arenas. Antonius, who saw little in Octavianus that was threatening, continued to court powerful interests for his own ends. As Caesar's assassins had fled and both Antonius and Octavianus wanted revenge, the two entered into a pact of convenience with Marcus Aemilius Lepidus to form the Second Triumvirate (the first had been made up of Julius Caesar, Cnaeus Pompeius, and M. Licinius Crassus). The threesome chased the assassins, Marcus Junius Brutus and Gaius Cassius Longinus, to Macedon, where the Second Triumvirate was victorious after two battles at Philippi in March 42 B.C. In the struggle, a force commanded by Octavianus had been defeated by Brutus, only to be saved by Antonius.

Lepidus was then dispatched to North Africa in the hopes that he would fade away; after he failed in a bid to conquer Sicily in 36 B.C., he did just that.

Antonius, however, had much more political support as well as his military reputation. Hoping to strengthen his position, Octavianus named Antonius to administer Rome's eastern provinces while arranging the marriage of his own sister Octavia to Antonius. In Rome, Octavianus proceeded to ingratiate himself with the Senate as well as to draw to himself talented and loyal generals. Antonius, while traveling about the east, met and fell in love with Cleopatra VII, queen of Egypt. She had earlier been Julius Caesar's lover and now became Antonius's. Cleopatra was an intelligent ruler who saw an alliance with Caesar, and later with Antonius, as a way to keep Egypt free from Roman domination by becoming an ally. Together, however, they grew inordinately ambitious. Antonius married Cleopatra (without divorcing Octavia first) and granted large landholdings to her and the children they proceeded to have. This was both an insult and a threat to Octavianus, who began to implement plans to bring Antonius down.

Antonius, meanwhile, was gathering support of his own. He named his own supporters to rule the eastern provinces, client kings who owed their position to him rather than to Rome. In a bid for Greek support, he and Cleopatra then declared themselves to be the incarnations of Dionysus and Aphrodite. Antonius launched

The battle of Actium. Fifteenth-century painting by Neroccio de Landi. (Corbis/North Carolina Museum of Art)

an invasion of Parthia, Rome's troublesome Persian neighbor, in the summer of 36 B.C., probably to give himself an even greater power base. The invasion failed, however, setting back Antonius's ambitions for 2 years. The loss of 20,000 to 30,000 men in the campaign meant that he had to replenish his forces at Egyptian expense, making him even further indebted to Cleopatra. In 32 B.C., Antonius sent a list of demands to the Roman government through two of his allies, Gaius Sosius and Gnaeus Domitius Ahenobarbus, the consuls serving for that year. Although they did not deliver the message as intended, Sosius made a speech critical of Octavianus. He responded by reading to the Senate a copy of Antonius's will (which may or may not have been real), which was a virtual surrender of Roman authority in the east to Cleopatra. The two consuls and some 300 senators fled to Antonius; the remaining senators rallied around Octavianus's demand for war.

The Battle

Antonius marched with nineteen legions, containing some 80,000 infantry and 15,000 cavalry, into Greece in the winter of 32–31 B.C.; eleven more legions were stationed in garrisons along the eastern Mediterranean coastline as far as Egypt. This seemed to be preliminary to an invasion of Italy itself, and Octavianus certainly portrayed it as such in his propaganda, but it probably was a move designed to forestall Octavianus's invasion of the eastern provinces. Antonius also commanded a force of 480 ships. His position on Greece's west coast at Actium (modern Punta) was strong, and he had a fairly secure supply line back to Egypt. The same could not be said for Octavianus as he marched. Maintaining his legions (73,000 infantry and 12,000 cavalry) in the field was expensive, and the taxpayer in Rome, often divided in loyalties, had to bear the burden. Octavianus's force crossed the Adriatic Sea early in 31 B.C. and marched down its east coast. In the meantime, Octavianus's chief general, Marcus Vipsanius Agrippa,

sailed more than 400 ships to southern Greece, where they very successfully raided Antonius's rear cantonments, cutting his lines of supply.

Octavianus marched to a point about 5 miles north of Actium and established a camp on the neck of a peninsula dividing the Ionian Sea from the Gulf of Ambracia. Antonius's camp at Actium was on a peninsula as well, across the straits separating the above bodies of water, but he crossed over to the end of the opposite peninsula and established a base there under the command of his chief subordinate, P. Crassus Candidius. The two adversaries spent the summer watching each other, as Antonius's men began to suffer from the lack of supplies. Finally, Antonius and Cleopatra decided on a naval battle. They gambled that their much larger ships, *quinqueremes,* would be able to overpower the smaller ships that Octavianus possessed. If they failed, then the ships would sail for Egypt, and the troops under Candidius would fight their way out to join them.

By the day of battle, 2 September 31 B.C., the two fleets were roughly equal in number. Octavianus's fleet faced the straits in three divisions side by side. Antonius deployed his fleet in a matching formation, with Cleopatra in command of a reserve of sixty ships. The battle was hard to fight for both sides. Antonius's huge quinqueremes were too stoutly built to be rammed successfully (the primary method of fighting at that time), but too slow to do much ramming themselves. Octavianus's ships, therefore, could not afford to close on the enemy because the larger ships also carried large numbers of soldiers whose javelins and arrows would do serious damage by firing down on Octavianus's smaller ships. Thus, the two sides sparred for position most of the day. Agrippa, commanding the left division, attempted to row around Antonius, in command of his own right flank. As the two drifted northward trying to flank each other, a gap appeared in the center of the two lines. Octavianus's subordinate general Lucius Arruntius drove into the gap with his division and threw the Antonians into disarray.

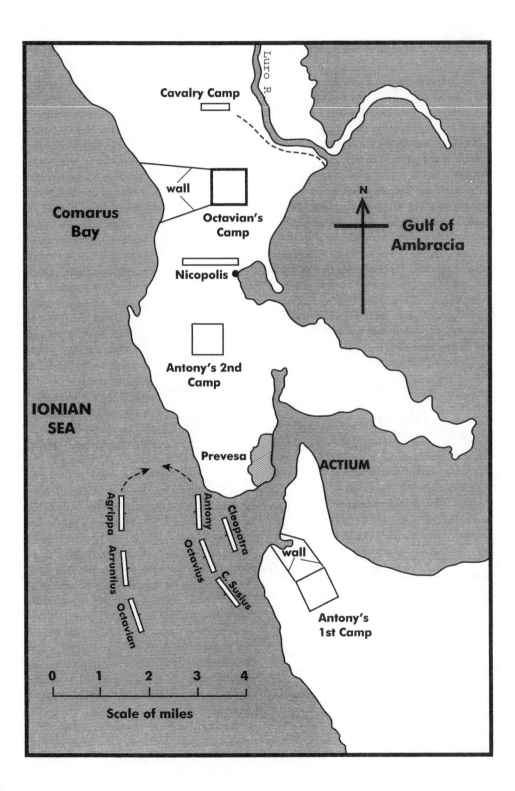

Seeing the battle beginning to go against them, Cleopatra decided not to be captured. Had she committed her reserve to plug the hole, the day probably would have been saved. Instead, she drove her 60 ships through the gap and rowed for Egypt. Seeing this move, Antonius immediately disengaged his own ships and sailed after her with 40 ships. This left the remainder of his fleet without a commander, badly outnumbered, and exhausted at the end of a day of rowing and backing the huge vessels. The onset of a storm in midafternoon was too much to bear. Their disarray turned to panic, and the remnants of Antonius's force began to surrender some 350 ships.

Results

Although Antonius was making his way quickly south in pursuit of Cleopatra, the army he left behind had no idea as to the outcome of the battle. When they learned of it, Candidius attempted to fight his way out, but the vast majority of his troops defected instead. News of Octavianus's victory at sea and on land spread quickly, and the "loyal" support of Antonius's client kings never materialized. The following summer, 30 B.C., Octavianus led an army through Syria toward Egypt. Most of the garrisons surrendered to him or fled as he marched south, while garrisons in posts west of Egypt surrendered to Octavianus's General Lucius Scarpus as he marched on Alexandria from Cyrene (in modern Libya). Antonius managed to put up a defense at Alexandria, but he was too badly outnumbered. Cleopatra, who had secretly sent peace feelers to Octavianus after Actium, was taken prisoner after Antonius committed suicide. Cleopatra did likewise, rather than suffer the humiliation of a public display in Rome.

With the only serious opposition removed, Octavianus was now regarded as the unchallenged ruler of Rome. He promised the Senate that he would respect the laws and traditions of the Roman Republic and made much of going through the motions. In reality, the First Citizen (as he styled himself) was the first emperor of Rome, and the far-flung possessions of Rome, from Spain to Mesopotamia, became recognized as the de jure Roman Empire, which they had long been de facto. The population, which throughout its long history had struck down anyone who pondered making himself king, readily accepted Octavianus as emperor. Indeed, he soon began calling himself Augustus in recognition of his position. When he died after a 41-year reign, the position of Caesar remained in the family, completely overthrowing any pretension of a republic.

Augustus also assumed control of Rome's territories. He allowed the Senate to rule in the Italian peninsula, but the governors of the provinces answered to him, and it was in the provinces that the Roman legions were based. The guise of republican rule was maintained while Augustus ruled in actuality. Further, the army, which had long been recruited on an as-needed basis, became at this time a standing force, allowing for long-term enlistment and increased professionalism. That not only further solidified Augustus's power, it made for a military that was for centuries to come a virtually unbeatable fighting machine. A standing army needed permanent bases, and the forts and camps that sprang up throughout Europe became the foundation of many of today's modern cities.

More importantly for Rome, the acquisition of Egypt proved immensely valuable. Long a rival or ally, it now became a possession, and the immense wealth it possessed became Roman wealth. Just as importantly, its agricultural production became Roman as well, and the bulk of grain for the Roman Empire for the next four centuries came from northern Africa. Rome's possession of Egypt also confirmed Rome as the sole sea power of the Mediterranean, so trade could move easily for centuries without threat from anyone except the occasional pirate. Free trade and military power made Rome fabulously wealthy, and the Pax

Romana that ensued took Roman civilization throughout the western world.

References: Cassius Dio. *The Roman History: The Reign of Augustus.* Translated by Ian Scott-Kilvert. New York: Penguin, 1987; Fuller, J. F. C. *A Military History of the Western World,* vol. 1. New York: Funk & Wagnalls, 1954; Gurval, Robert. *Actium and Augustus: The Politics and Emotion of Civil War.* Ann Arbor: University of Michigan Press, 1995; Porter, Barry. "Actium: Rome's Fate in the Balance," *Military History* 14(3), August 1997; Syme, Ronald. *The Roman Revolution.* Oxford, UK: Clarendon Press, 1939.

TEUTOBURGER WALD (TEUTOBURG FOREST)

A.D. 9

FORCES ENGAGED

Roman: 17th, 18th, and 19th Legions, plus auxiliary cavalry, totaling 15,000 to 18,000 men. Commander: Quinctilius Varus.

German: 20,000 to 30,000 men. Commander: Arminius (Hermann).

IMPORTANCE

Roman defeat marked the end of the empire's expansion into northern Europe, as both the German population and territory proved unconquerable.

Historical Setting

Although Julius Caesar conquered Gaul for Rome in the 50s B.C., he did little more than establish some garrisons along the eastern frontier to try to keep the German tribes at bay. The Germanic tribes were seminomadic and warlike, occasionally raiding across the Rhine River into Gaul. From the Marcommani in the area of modern Austria to the Frisians on the North Sea coast, the tribes called no one other than the strongest military leader master. This situation persisted until 12 B.C., when Caesar Augustus ordered forces across the Rhine to protect Gaul and establish Roman hegemony. Under the leadership of Tiberius, Romans managed to cross the Rhine and stay the winter in A.D. 4, but they were in no way secure.

Germany was unlike Gaul, in that there were no cities or even large towns for the Romans to capture and use as bases. Thus, Romans could make war on individual tribes but could not establish themselves in an administrative center. Still, after a few years of campaigning, the Germans seemed to have accepted the Romans as neighbors, if not as overlords. The Romans, however, took the relative peace to mean that they were gaining the upper hand. Thus it was that in A.D. 9. Quinctilius Varas was assigned to the governorship of Germany. A veteran of both military action and the governor's post in Syria, he was primarily an administrator rather than a soldier. He tried to not only enforce Roman law but to collect taxes. In a metal-poor society such as Germany, money for taxes was hard to come by and not willingly paid. That demand for taxes, so easily collected in Syria, plus the cavalier attitude that Varus exhibited toward the Germans, proved his undoing.

On Varus's staff was Arminius, a young German of the Cheruscan tribe. He, like many other Germans, had hired himself out to the Romans for service in auxiliary forces in campaigns in southeastern Europe. As an officer in Roman service, he distinguished himself and was not only granted Roman citizenship but granted the title of equestrian, a member of the upper classes. This impressed him little, but it did give him a first-hand view of the Roman way of war. Arminius chafed at the Roman administration attempting to govern his land and plotted to remove it. Although most other Germans felt the same way and he therefore had a large population upon which to draw, he had trouble within his own family. He had courted Thusnelda, daughter of Segestes, a Cheruscan chieftain who served Rome. When Segestes rebuffed Arminius's request for marriage to Thusnelda, Arminius eloped with her. This infuriated his new father-in-law, who swore vengeance.

Arminius, however, did everything he could to prove his loyalty to Varus, so any threat or warning that Segestes may relate, Varus refused to consider, thinking it merely retaliatory action over the loss of his daughter. Throughout the summer of A.D. 9, Arminius brought German leaders to Varus to ask his advice and settle their disputes. All of this flattered Varus's vanity and proved to him Arminius's devotion. Thus, when Varus began to gather in his camp on the Weser River in preparation for a return to winter quarters on the Rhine, he felt no compunction about having Arminius plan the move. As the autumn approached, Arminius began laying his trap. On his direction, small revolts against Roman garrisons broke out. Arminius suggested that Varus alter his route back to the Rhine to put down these rebellions, a move that certainly would take little effort. Varus agreed.

The Battle

Varus had on hand three legions, all veterans of the wars against the Germans. They numbered some 15,000 to 18,000 men, including a force of cavalry. However, another 10,000 camp followers (soldiers' family members, tradespeople, etc.) were involved with the move as well. Their wagons, coupled with those carrying the soldiers' supplies and equipment, meant a long column. The route Arminius suggested wound through a heavily wooded region known as the Teutoburger Wald, or Teutoburg Forest. It wound alongside Wiehan Ridge and Kalkriese Mountain to the west, with a large swampy area to the north. Once the column was under way, Arminius left, supposedly to scout ahead. He immediately took command of all the tribes that had rallied to his cause, between 20,000 and 30,000 men. It is impossible to determine his exact numbers because no contemporary German account exists. Suffice it to say, the motivation was there, but the supply sources were not, so the German forces probably waxed and waned through the campaign.

Exactly where the fighting took place has been a mystery for almost 2,000 years. The accounts of Roman historians Tacitus and Cassius Dio significantly postdate the battle, and their accounts are pieced together from evidence discovered later by a punitive expedition led by Germanicus. What seems clear is that the route that the Romans took wound through terrain both forested and rugged, narrow defiles where traditional Roman tactics could not be used. To make matters worse, high winds and heavy rains made footing treacherous, and broken (or cut) branches often blocked the way. The Germans, armed primarily with short spears, harassed the column constantly, causing severe losses. When the Romans emerged into a clearing late on the first day, Varus ordered a camp established. Here the Romans erected their traditional fieldworks, a barricade and ditch around their position. This kept the Germans at bay, for Arminius made sure that no serious attacks were launched against this strong position. He had seen the Roman army at work often enough to know that they could hold such ground indefinitely and inflict serious casualties on an attacking force.

The next morning Varus ordered many of the wagons burned, hoping to speed the column. It had little effect. Once away from their fieldworks and back into the wooded terrain, the Germans once again inflicted severe casualties. This served to both demoralize the Romans and make their already confused line of march even more confused. It is not certain if the Romans withdrew to their earlier camp or tried to erect a new one that next evening. Either way, it was insufficient to stop the now aroused and confident Germans. On what is thought to have been the final day of battle, the Roman cavalry broke away from the main body, but failed to reach safety. The press of German warriors proved too great for the encamped Romans to withstand. Varus apparently died by his own hand after receiving a serious wound. Recent excavations suggest that the battle took place more to the north of traditionally accepted sites because discoveries of large amounts of Roman coins bearing Varus's portrait imply that this was the money used for paying his troops. Weaponry unearthed around what appears to have been a hastily erected earthwork mainly appears outside the rampart, giving the impression that the Romans made a last dash for freedom. Only a handful of soldiers escaped the carnage and reached the nearest Roman base at Aliso. By that time, the battle was over and the Germans were more interested in loot than in continued combat. Those Romans that decided on surrender regretted their decision because the Germans sacrificed the prisoners to their gods.

Results

Arminius managed to maintain some unit cohesion and press on toward Aliso, which he besieged. It withstood his assaults, however, but the garrison quickly abandoned the position upon Arminius's withdrawal. They retreated even farther westward to Vetera on the Rhine, where another legion was stationed. The Germans did not attack there. Arminius kept his position as combat commander for the western German tribes and led them against Drusus Germanicus's punitive expedition 5 years later. Germanicus's four legions made some serious inroads into German lands during their two-year campaign, but it was not a serious attempt at conquest and occupation. At Idistaviso, east of Varus's last stand, Roman and German forces fought to a draw. Although the Roman army still maintained its legendary discipline and valor, the Germans matched them in bravery and by then possessed almost equal weaponry, much of which had been taken from the corpses at Teutoburger Wald. By that time, Augustus was dead and Tiberius ruled in Rome. He overruled Germanicus's request for another year's campaigning, during which the Roman general was convinced he could have brought Arminius and the Germans to heel.

When news of the defeat of three legions at Teutoburger Wald reached Rome, Augustus was thrown into a panic. He was convinced that there were insufficient Roman forces to stand against a concerted German push toward Italy. He immediately called for volunteers to defend the homeland. When few responded, he instituted conscription to build legions of freed slaves and retired veterans. He dispatched Tiberius, his adopted son and heir, to shore up the frontier defenses. He need not have worried. Although Arminius had performed well in organizing the tribes for a single battle, he lacked the power to unite the tribes for either offense or defense. The Germans returned to their isolationist ways, responding to Arminius only when Germanicus arrived. Gaul was threatened by no more than the occasional raids it had always suffered; Italy was not threatened at all.

The Roman defeat at Teutoburger Wald signaled the high-water mark of the Roman Empire in the north. In spite of Germanicus launching his attacks, the Romans had given up on the concept of occupying the land east of the Rhine. Even when fighting between the tribes flared up, the Romans did not take advantage of it, nor did they try again when Arminius was assassinated in A.D. 21. The lack of strongholds and a road network, the rugged countryside, the inability to live off the land, and the warlike nature of the Germans all contributed to Tiberius's decision to leave Germany alone. The long-term consequences of that decision are felt to this day. North-central and northeastern Europe remained free of Latin culture and law for several hundred more years. Not until the northern European tribes migrated into the Roman Empire, aiding in its downfall in the fourth and fifth centuries, did those populations adopt any major aspects of Latin culture. When they did, it was to enhance rather than replace their own mores. By missing the Roman "civilizing" influence, the Germanic languages survived. The populations migrated not only into the Roman Empire but also farther west into Britain. There the Anglo-

Saxon culture took over, swamping most of the influence Rome had had since the times of Julius Caesar.

The Roman military suffered its first major setback in centuries. The legions that had built an empire from Spain to Syria were unable to conquer these barbarian tribes. As so many disciplined armies have learned through history, the need for coordination and unit cohesion serves them only in open country. The guerrilla tactics that the Germans employed paralyzed or scattered the Romans, as they could not stand together in ranks. The Romans did not adapt their tactics, but instead avoided Germany altogether; as Edward Creasy wrote, "Roman fear disguised itself under the specious title of moderation."

Arminius in modern times has come to represent German nationalism, in spite of the fact that he did not unify the tribes but for a few temporary instances. In the late nineteenth century, a giant statue of him was raised on a hillside near the town of Detmold. Although his role in German unity may be overestimated, his defeat of Rome cannot be. Germany and Britain, at least, owe him a debt for their place in history.

References: Cassius Dio. *Dio's Roman History.* Translated by Earnest Cary. New York: Macmillan, 1924; Creasy, Edward S. *Fifteen Decisive Battles of the World.* New York: Harper, 1851; Dorenberg, John. "Battle of the Teutoburg Forest," *Archaeology Magazine* 45(5), 1992; Tacitus. *The Annals of Imperial Rome.* Translated by Michael Grant. London: Penguin, 1974.

BETH-HORON

October 66

FORCES ENGAGED

Roman: 30,000 infantry and 6,000 cavalry. Commander: Cestius Gallus, governor of Syria. Jewish (Judean): Approximately 14,000, principally light infantry, minimal cavalry. Commanders: Niger of Peraea, Silas of Batanaea, and Simon bar Gioras. Chief of Staff: Eleazar ben Simon.

IMPORTANCE

The extraordinary Jewish military victory against an overwhelming Roman punitive force convinced the skeptical majority of Jews that compromise was neither possible nor necessary because God would see the Jews through to victory. This proved to be a fatal delusion for the Jewish nation, inciting them to launch a general uprising.

Historical Setting

War between the ancient Jews and the Romans seems, in retrospect, almost a foregone conclusion. Since the first direct Roman influence in the area, that of the consul Pompey in 63 B.C., the worldly Romans and the religious Jews had too little in common to ever live together peacefully. Pompey's support of one claimant to the Judean throne over his brother led to a long series of incidents in which the ruling power of Rome offended the Jews. For the next century, Rome installed one ruler after another, each loyal to his benefactor to the detriment of the locals. Under the reign of King Herod (43–4 B.C.), foreign culture, especially foreign religious practices, became an everyday and much resented part of Jewish life. Herod's Hellenistic views, as well as his brutal actions toward anyone he perceived as a threat, provoked an orthodox reaction led by the Pharisee sect—pious legalists with a reverence for the Torah as it applied to all facets of everyday life.

During Herod's reign, banditry proliferated, with outlaw bands increasingly more daring and more political. For a time, Caesar Augustus heeded the complaints of the Jews and allowed Judea and Samaria theocratic sovereignty under a Syrian governor. The first few procurators looked as if they sincerely wanted to alleviate Jewish grievances, but local gangs of highway bandits, violent pseudoreligious groups, and a grassroots resistance, commonly termed the Zealots, complicated these efforts. Before long, unwittingly exacerbating the problem, the emperor and senate assigned third-rate administrators to Judea. The notorious Pontius Pilate is the first of a series of boorish officers sent to Caesarea. His provocations included blatant display of imperial icons within Jerusalem, a well-known offense to Jewish religious strictures; expropriation of Temple funds (albeit for an aqueduct that would serve Jerusalem's citizens); and the bloody suppression of the ensuing protests. Pilate's assault on a Samaritan religious pilgrimage resulted in his removal. In A.D. 39–40, Gaius Caligula ordered his statue to be placed in the Jewish Temple in Jerusalem, a flagrant provocation that only the brave insubordination of Petronius, the legate in Syria, prevented from escalating to a national uprising. From this point on, it was obvious to many Jews, leaders as well as common folk, that a showdown with Rome was inevitable.

Claudius attempted to preserve Roman influence in Judea by restoring a king to Judea, Herod Agrippa I, a direct heir of Herod the Great. Agrippa I was a ray of hope, a king who genuinely respected and honored Jewish customs and was an able diplomat. Unfortunately, he died after only 3 years in office. Thus ended the last hope of Judean autonomy. Agrippa had aroused Roman suspicions when he began strengthening the outlying walls of the Temple defenses and he called for a congress of Near Eastern rulers. Upon his demise, inept Roman administration resumed with the appointment of a stupid instigator, Cuspus Fadus, as procurator. There ensued a succession of venal, insensible local representatives whose brutish provocations encouraged the expansion of the Zealot groups. Symptomatic of the general unrest was the rise of numerous avowed messiahs, or deliverers, along with a general expectation that the "end of days" was near, when scriptural prophecies of a world ruler emanating from Jerusalem would be fulfilled. It appears that at least some of the ruling class—minor priests and notables—of the Pharisee sect were sympathetic to the Zealot program.

Zero hour arrived during the incredibly incompetent reign of procurator Gessius Florus.

Six years earlier, a power struggle between the Jews and gentiles (Greeks) in the Roman administrative center, Caesarea, led Nero to rule in favor of Greek dominance. By 66, the rioting between the two groups reached an intolerable level. Florus accepted a Jewish bribe to intervene and then did nothing as the Jews got the worst of the violence. He compounded his avarice by confiscating funds from the sacred Temple treasury to pay alleged arrears in Jewish taxes due the Romans. Florus arrived with troops in Jerusalem; in a vindictive mood, he insisted that the populace turn out to greet two of his cohorts sent to Jerusalem as reinforcements. When the crowds saluted the incoming troops at the behest of their dignitaries, Florus ordered his troops to contemptuously ignore them.

This affront incited the Jewish populace to further rioting and a fierce counterattack, generating widespread carnage. In May 66, the captain of the Temple, Eleazar ben Simon, threw an open challenge at Rome by halting the sacrifices regularly offered on behalf of the Roman emperor. This decision, according to Flavius Josephus, amounted to a declaration of war. Infighting among Jewish factions commenced, some favoring restoring the Imperial Temple sacrifices as a last-ditch concession to avert armed conflict. Agrippa II, Roman representative for the adjoining territories, sent troops to assist his Roman patrons to restore order, but they were repelled by the Jewish mobs, now forged into a makeshift army. The Roman garrison of the Antonia Fortress, overlooking the Temple compounds, was cut off and then treacherously slaughtered during a supposed amnesty. At this point, all-out rebellion was afoot, but the voices of moderation were still received in council.

The Battle

Procurator Gessius Florus sent an urgent request for assistance to his immediate commander, Cestius Gallus, the legate of Syria, who commanded the four-legion regional strategic

FLAVIUS JOSEPHUS: JUDEAN COMMANDER AND ROMAN WAR HISTORIAN

The enigmatic Jewish-Roman "general" and historian Flavius Josephus (A.D. 37—c. A.D. 98) participated in, observed, and then chronicled the Jewish War. It was the fate of future generations that this self-seeking, crafty individual would be virtually the sole source of information on the conflict. The central controversy turns on whether he is a traitor to the Jewish cause (the predominant viewpoint) or one who tried to preserve his people's way of life both during and after the cataclysm.

Josephus was an exceptionally resourceful but otherwise representative highborn Jewish male of the priestly class, thoroughly rooted in Jewish pharisaical practice and belief and also well versed in the classical Greco-Latin learning of the ruling Romans. A patriotic Jew, Josephus both feared and admired Roman military supremacy, which he saw first hand as a young man on a visit to Rome just after the great fire of 64. Josephus acted as an envoy seeking the release of some lower priests imprisoned for some trivial offense.

Josephus was a pragmatist who saw no hope in resisting Roman rule. His realism starkly contrasted with the mystical fatalism of many of the other Jewish leaders. Because of his priestly lineage and evident intellect, he became a natural, albeit reluctant, military leader of the rebellion, the causes of which his history fails to explain in any depth. He clearly had no sympathy with the rebels, whom he consistently denigrates as bandits, thugs, and worse, blasphemous defilers of Judaism. His disdain is less the attitude of an arrogant, reactionary elitist than that of a person truly horrified by the calamity that befell his nation. Josephus consistently tried to find a middle ground, satisfying both the imperial needs of Rome and the dignity and integrity of the Jewish way of life.

He opposed the uprising against Rome; however, in the climate of the terror after the early, unforeseen success against Cestius Gallus, he would have been executed had he confronted the fanatical Jewish leaders. After an initial victory, the Jewish leaders were reduced to defending their fortified cities against the Roman armies of Vespasian and his son Titus. Josephus, designated by the rebels as the governor-general of Galilee, engaged in a double game. The priestly Jerusalemite war council wanted Josephus to feign forging an army from the disparate bands of hotheads, but only to mollify the insurgents while the junta tried to hammer out a truce with the Romans. Instead of consolidating the defenses of Galilee, Josephus was mainly preoccupied with duping and defeating those who suspected ulterior motives. Nevertheless, he ultimately managed to mount a semblance of resistance as the Romans advanced. Josephus defended besieged Jotapata, persistently frustrating the more numerous and better-armed Romans through a variety of clever stratagems. However, Jotapata finally fell, and Josephus, through trickery, managed to survive a suicide pact among the few survivors. After his surrender, Josephus befriended Vespasian and Titus through flattering prophecies about their ultimately becoming emperors (which later proved accurate). The Roman generals spared him, and Josephus became an interpreter and intelligence analyst for the Romans and witness to their destruction of Judea, including Jerusalem in A.D. 70. After the loss of Jerusalem, Josephus accompanied his captors to Rome, where he stayed for the rest of his life and wrote *The Jewish War* (75?) and *Jewish Antiquities* (93?), among other works. Josephus's war history lacks impartial analysis of the causes of the Jewish rebellion or of the civil war among Jewish factions, which, in part, hastened the fall of Jerusalem. The astute, practical Josephus, and his moral compromises, shine through his works, leaving the reader to decide whether he was a despicable traitor or an admirable realist. *The Jewish War* is a well crafted, if not quite candid, account of Rome's campaign against Judea—through the eyes of the Jewish priest, general, Roman captive, and court historian. It describes the key first-century events in Judeo-Christian culture. Without Josephus's account, that epoch would be a blank page in our history books.

reserves in Antioch. Despite the gravity of the situation, it took Cestius 3 months from the date he received Florus's report to concentrate his expeditionary force. The muster consisted of the XIIth Legion, Fulminata (Thunderbolt), as the core, with some 4,800 men, augmented by *vexillationes*, consisting of 2,000 men from each of the other three legions, for a total of 11,000 infantry. Additionally, Cestius assembled four *alae* of cavalry—in all likelihood 2,000 horse—and six *cohortes* of auxiliary infantry, totaling about 5,000 men.

Allied monarchs offered a special counterforce, conceivably on the assumption that the hilly terrain of Judea and Galilee would favor the native slingers and javelin throwers mounting hit-and-run attacks—what would now be called light infantry or skirmishers. Cestius, if he were intelligent enough, would have cherished these special forces. Kings Antiochus IV of Commagene and Sohaemus of Emesa contributed soldiers totaling about 5,000 cavalry and 8,500 infantry. The total force thus gathered numbered about 32,000. En route from Antioch to Ptolemaïs on the coast near present-day Haifa, the township, or *toparchy*, militias in predominantly Greco-Syrian areas contributed another 2,000 troops, not well disciplined but eager to fight Jews.

Cestius then moved this large task force to Chabulon (Cabul), on the border of Ptolemaïs and Galilee, where he commenced a deliberate terror campaign. Some townspeople were slaughtered; the rest fled while the soldiers looted and burned the town and surrounding villages. The legate Placidus was left at Ptolemaïs with two infantry cohorts and a cavalry *ala*, while Cestius continued his "pacification" campaign, designed to intimidate the populations both en route to Jerusalem and in his rear so that they would neither aid nor harbor the expected Jewish resistance. The latter largely consisted of perhaps a dozen independent makeshift gangs operating with 2,000 or so members. Cestius placed the legate of the XIIth Legion, Caessennius, in charge of operations in Gali-

lee. Caessennius proceeded to march to Sepphoris, a strategically key city in Galilee with a strong pro-Roman element. The rest of Galilee followed suit. Some of the insurgent units moved off into the rebel mountain strongholds of Asamon and Jebel al-Deibedeh to the northwest, pursued by an *ala* of cavalry. The Romans lost 200 men; the Jews lost 2,000.

Meanwhile, Cestius led a detachment down the coast toward Caesarea while detaching other units, by land and sea, to demolish Joppa on the Judean coast, with the naval vessels isolating the port in support of the land operation. The town was razed and 8,000 of its inhabitants slain. Another column was sent to deal in the same way with Nabatene (Narbata) and the adjoining villages. The force continued down the coast from Caesarea to Antipatris, splitting off a contingent to deal with the nearby rebel stronghold at the Tower of Aphek, which proved to be abandoned. It and the surrounding villages were razed.

The coastal columns rejoined Cestius's main force at Caesarea along with the troops that had ravaged Joppa and Nabatene to regroup for the offensive toward Jerusalem.

With Galilee and the entire Judean coast in his hands, Cestius might have reasonably determined that he could wrap up the campaign in 3 weeks or so, before the October rains rendered the roads impassable. His regenerated force then moved into Judea proper, entering Lydda and burning the abandoned town along with fifty Jewish stragglers. A detachment was split off to Aphek (Mejdel Yaba), where they dispersed a concentration of insurgents.

Up until this time, the Jewish resistance seemed disorganized, and it often simply appeared to have melted away, confirming Cestius's hunch that his terror campaign had intimidated the Jews. The Romans continued to advance along the road to Jerusalem, to the point where it leaves the plain at Emmaus (Emwas or Nicopolis) and twists up into the hills through the notorious gorge at Beth-horon. They bivouacked overnight at the citadel of

Gabao (Gibeon or Jib), lying just over 6 miles northwest of Jerusalem.

Rashly, thanks to the good fortune and light resistance he had encountered thus far, Cestius set out the next morning in haphazard marching order, allowing his baggage train with its accompanying escort to lag behind, detached from the main body. He failed to reconnoiter in conformity with the usual Roman doctrine. Conversely, the Jews made excellent use of the heights neglected by Cestius's columns. From those heights, the Jewish sentries accurately discerned the layout and order of battle of the Roman forces. The Jews set up a comprehensive ambuscade along the crests. Although it was a Sabbath, the Jews poured out of Jerusalem and attacked the vanguard of the Roman column just as it was redeploying from marching to battle formation.

Aided by an assemblage of Jewish fighters from Adiabene, Niger of Peraea and Silas of Batanaea, seasoned defectors from Agrippa II's army, led the forces attacking the forward elements. Simon bar Gioras, a coarse but charismatic guerrilla chieftain, simultaneously led the attack on the rear guard where it was lumbering through the Beth-horon Pass. The Romans suffered considerable losses—515 killed (400 infantry, 115 cavalry) compared with 22 Jews killed—and, portentously, forfeited many mules needed to transport the baggage and equipment. However, they were able to recover, inasmuch as the forward elements disengaged in good order and wheeled about to assist the main body, while the Jews were not sufficiently well organized to counterattack the Romans once the legions had re-formed into their versatile battle dispositions. Cestius was able to regroup and withdraw to the main camp at Gabao.

The Romans mustered and advanced again toward Jerusalem in search of supplies. Cestius swept aside Jewish skirmishers and set up camp on Mt. Scopus, less than a mile outside of the city. Under the notion that the Jews were wracked with internal strife and could not repeat their success at the defile of Beth-horon,

Cestius was in no hurry to attack. During the hiatus, King Agrippa II sent emissaries to offer to broker an amnesty for the rebels, but the Jews killed one intermediary and wounded the other. For 3 days, Cestius sent out foraging parties to collect grain—manifesting his concern for his dwindling provisions—while he vainly awaited signs that the Jews within the walls were wavering. The next day, 15 October, he entered the Jerusalem outskirts and observed the rebels withdrawing behind the secondary city wall, where they occupied the prepared defenses. The Romans burned the suburb of Betheza in the hope that this demonstration of Roman ferocity would dampen the zeal of the Jews. Skirting the Antonia Fortress, Cestius shifted toward the wall opposite Herod's palace on the west side of the city. Josephus states that, had Cestius pressed his attack at that moment, Jerusalem would have been his. This seems probable, but his explanation that the procurator Gessius Florus bribed certain commanders not to attack so that general prolonged warfare would ensue, obscuring the procurator's misdeeds, is spurious.

The Roman task force pressed the attack for another 6 days, ultimately leading a picked force headed by archers to attack the north side of the Temple compound near the Antonia Fortress. Then, Cestius suddenly abandoned offensive operations. The onset of winter, the unexpected skill and boldness of the guerrillas at Beth-horon Pass, and his shortage of supplies and baggage mules all contributed to his decision.

Having learned nothing from his previous experience at Beth-horon Pass, during his evacuation Cestius neglected to post pickets on the hilltops overlooking the narrowest parts of the gorge, allowing the emboldened Jews to play cat and mouse with them all the way to his encampment at Gabao. Sundown saved Cestius from further catastrophe. The Romans loitered there fruitlessly for 2 days while more Jewish fighters took up blocking positions along the heights lining the road to the coast. Selected Jewish forces barred the exit of the Romans from

JEWISH REBELS: ZEALOTS, BANDITS, SICARII, ETC.

Thanks to Josephus's well-known bias against the Jewish insurgent groups, we have a very skewed picture of their origins, objectives, and role. Reading between the lines, we get an idea that there was a more or less continuous presence of paramilitary bands, borderline criminal and seditious vagabonds, since the time of the Maccabee rebellion in the mid–second century B.C. The groups are not homogeneous; nevertheless, all seem to have found more in common with the offshoot Pharisee faction than the priestly Sadducee establishment. During the Maccabee uprising, the holy men spurring on the warriors were known as Hasidim. They continued to play a role as a rudimentary form of Pharisee throughout the time of the later Hasmonean rule, as the leaders became more Hellenized (capitulating to cosmopolitan fashion instead of behaving piously) and corrupt. They were persecuted during the time of John Hyrcanus II and Alexander Jannaeus (mid–first century B.C.), and it is believed that at this time they formed outlaw bands, loosely identified with common criminal gangs. Queen Alexandra, the last Hasmonean ruler, tried to make a rapprochement with them, but, when she died, the ineptitude of her successors left the door open for Roman intervention and domination.

During the reign of Herod the Great, these gangs became endemic, to the extent that Herod's army spent much of its time hunting them down, fairly successfully. The outright conversion from Robin Hood–like underground opposition groups to political insurgents occurred in reaction to the conversion from client kingdom to full province after the death of Herod. In opposition to the census imposed by the Syrian legate Quirinius in A.D. 6, according to Josephus, a "Fourth Philosophy"—after Sadducee, Pharisee, and Essene—was formed by one Judas of Galilee, associated with another leader, Saddok. The movement recognized no master but God. Thus, no temporal being nor other deity could require payments, prayer, or any other form of homage from a Jew, especially a Jew in the land bequeathed to his people by Yahweh. Overlaying the matter of religious defilement, the small landholders were being crushed by the fiscal burdens of Roman taxation, Temple tithes, and a general downturn in the economy. Many lost their lands to foreclo-

the pass, while others assaulted down the slopes, covered by a devastating and unanswered hail of arrows, the Roman cavalry being immobilized in the crevasse. Captured Roman catapults inflicted further casualties and chaos on the disordered Roman force. To extricate his more mobile units, the Roman commander had to abandon what was left of his baggage train and rear guard. The XIIth Legion lost 5,300 infantry and 480 cavalry, as well as all their pack animals and artillery, which was to serve well the Jews of Jerusalem during Titus's siege operations 4 years later. Fulminata also lost its eagle (the legion's standard) to the Jews, a stigma that only a stunning victory could erase. By the time that the remnants of Cestius's battered force staggered back into Syria, the insurgents controlled all of Jerusalem, most of Judea, and a foothold in Fort Machaerus in southern Peraea.

Results

The unexpected Jewish victory convinced many ambivalent Judean moderates to join the ranks of the outnumbered, though relentlessly vigorous, war party, thereby frustrating an impending compromise with the Romans and ensuring that there would be a cataclysmic war. Had the Jewish insurgents been routed, it is likely that those still influential moderates in favor of rapprochement would have prevailed, forestalling the rebellion. As it occurred, many borderline collaborators were driven from Jerusalem to take refuge in the Decapolis cities or with Agrippa's forces. Others flocked to the rebel cause, out of fear, momentum, or the renewed certitude that God favored their cause. The conflict would signify the beginning of the end for the sovereign Jewish nation.

sure and had to become common laborers on the grounds they formerly owned. Employment became so scarce after the completion of Herod's vast make-work Temple project that his successors had to inaugurate a street-paving project so these men would not be left jobless. Both piety and poverty were driving many into the arms of the protoguerrilla gangs. Though Josephus is inconsistent about the origins and development of the Zealots, there is no real sense that they represented a single organization with a continuous tradition. Reading him between the lines, in conjunction with his modern interpreters, one sees that there were many groups with varying agendas. The *sicarii,* or daggermen, for example, were urban terrorists who stalked upper-echelon Jewish collaborators and stabbed them with curved daggers concealed beneath their cloaks. Their connection with other mainstream Zealot organizations is nebulous. They were engaged at several points, in internecine fighting with the more moderate factions of the resistance and were believed to have been the group that conducted the generally misinterpreted "last stand" at Masada Fortress.

At the onset of the Jewish War, there were a number of guerrilla bands, operating in Galilee as well as Judea. Among the leaders of these groups, John of Gischala became prominent in Galilee and Simon bar Gioras took a leading role in Judea. Eleazar ben Simon, the captain of the Temple who signaled the start of the revolt with his refusal to authorize sacrifices on behalf of the Roman emperor, may also have led a Zealot coterie.

There may have been a dozen or more guerrilla bands operating with 1,000 to 3,000 members. They were armed with spears, swords, javelins, slings, and throwing darts. They were lightly armored, if at all. Command structure was simple, and there does not appear to have been any formal chain of command. The war council in Jerusalem had to deal directly with the guerrilla chieftains, as there was no centralized staff system. Leadership was thus charismatic and dependent upon the active involvement of the chieftain. The men in the ranks had no special loyalty to the powers in Jerusalem, only to their commander. Josephus's assertion of assembling, arming, and training an "army" of 60,000 in Galilee based on the Roman model appears largely to have been wishful thinking.

Nero appointed Vespasian, a grizzled veteran of the uprisings in Britannia, as commander of a punitive expedition to pacify Judea. While Vespasian was carefully marshaling his forces, a conference of the more sympathetic priests and gentry formed a war council to prepare to meet the impending Roman counteraction. Greater Judea was divided into defense commands, five "generals" being appointed to organize their respective regions. A few abortive assaults on the vestigial Roman forces proved ineffective—notably a fiasco at Askalon —while Flavius Josephus clumsily attempted to hammer together a coalition of conflicting gangs in Galilee, where the first blow was expected. Josephus temporized, neglecting to adequately consolidate and fortify strategic towns, while trifling fruitlessly with an "army" on the Roman model.

When Vespasian invaded, he easily overran Galilee and made inroads into Judea by using friendly Samaria as a springboard. A bitter Roman succession struggle in the year 69 suspended operations for a year and a half, during which time internecine strife among the competing Zealot factions left Jerusalem in disarray. Intelligence of the Jewish disorder encouraged Vespasian's son Titus to mount a determined blockade and envelopment of Jerusalem. The capital was overrun in 70, after the burning of the Holy Temple. Isolated fortresses held out for another 3 years. The decimated Jews were stripped of all temporal power in Judea, which was renamed Syria Palaestina, a pointed reference to the ancient enemies of the Jews, the Philistines.

The Roman governor allowed Talmudic scholars to set up a national academy at Jamnia to codify and teach the tenets of pharisaic Judaism. The rabbinical center was politically quiescent, as was the Jewish multitude remaining in Palestine, that is, until A.D. 132, when an avowed messiah, Simon bar Kochba, sponsored by the great spiritual leader and scholar Rabbi Akiva, led another quixotic Jewish uprising that ended with the uprooting of the Judaic remnant and the great Diaspora. Judaism continued in a new form, no longer centered on Temple worship nor tied to any one place. There would be no Jewish homeland until 1948, with the establishment of Israel at the site of ancient Judea.

—*Jim Bloom*

References: Farmer, W. R. *Macabees, Zealots, and Josephus.* New York: Columbia University Press, 1956; Jones, A. H. M. *The Herods of Judaea.* Oxford, UK: Clarendon Press, 1967; Rhoads, David M. *Israel in Revolution: 6–74 C.E.* Philadelphia: Fortress, 1976; Sheldon, Rose Mary. "The Great Jewish War against Rome: Taking on Goliath," *Military and Naval Forum Proceedings* 3(9): 15–29, March 1996; Smallwood, E. Mary. "The Jews under Roman Rule from Pompey to Diocletian: A Study in Political Relations," in *Studies in Judaism in Late Antiquity,* Jacob Neusner, ed. Leiden: Brill, 1981.

MILVIAN BRIDGE

27 October 312

FORCES ENGAGED

Gallic: Approximately 50,000 men.
Commander: Constantine.
Italian: Approximately 75,000 men.
Commander: Maxentius.

IMPORTANCE

Constantine's victory gave him total control of the western Roman Empire, paving the way for Christianity as the dominant religion for the Roman Empire and ultimately for Europe.

Historical Setting

Rarely has the course of events followed such a convoluted path to a single decisive event as those that took the forces of the western Roman Empire to the battle at Milvian Bridge. In the 49 years between 235 and 284, Rome was ruled by no less than 26 emperors. Almost anyone with the support of a legion or two battled for, seized, and lost the position of supreme ruler of the Roman Empire. Finally, in 284, Diocletian seized and kept power. Although a soldier from Illyria (along the eastern Adriatic coast), Diocletian, once in power, spent most of his time trying to institute reforms that would stabilize the empire. This involved increased taxation, but the collection was done in a much more equitable fashion than in previous decades. The money was spent on increased bureaucracy and military to the point that some believed there to be more employees of the government than there were taxpayers.

While that did bring about a much more stable atmosphere, Diocletian's most serious reform involved the system by which the empire was ruled. Realizing that no one man could possibly manage everything from Britain to Persia, Diocletian introduced a tetrarchy, rule by four men. Basing his capital in Nicomedia, at the western end of the Sea of Marmora, he appointed a co-emperor, Maximian, to rule from Italy. Both Diocletian and Maximian would hold the title of augustus. Each man appointed a subordinate, called a caesar, to assist them in ruling their respective halves of the empire. Diocletian named Galerius as caesar in the east, and Maximian named Constantius as caesar in the west. The caesar was to replace the augustus upon his death or retirement and then name a replacement caesar for himself. This was meant to ensure a regular succession, which had not existed for many decades.

When Diocletian decided to retire in 305, he convinced Maximian to do so as well. As planned, Constantius and Galerius rose to

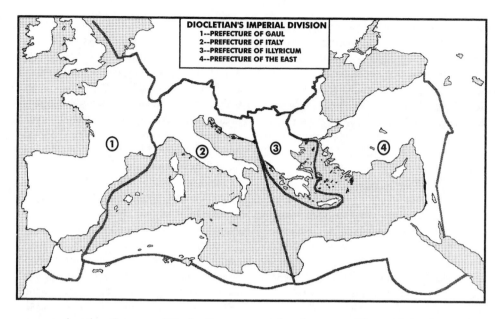

DIOCLETIAN'S IMPERIAL DIVISION
1--PREFECTURE OF GAUL
2--PREFECTURE OF ITALY
3--PREFECTURE OF ILLYRICUM
4--PREFECTURE OF THE EAST

augustus, but then they named Flavius Severus as caesar in the west and Maximinus Daia in the east, respectively. Naming those two as caesars seemed a slap in the face to the two who thought that by birth they should have had the positions: Constantine, as son of Constantius, and Valerius Maxentius, as son of Maximian. That resentment came to a head when Constantius died in 306. His army, based in Britain and Gaul, named Constantine not just caesar but augustus, although Constantine declined the higher title. He was confirmed as caesar, but Severus, as acting caesar, became augustus in the west. Unfortunately, troops in Italy named Maximian's son Maxentius as augustus, ignoring Severus who was next in line. That resulted in a civil war between 306 and 307 in which Severus was finally executed and Maxentius took the western augustus title, but ceded it to his father Maximian who came out of retirement to reoccupy the throne.

Rather than leave well enough alone, Galerius in the eastern empire refused to recognize either Constantine or Maximian as western augustus. Instead, Galerius named one of his generals, Licianus Licinius, as augustus to replace Severus, and he invaded Italy to enforce that appointment. During the invasion, Maxentius forced his father out of power and named himself western augustus. To make matters even more confusing, Galerius's nephew Maximinus Daia sought and received the title of augustus as well. Thus, six men held the title originally intended for two, while the post of caesar remained vacant. Diocletian finally stepped in, calling a conference in 308 at Carnuntum (modern Hainburg, Austria). Each man except Maximian (retiring a second time) was allowed to retain the title of augustus and was given control over separate regions of the empire.

Diocletian's mandate lasted but 2 years. Maximian, fleeing from his son to the court of Constantine in Gaul, tried to overthrow his host in 310. For his trouble, he was taken prisoner and allowed to kill himself. When Galerius died in 311, once again four men reigned, all as augustus and none as caesar: Constantine in Gaul, Maxentius in Italy, Licinius in the Balkans, and Maximinus Daia in the east. Had Constantine formally ceded the title of augustus and held that of caesar, Maxentius may never have felt the need to go to war against him. Maxentius, however, was a tyrannical ruler who spent lavishly on himself and his Praetorian Guard while abusing the common people; such men see conspiracies everywhere, and Maxentius suspected Constantine of plotting against him. Determined to rule the western half of the empire alone, in 311 Maxentius began preparations for an invasion of Gaul.

The Battle

Learning of Maxentius's intentions, Constantine decided to strike first. He had some 100,000 troops under his command, but more than half had to be left to protect the German and British frontiers. In the early spring of 312, Constantine marched his army of 40,000 through the melting alpine snow into northern Italy. Maxentius sent troops northward under a variety of generals, whom Constantine

proceeded to defeat at Susa, Turin, and Milan, each of his victories coming over superior numbers. Maxentius sent his best general last; Ruricius Pompeianus too was defeated at Brescia and Verona. As he fought his way south, Constantine maintained a fairly stable number in his army, picking up recruits from the countryside and his defeated enemies. As he approached Rome, his force numbered about 50,000 men. Maxentius, locked up in Rome, commanded about 75,000.

The events that occurred just outside Rome are the stuff of legend. Maxentius misread the omens he received. He was advised via the Sybilline books concerning the upcoming battle "that on that day the enemy of Rome should perish" (Dudley, *The Romans,* p. 270). Convinced that Constantine and not he himself was the enemy of Rome, Maxentius led his army out from behind the Roman Walls of Aurelian onto the plains near the village of Saxa

The Great Battle of the Milvian Bridge. *From the* History of Constantine the Great. *Tapestry after a painting by Peter Paul Rubens, eighteenth century. (Corbis/Philadelphia Museum of Art)*

Rubra, deploying them with the Tiber River at his back.

Constantine also received an omen. The day before the battle, it is said that he had a vision. This vision has been described in a variety of ways, depending on one's source. Durant's description, citing the contemporary source Eusebius, says that Constantine saw in the sky a flaming cross, upon which was written the Greek words *en tutoi nika*, "in this sign conquer." The following morning, Constantine heard a voice instructing him to place upon his soldiers' shields "the letter X with a line drawn through it and curled around the top—the symbol of Christ" (Durant, *Caesar and Christ*, p. 654). Most sources put the wording on the cross as Latin: *in hoc signo vinces*. Dudley (*The Romans*, p. 270) states that Constantine had a dream before the battle in which he was told to place the Greek letters *chi* and *rho* (the sign of Christ) on his army's shields.

Constantine had in his army a number of Christians, as well as followers of the equally popular Mithra cult. The followers of Mithra used a cross of light as symbolic of the Unconquerable Sun, a sign of their god. Constantine had also long been a believer in the cult of Apollo, the sun god. At any rate, Constantine later told Eusebius that he vowed before the battle to convert to Christianity if he was victorious.

Details of the battle are sketchy. It seems that both sides placed infantry in the center and cavalry on the flanks. Constantine commanded one of the cavalry wings and led the charge. His Gallic cavalry was more mobile than the heavily armored Roman cavalry under Maxentius, but was heavier than the lightly armed North African cavalry auxiliaries. Thus, it was able to outfight both and crush Maxentius's flanks. Among the infantry, this caused much panic, and only the Praetorian Guard stood their ground against the attacks of Constantine's infantry. They were overwhelmed and died where they stood. The rout of the remainder of Maxentius's force had but one escape route, that of the Milvian Bridge

across the Tiber. It was so crowded and the troops so desperate that not even Maxentius could get onto it. He tried to swim across, but the weight of his armor dragged him to his death. His body was brought to the surface the next day.

Results

Maxentius's death meant that Constantine was the sole ruler of the western Roman Empire. Just before he launched his invasion, Constantine had concluded a truce with Licinius. The agreement included the promise of marriage to Constantine's sister for Lucinius's impassivity during the campaign. Licinius was as good as his word, and once the situation had settled down, he and Constantine met in Milan in February 313. There the two issued the Edict of Milan concerning religious tolerance. "I, Constantine Augustus, and I, Licinius Augustus, met under good auspices in Milan, we discussed everything bearing on public advantage and security. First, we considered regulations should be framed to secure respect for divinity on these lines: that the Christians and all other men should be allowed full freedom to subscribe to whatever form of worship they desire, so that whatever divinity may be on the heavenly throne may be well disposed and propitious to us, and to all placed under us" (Dudley, *The Romans*, p. 271). Constantine seemed to be hedging his bets here, but as time went by he became more solidly supportive of Christianity.

Constantine was soon back in the field, campaigning against hostile Germanic tribes, while Licinius fought and defeated Maximinus Daia. This defeat placed Licinius in control of the eastern Roman Empire. For the next 11 years, the two alternately supported and fought each other. When Constantine defeated Licinius at a battle in 314 and took from him control of almost everything in Europe, Licinius responded by persecuting Christians in the east. He maintained his pagan ways as Constantine became more Christian, until a final showdown between the two resulted in Licinius's defeat in 323; he was executed the following year.

The city of Rome, which had become an increasingly less important city, lost its title as capital of the empire when Constantine established the city bearing his name, Constantinople. Over time, it became not only the political center of the empire but rivaled Rome for centuries as headquarters of the Christian faith. It was Constantine's victory outside Rome in 312, however, that put the Christians in a position to be arguing over where the power in their church should rest. The ban on persecution issued in Milan gave the Christians the first breathing room in their history. By 325, they were virtually guaranteed preeminence, for in that year Constantine summoned the Council of Nicea. There leaders of the Christian church branded certain beliefs to be heresies; unfortunately for history, Constantine blamed the Jews for Christ's death, setting in motion centuries of pogroms.

The depth of Constantine's conversion has been debated since his own day. The primary source for his statements of faith come from the contemporary Christian historian Eusebius, who was more than a little biased. Certain later statements attributed to the emperor give conflicting views. Constantine rarely followed Christian rituals, and, even though he expressed some religious views at the Council of Nicea, he was more interested in maintaining order than leading the church. His mother was a strong convert and certainly had some influence on him, but, whether he was a Christian by conversion or for political ends, the Christian Church benefited. Other religions soon found themselves persecuted just as harshly by the Christians as the Christians themselves formerly had been. Whatever the merits and drawbacks of later interreligious strife, the fact that Christianity is the dominant faith in Europe today is directly traceable to Constantine.

His foundation of Constantinople set up the division of the Roman Empire into two formal halves. The Eastern Roman Empire grew in power and wealth, later being titled the Byzantine Empire. It stood until overthrown by the power of Islam in 1453. The Western Roman Empire sunk into mediocrity, with occasional glimpses of its former glory when a passing tribe exercised enough power to establish any stability there. Ultimately, Rome came to be a religious rather than a political capital, and its later power emanated from the papacy rather than from the emperor.

References: Dudley, Donald. *The Romans.* New York: Alfred A. Knopf, 1970; Durant, Will. *Caesar and Christ.* New York: Simon & Schuster, 1944; Eusebius. *The History of the Church from Christ to Constantine.* Translated by G. A. Williamson. New York: Dorset Press, 1984 [1965]; Gibbon, Edward. *The Decline and Fall of the Roman Empire.* Abridged by Frank Bourne. New York: Dell, 1963; Grant, Michael. *Constantine: The Man and His Times.* New York: Charles Scribner's Sons, 1994.

ADRIANOPLE
9 August 378

FORCES ENGAGED
Gothic: 50,000 infantry and 50,000 cavalry.
Commander: Fritigern.
Byzantine: 40,000 infantry and 20,000 cavalry.
Commander: Emperor Valens.

IMPORTANCE
Adrianople marked the arrival of the Goths as serious participants in western European history and altered warfare from infantry to cavalry dominance for the next thousand years.

Historical Setting

After the death of Constantine in 337, the Roman Empire saw the return of sibling struggles for total control. Constantine had hoped that his three surviving sons would be satisfied with one-third of the empire each (western Europe, southeastern Europe, and the east), but such was not to be. Who fought and killed whom, and who succeeded whom, in the three major regions of the Roman Empire is too convoluted to follow. Suffice it to say that, as soon as his three sons were killed (none died of old age), they were followed not by blood relations but by generals from their armies. The general who finally rose to the top, in 364, was Valentian I, a man of humble birth but well above average military skill. He focused on shoring up the frontier along the Danube River, so, to keep the eastern part of the empire in friendly hands, he appointed his brother Valens to the position of co-emperor and placed him in Constantinople. Valentian died in 375 and was succeeded by his 16-year-old son Gratian, who was much too young and inexperienced to hold any sway over his uncle.

Valens was not the man to be emperor at this point. The Middle East was as turbulent as ever, with Byzantine forces trying to keep down the Persians under Sapor II. Paying more attention to the east than to his own backyard, Valens was unready for the war that broke out with the Goths. The Goths originated in Scandinavia, but wandered into northeastern Europe, spent a number of generations in eastern Russia, and finally appeared in the Balkans in the early third century. The Goths were not merely roaming about looking for a place to live, but active in raiding and pillaging as they migrated. By 270, they had cut a swath through the Balkans as far as Greece before they were finally defeated at the battle of Naissus. After that loss, they entered into an alliance with the Roman Empire and for the next hundred years remained peaceful. The Goths provided large numbers of recruits for the Roman/Byzantine armies as the citizenry of the Roman Empire, both east and west, dwindled in both population and motivation.

The Byzantines had defeated and allied themselves with the Visigoths, the western segment of the Gothic population. The Ostrogoths, or eastern segment, continued to live in Russia until they began to feel the pressure, in the early 370s, of the Huns, pressing against the Ostrogoths in their own aggressive migration from China. Defeated in their attempts to beat back the Huns, the Ostrogoths moved west into lands populated by their cousins, the Visigoths, who in turn pushed the more distant Visigothic tribes into the Danube River valley, the traditional northeastern border of the Roman Empire. When the Visigoths reached Byzantine territory, they asked permission to stay, to which Valens responded positively, under certain conditions. Valens told them that every male under military age had to be given up as a hostage and that all their weapons had to be handed over to Byzantine officials. Had he treated them with the same respect he had the Goths who had lived on Byzantine lands for decades, he might have had another vast pool of soldiers upon which to draw for his armies. Instead, Valens looked on them with some contempt, as previous campaigning he had conducted against these newly arrived Visigothic tribes gave him a low opinion of their abilities and character.

Valens in 377 marched against the Persians, leaving two poorly chosen subordinates in charge of collecting weapons: Lupicinus and Maximus. These two decided to enrich themselves at Gothic expense, taking bribes of money and the sexual favors of the warriors' wives and daughters in return for allowing them to keep their weapons. When the Ostrogoths arrived and also pleaded for sanctuary, they were refused. They crossed the Danube anyway, screened by the Visigoths who were already dealing with the Byzantines. Finally pressed too far in the demands for bribes, the Visigothic leader Fritigern conspired with the Ostrogoths to present a solid alliance in the face of official greed. When Lupicinus and Maximus attempted to assassinate Fritigern, killing instead his co-commander Alavius, the Goths went to war.

The Battle

Outraged by the assassination, Fritigern led his men against a Byzantine force at Marianopolis (in eastern Bulgaria), defeated them, and then joined with Ostrogoth forces under Alatheus and Syphax in the region between the Danube and the Black Sea. Valens was quick to respond. Concluding a quick truce with the Persians, he sent forces north under his generals Saturninus, Trajan, and Profuturus, who proceeded to back the Goths into a marshy area near the mouth of the Danube. The battle was inconclusive, but Fritigern managed to extricate his force through the marshes. In this battle, the Goths employed their standard defensive tactic, circling their wagons into a large laager and fighting from inside with occasional sallies against their attackers. This presaged similar tactics used almost a thousand years later by Jan Zizka of the Hussites in Bohemia and then the Boers of South Africa in the late nineteenth century.

Having escaped the Byzantines and aided by nomadic horsemen from the east, the Goths began looting the countryside north of Greece. Valens marched to Thrace, on the Black Sea northeast of Greece, while appealing for reinforcements from his nephew Gratian in Italy. He needed them because in 378 the Goths were

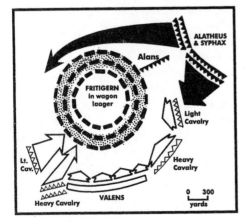

raising reinforcements of their own by entering into alliances with a few Germanic tribes, thereby disrupting the entire northern frontier of the Roman Empire. German uprisings along the Rhine forced Gratian to lead his forces into Gaul. There he severely punished forces of the Allemani and Franks and then marched down the Danube River valley toward his uncle's position. In the meantime, Valens's generals were successfully beating back the Goths from Thrace in the summer of 378.

The Goths retreated toward the city of Adrianople, on the Maritza River west of Constantinople and centered in the peninsula formed by the Adriatic Sea, Black Sea, and Dardanelles. There the Visigoths, under Fritigern, established themselves in their wagon-camp defensive position, while the Ostrogoths (supplemented by other eastern cavalry such as Alans and Sarmatians) foraged the region for supplies to feed the population of perhaps 100,000 warriors and 200,000 women and children. The Visigoths acted primarily as infantry, whereas the Ostrogoths and their allies operated mainly as cavalry, under the direction of the Ostrogothic chieftains Alatheus and Syphax. Valens had replaced his earlier generals with an Italian named Sebastiani, who took a smaller force of soldiers and trained them under his own direction. He believed that the bulk of the Byzantine army was weak, and so a smaller, more disciplined force seemed to him better able to inflict serious damage. After scoring some successes with guerrilla raids against the Goths, Sebastiani recommended to Valens a continuation of that strategy rather than engaging in a full-scale battle. He was sure that the Goths could not support themselves for long and would soon negotiate a withdrawal eastward, which would put them in the path of the Huns and therefore solve Valens's problem. Valens disregarded that sound advice because news of Gratian's victories against the Germans had aroused his jealousy. To restore his own reputation, Valens needed not only a victory but a quick one before Gratian's reinforcements

---

"PRIDE GOETH BEFORE A FALL."

Valens is the true villain of this piece, from the Roman Empire's point of view. He was too willing to respond to the will of the public rather than to the wiser counsel of his general, Sebastiani. In the first place, Valens bowed to public pressure to march against the Goths himself, rather than allow Sebastiani to maintain his effective strategy of harassing and starving the Goths into submission. Gibbon writes in *The Decline and Fall of the Roman Empire:* "the citizens, who are always brave at a distance from any real danger, declared, with confidence, that if they were supplied with arms, *they* alone would undertake to deliver the province from the ravages of an insulting foe. The vain reproaches of the ignorant multi-

tude hastened the downfall of the Roman empire; they provoked the desperate rashness of Valens, who did not find, either in his reputation or in his mind, any motives to support with firmness the public contempt. He was soon persuaded by the successful achievements of his lieutenants to despise the power of the Goths" (p. 472).

Once arrived at Adrianople, against the advice of Sebastiani, Valens gave in to his own views of the popular reputation of his nephew Gratian. Determined to prove himself to himself and to the public, Valens rejected the suggestion to wait for reinforcements, and the resulting balance of numbers against him in the battle (100,000 to 60,000) proved his folly.

---

arrived to rob him of his glory. Besides, he still believed the Ostrogoths to be overrated soldiers.

Upon hearing of Valens's approach, Fritigern sent a negotiating team. This was not to conclude a peace treaty, but to buy time for the cavalry to return from their foraging expedition. Valens refused to talk. On 9 August 378, he marched his 40,000 infantry and 20,000 cavalry out of Adrianople and some 8 miles to the Gothic wagon camp, arriving there about noon. Again Fritigern sent out envoys to ask for peace, again in order to buy time. He also set afire the crops in the area. Valens at first gave the impression he was willing to talk, but in reality he was also buying time in order to deploy his forces. As the day was already extremely hot, the Byzantine soldiers exhausted by their march, and the Gothic laager well situated and difficult to assault, Valens was glad for the opportunity to rest his men a few hours and reconnoiter the opposition.

As Valens's emissaries approached the Gothic camp, their escorting Iberian archers inexplicably launched some arrows into the Gothic camp and then turned and fled. This naturally provoked the Visigoths, and, unfortunately for Valens, it also coincided with the arrival of the Ostrogothic cavalry, some 50,000

strong. Led by some Alans, the cavalry swooped down on the Byzantine ranks, still attempting to deploy for battle. The Byzantine cavalry on the right flank faced the attackers and gave them a good fight. As this was happening, more Byzantine cavalry moved up on the left flank in order to possibly flank the Gothic position, but they were unsupported by infantry and too weak and exposed to do much damage.

It was the cavalry fight on the Byzantine right wing where the battle was decided, and, when that flank broke, the Ostrogoths pounded down on the disorganized infantry. Unable to completely deploy, the infantry was similarly unable to put up a defense. Instead, they were quickly surrounded and hard-pressed by the cavalry, which kicked up such dust that the infantry could not see. They were so confined by the ever-tightening circle of horses that the primary chronicler of the battle, Ammianus Marcellinus, says that the infantry forces could not even draw their swords, or wield them if the could draw them. Into the mass of infantry, the Ostrogoths poured a relentless shower of arrows. The situation then got worse for the Byzantines because Fritigern at this point opened his laager and moved his infantry into the fray. The longer slashing sword that they carried, as well as the battle-axes that they wielded, slaughtered thousands of Byzantine infantrymen. Not until sufficient numbers of them had died were the survivors able to have enough room to maneuver themselves and break out of the ring.

Valens himself stood at the rear of the battle, among his reserves, and fought alongside them when the Gothic soldiers reached them. They too were ultimately unable to withstand the huge numbers of Goths and were beaten back, Valens falling in the battle, badly wounded. By most accounts, he was carried to a peasant's hut, which was surrounded that evening and set afire by the Goths, not knowing that the emperor was dying in the flames. Valens was the highest profile casualty of the battle, but most of his top commanders died as well, along with probably 40,000 of his soldiers. Gothic casualties are unrecorded, but almost certainly were fairly light.

Results

Not since the great Carthaginian general Hannibal had destroyed a Roman army at Cannae in the Second Punic War had the Roman Empire suffered such a defeat as this. Not since the German tribes under Arminius destroyed two legions in the Teutoburg Forest in A.D. 9 had the Roman Empire felt such terror. To many, it seemed as if the barbarians, long nibbling away at Roman frontiers and society, were now in the ascendant. A better-organized Gothic force may have been able to take over the Eastern Roman Empire at this point, but, for all their skill on the battlefield, they had no siege machinery. Thus, Constantinople probably would have survived. Still, the Goths were able to return to their rampage through southeastern Europe. Valens was immediately succeeded by Theodosius, who began to reorganize and retrain the military. Within 5 years—with Gratian's support—he beat back his enemy, cleared the region around the west coast of the Black Sea, and forced the Goths back across the Danube, although those that swore loyalty were permitted to settle in the lands that they had once pillaged. Over the next decade, Theodosius continued the practice of defeating Goths and then allowing them to either settle in his lands or join his army. This meant an even bigger change in the Eastern Roman army than ever. For a thousand years, Rome and its possessions had been both won and defended by the legionaries, highly trained heavy infantry whose discipline outmatched almost any opponent. Even when Germanic recruits were taken into the Roman army, it remained primarily an infantry force. After the battle of Adrianople, and with the ensuing recruitment of Goths into the military, the army of the Eastern Roman Empire became predominantly cavalry. Because cavalry, especially from the east, was also primarily archers, their ability to attack at long range severely limited the power of the infantry formations. Thus, the horse soldier became the dominant military figure in Europe for the next thousand years. Not until the fifteenth century is the cavalry overturned by missile weapons: the longbow and crossbow.

Although Theodosius was able to maintain fairly good relations with the Goths, upon his death in 395 the next able leader to arise was Alaric the Goth. He proceeded to lead his people through southeastern Europe until finally he entered Italy itself. In 410, after three sieges, he captured and sacked Rome. At that point, it was already a lesser city, as Ravenna was then the seat of government. However, that Rome had not fallen to attack since the seventh century B.C. had greatly symbolic implications. The Ostrogoths settled into Italy, whereas the Visigoths moved through Gaul and into Spain. Thus, the Western Roman Empire collapsed and became Gothic in culture if not in political unification. Gothic though they many have been, the population adopted much of Roman culture. Adrianople thus spelled the end of the Western Roman Empire, while it spelled the beginning of the cavalry as Europe's main military arm.

References: Ammianus Marcellinus. *Ammianus Marcellinus*. Translated by John Carew Rolfe. Cambridge, MA: Harvard University Press, 1950 [1935–1939]; Fuller, J. F. C. *A Military History of the Western World*, vol. 1. New York: Funk & Wagnalls, 1954; Heather, Peter. *Goths and Romans*. Oxford, UK: Clarendon Press, 1991; Oman, Charles. *The Art of War in the Middle Ages*. Ithaca, NY: Cornell University Press, 1953 [1885]; Thompson, E. A. *Romans and Barbarians*. Madison: University of Wisconsin Press, 1982.

CHÂLONS
c. 20 June 451

FORCES ENGAGED
Roman/Visigoth: Unknown. Commander: Aetius.
Huns/allies: Unknown, probably approximately 100,000. Commander: Attila.

IMPORTANCE
Roman defeat of the Huns stopped the Asian spread westward, setting up the collapse of Attila's empire 2 years later.

Historical Setting

The population called Huns by Europeans emigrated from Asia, where they were probably called the Hsung-nu of modern China. Their origins are impossible to define accurately, but it is supposed that they were a forerunner of the Mongols and were possibly the reason the first section of the Great Wall of China was built. Unable to expand into the more settled regions of China, the Hsung-nu migrated westward over several centuries, driving other populations before them. Other peoples of similar stock may have populated as far as Finland, and the "barbarian" invasions that aided in toppling the Roman Empire were both racially similar to and driven westward by the Hsung-nu. They spread over a vast area and fought everyone with whom they came in contact, defeating and de-manding tribute from tribes south of the Caucasus that were part of the later Persian Empire. After they crossed the Don River in modern Russia in 375, these nomads came to be called "Huns," and their arrival put pressure on the Alans, Goths, and other eastern European tribes. Through the latter part of the fourth century into the first quarter of the fifth, they conquered territory north of the Danube as far west as modern Germany, with occasional raids against the Eastern Roman Empire's capital of Constantinople.

Like the Scythians before them and the Mongols after them, the Huns were nomadic horsemen bound by kin to each other, but traveling primarily in small bands to maximize grassland for their horses. Not until the fifth century did they seem to recognize a monarch over the entire population, and that was Rua. In the 420s and 430s, he led the unified Hun forces against the power of the Eastern Roman Empire as well as against the Goths and other populations inhabiting the Balkan region. After losing an army to the Huns, the Eastern Roman Emperor, Theodosius II (408–450), paid them tribute amounting to 350 pounds of gold per year.

When Rua died in 433, he was succeeded by two of his nephews, Bleda and Attila. For a time, the Huns raided little, seemingly consolidating their gains, but that changed in 441 when Attila led them on an invasion of southeastern Europe, where they sacked cities and ravaged the countryside as far as modern Yugoslavia. After a yearlong truce, the Huns attacked again, bypassing major fortified cities and marching on Constantinople. Another defeat forced Theodosius to increase the payment of tribute up to 2,100 pounds of gold annually. Apparently unwilling to share power, in 445 Attila murdered his brother Bleda. With sole leadership now in his hands, Attila looked west. After another quick campaign against Constantinople secured his rear, he faced his armies toward Gaul and the Italian peninsula.

The forces of western Europe were in disarray. Valentinian III, the Western Roman

Emperor, faced threats to the remnants of the original Roman Empire from Gaiseric, king of the Vandals, operating out of North Africa, as well as Theodoric, king of the Visigoths, who ruled the area of southern Gaul (France). Theodoric was also hostile to the Vandals, for Gaiseric had just repudiated his marriage to Theodoric's daughter and returned her, maimed, to her father. In 450, Attila planned to play these rivals against each other and defeat them one at a time. Further, he thought to use as an excuse for invading western Europe the proposal that he had received some years earlier from Valentinian's sister Honoria who, in a fit of pique against her brother, asked for aid from Attila. Attila's response was to claim this proposal to be one of marriage, which (he claimed) meant that half the Western Roman Empire should go to him as dowry. To give him even further cause for his invasion, a succession dispute among the Ripaurian Franks of northern Gaul led the two rival claimants to seek aid. One sought help from Attila; the other, from the commander of the Roman army, Aetius. Aetius for the previous three decades had campaigned against various tribes in Gaul, but in his youth had lived among the Huns in Rua's court. Attila had probably hoped his old friend would not seriously fight against him, but Aetius's vow to aid one claimant gave Attila the excuse he needed to aid the other.

In 451, however, Attila heard from Constantinople that the new emperor, Marcian, would no longer pay the annual tribute. The Hun monarch sent delegations to Constantinople and to Valentinian at Ravenna (capital of the later Roman Empire), demanding that he be granted his demands for gold from the former and Honoria from the latter. As he was facing west, and had as an ally one of the Frankish princes to allow him easy passage across the Rhine, Attila decided to deal with Marcian later. Attila's army was enlarged by the absorption of tribal forces of northern Europe that had been conquered by the Huns, but it is almost impossible to know how many men marched with

him. Contemporary sources say it was as many as 500,000, but modern historians suppose probably no more than 100,000 (Dupuy and Dupuy, *Encyclopedia of Military History*, p. 174).

The Battle

In the spring of 451, Attila and his army crossed the Rhine River along a wide front. His far left flank advanced along the Moselle River toward Metz, the center toward Paris and then Orléans, and the right wing swung wide toward Arras. They devastated the countryside, sacking and burning every city they approached. Paris was saved, according to legend, by the prayers of a young girl who motivated the citizenry and who was later beatified as St. Genevieve. In May, Attila began laying siege to Orléans. Sangiban, king of the Alans and located at Orléans after his defeat by Aetius in 442, promised Attila that he would surrender the city. When Aetius learned of that, he marched for the city.

Aetius had a difficult time raising troops. For all his campaigning in Gaul the previous 30 years, he had depended on hired foreign troops, often Huns. They abandoned him for Attila, and Aetius had to use every inducement to get men in the ranks. He appealed to Theodoric to join him, in spite of the longstanding rivalry with Rome, and, as Aetius marched toward Orléans, Theodoric joined him, seeing Attila as the greater enemy. The two joined with Sangiban who reluctantly combined his troops with theirs, as he had no love for Aetius, but had not been able to reach Attila in time. Contemporary accounts of the conflict (Gregory of Tours, *History of the Franks*) tell the story of Anianus, bishop of Orléans, getting a message to Aetius that the city could not hold out past 14 June. Just as the Huns were on the verge of creating a breach in Orléans' walls that day, lookouts sighted Aetius's army arriving. After a brief encounter, Attila withdrew his besieging force northward, calling his distant right and left wings to join the main body. He left a rear guard of the Gepid

Attila, the "Scourge of God." (Library of Congress)

tribe at the Seine River to cover his withdrawal, but Aetius destroyed it in a night attack in which all 15,000 of the Gepids were reported killed or wounded.

The position that Attila chose was a broad plain with the Marne River along his right flank. The exact site of the battle is disputed, but contemporary sources describe the Catalunian Plain in such terms that it lies somewhere in the Champagne region of France in a triangular area bounded by Troyes, Méry-sur-Seine, and Arcis, with the nearest major town being Châlons-sur-Marne. The Hun leader faced his army north; he commanded the Hun troops in the center, placed his Ostrogoth forces to his left under Walamir, and positioned the Gepids and other allied tribes under Ardaric on his right. Aetius placed Theodoric and his Visigoths opposite their Ostrogothic kin while he commanded a mixed lot of Franks, Burgundians, and other tribes on the left. Sangiban was placed in the center with his Alans. Given Sangiban's unreliability, this seems a risky move, but Aetius apparently hoped that by placing Sangiban between himself and Theodoric they could keep an eye on him.

The exact date of the battle is uncertain, with 20 June being proposed as the earliest and 27 September as the latest. Not knowing how many Visigoths marched with Theodoric, it is impossible to estimate the number of forces under Aetius, but it is assumed that, before the Visigoths joined him, the Roman general was able to muster only some 50,000. The morning of the battle there was some fighting on the Hun left flank over possession of a small hill, which finally came into the possession of the Visigoths under Thorismund, Theodoric's son. Attila dispatched some of his forces in the center to aid the Ostrogoths on the left flank and then around noon ordered the remainder of his Huns to attack the Alans directly to their front. Rather surprisingly, the Alans gave a fairly good account of themselves, withdrawing slowly under intense pressure. Aetius made little headway against the Gepids on his end of the battlefield, but Theodoric's forces on the Roman right

flank beat back the Ostrogoths and then turned to attack Attila, whose forces in the center were now separated from his flanks. Seeing the danger, Attila ordered a withdrawal to his base camp, which he reached by nightfall after a battle that lasted all afternoon. Once there, the superior Hun archers beat back any Roman assaults.

In the hours after the battle, many in Aetius's army stumbled about in the dark. When first light arrived, both sides were able to view the carnage of the previous day's fighting, and neither seemed eager to renew it. Thorismund confirmed that morning that his father was killed in the battle, and he was immediately proclaimed the new king of the Visigoths. Rather than attack the strong Hun position, he and Aetius decided on a siege. From the Hun camp, there were occasional intimations of a renewed attack, but these were little more than attempts at psychological harassment because the Huns had lost a significant number of men and Attila was not willing to reopen the battle. Just as the numbers of men engaged in this battle is unknown, so are the casualties. Contemporary sources state that they were between 165,000 and 300,000, but, because that would almost equal the total number of troops estimated at Châlons, both numbers are regarded as gross exaggerations.

Results

Although Aetius and Thorismund decided on a siege, Aetius soon began to think better of the idea. Although the Huns were beaten and on the defensive, Aetius began to consider the potential threat that Thorismund posed. He had distinguished himself in combat and was commanding a well-organized army flushed with victory, whereas Aetius commanded a haphazard force of mixed tribal and ethnic makeup. If Attila was completely defeated, Aetius reasoned, what reason would Thorismund have to maintain the alliance between Visigoths and Romans? Aetius instead urged Thorismund to return home, to protect his claim to the throne from any brothers that might claim it while he was off at war. This Thorismund did, leaving a gap in the ranks laying siege. Rather than attack this opening, Attila reasoned that it may have been a trap and decided instead to exploit his enemy's weak position and retreat. He led his forces across the Rhine, and Aetius did not follow. Fuller (*A Military History of the Western World*, vol. 1, p. 297) goes so far as to propose that Aetius actually met with Attila the night after the battle and worked out a mutually beneficial arrangement.

Hurt though he was by the defeat at Châlons, Attila was not yet broken. The following year, 452, he was once again demanding to marry Honoria, and this time he invaded the Italian peninsula to force that wedding. Hun forces pillaged their way southward from the Alps, causing at least as much devastation as they had the previous year in northern Gaul. Aetius could not gather an army strong enough to challenge him, and Emperor Valentinian retreated from Ravenna to Rome. Unable to fight Attila, Valentinian tried bargaining. He sent Pope Leo I to negotiate with Attila, and the two met at the Mincio River. What was said in the meeting was not recorded, but Attila turned and marched his army out of Italy. Probably Leo noted the lack of fodder for Hun horses as well as the widespread disease that was spreading across the region as a result of the destruction the Huns inflicted. That, coupled with the news that Emperor Marcian had sent an army to attack Attila's capital, probably convinced the Hun leader to take his army elsewhere.

Although the defeat at Châlons did not break Attila's power, it hurt it so significantly that his invasion of Italy was not nearly as strong as he had planned (which may be another reason for his withdrawal). Although planning to continue his campaigns, Attila died in 453. His sons divided the empire and immediately proceeded to fight among themselves, destroying what their father had wrought. Subject tribes declared their independence, and the Gepids dealt the Huns a severe defeat in 454 at the River Nedao, whose location is unknown. Within two generations, the remaining Huns were isolated in the region that ultimately took its name, Hungary, from them.

By halting Hun expansion, the battle at Châlons kept Attila from dominating western Europe. Aetius's force was thrown together at the last minute; if it had been defeated, there was really no other organized population that could have withstood the Huns. Although this only temporarily kept the Western Roman Empire from totally collapsing, it preserved the Germanic culture, which came to dominate Europe once Rome was finally politically powerless. It was the Germanic society that survived into the Middle Ages, adapting Latin mores to its own use rather than being overwhelmed by them. Thus, the Europe of the Middle Ages was dominated by various Germanic cultures, stretching from Scandinavia through central Europe and over to the British Isles.

Attila's defeat also helped the Roman Catholic Church to become the dominant political as well as religious force of Europe. Called by Europeans the "Scourge of God" to punish them for their sins, Attila, though defeated by Aeitus, had been virtually banished by Pope Leo. Papal power from a political as well as religious standpoint dates from this time. Plus, who were the heroes of Paris and Orléans but people who called on God for deliverance? As much as any military force, the Catholic Church was portrayed as the savior of Europe, and its power remained virtually unchallenged until Martin Luther in the sixteenth century.

References: Creasy, Edward S. *Fifteen Decisive Battles of the World.* New York: Harper, 1851; Fuller, J. F. C. *A Military History of the Western World*, vol. 1. New York: Funk & Wagnalls, 1954; Gregory of Tours. *History of the Franks.* Translated by Ernest Brehaut. New York: Columbia University Press, 1916; Jordanes. *The Gothic History of Jordanes.* New Haven, CT: Yale University Press, 1915; Thompson, E. A. *A History of Attila and the Huns.* Oxford, UK: Clarendon Press, 1948.

TRICAMERON
Mid-December 533

Historical Setting

Justinian came to the throne of the Eastern Roman, or Byzantine, Empire in 527. A soldier like his uncle Justin, whom he succeeded, he did not command in the field once he assumed the throne, but had the services of one of history's outstanding generals, Belisarius. He first came to notice when, as a general of only 24 years of age, he carried out a successful campaign against the Persian Empire during 529–530. Belisarius was back in Constantinople in 532 when Justinian faced his greatest domestic challenge, the Nika riots, which perhaps were the original model of all successive public disorders concerned with sporting events.

Two major chariot teams were supported by factions, the Blues and the Greens, with both political and religious goals. The Blues, with the support of Justinian, were made up of Orthodox Christians; the Greens, supported by Empress Theodora, were made up of Monophysites, a sect with a heretical view of the divinity of Jesus. Because both royal personages backed their own team, this tended to keep the peace between them. But in January 532 the two factions, for whatever reason, attempted to overthrow Justinian and replace him with Hypatius, nephew of Justin's predecessor. Justinian by all accounts was prepared to run for his life, but Theodora stiffened his resolve. Belisarius was assigned, with the eunuch Narses, to end the riots by whatever means necessary. Narses took money to bribe the Blue leadership, while Belisarius took troops to the Hippodrome, the main sporting arena, and slaughtered about 35,000 rioters.

Once Justinian was firmly back in control, Belisarius was able to return to the military campaign he had been organizing. Justinian had received an appeal from Hilderic, king of the Vandal empire in North Africa. Hilderic had recently been overthrown by Gelimer, and, as vassal of the Byzantine Empire, Hilderic sent for aid from his master. Justinian, who had been looking for a reason to launch an invasion of Italy in order to reunite the two halves of the Roman Empire, saw this as a perfect excuse to place soldiers in the central Mediterranean. Justinian also hoped to rid Italy and Europe of the Arian sect of Christianity, which also challenged orthodox dicta on the divinity of Christ.

Justinian had serious goals in all aspects of his political and religious life, but he rarely felt comfortable in spending the necessary funds to accomplish those goals. Belisarius in his campaign in North Africa was given but 15,000 men to conquer the entire Vandal empire. The soldiers serving the Byzantine Empire in the sixth century were certainly not in the mold of the traditional Roman legionary, the citizen-soldier. Instead, the army was made up of three types of troops: *numeri, foederati,* and *bucellarii.* The numeri were supposed to be the citizen-soldiers of yore but by this time were not well trained, equipped, or motivated; even slaves were recruited. The foederati were mercenary units made up of any man who wanted to fight and were recruited from all the ethnic groups with which the empire had contact. The bucellarii were private armies owned and operated by the wealthiest of the Byzantines, but the units were also on call when the emperor needed them. Thus, the 10,000 infantry and 5,000 cavalry that Justinian sent with Belisarius were hirelings with no bonds to the empire other than pay. But because pay was often in the form of loot, following a winner was even more important than merely hiring out one's services.

In late June 532, Belisarius launched his expedition, transported on 500 ships with another 92 warships for escort. Weather slowed the trip, but they finally made landfall in Sicily, where they had made previous arrangements with the queen of the island, Amalasuntha, for their landing. There Belisarius learned that the Vandal fleet, of which he was rightly afraid, was engaged in supporting the suppression of a rebellion in Sardinia. Belisarius quickly aimed south for Caputvada (modern Ras Kapudia in Tunisia). He landed there in September, established a base camp, and distributed a proclamation assuring the locals that he had no quarrel with them, only with Gelimer. When all was ready, Belisarius marched north toward the Vandal capital city of Carthage.

The Battle

The Byzantine force reached Ad Decimum, the road marker 10 miles from Carthage, on 13 September. Gelimer had originally hoped to delay Belisarius until reinforcements could arrive from Sardinia, but when he learned the paucity of his enemy's numbers he decided to attack. He directed his brother Ammatus to attack from Carthage when the Byzantines were in a defile marching north from Ad Decimum. Gelimer would command a force attacking from the rear, while a third force under Gelimer's nephew Gibamund was to strike the enemy's left, or western, flank. This was a good plan, given the ability to communicate, but in the sixth century it depended on timing that was extremely difficult to pull off.

That timing was the key to the Vandal defeat. Ammatus attacked too soon and was killed as his troops were driven back by Belisarius's advanced guard, 600 men under command of John the Armenian. The flank attack ran into a

body of Huns that Belisarius had placed on his left to guard against such an eventuality; it too was driven back with heavy loss. When Gelimer arrived on the scene, he was not only too late but he had lost his way and attacked not the rear of the column but its front, which was separated by a large gap from troops in the Byzantine rear and totally uncovered by the advanced guard, which was making its way to Carthage to gather all the loot they could. Gelimer's attack drove the front of Belisarius's army back, and a bold pursuit could well have broken the Byzantines. Instead, Gelimer discovered his brother's body and stopped everything until it could be buried. That gave Belisarius all the time he needed to rally his troops, which attacked and drove the Vandals off in confusion.

Belisarius marched into an undefended Carthage on 15 September and proceeded to repair its fortifications. Gelimer meanwhile retreated 100 miles west and sent for his brother Tzazon to bring his troops from Sardinia. Once reinforced, Gelimer marched on Carthage, stopping about 18 miles west at the village of Tricameron. Gelimer's spies learned that the Huns with the Byzantine army were discontented and therefore open to suggestion. He contacted them and offered great rewards if they would turn on their compatriots in the midst of the next battle. Belisarius learned of this and, unknown to Gelimer, outbribed him. The Huns listened to Belisarius, but could they be trusted if the battle was not going well?

In mid-December, Belisarius decided to take the battle to the Vandals, rather than await their attack and possibly lose his advantage with his Huns. They were marching against a force at least three times their own number, but Belisarius gave them a first-class warm-up talk, finishing with: "For not by numbers of men, nor by measure of body, but by valor of soul is war wont to be decided" (Procopius, *Procopius*, vol. IV, I, pp. 15–16). With these words, the army marched out of Carthage toward the Vandal camp. Belisarius sent most of his cavalry, about 4,500 horse commanded by John the

THE EMPEROR AND HIS GENERAL

It is safe to say that no general has ever been so successful and so underappreciated as Belisarius. Almost no general has accomplished more, with less, than he did, and yet Justinian was constantly afraid of his commander's popularity. In a society in which assassination was a recognized form of advancing to the throne, anyone with military support was a potential rival. That is one reason why Justinian never put large armies under Belisarius's command. Belisarius, however, never did anything to give the impression that he had ambitions beyond his station. It is surprising, perhaps, that he did not try for the throne in sheer frustration with his treatment.

Here is a catalog of Belisarius's accomplishments and Justinian's reactions:

529–531: defeated Persian Empire armies; recalled to lead invasion of Africa.

533–535: defeated Vandals; recalled because of jealousy.

535–536: led invasion of Sicily and Italy; recalled to suppress rebellion in Africa.

536–541: campaigned against Goths in Italy, so impressing them that they offered him the position of emperor in the west, which he refused; recalled to fight Persians.

542–544: defeated Persians; recalled to command in Italy.

544–549: returned to Italy to restore Byzantine authority; replaced by Narses in 551.

549–554: retired in Constantinople.

554: called out of retirement to reconquer southern Spain for Byzantines; retired again.

559: called out of retirement to defend Constantinople with less than 1,000 men against 7,000 invading Bulgars, was victorious, and retired for the final time.

Armenian, forward and marched his infantry and the remaining 500 cavalry behind. They camped well short of the Vandal stockade at Tricameron.

Learning of the Byzantine approach, Gelimer assembled his troops, almost all cavalry, and rode toward Belisarius. Instead, he ran into John's cavalry, dismounted and preparing lunch. Rather than attack, as he should have, Gelimer deployed his men and waited for the Byzantine cavalry charge. John obliged him, forming his men into three squadrons, a mirror image of the Vandal formation, although considerably smaller. Belisarius, alerted to the situation, rode forward with the remaining 500 cavalry, having the infantry maintain a steady march. After facing each other for a time, John opened the battle by leading a small force of picked men forward into the Vandal center, which was commanded by Tzazon. John's forces were beaten back but not pursued. John repeated the attack with a bit larger force and again was turned back. The third time, he led a force somewhat larger yet, and in the combat that followed Tzazon was killed. As soon as that news reached the remaining Byzantine cavalry, they all charged the center, which was collapsing because of Tzazon's death. With the upper hand displayed, the Huns decided that the Vandals could not win, so threw in their lot with John and proceeded to ride down as many Vandals as they could.

Gelimer retreated to his fortified camp, there to make a stand. By this time, the Byzantine infantry had arrived, still fairly fresh because of the measured pace of their advance. As the infantry formed up outside the walls of Gelimer's camp, Gelimer lost his nerve. Without a word to anyone, he mounted his horse and dashed westward. Seeing their king in flight after witnessing his brother's death, the Vandal army fell apart and followed. The Byzantine soldiers walked into the well-stocked Vandal camp and proceeded to loot it thoroughly. Had Gelimer found some courage, turned his forces, and attacked his own camp, the completely disorganized Byzantine troops would have been easily overrun and slaughtered, too busy with their pillage to worry about watching for a returning enemy. Belisarius knew the danger, but could not stop his men. Luckily, Gelimer had no courage.

Results

In numbers of casualties, the battle at Tricameron was relatively minor: some fifty Byzantines fell in the opening battle against about 800 Vandals. The meeting at the Vandal camp was not really a battle. Gelimer surrendered to Belisarius in March 534 and was taken back to Constantinople with a large number of his troops. Belisarius accompanied Gelimer to the capital because the successful general had aroused Justinian's jealousy and the emperor wanted him back where he could keep an eye on him. It was a pattern that Justinian repeated constantly throughout his life, possibly because of the suggestions of Narses, who exerted influence on Justinian second only to that of Empress Theodora. Belisarius was back in Africa a few years later to put down a rebellion against his successor, and then he led the Byzantine invasion of Italy in 535.

Belisarius's victory at Tricameron and the resulting surrender of Gelimer ended the Vandal empire. The Vandals were one of the northern European barbarian tribes that took advantage of the weakness of the Western Roman Empire in the fourth and fifth centuries. They had campaigned through Spain and then drove out the Visigothic kingdom in northern Africa, reestablishing the first independent empire there since the destruction of Carthage in the third century B.C. For Justinian, this victory was a major step on the road to reuniting the two halves of the Roman Empire. With control over northern Africa, he could use it as a base for operations against the Ostrogothic kingdom in Italy. That campaign began in 535, and once again Belisarius was victorious, although once again his emperor gave him a minuscule number of men to accomplish it. The war against the Ostrogoths lasted until the Byzantine victory at Taginae (modern Gubbio, Italy) in 552 broke their power. Belisarius, who had conquered much of the peninsula and showed his standard brilliance on the battlefield, was once again recalled to Constantinople, and Narses won the battle at Taginae and oversaw the reduction of the last remaining Ostrogothic strongholds.

Justinian by his victories took the Roman Empire back to its position as master of the Mediterranean, but that was short-lived. His governors in Italy were so corrupt and the countryside so devastated by almost two decades of war that the population welcomed yet another invader, the Lombards, and then the Franks. Justinian did, however, destroy the Ostrogoths, the one population of serious Arian Christians. With their end came the end to the Arian heresy, so Justinian did indeed kill two birds with one stone. In spite of his vision, Justinian's innate weakness was responsible for not initiating just rule in Italy and possibly keeping Italy under Byzantine rule for generations.

References: Barker, John. *Justinian and the Later Roman Empire.* Madison: University of Wisconsin Press, 1966; Browning, Robert. *Justinian and Theodora.* London: Weidenfeld & Nicolson, 1971; Fuller, J. F. C. *A Military History of the Western World,* vol. 1. New York: Funk & Wagnalls, 1954; Procopius. *Procopius,* vol. IV. Translated by H. B. Dewing. New York: Putnam, 1916; Treadgold, Warren. *Byzantium and Its Army, 284–1081.* Stanford, CA: Stanford University Press, 1995.

BADR

15 March 624

FORCES ENGAGED

Medina: Approximately 300 men.
Commander: Mohammed.

Mecca: Approximately 900 men.
Commander: Abu Sufyan.

IMPORTANCE

Mohammed's victory confirmed his authority as leader of Islam; by impressing local tribes that joined him, the expansion of Islam began.

Historical Setting

In the early seventh century, a young man of the city of Mecca began having visions and hearing voices, both of which he took to be divinely inspired. Although he was illiterate, in the visions he was able to absorb the writing on a quilt that was being pressed upon him, thus having the words imprinted on his heart. These words became the verses of the Koran, the holy book of Islam. Mohammed attempted to share his experiences with his fellow citizens of Mecca, but met opposition. At the time, Mecca was a key trading center in Arabia, halfway between Christian and Jewish trade centers and affected by both, economically and socially. When Mohammed's teachings criticized some of the business practices of Meccan merchants, led by the ruling clan of Quraysh, they put pressure on his clan to silence him. The clan leader, Mohammed's uncle Abu Talib, refused to comply; in return, his clan was subjected to economic boycott. As time passed, more direct threats were leveled against Mohammed.

Why these merchants would fear Mohammed is a matter of speculation, but probably they thought that he would come to be accepted by the population as a wise man whose pronouncements against them could hurt profits. They also feared the political repercussions of Mohammed's increasing popularity because, if he became involved in Meccan government, he could seriously harm their business. Thus, they conspired to silence or expel him. When Abu Talib died in 619, his successor was less tolerant of Mohammed's troublemaking.

In 620, Mohammed met some citizens of Medina, about 200 miles north of Mecca. They were impressed with his personality and character and asked him to move to Medina and act as an arbitrator in a series of feuds that had occurred over the previous several years. He declined at first, but the following year a dozen Medinans swore to recognize him as God's prophet. Mohammed still hesitated, sending some associates to Medina to look over the situation there. When seventy-five Medinans in 622 offered to follow him in battle as well as in the faith, he was convinced to move. He had been sending his Meccan followers out of the city to Medina for some months without alerting the Meccan business leaders to his plans. By the time they learned of his intention to escape to Medina, where they could not keep an eye on him and from where he could build an alternate power base, he had slipped away in the night.

In Medina, Mohammed's strength of will brought many of the inhabitants into the faith, although some of the city's Jewish and pagan citizens held aloof. Unable to farm in the limited arable land of the oasis at Medina, and used to a life of trade, Mohammed and his emigrant followers from Mecca decided to make a living by raiding the caravans of their erstwhile Meccan associates. Through the latter part of 623, Mohammed sent out increasingly larger bodies of men to attack Meccan caravans, but apparently spies in Medina alerted the targets and most of them escaped attack. In January 624, Mohammed sent out a small band with sealed orders, successfully thwarting the spies. His orders were for the twelve men of the raiding party to attack a small caravan bound from Yemen to Mecca. They located it and then, acting as pilgrims, joined it. Mohammed's men faced a problem. They were currently in a month held as holy in Arabia, during which fighting was not supposed to occur. If they accompanied the caravan until the holy month was over, they would be in the holy city of Mecca, where fighting was also banned. They decided to violate the first stricture rather than the second and overpowered the guards, killing one and taking two others prisoner.

Criticized for this violation of sacred practice, Mohammed responded that the persecution of Moslems by the merchants of Mecca was a greater sin than violating the holy month, therefore it was permissible. In Mecca, however, the raid was intolerable. A caravan going from Gaza to Mecca and that was owned and led by Abu Sufyan, the leading Quraysh merchant, was the bait with which the Meccans hoped to lure Mohammed and his followers into a decisive battle. Indeed it did, for Mohammed organized a force of some 300 men to attack this caravan; he led his force out of Medina in early March 624. They were primarily infantry, possessing only 70 camels and 2 horses for the entire column; they took turns riding and walking. Learning of this threat, Abu Sufyan sent word to Mecca for aid, and almost 1,300 men responded under the command of Abu Jahl. His force was much better equipped and armed, with 700 camels and 100 horses, as well as some 600 infantry wearing mail.

The Battle

Abu Sufyan, learning by personal reconnaissance the location of Mohammed's force, diverted his caravan along another route and made his way safely to Mecca, from where he sent word to Abu Jahl of his arrival. Some of the relief force decided that there was no reason to stay in the field, so about 400 men defied Abu Jahl and returned home. He was unwilling to do the same, for he was determined to defeat Mohammed and exterminate the threat to Mecca's economic preeminence. He announced that the remaining men would go to the wells at Badr, about 25 miles southwest of Mecca, to celebrate the safe return of the caravan.

It was at Badr that Mohammed's men were waiting. Learning from captured scouts of Abu Jahl's approach, Mohammed called a council on the evening of 14 March 624. He received the ready support of his Meccan followers, called the Emigrants, but wanted to know the strength of the faith of his Medina followers, called the Helpers. When they too swore allegiance as powerfully as did the Emigrants, Mohammed was satisfied with the determination of his men and assured them that the battle would be theirs. Upon the advice of his second-in-command, Abu Bakr, Mohammed placed his force around the well closest to the Meccan force and stopped up the other wells in the area. They then waited for battle. That night it rained; according to the Koran, this was to cleanse the Moslems as well as solidify the sandy ground for the battle. It is reported that the Moslem force all slept peacefully except for Mohammed, who spent the night in prayer.

As Abu Jahl's force approached Badr, they were nearing the limit of their own water supply, and they encountered Mohammed's force on rising ground overlooking the one remaining well. Mohammed was seated under a tent overlooking the battlefield and had ordered his men not to attack until he gave the signal; instead, they were to counter the Meccan attacks with arrows. The battle started, however, with the approach of three Meccan warriors, who challenged the Moslems. When three soldiers stood up to face them, the Meccans rejected them and called for members of Mohammed's clan to fight. Ubaidah bin Al-Harith, as well as Mohammed's uncle Hamza and cousin Ali responded. Hamza and Ali quickly killed their challengers and then went to Ubaidah's aid. He too was victorious, but so badly wounded that he died a few days later. Ubaidah thus has the distinction of being the first martyr to Islam. A few other individual duels followed and then the Meccan force attacked.

True to their orders, the Moslems stood on the higher ground and pelted the attackers with arrows. Mohammed, meantime, had another vision in which he was assured not only of victory but of divine assistance in the form of mounted angel warriors. He awoke from this and then picked up a handful of sand or gravel, saying "Confusion seize their faces" (*The*

Koran, 8:17). At this point, it is reported that a sandstorm appeared and struck the Meccans. Later, prisoners reported having been overwhelmed and captured by warriors on horseback, in spite of the fact that the Moslem forces possessed only two horses. This has been attributed to the angelic intervention. Whatever the case, the Meccan attack was faltering and Mohammed ordered his men forward. Meccan forces broke and ran, leaving behind seventy dead and another seventy prisoners. Among the dead was Abu Jahl, wounded in the fighting and then beheaded when he refused to acknowledge Allah as the true victor of the battle. Abu Jahl's given name was Amru bin Hasham, called by the clan of Quraysh Abu 'Ihoem, Father of Wisdom. He has been better known since his death by the Moslem epithet Abu Jahl, Father of Folly.

Results

The Moslem victory at Badr marked Mohammed's real arrival as a political leader in addition to his already established role as a religious figure. By defeating a force three times the size of his own, his military acumen took on a new luster. In reality, he used good tactics by holding high ground with rested troops against tired and thirsty attackers. As for the timely sandstorm and angelic intervention, we have only the Koran for this account; secular commentary cannot confirm or deny that aspect of the battle. Whatever the details, Mohammed's men did win at Badr.

This proved a major psychological defeat for Mecca, which lost a number of its leading citizens as dead or prisoners, which were ransomed. Mohammed's followers divided the loot of Abu Jahl's army equally among all the men present, no matter their roles as combatants or guards that did not fight. That decision did not sit well with some of the soldiers, but Mohammed's decision for equal distribution was confirmed a year later. At the battle of Uhud, just outside Medina, on 23 March 625, Moslem forces were bested on the battlefield. In spite of that, the Meccans withdrew, and the battle did not harm Mohammed's reputation. Unable to discern how they could have been beaten with Allah on their side, Mohammed told the Moslems that it was divine punishment for the desire for loot.

The mere fact that the Meccans did not press their advantage that day actually reinforced Mohammed's mystique because it made the Meccans appear afraid. During the battle, Moslem infantry had outfought the attackers, but superior Meccan cavalry proved the decisive factor. A year later, a force from Mecca once again attacked and besieged Medina. Although they brought 10,000 to 13,000 men and 600 cavalry, Mohammed was again victorious. He dug an extended ditch before his position, making a cavalry charge impossible. The Arabs, unaccustomed to siege warfare, soon lost interest and went home. Mohammed's reputation was again enhanced. In 630, Mohammed's army captured his former home of Mecca, and the focus of Islam was transferred to that city. It proved the crowning achievement for Mohammed as a political, military, and religious leader, but he lived only 2 more years. Dead in 632, he was succeeded by Abu Bakr, who crushed any opposition to his reign as caliph by 633.

It was Badr that started it all. Prior to that battle, Mohammed was a religious leader with a limited following, and he engaged in nothing more than harassing raids against his enemies in Mecca. They feared his potential, however, and in that they were correct. After Badr, Mohammed was able to consolidate his power in Medina by crushing or exiling opposing factions, primarily Jewish clans that had maintained commercial ties with the Quraysh clan. He also began attracting support from outlying Bedouin tribes, whose aggressive nature enhanced his military forces. Abu Jahl went into the battle of Badr with the intent of killing Mohammed and stifling his religion. A Meccan victory would probably have accomplished that.

Instead, Islam began its expansion across Arabia, the Middle East, North Africa, southeastern Europe, and Asia. Badr is one of those battles in which the number of men actually involved in the fighting was small, but the effects were enormous.

References: Balyuzi, H. M. *Mohammed and the Course of Islam.* Oxford, UK: G. Ronald, 1976; *The Battle of Badr.* <www.islaam.com/ilm/battleof.htm>; Holt, P. M., Ann K. S. Lambton, and Bernard Lewis. *The Cambridge History of Islam,* vol. 1. Cambridge, UK: Cambridge University Press, 1970; Irving, Washington. *Mahomet and His Successors.* Madison: University of Wisconsin Press, 1970 [1868]; *The Koran.* Translated by N. J. Dawood. Hammondsworth, NY: Penguin, 1974.

CONSTANTINOPLE

August 717–15 August 718

FORCES ENGAGED

Byzantine: Unknown. Commander: Emperor Leo the Isaurian.
Moslem: 210,000. Commander: Muslama.

IMPORTANCE

By turning back the Moslem invasion, Europe remained in Christian hands, and no serious Moslem threat to Europe existed until the fifteenth century. This victory, coincident with the Frankish victory at Tours (732), limited Islam's western expansion to the southern Mediterranean world.

Historical Setting

Mohammed the Prophet had a public career of 10 years, 622–632. He died without publicly naming a successor, and his close associate Abu Bakr was elected to succeed him. His time in power was only 2 years. Upon his death, Omar reigned as caliph, or deputy, the religious and political head of Islam. For 10 years, Omar oversaw the spread of Islam into Byzantine territory, Persia, Syria, modern Iraq, and Egypt. It spread farther under the caliphate of Othman (644–656), ultimately reaching the Atlantic shore of North Africa, as well as Armenia and Afghanistan in the east. Othman was assassinated, however, and thereafter Islam split into two major factions: the followers of Mohammed's nephew Ali became the Shi'ites, and the supporters of the Syrian governor Muawiya started the Sunni faction. Muawiya finally came to exercise control by establishing the Umayyad dynasty, which ruled from Damascus between 661 and 750.

Muawiya aimed to see the downfall of the Christian Byzantine Empire because reportedly whoever was involved in the capture of the capital city of Constantinople would have all his sins forgiven. Intermittently between 674 and 678, Moslem forces attempted to capture the city, both by land and sea, but the double walls protecting it proved too formidable. Muawiya signed a peace treaty with the Byzantine emperor that called for an annual tribute from Damascus to Constantinople. For the next 30 years, the forces of Islam carried the faith as far as Spain and India, but the lure of Constantinople, the key to Europe, always beckoned. Caliph Walid (705–715) organized the forces necessary to seize the city, but died before the project could be launched. Thus, his successor Suleiman sent men and ships to the Byzantine capital in 717.

The Byzantine Empire had suffered through a chain of lackluster emperors since the last assault. As the Moslems were gathering their strength, the emperor was Anastasius. He came to the throne in 713 and was in the market for able soldiers to defend his realm. In his army served a general named Conon, better known as Leo the Isaurian. (He was probably from Syria rather than the Anatolian province of Isauria, modern Konia, however.) He had served the empire since 705 and in 716 was assigned to command the *theme,* or district, of Anatolia. He harassed the approaching Moslem soldiers as they marched out of

Syria toward Constantinople and then took the throne from Anastasius in March 717. Leo III, as he was crowned, immediately set about laying in as many provisions as he could for the siege he knew was coming, a daunting task for a city of perhaps half a million people. He also oversaw the repairs and strengthening of the city's two defensive walls and the placement of weaponry to beat back attacks from land or sea.

Caliph Suleiman named as commander of his forces Muslama, who led an army of reportedly 80,000 men through Anatolia toward the Byzantine capital. His plan was to invest the city from the western (landward) side, while a massive Moslem fleet kept any supplies from reaching the city. That fleet numbered some 1,800 ships, carrying another 80,000 men under the command of a general named Suleiman, not to be confused with the caliph. The Moslem fleet was to be divided into two divisions, one to blockade the Dardanelles (or Hellespont) and keep any relief from coming to Constantinople from the Mediterranean, while the second fleet blocked the Bosporus to the north, keeping out any relief from Black Sea ports. Muslama crossed his men over the Hellespont in July 717 and divided his forces: he commanded the main body that began the siege of the city, while a detachment was sent to Adrianople to keep an eye on the Bulgars, a population that had been pillaging through southeastern Europe and had attacked Constantinople in 712.

The Battle

Muslama threw an attack against the walls immediately upon his arrival but it was easily beaten back. That convinced him that a frontal assault was indeed futile, so he began digging trenches to prevent any breakout from the city. Most of the fighting, therefore, took place on the water. Suleiman left part of his navy at the Dardanelles, as ordered, and led the remainder northward to take up station on the Hellespont. As they approached Constantinople, however, the leading ships were caught in a swift and unfamiliar current that began to tangle them. Seizing his opportunity, Leo quickly lowered the chain that protected the Golden Horn, the upper harbor of the city, and dashed out into the Moslem fleet before they could form into line of battle. By using Greek fire (see sidebar), his ships quickly destroyed or captured a large number of Moslem ships; the rest retreated. Suleiman feared sailing past the city now because another such lightning assault could destroy the remainder of his fleet. Thus, the northern avenue of aid was kept open for a time.

The Moslem effort was off to a bad start, and soon bad news came from home. Caliph Suleiman had died of a stomach ailment (probably brought on by overeating) and he had been replaced by Omar II, not known for his military acumen. For the next several months, little happened, as is the nature of many sieges. More bad luck befell the Moslems during the winter. It was much colder than usual during the winter of 717–718, and snow lay on the ground for more than 3 months. For an army born and raised in Arabia and Egypt, this was disconcerting at best, deadly at worst. Delays in the delivery of supplies from Egypt, coupled with the bad weather, meant the deaths of thousands of besieging soldiers.

The Moslems had planned to take the initiative in the spring of 718 with the arrival of a new fleet from Egypt and 50,000 reinforcements. The 400 ships of the fleet from Egypt snuck past the Byzantine fleet in the Golden Horn at night, thus avoiding a naval battle, and stationed themselves at the Hellespont. That cut off the flow of supplies and would eventually have spelled the city's doom, but Leo's navy again saved the day. He was aided by the desertion from the new Egyptian fleet of large numbers of crew members who were Coptic Christians pressed into service by the Moslems. Learning of the Moslem fleet's disposition, Leo launched a surprise attack in June that caught the Moslem fleet completely unawares. The Greek fire once again caused both destruction and terror, and the Christian crews deserted wholesale to the welcoming Byzantine forces. The northern blockading fleet was destroyed, and Leo's victory was followed by an attack on Moslem forces on the Asian side of the Sea of Marmora, opposite the capital. That attack was also so unexpected that the defenders were slaughtered by the thousands.

Leo at this point proved himself to be as able a diplomat as a general. He sent to the Bulgars envoys who persuaded the Bulgar king, Tervel, to attack the Moslem army from the west. Tervel's Bulgars in July drove the Moslem holding force past Adrianople and attacked Muslama's forces in the rear, defeating them badly and inflicting some 22,000 casualties. This new threat was reinforced by the rumor that the Franks had sent an army across Europe to

---

GREEK FIRE

One of the great mysteries of classical age technology is the composition of Greek fire. First mentioned in relation to Archimedes in the Peloponnesian War, it appears occasionally in the accounts of naval and siege warfare for more than a thousand years. Although always kept a secret by whomever employed it, one would assume that the recipe would in some way have been leaked, or recorded for modern historians to discover, but none has ever been recovered. The best discussion of it is probably in Edward Gibbon's classic work, *The Decline and Fall of the Roman Empire,* vol. 6:

The historian who presumes to analyse this extraordinary composition should suspect his own ignorance and that of his Byzantine guides, so prone to the marvelous, so careless, and in this instance so jealous, of the truth. From their obscure and perhaps fallacious hints, it should seem that the principal ingredient of the Greek fire was the naphtha, or liquid bitumen, a light, tenacious, and inflammable oil which springs from the earth and catches fire as soon as it comes in contact with the air. The naphtha was mingled, I know not by what methods or in what proportions, with sulphur and with the pitch that is extracted from evergreen firs. From this mixture, which produced a thick smoke and a loud explosion, proceeded a fierce and obstinate flame, which not only rose in perpendicular ascent, but likewise burnt with equal vehemence in descent or lateral progress; instead of being extinguished, it was nourished and quickened, by the element of water; and sand, urine, or vinegar were the only remedies that could damp the fury of this powerful agent, which was justly denominated by the Greeks the liquid or the maritime fire. For the annoy-ance of the enemy it was employed with equal effect, by sea and land, in battles or in sieges. It was from the rampart in large boilers, or launched in red-hot balls of stone and iron, or darted in arrows and twisted round with flax and tow, which had deeply imbibed the inflammable oil: sometimes it was deposited in the victims and instruments of a more ample revenge, and was most commonly blown through long tubes of copper, were planted on the prow of a galley, and fancifully shaped into the mouths of savage monsters, that seemed to stream of liquid and consuming fire. This important art was preserved at Constantinople, as the palladium of the state; the galleys and artillery might occasionally be lent to the allies of Rome; but the composition of the Greek fire was concealed with the most jealous scruple, and the terror of the enemies was increased and prolonged by their ignorance and surprise. In the treatise of the Administration of the Empire the royal author [Constantin] suggests the answers and excuses that might best elude the indiscreet curiosity and importunate demands of the barbarians. They should be told that the mystery of the Greek fire had been revealed by an angel to the first and greatest of the Constantines, with a sacred injunction that this gift of heaven, this peculiar blessing of the Romans, should never be communicated to any foreign nation; that the prince and subject were alike bound to religious silence under the temporal and spiritual penalties of treason and sacrilege; and that the impious attempt would provoke the sudden and supernatural vengeance of the God of the Christians. By these precautions, the secret was confined, above four hundred years, to the Romans of the East; and, at the end of the eleventh century, the Pisans, to whom every sea and every art were familiar, suffered the effects, without understanding the composition, of the Greek fire.

assist their fellow Christians. The Moslems had not yet fought the Franks, but had heard that they were a formidable military power. At this news, Caliph Omar decided enough was enough. On 15 August 718, Muslama led his army away from the walls of Constantinople.

Results

The defeat at Constantinople was the first disastrous loss the armies of Islam had suffered. They had lost battles here and there, but never such an overwhelming catastrophe. Of the 210,000 men who took part in the land and naval action, it is reported that only 30,000 of them actually saw their homeland again. Of the more than 2,000 ships that are supposed to have been involved, only 5 supposedly made it home.

Had Muslama's armies captured the city, the continuing route into eastern Europe would have been virtually unguarded. Until one reached the armies of western Europe, little organized resistance could have been mounted against hordes of Moslem troops. Constantinople, as the seat of political, religious, and economic power in the Christian east, probably would have become the center of Islam. The Eastern Orthodox Church could well have disappeared, with untold consequences in eastern Europe and Russia. Sea power would have been completely in Moslem hands, for no European population at this time possessed a significant navy and none would before the Vikings a century later. Even with the Frankish victory at Tours 15 years afterward, Islam could well have become the dominant European, and therefore world, religion.

As it was, the strength of Islam remained potent, but at a distance. Its rapid spread through Byzantine lands in the Middle East was upsetting not only to the emperors but to the religious leaders, who saw many people accepting Islamic conquest with open arms. The Byzantine administration was well known for both its high taxation and its strict enforcement of Orthodox religious beliefs. Islam was a pleasant alternative, for it was religiously tolerant, and even the taxes that a non-Moslem was obliged to pay were significantly less than those levied by Constantinople. The spread of the Moslem faith, however, was more troubling, and the Orthodox Church began to take steps to change itself in such a way as to appeal to Moslems. The primary way in which that change manifested itself was the beginnings of iconoclasm, a rejection of icons or pictures in worship. Islam banned any pictorial representation of life as being a challenge to the power of God as Creator. For a time, the Orthodox Church banned them as well, which created a serious problem with the Roman Catholic Church. In Europe, a church hierarchy dealing with a less literate population needed icons for teaching purposes. The rivalry between the two centers of religion, Rome and Constantinople, intensified. Not until the twelfth century Crusades would there be any serious cooperation between the two factions of Christianity.

The Byzantine victory insulated Europe from Islam, but also from almost all outside influences. Although the knowledge of the Hellenistic culture of the east survived and in many ways flourished in the Middle East and Africa, Europe entered into the Dark Ages. Militarily, Europe could protect itself from invasion, but culturally progress was slow. Not until the Crusades and the resulting revival of trade with the east was the old knowledge rediscovered, and the Renaissance was the result. It is interesting to speculate what Europe may have been like had Constantinople fallen in 718 instead of 1453.

References: Fuller, J. F. C. *A Military History of the Western World,* vol. 1. New York: Funk & Wagnalls, 1954; Gibbon, Edward. *The Decline and Fall of the Roman Empire,* vol. 6. New York: Gallery Press, 1979 [1737]; Oman, Charles. *The Byzantine Empire.* London: T. F. Unwin, 1892; Treadgold, Warren. *Byzantium and Its Army, 284–1081.* Stanford, CA: Stanford University Press, 1995.

TOURS (POITIERS)

October 732

FORCES ENGAGED

Franks: Unknown. Commander: Charles Martel.
Moslems: Approximately 80,000. Commander:
Abd er-Rahman.

IMPORTANCE

Moslem defeat ended the Moslem's threat to
western Europe, and Frankish victory established
the Franks as the dominant population in western
Europe, establishing the dynasty that led to
Charlemagne.

Historical Setting

During 717–718, Moslem forces tried and failed to capture Constantinople, capital of the Byzantine Empire. That was a major setback for the Moslems, whose forces (intent on spreading their faith) had been virtually unstoppable in conquests that spread Islam from India to Spain. Although that defeat kept the followers of Mohammed out of eastern Europe for another seven centuries, it must have motivated other Moslems to attempt to spread the faith into Europe via another route: North Africa into Spain into western Europe.

Moslem forces had spread across the southern Mediterranean coast through the later decades of the seventh century and in the process of converting their conquered enemies absorbed them into the armies of the faithful. In North Africa, some of the most ardent converts were Moors (called Numidians by the Carthaginians of Hannibal's time), the Berbers of modern Morocco. In 710, Musa ibn Nusair, Moslem governor of the region, decided to attack across the Straits of Gibraltar and raid Spain. Without ships, however, he turned to Julian, a Byzantine official, who loaned him four ships. Julian did this because of a grudge he bore against Roderic, the Visigoth king that ruled in Spain. With four ships able to carry 400 men,

Musa launched a raid that netted him sufficient plunder to whet his appetite for more.

In 711, he ferried 7,000 men across the straits under Tarik ibn Ziyad. Although this was originally intended to be simply a larger raid, Tarik's victory over Roderic opened the Iberian peninsula to Moslem troops. Within a year, Musa was back in command and master of Spain. Recalled to the Middle East by the caliph, Musa's successor, Hurr, pushed deeper into Spain and through the Pyrenees into the province of Acquitaine during 717–718. Over the next several years, Moslem power ebbed and flowed through southern, central, and even northern Gaul (France).

The arrival of the Moslems was fortuitously timed, as internal feuds divided the population of Gaul. The dominant population, the Franks, were in a slump. Upon the death of Pepin II in 714, the Frankish throne was disputed between Pepin's legitimate grandson and illegitimate son. Eudo of Acquitaine saw an opportunity to escape Frankish domination, so he declared his independence and received in return the wrath of Charles Martel, Pepin's illegitimate son who finally succeeded to the throne in 719. After defeating Eudo, Charles then turned toward the Rhine River to secure his northeastern flank. He made war against the Saxons, Germans, and Swabians until 725, when Moslem successes in southern Gaul diverted his attention.

While Charles was off fighting in Germany, Eudo feared for his future because he was located between aggressive Moslems to the south and a hostile Charles to the north and east. Eudo entered into an alliance with a renegade Moslem named Othman ben abi Neza, who controlled an area of the northern Pyrenees. That alliance provoked Abd er-Rahman, Moslem governor of Spain, who marched against Othman in 731. After defeating him, Abd er-Rahman decided to drive deeper into Gaul, spreading Moslem influence and, more importantly, looting the wealthy Gallic countryside. He defeated Eudo at Bordeaux and proceeded north toward Tours, whose abbey was reputed to hold immense wealth. To spread as much terror and accumulate as much loot as possible, Abd er-Rahman divided his army, probably some 80,000 strong, into several columns and sent them pillaging.

Eudo fled to Paris, where he met with Charles and begged his aid. Charles agreed on the condition that Eudo would swear loyalty and never again try to remove himself from Frankish dominion. With that promise, Charles gathered together as many men as he could and marched toward Tours.

The Battle

The army that Charles amassed was probably some 30,000 men, a mixture of professional soldiers whom he had commanded in campaigns across Gaul and Germany and a mixed lot of militia with little weaponry or military skills. The Franks were hardy soldiers that armed themselves as heavy infantry, wearing some armor and fighting mainly with swords and axes. How much the Franks depended on cavalry has been disputed, for infantry had long dominated the European battlefield, and cavalry was only at this time becoming common. The strength of both infantry and cavalry was their determination in battle, but their weakness was their almost complete lack of discipline. Further, Charles lacked the wherewithal to maintain any sort of supply train, so his army lived off the land.

The army he marched to face was made up primarily of Moors who fought from horseback, depending on bravery and religious fervor to make up for their lack of armor or archery. Instead, the Moors fought with scimitars and lances. Their standard method of fighting was to engage in mass cavalry charges, depending on numbers and courage to overwhelm any enemy; it was a tactic that had carried them thousands of miles and defeated dozens of opponents. Their weakness was that all they could do was attack; they had no training or even concept of defense. They, like the Franks, lived off the land.

The two armies approached each other in the early autumn of 732. Abd er-Rahman's army had succeeded in plundering many towns and churches, and they were overwhelmed with their loot. They met in an unknown location somewhere south of Tours, between that city and Poitiers. Abd er-Rahman was surprised by the arrival of the Franks. Exactly how large the opposing forces were is the point of much disagreement. The Moslem army is numbered by modern writers as anywhere from 20,000 to 80,000, whereas the Frankish army has been described as both larger and smaller than those numbers. Abd er-Rahman faced a dilemma: to fight, he would have to abandon his loot, and he knew that his men would balk at that order. Luckily for him, Charles did not attack, but merely kept his distance and observed the Moslems for about a week. Abd er-Rahman used that break to send men south with the loot, where they could recover it after they beat the Franks. In the meantime, Charles was awaiting the arrival of his militia, whom he used primarily as foragers for his fighting men and less as fighters themselves.

After 7 days of waiting, watching, and certainly a bit of probing by both sides, Abd er-Rahman felt his loot sufficiently safe to focus on the battle. The exact date of the battle is unknown, although some sources (Perrett, *The Battle Book*) name 10 October. Charles knew the nature of the Moslem fighting style, and he had just the troops to counter it. As the Moslems massed to launch their charge, Charles formed his men into a defensive square made up primarily of his Frankish followers, but supplemented with troops from a variety of tribes subject to the Franks. No detailed account of the battle exists, but later reports relate that the Moslem cavalry beat unsuccessfully against the Frankish square, and the javelins and throwing axes of the Franks inflicted severe damage on the men and horses as they closed. The Moslems, knowing no other tactic, continued to attack and continued to fail to break the defense. Isidorus Pacensis wrote about the staunch Frankish square: "The men of the North stood motionless as a wall; they were like a belt of ice frozen together, and not to be dissolved, as they slew the Arab with the sword. The Austrasians [Franks from the German frontier], vast of limb, and iron of hand, hewed on bravely in the thick of the fight." It was this display of strength that earned for Charles his nickname Martel, or "the Hammer." Eudo, fighting with Charles, led an attack that turned the Moslem flank; they either panicked or feared for their loot. Creasy (*Fifteen Decisive Battles of the World*, p. 166) quotes a Moslem source: "But many of the Moslems were fearful for the safety of the spoil which they had stored in their tents, and a false cry arose in their ranks that some of the enemy were plundering the camp; whereupon several squadrons of the Moslem horsemen rode off to protect their tents." The departure of some of the cavalry apparently had a bad effect on the rest, and the Moslem effort collapsed.

At day's end, the Moslems withdrew toward Poitiers. Charles kept his men together and did not pursue, thinking that the battle would resume the following day. In the night, however, the Moslems learned that Abd er-Rahman had been killed in the fighting, so they fled. When the Franks found the Moslem camp empty of men the next morning, they contented themselves with recovering the abandoned loot. No accurate casualty count for either side was recorded.

Results

Survivors of Abd er-Rahman's army retreated back toward Spain, but they were not the last Moslems that ventured across the Pyrenees in search of easy wealth. They were, however, the last major invasion. Pockets of Moslem power remained along the southern frontier and Mediterranean coast until 759, but, for the most part, Islam settled into Spain and went no farther. Although the effectiveness of Charles Martel's tactics was certainly a factor, it was internal

struggles within Islam that limited continued expansion. When factional fighting broke out in Arabia, the effects spread throughout the Moslem empire. This not only divided the fighting forces, it also isolated the Moslem occupants in Spain from any religious leadership from the Middle East. Thus, consolidation seemed preferable to expansion.

Had the Moslems been victorious in the battle near Tours, it is difficult to suppose what population in western Europe could have organized to resist them. On the other hand, Abd er-Rahman's force was rather limited, and the religious schism that flared soon after the battle could well have stopped his campaigning as effectively as did the Franks. Thus, whether Charles Martel saved Europe for Christianity is a matter of some debate. What is sure, however, is that his victory ensured that the Franks would dominate Gaul for more than a century. For a couple of centuries, the ruling Merovingian dynasty had produced young, weak kings that ceded much of their ruling power to men who held the position of majordomo, or mayor of the palace. As the representative from the king to the aristocracy, the majordomos were able to coordinate public activity more than order it. By the time of Pepin II, however, the role of the majordomo was virtually indistinguishable from that of the king, and the monarch ruled in name only. Indeed, Charles was majordomo without a king, and upon his death in 741 his sons claimed kingship and divided the realm between them. During this same period, the aristocrats began exercising hereditary rights to their lands, rather than receiving their positions at the king's pleasure. This was the start of the feudal era, which dominated European society for centuries. To exercise control over these aristocrats, Charles Martel also granted land in payment for military service rendered, but to acquire that land he had to take it from the greatest landowner, the Catholic Church. That earned him the displeasure of Rome, but similar actions on the part of Charles's grandson actually brought the military power of the Franks and the religious authority of the church closer together. His grandson was also called Charles, later termed "the Great," or Charlemagne. Under his rule, the Franks rose to their greatest power both politically and militarily.

The nature of the European military changed after this battle. The concept of heavy cavalry was forming in the eighth century. The introduction of the stirrup made stability on horseback possible, and stability was vital for both carrying an armored rider and using heavy lances. The age of the armored knight, a fighting machine that was both the result and the foundation of feudalism, was being born. Although infantry remained key to winning European battles, it was paired with or subordinated to cavalry from this point until the fifteenth century.

Thus, the establishment of Frankish power in western Europe shaped that continent's society and destiny, and the battle of Tours confirmed that power.

References: Creasy, Edward S. *Fifteen Decisive Battles of the World.* New York: Harper, 1851; Dupuy, R. Ernest, and Trevor Dupuy. *Encyclopedia of Military History.* New York: Harper & Row, 1970; Fuller, J. F. C. *A Military History of the Western World,* vol. 1. New York: Funk & Wagnalls, 1954; Gregory of Tours. *History of the Franks.* Translated by Ernest Brehaut. New York: Columbia University Press, 1916; Oman, Charles. *The Art of War in the Middle Ages.* Ithaca, NY: Cornell University Press, 1953 [1885].

PAVIA
773–774

FORCES ENGAGED

Frankish: Unknown. Commander: Charlemagne.

Lombard: Unknown. Commander: Desiderius.

IMPORTANCE

The defeat and consequent destruction of the Lombard monarchy rid Rome of its most persistent threat to papal security, laying the groundwork for the Holy Roman Empire.

Historical Setting

The relationship between the pope and the kingdom of the Franks started in 756. Pepin III, known variously as "the Short" and "the Great," responded to a call from Pope Stephen II to save Rome from depredations by the Lombards, the population that dominated the northern Italian peninsula. The amity upon which this response was based rested on Stephen's support of Pepin's deposition of the last king of the Merovingian dynasty, Childeric III, in 751, and the blessing for that action that Stephen bestowed upon Pepin in 754. This began close ties between politics and religion in the Frankish lands, for Pepin and his heirs were to hold the title of *patricius Romanus* and protect the Catholic Church from spiritual and temporal threats. Thus, in 755, Pepin marched his army into Italy to capture the city of Pavia and stop the aggressive actions of the Lombard King Aistulf. As soon as he returned to France, however, Aistulf was again threatening Rome. Pepin was back in 756, defeated Aistulf again, and is reported to have promised the pope possession of a large amount of the Italian peninsula. When Aistulf died shortly thereafter, he was replaced by Desiderius, who promised to respect papal authority and possessions. That he did not do.

Upon Pepin's death in 768, his realm was divided between his two sons, Carloman II and Charles. The two apparently got along well with each other. Although the Lombards continued to harass successive popes, for a time the Franks and Lombards enjoyed friendly relations. At the urging of his mother, Charles in 770 divorced his wife in order to marry Desiderata, daughter of the Lombard king. Charles returned Desiderata to her father a year later for unknown reasons; possibly she was presumed infertile. That did nothing to endear Charles to Desiderius. In 771, Carloman died, leaving Charles sole king of the Franks. Carloman's wife left for Lombardy, however, seeking shelter in the king's court, and Desiderius began pushing Carloman's son as the rightful Frankish monarch.

Meanwhile, Charles's relations with Rome had been strained because Pope Stephen III criticized him for his marriage to Desiderata. When Charles ignored the criticism, Stephen grew closer to Desiderius, allowing Lombard appointees to hold important places in the Roman government and to persecute any opposition. Stephen died in 772 and his successor, Hadrian I, quickly cleaned house of these aggressive Lombards. That provoked a violent response. Desiderius, while sending messages requesting an audience with the pope, sent his troops into ever-deeper invasions of papal territory, until the town of Otriculum fell, a mere day's march away from Rome. Hadrian called out what troops he could and sent to Charles for assistance.

Hadrian's emissary traveled by sea to Marseilles because Desiderius had troops blocking all overland routes into France. The emissary finally reached Charles, who was holding court in Thionville on the Moselle just north of Metz, and delivered this message: "They would attack us by land and water, conquer the city of Rome and lead ourselves into captivity.... Therefore we implore you by the living God and the Prince of Apostles to hasten to our aid immediately, lest we be destroyed" (Winston, *Charlemagne*, p. 107). The note contained a list of all the people supposedly allied to Desiderius, many of whom threatened Charles's authority in one way or another. Charles sent envoys to Rome and Lombardy to offer a diplomatic solution, but at the same time he readied his army. When he received confirmation of Desiderius's aggression, as well as the Lombard king's refusal of a large monetary payment for the return of the cities he had taken from the pope, Charles's troops were mobilized and on the march in early summer 773.

The Battle

The size of Charles's army is unknown. Not only in this campaign, but in virtually all his military actions, this is the case. Although some sources claim that he could muster only several thousand knights, others propose an ability to field a force of 100,000 cavalry and infantry. Whatever the size, he divided it in half for the passage through the Alps into Italy. His uncle Bernard led half the army through the St. Bernard Pass, while he led his contingent through the Dora Susa by Mount Cenis farther west. They passed easily over the highest point and began winding their way down the valley toward open land, when they ran into a fortification blocking their way garrisoned by Desiderius's army. An assault failed to break through, so Charles entered into fruitless negotiations while his men grumbled. He finally gave permission for a small force to scout a possible alternate route. One was found, possibly by luck or (according to tradition) via the efforts of a Lombard minstrel who defected and was handsomely paid for turning coat. Whatever the method, when a band of cavalry appeared on the Lombard flank, the defenders panicked and fled for the walled city of Pavia, southwest of Milan. It is also possible that they learned of the approach of Bernard from the east and that motivated their flight. Charles's unhappy men gorged themselves on the riches of the abandoned Lombard camp and soon marched to Pavia, where the siege began in September 773.

That Charles had sufficient men to surround the city for 10 months implies a rather large force, especially because he was able to march away from the siege in order to spend Easter in Rome. Although they had no siege engines to batter the walls, they had the resources at harvest time of the fields surrounding the city. Unprepared for a siege, the defenders had not stocked the city well. Not only was Desiderius locked up inside but his son Adelchis had fled to hide behind the stronger city walls of Verona, there to watch over Carloman's wife

CHARLEMAGNE'S ARRIVAL BEFORE PAVIA

Although the number of men with Charlemagne on his invasion of Italy is unknown, one of his biographers wrote a powerful description of the army as it approached the city of Pavia, where Desiderius had retreated to make his stand. This account was written by Notker the Stammerer for Charlemagne's great-grandson, called Charles the Fat, in the late ninth century. Notker's story deals with a traitor to Charlemagne's cause, one Otker, who had placed himself in the service of the Lombard king. Otker and Desiderius were in a watchtower when the vanguard of the army of the Franks emerged into view.

As soon as the baggage trains came into sight, moving even more quickly than those of Darius or Julius Caesar, Desiderius said to Otker: "Is Charles in the midst of that vast array!" "Not yet, not yet," answered Otker. When he perceived the army itself, collected together from all the nations of Charlemagne's vast Empire, Desiderius said sharply to Otker: "Now Charles is advancing proudly in the midst of his troops." "Not yet, not yet," answered Otker. Desiderius then flew into a panic and said: "If even more soldiers come into battle with him, what can we possibly do!" "When he comes," said Otker, "you will see what he is like. I don't know what will happen to us." As they spoke together, the sovereign's escort appeared, tireless as ever. When he saw them Desiderius was stupefied. "This time it really is Charles," said he. "Not yet, not yet," said Otker once more. After this the bishops came into sight, and the abbots and the clergy of Charlemagne's chapel, with their attendants. When he saw them Desiderius longed for death and began to hate the light of day. With a sob in his voice he stammered: "Let us go down and hide ourselves in

the earth, in the face of the fury of an enemy so terrible." Otker, too, was terrified, for in happier days he had been in close contact with the strategy and the military equipment of the peerless Charlemagne, and he knew all about them. "When you see the fields bristle as with ears of iron corn," he said, "when you see the Po and the Ticino break over the walls of your city in great waves which gleam black with the glint of iron, then indeed you can be sure that Charlemagne is at hand." He had not yet finished his words when from the west a mighty gale and with it the wind of the true north began to blow up like some great pall of cloud, which turned the bright daylight into frightful gloom. As the Emperor rode on and ever on, from the gleam of his weapons dawned as it were another day, more dark than any night for the beleaguered force.

Then came in sight that man of iron, Charlemagne, topped with his iron helm, his fists in iron gloves, his iron chest and his Platonic shoulders clad in an iron cuirass. An iron spear raised high against the sky he gripped in his left hand, while in his right he held his still unconquered sword.... His shield was all of iron. His horse gleamed iron-coloured and its very mettle was as if of iron. All those who rode before him, those who kept him company on either flank, those who followed after, wore the same armour, and their gear was as close a copy of his own as it is possible to imagine. Iron filled the fields and the open spaces. The rays of the sun were thrown back by this battle-line of iron.... When therefore Otker, who had foreseen the truth, with one swift glance observed all this, which I, a toothless man with stammering speech, have tried to describe, not as I ought, but slowly and with labyrinthine phrase, he said to Desiderius: "That is Charlemagne, whom you have sought so long." As he spoke he fell half conscious to the ground.

and children. Charles left the bulk of his force at Pavia and led a small contingent to Verona, which gave in without a fight. Adelchis fled to Constantinople, while Charles's sister-in-law entered into his keeping and vanished from history. Through the latter months of 773 and into the first months of the following year, Charles rode around the environs of Pavia establishing his authority. In the meantime, none

of Desiderius's subordinates in other cities made any attempt to relieve him, and apparently he made no attempt to break out.

"It was now the tenth month of the siege: disease and probably famine were pressing the defenders hard: and Desiderius, who had never been a popular sovereign, heard on every side of the defection of his countrymen. At length on a certain Tuesday in June (774) the city opened the gates to her conqueror" (Hodgkin, *Charles the Great*, p. 101). Charles accepted the homage of the Lombard aristocracy and named himself king of the Franks and the Lombards. Desiderius was sent with his family to northeastern France, where he was invited to enter a monastery; by most accounts, he took well to religious life.

Results

With Desiderius removed from the Lombard throne, there was a major power shift in Italy. Hadrian and Charles were well-matched to share an unusual arrangement: Hadrian wanted political power in Italy, which he could not wield without Charles's army; Charles was a Christian knight who wanted to do God's work, but without any real oversight. These aims seem at first to be at cross-purposes, but apparently the two men reached an understanding of where their respective authorities lay. During Charles's Easter 774 visit to Rome, the two men treated each other as equals, but Hadrian was able to wring from Charles confirmation of the pope's possession of large amounts of land in Italy (most of the peninsula, actually) granted to Pope Stephen II by Pepin. As king of the Lombards, Charles controlled much of that land, but much of it was still occupied by forces of independent nobles or the Byzantine Empire, leftover forces from Belisarius's conquests during Justinian's reign. Thus, it was not all Charles's land to grant, and whether Hadrian expected him to conquer the remainder of it for Rome is a question that has never been answered. As Charles spent most of his reign north of the Alps in campaigns against his enemies there, he apparently never had any serious intention of being on hand as Hadrian's enforcer. Still, he had the pope's blessing and fought to spread both Christianity and the borders of his realm with equal diligence.

Pope Hadrian died in 795 and was succeeded by Leo III. Leo was unpopular with the citizens of Rome, who accused him of a variety of crimes. Following a failed assassination attempt in 799, Leo fled Italy for Aachen, where Charles had established his capital. Leo demanded that Charles restore him to the papal throne. Charles sent him back to Rome with an armed escort and then followed along himself, arriving in December 800. He obliged Leo to publicly swear that he had done nothing wrong and was reconfirmed as pope. Leo's response changed Europe for centuries. On Christmas Day, Charles went to St. Peter's Basilica to celebrate mass. He knelt before the altar to pray, and, as he raised his head, Leo placed a crown on it with the words, repeated three times: "Hail to Charles the Augustus, crowned by God the great and peace-bringing Emperor of the Romans."

There has been widespread speculation over the motivations of both Charles and Leo in this coronation. Charles seems to have been eager to hold a position equal to that of the ancient caesars, but his contemporary biographer, Einhard, claims that, had Charles known what Leo was going to do, he would not have gone to church that day. One can only suppose that, although he wanted to be emperor of a latter-day Roman Empire, Charles wanted it on his own terms. Leo, by initiating the ceremony, placed himself in the equation. Although Leo paid homage to Charles, now Charles the Great (Charlemagne in French, Karl der Grosse in German), the coronation was performed by the head of the Catholic Church. Thus, who was the superior: the emperor or the man who made him emperor? Leo, possibly humiliated by the public oath that Charles had made him swear, could have been saying that only the pope could make an emperor, no matter how much the pope depended on that emperor's temporal power. In their lifetimes, both men benefited: "The coronation had results for a thousand years. It strengthened the papacy and the bishops by making civil authority derive from ecclesiastical conferment. . . . It strengthened Charlemagne against baronial and other disaffection by making him a very vicar of God; it vastly advanced the theory of the divine right of kings" (Durant, *The Age of Faith,* p. 469).

The coronation had effects far outside the kingdom of the Franks. The Byzantine Empire was just beginning to feel the press of Islam against its borders, and, with Charlemagne's coronation, the eastern emperor found the old Roman Empire threatened from a new quarter. Charlemagne's coronation had come at a time of political upheaval in Constantinople because Irene was trying to rule as empress after deposing her son. By the time she was forced out of power and replaced by Nicephorus I in 802, the reestablished Western Roman Empire was a virtual fait accompli. The next emperor in Constantinople, Michael I, accepted the inevitable by addressing Charlemagne as "brother," that is, equal. The situation also further alienated the Roman Catholic and Eastern Orthodox Churches because each emperor championed his own faith.

Charlemagne's victory at Pavia, by making him the major military power in Italy and placing him in a partnership with the pope, put him in a position to establish a dynasty whose role was defender of the faith: "the coronation established the Holy Roman Empire in fact, though not in theory" (Durant, *The Age of Faith,* p. 469). When the dynasty faded from power in the tenth century, that political entity came into official being under Otto I in 962.

References: Durant, Will. *The Age of Faith.* New York: Simon & Schuster, 1950; Einhard, and Notker the Stammerer. *Two Lives of Charlemagne.* Translated by Lewis Thorpe. New York: Penguin, 1969; Hodgkin, Thomas. *Charles the Great.* Port Washington, NY: Kennikat Press, 1970 [1897]; Lamb, Harold. *Charlemagne.* Garden City, NY: Doubleday, 1954; Riché, Pierre. *The Carolingians.* Translated by Michael Idomir Allen. Philadelphia: University of Pennsylvania Press, 1993; Winston, Richard. *Charlemagne: From the Hammer to the Cross.* Indianapolis, IN: Bobbs-Merrill, 1954.

LECHFELD
9 August 955

FORCES ENGAGED
German: Approximately 10,000 men.
Commander: Otto of Saxony.
Magyar: Approximately 50,000 men.
Commander: Lél.

IMPORTANCE
Magyar defeat ended more than 90 years of their pillaging western Europe and convinced survivors to settle down, creating the basis for the state of Hungary.

Historical Setting

Aside from the legend of a Middle Eastern origin, the Magyars in reality seem to have had Finn-Ugaric origins with traces of Turco-Tartar elements. They had long practiced a nomadic lifestyle in central Asia and finally migrated westward past the Ural, Volga, Don, Dnieper, and at last the Danube Rivers. In this movement, they had to successively fight and defeat other nomadic tribes, such as the Bulgars, Khazars, and Petchenegs. It was finally the pressure of the Petchenegs and Bulgars who drove the Magyars into Europe. As they entered eastern Europe, they encountered the power of the Byzantine Empire, which hired them as mercenaries and introduced them to Christianity; likewise, Germanic kings hired them to aid in fighting the Slavs.

By the ninth century A.D., the Magyars had moved into central Europe under the leadership of Arpad. Under his direction, some 150,000 men entered the Hungarian plain; they defeated the Slavs and Alans, settled there, and used it as a base for further raiding into German and Italian lands. The Magyars became the permanent occupants of this region. Magyar soldiers under Arpad ranged successfully into Italy as far as Milan and Pavia in 899, finally leaving upon receiving sufficient bribes. The

Magyars fought in much the same style as the Huns and were precursors to the Mongol invasion of Europe. Employing mostly light cavalry and archers, they avoided close contact with their enemies, harassing them into exhaustion and then exploiting any openings. Unlike their Hunnish kin, the bows they employed were straighter than the standard curved bow of the steppe peoples. They also carried a slightly curved sword, which they adopted from the Alans, and at times they fought with a mace. The heavy cavalry developed in western Europe at this time did not at first succeed against the Magyars, but over time the westerners adopted some of the eastern tactics and began to have more success.

For a time, the Magyars allied themselves with various Germanic principalities and accepted bribes to leave one region alone or attack another. By 907, however, Magyar interest in Germany forced competing nobles into cooperation. Luitpold of Bavaria allied with Ditmar, the Archbishop of Salzburg. Their efforts proved futile as the Magyars defeated them at Presburg. In the 920s, the Magyars raided as far as the Champagne region of France, into northern Italy again, and as far as the Pyrenees. The Magyars created as much terror as the Vikings were doing from the north, but the Germanic nobles soon began to prevail against them. Henry the Fowler, king of Saxony, defeated the Magyars in 933 at Merseburg, inflicting 36,000 Magyar casualties. He and his successors began fortifying the frontier, and that lessened the frequency of the Magyar raids, while the Bavarians began to raid Magyar lands.

Henry's successor on the Saxon throne was Otto, a son by his second wife. Otto spent much of his early reign putting down rebellions while at the same time dealing with the troublesome Magyars. As late as 954, Otto was still defeating surly vassals, while the Magyars were organizing for a major offensive into western Europe.

In 925, the Magyars had formed an alliance with Hugh of Provence. They cooperated with him in campaigns against rival Italian rulers as well as the Moslem kingdom of Cordoba, which threatened to expand past the Pyrenees. In 954, the Magyars convinced Hugh to allow them free passage through his southwestern French province of Provence. With a force of between 50,000 and 100,000, the Magyars swept through Bavaria and through central France as far as the southeastern province of Aquitaine. Such an attack strengthened Otto in his appeals to the German nobility to rally around his standard and fight a common enemy. Otto, after suppressing an uprising by Conrad of Franconia, put an army in the field in the late summer of 954, but failed to locate and engage the Magyars.

The Battle

In 955, the Magyars once again rode into southern Germany. Their leadership consisted of two men: the civil leader of the Magyars was the *harka,* a position held by Bulcsú; the military commander's position was that of *gyula,* held by Lél. Their intent seems to have been to defeat the Germanic princes sufficiently to protect the extended frontiers that the Magyars wanted to maintain around their adopted homeland, which stretched from Transylvania in modern Rumania into Austria. They had devastated a large buffer zone around their lands to discourage invasion and apparently wanted to keep that buffer zone intact as well as make sure no neighbor was strong enough to restrain their raids into western Europe. They started their campaign in an unusual manner. Rather than engage in their standard light cavalry sweeps, they approached the city of Augsburg and prepared to lay siege. This they began on 8 August, but the siege was lifted after a single day with the news of Otto's approaching army. The Magyars moved to the nearby Lech River and set up camp.

Otto's army comprised units from Bavaria, Saxony, Franconia, Swabia, and Bohemia. Establishing their camp somewhat upriver from the Magyars, Otto ordered his men to fast the night before the battle in order to pray and purify themselves. Knowing that their force of 10,000 faced one five times their strength probably was sufficient to keep most of the men too nervous to eat anyway. They celebrated mass the following morning and then mounted and rode toward the Magyar army. The German force was comprised mainly of heavy cavalry, and they hoped to use their superior weight and mass to overwhelm the more numerous but lighter enemy. Henry the Fowler had accomplished just that in his victory 30 years earlier, and Otto hoped to repeat his father's victory.

Otto moved his men over rough terrain in a column of units broken down by their nationality. The leading three units were Bavarians, followed by Franconians led by the previously rebellious Conrad; Otto commanded the Saxons in the middle of the column, followed by two units of Swabians and the Bohemian cavalry in the rear. As they rode down the eastern side of the Lech, they failed to notice a force of Magyar cavalry riding in the opposite direction on the western side. This almost proved their undoing. The lighter Magyar cavalry crossed the river and swung down on the Bohemians in the rear, who were escorting the army's baggage train. This surprise attack scattered the Bohemians, and the two Swabian units to their front soon fled as well.

Caught between two large forces, Otto's army should have been crushed. They were not because of poor coordination between the flanking force and the main body of the Magyar army to his front. They also were aided by the Magyars themselves, who stopped their attack in order to loot the baggage train. This one mistake has cost innumerable victories for armies throughout history, yet it is a lesson that rarely seems to be learned. Otto ordered Conrad's Franconians out of column and to the rear, where they came quickly upon the dismounted pillagers and ran over them. Most of the Magyars fled with what they could carry, leaving behind what prisoners they had captured in their initial success.

With his rear now unthreatened, Otto deployed his force out of column into line, facing the main Magyar host. His knights began their charge in good order, presenting a solid heavy mass bearing down on the oncoming Magyar army. As the two armies headed for their collision, Otto is said to have shouted, "They surpass us, I know, in numbers, but neither in weapons nor in courage. We know also that they are quite without the help of God, which is of the greatest comfort to us" (Guttman, "Survival of the Strong"). This sounds more like a prebattle speech, but such is the nature of legend. As the two armies bore down on each other, the Magyars loosed a volley of arrows, but the knights raised their shields just in time to deflect most of them. Before the Magyars could let go another volley, the Germans were on them.

As Otto had hoped, the stability of his line made its weight overpowering, and the lighter armed and armored Magyars began to fall back. Lél ordered a portion of his cavalry to fall back in mock retreat, hoping to encourage the Germans to break their ranks in pursuit, but their discipline brought the Magyar ruse to naught. As the Magyars began fleeing the German onslaught, they had nowhere to retreat but into the Lech, where many drowned. Others fled to local villages, but the inhabitants either overwhelmed them or pointed out their hiding places to the German troops when they arrived scouring the area for prisoners. For 2 days, Otto's men rounded up the Magyar survivors. Many of them were executed, but the rest were sent home minus ears or noses.

Results

The opening attack on the German rear guard to the final rout of the Magyar army took 10 hours. That, coupled with the rounding up of stragglers, virtually destroyed this Magyar force, but another, larger army remained in the east in defense of the homeland. Otto decided against invading, but he had no need to do so. This serious defeat changed the attitude of the Magyar population. Seeing that a strong and united Germany stood against them, they realized that their days of raiding were over. Unlike the Huns previously or the Mongols later, the Magyars did not return to their eastern roots. The leaders who rose to power in the wake of the battle of Lechfeld were descendants of the great Magyar leader Arpad, and they established what became the kingdom of Hungary (from the Magyar word *Onogur*, Ten Arrows, an ancient tribal confederation). The population, which traditionally were animists, soon were converted to Christianity, and that brought them into the community of European nations.

At home in Hungary, they settled down to a more stable and civilized lifestyle under the leadership of Duke Geyza in the 970s. As Christianity replaced their Asiatic animistic and totemic beliefs, the Magyars began showing a toleration and acceptance of other cultures. King Stephen (997–1038) defended his homeland from takeover by the Holy Roman Empire and acquired from the pope the authority over a national church. Stephen oversaw the construction of monasteries and cathedrals and for his efforts and example was later canonized. The Magyar language became and remains the official language of Hungary; but for the battle at Lechfeld, it may have been the language of much of western Europe. For all their terrorism of the west, it was the Hungarians who defended western Europe from the Ottoman Turks as they fought to capture Vienna and expand the Moslem faith into Europe in the sixteenth century.

Otto received widespread recognition for his victory, being given the title "emperor" by the Byzantines and given the same title by Pope John XII in 962. Visiting Rome in that year, Otto reconfirmed the temporal power of the pope as Charlemagne had done almost two centuries earlier. Under Otto, however, the pope was to be a vassal of the Germanic king that took the title Holy Roman Emperor. Although the geographic entity of the Holy Roman Empire was fluid over the succeeding centuries, the position of emperor lasted until 1806. Otto was serious in his intent to control the pope, for in 963 he deposed John XII and replaced him with the more pliant Leo VIII. Leo was followed after his death in 965 by another of Otto's appointees, John XIII, after a military campaign into Italy crushing Roman opposition to the installation. The link between emperor and pope proved to be a tenuous one, with one alternately exercising authority over the other through the next several centuries, but the linking of the Germanic states and the Italian ones proved to be the primary power structure in Europe until the rise of Spain in the sixteenth century. Although Germany failed to unify under any single leader until 1871, Austria came out of this struggle as the state from which the Holy Roman Empire would be run.

References: Balász, György, and Károly Szelényi. *The Magyars: The Birth of a European Nation.* Budapest: Corvina Press, 1989; Guttman, Jon. "Survival of the Strong," *Military History* 8(2), August 1991; Markov, Walter. *Battles of World History.* New York: Hippocrene Books, 1979; Vambery, Arminius. *Hungary in Ancient, Medieval, and Modern Times.* Hallandale, FL: New World Books, 1972.

HASTINGS
14 October 1066

FORCES ENGAGED
Norman: 2,000 cavalry and 5,000 infantry. Commander: Duke William of Normandy.

English: 2,000 housecarls and 5,500 militia. Commander: King Harold Godwinsson.

IMPORTANCE
William's victory placed a foreign ruler on the throne of England, introducing European rather than Scandinavian society onto the isolated island. This was the last successful invasion of England.

Historical Setting

When King Edward the Confessor died in January 1066, his succession was disputed. The *witan,* the governing council of English nobles and religious leaders, named Harold Godwinsson as the next king because he was the strongest of the nobles and his sister was Edward's wife; further, Edward on his deathbed apparently named Harold as his successor. Almost immediately, a challenge to this announcement came from across the English Channel. Duke William of Normandy claimed that Edward had years earlier named him as successor. Edward had spent 30 years in Normandy before his ascension to the English throne and was heavily influenced by that long stay, introducing many aspects of Norman society into England. While staying in northern France years before (date unknown), Harold had agreed to support William's claim, but that made no difference to the witan and Harold was prepared to uphold their decision. William prepared to invade England to enforce his claim. To make the succession race even more heated, Harold's brother Tostig laid claim as well and had the support of the king of Norway, Harald Hardrada.

As the only accounts of the Norman invasion of England are from the Norman point of view, it is impossible to know exactly who, if anyone, was in the right. William convinced Pope Alexander II, however, of the justice of his cause by slandering the strength of Harold's commitment to Rome. Harold's commitment had never been anything less than wholehearted,

Norman cavalry attacks a hill defended by the Saxon infantry. Detail from the Bayeux Tapestry. Musèe de la Tapisserie, Bayeux, France. (Erich Lessing/Art Resource, New York)

however, so no one knows why the pope accepted William's account without consulting Harold, but papal approval of the invasion resulted in a much stronger response from the nobles of northern France in joining William's cause. Through the spring and summer of 1066, William organized his invasion force.

The first defense of Harold's throne took place against Tostig, however, who (with his Viking allies) raided the Isle of Wight in May 1066. He landed along the east central coast of England the following month, but was beaten by Edwin of Mercia and fled to Scotland. There Tostig welcomed the arrival of forces brought by Hardrada, and together they landed in northern England on 18 September, defeating a local force at the battle of Gate Fulford. This attack in the north put incredible pressure on King Harold and his army.

The strength of Harold's army were the housecarls, trained heavy infantry wearing chain mail and fighting with long-shafted axes adapted from the Vikings. These were very good soldiers, but their supporting units were the *fyrd,* the militia. All males of fighting age were part of the fyrd and owed the king a certain number of days per year for military service, whereas the housecarls were more permanent soldiers. Still, the fyrd were not to be despised, for they had been defending England for 200 years from Viking raids and knew how to fight. When Harold learned that William was gathering forces in Normandy for an invasion, and then Tostig raided the Isle of Wight off England's southern coast, Harold called out the fyrd. He kept them under arms in southern England to be available when William arrived, yet, when he learned of the attack by Tostig and Hardrada, he had to march north to deal with them. This he did at Stamford Bridge (9 miles northeast of the town of York) on 25 September, marching the 200 miles to the battleground in a mere 5 days. This was an extremely hard-fought battle, and Harold's casualties numbered 1,000 housecarls, one-third of all upon which he could draw. (Casualties among

the fyrd are unknown.) Both Tostig and Harald Hardrada were killed in the battle, and Hardrada's son swore never to attack England again. This ended the Scandinavian threat to England's independence, but it cost Harold's army dearly in soldiers and stamina. On 1 October, Harold learned that William's force had landed.

After a long delay waiting for favorable winds, the Norman force finally arrived along the south coast of England. Although William originally intended to land on the Isle of Wight and establish a base there, the poor Norman navigational ability could not contend with contrary winds. Thus, William's men landed much farther east near Pevensey. After a few days of pillaging the countryside, William aimed his force toward Hastings. While on his way, he almost literally ran into Harold's army, newly arrived from York.

The Battle

Harold's men made another forced march back to London, where he spent a few days resting his men and gathering more troops. On the evening of 13 October, Harold's men occupied Senlac Hill, overlooking William's army. Many of the fyrd had either marched north and fought at Stamford Bridge or remained in the south and fought William's Normans. Either way, many had gone home as their annual duty had expired. Thus, Harold did not have as many men as he had hoped, and those that he had were exhausted. They did have the element of surprise, however, for they appeared almost magically in front of the Normans much sooner than William had thought possible. Rather than start fighting late in the day, however, the two sides encamped and waited for morning.

Harold placed his men in a strong formation along the crest of Senlac Hill and stretched in a line that curved back somewhat on the flanks. Knowing that the strength of the Norman army was its cavalry, Harold could hardly be in a better position. His men were used to close-in fighting, and their almost impenetrable wall of shields could easily thwart any attempt to send the cavalry up the hill against them; any horses, however strong, would be at a serious disadvantage by the time they reached the crest of a fairly steep hill. Harold's force numbered at best some 2,000 housecarls aided by more than 5,000 militia, although some sources (Fuller, *A Military History of the Western World,* pp. 373–374) count the militia at no more than 2,000 to 3,000. Maintaining their defensive line without a break in discipline was Harold's most difficult task.

The Norman army contained about 2,000 cavalry. These were mainly of the nobility, or at least the most economically advantaged, and wore metal helmets and chain mail. One of the main keys to Norman warfare was the recent introduction of the stirrup, which allowed a knight to stay on his mount when he used his heavy lance on an enemy. William's goal was to get the English army in the open so that cavalry could operate effectively, just as it was Harold's goal to stay on top of that hill to neutralize the cavalry. The rest of William's army, perhaps 3,000 to 5,000 men, was made up of infantry that resembled that of the English, al-though the sword was their preferred weapon rather than the ax. They also hurled javelins (as did the English) and were supported by archers. The battle of Hastings saw the first combat use of the crossbow, as well as the traditional bow and arrow.

The battle started in late morning with the Normans closing to within about 200 yards to launch their arrows. This they did with little effect, for the uphill angle arced the arrows and crossbow bolts over the English or down onto their shields. When this proved unproductive, the infantry were ordered up the hill, but neither they nor the cavalry made much impression on the English shield wall. In their withdrawal, however, the less disciplined troops of the fyrd began a pursuit, which weakened the virtually fortresslike front that Harold's army had presented. That, coupled with a rumor that William had fallen, disheartened the Norman force. William's appearance, helmetless so all could identify him, rallied the troops. Those militia that had chased the retreating Normans down the hill found themselves isolated and soon destroyed. The English line tightened up and repelled the next assaults by William's cavalry.

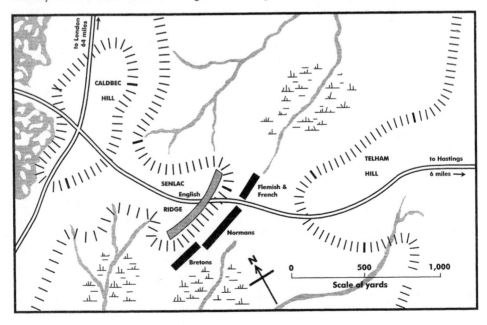

Making no headway against Harold's steadfast housecarls, William in desperation tried deceit. He ordered his men to feign panic and retreat. This time the temptation was too great for more of the English militia. Perhaps they had thought an earlier charge on the heels of the retreating Normans may have broken them completely, or perhaps they were just tired of accepting all the punishment and now felt like inflicting it. Whatever the reason, Harold could not hold them in place, and many of his troops began pursuing the Normans down the hill. This took them onto the open ground where William wanted them, and now his cavalry could do its work. They turned and charged back into the English, who could not stand the attack and were cut down as the earlier pursuers had been. Harold, however, still remained with his best men atop Senlac Hill.

William once again brought in his archers, who faced no return fire because the English had no archers of their own. The English huddled down behind their shields, turtle style, but a chance arrow broke through and struck Harold in the eye, killing him. This broke English morale, and the remaining militia fled, leaving only the remaining exhausted housecarls. William threw in his entire force, and the English had no choice but retreat. At nightfall, the Normans commanded the hilltop.

Results

William's army occupied Hastings, then took Dover, and then marched on London. As the bulk of the fighting men had been against Harold, no serious force stood in its way. It was a surly population that William faced upon occupying London, but he soon did more to make the population hate him. William forced the witan to name him king, and then he went about proving he held the throne. He brought more troops and supplies from Normandy and proceeded to conquer England, making local nobles swear loyalty to him or replacing them with Norman aristocrats. All across England,

Norman castles sprang up, acting as both a defensive position in which the Norman noble lived and a base from which he imposed his will upon the conquered. Not since the days of the Roman Empire had England been so thoroughly beaten and subjugated. Wales, Scotland, and Ireland were not much longer free from Norman dominance; within a matter of decades all were occupied. All of this gave William the nickname the Conquerer, by which he has been known to history.

The Norman conquest completely altered the nature of England. Dominated by the Saxons since the Roman Empire fell more than five centuries earlier, England had made but little progress in relation to the rest of Europe. From 1066 that changed. The feudal system that had been developing in France since the days of Charlemagne in the eighth century became the basis of English society and politics as well, although adapted somewhat. Before the invasion, England had been a loose confederation of nobles more than a country; afterward it became a real kingdom. This meant a country going in one direction, able to focus on its internal needs as well as foreign relations from a single point of view. The unification that William accomplished strengthened that concept, for the British Isles had been occupied by multiple Scandinavian and north European populations, usually antagonistic to each other.

William made himself a king and then implemented his own brand of feudalism. In the traditional feudal system, nobles swore fealty to a king and in turn had underlings swear fealty to them, thus creating the potential for divided or conflicting loyalties. In England, only the king could award lands in return for service and loyalty, so he remained the primary power and focus of national politics. That power held by one man centralized the direction of government, but also laid the foundation for future reforms: when King John as absolute monarch attempted to act as such, he found himself facing a hostile group of nobles that forced him to sign the Magna Carta. Thus, the future of the English constitutional system found its basis in William's monarchy. However, although William had imposed a Norman legal structure, he also adapted it to local English law from the previous Saxon occupation; together they laid the foundation for the English constitutional system.

Devastating as the short-term consequences of the Norman invasion were—and William destroyed large amounts of the countryside while imposing his will—in the long run, the nation of England was created, with all the ramifications that has had on the course of world history.

—Michael Forbes

References: Creasy, Edward S. Fifteen Decisive Battles of the World. New York: Harper, 1851; Freeman, Edward. The History of the Norman Conquest of England. Chicago: University of Chicago Press, 1974; Fuller, J. F. C. A Military History of the Western World, vol. 1. New York: Funk & Wagnalls, 1954; Furneaux, Rupert. The Invasion of 1066. Englewood Cliffs, NJ: Prentice-Hall, 1974; Howarth, David. 1066: The Year of the Conquest. New York: Viking Penguin, 1977.

MANZIKERT
1071

FORCES ENGAGED
Byzantine: Approximately 40,000.
Commander: Romanus IV Diogenes.
Turkish: Approximately 40,000.
Commander: Alp Arslan.

IMPORTANCE
Byzantine defeat severely limited the power of the Byzantines by denying them control over Anatolia, the major recruiting ground for soldiers. Henceforth, the Moslems controlled the region. The Byzantine Empire was limited to the area immediately around Constantinople, and the Byzantines were never again a serious military force.

Historical Setting

By the middle of the eleventh century A.D., the Byzantine Empire was well past its prime, although still a force with which to be reckoned. A series of weak and short-term emperors and empresses had frittered away the empire's wealth while ignoring its frontiers and defenses. Although the Byzantine army, which trained and fought upon proven standards, was probably the best organized army of its day, it was irregularly led and the quality of its recruits had dropped markedly. The manuals *Strategicon* from the sixth century and *Tactica* from the early tenth century were the bases of a workable and working military philosophy, but the sturdy Anatolian peasant upon which the empire had long depended for its soldiery was no longer providing the core of the army. Foreign recruits or mercenaries made up the majority of the army. Although some of these were outstanding fighters, such as the Varangian Guard, few were tied to the empire in any way but monetary. Only the lack of an organized rival kept the Byzantine army the premiere force of the time, and the tenuous nature of the force's composition meant that it could not really stand to be seriously challenged or badly commanded.

The empire had for two centuries been pressed along its southeastern front by the power of Islam. It had lost much of its territory in that direction, but by the time of Manzikert still held Asia Minor and the southern Balkans. When not fighting back the Moslem threat, the Byzantines made war in Europe against a variety of populations, most of whom had arrived in southeastern Europe during and immediately after the fall of the Western Roman Empire. Serbs, Magyars, Petchenegs, Cumans, and others were constantly causing the empire's European frontiers to shift. They, also, were too few in number or too disorganized to do more than eat away at Byzantine power. Although the government in Constantinople needed to deal with them, the judicious use of bribery, diplomacy, or the threat of force kept that front sufficiently quiet that the government could focus most of its attention on the Moslems.

Along the far eastern reaches of the Byzantine Empire, acting as something of a buffer against the Moslems, was the region of Armenia. It was an area rich in natural resources and situated to take advantage of trade from Asia or up from Egypt. It was a wealthy region populated by inhabitants fiercely independent and difficult to subdue. Its wealth and resources made it attractive to generations of passing raiders and potential conquerors, and its location put it squarely in the path of the rising power of the Seljuk Turks, who appeared from the steppes of central Asia as another in a seemingly inexhaustible series of nomadic horsemen. What made them different was their conversion to the Sunni sect of Islam and that, instead of raiding and moving on, they stayed and established a government. By 1040, they ruled Persia and occupied Baghdad. This put them into a rivalry with the Egyptian Fatimid dynasty, which practiced Shia Islam and whose possessions included the Levant and the western coast of the Arabian peninsula. Their control of Syria gave them access to lucrative trade, so for reasons of wealth, power, and religion, the Seljuks and Fatimids seemed bound to clash. The Fatimid alliance with Constantinople, however, ensured a continuing Byzantine interest in any conflict. Further, the Byzantine desire to acquire the wealth of Armenia would put them in the way of possible Seljuk territorial desires as well.

In 1065, Alp Arslan became leader of the Seljuk Turks. Arslan was both a good general and a good administrator, and under his rule the Seljuks prospered. He succeeded Tughril Bey, who had brought Baghdad, Mosul, and Diarbekir under Seljuk sway. Arslan extended the boundaries of the Seljuk domain, campaigning against Georgia and laying siege to the Armenian capital of Ani. He captured the city after a siege in 1064 and laid the city waste, as he planned to do with most of Anatolia. By denuding it of cultivated land, he could have the grassland so beloved of steppe people for the grazing of their horses. Thus, Arslan put himself and his people into the line of sight of the Byzantine government, which came under the control of Romanus IV Diogenes in 1068. Although Romanus was a general with some previous successes in the Balkans, the army was not happy with him, and the influential Varangian Guard distrusted him for the favoritism he extended toward native-born troops.

Romanus's ambitions faced toward Armenia. He quickly massed the Byzantine army and attacked the Seljuks, who had just plundered the west-central province of Phrygia. Romanus surprised them at Sebastea (modern Sivas) and

Battle between the cavalry of the Byzantines and the Seljuks. Scylitzes Chronicle, *eleventh century. Biblioteca Nacional, Madrid, Spain. (Werner Forman/Art Resource, New York)*

drove them from the field, capturing all their plunder and freeing all their prisoners in the process. He then drove southward toward Aleppo, raiding there and returning to Anatolia via Alexandretta.

In 1069, Romanus resumed his campaign against the Seljuk Turks, clearing them out of the western province of Cappadocia, but he was forced to retreat after a defeat at Khilat, near Lake Van. He fought Arslan a few months later at Heraclea (Kybistra) and defeated him, but the Seljuk leader was able to break out of a trap and escape to Aleppo. In 1070, Romanus had to deal with the Normans in the west, so he placed his eastern forces under his nephew Manuel Comnenus. Manuel lost to Alp Arslan's brother-in-law, Arisiaghi, and was taken prisoner, but entered into machinations with his captor, who contemplated seizing power from Alp Arslan. Manuel convinced Arisiaghi to go to Constantinople to negotiate with Romanus, which he did by entering into an alliance. When Alp Arslan demanded Arisiaghi's extradition and was refused, he went again to war.

The Battle

Alp Arslan led his army north of Lake Van to Manzikert, which he besieged and captured. He marched then to Edessa and then, failing to capture the city, returned to Persia. Romanus was soon in the field after him. Early in 1071, Romanus gathered his forces, but the exact number is unknown. Contemporary Moslem sources cite numbers between 200,000 and 400,000, but those are certainly outrageously high. It was "considerable" in size, according to J. F. C. Fuller, and probably was larger than that fielded by the Seljuks, at least at first. By the time battle was joined, they were probably roughly equal. The trouble with the army was not its size but its discipline and loyalty, both of which were lacking. Romanus had difficulty demanding the allegiance of some German mercenaries and had to contend with the widespread pillaging in which many troops engaged

despite orders to the contrary. Further, and more dangerous, was the conspiracy against him conducted by his wife, the Empress Eudocia, and her son Michael VII. Key officers in Romanus's force were in league with them and that would prove his ultimate undoing.

Romanus paused in Theodosiopolis (Erzerum) to finish his planning. He was sure than Alp Arslan was in Persia, so Romanus decided to retake Manzikert and capture the city of Khilat some 30 miles to the south to establish a base of operations to launch his campaign into Persia. He led the column to Manzikert while assigning Khilat to Frankish mercenaries under the command of Roussel de Bailleul. As the garrisons defending the two cities were not large, this plan should have proceeded nicely. However, Romanus did not know that Alp Arslan was not in Persia but in Syria, where he was preparing to fight the Fatimids. When he learned of the Byzantine advance, Arslan gathered together what forces were handy and marched to Mosul. There he added another 14,000 men and then marched northeast to Khoi, where he received reinforcements from Azerbaijan. Now with some 40,000 men, he marched west toward Lake Van and then skirted the southern shore to approach Khilat from the south.

Romanus quickly captured Manzikert and then weakened his own force by sending reinforcements to Bailleul and a foraging party of 12,000 to Georgia. How many men Bailleul commanded is unknown, but when Arslan appeared seemingly out of nowhere on 16 August 1071, Bailleul retreated. He did not withdraw toward Manzikert and Romanus, however, but instead marched northwest away from both armies. He was almost certainly involved in the conspiracy with Empress Eudocia because this was poor tactics; further, he did not send word to Romanus of his move. Khilat rapidly fell to the Seljuks, and Arslan immediately pushed on toward Manzikert. Romanus meanwhile marched to Khilat, unaware that he was about to run headlong into his enemy.

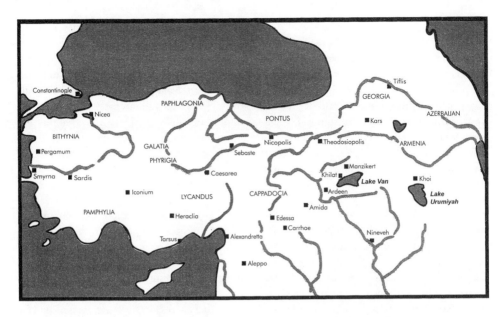

When his advanced guard ran into the main Seljuk body, Romanus immediately sent for Bailleul to come to his aid, a futile errand. In spite of that, Romanus did not lack for confidence. He depended on the tactics proven over centuries, whereby the more heavily armed and armored Byzantines had often prevailed over the swifter and more lightly armed nomadic cavalry. Thus, when Arslan offered peace terms, Romanus rejected them out of hand, demanding Arslan's surrender and a promise that the Turks would never again invade the empire. With neither side agreeable, both prepared for battle.

The standard Byzantine tactic for fighting the Turkish light cavalry was to maintain steady lines with their heavy infantry and cavalry and then push the enemy against some terrain feature where the enemy's maneuverability could not be used. Early in the battle, the Turkish tactics of lofting arrows from long range had the desired effect of hurting the Byzantine horses and provoking sufficient fear in the Kipchak and Petcheneg mercenaries that they abandoned the field. As his cavalry was diminishing because of the archery, Romanus ordered his lines forward. This disciplined maneuver had the desired effect, for the Seljuks retreated past their camp. This advantage failed to hold, however, because the Turks had plenty of open area into which they could retreat, and retreat they did until the day was almost gone.

As darkness approached, Romanus found himself in a dilemma. To push forward would gain nothing, but it was too late in the day to return unhindered to his own camp. With little choice, he ordered his lines to fall back, and the Seljuks were quick to face about and harry the withdrawing infantry. As the enemy approached, Romanus ordered his lines to turn and face them, but only the line nearest the enemy heeded him. The rear line continued to retreat, whether through ignorance of the order or (more likely) out of design. The line that continued to retreat was commanded by Andronicus Ducas, whose noble father was one of Romanus's bitterest enemies. He reached the Byzantine encampment, leaving behind Romanus who, with a much smaller force, could not stand. The Seljuks quickly enveloped the remaining Byzantines and demolished them. Romanus's men fought hard, but they had no chance. By the time darkness was complete, so was Alp Arslan's victory.

Results

Romanus was one of the few survivors, and he was taken captive to Arslan. The sultan treated him with the utmost courtesy and concluded a treaty whereby Romanus would return to Constantinople and raise a ransom to be paid over 50 years. It was a debt that was only partially paid. While in captivity, Romanus lost his throne to Caesar John Ducas, Andronicus's father. The empress, for all her plotting, found herself in a nunnery while Ducas ruled as regent over her son Michael VII. Romanus gathered some loyal troops and challenged Ducas, but met defeat a second time at Doceia. Captured by Andronicus, Romanus was blinded so traumatically that he soon died of his wound. Before his death, however, he had gathered the first payment of his ransom and sent it to Alp Arslan.

Edward Gibbon wrote of Manzikert: "The Byzantine writers deplore the loss of an inestimable pearl: they forgot to mention that, in this fatal day, the Asiatic provinces of Rome were irretrievably sacrificed" (Gibbon, *The Decline and Fall of the Roman Empire,* vol. 6, p. 243). From this point forward, the Turks dominated Asia Minor as well as much of the Middle East. The Seljuks soon gave way to the Ottomans, but it was the Seljuk victory and their plan for devastation that irrevocably changed the face of Anatolia. Alp Arslan's forces were once again on the offensive in 1072, but he was soon assassinated by his son, Malik Shah. Malik completed what his father had begun, which was the destruction of every Anatolian city, town, and farm and the execution of everyone in them. Hundreds of thousands of Byzantine citizens were killed or sold as slaves, and Asia Minor was for generations afterward a wasteland. The Turks accomplished what seemed to be the traditional goal of the steppe nomads, to have as much grassland as possible for their horses. Physically, the region was never the same.

Politically, the Byzantine Empire did not fall, but a huge portion of its remaining territories was lost. The peasants of Anatolia had provided for the bulk of the stolid fighting men of the Byzantine army, but they never would again. The Byzantine Empire, which was already overly dependent on foreign troops, became completely so. This meant that, as in the late Western Roman Empire, power came from the loyalty of the military rather than from administrative ability or vision. The Byzantine line of succession was almost never a line at all, for the prevailing philosophy was that, if an emperor was overthrown, he had lost God's favor and therefore should no longer rule. This meant that "might became right," resulting in a series of short-term rulers. Unable to maintain any consistency in any area of government, the Byzantine Empire became progressively weaker as the Normans took away territory in the Mediterranean. The resulting weakened empire could not defend itself from the successive nomadic tribes that harried its European possessions. In less than a quarter century after Manzikert, Constantinople appealed to the west for aid. The result was the first of the Crusades.

References: Canard, M. "Byzantium and the Moslem World to the Middle of the 11th Century," in J. Hussey, ed. *Cambridge Medieval History,* vol. IV. Cambridge, UK: Cambridge University Press, 1966; Friendly, Alfred. *The Dreadful Day: The Battle of Manzikert, 1071.* London: Hutchinson, 1981; Fuller, J. F. C. *A Military History of the Western World,* vol. 1. New York: Funk & Wagnalls, 1954; Gibbon, Edward. *The Decline and Fall of the Roman Empire,* vol. 6. New York: Gallery Press, 1979 [1737]; Jenkins, Romilly J. H. *Byzantium: The Imperial Centuries, A.D. 610–1071.* Toronto: University of Toronto Press, 1987.

JERUSALEM
9 June–18 July 1099

FORCES ENGAGED

Crusader: 1,250 knights and 10,000 infantry.
Commander: Duke Godfrey de Bouillon.

Moslem: Approximately 20,000 men.
Commander: Emir Iftikhar.

IMPORTANCE

This crusader victory marked the high point of the European attempt to establish its rule in the Holy Land. The Crusade also began the return of strong papal influence over political affairs in Europe.

Historical Setting

The latter part of the eleventh century saw the occurrence of two major struggles, one dealing with the Catholic Church in Europe and one with the Byzantine Empire. In Europe, the pope was trying to beat back a challenge by the Holy Roman Emperor as to which would reign supreme in both European politics and religion. Although officially protector of the church, the Holy Roman Emperor at times assumed the role of dictator, attempting to name the pope as well as lower-ranking officials in the Catholic Church hierarchy. Thus, the pope was looking for something to increase his prestige in the eyes of European nobility. In the Byzantine Empire, the Seljuk Turks, who had been gradually consolidating their power through the Middle East, scored a major victory over the weakening Byzantines at the battle of Manzikert in 1071. That battle put almost all of Asia Minor in the hands of the Turks, and the capital at Constantinople seemed destined to become a target.

These two problems dovetailed nicely for both pope in the west and emperor in the east. Byzantine Emperor Alexius Comnenus brilliantly played off his opponents while restocking the treasury. He could thus afford to pay for European troops if they would come to his aid. He appealed to Pope Urban II, claiming that the Moslems were barring Christians from holy sites in Palestine. Indeed, the routes were closed, but more through a lack of cooperation among Moslem factions rather than through anything intentional. Still, it was a religious focal point upon which Urban could hopefully rally his European flock. This would increase his status, spread Christianity, make the Eastern Orthodox Church indebted to Rome, and take feuding nobles out of Europe and focus

their warlike natures on infidels rather than each other. Earlier popes had granted religious sanctions for campaigns against Moslems in Spain, so the concept of holy war was familiar in the west.

The response was greater than either Urban or Alexius had hoped. All across Europe, people flocked to the cause, and for a number of reasons. Some had a true desire to spread the faith; some wanted to receive the Church's promised forgiveness of sins. Others merely went for the adventure or the potential fortune in loot or land. Younger sons who stood to inherit nothing upon their father's death saw this as an opportunity for advancement that they might never achieve on their own. Unfortunately, no one had any real conception of the difficulty involved. Tens of thousands of poor people joined the People's Crusade behind the religious zealot Peter the Hermit. They managed to forage their way through eastern Europe and into Asia Minor, but, with no military training and precious little weaponry, they were slaughtered by the Turks. A worse fate befell the German Crusade. After killing any Jew they found at home, they marched for Constantinople via Hungary, but they never made it through that country because they were dispersed by Hungarian troops. Neither of those did anything to inspire Byzantine confidence, but they had more to fear when the warriors actually got organized and began their march. Fearing that they might find his capital city too rich to pass without looting, Alexius forced each passing crusader army to swear fealty to him to obtain passage across the Bosporus and supplies for the expedition. After some violence, he was able to save his city from the more rambunctious crusaders, and they finally passed through into Asia Minor.

Before reaching the Holy Land itself, the crusaders had to capture Turk strongholds at Nicaea and Antioch. Nicaea fell 19 June 1097 after a monthlong siege. Battles at Dorylaeum (modern Eskisehir), Inconium (Konia), and Heraclea (Eregli) took the crusaders to the northeastern corner of the Mediterranean at the Turk stronghold of Antioch by October. Not until early June 1098 did the city fall after two relief armies were beaten back. The crusaders almost immediately found themselves besieged, but a bold sally in late June drove off the attacking Moslem army. The victors then squabbled among themselves for 6 months over what to do next. One of the main generals, Duke Bohemund of Taranto, stayed in Antioch and established his own principality. The remainder marched onward for Jerusalem, leaving in January 1099. A fleet from Pisa sailed alongside the force, carrying their supplies, until they reached the town of Arsuf. At that point, the crusaders turned and marched inland to Jerusalem.

The Battle

Some 12,000 soldiers remained by this point, with Duke Godfrey de Bouillon of Lorraine in command, assisted by Count Raymond of Toulouse and King Tancred of Sicily. The force defending the city numbered probably 20,000, under the leadership of the Emir Iftikhar. Jerusalem was out of the territory controlled by the Seljuk Turks and in a region under the control of the caliph of Cairo. The Moslems there were of the Fatimid sect, followers of the Prophet's

daughter as the true ruling lineage down from Mohammed. They were therefore more Arab in their ethnicity than Turkish. It mattered little to the crusaders, for one infidel seemed much like another to them.

The siege began on 9 June 1099. There were too few crusaders to fully encircle the city, so the only way to take the city was by storm rather than via starvation. Indeed, the besiegers suffered a more severe water shortage than did the defenders. The Moslems had poisoned the cisterns and wells outside the city before the crusaders' arrival, and the June sun beat upon them unmercifully. On 12 June, they launched their first assault; it proved disastrous. New machines were necessary to reduce or overcome these walls, yet little wood was available. On 17 June, however, the necessary materials arrived aboard six ships, which had docked in the recently abandoned port of Jaffa. Genoese engineers assisted the crusaders in the construction of mangonels (or trebuchets), a long arm with a sling on one end and a massive counterweight on the other. Along with siege towers and scaling ladders, the besiegers hoped to destroy or climb the walls.

On the night of 13–14 July, a second assault took place. It had little success, but on 15 July a siege tower was finally placed against the

The Conquest of Jerusalem. *Predella, fifteenth century, in the collection of the Museum voor Schone Kunsten, Ghent, Belgium. (Scala/Art Resource, New York)*

city wall. The gangplank fell and a bridge into the city was created. The Moslem defense crumbled almost immediately. Some retreated to the El Aqsa mosque, but they were hotly pursued by the Sicilian, Tancred. He promised mercy, but little was extended once the crusaders had the city in their control. Although he tried to protect those in the El Aqsa mosque, a killing rage was on the vast majority of the invaders, and almost the entire population of the city was put to the sword. One chronicle reported that within the El Aqsa the blood was knee deep. Raymond of Agiles reported that "wonderful things were to be seen. Numbers of the Saracens were beheaded ... others were shot with arrows, or forced to jump from the towers; others were tortured for several days and then burned in flames. In the streets were seen piles of heads and hands and feet. One rode about everywhere amid the corpses of men and horses" (Durant, *The Age of Faith*, p. 592).

The Jewish citizens fared no better. European Christians had long blamed the Jews for killing Christ, so there seemed to be no reason to spare them either. Most were burned to death inside the city's main synagogue. Afterward, the "victors flocked to the church of the Holy Sepulcher, whose grotto, they believed, had once held the crucified Christ. There, embracing one another, they wept with joy and release, and thanked the God of Mercies for their victory" (Durant, *The Age of Faith*, p. 592).

Results

Once the frenzy had passed, Godfrey de Bouillon was named Guardian of Jerusalem and Defender of the Holy Sepulcher; he refused to be named king of Jerusalem. The crusaders had little time to enjoy their victory, for a 50,000-man relief force was on the way from Egypt. Although Godfrey could muster only 10,000 knights and infantry to face them, the crusaders won a fairly easy victory at Askelon on 12 August 1099. Unlike the Turks, whose steppe heritage was to harry an enemy with archers

mounted on horseback, the Egyptians fought in the more traditional Moslem fashion. They depended on speed and fanaticism to overwhelm their enemy in one mad rush. Against the discipline of the European infantry and the heavy cavalry of the knights, the Moslems were like a wave breaking on a rock; the crusader charge that overran the Moslem camp pushed much of that army into the sea.

After Askelon, the First Crusade was over. Most of the participants returned to Europe, but those that had staked out claims after victorious sieges stayed behind. Crusader principalities were established at Antioch under Bohemund, Edessa (about 100 miles northeast of Antioch) under Baldwin de Bouillon, and Tripoli under Raymond of Toulouse, all supposedly under the authority of Jerusalem. When Godfrey died just a year after the fall of Jerusalem, his brother Baldwin succeeded him and assumed the title of king. He ruled only with the consent of his subordinates, who acted virtually independently within their "counties." Baldwin also ceded control of most of the ports to the Genoese and Pisans in return for a steady flow of supplies from Europe. A European-style feudal system was imposed that made most of the locals, including Christians, long for the return of Moslem rule.

These isolated fiefs survived for almost 50 years only because the Moslems themselves were too disorganized to mount an effective offensive against them. Still, the Europeans did prove difficult enemies even when an effective Moslem campaign could be mounted. In the first half of the twelfth century, one sees the establishment of military orders of monks, dedicated to serving the church and protecting pilgrims visiting holy shrines. In 1119, eight knights followed Hugh de Payens to establish an order based in the area around Solomon's Temple in Jerusalem, and these came to be known as the Knights Templars. The following year, the staff of a hospital in Jerusalem that had operated since 1048 organized themselves as the Knights of the Hospital of St. John, or the Knights

LIMITED WARFARE

The nature of feudalism was such that, although a lord could have a number of vassals who had sworn fealty to him, just as the king had a number of lords who had done the same, keeping the fighting to a minimum between kings, between lords, or between vassals was no easy task. After all, one of the primary reasons that feudalism existed was to have a ready supply of trained forces in time of crisis. "Every baron claimed the right of private war against any man not bound to him by feudal ties, and every king was free to embark at any time upon honorable robbery of another ruler's lands. When king or baron went to war, all his vassals and relatives to the seventh degree were pledged to follow him for forty days" (Durant, *The Age of Faith*, p. 571).

In spite of all that, for the most part it was not the soldiers who suffered. Aristocrats were too valuable to kill because ransom could be collected on prisoners, but only revenge came from killing. Therefore, the countryside that had to endure the multiple passings of armies bore the brunt of the death and destruction; pillage was often the only pay one might receive for time on campaign. Beasts of burden often were killed or stolen, leaving the peasants with work more back-breaking than usual. In an attempt to keep the numbers of parishioners from falling too far, the Catholic Church attempted to protect the general population from the ravages of war. Between 989 and 1050, various popes and church councils decreed a *Pax Dei*, or Peace of God, threatening excommunication for anyone who made war against noncombatants. French churches after 1027 called for a *Treuga Dei*, or Truce of God. Under this, no fighting could take place during harvest (15 August–11 November), on holy days, or on certain days of every week. Usually this meant no warfare between Wednesday evening and Monday morning. In its final form, the Truce of God limited warfare to 80 days per year.

Oddly enough, this did have significant effect. Private wars decreased as international wars increased. Knights who needed to prove themselves in battle, finding less and less opportunity for doing so in Europe, quickly joined the ranks of men marching off on the First Crusade. As the rules laid down by the church applied only to Christians, Moslems were fair game for any type of fighting and killing one could imagine.

Hospitalers. Although these two orders despised each other, they both carried out the same tasks of protection of pilgrims; later they began to make war on the Moslems.

All of this, the feudalism, the attacks, the persecution, all motivated the Moslems (finally) into a response. In 1144, the Prince of Mosul, Zangi, counterattacked and recaptured the city of Edessa. After his assassination, the more aggressive Nur ed-Din continued the war against the European Christians. That provoked the Second Crusade; many more followed as the ancient crossroads of history saw innumerable armies and battles over the following two centuries.

In Europe, the establishment of Christian strongholds in the Middle East had more than religious effects. The Genoese and Pisans, possessing the strongest navies of Europe, entered into a long period of trade with their former enemies. The wealth of the east that had lured many young aristocrats to the Crusade was based on a number of luxury goods that Europeans would pay dearly to have. Silks from China and spices from India and Indonesia became high-demand items among Europe's aristocrats. Forget religion; the money was too good to be picky about one's trade partner. The city-states of the Italian peninsula became the centers of wealth. When the religious fervor died down and trade could be carried on peacefully, Italy's rise to international power followed. The money made on trade with the east, as well as the knowledge gained from Moslems who had saved ancient scientific and literary works long forgotten in Europe, became the foundation for the Renaissance. That the Renaissance proved to provide a rationalist challenge to the faith of the Catholic Church was an ironic result of the Crusades.

References: Armstrong, Karen. *Holy War: The Crusades and Their Impact on Today's World.* New York: Doubleday, 1991; Billings, Malcolm. *The Cross and the Crescent.* New York: Sterling, 1990 [1987]; Durant, Will. *The Age of Faith.* New York: Simon & Schuster, 1950; Riley-Smith, Jonathan. *The First Crusade and the Idea of Crusading.* Philadelphia: University of Pennsylvania Press, 1986; Runciman, Sir Steven. *The First Crusade.* New York: Cambridge University Press, 1992 [1980].

HATTIN
4 July 1187

FORCES ENGAGED

Moslem: 18,000 to 20,000 men. Commander: Saladin.
Crusader: 1,200 knights and 18,000 infantry. Commander: King Guy of Jerusalem.

IMPORTANCE

Saladin's victory ended the European domination of the Holy Land.

Historical Setting

At the end of the eleventh century, the First Crusade had won for European Christians the strip of coast along the eastern Mediterranean. From Antioch in the north to Gaza in the south the Holy Land was under European command, but not necessarily under its control. The imposition of feudalism in the region had alienated even the Christian inhabitants, while persecution of Islam and Judaism had angered the remainder. Living in a land populated by enemies, the only way the crusaders could have maintained their position was through close cooperation. However, the rivalries that had existed in Europe between aristocrats were merely transplanted to the Middle East, and fighting among the Europeans was as common as Christian-Moslem clashes.

Luckily for the Europeans, the Moslems were just as divided. Since the death of Malik Shah, Sultan of the Seljuk Turks, in 1092, rival claimants to his throne, as well as rival sects within Islam, had kept any serious challenge to the crusaders from forming. This changed in 1127, however, with the rise to power of Imad ed-Din Zangi of Mosul, who began reuniting Moslems under his banner. After conquering Syria, he aimed at the northernmost crusader city, Edessa, which he captured on Christmas Day in 1144. Two years later, Zangi was assassinated, but his son Nur ed-Din continued his father's work.

The fall of Edessa awoke yet another Crusade in Europe, organized at the urging of Bernard of Clairvaux. This Second Crusade was led by Emperor Conrad III of Germany and King Louis VII of France. Armies led by these two encountered serious difficulties in Asia Minor, but finally reached the crusader lands, called "Outremer" in Europe, in 1147. There the two Europeans joined forces with King Baldwin III of Jerusalem. It proved a short Crusade. An attempt to besiege Damascus in 1148 collapsed when the local forces accepted bribes to lift the siege. This so disgusted the Europeans that they went home. Encouraged, Nur ed-Din stepped up his attacks on crusader fortresses. He defeated Raymond of Antioch in 1149 and in the following year consolidated his hold on the county of Edessa. By capturing Damascus in 1154, Nur ed-Din placed himself in the city that was the key to the Middle East.

In control of the northern flank of Outremer, Nur ed-Din looked longingly at the southern flank, Egypt. He sent one of his generals, Asad ud-Din Shirkuh, to Egypt in 1163. His supposed intention was to aid the deposed Egyptian Vizier Shawar ibn Mujir in the suppression of a rebellion, but the Egyptians soon learned of Shirkuh's intention to seize the entire country for his master. Proving that politics makes strange bedfellows, the vizier appealed to King

Malric I of Jerusalem for aid. The combined Egyptian-crusader army defeated Nur ed-Din near Cairo in 1167, and the crusaders established a base there for a continuing campaign against Moslems holding Alexandria. The garrison there was under the command of an up-and-coming leader, Salah-al-Din Yusuf ibn-Ayyub, better known as Saladin.

Saladin was Nur ed-Din's lieutenant, but with greater vision. Although not at first interested in a military life, he became one of the best military minds of the medieval period. He also had a grand political sense. In 1171, he overthrew the reigning Fatimid dynasty in Egypt and placed the country under the spiritual leadership of the caliph of Baghdad, a Sunni. At the same time, he became the virtual master of Egypt. He consolidated his power for 3 years and then began expanding it when Nur ed-Din died in 1174, leaving behind an 11-year-old heir. That same year, King Almaric of Jerusalem died, also leaving an 11-year-old heir. The disputes over who would serve as regents to the young rulers created sufficient confusion in both Seljuk and crusader camps that Saladin was able to exert his claim to power. He marched for Damascus; occupying that city in November 1174, he then aimed at Aleppo, which would give him all of Syria.

Threats to his lines of communication back to Egypt kept him from his prize in 1175, but the following year the crusaders were dealt what proved ultimately to be a killing blow. Byzantine Emperor Manuel had been regaining control over Asia Minor, but was defeated in 1176 by Kilij Arslan II, the Seljuk Sultan of Rum, in central Asia Minor. The defeat at Myriocephalum was a second Manzikert, forever crushing any Byzantine dream of expansion southward or eastward from Constantinople. It also meant that the Europeans had no nearby source of supply. Thus, the crusaders were even more isolated than before. After desultory fighting with Saladin, a truce was signed in 1180.

Throughout the 1170s and 1180s, a succession struggle for the throne in Jerusalem dominated the interests of the crusaders. The struggle was so complicated that only an extended soap opera could describe it. By 1187, two major factions emerged. Guy de Lusignan became king of Jerusalem, and most of the knights swore fealty to him. His only serious rival was Reynald of Châtillon, who was lord of the castle at Kerak on the Mecca-Damascus road. By attacking Moslem caravans and then launching a raid on Moslem towns on the Red Sea, Reynald provoked Saladin's anger. When Guy would not punish Reynald for violating a truce, Saladin declared a holy war and invaded.

The Battle

Although Guy de Lusignan was king of Jerusalem and technically supreme European leader in Outremer, his vassals exercised a lot of independence. Rather than support Reynald's outrageous behavior, Bohemond of Antioch and Raymond of Tripoli renewed the truce with Saladin. Believing Guy unfit to rule, Raymond secretly conspired with Saladin to oust him. Learning of the plot, Guy's advisors convinced him to rally the crusader forces and attack Raymond, currently at his wife's castle at Tiberius, on the west side of the Sea of Galilee. After a skirmish between some of Saladin's troops and a deputation from Guy to Raymond, Raymond decided he could not in good conscience side with a Moslem against other Christians. In May 1187, Raymond left his wife in charge of the castle at Tiberius while he went to make his peace with Guy. While meeting with Guy in the port city of Acre, news came that Saladin's army of perhaps 20,000 had begun to lay siege to Tiberius.

Although it was his wife in danger, Raymond counseled against an immediate relief. Knowing the supply situation inside the castle, he argued that it would be best to let Saladin's force go hungry in the countryside before launching an attack against him. Besides, the height of the summer's heat was approaching. Guy's more aggressive counselors argued for immediate action; honor demanded no less. Guy ordered all the fighting men in Outremer to be assembled, and the fortresses and castles were stripped of their garrisons to do so. In late June, 1,200 knights and 18,000 infantry marched for Tiberius. On 2 July, they encamped at Sephoria, roughly halfway from Acre to Tiberius. Again Raymond approached Guy and counseled caution, claiming he was willing to sacrifice his family for the good of the Christian cause. Again, more aggressive advisors won out.

Early in the morning of 3 July, the army began marching east, not so much in search of battle as water; Raymond had told Guy that only one spring existed along the line of march and there was nothing for forage. They marched into the Jebel Turan hills. When Saladin was alerted to this advance, he exulted, for he knew his heavily armed and armored enemy would parch themselves on the way. He immediately dispatched light cavalry to harass the crusaders. When the Knights Templars and Knights Hospitalers in the rear guard were attacked, the column stopped in the middle of a dry and barren land. At this, Raymond bemoaned the fate of his army and his entire cause: "Alas, alas, Lord God! The war is over; we are dead men; the Kingdom is undone!" (Fuller, *A Military History of the Western World*, vol. 1, p. 426).

The crusaders bivouacked near the town of Hattin under two high mounds called the Horns. Sunset brought little relief, for what water the troops had brought had long since been drunk, and the Moslems kept up a barrage of arrows into the camp throughout the night. To make bad matters worse, the Moslems set afire the scrub brush upwind of the camp, and the crusaders and their horses had to breathe smoke all night. The following morning, Saladin continued to torture the Christians. Refusing to close with them, he instead brought up new stocks of arrows to keep up the barrage. The heavy cavalry charged in an attempt to break up the harassing fire, but in doing so separated themselves from the support of the

Crusaders battle Turks at Dorylaeum during the First Crusade, 1097. (Archive Photos)

infantry, which retreated in increasing panic up the slopes of the Horns.

Guy did what he could to rally his men. He raised up the True Cross and that infused his troops with spirit. They launched repeated attacks down the hill into the Moslem ranks, failing to break them but giving Saladin pause, for he knew the potential for Christian fanaticism.

Raymond organized a last charge as Guy's camp was being overrun. He gathered as many cavalry as he could and charged toward the enemy force commanded by Saladin's nephew, Taki-el-Din Omar, who decided discretion was the better part of valor and opened a gap in his ranks for the crusaders to ride through. They were the only ones to escape. Surrounded and outnumbered, but more importantly dying of thirst, the infantry could do nothing but surrender or die.

Results

Exact losses suffered in this battle were not recorded, but certainly the crusaders inflicted

...TRY, TRY AGAIN

The crusader defeat at Hattin was hardly an atypical incident. Only the First Crusade really had any success in acquiring control over the Holy Land. Once the Holy Land was lost after Saladin's victories, successive attempts to reestablish European dominance failed miserably. Here's the record:

- People's Crusade (April–October 1096): The People's Crusade was an abortive mass movement following the mystic leader Peter the Hermit. Those that did not starve along the way were easily defeated and killed in their one and only encounter with Moslems in Anatolia.
- First Crusade (1096–1099): The First Crusade established European dominion in the County of Edessa, the Principality of Antioch, the County of Tripoli, and the Kingdom of Jerusalem. European control lasted until Saladin's victories in 1187.
- Second Crusade (1147–1149): Reports of the fall of Edessa provoked a European response to regain the lost territory at the northern end of crusader lands. Dissension between Europeans and the crusaders based in the Holy Land spelled the end of the Crusade.
- Third Crusade (1189–1192): The Third Crusade was called to recover Jerusalem after Saladin's victories. Kings Frederick Barbarossa of Germany, Louis Phillipe of France, and Richard I of England participated. Barbarossa died along the way. Arguments between Louis and Richard destroyed any chance of a cooperative effort. Louis abandoned the Crusade and went home. After Richard scored minimal successes and failed to capture Jerusalem, he signed a treaty with Saladin and went home. He was taken prisoner and held for ransom in Germany.
- Fourth Crusade (1202–1204): Disputes with Venetians over transport costs ended in crusaders hiring themselves out to reconquer territory across the Adriatic lost to Venice. The attempt to get involved in a succession dispute in Constantinople led to the sack of that city by the crusaders. This Crusade never fought any Moslems over the Holy Land.
- Fifth Crusade (1218–1221): Pope Innocent III called for a Crusade against Egypt. This was led by King John of Jerusalem and was primarily made up of troops from northern Europe. The crusaders captured the Egyptian city of Damietta after a siege of a year and a half, but they were decisively beaten at the Ashmoun Canal after rejecting reasonable peace offers.
- Sixth Crusade (1228–1229): The Sixth Crusade was one of the few successful operations in spite (or because) of the fact that no fighting took place between Christians and Moslems. Instead, King Frederick II of south Italy negotiated possession of Jerusalem, Bethlehem, and Nazareth. The only fighting was between Frederick's troops and those of Pope Gregory, who had earlier excommunicated Frederick for delaying the start of the Crusade. Frederick regained his lands and made peace with the pope.
- Seventh Crusade (1248–1254): Moslem reoccupation of Jerusalem inspired France's King Louis IX to try and recapture it. He decided to try from the south, so he invaded Egypt first. He captured Damietta but failed in his attempt to capture Cairo. The remnants of his starving army were ransomed for 800,000 pieces of gold.
- Aragonese Crusade (1269): King James of Aragon in Spain reluctantly launched this campaign under pressure from the pope. James was driven off by heavy storms and failed in his attempt to land in Asia Minor.
- Eighth Crusade (1270): After his ransom was fully paid, Louis IX felt justified in renewing his Crusade. Instead of going to the Holy Land directly, he sailed to Tunis, on the mistaken information that the ruler there was interested in converting to Christianity. When that proved incorrect, Louis laid siege. An epidemic killed a large part of the invading force, including Louis. His brother negotiated some tribute and left.
- Crusade of Peter I of Cyprus (1365–1369): This Crusade consisted of harassment of the Moslem Mediterranean coast and the capture and sack of Alexandria. It ended with Peter's assassination.
- Crusade of Nicopolis (1396): Pope Boniface IX called for a Crusade against Moslem expansion in the Balkans. French knights made up the bulk of the force that responded, but they were soundly defeated by the Turks at Nicopolis in Bulgaria.
- The Last Crusade (1443–1444): King Ladislas of Poland organized a group of Hungarians, Poles, Bosnians, Wallachians, and Serbians. Their plan was to expel the Moslems under Murad II from the Balkans. A Venetian fleet was to ferry the crusaders from Varna to Constantinople and then stop any Moslem reinforcements from crossing the Bosporus. The fleet failed, and Murad's army crushed the crusaders at Varna.

some heavy casualties on the lighter-armed Moslems during their attacks from the hillside. It was all for nought. The crusader army was virtually annihilated. Only Raymond's breakthrough saved any of them from death or capture. Saladin was both merciful and just. King Guy he treated almost as a guest, whereas Reynald he executed after a loud confrontation. Knights Templars and Hospitalers were likewise executed for their aggressive policy toward Islam.

Tiberius surrendered a few days later. It, like every other crusader castle in the Holy Land, was at this point virtually undefended because the army had been made up of the collected garrisons. The True Cross, or what the crusaders deemed to be the actual instrument of Christ's crucifixion, fell into Moslem hands. That was the greatest of all blows to Christian Europe. It marked, in reality, the handing over of power in the Middle East. Although a number of Crusades were launched after the disaster at Hattin, none ever seriously threatened Islam's hold on the region. Coupled with the Byzantine defeat at Myriocephalum, Hattin meant that neither the Orthodox nor Catholic Church would control the shrines sacred to their faith. Jerusalem, the holiest of cities, fell to Saladin within 3 months. Unlike in the capture of the city by the soldiers in the First Crusade, Saladin demanded little ransom (ten pieces of gold per man) and immediately set about restoring the city's markets so the money for ransoms could be paid. When the poorest citizens could not scrape together the money, Saladin's brother asked for a thousand of them as slaves; granted the request, he immediately set the slaves free. Such actions, sorrowfully, never led to a positive relationship between Christianity and Islam.

Future Crusades became increasingly secular rather than religious. European armies, particularly Norman ones, spent more time fighting the Byzantines than the Moslems. The foundation for any cooperation that may have been laid during the First Crusade crumbled after Hattin. The Fourth Crusade actually ended up being a commercially sponsored enterprise operated by Venice. It captured and sacked Constantinople rather than Egypt, its original target.

There were, however, some positive aspects for Europe. A sense of unity prevailed for a time under the banner of the church. France, a struggling set of dukedoms and principalities, began unifying into a single country, although it would be fought over by internal and external factions for a long time to come. Although the Templars and Hospitalers suffered a severe decline, the Teutonic Knights (another military order of monks) went to work fighting the church's enemies in eastern Europe and in so doing laid the foundations for the countries of both Poland and Germany. The Catholic Church, in spite of its decreasing influence over the crusaders, enjoyed a power rarely exercised before or since. Unfortunately for the church, the power corrupted. The sale of indulgences and the exaction of tithes led away from spirituality and into worldliness, which people such as Martin Luther would later use as justification for the Reformation.

Perhaps most important of all the results was the spirit of adventure that ensued. Travel to faraway lands carried the imagination to new frontiers, as well as brought new trade goods to Europe. Both the desire for wealth and the need "to boldly go where no one has gone before" sparked the intellectual search for frontiers of the Renaissance and the physical travel west to the Americas.

References: Armstrong, Karen. *Holy War: The Crusades and Their Impact on Today's World.* New York: Doubleday, 1991; Ehrenkreutz, Andrew. *Saladin.* Albany: SUNY Press, 1972; Fuller, J. F. C. *A Military History of the Western World,* vol. 1. New York: Funk & Wagnalls, 1954; Regan, Geoffrey. *Saladin and the Fall of Jerusalem.* New York: Croom Helm, 1987; Smith, Jonathan Riley. *The Crusades.* New Haven, CT: Yale University Press, 1987.

SECOND BATTLE OF TARAORI
1192

FORCES ENGAGED

Moslem Afghans: 120,000 men, primarily cavalry.
Commander: Mohamad of Ghor.
Rajputs: Unknown.
Commander: Prithvaraja, Amir of Delhi.

IMPORTANCE

Although Islam had been introduced into India
several centuries previously, after this battle a
Moslem ruled India, especially northern India,
until the fall of the Moghul dynasty in 1857.

Historical Setting

The first time a Moslem set foot in India was
shortly after Mohammed the Prophet established the faith. The original practitioners of
Islam that visited India were merchants, whose
voyages along the northern rim of the Arabian
Gulf had been taking them to India for some
years. Not until the reign of the caliph Omar,
second successor to Mohammed, was a military expedition launched (637), not only to
spread the faith but also to pillage the Indian
wealth, of which the merchants had so long
spoken. For the next several decades, only raids
were conducted, with no intent at conquest or
colonization. In 712, however, Chaldaean governor Al-Hajjaj sent his 17-year-old cousin
Mohammed ibn Kasim to establish a Moslem
presence in India. He invaded the province of
Sind, bordering the mouth of the Indus River.
After some brilliant campaigning, he succeeded
in conquering the region, but it proved poor in
both economy and prospects. Unsupported to
any great extent from home, however, the
colony slipped from the notice of those who
had dispatched it. A few centuries later, Moslem families still dominated the government of
Sind, but had become Indianized and had

spread neither their faith nor their power into
the Indian interior.

The Moslem conquest of India had to come
from a population other than the Arabs. The
group that seriously embarked on military forays into India were the steppe Turks who, after
establishing themselves in Persia and Afghanistan, looked southeast toward the fabled wealth
of the subcontinent. The leader of this wave of
Moslem invaders was Mahmud of Ghazni. His
father Sabutagin had raided into northern India, but his death in 997 ended his dreams of
conquest. Mahmud picked up his father's ambition and in 1000 launched the first of sixteen invasions of the northern Indian region of
Hindustan. His goals were religious as well as
economic because, as the Turks were fairly recent converts to Islam, they were the most ardent, and Mahmud wanted to spread the faith
and destroy the idols of Indian religions, which
he considered blasphemous. Over the following 26 years, he launched sixteen invasions. His
religious zeal led him to destroy every Hindu
temple or shrine he could find, earning him
the epithet "Idol Breaker." He also looted the
treasuries and temples he destroyed, and his
capital city of Ghazni for a time was one of the
wealthiest in all the world. "A great soldier, a
man of infinite courage and indefatigable energy of mind and body, Mahmud was no con-
structive or far-seeing statesman. We hear of
no laws or institutions or methods of government that sprang from his initiative" (Lane-
Poole, *Medieval India under Mohammedan Rule,*
p. 23). Thus, Islam showed its aggressive side
without the magnanimity that often accompanied it. That was left to Mohamad of Ghor.

Mahmud's descendants spent his wealth on
knowledge, culture, and ease, and, although
their rule was beneficent, it was not always wise.
Early in the twelfth century, Ghazni was challenged by the growing power of Ghor, a fortress town in the Afghan mountains. They
traded victories and defeats for a time, until
two brothers in Ghor established their su-

premacy. Ghiyas-ad-Din captured Ghazni and set his brother Mu'izz-ad-Din on the throne in 1174. Ghiyas returned to Ghor to rule, but his brother, who came to be called Mohamad of Ghor, set out to establish his own power in India.

Mohamad's first task was to conquer the old Arab region of Sind. This he accomplished by 1182. Three years later, he captured the last descendant of Mahmud, thereby placing himself in charge of the Punjab, that region of northwestern India bordering Afghanistan through the Khyber Pass. It comprises the westernmost part of that region known as Hindustan, which parallels the Himalayas from Afghanistan eastward to the Bay of Bengal. Mahmud's successors had come to rely strongly on locally recruited Hindu troops, but Mohamad was determined to employ only Turks and Afghans, solid Moslems he could trust to carry out a holy war against the Hindus. The most powerful of the Hindu tribes at the time were the people of Rajputana, a rugged region just south of the Punjab. The Rajputs had developed a feudal system like that of western Europe, and they were therefore loyal and disciplined fighting men. They also had no love for Moslems. Their king, Prithvaraja, was an able commander who made Mohamad pay dearly for whatever lands he might conquer in India.

The Battle

In the winter of 1190–1191, Mohamad returned to India with the intent of conquering as much of the northern part of the subcontinent as possible. He quickly captured the fortress town of Bhatinda and established a garrison of 1,200 cavalry under the command of one of his best generals, Qazi Ziya-ud-din. As Bhatinda was in Rajputana, it is not surprising that Prithvaraja immediately responded. The site where the two rivals fought was near Panipat, site of so many battles in Indian his-tory. This particular battlefield has been called variously Tarain, Narain, and Taraori, with the third being slightly more widely used (although Tarain seems the most accepted in the latest accounts). Never had Mohamad's troops faced such a well-trained foe, and in 1191 (no particular date has been recorded) the Rajputs had the upper hand. No numbers have been recorded either, but all accounts say that the Rajputs outnumbered the Moslem army. Using the standard steppe tactics, Mohamad launched his cavalry at the enemy center to harass it with archery fire, but the Rajputs not only stood firm but responded with flanking movements of their own that repeatedly forced the Moslems to retreat. Believing he needed to perform some personal act of bravery to save the day, Mohamad himself led a charge that was met by Prithvaraja's brother, Govind Rai, the viceroy of Delhi. Mohamad attacked "and shattered his [Govind Rai's] teeth with his lance," but, as he was dying, Govind Rai had pierced Mohamad's arm with his javelin. This wound was serious, and Mohamad was unhorsed and bleeding profusely. He was rescued by one of his soldiers who, riding double in the saddle, escaped with his commander.

Mohamad rejoined his retreating forces and was placed on a litter, and the army retreated to Ghor. The Rajputs, rather than pursuing, laid siege to Bhatinda. It took 13 months before they were finally able to recapture the town. Back in Ghazni, Mohamad quickly recovered and began planning his next campaign, looking to gain revenge for the loss. He returned the following year. One source claims that he led a force of 12,000, but that seems entirely too small. Other sources that number the army at 120,000 Afghans, Turks, and Persians are probably nearer the mark.

The rematch took place on the same battlefield; again, no exact date is recorded. This time, Mohamad was careful not to allow his troops to close with the Rajputs. He divided his force into five divisions. Four of them he sent to attack the Rajput flanks and, if possible, attack their rear. Anytime the Rajputs pressed them, they were to feign panic and retreat. After fighting for most of the day and failing to break the Rajput ranks, Mohamad began withdrawing his entire force. Again, he feigned panic, and this time the Rajputs took the bait. The fifth division of 12,000 cavalry that he had held in reserve under his own command was still fresh, and they attacked headlong into the fatigued Rajputs who were less than coordinated because of their desire to crush what they presumed was a defeated enemy. This attack broke the Rajput pursuit and sent them fleeing; the remainder of the Moslem force turned and rode the Rajputs down. Seeing his army disintegrating, Prithvaraja abandoned his elephant and mounted a horse for a quicker escape, but the momentum of the Moslem charge carried his pursuers quickly to him. He was captured a few miles away and then executed; most of his subordinates died in the battle as well.

Results

"The result of this victory was the annexation of Ajmir, Hansi, and Sirsuti, ruthless slaughter and a general destruction of temples and idols and building of mosques" (Lane-Poole, *Medieval India under Mohammedan Rule*, pp. 37–38). That was the short-term effect, but Mohamad was not through fighting. For the next few years, his armies conquered eastward, mainly under the command of Kutab-ad-din, a slave that Mohamad placed on the throne as sultan of Delhi. Mohamad himself returned from Afghanistan periodically to lead his armies, but Kutab-ad-din was primarily responsible for the spread of Moslem power through northern India. Kutab-ad-din turned his attention to pacifying regions to the west and southwest of Delhi while another general, Mohammad Bakhtiyar, led Moslem forces all the way to Bengal (1202), completing the conquest of Hindustan. His forces occupied the province of Bihar in 1193, the center of Buddhism in

India. The Moslems quickly killed or scattered the Buddhists, the survivors fleeing to Nepal or Tibet. Thus, Buddhism as a widely practiced faith came to an end in India, instead making its mark in central Asia and China.

Mahmud of Ghazni became the better known of the two invaders of India because he established such an impressive capital with his loot and, with his heirs, became a patron of the arts. Mohamad of Ghor, however, is the man who really established the rule of Islam in India. Although, as mentioned, much more fighting was necessary for that rule to be secured, after Prithvaraja's defeat there was no serious army that could withstand the Moslems. The Rajputs came under nominal Moslem control, but were never converts to the faith and, retaining their martial culture, were constant thorns in the side of the Moslem rulers that followed.

Mohamad, rather than being satisfied with his Indian conquests, was too much the Afghan Turk to abandon dreams of establishing power in Persia and the Middle East. He failed in that effort, however, being dealt a severe defeat during his invasion of Khwarizm (modern Khiva) in 1203. That broke the power of his clan in Afghanistan and left Kutab-ad-din without a master. In 1206, he declared a new government and established what history has come to call the Slave dynasty of Delhi. They ruled northern India along Islamic lines until 1290, when they were overthrown by the invasion of Mongol forces. That in turn established the Moghul dynasty, which ruled until officially deposed by the British in 1857. Thus, for eight centuries, India has been a religiously divided country, which lived under a Moslem government while the bureaucracy and most of the major landholders (paying tribute or taxes) remained Hindu. Differences were in the main suppressed during British rule, but the two faiths rarely got along well. With the independence of India in 1948, long-standing hostility forced the creation of Moslem Pakistan, which has been at odds with predominantly Hindu India ever since.

References: Dunbar, Sir George. *A History of India from the Earliest Times to the Present Day*, vol. 1. London: Nicholson & Watson, 1943; Haig, Sir Wolseley, ed. *The Cambridge History of India*, vol. 3. Delhi: S. Chand & Co., 1965; Kar, H. C. *Military History of India*. Calcutta: Firma KLM, 1980; Lane-Poole, Stanley. *Medieval India under Mohammedan Rule*. New York: Kraus Reprint, 1970 [1903]; Narvane, M. S. *Battles of Medieval India*. New Delhi: APH Publishing, 1996.

BOUVINES
26 July 1214

FORCES ENGAGED

French: 11,000 cavalry and 25,000 infantry. Commander: King Philip II Augustus.

Germanic: 11,000 cavalry and 60,000 infantry: Commander: Emperor Otto IV.

IMPORTANCE

Philip's victory virtually created the nation of France, whereas Otto's defeat led to a weakening of the Holy Roman Empire and Germany's long-lasting dissension. English King John's inability to muster support for the campaign led to his weakening via the Magna Carta.

Historical Setting

The background to the battle of Bouvines is a complicated tale of religious and royal ambition involving King John of England, King Philip II of the Ile de France, Holy Roman Emperor Otto IV, and Pope Innocent III.

The Holy Roman Empire (covering much of central Europe) had lost much of its papal favor by the late twelfth century, and the position of emperor was weakened by the ambitions of numerous Germanic princes. The family of Hohenstaufen held the throne, but, after the death of Frederick Barbarossa on the Second Crusade, his successors had difficulty maintaining order. His son Henry V had an undistinguished reign followed by a succession

struggle in 1197 between Otto IV and Henry's son, the 4-year-old Henry VI. Henry V had married the daughter of the Norman king of Sicily, and Henry VI was born and raised on that island. Upon Henry V's death, Pope Innocent III responded to the emperor's last will and testament and made the young heir his ward. Henry VI grew up under loose supervision and with little direct support, but made himself an intelligent young man.

Pope Innocent III wanted to make the power of the papacy dominant in Europe. He enforced his will on a number of kings by threatening excommunication of either the monarch or his entire population. He also employed the Lombards, Europe's bankers, to collect taxes and handle the church's money, leading to immense wealth. In 1209, Innocent gave his blessing to Otto as Holy Roman Emperor, to the general but not complete support of the Germanic people. Otto had the support of England's King John, who wanted a continental ally to aid him in his ambitions in western Europe.

King John, son of Henry II of England and uncle of Otto, was an unpopular monarch. He raised taxes too often to support usually unsuccessful wars. He had inherited from his father large holdings on the continent, obtained through his father's marriage to Eleanor of Acquitaine as well as military conquest. This so-called Angevin Empire consisted of what is today the western half of France. Poor leadership and egotism did nothing to endear John to the nobility, and his attempt to place a friend in the position of archbishop of Canterbury got him excommunicated. This did little to inhibit his ambitions, however, and he plotted to take over all of modern France by making war against the rising power of Philip II of the ruling House of Capet in Paris.

Philip came to the throne at a key time. His forebears had managed to hold the area around Paris, the Ile de France, and at the same time acquire neighboring lands through feudal relations or quick action when other families had no surviving male heirs. William of Normandy, conqueror of England in 1066, was a vassal of the Capetian dynasty, and thus, theoretically, he and his descendants were bound to follow the orders of a French king.

In 1199, these disparate story lines began to come together. John (temporarily in the pope's good graces) obtained a divorce from Isabel of Gloucester and married Isabella of Angoulême, betrothed to the count of Lusignan. This upset nobles in both England and France, the continental aristocracy appealing to Philip for redress. Philip ordered his "vassal," King John of England, to appear in Paris to explain himself. He refused. In response, Philip went conquering, gaining Normandy from English control in 1204 and following it up with Brittany, Anjou, Maine, Touraine, and Poitou over the next 2 years. He implemented a strong administration in his new lands and gained the support of most of the nobility. Not surprisingly, these conquests did nothing to make King John happy.

In 1212, Otto declared war on the southern Italian Kingdom of the Two Sicilies to expand the power and possessions of the Holy Roman Empire and to eliminate his possible rival, Henry VI, now a bright and resourceful young man. This aggression threatened to totally surround Rome with Otto's Germanic power, so Pope Innocent responded by excommunicating Otto and crowning Henry the new emperor. Philip, wary of Otto's ambitions, supported the pope's nominee. Philip had often had his own troubles with the pope, but for a time they worked toward a common purpose. John, hoping to regain his lost lands on the continent and maintain his country's wool trade with Flanders, allied himself with his nephew Otto. John, however, found his disgruntled nobles unwilling to follow an excommunicant into a war against the pope, so he was forced to patch up his differences with Innocent by swearing to place all of England under papal vassalage.

The Battle

As it turned out, John posed no threat at all. He went to Acquitaine but could rouse no support for his war. Philip dispatched his son Louis to keep an eye on that quarter while he led the bulk of his forces to meet the Germanic threat. Otto had combined with the counts of Flanders and Boulogne as well as the princes of the Netherlands. Philip hoped to gain control of Flanders and its profitable wool trade, denying it to John. Thus, Philip marched against a formidable array of nobility who collectively fielded a force of 6,000 knights and 18,000 infantry.

Philip's own forces consisted of some 7,000 knights and 15,000 infantry. He marched into Flanders to avert an invasion of his own lands. Between the towns of Lille and Tournai was a bridge at Bouvines, where the two armies met. Hearing rumors of some dissension within his own ranks, Philip ordered a meal served to all his nobles. Likening it to the Last Supper, Philip asked if there were any who would betray him. All the nobles stood before him and ate, pledging their allegiance with the words, "We will have no other king but you! Now ride boldly against your enemies, and we are prepared to die with you" (Masson, *Medieval France,* p. 74).

The two armies faced each other for a matter of hours, and then Philip began to withdraw toward the bridge in response to Otto's movement to try and place himself athwart Philip's line of communications back to Paris. Seeing the French withdrawal, Otto hastened forward without awaiting nearby Flemish and German reinforcements. The withdrawal was a ruse, bringing the imperial forces into flat terrain where Philip's better-trained cavalry could operate.

The battle (27 July 1214) opened with some infantry from Soissons attacking the imperial right flank, where Flemish knights were stationed. They at first disdained to fight the attacking commoners, but a call of "Death to the French" motivated them to engage. The French royal household cavalry rode in support of the Soissons infantry and a melee ensued. Philip was in the thick of the battle, leading the bulk of his knights in attacks on the imperial center while the imperial cavalry was en-

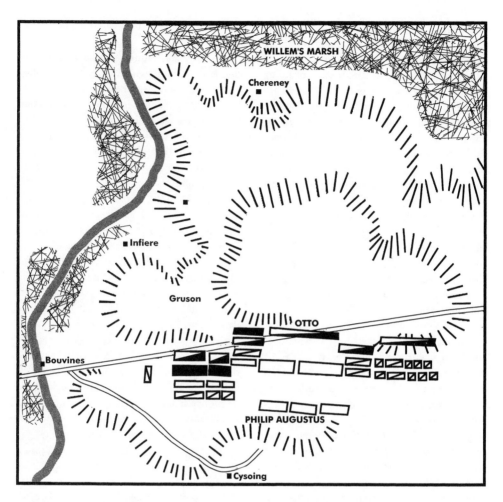

gaged on the flanks. The fighting in the center was intense, with Philip at times in direct danger, but the Germans fell back. Otto, also in the midst of the fighting, abandoned the field while the battle was still in doubt. With his retreat, the army began collapsing. Only on the imperial right did the line hold for a time. There Count Renaud of Bourgogne led a determined force of Englishmen. The count formed his pikemen in two concentric circles, out of which he and his knights would charge, engage, and then retreat inside. Finally, unhorsed outside the circle, Renaud's resistance ended.

The French casualties were relatively light, but the imperial forces suffered much more heavily. In a time when a lot of the fighting between knights was more formal than mortal, Bouvines proved an exception. Along with an unknown number of infantry, 170 knights lost their lives; 140 knights and 1,000 infantry were captured. The fact that both commanders, Philip and Otto, were in the thick of the fighting and in imminent danger was a common occurrence in medieval battles.

Results

For the Holy Roman Empire, a change on the throne was in order. Otto, deposed after the defeat, was replaced by Innocent's nominee,

Henry VI. This, however, proved to be a hollow victory for the pope. Henry, born and raised in Sicily, disliked the cold climate of Germany and spent only 4 years there. Instead of ruling the empire with papal support, he instead appointed a number of local nobles to oversee various aspects of the central European scene, and he returned to the Mediterranean. This lack of direct oversight resulted in intense squabbling among the ambitious German princes and a virtual guarantee that none of them could exercise authority over another. What could have been, in the hands of an able and far-seeing ruler, a united Germany became the multitude of petty states that saw little unification before Bismarck's regime in the latter part of the nineteenth century. Although the Holy Roman Empire remained a political entity, it exercised little real power.

Philip proved to be the big winner in this. Whatever dissension there might have been before the battle ceased to exist afterward. Philip's return to Paris was marked by a week-long celebration that went far toward earning him the title granted by his chaplain: Augustus, the name by which French historians have always called him. With both eastern and western threats gone, Philip gained control of even more land, incorporating the towns of Amiens, Douai, Lille, and St. Quentin, giving him a border on the Rhine River. Coupling that with the lands he had earlier taken from John, the territory under his direct control tripled during his reign. This created a country where before had been a collection of provinces. "The victory at Bouvines marked the commencement of the time at which men might speak, and indeed did speak, by one single name, of *the French*" (Masson, *Medieval France*, p. 77). Philip's administration, based on hiring local intelligentsia to handle his affairs, increased the crown's wealth and control. He increased the power of the courts by the appointment of lawyers rather than ecclesiastics, and he encouraged the expansion of trade by granting wide privilege to the merchant class. The power of the nobility decreased as the power of the monarch grew.

In England, John's inability to regain his continental holdings, as well as his continued rivalry with the nobility, had the opposite result. "The nobles resented his inordinate taxation for disastrous wars, his violations of precedent and law, his bartering of England for Innocent's forgiveness and support. To force the issue, John required of them a scutage—a money payment in lieu of military service" (Durant, *The Age of Faith*, p. 675–676). In the days of Henry I, the nobles had obtained certain delineated rights, and, in the face of John's continued demands for money, they returned with a demand of their own. In 1215, they forced John to sign the Magna Carta, the basis of England's law ever since. The king of England from that point forward would never rule absolutely. The rule of Parliament, although still a long time in coming, can be traced to that day.

Because of the battle at Bouvines, France had the basis of an absolute monarchy that lasted until the French Revolution in 1789; England saw its monarch similarly restricted in his power; and Germany saw itself without nationhood or monarch for more than six centuries.

References: Baldwin, John. *The Government of Philip Augustus.* Berkeley: University of California Press, 1986; Bradbury, Jim. *Philip Augustus: King of France, 1180–1223.* London: Longman, 1998; Durant, Will. *The Age of Faith.* New York: Simon & Schuster, 1950; Masson, Gustave. *Medieval France.* New York: Putnam, 1888; Perrett, Bryan. *The Battle Book.* London: Arms and Armour Press, 1992.

AIN JALUT
3 September 1260

FORCES ENGAGED

Mamluk: 120,000 men. Commander: Baybars.
Mongol: 20,000 to 30,000 men.
Commander: Kit-Boga.

IMPORTANCE
Mamluk victory ended the Mongol threat to
dominate the Middle East.

Historical Setting

By 1219, the Mongols under Genghis Khan
had spread their influence as far as the Caspian
Sea. There, the Shah of Khwarizm offended the
Great Khan by declining to extradite one of his
governors for the death of two Mongol merchants. This provoked an invasion and the destruction of Khwarizm and led to the Mongol
onslaught into the Middle East. Four Mongol
armies engaged in the punishment: Genghis led
one army that burned Bokhara, Samarkand,
and Balkh; his son Juchi defeated the Shah's
forces at Jand, reportedly killing 160,000 men
in the victory; another son, Jagatai, captured
and sacked Otrar; yet another son, Tule, led
70,000 men through Khorasan and pillaged
everywhere he went. All the armies proceeded
undefeated, capturing and despoiling Merv,
Nishapur, Rayy, and Herat.

Genghis returned to Mongolia, but the
steppe horsemen stayed. After Genghis's death,
his successor Ogadai sent 300,000 men to put
down a rebellion launched by Jalal ud-Din, who
was defeated at Diarbekr in northern Persia. In
the wake of the victory, the Mongols proceeded
to pillage Armenia, Georgia, and upper Mesopotamia. In 1234, Genghis's grandson Hulagu
led a force into Iran to defeat the Assassins at
Alamut and then turned his men toward
Baghdad. Although Hulagu was a Buddhist, his
primary wife was Christian and he carried on
his grandfather's policy of religious toleration.
Therefore, his attack on Baghdad was intent
on conquest, not religious persecution.

Hulagu drew on the assistance of troops
from the Golden Horde (the Mongol dynasty
based in modern Russia) to capture Baghdad.
Caliph Al-Mustasim Billah refused to offer allegiance to Hulagu, but he also failed to heed
his generals' warnings to strengthen the city's
weakened walls and military. The caliph depended on his religious authority to draw sufficient defensive forces, but that prestige had
long ago faded and he had to choose between
the Mongols and the Mamluks, slave soldiers
who had come to power in Egypt and whom
he had long scorned. Too late he looked to his
city's defenses; in 1258, the Mongols breached
the walls and proceeded to spend 8 days sacking the city. Baghdad lost most of its several
hundred thousand inhabitants, plus its libraries, universities, mosques, and treasures. Never
again would it serve as the intellectual capital
of Islam.

The destruction of Baghdad had religious
significance that Hulagu never intended. On
the one hand, his Christian wife urged him to
ally himself with the crusaders based in Syria.
On the other hand, his relative Birkai, chief of
the Golden Horde, had converted to Islam and
refused to aid him any longer; indeed, he offered aid to the Mamluks of Egypt in an Islamic coalition. Hulagu, with the assistance of
crusader forces in Palestine, took Aleppo on 25
January 1260 and Damascus on 2 March. "Of
the old heartlands of Islam, only Egypt and
Arabia remained inviolate—and the way
seemed open for the Mongols, firmly established in Damascus, to continue their irresist-
ible advance" (Holt et al., *The Cambridge History
of Islam*, vol. 1, p. 212). Hulagu was aiming for
Jerusalem when news came to him that changed
the fate of the Middle East. The Great Khan
Mangku had died, and it was Hulagu's duty to
return to Mongolia. Although advised by his
wife, generals, and the crusaders not to go,
Hulagu left for home. He left behind a contingent under Kit-Boga.

In Egypt, the new sultan, Kotuz, and his
brilliant general, Baybars, had been preparing
for battle ever since they had executed Hulagu's
emissary, who arrived with the message: "This
is the word of him who rules the earth. Tear
down your walls and submit. If you do so, peace
will be granted you. If you do otherwise, that
will happen which will happen, and what it is
to be we know not. The Sky alone knows"

(Lamb, *The March of the Barbarians,* p. 244). They took advantage of Hulagu's withdrawal and marched toward Syria. Not all the crusaders had allied with the Mongols, and Kotuz was able to gain safe passage and supplies from the Frankish troops in the port city of Acre. While there, the Mamluks learned of Kit-Boga's advance into Galilee, so they marched southeastward to intercept the Mongols.

The Battle

Hulagu had marched homeward with the bulk of the Mongol army, leaving Kit-Boga with a minimal rear guard, described in various sources as between one and three *toumans,* the standard cavalry division of the Mongol military, thus totaling 10,000 to 30,000 men. The

Mamluk general Baybars had gathered together not just the Mamluk soldiers of Egypt but also Bedouins, members of the semibarbarous Hawwarah tribe of Upper Egypt, and fugitive Turcomans and Arabs. In total, the Mamluk army that marched out of Egypt numbered as many as 120,000 men. In a battle of equal numbers, the Mongols would certainly have had the advantage, but Kotuz hoped that his numerical superiority would overcome the well-known prowess of the steppe horsemen.

The two forces converged on the Plain of Esdraelon at Ain Jalut (Goliath's Well) on 3 September 1260. The standard Mongol force was comprised of approximately 40 percent heavy cavalry, armored and employing the lance as their primary weapon; the remainder of the force was light cavalry, using mainly the com-

---

MAMLUKS

The Koran states that the only legitimate sources of slaves are the children of slaves and prisoners of war. It was via the second route that most of the slaves that lived under early Islam came to be enslaved. As slaves were used for every conceivable purpose, perhaps it is not surprising that the rulers of Egypt used them as soldiers, or *ghulams.* The Fatimid (909–1171) and Ayyubid (1171–1250) dynasties of Egypt built armies of slave soldiers and, as happened in other areas of slavery, those most talented rose in power and influence, in spite of their slave status. As trustworthy eunuchs rose to positions of political power as advisors to royalty, so did slave soldiers rise to command armies under the caliphs and viziers.

The Mamluks fought well and bravely under their Moslem masters, but in the mid–thirteenth century they took power for themselves. The final Ayyubid sultan, al-Salih, died in 1249 but his wife Shajar-al-Durr kept his death secret for a time and gave orders in his name. When she was discovered, rather than remove her, the Moslem leaders in Cairo paired her with the Mamluk general Aybak. Although they married, she continued to rule and had Aybak assassinated, but not until after a son had been born. Aybak's

female servants killed Shajar-al-Durr in 1257, and the surviving son became the first of the Mamluk dynasty. The dynasty lasted more than 265 years and occasionally saw brilliant leaders as well as a renaissance in the arts.

After 1381, a second ruling family, the Burjis, rose to power from Mamluk descendants. The Burji dynasty, although it lasted another 136 years, was rocked by almost constant palace intrigue and assassination. During this time, the sultans spent lavishly, and Cairo became the richest city in the Mediterranean world, but the instability of the succession spelled its doom. Selim I of the Ottoman Empire defeated the Mamluk armies in 1517, after which Egypt became a vassal state ruled by a Turkish governor. Still, the Mamluks retained some influence in government, serving under the Turkish pasha and still held command positions in the army. When, in 1798, Napoleon Bonaparte arrived to attempt the conquest of Egypt, a Mamluk army fought him. They were defeated at the Battle of the Pyramids, but, after the French withdrew, the Mamluks tried to regain the throne. The Turks defeated them in 1805 and again in 1811, breaking Mamluk power for good.

pound bow, although also carrying javelins. The doctrine under which they had fought since the time of Genghis Khan was that of attack. Kit-Boga was not about to tamper with decades of success. Although outnumbered approximately four to one, he launched his light cavalry forward and ordered the heavy cavalry to strike the Mamluk left flank. The incredible discipline that had built the Mongol Empire exerted itself, and the Mamluks were soon in full retreat. Baybars, however, was prepared.

Baybars was somewhat typical of the slave soldiers that made up the Mamluk regime. Born a Kipchack Turk, he was captured by the Mongols as a youth and then captured again and sold to a Mamluk emir in Egypt. Thus, he incorporated the knowledge of two military philosophies and could implement both as needed. At Ain Jalut, he played the Mongol game of luring an attacker with a retreat. By all accounts, the Mamluk withdrawal was not a ruse but a true retreat under the power of the Mongol attack, but Baybars had apparently anticipated it. He had placed himself and a large force of Mamluks in the hills bordering the valley into which the Egyptian force was driven. From those hills, he threw his own men upon the flanks and rear of the Mongols, and the full weight of Egyptian numbers proved too great for the Mongols to repel. The entire Mongol force was killed or captured, while the Egyptian army's losses, though unrecorded, were probably moderate.

Results

Kit-Boga was taken before Kotuz. He responded calmly to the Mamluk scorn heaped upon him, promising that a force as small as his was as nothing to the Mongol Great Khan and that the day would come when his defeat would be avenged and Egypt would be destroyed in retribution. Again, he based his statement on decades of Mongol successes, but yet again he was proven wrong. On his way home to the Mongol capital at Karakorum to elect the new Great Khan, Hulagu learned that Genghis's grandson Kubilai had been elevated to that position. At the same time, word reached him of Kit-Boga's defeat. He turned to avenge his subordinate's death, but never did. The rivalry with the Golden Horde mentioned above caused him to look that direction first, for he could not reinvade the Middle East with a hostile army at his back.

Baybars soon assassinated Kotuz for not sufficiently rewarding him for the victory at Ain Jalut. Baybars was a popular figure with both the army and the public, so this action occasioned little comment. Baybars knew that Kit-Boga's defeat was indeed potentially nothing more than a minor setback for the Mongol Empire, so he decided to take active measures to prepare for Hulagu's almost certain return. He marched into Syria and evacuated the population while employing a scorched-earth policy, designed to deny an invading cavalry necessary forage and supplies. He also convinced the crusaders to remain neutral rather than follow the mistaken path of alliance that some of their fellows had done with Kit-Boga. As it turned out, these actions proved unnecessary.

The election of Kubilai to the position of Great Khan was not without opposition. His younger brother Arik-Buka challenged the decision. Hulagu supported Kubilai, and that was a factor in arousing Birkai, Khan of the Golden Horde, to approach Baybars about an alliance. Baybars's response was quick and flowery, flattering Birkai and convincing him of Hulagu's intention to destroy their religion, Islam. When Hulagu readied his army to avenge Kit-Boga in 1262, he was forced to stop his advance upon receiving word of an army of the Golden Horde riding south from the Caucasus. He turned to face it and attacked Birkai's army on the Terek River. The two forces fought each other almost to exhaustion and neither was able to gain the upper hand. Hulagu retreated to Persia and hoped to rekindle his alliance with the crusaders, but his death in 1264 ended that idea. His son Abaka marched for Egypt in 1281, but was met in Syria and defeated by Kalawun, Baybars's successor, at the battle of Homs. The Mongols retreated across the Euphrates and established the dynasty of the Il-Khans.

The Mongol invasion of the Middle East was relatively short, the actual fighting taking place over approximately four decades. It proved decisive in confirming the Moslems as the dominant influence in the region because the Mongols and crusaders never cooperated as fully as they might have. Kit-Boga's defeat at Goliath's Well, although a relatively small battle in itself, proved to be the Middle Eastern version of the Moslem defeat at Tours, France. As Christian Europe held back the forces of Islam there, so Moslem Egypt turned away the forces that could have ended their hold on the Middle East, possibly driving them back to the deserts of Arabia and the Sahara. The Mongols exercised the well-known tactics of destruction and terror, killing hundreds of thousands of people and destroying much of Islam's literature and scientific writings, although the Il-Khans did strive to renew that intellectual atmosphere in their short-lived dynasty.

The confirmation of the Mamluk dynasty after Ain Jalut revitalized Islam. It did not go unnoticed by contemporary observers that the Mamluks were themselves originally men of the steppe, and the military prowess thus exhibited emboldened the Moslems to continue the spread of their faith to the northeast. The Mongols that established the Persian Il-Khan dynasty later converted to Islam, giving the faith a powerful presence on the frontier with Asia.

References: Allsen, Thomas. Mongol Imperialism. Berkeley: University of California Press, 1987; Holt, P. M., Ann K. S. Lambton, and Bernard Lewis. The Cambridge History of Islam, vol. 1. Cambridge, UK: Cambridge University Press, 1970; Kwanten, Luc. Imperial Nomads. Philadelphia: University of Pennsylvania Press, 1979; Lamb, Harold. The March of the Barbarians. New York: Literary Guild, 1940; Muir, William. The Mameluke, or Slave Dynasty of Egypt. London: Smith, Elder & Co., 1896.

HSIANG-YANG
1268–1273

FORCES ENGAGED
Mongol: 60,000, plus auxiliaries.
Commander: Liu Cheng.
Sung: Unknown. Commander: Lü Wen-huan.

IMPORTANCE
Mongol victory broke the main defense of the southern Sung dynasty, leading to the establishment of the Yüan dynasty.

Historical Setting

The Sung dynasty in China began in 960, succeeding the T'ang dynasty. For a time, the Sung controlled territory stretching from the southern reaches of modern Manchuria to the northern borders of Vietnam, with their power extending westward 1,000 miles from the China Sea. In 1127, they lost their northern lands to the Jurchen Mongols and concentrated their authority in the richer southern China by building a new capital city at Hangchow, at the mouth of the Yangtze River. The Southern Sung dynasty came to be regarded as something of a golden age in China, with expanding trade routes bringing in immense wealth as well as from Annam a new type of rice, which led to improvements in agriculture. Culturally, they reintroduced an interest in Confucianism, which had gradually been losing popularity to Buddhism and Taoism; that in turn led to a new form of bureaucracy, with examinations on Confucian principles becoming the basis of gaining a position in the civil service, a practice that was maintained almost until the twentieth century.

Unfortunately, the Sung dynasty was not blessed with a sufficiently strong military to be as aggressive as earlier dynasties, or even strong enough defensively to beat back the Jurchens in the early twelfth century or the Mongols under Genghis Khan that threatened their security a century later. Genghis was recognized as ruler in the north when his forces captured Beijing in 1215. He then made war on the Hsia population to the west, conquering them in 1227, the year of his death. His son Ogadai continued the conquest of the rebellious northern territories. In the process of finally subduing the Jurchens, Ogadai's nephew Tului gained safe passage through Sung lands to complete a wide encircling movement that led to the Jurchens' ultimate demise. In return for that cooperation, the Sung asked for a reward of some of their lost northern territory. When the Mongols refused, the Sung forcibly annexed the province of Honan, setting off a war with the Mongols that lasted 35 years.

Most of the fighting against the Sung was directed by Ogadai's nephews Mangu and Kubilai. They both had successes against the Sung in the 1250s, but the invasion was put on hold because of internal political problems. Mangu succeeded Ogadai as the Great Khan, but his reign was short. His death in 1260 provoked a civil war between one Mongol faction that named Kubilai as Great Khan and a second group that supported his brother Arik-Buka. The two groups fought for 4 years before finally Kubilai held the throne unopposed. With his position secure, Kubilai returned to his war against the Southern Sung. Although Kubilai hoped to conquer them quickly and easily, some Sung strongholds and generals made that hope a vain one.

The man that Kubilai put in charge of the invasion was a Sung defector, Liu Cheng. This was a wise move because not only did Liu Cheng possess an intimate knowledge of the primary target cities that the Mongols would have to capture, but he also had experience with naval warfare. This was an aspect of fighting with which the Mongols had no knowledge and was one of the main strengths of the Sung military. That knowledge, coupled with the sheer numbers of the Mongol land forces, proved a potent combination. The key fortress upon which Kubilai focused was Hsiang-yang, on the Han River. This city, with the almost equally strong city of Fan-cheng directly across the river, controlled the main route of access to the Yangtze River valley, which the Mongols needed to control to reach the Sung capital at Hangchow. It proved to be one of the most difficult fortresses that the Mongols ever had to attack.

The Battle

During the period of the Mongol internal struggles, the Sung had begun to prepare for the invasion. The primary figure in this preparation was the prime minister, Chia Ssu-tao. His activities are the subject of some dispute, for the official Chinese chronicles paint him as a self-centered, grasping, and corrupt official whose policy was to mislead his emperor as to the potency of the Mongol threat while enriching himself and his cronies. Less biased observers describe him in a more favorable light, believing that his unpopularity came from his increased taxes for military operations. Whatever the truth of the matter, the fortress at Hsiang-yang was prepared for the arrival of the Mongols. The city's commander, Lü Wen-huan, had a strong fortress to defend, supplies that would last for years, as well as contact via a series of bridges with the city of Fan-cheng across the Han. All of that made his city a tough one to invade.

Kubilai sent 60,000 veterans under the command of Liu Cheng, and they began their investment of the city in March 1268. The Mongols had built their Asian Empire on massive cavalry forces, which were of absolutely no use at all in besieging a city. Since the days of Genghis, however, the Mongols had been quick to adopt the technology of whatever population they conquered, so they had besieged cities before. They quickly built 10 miles of fortified lines surrounding the city, but also had to build a fleet to stop any succor reaching the city by river. The Mongols began to fortify the towns of Po-ho-k'ou and Lu-men Shan, downriver from Hsiang-yang, in order to harass any relief fleet sailing up from the Yangtze. The city continued to receive aid from Fan-cheng, however, so in October Kubilai ordered another force, under A-chu, to surround that city. Their arrival created a panic in Hsiang-yang, and the Sung forces attempted a sally against them on 6 December. It was a disaster, and never again did the defenders leave the city.

Even with Fan-cheng surrounded, the siege was irregular in its effectiveness. "Although the Mongol army was constantly reinforced by bodies of fresh troops, and notwithstanding that Kubilai himself devoted much of his attention to the subject, the siege of the Sung stronghold made very little progress. Several times were his generals compelled to change their position, to extend their lines at one point and to curtail them at another" (Boulger, *The History of China*, vol. 1, p. 335). Time dragged on with neither side seemingly willing to back down. In February 1269, Kubilai sent an emissary to the siege to report to him on its progress and to make recommendations for improvement. That resulted in an extra 20,000 men to strengthen the downstream fortifications. A Sung attempt at resupply came in August 1269, with 3,000 boats, but it was easily thrown back. In April 1270, Liu Cheng and A-chu asked for another 70,000 men and 5,000 ships; Kubilai dispatched the new batch of reinforcements to the siege just as Chia Ssu-tao launched another major resupply effort in October 1270; it too failed to break through.

The only minor success that the Sung relieving forces scored was in September 1272. Two forces, one with supplies and one of warships, made their way down a tributary of the Han. While the warships pinned down the Mongol fleet, a number of the supply ships along with 3,000 men slipped past the battle and into Hsiang-yang. They brought some necessary supplies, including salt, but then tried to cut their way back out of the encirclement. Apparently one of their number defected to the Mongols and alerted them to the breakout, and the 3,000 sailed into a trap that annihilated

them. The lines around the city tightened somewhat after this incident.

The deciding change in the battle came from well outside China. Increasingly frustrated with the lack of progress, Kubilai responded to the suggestion of one of his military advisors, Arigh Khaya, and sent word to his nephew Abakha, in control of the Mongol domain in Persia. In late 1272, two Persian engineers, Ismail and Ala al-Din, arrived. These two were skilled in the construction and employment of siege machinery. After surveying the situation, the two oversaw the construction of a mangonel and a catapult. The rock-throwing machines were deployed in March 1273 against Fan-cheng, and within a few days sufficient damage had been done to allow a successful assault against the city. "The battle raged from street to street, from house to house; and, when there was no longer any possibility of continuing the contest, the officers, sooner than surrender, slew themselves, in which they were imitated by their men. The Mongols had indeed captured Fanching [sic], but their triumph was only over a city of ruins and ashes" (Boulger, *The History of China*, vol. 1, p. 338). When Fan-cheng fell, Lü Wen-huan realized that his city could not survive a similar attack. After some preliminary bombardment, the Mongols offered generous terms. Lü Wen-huan accepted them and also accepted an offer to serve in Kubilai's army.

Results

Although the fall of Hsiang-yang did not destroy the Sung dynasty, it turned the tide of the Mongol war against it. The Sung emperor and his court had consistently rejected any Mongol emissaries, confident in their defenses. With the Han River now open to the Yangtze, the Mongol army had a clear path toward Hangchow. Prime Minister Chia Ssu-tao went to the field to take over command of the Sung armies in a desperate attempt to save his reputation, position, and emperor. Instead of mounting a major expedition earlier against the besieging Mongols, during which he could have cooperated with a coordinated sally from the city, he now had to face a large, unified invading army under a new commander. Responding to the advice of one of his primary Chinese advisors, Kubilai had placed all of his southern army under a single general, Bayan. Grandson of Genghis's most gifted subordinate, Subotai, Bayan apparently had inherited all of his forebear's military talent. He had campaigned with the Mongols in Persia and the Middle East and had Kubilai's compete confidence.

Bayan moved downstream with a growing army. He demanded the surrender of every town he encountered in the traditional Mongol manner: surrender to leniency or fight to the death. Lacking faith in the imperial court, many Sung commanders chose the former alternative. The Sung emperor Tu-tsung died in August 1274 and was succeeded by a 4-year-old son. Power was therefore in the hands of Empress Hsieh, Tu-tsung's wife, but she was little equipped to exercise that power. Bayan defeated Chia Ssu-tao's 130,000-man army in mid-March 1275, and the final bar to Hangchow had been removed. Even more cities now surrendered without a fight, and the Sung government was virtually powerless to resist. The Empress Hsieh tried negotiations, but, after so many earlier rejections and with momentum irresistibly on his side, Bayan would accept nothing less than unconditional surrender. With the Mongol army at Hangchow's gates, she finally conceded in late January 1276.

Sung loyalists in the south, led by the talented general Chang Shih-chieh, continued for some years to offer up alternate emperors and fight the inevitable. The Mongols pressed on with their occupation of southern China, harrying the remnants of the Sung resistance. The death knell finally tolled 3 April 1279 in a large naval battle off the coast near Canton, when Chang Shih-chieh abandoned his defeated flotilla by jumping into the sea with the last pretender to the Sung throne in his arms.

Kubilai Khan, however, had announced the end of the Sung dynasty in the midst of the siege of Hsiang-yang; in 1271, he declared the institution of the Yüan dynasty. Although it proved relatively short-lived, Kubilai's government was not without positive accomplishments. He realized the superiority of Chinese administration over that of the traditional Mongol state and adapted his population to that of the conquered. The efficient civil service that the Sung had established remained in place, and the trade routes that they had used were reopened. What Kubilai's dynasty did was to permit the uninterrupted flow of Chinese culture and bureaucracy and gave to it a unified empire larger than it had ever encompassed. After Kubilai's death in 1294, his successors ruled badly and fought among themselves. The resulting discontent provoked a rebellion that by 1368 chased the Mongols westward past the Great Wall and founded the Ming dynasty. The enlarged territory that Kubilai had left to China, however, remained (for the most part) the China that exists to this day.

References: Boulger, Demetrius Charles. *The History of China,* vol. 1. Freeport, NY: Books for Libraries Press, 1972 [1898]; Ch'i-ch'ing Hsiao. *The Military Establishment of the Yuan Dynasty.* Cambridge, MA: Harvard University Press, 1978; Kwanten, Luc. *Imperial Nomads.* Philadelphia: University of Pennsylvania Press, 1979; Rashid al-Din Tabib. *The Successors of Genghis Khan.* Translated by John Andrew Boyle. New York: Columbia University Press, 1971; Rossabi, Morris. *Khubilai Khan: His Life and Times.* Berkeley: University of California Press, 1988.

HAKATA BAY
November 1274 and June–August 1281

FORCES ENGAGED

Japanese: Unknown.
Commander: Hojo Tokimune.

Mongol: 50,000 in first invasion; possibly 140,000 in the second. Commander: Kubilai Khan; field commanders unknown.

IMPORTANCE
The destruction of the Mongol fleets guaranteed
Japanese independence, yet created a power
struggle in the Japanese military government that
led to the military's dominance over the emperor.

Historical Setting

In 1259, Kubilai Khan, grandson of Genghis
Khan, established himself as the first monarch
of the Yüan dynasty in China. As he was in the
process of imposing Mongol rule over all of
China, only the crumbling Sung dynasty in
southern China remained as yet unconquered.
With Mongol hegemony in place over Korea,
Kubilai looked at the island nation of Japan as
his next target. In 1268, he sent envoys to the
Japanese government, demanding recognition
of his suzerainty over Japan. The alternative,
Kubilai was clear in pointing out, was war.

The Japanese leadership at the time was in
the hands of an 18-year-old, Hojo Tokimune.
He was head of the *bakufu*, the military administration that ruled in the name of the emperor. The threat could not be treated as anything but genuine; Japanese contacts in Korea
and ship captains from the Sung ports assured
the bakufu of the aggressive Mongol nature. Not
wanting to directly provoke the Great Khan,
the bakufu decided to send no response to the
demand and spend the interval before Mongol
invasion in preparing a defense of the country.

In the capital city of Kamakura, Hojo ordered his vassals in the western provinces to call
out their retainers and prepare for invasion.
Those lords with lands on the western coast
were to have their forces stand guard along the
beaches, and those forces would be replaced by
periodic rotations of armies from inland fiefs.
From the time of the expulsion of the Mongol
envoys to Kubilai's invasion was 5 years; keeping his samurai warriors at a constant state of
readiness was a major accomplishment of Hojo.
He was aided, however, by religious leaders in
Japan, notably a Buddhist priest named
Nichiren. He loudly criticized Hojo for following the teachings of the Zen Buddhist priest

Bukkô, an exile from the Mongol regime in
China. Nichiren claimed the need for a Japan
united in one faith, his Lotus Sutra, or the gods
would punish the country. Such rivalry among
religious orders kept the population focused on
the threat of foreign invasion.

In 1274, Kubilai began to amass ships in
Korean ports, possibly 900 ships being collected
to transport as many as 40,000 soldiers, primarily Mongol, but with Korean and Chinese
auxiliaries. Whether this was an actual invasion
or merely a reconnaissance-in-force is difficult
to determine. Its first actions were certainly
sufficient to argue for invasion: the fleet set sail
for the island of Tsushima, roughly halfway
between the southern Korean coast and the
western shore of the Japanese island of Kyushu.
The Mongols landed on the island, quickly
wiped out its small defense force, and then proceeded to the smaller island of Iki, a mere 12
miles from Kyushu. The smaller defense force
there put up even less resistance, although Japanese legend has it that the stubborn bravery of
the samurai provoked rage in the Mongols
rather than admiration.

The Battle

On 18 November 1274, the fleet appeared off
Kyushu's Hakata Bay, and the following day the
Mongols landed men ashore. They quickly captured the town of Hakata and were soon engaged by the samurai force on duty. Rather than
awaiting reinforcements that had been dispatched, the warriors at the site threw themselves at the Mongols and found themselves
hopelessly outnumbered and outmatched. The
standard practice of Japanese warfare involved
individual combat, in which the mettle and skill
of a warrior with a sword could be displayed.
The Mongols, true to their steppe heritage,
fought on horseback, launching clouds of arrows at a distance into the enemy mass. The
Mongols also employed some sort of catapult
that threw metal balls that exploded on contact, although probably more firecracker than

bomb. Still, the noise and burns they created certainly dismayed the Japanese as well as caused a number of casualties. Even the invading infantry did not fight in Japanese style, instead operating in a phalanx-type formation whose spears kept Japanese attacks at bay.

In spite of their lack of success, the Japanese did inflict a significant number of casualties on the Mongols. How many is unknown, but, when the samurai force abandoned the field and withdrew into the earthworks and fortifications of Dazaifu, a few miles inland, the Mongols did not pursue. The massive number of arrows that they had let fly during the battle, the unfamiliarity with the terrain, the expectancy of reinforcement for the defenders, as well as the number of men killed and wounded, convinced the Mongols to spend the night aboard ship, rearming and regrouping. It proved a fateful mistake because that night a gale blew up and caused many of the ships to sink, which brought about the loss of perhaps one-third of the invasion force. The lack of naval experience for the Mongols certainly argued against their staying on ship in hostile waters, and it can be assumed that the Korean captains pressed such a point home as well. Thus, the remaining ships returned to Korea.

The bakufu, in analyzing the performance of their troops during the invasion, realized that it was nature rather than force of arms that had saved their country. Hojo rightly assumed that Kubilai would not take such a defeat lightly and would send another army against the islands, so Hojo ordered a redoubling of the nation's defense efforts. Although all of southern Honshu, the largest island of Japan, and the western coast of Kyushu were potential targets, Hakata Bay seemed the most likely location for a return match. Thus, Hojo ordered a wall to be constructed along the entire length of the shoreline. To motivate the population, Hojo ordered that anyone who performed well in fighting the Mongols, whether or not in the service of a feudal lord, could find himself rewarded by the government. Just as a similar promise of reward and advancement had motivated the population of Europe to join the Crusades less than a century before, so the population of Japan responded to the call.

In the meantime, Kubilai was indeed angered by the failure of his invasion force, but he was so involved in crushing the last remnants of the Sung in southern China that he had to postpone his retribution. He immediately sent more envoys to Japan, making the same demands that his first emissaries had made. Rather than send them away without a response, Hojo began beheading them instead. This continued until 1279, when Kubilai finally stopped sending them.

In Japan, the bakufu decided not only to beef up the defenses along the coastline but also to begin construction of a navy of their own. They would need all the assistance they could muster because, when Kubilai once again turned his attention to the Japanese, he had at his disposal not only the Korean navy but also the ships and sailors of the recently defeated Sung. Thus, he began amassing two invasion fleets and armies. In Korea, once again some 900 ships were gathered, crewed by 17,000 sailors, transporting 10,000 Korean soldiers and another 15,000 Mongols and Chinese. This collection of military might was named the Eastern Route Army. The Southern Route Army, organized south of the Yangtze River, was reportedly 100,000 men and was to be transported on as many as 3,500 ships. The two were supposed to combine forces at Tsushima and sail for Kyushu.

The Eastern Route Army departed Korea on 22 May 1281 and landed men ashore at Tsushima on 9 June. Although the Japanese defense force had been enlarged since the previous assault, these later defenders were again outnumbered and annihilated. A similar fate once again befell Iki on 14 June. The Mongols quickly sailed on to Hakata Bay, where they arrived on 21 June. The Southern Route Army had not yet completely organized itself and was thus well behind schedule. Rather than wait for them, the Eastern Route Army proceeded with the invasion. The first squadron of ships sailed past Hakata Bay toward the main island of Honshu, but that was merely a diversion, which the Japanese did not follow up.

The primary Mongol force sailed into Hakata Bay and landed men along the Shiga peninsula, which blocks half the mouth of the bay from the north. The shoreline wall had not been extended so far, so the Mongols were in a position to flank the Japanese defenses. Rather than allow that to happen, Japanese warriors blocked the route with waves of attackers, a foretaste of the banzai charge of World War II. It worked, and the Mongols were unable to break out of their beachhead. The limited beach space available to the Mongols because of the wall kept them from mounting a major assault, so the Japanese were able to engage in some offense of their own. At night, the small boats

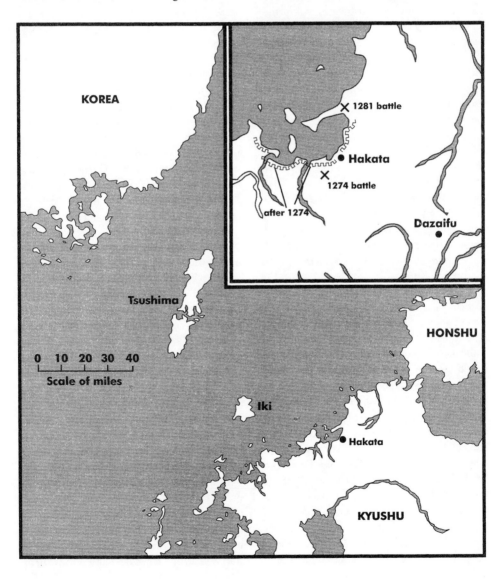

that the Japanese had been constructing since the last invasion were sent out among the invasion fleet. Containing only a handful of samurai on each, the craft crept alongside the larger Korean ships in the darkness. In silence, the samurai would swarm aboard, kill as many sleeping Mongols as they could, reboard their boats, and escape. This harassing tactic proved so effective that the Mongols withdrew their navy to Tsushima. There they awaited the arrival of the Southern Route Army, but in the meantime the close quarters and summer heat created an epidemic that killed some 3,000 men. The first ships of the Southern force sailed into view on 16 July; by 12 August, the two fleets were completely merged and the invasion was on.

Faced with overwhelming force, the Japanese population did what men and women have always done in times of extreme emergency: they prayed to their gods for deliverance. It is said that a nation in prayer can work miracles, and one appeared on 15 August 1281. According to Japanese accounts, a small cloud appeared on the horizon and grew into a massive storm. The tempest that struck the Tsushima Straits blew for 2 days and destroyed most of the combined Mongol navy. Mongol sources do not give numbers, but the contemporary Japanese accounts claim that no more than 200 ships survived being sunk at sea or blown ashore; 80 percent of the troops were either drowned or killed by Japanese troops on the beaches.

Results

Kubilai Khan began to make plans for a third invasion, but abandoned them in 1284 when he began to have problems in Southeast Asia. The war seemed to have done minimal damage to the Mongol empire. The Chinese contingent of the Mongol army bore the brunt of the loss; 12,000 Chinese were made slaves by the Japanese. The Mongols lost their share of men and ships, but little else. Mongol pride was hurt, in that Japan now held the distinc-

tion of being the only state in the Orient that did not pay tribute to them.

Oddly, the Japanese victory did more harm than good to the Hojo rulers. When the Mongols first arrived, the government appealed to Heaven for help. Throughout the empire, prayers were offered, liturgies were chanted, and incense was burned in the temples. The priesthood took credit for the Japanese victory over the Mongol invaders, even claiming that they were responsible for the timely storm that saved the nation. Many of the priests expected and were given huge rewards for their help in the campaign. That brought resentment among the soldiers who fought so hard for victory and whose payment for services was very small in comparison. The victory over the Mongols brought no wealth to the victors, since the invading forces had left no land as spoils of war to be divided among the bakufu, the military leaders who were the major landowners. This lowered their prestige. Because the bakufu had little trust in the Mongols, they did not relax their precautions for another invasion for another two decades. This put a great financial burden on the Japanese government and further demoralized the warriors who continued to look for their reward. All of that eventually led to the downfall of the Hojo family.

The inability of the Mongols to establish a foreign regime in Japan meant that the islands could remain isolated from outside influence. When Europeans began arriving in the sixteenth century, the perceived threat to the stability of Japanese society convinced the government to reject almost all foreign visitors and trade. Not until the middle of the nineteenth century was Japan opened to the outside world when a U.S. fleet under the command of Commodore Matthew Perry forced the acceptance of a U.S. ambassador. Other western embassies followed, and the Japanese, realizing the drastic technological gap between themselves and the rest of the world, began to accepted foreign trade. The centuries of isolation, and the conservatism of the culture that had been

KAMIKAZES

It was a recollection of the thirteenth century salvation that brought about the rebirth of the kamikaze, destined to attempt to save Japan from foreign invasion almost seven centuries later.

Between the years of Hakata Bay and World War II, Japan developed a society dominated by the military and its values. For a war such as that fought in the Pacific between 1941 and 1945, dominated by naval operations and their accompanying air arms, the Japanese needed—but did not possess—numeric superiority in ships and aircraft. Thus, they were doomed from the start, and Japanese warriors have never been more prone to extreme actions than when faced with imminent defeat. The virtually inbred creed that no soldier surrenders, that death for one's country and emperor is far preferable to surrender or defeat, almost guaranteed that the Japanese would sooner or later engage in desperate measures.

In the first offensive ground combat on Guadalcanal, in the Solomons Islands northeast of Australia, U.S. Marines faced what came to be called banzai charges. Banzai (literally "10,000 years") was the cry to the emperor not only for his long life but for his soldiers' commitment to die for him. What came to be a common occurrence for Marines to witness was emulated by Japanese pilots starting in 1944. The first recorded intentional suicide attack by a Japanese pilot was in May of that year off the coast of New Guinea. Prime Minister Tojo in the Japanese cabinet had already ordered preparations for special attack units. The first serious call for self-sacrificial attacks, however, came from lower-ranking officers who felt the personal need to employ special measures to meet the increasingly desperate straits that the Japanese army and navy were up against in the face of superior U.S. numbers in both aircraft and ships.

In the summer of 1944, the Aerial Research Department of Tokyo's Imperial University began designing a rocket-propelled aircraft called *ohka* (cherry blossom) with a warhead in the nose. The pilots trained to fly these rocket bombs were called Thunder Gods. The ohka were not mass-produced (only a few hundred were made), so the vast majority of airborne kamikaze attacks were made by regular aircraft, both bombers and fighters. These made their initial appearance during the U.S. invasion of the Philippines in October 1944.

The pilots who volunteered for kamikaze missions did so from a sense of duty and usually had a lot of time to think about their decision because almost no one was sent off immediately upon volunteering. In some cases, the pilot waited weeks or even months before his assignment came. Before his mission, the pilot donned a white head scarf *(hachimaki)* with the rising sun emblazoned in the center. Many pilots also wore a ceremonial waist sash *(senninbari)*, called "thousand-stitch belts," in which 1,000 women in Japan had sewn one stitch each to show the widespread support for the pilot. Before the mission, the pilot was served a ritual cup of water or sake, rice wine. There were survivors of these missions. Although some sources tell of pilots returning with mechanical difficulties and being shunned by their compatriots, other sources report that, if no target was found, the pilot was supposed to return to base.

In January 1945, the Japanese army and navy chiefs of staff submitted a plan to the emperor to require all the armed forces to engage in suicide tactics. The emperor disagreed. By February, the large number of early volunteers was beginning to dry up, and kamikaze pilots began being drafted. Only a few attacks took place during the Iwo Jima campaign during February–March 1945, but, when U.S. forces landed on Okinawa in April, the full force of the special attack units was felt. Fifteen ships were sunk and another fifty-nine damaged, with a total loss of more than 48,000 Americans killed and wounded during the Okinawa campaign. The final attack took place on 13 August, only 2 days before the emperor announced Japan's surrender. Japanese navy pilots who died in the attacks numbered 2,525; Japanese army pilots who died numbered 1,388.

Although the aerial kamikazes were the best known of the suicide units, there were also small submarines fitted out for one-way trips against U.S. shipping. These were called *kaiten*, or Heaven Shifter, in the hopes that they could shift the fate of Japan's forces. Individual soldiers are reported to have laden themselves with explosives and jumped on tanks to disable them. Plans were also under way to encourage the civil population of Japan to assume a suicidal role when the U.S. invasion came. They were designated the *Ichioku Tokko,* or "hundred million as a Special Attack Force." Many believe that only the shock of the two atomic bombs in August 1945 was sufficient to overcome the duty that many of Japan's population were preparing to undertake.

created, kept the Japanese suspicious of foreign ways and leery of foreign, especially European, motives.

To Japan, the avenging hurricane that destroyed the Mongols came to be termed kamikaze, Divine Wind. The legend grew over the centuries, to be revived in the 1940s. Hoping to create a Divine Wind to save their empire, Japanese pilots used suicide tactics during the U.S. invasion of the Philippines in October 1944 and continued them until the final surrender almost a year later.

References: Cook, Theodore. "Mongol Invasion," *Military History Quarterly* 11(2), Winter 1998; Kwanten, Luc. *Imperial Nomads.* Philadelphia: University of Pennsylvania Press, 1979; Mason, R. H. P., and Caiger, J. G. *History of Japan.* New York: Free Press, 1972; Sansom, George. *A History of Japan, 1334–1615.* Stanford, CA: Stanford University Press, 1961; Turnbull, Stephen. *The Samurai: A Military History.* New York: Macmillan, 1977.

BRUSA
1317–1326

FORCES ENGAGED
Byzantine: Unknown. Commander: Unknown.
Turkish: Unknown.
Commander: Osman I and then Orkhan.

IMPORTANCE
The capture of Brusa established Osman I (Othman) and his successors as the major power in Asia Minor, beginning the Ottoman Empire.

Historical Setting

The peoples known as Turks originated not in the Turkey of today but in Turkestan in central Asia. In the middle of the sixth century A.D., they formed themselves into a large tribal confederation and then shortly thereafter split into eastern and western factions. The eastern Turkic tribes interacted strongly with the Chinese, most notably the T'ang dynasty, and alternately aided or were defeated by the Chinese. The western Turkic tribes, however, were better known as conquerors for their occupation of territory stretching from the Oxus River to the Mediterranean Sea.

Their first major entry into western history came with their contact with Arabs spreading Islam past Persia and toward central Asia. The pastoral Turks became exposed to the civilizations of Persia and the Byzantine Empire and began a gradual conversion to western religions, mainly but not exclusively Islam. Soon Turkic soldiers served in Moslem armies, either as volunteers or as slave soldiers, forerunners of the Mamluks or the Janissaries of the Ottoman Empire. They soon became ghazi, or border warriors, hired by Moslem governments to protect the northeastern frontier. At this point, the western Turks also split, the eastern faction becoming the Ghaznavids and the western becoming the Seljuks.

Most of the Turks embraced the more orthodox Sunni branch of Islam, and they spread the faith as well as practiced it. Based out of the city of Ghazna (some 90 miles southwest of modern Kabul, Afghanistan), the Ghaznavids in the tenth and eleventh centuries spread their power and religion eastward into India. Their most notable achievement was the introduction of Islam into India, though their use of forced conversions often made them more feared than welcomed. They were defeated not by Indian resistance but by the Seljuks.

Named for its first major leader, Seljuk or Selchuk, the western Turkic tribes also served Moslem governments. Their position on the Asian frontier attracted growing numbers of Islamicized Turkic tribes, and soon the land grants ceded by the Moslems proved inadequate for the needs of so many pastoral people. Their growth in numbers gave them an increased military strength as well as a growing need for grazing lands. As the Moslem Buyid dynasty grew weak and the Ghaznavids looked toward

India, the Seljuks found conquest of the lands west of Persia relatively simple. They defeated the Ghaznavids in 1040 and then occupied Baghdad in 1055. They did not take the city to pillage it but to return it to Sunni control from the less orthodox Shi'ites. The marriage of the Seljuk chief to the sister of the caliph, and his resulting promotion to the position of sultan, established the Seljuks as the premiere military and political force in the Middle East.

Filled with religious zeal, the Seljuks conquered Armenia, the Levant, and into Asia Minor; Malik Shah, the most successful Seljuk military leader, scored a major victory over Byzantine forces at Manzikert in 1071. In spite of their desire to reestablish the Sunni sect of Islam, the Seljuks did not undertake the practice of forced conversions, which the Ghaznavids did in India. Though they made subjects of Christians and Jews, they did not persecute them; the Seljuks followed Mohammed's teachings of religious tolerance. Once established in Asia Minor, they chose as their capital city Konia, a site occupied since the Hittites at the dawn of recorded history. It became a center for culture and learning. The orthodoxy of the Sunni Seljuks frightened Europeans, who rejected peaceful interaction in favor of militant Christianity and mounted the Crusades. Although the Crusades brought about no lasting European presence in the Middle East, and the Seljuks remained in power, they finally were doomed to destruction in the same manner that brought them to power: invasion from central Asia, the Mongols of the thirteenth century. Their occupation of Asia Minor ultimately weakened the Byzantine Empire to the point that it fell to the successors of the Seljuks, the Ottoman Empire.

The Campaign

The formation of the Ottoman Empire was very much a matter of timing and location. In the late thirteenth and early fourteenth centuries,

the power of the Mongols had waned, as had that of the Byzantine Empire. In the region in and around Asia Minor, a power vacuum formed. The people living in Asia Minor were basically still a steppe society, uncomfortable with a settled lifestyle and militarily aggressive. Such a combination had served to keep the Seljuks from ever establishing an extended dominion; attempts by political leaders to convince the people to settle down and pay taxes resulted in rebellion. The Turks followed strong leaders, no matter their birth, and, for a strong leader to maintain his following, he needed conquests to keep his people occupied and provide operating capital.

Osman I (or Othman) became the main prince of Asia Minor who attracted warriors. His land, awarded to him in 1290 for service to the Seljuks, was based on the town of Sorgut, supposedly established as a regional stronghold by Hannibal. Sorgut was located southeast of Constantinople, fairly near the Sea of Marmora. This meant that Osman's lands abutted the frontiers of the Byzantine Empire. That location was the primary reason that warriors flocked to his banner; fighting Christians was more honorable and lucrative than fighting fellow Turks. Osman's campaigns against the Byzantines were at times mere raids for loot and at other times intentional territorial acquisitions, and they both attracted the attention of Constantinople. Of all the Asia Minor princes, Osman was deemed the greatest threat.

Osman focused his attentions on three primary targets: Nicaea (modern Iznik), Nicomedia (modern Izmit), and Brusa (modern Bursa). He first laid siege to Nicaea in 1301. This action attracted the attention of the Byzantine emperor Andronicus II to him. The Byzantine government dispatched a force of 2,000 men to relieve the siege, but Osman ambushed and destroyed them at Baphaeon. The local population evacuated the countryside and fled to Nicomedia. The emperor hired some Alan mercenaries to deal with Osman, but they too were defeated (1302 and 1304). Osman was unable, however, to overcome either Nicaea or Nicomedia, so he returned to raiding.

Brusa had once been a town as important as Nicaea and Nicomedia, but after the invasion of the Goths in the third century only the latter two were restored under Byzantine rule. Just before Constantine established the empire and Nicaea was still the regional capital, Brusa had its walls restored. It was such a good job of reconstruction that, when Osman began his siege in 1317, the town held out for more than 9 years. As to the details of the siege of Brusa, almost nothing exists. It was a long siege, and that is about all that can be said, other than some sources say it may have been intermittent rather than continuous. When it fell on 6 April 1326, Osman lay dying, so he never saw the inside of the city. His son, Orkhan, became the second leader of the dynasty that became known as the Ottomans. Upon his occupation of the city, he named it the capital of the emerging Ottoman Empire. Whatever damage that had been inflicted during the siege was quickly repaired and the town's former elegance was restored. It became "a great city with fine bazaars and broad streets, worthy of the greatest of the Turkmen kings" (Muller, *The Loom of History,* p. 301).

Results

Although Osman was the father of the ruling line, it was Orkhan who really established the power of the Ottomans. He succeeded in capturing Nicaea in 1331 after beating back a Byzantine relief force and then he took Nicomedia in 1337. All of this served to attract even more warriors to the Ottoman cause. Although there were occasional periods of peace (Orkhan married a Byzantine princess), for the most part the Moslem Ottomans and the Christian Byzantines were at odds. Orkhan's son Suleiman led troops across the Dardanelles to conquer Thrace, and the empire's capital was transferred from Brusa to Adrianople. In 1453, another of Osman's descendants, Mehmet, captured Constantinople. He renamed the city Istanbul and it remained the capital of the Ottoman Empire until its demise in 1919.

The Ottomans succeeded where the Seljuks failed because they were able to overcome their nomadic heritage. "The astonishing achievement of the Ottomans was breaking the cycle of birth, short life, then dissolution that characterized the earlier nomadic empires" (McCarthy, *The Ottoman Turks,* p. 36). This was the result primarily of the uncanny abilities of the first nine Ottoman sultans, who put together a 200-year chain of able rulers. By maintaining war against the Byzantines, then the Christians of southeastern Europe, and then the Shi'ites of Persia, the Ottomans were able to harness the warlike nature of their people. However, by adopting Christian/European advisors, military advancements, and technology, they gradually introduced a more settled lifestyle. The sultan ruled from the capital, and the provinces pretty much ruled themselves, but a common culture, religion, and economic life held the population together. Osman's life of warfare against the Byzantines and his legacy of wisdom and strength in leadership turned the city of Brusa into an imperial capital and then, when it was left behind for bigger and better power centers, a beautiful city: "The successors of Orkhan beautified and sanctified the city by building mosques and tombs, the earliest Ottoman shrines" (Muller, *The Loom of History,* p. 301).

References: Koprulu, Mehmet. *The Seljuks of Anatolia.* Translated by Gary Leiser. Salt Lake City: University of Utah Press, 1992; McCarthy, Justin. *The Ottoman Turks.* New York: Longman, 1997; Muller, Herbert. *The Loom of History.* New York: Harper & Brothers, 1958; Parry, V. J. *A History of the Ottoman Empire to 1730.* Cambridge, UK: Cambridge University Press, 1976.

CRÉCY
26 August 1346

FORCES ENGAGED

English: Approximately 11,000 men,
including 3,900 men-at-arms.
Commander: King Edward III.

French: Approximately 60,000, including 12,000
to 20,000 knights. Commander: King Philip VI.

IMPORTANCE

Victory of the English marked their arrival
as an international army of note and began the
long decline of the cavalry as the dominant
force in the military.

Historical Setting

When French King Charles IV died without a male heir in 1327, the ruling line of Capet came to an end. Although English King Edward III was a more direct descendant, he at first conceded the throne to the favorite of the French nobility, Philip Valois. He paid homage to him as Philip VI in return for a guarantee of continued English possession of the Duchy of Acquitaine, just north of the Pyrenees and that had come into English possession when Eleanor of Acquitaine married English King Henry II in the previous century. By 1340, however, Edward changed his mind and decided to lay claim to the French throne. By this time, the English and French had begun fighting what came to be called the Hundred Years' War (actually intermittent fighting between 1337 and 1453). The reasons for war were the Anglo-French rivalry over the wool trade centered in Flanders, as well as French support for Scottish rebellions against England.

The first major English victory came at the naval battle of Sluys in 1340, wherein Edward's longbowmen aboard some 150 vessels slaughtered a French force aboard 190 ships. The battle led to no strategic advantage, but did prove the worth of the longbow against armored troops. Unfortunately for the French, they failed to grasp that. Thus, when Edward committed troops to France over the next few years, he held a tactical advantage that the French failed to appreciate.

Edward reigned over a country that was much poorer than France in terms of money, but the nature of his army was vastly superior to that of the French. For the previous few centuries, the dominant practice of feudalism bound all the adult males of the realm to a term of service for their lords, who in turn gave that service to their king. This could produce large armies, but rarely ones that were well trained or motivated. Edward, on the other hand, introduced the system of indenture, whereby his nobles recruited men well versed with their weapons and paid them. Thus, the English army became professionals, and were recruited on the basis of talent with arms rather than being levied from the masses. In combat against the Scots, Edward's army solidified its professionalism and gained valuable experience. The armies he committed to France were made up of veteran soldiers, and they faced mixed forces of French noble knights and, at best, semi-trained peasants.

Edward had troops based in Acquitaine, and they faced an invading French force in the spring of 1346. To relieve pressure on his men, besieged in Aiguillon, Edward marshaled his forces to threaten northern France. Edward's army of some 15,000 men arrived on the Normandy coast on 13 July 1346. Normandy was unprepared for war and the loot was enormous. Edward launched a *chevauchée,* something like an attacking scorched-earth policy. His intent was to pillage the countryside of everything valuable and spread terror through rape, torture, and killing, thereby inflicting a terrible dread on the population. It was immensely successful, with all his men getting their fill of wealth and depravity. His army terrorized their way to Paris, but did not attack the city. Philip was massing his own force on the outskirts of town, so Edward withdrew northward, burning and destroying as he went. Philip almost caught up to him near Abbeville near the mouth of the Somme River, but the English managed to locate a ford just before the tide swelled the river, leaving the French on the far side.

The Battle

Edward encamped his troops at Crécy-en-Ponthieu, where they rested in the wake of their recent narrow escape. They replenished their stocks of food and wine from local houses and shops. Edward also deployed his men in a strong defensive position: his northern left flank was anchored on a stream, the Maie, while his right rested on the immense Crécy Forest. The only avenue of attack was across a downward slope into the front of the English position, providing an open field of fire for the English longbowmen.

Edward's army by this time had dwindled down to about 11,000: 2,000 knights and men-at-arms, 500 light cavalry, 7,000 English and Welsh longbowmen, and 1,500 skirmishers armed with long knives. He deployed his men thus: 4,000 on the right commanded by 16-year-old Prince Edward (called the Black Prince); 800 men-at-arms in the center with 2,000 archers on either side; the knife-wielding skirmishers in the rear; on the left, another 500 men-at-arms with 1,200 archers arrayed on either side of them; and, under the command of Edward, a reserve of 700 men-at-arms, 2,000 archers, and the rest of the skirmishers. Having deployed his men, Edward circulated among them with words of encouragement that seemed to have great effect, and then he allowed the men to eat and drink their fill. Placing himself in a mill overlooking the battlefield, Edward received word of the French approach at noon on Saturday, 26 August 1346.

The French host, rather than being an army, was more a swarm with little discipline or coordination. Philip had sent a few knights ahead of his troops to reconnoiter, and they returned with news of the English position.

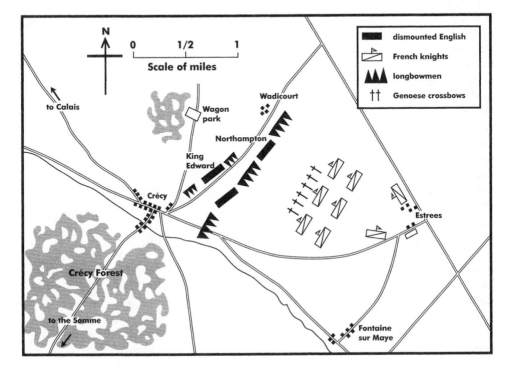

They counseled that Philip draw his men up before the English, stay the night, and then attack on the following morning. Philip agreed, but many of his nobles did not. As they and their retainers approached Crécy, they were intent on closing as soon as possible. This was based both on their desire to cover themselves in glory as well as to get the highest-ranking English prisoners for themselves. Rank equaled wealth, and the ransoming of prisoners was a profitable enterprise in those days. Further, the nobles considered themselves more allies than vassals of the king, so responding to orders was not to their liking.

The first French contingent that arrived on the battlefield was commanded by the nearly blind King John of Bohemia, still a fearsome warrior in spite of his sight difficulties. He was accompanied by Charles, Comte de Alençon, who was Philip's brother. In the English camp, trumpets sounded, and the men returned to their positions as the French forces spread out before them. They began to deploy at about 1600 hours, and the French troops continued to come up over the next 2 hours. In the front came 6,000 to 8,000 crossbowmen from Genoa, the only professional troops among the French army. Behind them massed the armored knights, jockeying for position. Rather than spend the night scouting out the field and resting from the day's march, the impetus of the French movement meant battle that day. At 1800 hours, a quick, heavy rainstorm struck, but broke after several minutes of soaking the field. In its wake, the sun returned to a clear sky, but it was setting directly behind the English. What light remained in the day was in the French soldiers' eyes.

The Genoese opened the battle by advancing toward the English and loosing a shower of quarrels. They were launched at too great a range to be effective, but from a distance that put them well within range of the longbow. The English launched the first volley of arrows, and great gaps appeared in the Genoese ranks. Firing as many as five arrows a minute—as opposed to no more than two per minute for the crossbow—the English bowmen dealt a terrible slaughter. After several volleys, the surviving crossbowmen broke and ran. The French knights expected nothing less of commoners, and were glad that the time had now come for them to enter the fray. Riding through and over the Genoese, the first wave of French heavy cavalry swarmed toward the English lines. Long before the French cavalry could close with their enemy, the English arrows were piercing their armor and slaying their mounts. Dozens of knights fell and the rest drew back. The longbowmen's deployment allowed them to pour a heavy crossfire into the mass of men and horses, and the dismounted English men-at-arms were unharmed.

Undaunted, the French nobles rallied and charged again, and again were slaughtered and driven back. Through the waning hours of the day twelve to fifteen cavalry charges were launched. Some indeed managed to break through the hail of arrows and close with their English counterparts, and at times the fighting was fierce. The cavalry could not get to the bowmen, however, because they were safe behind an array of sharpened stakes. Among the nobles, the dismounted English fought shoulder to shoulder with their recruits, and with spear, sword, and battle-ax inflicted many more French casualties than they themselves suffered. On the English right flank, the troops commanded by Prince Edward, a mere 16 years old, engaged in some of the most difficult combat of the day. When pressed for reinforcements, his father the king is said to have replied, "Let the boy win his spurs." He did so.

Results

Darkness finally brought the fighting to an end. Edward ordered his men to stand their ground for the night. This did not keep many of the spearmen from breaking ranks and finishing off some of the wounded nobles in order to plunder their bodies for jewelry. This exasperated

dieu. Qui eust peu pren
dre partie des condicions du
Roy nre maystre et partie des
siennes / on en eust bien fait
vng prince parfaict / Car
sans nulle doubte le Roy en
sens le passoit de trop / et la
fin la monstre par ses œuures.

▪ Icy parle par Incident
des guerres qui furent en
Angleterre ou mesme temps.

E me suys oublie
en parlant de ces
matieres precedētes
de parler du Roy
Edouard dangleterre / Car ces
trois seigneurs ont regne dūg
temps grandz Cestassauoir
nre Roy et led Duc de bour
gongne et led Roy Edouard.
Je ne vous garde point loirde
descrire qui sont les hystones
ny nomme les armees ny
proprement le temps que

King Edward III of England at the Battle of Crécy. From Mèmoires de Phillipe de Commines, *Ms. 18, fol.
73v. Early sixteenth century. Musèe Dobrèe, Nantes, France. (Giraudon/Art Resource, New York)*

Edward and his nobles, for it meant that many fewer Frenchmen to be held for ransom. The following morning, the tail of the French army caught up to the body and tried its hand at the English, but were quickly driven off. With Philip in retreat, Edward and his men then left their positions and explored the battlefield.

Approximately 1,500 French knights were killed or captured, and another 10,000 foot soldiers lay dead. The English casualties numbered less than 100, and many of them were the insubordinate spearmen who tried to reap their rewards before the battle was completely over.

AGINCOURT

The English and their longbows continued to decimate the French aristocracy, and the French continued sending their knights into combat. The battle of Crécy marked the beginning of the decline of the armored knight, but the battle of Agincourt marked the last gasp. The Hundred Years' War had seen combat intermittently since 1337, with a large pause in the middle of the fourteenth century because of the arrival of the bubonic plague. England had had little success in establishing primacy in France, but King Henry V decided to try again. English nobles were squabbling among themselves, and Henry decided that a war would quiet domestic bickering. After engaging in negotiations designed to make the English seemed the injured party, Henry launched his invasion in 1415.

He landed in France with 10,000 to 11,000 men, but after several months of campaigning that number had dwindled by at least 3,000. Although he finally was able to capture the fortress city of Harfleur, the swampy terrain in the region provoked an outbreak of amoebic dysentery in his army. Had the city held on another week or two, Henry would probably have abandoned the siege. Once he had garrisoned the newly captured city, however, he marched the rest of his men through the early autumn rains toward Normandy. The forces of French King Charles VI were soon in pursuit, and the two armies met near the village of Agincourt in late October 1415. The French army of some 40,000 spent the night before the battle partying in their plush pavilions, while Henry's ragged and ailing troops camped in the rain. On the morning of 24 October, the English army of less than 6,000 lined up across the muddy field from the thousands of French noble knights, most of them mounted in the first ranks.

When the French would not attack, Henry ordered his men forward. They stopped 200 yards short of the French force and proceeded to drive pointed stakes into the ground at an angle toward the French, who did nothing to harass them. Once deployed, Henry ordered his archers to do their work, and they did. As the yard-long arrows fell out of the sky through the armor of the mounted knights, they rallied themselves to charge. The rain of arrows after the days of rainfall equaled a battlefield littered with the corpses of horses and men unable to gain solid footing. When the cavalry failed, the knights decided to close on foot.

Sinking into the muck because of the weight of their suits of armor, the nobles made slow progress and were slaughtered by the longbows every step of the way. When finally they closed with the English, their valor and numbers almost prevailed, but Henry's knights fought just as valiantly. As the French fell in the mud in the narrow battlefield, piles of men grew. The archers, unable to wield their bows at such close range, entered the fray on foot, killing downed knights by sliding daggers through faceplates or any chink in the armor. It is said the bodies were piled higher than a man's head. At the end of the day, the rain, the mud, the arrows, and the desperation of the outnumbered English spelled French doom. The execution of many of the prisoners cost the English multiple fortunes in ransom, but a potential counterattack had to be faced and the huge number of prisoners could not be guarded if the enemy reserve attacked the rear as expected. The death of so many French nobles, between 7,000 and 10,000, spelled the demise of French chivalry. Never again would knights be the mainstay of European armies.

The English victory at Crécy had little long-standing effect on the Hundred Years' War. It did allow Edward to withdraw unopposed to Calais, which he proceeded to besiege. It took a year, but he finally occupied that coastal city, and it remained in English hands for the following two centuries. Although strategically the battle may have been only of passing importance, it had two major effects.

First, the English army became recognized as a force of some repute. Since at least the days of William the Conqueror and Hastings, the French had dominated European warfare because they had the greatest number of nobles, and the mounted knight was the primary component of medieval armies. The English had not fought any army of distinction. The continental military men considered victories over the Welsh and Scots as nothing to brag about, but it was those wars that laid the foundation of Edward's victory at Crécy. The concept of indenture meant the introduction of troops that trained with their weapons and fought for pay and whatever loot they might acquire in the process. The fact that the longbowmen by law were required to practice with their weapons every weekend meant that Edward and his nobles had a vast pool of talent upon which to draw, and they could therefore sign up the best archers rather than take whatever was available as the French lords did. Local recruiting also meant stronger unit cohesion, and the English noble's willingness to train and fight alongside his troops meant a vastly higher morale than could be built in the French ranks. From 1346 onward, English arms could no longer be discounted.

The second major result of this battle was the signal that the days of the supremacy of the mounted knight were numbered. The heavy horses bred for carrying a man in armor were so expensive that only the nobles could afford them. The large number of nobles in France meant that this armored fighting machine could overwhelm most smaller and lighter enemies. Less wealthy opponents could pay for neither horse nor armor, and thus could not compete. The introduction of the longbow changed all that. Able to pierce armor at more than 200 yards, the longbow meant that the mounted knight became little more than a large target. It would take a long time for the French to finally accept this reality, for Henry V's army at Agincourt in 1415 repeated the tactics and results of Crécy. The commoner with a missile weapon now had the ability to overcome a noble. That in itself brought a new public view of the nature of feudalism; when gunpowder weapons appeared in the following century, armored knights became an anachronism that neither aristocrats nor generals could afford.

References: Allmand, C. T. *The Hundred Years War: England and France at War.* Cambridge, UK: Cambridge University Press, 1988; Fuller, J. F. C. *A Military History of the Western World,* vol. 1. New York: Funk & Wagnalls, 1954; Sumption, Jonathan. *The Hundred Years War: Trial by Battle.* Philadelphia: University of Pennsylvania Press, 1988; Vale, Malcolm. *English Gascony, 1399–1453.* London: Oxford University Press, 1970; Wailly, Henri. *Crecy, 1346: Anatomy of a Battle.* Poole, Dorset: Blandford, 1987.

ORLÉANS
12 October 1428–7 May 1429

FORCES ENGAGED
French: Garrison: 2,400 soldiers and 3,000 armed citizens. Commander: Jean Dunois, comte de Longueville. Relieving force: 4,000 soldiers. Commanders: Duke of Alençon and Jeanne d'Arc.
English: 5,000 soldiers. Commander: Earl of Salisbury until his death and then the earl of Shrewsbury.

IMPORTANCE
Jeanne d'Arc's leadership inspired the dispirited French nation; English impetus halted, and the French began to gain the advantage in the Hundred Years' War.

Historical Setting

During the course of the Hundred Years' War, the momentum shifted back and forth between the combatants. Edward III's victories at Sluys and Crécy gave England the early advantage, but during the middle part of the fourteenth century the spread of the bubonic plague halted fighting and robbed either side of any advantage. For the several years that the Black Death ravaged France and England, major societal changes occurred. As farmers either died from the plague or fled the countryside for the cities, feudal lords saw their incomes fall rapidly. The cities, on the other hand, began to enjoy a blossoming economy. The fear of death encouraged many citizens to pay for extravagant sundries to enjoy their last days on earth, and merchants and artisans grew rich. As the cities gained in wealth and the manors declined, the king began courting the financial support of the townspeople for his royal projects, including warfare. Soldiers thus became paid employees rather than feudal pawns, and the aristocrats' fortunes further waned.

More importantly from a social point of view, the unexplained epidemic meant that many people turned to the church for answers and solace. Thus, the power of the church also grew as more of the population became increasingly religious. Some viewed the plague as the wrath of God, whereas others blamed the traditional scapegoats, the Jews. In France, blame was laid on the English. Whatever the cause, people believed that the deliverance had to come from God.

While the plague raged, the war took a back seat, and English gains melted away. By default, momentum shifted to the French. When Henry V came to the throne of England in 1413, he claimed the French throne just as Edward had done. After his victory at Agincourt in 1415, he was able to wrest the throne away from the heir of Charles VI and for a few years reigned as king of England and France. His untimely death in 1422 reopened the question of the succession to the French throne. The English named Henry's infant son as rightful king, whereas the French supported Charles VI's son as King Charles VII. He certainly had the proper bloodline for claiming the throne, but unfortunately he had nothing else. While officially claiming the throne, he did nothing to actually rule, for he was an incredibly weak character. Thus, while Charles vacillated, the regent for England's Henry VI, the duke of Bedford, proceeded to reestablish English dominance in France. Aided by an alliance with the powerful Duchy of Burgundy, Bedford placed all of France north of the Loire under English control. Everything seemed to be going England's way, and the decades of war, plague, and poor leadership all conspired against France. The people of France could only pray for a miracle to deliver their country.

Enter Jeanne d'Arc. Born to a well-to-do common family in the eastern province of Lorraine, Jeanne lived a fairly normal life until she reached her teen years. At age 13, she began hearing voices, which she was convinced came from Saints Margaret and Catherine (earlier queens of France) and the archangel Michael. At age 17, she was told by the voices that she was chosen to assist in France's liberation and force the useless Charles VII to actually take control of France.

The Battle

Jeanne's heavenly directive coincided with Bedford's latest offensive against the French. With almost all of northern France under his control, Bedford aimed to conquer Armagnac, the lands south of the Loire. His first target was Orléans, one of the fortress cities that lined the river. English forces commanded by the earl of Salisbury arrived at Orléans on 12 October 1428 and proceeded to surround the city as best they could. They numbered only about 5,000. Their first objective was to seize the fortified bridge across the Loire. This they did on 24 October, but Salisbury was killed in the at-

Jeanne d'Arc. From Antoine Dufour, "Vie des femmes cèlèbres." Ms. 17, French, c. 1505. Musèe Dobrèe, Nantes, France. (Giraudon/Art Resource, New York)

tempt. His temporary successor was the earl of Suffolk, but he was replaced in December by John Talbot, earl of Shrewsbury. The English maintained a steady artillery barrage against the city, but the cannonballs were made of stone and hence did not harm the thick stone walls much. The size of the besieging force meant that a secure investment of the city was impossible, and the English built small forts to protect their hold on the bridge as well as their encampments. Occasional forays by the French netted some supplemental supplies during the siege, but by the spring of 1329 the condition of the besieged was getting desperate.

It was Orléans that Jeanne was supposed to relieve. Through her uncle, a soldier, she managed to gain an escort to Chinon, where she finally gained an interview with Charles after a month's grilling by church and military personnel. Why Charles should have granted a teenage girl command of an army is a question that has never been answered, but his personal vice of visiting soothsayers may have influenced his decision to deal with someone who heard voices from the beyond. She was assigned co-commander, along with the duke of Alençon, of a force of 4,000. As they approached Orléans, Jeanne sent a letter to the English demanding their withdrawal; not surprisingly, it was ignored. Commanded by her voices to enter the city from the north, she had to overcome the wishes of the other officers, who feared challenging the English directly. She convinced them to ferry her and the army across the Loire to the north bank, between the city and the English camp at St. Loup. She marched her troops north, waited a night, and then marched them back to the city on 29 April 1429 and through the gate she had been instructed to use. She had so far followed her instructions against little enemy opposition.

For a few days, little happened because the defenders within Orléans did not want to attack the English. She assured them of God's leadership and protection; when she heard of English reinforcements approaching, she celebrated, ordering that she be alerted as soon as they arrived or she would behead the comte de Longueville, commander of the Orléans garrison. On 1 May, after a short truce, she jumped up from her slumber and announced that it was time to attack. She quickly donned her armor and mounted her white horse, riding out of the city. She found that a French sally against the fort at St. Loup was taking place and not going well. She dashed to the battle, rallied the French, and the fort fell. The French lost two dead, whereas all the English defenders were killed in the battle. She commanded the entire army to praise God and confess their sins and proceeded to banish all prostitutes following the army. She allowed no fighting the following day, the Feast of the Ascension, but announced that the English would be gone within 5 days. Another appeal to the English to withdraw was met with obscene shouts, so she had no choice but to prepare for battle.

On 5 May, Jeanne led a sortie out the south gate of the city, which led to the bridge whose southern end the English had captured in the first days of the siege. She bypassed the bridge and led her troops across the shallows to an island in the Loire and then used a boat bridge to reach the southern bank. The French quickly captured a fort at St. Jean le Blanc and then marched toward the larger fort at Les Augustins, near the bridge. The fight for that fort was difficult and costly for both sides, but Jeanne led a charge that swept an English sally back into the fort and ultimately into French hands. On 6 May, the French assaulted Les Tournelles, the towers at the southern end of the bridge. In the midst of the fighting, Jeanne was struck by an arrow and carried from the field. It turned out to be little more than a flesh wound, and by late afternoon she was back in the fight. After 10 minutes of prayer, she led her exhausted troops in an attack on another English sortie that quickly retreated into the towers.

On 7 May, a French knight took Jeanne's banner and made for Les Tournelles. She tried to stop him, but, when the French soldiers saw her banner, they rushed to follow it. Bringing assault ladders, they scaled the walls with Jeanne in the lead. The 400 to 500 English defenders tried to flee, but died as the burning bridge, which was their escape route, collapsed. The next day the English abandoned the siege, and

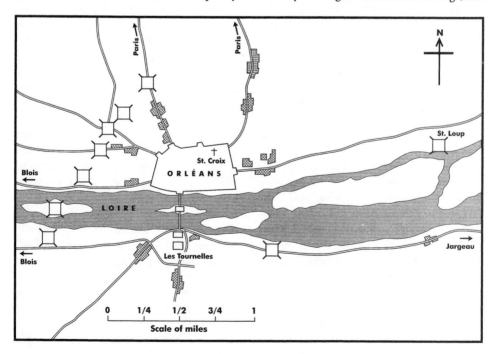

the French troops reentered Orléans after killing or capturing all the English troops left on the south side of the river. When the English destroyed their camps and marched away on 9 May, many French soldiers wanted to attack the retreating column, but Jeanne forbade it. It was Sunday, and only fighting in self-defense was allowed. On Monday, they did strike at the English and captured some artillery and supplies.

Results

When Charles heard of the relief of Orléans, he took complete credit, never mentioning Jeanne in his missives. The French citizenry knew who really won the battle, however, and the numbers of the French army swelled. Jeanne led attacks against English garrisons in towns throughout the region and liberated a number of towns. On 18 June, she led a charge against Shrewsbury's army, lately reinforced by 1,000 mercenaries. Her 6,000 troops inflicted 4,000 English casualties as the enemy was routed. The next day at the battle of Patay, the French surprised an English ambush and routed them yet again; Shrewsbury was captured. "[B]eyond the local decisions at Orléans and Patay, an answer had at last been found to that English system of war which enabled the smaller nation to bring France to the edge of national collapse. Most obviously the solution lay in the release of moral forces. *In hoc signo vinces* can be quite as useful a military weapon as a sword or a cannon" (Pratt, *The Battles That Changed History*, p. 128).

Joining with Charles, Jeanne urged him to make his way to Reims to be crowned king of France. She led the force that escorted him, capturing without a fight the city of Troyes from a Burgundian garrison. Reims also was under Burgundian control and the French had no siege equipment, but Jeanne was undaunted. She told her troops to "advance boldly and fear nothing," and that city also surrendered without opposition. Charles was duly crowned king on 16 July 1429.

Jeanne led an attack on Paris, also held by Burgundian forces, although she heard no voices directing her to do so. She was wounded in the leg during the fighting, and Charles ordered the French to retreat. After disbanding his army, only a few hundred men of Jeanne's personal unit campaigned with her in 1430, and their numbers were too few to accomplish the heavenly directives she received. She fell prisoner to the Burgundians, and Charles refused to ransom her. Sold to the English, she was tried as a witch. The trial was a sham that resulted in her execution at the stake on 30 May 1431. In spite of the stacked deck against her, the prosecution could find not one witness to speak against her.

Jeanne d'Arc is better known outside France by her English appellation Joan of Arc. Much about her short life and career, although well documented, remains mysterious. What caused the voices she heard and the bright lights that accompanied them, which only she could hear and see? Whatever may be the actual cause, the heavenly explanation is the only one that matters. Everyone in France knew of her voices, and in a time of religious intolerance of anything uncommon, she convinced experts and laypeople alike that she was indeed blessed. A population newly emerged from the horror of the Black Death and intent on following God's will saw her as a divine emissary. Clad in a white-enameled suit of armor, riding a white horse, carrying a white and blue banner emblazoned with two angels and the words "Jhesus Maria," called *La Pucelle* (the Virgin) by her troops, everything about her spoke of holiness. For a citizenry that had believed that only a miracle could rescue France, Jeanne was it. Nothing else explains why hardened veterans would not only follow her into combat but accept without complaint her demands that they neither curse nor visit prostitutes.

Jeanne's strategy changed the fortune of this war. She began reversing the tactics practiced by the French throughout the conflict, tactics of frontal assault against prepared

---

GOD'S AGENT?

Whatever was the cause of Jeanne d'Arc's voices, the record of her activities certainly suggests that, if she was not divinely inspired, she was very lucky.

She convinced her uncle, a soldier, to take her, a "mere girl child," to the local garrison commander. She convinced the garrison commander to provide her with a military escort to see the Dauphin, Charles. She and the military escort rode for 11 days through enemy territory without being stopped. After a month of questioning by clerics who could find no reason to doubt her story, she was allowed to see Charles. He exchanged clothes with one of his courtiers and hid among the crowd at court, yet when she entered the room she walked straight up to him and addressed him as the king. After 5 minutes of private discussion, she convinced him to provide her with an army.

When she left for Orléans, she sent a message to the members of St. Catherine's Church in Ferbois to dig under its stone floor near the altar, where they would find a sword. They did. She had never been to the town, and no one in Ferbois had any notion of such a relic under their church. Although she ate little, she comfortably wore a suit of armor, sometimes for days at a stretch. Veteran soldiers followed her and took

her orders, in spite of the fact that she was a 17-year-old girl with no military experience.

When her troops needed to float upriver past the English positions in order to cross the Loire, the winds as well as the current were against them. On her word, the winds shifted direction and picked up force, driving her flotilla upriver. Against the advice of the other officers, she followed her directive to enter Orléans by the north gate; although the English army originally barred the way, when she approached they were elsewhere. In the wake of her first battle, she cried over a wounded Englishman, holding him as he died. She predicted that her enemy would abandon the siege within 5 days, and that came to pass.

She survived numerous battles, although she never wielded a weapon, just her banner. Her mere presence and personality were sufficient to force the surrenders of two cities without a fight.

More than 600 witnesses had their testimony recorded at her trial, and not one negative comment was made. Thirty-nine of forty-two prosecuting attorneys begged the court for clemency. In spite of being abandoned by the king she had made, she never said a word against him nor showed the slightest public hint of despair.

English lines. As long as she kept to that plan, French forces won. More importantly, as mentioned earlier, as much as the loss of troops in the field, it was the shift in morale that secured the English defeat. After Orléans and Patay, the fortunes of the English in France began to wane. The war itself dragged on for more than 20 years, but after Orléans the fate of France seems to have been sealed. Considering the lack of leadership provided by Charles, it is amazing that the French fighting spirit survived Jeanne's death. But infighting among the English and Burgundians proved as helpful to France as Jeanne, the Maid of Orléans. Few in France doubt the wisdom of her sanctification by the Catholic Church in 1920.

Had England prevailed and established a long-term dominant presence in France, how would that have changed the course of events? Possibly as much as did the Norman invasion of 1066. The administration that the British had begun to operate in northern France was made up primarily of French bureaucrats. Acceptance of French advisors and functionaries by the English monarchs could well have had more influence in England than the English would have had in France, which could have affected the entire process of democracy in England and its possessions.

References: Fuller, J. F. C. *A Military History of the Western World,* vol. 1. New York: Funk & Wagnalls, 1954; Gies, Frances. *Joan of Arc: The*

Legend and the Reality. New York: Harper & Row, 1981; Pratt, Fletcher. *The Battles That Changed History.* Garden City, NY: Doubleday, 1956; Sumption, Jonathan. *The Hundred Years War: Trial by Battle.* Philadelphia: University of Pennsylvania Press, 1988; Wheeler, Bonnie, and Charles T. Wood, eds. *Fresh Verdicts on Joan of Arc.* New York: Garland, 1996.

CONSTANTINOPLE

February–May 1453

FORCES ENGAGED

Turkish: 90,000 men. Commander: Sultan Mohammed II.
Byzantine: Less than 10,000 men. Commander: Emperor Constantine XI Paleologus.

IMPORTANCE

This battle accomplished the final destruction of the Byzantine Empire and opened Europe to the spread of Islam. It also marked the arrival of the Ottoman Turks as the dominant Moslem faction until the twentieth century.

Historical Setting

When Constantine the Great established the city of Constantinople as his capital in 323, he occupied the former city of Byzantium, which had controlled for centuries the straits separating Asia and Europe. The Sea of Marmora is flanked northeast and southwest by the Bosporus and the Dardanelles, two narrow passages that link the Mediterranean and the Black Seas. Unless one plans to go completely around the Black Sea, the only way from Europe into Asia Minor is across one of those straits, and Byzantium/Constantinople/Istanbul has therefore been an extremely strategic possession for both land and naval warfare, as well as overland and maritime trade.

As Rome faded and Constantinople rose in power, Constantinople became the seat of the Eastern Roman, or Byzantine, Empire. It

was not only the political capital of much of the Mediterranean and Middle East, it was the seat of the Greek Orthodox Church, rival to the power of the pope in Rome for the souls of Christians everywhere. In the end, it was the religious rather than political differences that spelled Constantinople's doom.

In the seventh century, Mohammed the Prophet founded Islam. Claiming his divinely inspired teachings, the Koran, to be the successor to the Bible and the fulfillment of God's plan for humanity, he oversaw the spread of his faith by both proselytization and warfare. By coincidence (or divine intervention) Mohammed arrived on the scene in Arabia just as the two major Middle Eastern powers, Persia and the Byzantine Empire, had fought each other to an exhausted standstill. Mohammed was therefore able to undertake a massive territorial acquisition hand in hand with the spread of his faith, and both Persia and the Byzantine Empire suffered major losses of real estate, as well as major losses of converts to Islam who found it less oppressive than the ultraconservative Orthodox Church.

For 700 years, the forces of Islam and Orthodoxy struggled against each other, with both sides trading ascendancy. By the fifteenth century, however, the Byzantine Empire had shrunk to almost nothing: Constantinople and a handful of Aegean islands. An earlier threat to the city by Islam had resulted in the Crusades in the twelfth century, but those too had ended in further alienation between the Catholic and Orthodox Churches. When in 1452 Sultan Mohammed II, son of Murad II, decided that Constantinople needed to be his, European response to pleas for help were almost entirely negative. England and France were just winding down their own costly Hundred Years' War. Germanic and Spanish princes and kings hinted at aid but sent nothing. Only in Italy was there any positive reaction. Genoa and Venice did not want to see Constantinople fall into the hands of Arab merchants, and

Rome promised aid if the Orthodox Church would submit to papal will. To save his city, Emperor Constantine XI Paleologus would make any bargain, so he agreed to Rome's demand; it netted him a mere 200 archers for his meager defenses. Constantine's decision was not a popular one among many Byzantines, who opined that they preferred Turkish domination to Roman.

In the spring of 1452, Mohammed II sent 1,000 masons to the Bosporus to begin construction of a fort with which to cover the transport of his men across the straits. Constantine could do little more than lodge a protest because he numbered among his citizens a mere 5,000 native and 2,000 foreign soldiers. He did, however, have tradition on his side, for the triple walls that blocked the city from the landward side had withstood twenty sieges in the city's history, even though they were at this point not in the best of repair. He also had, as of January 1453, the services of the Italian soldier of fortune Giovanni Giustiniani, who arrived with 700 knights and archers. Giustiniani was well known in Europe for his talents in defending walled cities. Unfortunately, Mohammed also had some European assistance in the form of a cannon maker named Urban from Hungary, who provided the Moslem army with seventy cannon, including the "Basilica," a cannon 27 feet long and firing stone balls weighing upward of 600 pounds. It could fire only seven times a day, but did significant damage to anything it struck, including the city walls.

The rest of Constantinople was defended by a single wall that ran the circumference of the city's seaward sides. As Mohammed had chosen to cross his men to the north, across the Bosporus, the southern approach was open to the Mediterranean. The primary harbor inlet, called the Golden Horn, was protected by a chain boom across its mouth backed by twenty-six galleys. Thus, the route for relief was open, if indeed any would be forthcoming.

The Battle

Mohammed II arrived before Constantinople's walls on 6 April 1453. He led 70,000 regular troops and 20,000 irregulars called Bashi-Bazouks, who were fighting only for the loot they might gain when and if the city fell. The premier troops were the Janissaries. These were slave soldiers taken captive in their youth from Christian families and raised in a military atmosphere to serve the sultans. They were heavily armored and highly skilled, and at Constantinople they were beginning to use personal firearms for the first time. Mohammed's first act was to seize the town of Pera across the Golden Horn from Constantinople. At first it was little more than symbolic, but had serious ramifications later. He then arrayed his forces on the city's western face and prepared for the siege. The northern end of the city was protected by a single wall, near the imperial palace. It was there, in a section called the Blachernae, that Constantine placed the greatest portion of his men.

On 18 April, Mohammed decided that the previous 12 days' cannonade had softened up the defenses sufficiently for an assault. A narrow breach in the walls was easily defended, and the Byzantine troops killed 200 attackers and drove off the remainder without loss to themselves. On 20 April, lookouts on the seawall saw the sails of four ships approaching from the south, three Genoese transports with men and supplies from Rome and a Byzantine ship hauling corn from Sicily. After a hard fight with the Moslem fleet, they managed to break through, clear the boom, and enter the Golden Horn. Mohammed decided he had to control the harbor, but he could not pass the chain boom. He therefore ordered ships to be dragged overland, through the town of Pera, to the harbor. It was a monumental feat of engineering, and on 22 April, thirty Turkish ships were in the Golden Horn. The Byzantine counterattack was betrayed by an agent of the sultan and managed to destroy only a single Turkish ship. In spite of this Turkish accomplishment, the presence of the ships in the Golden Horn had little effect on the siege.

Mohammed continued his cannonade against the walls, and by 6 May had opened another breach at the Gate of St. Romanus, where the Lycus River enters the city. Giustiniani, rather than trying to repair the wall under fire, instead built a new one just behind the breach. When the Turks attacked on 7 May, their 25,000 men were thrown back after 3 hours of fighting. On 12 May, another breach in the wall at the Blachernae was assaulted and only quick reinforcement by Constantine and the Imperial Guard was able to stem the tide. Mohammed

then tried undermining the walls, but Constantine had on his staff Johannes Grant, who managed to locate each of the mining attempts and either undermine the mines or destroy the attackers inside with explosives, flooding, or the incendiary Greek fire. None of the fourteen mines succeeded in damaging any walls.

Mohammed then determined to try scaling the walls. He had a siege tower constructed and rolled into place before the Charisius Gate, the northernmost opening in the city walls. Bombardment had destroyed one of the defending towers in the walls, and the siege tower was able to provide covering fire for Turks filling in the moat before the wall. In desperation, Constantine called for volunteers for an attack

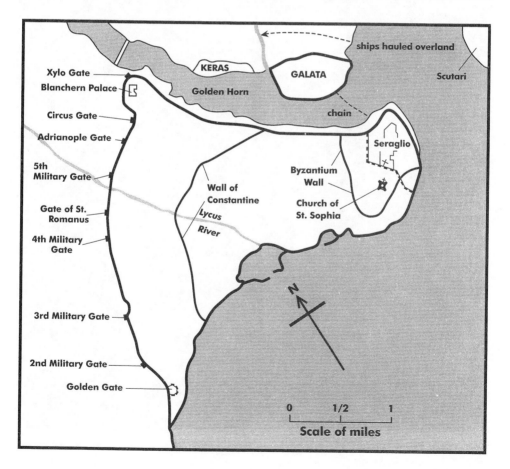

on the siege tower. It was unbelievably successful. Surprising the Turkish guards, the Byzantines broke pots of Greek fire on the wooden
siege tower while their compatriots spent the
night rebuilding the city wall and its destroyed
tower. The next morning, Mohammed saw only
the charred remains of his assault machine smol-
dering before the newly reconstructed tower in
the city wall.

In both camps, officers argued the pros and
cons of the siege. The defenders were exhausted
and running out of supplies. In Mohammed's
camp, some factions were for ending the siege
before a rumored rescue fleet could arrive. Instead, Mohammed favored those who counseled continuation, and the sultan decided on
one more attempt before giving up. The most
serious damage to the walls had been inflicted
along the Lycus River entrance to the city, and
it was there that he proposed to launch his final assault. A spy in the Turkish camp alerted
Constantine to the plan, but could his dwindling force hold on for one more battle? The
attack started at 0200 on 29 May with the

Jacopo Palma, First Attack on Constantinople by the Turks in 1453. *Oil on canvas. Palazzo Ducale, Venice,
Italy. (Erich Lessing/Art Resource, New York)*

EASTERN EUROPE PROTECTS THE WEST

If ever Islam was going to make its way into western Europe, Mohammed II had the best opportunity of taking it there. In the wake of Constantinople's fall, he was able to extend his reach into the Balkans, but was unable to make serious progress once he ran into the Hungarian defenses, captained by John Hunyadi, around Belgrade. Later Ottoman leaders would pass that obstacle, aiming toward the capital of the Holy Roman Empire at Vienna. The countries of western Europe were almost continually at each other's throats, with modern countries such as Italy, Germany, and Spain not yet in existence, but instead being comprised of multitudes of squabbling princes and petty kings. Had any

Ottoman sultan over the next hundred years been able to capture Vienna, the major military force of Europe would have been removed. A century after the Ottomans seized Constantinople their greatest commander, Sultan Suleiman the Magnificent, failed to take Vienna in three tries: 1529, 1543, and 1566. Vienna was saved from the final Ottoman attack in 1683 not by any western European power, many of which by this time did have significant military strength, but by the Polish commander Jan Sobieski. Eastern Europeans kept western Europeans from Islamic rule, just as they stood before Eastern nomadic invasions of the Mongols in the thirteenth century.

Bashi-Bazouks hurling themselves against the Byzantine defenses. For 2 hours, the Byzantines killed them with arrows and firearms, but grew increasingly tired in the process. As soon as the first attack was repulsed, Mohammed threw in the second wave before the defenders could catch their breath. Even though these were regular troops with better discipline and equipment, the narrow breach provided the defenders with less area to cover, and they threw back that assault as well.

After another 2 hours of fighting, the Byzantine troops could barely stand, but they now had to face the third wave, made up of Janissaries. Fighting on adrenalin alone, Constantine's troops repulsed them as well. As this was going on, however, a small band of Turks found a small open gate and rushed a handful of men through before it could be closed. When they seized a tower near the Blachernae and raised the sultan's banner, the rumor quickly spread that the northern flank had been broken. Simultaneously, Giovanni Giustiniani was severely wounded. His evacuation badly hurt his men's morale and, coupled with the report from the north quarter, the defenders began to fall back. Mohammed was quick to exploit his advantage. Another assault

by fresh Janissaries cleared the space between the walls and seized the Adrianople Gate, through which the attackers began to pour.

Results

Constantine XI led his last remaining troops into the Turkish onslaught and died for his city and empire. He was joined by almost all his co-defenders as well as a huge portion of the civilian population, for the Turks went on a rampage, looting Constantinople. Mohammed II limited very little of the pillage, reserving the best buildings for himself and banning their destruction. He appropriated the Church of St. Sophia, and within a week the Hagia Sophia was hosting Moslem services. The Turkish flags flying over the city were seen by the thirty ships of a Venetian fleet sailing to Constantine's relief, which turned around and sailed home.

The looting finally subsided, and the bulk of the population that was not killed was enslaved, possibly numbering 50,000 people. The bastion of eastern Christianity, which had stood against all opponents, fell after more than 1,100 years as Constantine the Great's city. For Mohammed II, it was merely another step in the expansion of his domain, for he proceeded to conquer Greece and most of the Balkans during the remaining 28 years of his reign.

Western Europe, which had done so little to assist Constantinople and the remnants of the Byzantine Empire, was shocked that it fell after so many centuries of standing fast against everyone. In Rome, the Catholic Church was dismayed that they would now have no eastern Christians to convert, as they were all rapidly becoming Moslem. The Eastern Orthodox Church did survive, however, because Mohammed allowed a patriarch, George Scholarius, to preside over the church. It remained, therefore, a viable religion, but now far from the reach of the Catholic Church's influence. As such, its survival heartened others who chafed under the pope's rule. Within 60 years, Martin Luther was leading a major protest against the Roman Catholic Church. That protest started the Reformation.

The trading centers of Genoa and Venice quaked at the thought of having to deal with the hard-bargaining Arab merchants that now completely controlled all products coming from the Far East. The major cities of eastern Europe began to fear the Turkish armies approaching their gates, and for the next 450 years Austria in particular carried on a constant struggle with the Ottoman Empire. The Ottoman Turks, who had been slowly establishing themselves as the premier Middle Eastern Moslem power, now held that title firmly and controlled at their height almost as much as the Byzantine Empire had: the Balkans, the Middle East, and much of North Africa. They also exercised naval control of the eastern Mediterranean until 1571, when Christian naval forces won the battle of Lepanto.

Still, all was not negative for western Europe. The flood of refugees from southeastern Europe, especially Greece, brought thousands of scholars to Italy, further enhancing the peninsula's Renaissance. Italian merchants, shocked at the exorbitant prices that the Moslems charged as dealers for spices and silks from the east, soon began to search for other ways

to get those goods. Within 30 years, Portuguese ships were exploring the coast of Africa for ways to India and China, and the Genoese captain Christopher Columbus soon thereafter convinced the Spanish monarchy to finance his dream of establishing a new trade route to the east. Certainly the age of European exploration came much sooner because of Constantinople's fall.

References: Antonucci, Michael. "Siege without Reprieve," *Military History* 9(1), April 1992; Durant, Will. *The Reformation.* New York: Simon & Schuster, 1957; Fuller, J. F. C. *A Military History of the Western World,* vol.1. New York: Funk & Wagnalls, 1954; Norwich, John J. *Byzantium: The Decline and Fall.* London: Viking, 1995; Runciman, Sir Steven. *The Fall of Constantinople—1453.* Cambridge, UK: University of Cambridge Press, 1968 [1903].

GRANADA
June–December 1491

FORCES ENGAGED
Castillian: Unknown.
Commander: King Ferdinand.
Moorish: Unknown. Commander:
King Muhammed XI (Abu Abdullah, Boabdil).

IMPORTANCE
Ferdinand's successful siege brought to an end Moorish control over Spain, ending a conflict that had lasted almost 700 years.

Historical Setting

The Iberian Peninsula has long been the site of conflict as well as a source of warriors. Iberian mercenaries composed the bulk of the Carthaginian army, and, after Rome defeated Carthage and occupied the peninsula in the wake of the Second Punic War (late third century B.C.), it drew on the population there as well. Roman culture dominated what came to be called Spain until the fourth century A.D., when the Romans were defeated by the invading Vandals, who moved on through to North Africa. Then the Visigoths took over after their long wanderings from Scandinavia through Europe. Those barbarian invasions infused even more warrior blood into the population. Over time, however, even warrior societies begin to soften and the Visigoths fell prey to the power of Islam in the early eighth century.

Moslem forces spreading their religion moved westward from Arabia in the late seventh century, conquering everything from Syria to Morocco. In 711, Moslem troops crossed the Straits of Gibraltar into Spain and soon conquered the peninsula. They would have used that as merely a base for further expansion but for a major defeat in 732 at Tours, at the hands of Frankish forces under the command of Charles Martel, forebear of Charlemagne. That battle determined that the Pyrenees would mark the border between western Islam and Christian Europe, but the two religions could never leave each other alone. The Moslems settled into Spain: troops originating in Arabia settled into the fertile eastern regions of modern Andalusia and Aragon, Syrian forces occupied the southern region of Granada, North African Berbers were granted lands in the central hill country, and mercenaries grabbed whatever land was left.

In the far northern provinces along the Bay of Biscay, a few Christian fortress holdouts remained independent. Over time, the two sides entered into a tenuous peace. After the caliphate that had been established at Cordova in the eighth century collapsed in the tenth, there was enough dissension between the Moslem provinces that no unified effort was launched at the Christians. Except for the occasional holy war declared by fundmentalists like the Almohads or Almoravids in North Africa, the Moslems, or Moors as they were called in Spain, became less warlike. The fervor aroused by the Christian Crusades, starting at the end of the eleventh century, created the opposite effect among the Christians. Indeed, some of the motivation for the Catholic Church's call for a war against the Moslems in the Holy Land grew from successes scored by Christian forces in Spain.

The Christians took the offensive under leaders such as Rodrigo de Vivar, known to history by his nickname El Cid (from the Arabic Al Sayyid, meaning chieftain), and King Alphonso VIII of Castile. These men, for their own gain or for their faith, began picking off the Moorish provinces one by one, until in the late 1400s only the southern province of Granada remained in Moslem hands. The city of Granada was the capital of the province of the same name, and it was targeted for conquest by Ferdinand II, king of the recently united Christian provinces of Aragon, Castille, and Leon. He and his wife Isabella of Castile formed a formidable team, and together they were determined that they would unify Spain into a completely Catholic country, this movement taking the name of *Reconquista,* the reconquest. In the summer of 1491, Ferdinand and Isabella's army marched up to Granada, home of the famous Alhambra Palace, to begin the siege of the final Moslem stronghold.

On the other side, the Moslems were led by King Muhammad XI, born Abu Abdullah, but better known to the Spanish as Boabdil. His father, Abu Hassan, had submitted to the demand from Ferdinand to pay an annual tribute to maintain peace, but in 1478 reneged on the pledge. Occupied with a war against Portugal, Ferdinand was unable to turn his attention to this matter until 1481. Thus, Abu Hassan had had 3 years to recruit troops and allies in North Africa and he was ready for war. He struck the first blow, attacking and pillaging the town of Zahara at the end of December. Ferdinand's main commander, the marquis of Cadiz, responded by capturing the fortress at Alhama, near the city of Granada. He held the city against Abu Hassan's recapture attempt, and the Moors retreated to Granada. There Abu Hassan was deposed by his son Boabdil, and he retired with some supporters to Malaga.

This created two factions in the Moorish ranks, with only their fear of Christian expansion in common.

Boabdil's forces were commanded by his father-in-law, Ibrahim Ali Atar, a 90-year-old soldier. Through 1482, he gave Ferdinand all he could handle until he was killed in battle at Sierra de Rute, after which Boabdil fell into Ferdinand's hands. Boabdil was released on the stipulation that he would pay tribute and surrender hostages, including his own son. That resulted in a 2-year truce, but also in increased hostility against him in the Moorish community. Abu Hassan was not about to follow his son's lead, and he continued his war with the Christians, but upon getting sick was succeeded by his brother Muhammad ibn Sa'ad, known as al-Zagal. Al-Zagal rallied the faithful and continued the conflict, to which Ferdinand replied by instituting a campaign of *talas*, an offensive scorched-earth policy designed to deny al-Zagal any resources. By 1485, the Christians had spit the province of Granada in two. Boabdil was sent to reacquire the capital city from his uncle al-Zagal, but instead the two joined together.

Ferdinand attacked his erstwhile ally at Loxa, and a major battle and then siege ensued. When the city finally fell after an intense bombardment, Boabdil was once again Ferdinand's prisoner. The war continued against al-Zagal, however, while Boabdil reestablished his throne in the city of Granada. In 1489, Ferdinand was able to occupy most of the remaining Moorish strongholds and force the surrender of al-Zagal; that resulted in Boabdil requesting negotiations to determine a long-lasting settlement between Christian and Moor. For some reason, Boabdil broke off the talks in the summer of 1490 and went on the offensive, which brought about Ferdinand's siege of the capital.

The city of Granada is built on two hills, one crowned by the Alhambra, the other by the Alcazaba fortress. Between is a small valley through which runs the Darro River, and the city is built between the heights. A wall surrounded it, as was typical of the day, reportedly surmounted by a thousand towers. Ferdinand's troops surrounded the city, while he established his headquarters in the nearby village of Atqa.

The Battle

After a time of relatively passive siege, the two forces met in July 1491 in the wake of an exchange of insults. In the midst of a sally against the Spanish, a Moorish soldier had flung his spear toward the king's pavilion. That night, a number of Spanish troops snuck into the city and attached a copy of the Ave Maria, a prayer, to the door of a mosque. The following day, the same Moor who had thrown the spear, named Yarfe, rode his horse in front of the Spanish lines with the Ave Maria tied to its tail. This last incident took place during a visit to the front by Queen Isabella, who was escorted to a point near the city by a large force of cavalry and heavy infantry under the command of the marquis of Cadiz, Don Rodrigo Ponce de Leon. The Moors had opened the gates and deployed troops in response, but Isabella forbade her troops to engage, as she merely wanted to view the city and not be the cause of anyone's death. When, however, Yarfe desecrated the Ave Maria, Ferdinand acceded to the wish of one of his soldiers to engage in single combat.

The two armored knights fought on horseback and then on foot until, after an even struggle, the Spanish knight prevailed. During the combat, both armies had observed the rules of chivalry and refrained from interfering, but, once their champion was dead, the Moors attacked. Unable to maintain his queen's wish against fighting in the face of this onslaught, the marquis committed his troops. Artillery fired from the fortress at the Spanish, but their heavy cavalry broke the assault, and the Moors began to retreat behind the city walls, leaving behind 2,000 casualties.

In the wake of this victory, the Spanish suffered a disaster. That night, a candle in Queen Isabella's tent caught some curtains on

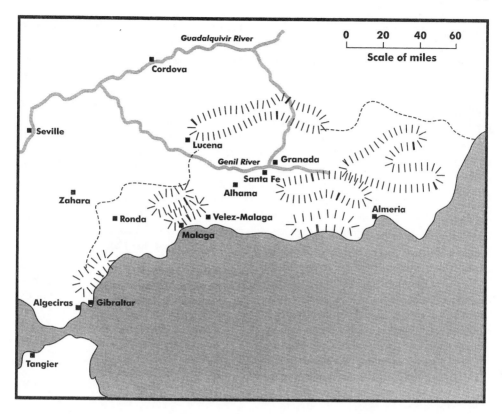

Guadalquivir River

Cordova

Seville

0   20   40   60
Scale of miles

Lucena

Genil River   Granada

Santa Fe

Zahara

Alhama

Ronda   Velez-Malaga

Almeria

Malaga

Algeciras   Gibraltar

Tangier

fire, and the result was a conflagration that burned down most of the Spanish camp. The following morning, to prove to the Moors that he was not really broken, Ferdinand paraded his troops before the city walls. Boabdil responded by sending his troops out of the gates into battle. A large number of skirmishes ensued until finally the Spanish gained the upper hand and the Moors once again retreated into the city. For the next 3 months, the Moors looked down on the Christian camp as it was rebuilt into a small, permanent town that came to be called Santa Fe. They watched and starved.

Results

In September, Boabdil called for negotiations and was presented with a list of demands, the Capitulations. It was extremely fair. There was to be no retribution against the inhabitants, and freedom of worship was guaranteed, as were locally elected magistrates and protection of Islamic culture. Those citizens that did not wish to remain in a Christian-ruled country were free to emigrate to North Africa, a trip for which Ferdinand's government would pay. That settlement was reached on 25 November 1491, but not scheduled to go into effect for another 2 months. When a small group opposed to the surrender began agitating for resistance, Baobdil asked for the transfer date to be moved forward. Thus, Ferdinand received the keys to the city from Baobdil's hand on 1 January 1492.

With the occupation of the city of Granada, the Reconquista was finished after a struggle of almost 800 years. Spain entered into a new era, both for herself and the world. Ferdinand's previous consolidation of the kingdoms of Spain under one monarch began the process of creating a nation, and, once this was a fact after

1492, a spirit of nationalism grew in Spain. That meant, regrettably, a spirit of intolerance for things not Spanish, and the promises that Ferdinand made to Baobdil and the Moors were soon forgotten. The aggressive Catholicism for which Spain became famous began in earnest, and both Moors and Jews suffered persecution, exile, and death. It is possible that such an expulsion of non-Christians solidified Spanish culture as well as population.

Spain's new nationalism was perfectly timed and placed. Located between the Atlantic and Mediterranean, Spain was positioned to take advantage of trade possibilities in both. Its neighbor Portugal had recently been exploring possible alternatives to overland trade with the Far East via the Arabs and Turks by exploring maritime routes around Africa. Spain's monarchs had an almost immediate opportunity to establish an alternate route themselves with the timely appeal of Christopher Columbus for ships to discover a western pathway to the Far East. The profits potential involved in bypassing Moslem dealers was a driving consideration, but so was the religious aspect. Rumors of Far Eastern Christian realms had long been extant in Europe. If they could be recruited to cooperate with European Christians, then a pincer attack on the Middle East could conceivably crush Islam and recover the Holy Land for Christianity. A combination of expanding wealth and religion was too much for Ferdinand and Isabella to forego. A divided Spain struggling with the Moors could never have engaged in such a project; a united Spain accepted the challenge and was victorious, establishing an international empire that resulted in immense wealth and power for Spain in Europe.

That empire, although incredibly profitable for Spain, resulted in the destruction of native civilizations in the Western Hemisphere. The conquistadors, the warrior class in Spain that had carried on the struggle against Islam for centuries, found themselves with little to do in Spain after the fall of Granada. Rather than have them idle about Spain, Ferdinand commissioned many of them to take their tal-

ents to the New World, and the resulting conquest enriched both warrior and king while causing the deaths of millions, primarily via European diseases. When or if a Moslem administration in Iberia would have undertaken such a venture, had Ferdinand not been successful, is impossible to surmise. As it was, Christianity and European values entrenched themselves in the Americas. A Moslem Spain engaging in similar explorations would certainly have been just as aggressive in spreading its faith to the New World as were the Spanish Catholics. The effects of a Moslem culture in that part of the world at that time would certainly have altered the entire world significantly.

References: Castlewitz, Donald. "Siege Forces a Kingdom," *Military History* 12(2), June 1995; Fernandez-Armesto, Felipe. *Ferdinand and Isabella.* New York: Taplinger, 1975; Fuller, J. F. C. *A Military History of the Western World,* vol. 1. New York: Funk & Wagnalls, 1954; Harvey, L. P. *Islamic Spain, 1250 to 1500.* Chicago: University of Chicago Press, 1990; Hillgarth, J. N. *The Spanish Kingdoms, 1250–1516.* Oxford, UK: Clarendon Press, 1976–1978.

TENOCHTITLÁN
26 May–13 August 1521

FORCES ENGAGED
Spanish/Allied: 86 cavalry, 118 crossbowmen and harquebusiers, more than 700 infantry, plus 50,000 Tlaxcalan allies. Commander: Hernán Cortés.

Aztec: Unknown. Commander: Cuauhtemoc.

IMPORTANCE
Capture of the capital of the Aztec Empire spelled its doom, as Spain became the dominant force in Central America for the next 300 years.

Historical Setting

Much of Central America was dominated by the Toltec peoples until their mysterious disappearance about A.D. 1200. The power vacuum that followed was coincident with the arrival of nomadic tribes from the north. One of them came to be known as Aztecs, or People from Aztlan, an unknown region to the north. They drifted into the valley of central Mexico and became subject to whatever power was able to achieve temporary hegemony. The Aztecs ultimately settled on the western side of Lake Texcoco, where they began to adapt themselves to the already established practice of building "floating gardens" of built-up silt. Here they established the city of Tenochtitlán in the middle of the fourteenth century. A second city, Tlatelolco, was built by a second Aztec faction. The two cities put themselves under the protection of rival powers: Tenochtitlán under Culhuacan, Tlatelolco under the Tepanecs.

Through the latter part of the fourteenth century, the Tepanecs came to dominate the valley, and they expanded their power across the mountains to the west to encompass an area of perhaps 20,000 square miles. This consolidation was accomplished by the Tepanec king Tezozomoc, but, after his death in 1423, the various city-states he had dominated began to rebel. Three powers joined together into a Triple Alliance to replace the Tepanecs, and one of those three were the Aztecs of Tenochtitlán. Despite the occasional disagreement, the three worked fairly well together and dominated central Mexico for 90 years. From 1431 to 1465, they consolidated their hold over the former Tepanec domain, and then they began a period of expansion. The Aztecs came to be the dominant partner in the triumvirate, but the three tribes collectively spread the empire from the Atlantic to the Pacific and as far southward as the modern-day border between Mexico and Guatemala. Only two tribes remained recalcitrant, and the Aztecs established garrisons along disputed borders and occasionally warred with the Tlaxaltecs and the Tarascans, although the Aztecs never subjugated them.

The Aztecs led the expansion for a number of reasons. Mainly they were expanding their trading routes while incorporating a larger tax base among the conquered peoples. They also fought for religious reasons. The Aztecs worshiped, among others, the god of the sun, Huitzilopochtli. The Aztec religion taught that history had moved in cycles, the end of which came with the destruction of the sun. To keep the god healthy and shining he required sacrifices to eat, and the Aztecs went conquering for sacrificial offerings. The pyramids that dominated the city of Tenochtitlán were large altars that saw the daily execution of prisoners of war. On days of special celebration, several thousand would be sacrificed. This need for offerings drove the Aztecs to conquest but did not create loyal subjects.

Once their empire was consolidated, the city of Tenochtitlán was expanded and beautified. The city reached a population of perhaps 200,000, which may have numbered one-fifth of the Aztec population; the total number of subject peoples might have taken the empire's population as high as 6 million. When Moctezuma II came to power in 1502, the Aztec empire was well established, and he was responsible for much of the lavish architecture and decoration in the capital city. Their sister-city Tlatelolco, which they took under their control in 1475, became the commercial center that contained the largest market in Central America, hosting perhaps as many as 60,000 people on market days.

The constant need for sacrificial victims created a resentment among all the subject peoples, and, when the Spaniards arrived, they were able to easily gain allies to assist them in their attacks on the Aztec Empire. In 1519, the Spanish conquistador Hernán Cortés landed on the coast of Mexico with 550 men and sixteen horses. He had heard reports of a powerful tribe known as the Aztecs who ruled a vast, rich empire located in a land far to the west of Cuba, his Caribbean base. Landing at the site of modern Vera Cruz, Cortés learned that the tribes subject to the Aztecs feared and resented their rulers. Seeing Cortés as a possible savior, they allied with the strange newcomers.

Among the peoples of Central America was a belief in a great white god, Quetzalcoatl, who

The meeting of Cortés and Moctezuma. (Library of Congress)

had visited the region in ages past and promised to return. Cortés was able to play on that belief because his horses, iron armor, and firearms were otherworldly items to the Aztecs and their subjects.

Cortés began his march into the interior in August 1519, gaining allies by reputation or by force. His major confrontation came with the Tlaxcalans. The Spanish and Tlaxcalans fought a number of battles throughout September, the Spanish firepower and cavalry on open ground allowing Cortés to slaughter large numbers of the natives. Tlaxcala finally surrendered to him in the middle of the month, and the inhabitants quickly saw that the Spaniards could prove vital in overthrowing the Aztecs. The Tlaxcalans warned Cortés that the route by which Moctezuma had asked him to travel, through the religious center of Cholula, was surely an ambush. When Moctezuma learned

that Cortés had avoided his ambush, the Aztec emperor was convinced that only a god could have had the foreknowledge of his plan. From that point forward, Moctezuma seemed to have ceded the initiative to the Spanish. Cortés and his men were welcomed into Tenochtitlán on 8 November, where they were amazed at the wealth the city contained.

The Battle

After a few weeks of discussions with Moctezuma, Cortés learned that an Aztec governor near the coast had attacked and killed some Spaniards near Vera Cruz. Cortés used that as an excuse to seize Moctezuma and began to rule through him. Knowing no other ruler, the Aztecs would follow no one of their own people who tried to make himself emperor in the face of Moctezuma's apparent surrender. Cortés, however, pushed his luck too far when he began dismantling the Aztec religion to introduce Christianity. That decision provoked extreme disquiet among the population. Then, to make matters worse for him, Cortés learned that a Spanish expedition from Cuba, sent by his main rival, the governor Diego Velazquez, had arrived off Vera Cruz. For a few weeks Cortés carried on a long-distance negotiation with the expedition's commander, Pánfilo de Narváez. By carefully leaking news of the immense wealth available, Cortés subverted many of Narváez's men. Sometime in the spring of 1520, Cortés led some 250 of his men to fight Narváez; the short battle went completely Cortés's way, and he quickly incorporated into his army the men sent to capture him.

When he left Tenochtitlán, Cortés had left in command Pedro de Alvarado, who began fighting the Aztecs in Tenochtitlán and found himself badly outnumbered and besieged in one of the palaces. Cortés marched back to Tenochtitlán at the head of a force of nearly 1,100 men. No sooner had he reestablished himself than all his work began to fall apart. Moctezuma refused to cooperate in any way and managed to secure the release of his brother, Cuitlahuac, claiming that the people would lay down their arms if Cortés displayed that act of good faith. Instead, Cuitlahuac was quickly elected emperor in Moctezuma's place by the war chiefs of the city, and, near the end of June, an assault was launched on Cortés's position. The massive amounts of javelins and arrows wrought havoc in the Spanish lines. Fire from cannon and harquebuses tore huge holes in the Aztec forces, but, employing human wave tactics, they broke through the palace walls and pressed the Spaniards hard. The nature of Tenochtitlán, a city crisscrossed by canals, made maneuver nearly impossible because the Aztecs controlled all the bridges. Cortés led sallies against the attackers, but was always overwhelmed and forced to retreat. "Men who had fought against the Moors declared afterwards that they had never faced such a fierce and determined enemy, and veter-

ans of the Italian wars said that even the French king's artillery was easier to face than these Indians" (Innes, *The Conquistadors,* p. 164). Soon every Spaniard not killed had been wounded. Cortés put Moctezuma on a rooftop to speak to his people, to convince them to stop fighting so that the Spanish could evacuate the city. After some discussion, the more warlike Aztecs prevailed, and arrows and stones were soon flying. Moctezuma was struck in several places and died 3 days later.

Cortés had large wooden towers built, hoping to give his crossbowmen sufficient height to control the streets, but the Aztecs were still too numerous. Even aided by a few thousand Tlaxcalans within the palace walls, Cortés was badly outnumbered. He enjoyed a small, hard-fought victory at the pyramid temple near his palace, but his only hope of survival was in escape. He fought his way for 2 days through the streets to the causeway to Tacuba and then had to capture the gaps in the road where eight bridges had been destroyed by the Aztecs. Slowly, the Spaniards captured each Aztec barricade and then tore it down to fill the gap in the causeway where the bridge had been; they then fought their way to the next barricade. Cortés thought he had bought a cease-fire when envoys promised to stop fighting if their high priest was released; in reality, the Aztecs needed him to perform the requisite ceremonies to install Cuitlahuac as emperor. The attacks started again, and the Spaniards were forced back to their palace. Hastily building a portable bridge, Cortés ordered a force of 150 of his soldiers and a few hundred Tlaxcalans to lay the bridge across the first gap in the causeway and then defend it while the bulk of his survivors crossed; they would then lay down fire for the second gap to be bridged. The evacuation took place on the night of 30 June–1 July, what the Spaniards called the *Noche Triste,* the Night of Sorrows. They managed to break out of the palace with almost all of their cannon, but their greed caused them to carry as much gold as they could, and that certainly slowed their escape.

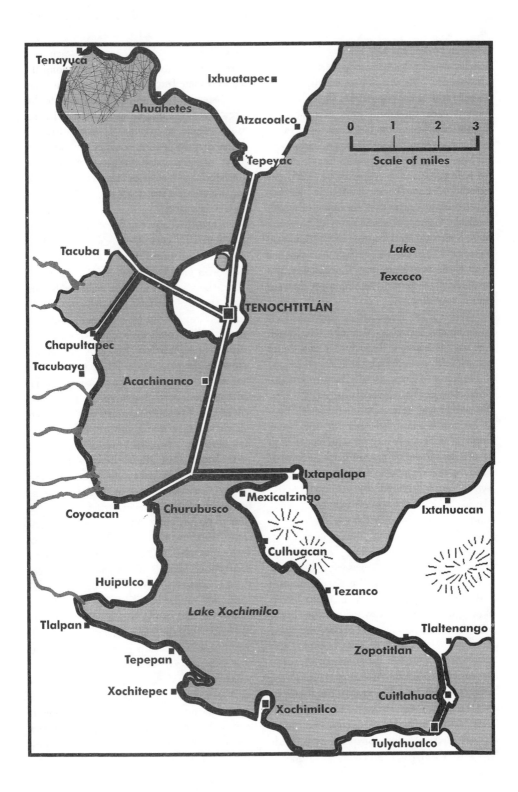

In the end, the Spaniards succeeded to escape, but all their artillery and most of their gold was lost, as were some 600 men and two-thirds of the sixty-eight horses. His Tlaxcalan allies lost perhaps 2,000 men. They made a stand at Tacuba and then escaped the following night northward. They were harassed constantly on their retreat to Tlaxcala.

Had the Aztecs continued to launch hit-and-run attacks on the Spaniards, Cortés's force would certainly have been wiped out. Instead, Cuitlahuac decided on a battle. Having fought the Spaniards only in the city, he had no idea what their cavalry could do in the open, but he learned the hard way. At the town of Otumba on 7 July, the two forces fought. Cortés had but twenty-two horses, but with armor and lances they were still formidable. By attacking the conspicuously dressed commanders, the Spanish were able to rob the Aztecs of their leadership; still, it was an all-day battle. No accurate count of Aztecs engaged exists, but there must have been many thousands. Spanish discipline defeated them. The day after the battle, the retreating Spaniards reached the Tlaxcalan border, and the Aztecs withdrew.

Cortés sent to Vera Cruz for all the gunpowder and cannon available. He spent the next several months rebuilding his force and, with Tlaxcalan assistance, pacifying the neighborhood and gaining allies. During this period, Cortés was aided by a benefactor of which he could never have conceived. An African slave who was with the Narváez expedition and afflicted with smallpox died in the town of Zempoala. The disease spread from that one man across all of Mexico, and the epidemic severely weakened Cortés's enemies. The germs ran rampant through Tenochtitlán, killing Cuitlahuac, who was succeeded on the throne by Cuauhtemoc, one of Moctezuma's sons-in-law.

Cortés spent his time wisely, sending ships to Jamaica to buy ordnance and horses. He also began the construction of thirteen small ships (brigantines) to operate on the lake upon which Tenochtitlán sat. By Christmas 1520, he was ready to march. By April 1521, his men were capturing one town after another along the shores of Lake Texcoco. After fighting their way completely around the lake, Cortés sent for his allies in order to make his final assault. By this time, he commanded eighty-six cavalry, 118 crossbowmen and harquebusiers, and more than 700 infantry armed with swords and pikes. Another 50,000 Tlaxcalans supplemented his army. Cortés divided his force into three columns, two to march counterclockwise around the lake and occupy Tacuba and Coyoacán, west of Tenochtitlán, and the third to capture Iztapalapa to the southeast. This would put them in control of the mainland end of the causeways entering Tenochtitlán. A fourth contingent was under the command of Cortés himself: the thirteen brigantines he had built to operate on the lake and deal with the canoe-borne Aztec warriors.

The attack got off to a bad start when one of the Tlaxcalan chiefs decided to defect. He was quickly executed for desertion, with the approval of the other Tlaxcalans. Then two of Cortés's commanders quarreled and refused to cooperate with each other; Cortés used all his diplomatic skills to ease the conflict between his subordinates. On 26 May, his first two columns were in position and destroyed the aqueduct that took water to the city. On 31 May, a swarm of Aztec canoes attacked Cortés's small flotilla. In the early morning hours, they rowed away from the attackers, but, when the dawn brought a friendly breeze, Cortés faced about and attacked. The cannon aboard his small ships did amazing damage; by day's end he was ruler of Lake Texcoco. The attack on the city was another matter, for the gaps in the causeways were now too large to be bridged. Unfortunately for the Aztecs, one gap was sufficiently wide for the Spanish ships to sail through and set up a crossfire on the defenders, forcing their retreat. A force of crossbowmen was able to enter the city and attack one of the temples, but was quickly forced back by overwhelming numbers of Aztecs.

The capture of the city of Mexico. Hand-to-hand combat with Aztecs, 1521. Engraving, 1870, in "Two Americas." (Library of Congress)

The battle went on for 10 weeks. Each day the Spaniards saw their fellows, taken prisoner by the Aztecs, sacrificed to the god of war atop the city's central pyramid. That steeled their resolve, and the lack of freshwater inside the city took its toll as well. The brigantines kept Aztec canoes inoperable while the Spanish worked their way up the damaged causeways. Occasional Aztec ambushes kept the Spanish at bay for weeks. The Aztecs also threw body parts of sacrificed prisoners at the attackers in an attempt to break their spirit. The siege also took place during the rainy season, dampening the Spanish spirits as they made but slow progress. A few Aztecs were able to slip out of the city and carry severed heads of Spaniards and their horses to neighboring towns in an attempt to drum up support, but a punitive expedition by a Tlaxcalan force brought in even more allies to the Spanish cause. Finally, the

Spanish were able to fill the gaps in the causeways and move ever closer to the city. In desperation, the Aztecs launched larger and larger attacks, which the Tlaxcalans beat back with enormous losses. Fighting went on street by street as the invaders gained more and more of the city. Finally, on 13 August, Cortés launched a massive attack on the final survivors defending Tenochtitlán. The last 15,000 defenders died in that fight, the handful of survivors fleeing in canoes. The Spanish and their allies occupied the Aztec capital, but it contained only rotting bodies.

Results

Although the Aztecs were in many ways more advanced than the Europeans, they lacked the necessary weaponry and resistance to foreign diseases to defeat their invaders. Although they created outstanding works of art and developed an extensive hieroglyphic writing system, their scientific knowledge was too limited. Even without the arrival of the Spaniards, it is questionable how much longer the tribes of Central America would have accepted the military dominance and religious practices of the Aztecs.

Cortés and the Spaniards who followed him completely dismantled Aztec society. Disease did its work, killing an estimated 90 percent of the population. However, the Spanish were intent on making this country their own rather than adapting themselves to it. One of the first goals of that plan was to ban the exercise of the Aztec religion, for human sacrifice and cannibalism could hardly be acceptable to staunch Catholics. With the new governing power completely in Spanish hands, if any citizens of New Spain had any idea of advancing themselves, learning the Spanish language was vital. Within a generation, the Aztec religion and language virtually ceased to exist. The Aztec culture, as reflected in their artwork, also disappeared. The Aztecs were reputedly expert goldsmiths, and most of their artwork in gold and silver was melted down into bullion for easier distribution as booty for the soldiers as well as ease of transport in the ships that took the wealth of the New World back to Spain.

King Charles in Spain recognized Cortés as the governor and captain-general of the land he had conquered, which came to be called New Spain. The immense wealth looted from Central America, coupled with that obtained in South America, made Spain the richest and most powerful nation on earth. With that financial foundation, the intensely Catholic Spanish king proceeded to spend that money in Europe on military power to enforce the will of the church, embroiled at the time with the new Protestant movement. For a century, Spain dominated Europe, but the defeat of the Spanish Armada at the hands of the English at Calais in 1588 began their decline from international preeminence to that of also-ran by the end of the nineteenth century.

References: Carrasco, David. *Montezuma's Mexico.* Niwot, CO: University of Colorado Press, 1992; Diaz del Castillo, Bernal. *The Discovery and Conquest of Mexico, 1517–1521.* Translated by A. P. Maudslay. New York: Harper, 1928; Innes, Hammond. *The Conquistadors.* New York: Alfred A. Knopf, 1969; Prescott, William H. *Conquest of Mexico.* Garden City, NY: Blue Ribbon Books, 1943; White, Jon Manchip. *Cortés and the Downfall of the Aztec Empire.* London: Hamish Hamilton, 1971.

PANIPAT
21 April 1526

FORCES ENGAGED
Moghul: Approximately 10,000 Afghans and 5,000 allied troops. Commander: Babur.
Hindustani: Perhaps 40,000 men and 1,000 (or 100) elephants. Commander: Sultan Ibrahim Lodi.

IMPORTANCE
Babur's victory established in India the Moghul dynasty, which lasted until its replacement by British colonial power in the eighteenth century.

Historical Setting

The roots of Babur's invasion of northern India in the 1520s lay in his ancestor Timur the Lame, better known to history as Tamurlane. In his destructive career, Timur had devastated every land he could, reaching from the Black Sea to India, which he looted in 1398. He left little in the way of an empire, for his actions focused more on pillage than long-term conquest. Thus, any claims of his heirs to Timur's lands was pretty tenuous. A century after Timur's death, Babur attempted to assert his right to rule from Timur's fabled capital of Samarkand. Babur's father was Turkish and his mother was Mongol; his people came to be called Moghul, from the Arabic word for Mongol. Babur managed to seize the throne twice, but could not hold it, pressured as he was by the powerful Uzbeks to his north. After a third try at seizing power in Samarkand in 1512, Babur settled for Kabul, in present-day Afghanistan, as his capital. His ambition was for more than a relatively small mountain kingdom, so he looked to the southeast, toward India, to fulfill his ambition for power.

In 1519, Babur made his first foray into the northwestern Indian region called the Punjab, which bordered Afghanistan, but this foray was no more than a raid. It did, however, whet Babur's appetite for more. His dream of reclaiming Timur's Indian conquest received some local assistance in 1524 thanks to bickering in the ruling family sitting on the throne in Delhi. Sultan Ibrahim Lodi was the ruler of northern India, called Hindustan, comprising the land from the Khyber Pass in the west to the Ganges delta in the east, with the Himalayas as its northern border and the central Indian mountains of the Deccan along the southern edge. Ibrahim was challenged by a number of his relatives, but the first to contact Babur was Ibrahim's uncle, Alam Khan Ala-al-din, who traveled to Kabul seeking military aid to seize the throne. Soon thereafter, Alam Khan's nephew, Punjabi governor Daulat Khan, also went to Kabul requesting aid for the same purpose. Babur led troops into the Punjab in 1524, ostensibly aiding one or the other of the two supplicants, but probably just to see what would happen. His troops seized the Punjabi capital city of Lahore, where Babur stationed a garrison. He then returned to Kabul for the winter, to recruit more troops and tend to his northern border dispute with the Uzbeks.

During the winter, Daulat Khan and his nephew Ghazi Khan raised an army of their own to expel the Moghuls. As this challenged Alam Khan's ambitions, he again went to Kabul to make a new deal with Babur: put down the threat of Daulat and Ghazi and then unseat Ibrahim in Delhi. As payment for his assistance, he would grant Babur control over the Punjab. Upon his return to Lahore, however, Alam approached Daulat and Ghazi about an alliance, although which of them would succeed Ibrahim on the Delhi throne is unclear. When Babur mounted his final expedition in November 1525, he learned of Alam's duplicity, but did not know if it was merely a ruse to neutralize Daulat. Thus, Babur marched his force into the Punjab certain that danger lay ahead, but sure of only two sources: Ibrahim in Delhi and a new threat, that of the princes of Rajputana, south of the Punjab, Hindus who saw an opportunity to depose a Moslem king in Delhi and possibly turn back a Moslem incursion from Afghanistan.

Alam's negotiation with Daulat was no ruse. He assigned Daulat and Ghazi to protect the Punjabi border while he attempted to seize Delhi. He tried and failed, withdrawing to his home in the hills. From there, he fled Babur's advance and rejoined Ghazi. Meanwhile, Ghazi and Daulat were also withdrawing before Babur's advance, fearful of testing his strength. Babur was able to link up with his garrison in Lahore in early January 1526. Word reached him that Daulat was gathering an army of 40,000, and that he had girded himself with two swords, indicating a fight to the death. Instead, his army scattered without a fight and Daulat threw himself on Babur's mercy. Ghazi fled to the hills, never to be heard from again. Alam Khan also surrendered himself to Babur's mercies, which he received. Babur realized that protecting a local leader and former enemy would ease his path with local princes. With the Punjab now secure, Babur aimed his army toward Delhi.

The Battle

Babur stayed to the Himalayan foothills until he reached the town of Panipat, about 90 miles north of Delhi. Using the town as an anchor for his right flank, he established a defensive position reminiscent of Turkish tactics in Anatolian battles. Babur scoured the countryside for wagons and, collecting about 700 of them, arranged them in a line with rawhide ropes tying them together. Behind the wagons, he arranged troops armed with matchlocks. The line of wagons was occasionally separated by gaps through which cavalry charges could be launched; other gaps held artillery, which Babur had adopted upon seeing its effects in battles earlier in his career. As the gaps in the line were so frequent, the position was not a solid front. It is probable that he did this on purpose to make his position seem less formidable, thus making it more attractive to attack. On the far left, he felled trees and laid them along a ravine in order to protect his flank from an encirclement. Thus, although outnumbered, he possessed gunpowder weapons, which his enemy did not. Allied with some local princes, Babur's army probably numbered around 8,000 to 10,000 Moghuls and another 5,000 local troops.

Sultan Ibrahim was in no hurry to close with Babur's army. His force leisurely made its way from Delhi toward Panipat, arriving on 12 April 1526. Babur's intelligence gathering re-ported his enemy to be 100,000 strong and possessing as many as 1,000 elephants. That number probably included camp followers as well, so the fighting force probably totaled only 30,000 to 40,000 men. Babur attempted to provoke an attack on his prepared position, but Ibrahim would have none of it. Light cavalry forays and arrow attacks failed to move Ibrahim, and Babur grew worried. His men were uncomfortable so far from home and in land that was much flatter than that to which they were accustomed. The longer it took to fight, the more uneasy many of the Afghans grew. Babur's force was too small to launch an attack, but to withdraw into the hills would force the abandonment of a prime defensive position.

After almost a week of inactivity, Babur grew bolder. On the night of 19 April, he ordered an attack by some of his Moghuls and a number of his allied auxiliaries, altogether probably 5,000 men. It was poorly coordinated, with the columns losing their way in the dark and

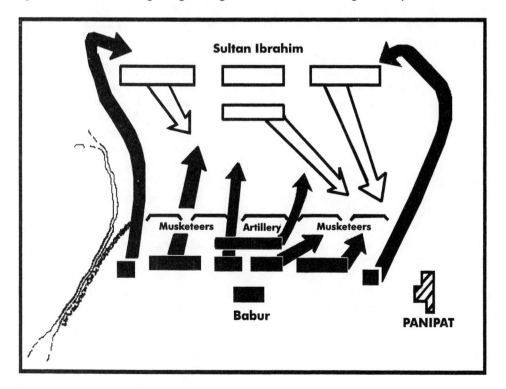

finding it impossible to coordinate any attack. When the sun rose on 20 April, the attackers were disorganized and exposed just in front of Ibrahim's lines. Fearing a major assault, Ibrahim ordered his troops to deploy. That action forced the raiding party to withdraw, harassed only lightly. The poor showing of this force apparently encouraged Ibrahim. At dawn on 21 April, Babur's scouts reported that the enemy was advancing across the open plain. Babur deployed his men. His plan was to use the firepower in the center of his line to hold Ibrahim's army in place. The rate of fire of the matchlocks and the artillery was so slow that, although they could do significant damage, they could not maintain a withering fire; that, too, Babur hoped would entice a frontal assault.

Although Ibrahim's force reportedly had 1,000 elephants, they played no part in the battle; probably the noise of the artillery was sufficient to unnerve them. Ibrahim's force deployed in traditional Asiatic formation: three units abreast with a centrally located vanguard. Not wanting to go around or through the town of Panipat, Ibrahim aimed his attack at the Moghul right flank where it joined the town. To accomplish this attempt to turn the Moghul right, the attackers began to move into an echelon formation. This disrupted their normal line-abreast style of march and cramped the soldiers into a smaller space than they were used to. This caused the front troops to hesitate just before contact, not sure whether to storm the end of the wagon line or wait to dress ranks. In that moment, Babur struck. His forces were deployed in a mirror image of Ibrahim's, with minor differences. Babur's center formation was subdivided into right and left halves, and he had small flanking cavalry units as well. He also held a cavalry reserve. All this was arrayed behind his wagon line. When Ibrahim's attack hesitated before the right flank, Babur dispatched his right center to support and then ordered his flanking units to ride around the enemy flanks and strike their rear, which was the stratagem he had planned from the beginning.

As the troops on Ibrahim's left pressed forward into the hesitating front lines, the press became too great for any movement. It also became a huge target for all the Moghul firepower, both gunpowder and arrows. Sensing a growing panic in the attackers, Babur ordered his left center to advance through the gaps in his wagon line. Pressed from three sides, Ibrahim's army could do little more than stand and die. By noon, they were doing all they could to break free from the mass and escape, leaving behind between 15,000 and 20,000 dead, including Ibrahim.

Results

Babur sent his cavalry after the fleeing enemy, and several princes were captured. All Ibrahim's elephant handlers quickly made their way to Babur, swore the allegiance of themselves, and offered the service of their animals. Babur dispatched his son, Prince Humayun, with a lightly burdened cavalry detachment to Agra to seize Ibrahim's treasury and hold it until he arrived. Babur made for Delhi, there on 27 April to assume the throne from which he proclaimed the new Moghul dynasty. He stayed in Delhi through the following Friday to hear his name mentioned in public prayers, the usual tribute to the sitting monarch. He then joined his son at Agra. When he arrived, Humayun introduced his father to the family of the Prince of Gwalior, 50 miles south of Agra. The family had been taking refuge in the fort at Agra while their father fought alongside Ibrahim. Humayun had treated them with all due respect and in return was given a huge diamond. Many believe this was the famous Koh-i-Noor, now part of the British crown jewels.

Many of Babur's victorious troops were eager to go home to Afghanistan to escape the oncoming heat of the Indian summer, but he delivered a stirring oration that convinced them to stay; indeed, Babur never saw Kabul again. His new neighbors were ready to challenge the authority of the new dynasty, and in March

OTHER PANIPAT BATTLES

Before Babur won fame and a throne at Panipat, his forebear Timur the Lame had won a victory on the same field in 1399. He crushed his opponent, the sultan of Delhi, and then proceeded to capture the undefended capital and loot it for 10 days. This victory was the source of Babur's claim to the throne a century and a quarter later.

Three decades after the foundation of the Moghul Empire in India was laid by Babur's victory at Panipat, its establishment was confirmed by his grandson Akbar. He was only 14 years old when the battle was fought on 5 November 1556, but he was ably assisted by an advisor named Bairam. Hemu, the general who took the throne in Delhi after Sher Khan's accidental death in 1545, led 100,000 men against Akbar's 20,000. Although the battle in its early stages seemed to belong to Hemu, when he was struck in the eye by an arrow, his army collapsed. Akbar incorporated many of the defeated enemy troops into his own army, which he organized along the lines employed by Sher Khan and Hemu. With this professional force, Akbar spread Moghul influence through the northern two-thirds of India. He became legendary for his wise leadership and thirst for knowledge. Unfortunately, his son had no such fine qualities and poisoned his father in 1605.

The final battle at Panipat occurred in 1761. By that time, the once might, Moghul Empire was a kingdom in name only. The last Moghul of any authority, Aurangzeb, died in 1707. Afterward, the throne was occupied by a series of weak figures. In the 1750s, the Punjab had been conquered by the Afghan leader Ahmad Shah, but, upon his return home through the Khyber Pass, the region had been conquered by the Marathas. They had once been a population of bandits and guerrillas, but by 1760 had transformed themselves into a disciplined army, well armed with European artillery. They raised the flag of religious war, Hindu against the Moslem Afghans, and in 1761 the two armies met at Panipat. The Marathas numbered 70,000 infantry and 15,000 cavalry under Sadasheo Bhao. The Afghan army was comprised of 40,000 infantry and 53,000 cavalry under the command of Ahmad Shah.

Both sides entrenched themselves and faced each other down for 2 months. Finally feeling the strain of hunger and failing to receive any receptive response to peace feelers, Bhao ordered an assault. The Hindus had the early advantage with their superior weaponry, and the Rohillas, Indian allies to the Afghans, began to buckle. Just as all seemed to be lost, Ahmad Shah ordered a concentrated cavalry assault on the Marathas that, at the end of an exhausting day, proved the difference. With the defeat of the Maratha army, the only serious military force in India was broken. Ahmad Shah, although victorious, was severely weakened by the battle and unable to follow up. Thus, the Moghul king, Shah-Alam, negotiated an agreement with the British East India Company, which gave him a pension in return for administrative control of much of Hindustan. Having defeated their only European rival, the French, at Plassey in 1757, the British assumed a position of power that no local or foreign power could challenge. Thus, Panipat was the scene of the beginning and the end of the Moghul dynasty.

1527 the armies of Rajputana tried to expand into Ibrahim's lands. At Khanua on 16 March, Babur with less than 20,000 men defeated a Rajput force five times that size under the command of Rana Sanga. With his southwestern frontier secured, Babur turned farther east and conquered as far as Bengal by 1529. He returned to Agra, from where he directed his subordinates to occupy various regions of his new domain and to suppress a few local uprisings. He also proceeded to improve Agra with parks, fountains, and new construction, as well as renovation of old forts and public buildings.

Babur died on 26 December 1530. All his adult life he had kept a chronicle of his activities, and he often referred to his large intake of alcohol and *majoud,* some sort of hallucinogenic drug (possibly hashish). Throughout his memoirs he mentions coughing fits and spitting up blood, so a hard life both in battle and in relaxation seemed to have conspired against him. He was but 45 years old.

Humayun succeeded Babur and for a time seemed an able ruler. He expanded his realm somewhat, but was challenged and defeated by East Indian forces led by Sher Khan. It seemed as if the Moghul dynasty was to be but two generations long, but Humayun's son Akbar redeemed the family name. Fighting at Panipat in November 1556, Akbar defeated Hemu, the general that had succeeded Sher Khan, and firmly reestablished the dynasty in the process. Akbar proved to be one of the best kings in all of Indian history, powerful in battle and wise in administration. Through his efforts, the northern two-thirds of the Indian subcontinent was united and extremely well run. His grandson Shah Jahan further enhanced Indian history and culture with the construction of the Taj Mahal. The last of the able Moghul leaders was Aurangzeb, who had the misfortune of ruling as the British seriously began to take an interest in India in the middle of the eighteenth century.

References: Babur. *The Babur-nama in English: Memoirs of Babur.* Translated by Annette Susannah Beveridge. London: Luzac & Co., 1921; Gascoigne, Bamber. *The Great Moghuls.* New York: Harper & Row, 1971; Lamb, Harold. *Babur the Tiger.* Garden City, NY: Doubleday, 1961; Lane-Poole, Stanley. *Medieval India under Mohammedan Rule.* New York: Krause Reprint, 1970 [1903]; Williams, L. F. Rushbrook. *An Empire Builder of the Sixteenth Century.* Delhi: S. Chand & Co., 1916.

VIENNA

27 September–14 October 1529

FORCES ENGAGED

Austrian: 16,000 troops and 72 guns.
Commander: Archduke Ferdinand.

Ottoman: Approximately 250,000 troops.
Commander: Sultan Suleiman.

IMPORTANCE

Turkish defeat at Vienna was the high-water mark of Ottoman expansion in Europe, signaling the beginning of a long decline in Ottoman power.

Historical Setting

Europe in the 1520s presented to a potential outside aggressor a wonderful opportunity, just as the weakened condition caused by Byzantine-Persian hostility had opened the door for Islam to break out of Arabia in the seventh century. More than weakness, however, it was political rivalry in Europe that made the continent vulnerable. Politically, King Francis I of France and Charles V, Holy Roman Emperor, argued and fought over land that today is the Franco-German frontier, as well as control over northern Italy. France had a powerful military based on artillery and heavy cavalry, with which it won a number of victories. Charles, as head of the Hapsburg family, controlled not only the Holy Roman Empire (which consisted of Austria and parts of whatever countries bordered it) but also Spain, whose military power was based on the *tercio,* a phalanx of pikemen supported by smaller contingents of soldiers, each armed with the harquebus, a matchlock musket. Against these formations, cavalry made no impression, and, when the two armies met at Pavia in northern Italy in 1525, France came up the loser. Ferdinand not only was defeated, he was taken prisoner. During and after his captivity, he plotted revenge and pondered on possible allies.

Although Charles was enjoying this military success, he was bothered by Pope Clement VII in Rome. Although technically the Holy Roman Empire was supposed to be the defender of the Catholic Church, just which was the senior partner in the equation had been a point of difficulty since Charlemagne took on the job in 800. Clement resented Charles for controlling so much of Italy because, before his accession to the papacy, Clement had been Giulio de Medici, a wealthy and powerful figure in his own right. Thus, Clement's attitude toward Charles meant not only a lack of political support but also a lack of religious support in dealing with the rise of the Protestant Reformation and the increasingly political activities of Martin Luther in Germany. Thus, Charles had his hands full with rivals in Rome, France, and central Europe.

Sultan Suleiman in Constantinople was not slow to see this. He was the ninth sultan of the Ottoman Empire, successor to a long line of able, resourceful, daring, and strongly religious rulers. He inherited an empire that stretched from the Persian frontier in the east to Morocco in the west, as well as much of the Balkans. He also inherited a military that in its own way was as impressive as anything Charles or Francis could put in the field. The pride of the Ottoman army lay in two arms: the heavy infantry and the artillery. Since the days of the second sultan, Ala ed-Din, the Ottoman government had accepted for taxes payment in kind in the form of male children of Christian families. They became slaves, were raised as Moslems, and from their youth trained as soldiers. They developed into a fearsome unit called the Janissaries, completely dedicated to their faith and their sultan and, in the service of both, ready to go anywhere and fight any enemy. The Ottoman Turks had also learned from western Europe the craft of casting artillery, and they had far outstripped their teachers. The Ottomans produced the largest guns of their day, and with them they captured Constantinople in 1453 after it had stood unconquered for more than a thousand years. Heavy siege guns were the Turks' specialty, and many cities became Ottoman possessions because of those weapons, just as many armies fell before the talent and élan of the Janissaries.

Although Suleiman was an open-minded and interesting political ruler whom the Europeans viewed as a man with whom they could do business, he was also caliph of all Islam, thanks to the recent acquisition of Egypt and deposition of the last spiritual leader. Suleiman was therefore bound by the tenets of his faith to spread Islam and convert the unbelievers or exact tribute from them. As such, he conducted campaigns against the Persians, and he also looked to extend his political and religious dominion into Europe. He was also contacted by the vengeful King Francis, who encouraged an invasion to threaten Charles's eastern front and correspondingly weaken his French frontier.

Suleiman's venture into Europe began in the summer of 1526 when he captured Buda and placed Hungary under his sway, promoting John Zapolya, governor of Transylvania, to the Hungarian throne as his tributary monarch. That throne was contested, however, by Ferdinand, archduke of Austria and king of Bohemia. While Suleiman was campaigning in Persia in 1528, a rebellion broke out in Hungary. Some of the rebellious factions claimed to be fighting for Ferdinand's cause. Once his Persian problems were settled—at least temporarily— Suleiman made ready to march on Ferdinand's home city of Vienna and add Austria and the Holy Roman Empire to his own Ottoman Empire.

The Battle

Suleiman led his army out of Constantinople on 10 April 1529. When Ferdinand heard of this, he called a council in Bohemia to gather an army. For the most part, his requests went unanswered. Lots of promises were made by Austria and Bohemia and the empire, but few troops actually arrived. Charles was busy with trouble in Italy and had to keep an eye on both Francis and Clement. In Vienna, meanwhile, the 250-year-old city walls, no more than 5 feet thick, were in many places badly in need of repair. They could not be mended with masonry, as there was no time, so for the most part dirt and the debris of the suburbs were used because the outlying houses were razed to open up a field of fire before the city walls. The official in charge in Vienna was Philip, count palatine of Austria. He was assisted in his job by two talented men, Graf Nicholas zu Salm-Reifferscheidt and William von Roggendorff. Graf Nicholas oversaw the wall repairs, gathered in as much food and ammunition as he could, and expelled from the city as many women and children as he could to ease the supply burden. During the siege itself, he oversaw the placement of the artillery, seventy-two guns of widely varying size and caliber. When the siege began, the city was defended by a garrison of 22,000 infantry and 2,000 cavalry. Between the garrisons that Suleiman had absorbed along his line of march, reinforcements commanded by his lackey King John Zapolya, and innumerable camp followers, the Ottoman force that stood before Vienna on 26 September 1529 was possibly as large as 350,000 people, although it included probably 80,000 Turkish soldiers and another 6,000 Hungarians.

The Ottoman advance had been a wonder to behold. Many of the Janissaries advanced up the Danube in boats, stopping with Suleiman for 5 days at Buda to recapture the city and massacre the defenders. News of that action, as well as the activities of some 20,000 *akinji* (ransackers) that were devastating the countryside all along the line of march, motivated the defenders in Vienna to fix their walls as best they could. The first contingent of Turks arrived in sight of Vienna on 23 September and skirmished with the Viennese cavalry. By 27 September, the city was surrounded, and Suleiman sent a delegation to demand its surrender. The delegation was comprised of four captured cavalrymen, fabulously dressed in Turkish clothing. The sultan stated that an immediate surrender would end in no occupation of the city but for a few functionaries, and he would have breakfast there on the morning of 29 September. Resist, and the city would be destroyed so thoroughly that no one would ever again find a trace of it. Graf Nicholas, de facto commander, sent back four richly dressed Turkish prisoners; they carried no answer at all, which was answer enough.

The fate of Vienna in reality lay neither in the city walls nor the attacking army, but in the weather. The summer of 1529 was the wettest anyone in southeastern Europe could remember, and the supply wagons, vital to supporting the immense force before Vienna, lagged far behind. Worse still for the Ottoman cause, the massive siege artillery also could not be moved along the muddy roads. The artillery that Suleiman had with him were 300 small pieces that lacked the destructive power necessary to break down even these old walls.

Suleiman's only alternative was to mine the city walls. This involves digging a tunnel from one's own protected trenches under the walls of the enemy and then filling the tunnel with gunpowder and exploding it. The collapsing tunnel would then collapse a section of wall. Such operations began immediately, but the defenders were lucky enough to learn the placement of the mines from a deserter. They quickly countermined, either digging their own tunnels under those being dug by the Turks in order to collapse them or digging at the same level, which resulted in underground battles, in which the defenders tended to be the more victorious. Not all of the mines could be discovered, however, and some of them worked. The breaches, which were occasionally large enough to ride several horses through abreast, could not be exploited. Behind the walls, the defenders had dug trenches and built wooden palisades from which they beat back the attackers. The breaches were held by the same stolid pikemen that had won the battles of western Europe, and the swords of the Janissaries were of little use in the cramped confines of the battle. A major battle in one breach on 12 October resulted in the Janissaries leaving behind 1,200 dead.

On the night of 12 October, Suleiman held a council of war. The supply wagons had not arrived, and the countryside was not providing nearly enough food to support his army. The city was proving unexpectedly tough. Winter was approaching. The defenders had won every encounter in the breaches that had been created, and the attackers' death toll was between 14,000 and 20,000, primarily Janissaries and aristocratic cavalry. For the first time in their history, the Janissaries complained that they were being sacrificed. To do just that had been their duty and indeed their entire life for nearly two centuries. Suleiman offered them a huge bonus for one more attack. On 14 October, another mine blew up, but the collapsing wall fell outward, creating such a pile of rubble that it was impossible for the attackers to rush the breach. The pikemen once again stood firm in the face of the Janissary onslaught, and once again they turned the attackers away.

That night, the Ottoman army struck its tents, which had covered the plain outside Vienna for as far as the eye could see. In massive bonfires, they burned everything that they could not carry and then threw their prisoners in the flames as well. The army marched away the next morning as it snowed.

Results

A relative handful of men saved western Europe from Ottoman invasion. At first it seemed that little had changed, however. John Zapolya still ruled in Suleiman's name in Buda, and Hungary was part of the Ottoman domain. Although Suleiman returned 3 years later to finish the job he had started, a spirited resistance at the town of Guns (modern Koszeg, Austria)

VIENNA, 1683

Although the first siege of Vienna marked the long downward slide of Ottoman power, that did not mean that later sultans had no ambition for glory. An Ottoman offensive in 1663 was turned back at St. Gotthard Abbey. That defeat was followed by the signing of the Treaty of Vasvar, which called for a 20-year truce while ceding Transylvania to the Ottomans.

The architect of that defeat was the grand vizier, Ahmed Kiuprili. He also oversaw a series of Turkish defeats at the hands of the Poles and Russians in the mid-1770s. He was succeeded by the sultan's appointee, Kara Mustapha, totally lacking in talent but a close friend, hunting partner, and possibly lover of the sultan. Kara Mustapha was overwhelmingly greedy, corrupt, and bloodthirsty. It was he who convinced Sultan Mehmet to authorize another assault on Vienna when the Treaty of Vasvar lapsed, although no one other than Mustapha was particularly motivated to fight.

Mehmet raised an army of 150,000 to 200,000 men and held a spectacle in Constantinople to mark the outset of the campaign, but a bad turn of weather gave the superstitious in the empire some foreboding. Like the expedition of 1529, this one brought few pieces of siege artillery, although Ottoman firearms were at this point superior to those of the defenders. The garrison inside Vienna numbered less than 15,000 and, like the earlier siege, the walls were once again in a state of disrepair. Vienna's salvation lay in Mustapha.

Vienna could not possibly resist his forces, Mustapha reasoned, but the way in which the city fell would determine his own fortune. If the city was sacked after an assault, the troops would split the booty. If, however, it fell through starvation or negotiation, Mustapha would be the primary beneficiary. Hence, he did not press his siege. That decision allowed reinforcements to gather and march to the city's relief. A mixed force of Austrians, Germans, and Poles under the command of the Polish leader Jan Sobieski arrived 12 September 1683, in the seventh week of the siege. Mustapha's three-to-one advantage did him no good as the Europeans thundered down from the surrounding hills. After an all-day battle, the Turks were on the run. For a time, Mustapha was able to convince the sultan that the defeat was not his fault, but, when the truth became known, Mustapha was executed by ritual strangulation. Never again did the Ottoman Empire seriously take the offensive, but survived the remaining two and a half centuries of its existence losing land to one neighbor or another.

and a major deployment of European troops under Charles V once again convinced him to return home. Another uprising in Persia diverted Suleiman's attention, so he made peace with Ferdinand and turned his armies eastward. He returned to Europe in 1541 to recapture Hungary from Ferdinand's invasion, but he went no farther.

Suleiman presided over the Ottoman Empire at its zenith, both in power and territory. After him, the long line of talented sultans ended. His son, Selim (called "the Sot"), had none of his father's talents. From Selim's rule forward the Ottoman Empire began a long decline until by the nineteenth century it was regarded by the world as "the sick man of Europe." Had Suleiman captured Vienna, he could have wintered there and proceeded the following season to invade Germany. Any sort of cooperative moves by France would have placed the Holy Roman Empire in a vise. That would have served Francis's aims in the short term, but he certainly overestimated his influence on the sultan. Islam could well have triumphed against a divided enemy.

Within the Ottoman military, the zenith passed as well. Vienna marked the beginning of the end for the Janissaries, for their once invincible front had been shattered. They could be beaten, and not only did their enemies know it, but so did the soldiers themselves. The bribe they were offered for that final attack was proof that their élan was no more. "The Janissaries themselves degenerated from the mighty force they had been. They used their power to improve their personal lives, at the expense of the state" (McCarthy, *The Ottoman Turks*, p. 164). "The Janissaries were to turn into unruly Praetorian guards, who made and unmade sultans, and this was perhaps inevitable. But even determinism must admit that Vienna started them down the long slide" (Pratt, *The Battles That Changed History*, p. 149). The elite force that had been the instrument of Ottoman expansion became the instrument of internal instability.

The decline in quality leadership after Suleiman was compounded by the success of the previous Ottoman line. The empire by the middle of the sixteenth century was too large to be efficiently governed by the overly centralized authority in Constantinople. Although the limits of the empire were (for the most part) as far as an army could march from Constantinople in one campaign season, that was still too large for the nature of imperial rule. Because their primary enemies at that time were the Holy Roman Empire and Persia, only two complete armies could maintain authority. To create them would mean an increase in cost and a corresponding decrease in quality, especially with the decline of the Janissaries. Thus, the Ottoman Empire could not expand its borders any farther. Conquest and booty had always been a major contributor to the economy. Over the following century, the Turks began to experience a rise in unemployment and banditry, which the weakening government could not successfully address. Unfortunately for the Ottoman Empire, Vienna spelled a change of fortune: just when a strong and visionary ruler was vital to maintain or expand the empire, the talent pool dried up.

References: Barber, Noel. *The Sultans.* New York: Simon & Schuster, 1973; Clot, Andre. *Suleiman the Magnificent: The Man, His Life, His Epoch.* Translated by Matthew J. Reisz. London: Saqui Books, 1989; McCarthy, Justin. *The Ottoman Turks.* New York: Longman, 1997; Parry, V. J. *A History of the Ottoman Empire to 1730.* Cambridge, UK: Cambridge University Press, 1976; Pratt, Fletcher. *The Battles That Changed History.* Garden City, NY: Doubleday, 1956.

CAJAMARCA
16 November 1532

FORCES ENGAGED

Spanish: Approximately 100 infantry and 67 cavalry. Commander: Francisco Pizarro.

Inca: Approximately 6,000 warriors. Commander: Atahualpa.

IMPORTANCE
Slaughter of Incan forces and capture of their king established the Spanish in power in Peru, the wealthiest region of South America.

Historical Setting

Francisco Pizarro was a conquistador, one of the warrior class that emerged in Spain during the wars between the Christians and Moors. After the Christians came to power in 1492, Spain was lucky enough to almost immediately sponsor Christopher Columbus, whose discovery (from the European perspective) of the Americas led to Spain being the most powerful nation on earth. Pizarro was a soldier in the expedition of Vasco Nuñez de Balboa to Panama in the 1520s, but found himself little richer for the experience. Hearing rumors of a land to the south with immense wealth and, like all conquistadors, fired by the stories of the success of Hernán Cortés in Mexico, Pizarro formed a partnership with three other men to explore the west coast of South America. His confederates were Diego de Almagro, Fernando Luque (the vicar of Panama), and Pedrarias Dávila (the governor of Panama). All were in their fifties by this time, and, if they were going to be rich, they needed to do something soon. Pizarro was more the soldier; Almagro, the supplier; and Luque, the diplomat. They entered into a contract with Bartolomé Ruiz, an experienced ship captain, to sail along the coast and find what they may.

Between 1524 and 1528, they suffered hardships, including disease and starvation, in their search for wealth. Ruiz had the greatest success, learning of an interior empire with fabled stores of gold. Almagro was more interested in exploring north of Panama and so was hesitant to supply Pizarro with men or materiel, so Pizarro returned to Spain to recruit backers. He found only a few, but his four brothers went in with him. They returned to Panama in December 1531 with 180 men and thirty horses and set sail for points south. They landed at the town of Tumbez on the coast of modern

Peru in the spring of 1532 and were joined by 100 men and fifty horses under the command of Hernando de Soto. As Cortés had done in Mexico with the founding of Vera Cruz, Pizarro established the settlement of San Miguel to use as his base. To his east, lay the formidable Andes Mountains and the storied Inca Empire.

The Incas ruled a vast empire stretching from modern Ecuador to about the site of Santiago, Chile, some 2,700 miles distant. The capital of this empire was at Cuzco. The head of government was the Inca, an American version of the pharaohs of ancient Egypt: both king and god. Like Moctezuma in Mexico, he ruled by force over a diverse population, but the Inca was much more forceful in his rule over his society, obliging all the conquered tribes to adopt the Incan language, Quichua, and incorporating defeated soldiers into his army. Also like Moctezuma, he was leader of the population's religious life, which was centered on worship of the sun. The most powerful Inca had been Huayna Capac, who conquered the Quito people of modern Ecuador and oversaw the construction of a highway system designed to facilitate trade and troop movements. Upon his death in 1527, he was succeeded by two sons. His legitimate heir, who took the traditional throne name "Cuzco, son of old Cuzco," was Huascar, who ruled from the capital city. Huascar had a half brother, Atahualpa, born of one of his father's concubines, a daughter of the defeated king of Quito. Huayna died in Quito; Atahualpa, apparently his favorite and the favorite of the military leaders, was by his side. Huascar, however, was the legitimate heir and in the administrative center at Cuzco when his father died, so he naturally assumed the throne. Whether the two were intended to rule cooperatively in a divided kingdom is unknown, but not surprisingly war soon broke out between the two. Atahualpa gained the upper hand; his generals defeated and imprisoned his brother in the temple at Cuzco in the spring of 1532. During the battle at Cuzco, Atahualpa had commanded reserve forces some 600 miles to the north in the city of Cajamarca.

The only records extant are those recorded by the Spanish, and they paint a gruesome picture of Atahualpa. He supposedly killed all his father's other sons, almost 200 of them, except for Huascar, who for some reason Atahualpa allowed to live. Atahualpa then is supposed to have slaughtered all of Huascar's family so no pretender could arise. How much of this actually happened is open to question, but one thing is clear: Atahualpa was just coming to power as Pizarro's men were landing some 250 miles to the north and establishing the town of San Miguel. News of that action reached Atahualpa in Cajamarca, and he apparently decided to stay there rather than retreat to the capital.

Pizarro's force departed San Miguel in September 1532. The climb into the Andes to reach Cajamarca was slow and difficult; although the location is near the equator, it was cold in the mountains and the rainy season had begun. Along the way, Pizarro received two delegations from Atahualpa, both of which brought gifts and extended a welcome. As some of the gifts were wrought from gold, Spanish spirits lifted. On 15 November, Pizarro's men crossed a pass and looked down on the town of Cajamarca; they entered it that day and found it deserted.

The Battle

The Spanish were equally impressed with the town and with the thousands of tents outside it where the Incan warriors were bivouacked. The center of the town was a triangular plaza, bordered on all sides by large halls that may have been government buildings. A stone fort overlooked the plaza, and all the buildings, public and private, were large and constructed of massive stonework. Above the entire city was yet another fort on the hillside, also triangular and seemingly hewn from the rock itself. The fact that Atahualpa ceded such a stronghold to men with firearms clearly indicates he had no idea with what he was dealing.

After a few hours in town with no sign from the Incan camp, Pizarro sent de Soto with twenty men on horseback to speak to Atahualpa. Pizarro ascended to the top of the fort, got a better look at the vastness of the Incan camp, and sent his brother Hernando and another twenty cavalry after de Soto. The Spanish rode unmolested into the tent city and up to the pavilion where Atahualpa awaited them. Atahualpa had been alerted that the aliens had horses (completely unknown in the Western Hemisphere). Although that may have reinforced the idea that these white people were emissaries of some divinity—as the Aztecs had believed—Atahualpa exhibited no anxiety in the presence of the Spanish or their animals. The two Spaniards extended an invitation for Atahualpa to visit Pizarro in Cajamarca. The reply, not from the Inca but from one of his aides, was that today was a day of fasting and tomorrow would be soon enough for a visit. The impression that Atahualpa gave was of a man who, divine in his own right, would give no concessions to anyone and that these Spaniards were, like everyone else, inferior beings. Still, forty riders in armor must have made an impression on him.

That night, the Spanish readied themselves for Atahualpa's visit. Knowing well how Cortés had seized power in Mexico by seizing Moctezuma, Pizarro planned to do exactly the same. Tensions ran high among the Spaniards, for they were surrounded by thousands of warriors and were a world away from any outside support. Pizarro was at his best as commander in calming his men and preparing them for the next day's encounter. The next morning, Pizarro deployed his men in the large halls fronting the plaza and waited for Atahualpa's arrival. They waited all morning before finally seeing a stirring in the Inca's camp. What caused the delay is a matter of speculation, although it was probably a council of war. As his best generals were still in Cuzco, overseeing his brother's captivity, one can only surmise the quality of advice Atahualpa may have received.

His men marched in a formal procession, some 6,000 strong, while the Inca himself was borne on a palanquin. Warriors were deployed along both sides of the 4 miles that the procession covered. As Atahualpa approached Cajamarca, there were no signs of activity within the town. About a half-mile from the town, the procession stopped. Atahualpa sent a messenger to Pizarro, stating that he would visit on the morrow instead of late on this day, 16 November. Pizarro's men had had their nerves stretched to the breaking point by the long day that they had spent in hiding, and Pizarro did not want to increase their anxiety by spending another night waiting. He sent a return message to Atahualpa, stating that food and entertainment had been prepared and awaited him. The message may have said something more provocative, however, to convince the god-king to respond to Pizarro's pressure; its exact contents are unknown. Whatever it said, Atahualpa's procession proceeded toward Cajamarca as the afternoon waned.

Although Atahualpa had informed the Spanish that he would enter their camp armed, as they had entered his, this apparently did not happen. In the society of the time and place, it was proper for enemy commanders to meet unarmed before a battle, and Atahualpa was doing no more than following protocol. As the procession entered the plaza, it divided into two columns so that the Inca's palanquin could be escorted to the center. Still, nothing stirred until the arrival of a Catholic priest, Father Valverde. Speaking through the same interpreter who had accompanied the Spanish from San Miguel, the Dominican friar began telling the Inca about Christ. Atahualpa listened passively for a time, but grew more upset as he realized the Spaniard was challenging his divinity and demanding he concede power to a foreign god and to a far-distant King Charles V. Atahualpa took the Bible from Valverde, broke its clasp to look inside, and then threw it to the ground in disgust. After fighting a war to seize his throne, he was not about to give it up on the word of some lackey of a foreign monarch.

Valverde picked up the Bible and fled. As soon as he was clear of the plaza, Pizarro gave a signal to his brother Hernando, who transmitted it to Pedro de Candia, who oversaw the two small cannon that Pizarro had ordered placed on the nearby fort. As the first cannonballs blew through the packed mass of Incan warriors, three columns of cavalry poured out of the halls bordering the plaza. Although it is reported that some of the Incan warriors carried slings or javelins under their clothing and therefore were not really unarmed, they could in no way resist a charge of heavy European cavalry. Lances and swords cut through virtually every warrior in the plaza; only a few managed to escape. Thus, the battle at Cajamarca was hardly a battle at all, but a massacre.

Pizarro fought his way through to Atahualpa's palanquin because he had to have the Inca alive. Indeed, Pizarro was the only Spaniard wounded in the entire melee, a sword cut coming from one of his own men caught up in the fury of the moment. No other native was taken alive. For whatever reason, the thousands of warriors outside the town did nothing to come to the rescue of their leader, either in the midst of battle or afterward.

Results

The next day, as Atahualpa's army either stayed in camp or began to drift away (those who were local levies only recently conquered), the Inca was plotting his release. Seeing the value the Spanish placed on gold, he offered to fill a room, 17 by 22 feet and as high as he could reach, roughly 7 feet. A second, smaller room was to be filled twice over with silver. Would that suffice for his ransom? Pizarro agreed that it would. Atahualpa sent messengers across his empire to gather the gold to a volume of more than 2,600 cubic feet. Pizarro and his followers soon saw the fruits of their labors being delivered. Sly as Atahualpa may have been in this plan, Pizarro was one step ahead of him. He had sent de Soto to Cuzco, where Huascar was prisoner and who, when he heard of the Spanish victory, sent word that he would like to work with them. He claimed that he knew the secret storehouses of his father's wealth, whereas his brother Atahualpa could only loot shrines and temples for pieces of gold. As Atahualpa's promise neared completion, Pizarro informed him of Huascar's offer to double the ransom. Atahualpa, who had been allowed attendants in his captivity, sent word secretly to his generals in Cuzco, who killed Huascar.

Pizarro was not happy with that and soon had to decide what to do with his captive. Although he had promised Atahualpa his freedom in return for the room of gold, when the task was accomplished, Pizarro instead brought his prisoner up on charges for Huascar's murder. Unsurprisingly, he was convicted. Sentenced to burn at the stake as a heathen, Atahualpa at the last moment accepted the foreign religion and died by strangling.

Pizarro nominated one of Atahualpa's brothers (apparently he had not had them all executed), Toparca, to be the new Inca. As they traveled to Cuzco to install him on the throne, Toparca died. As Pizarro marched on Cuzco, one of Huascar's surviving brothers appeared. This was Manco Inca, and he professed his loyalty to Pizarro and received the throne in return. Later, he plotted against the Spanish and raised a rebellion in April 1536. A battle was fought at the fortress of Sacsahuaman, outside Cuzco, but forces under Hernando Pizarro defeated them after a weeklong struggle. Francisco Pizarro also had to beat back a siege from his newly established capital at Lima, but, because the land around the town was flat, his cavalry quickly killed the native warriors.

The only threat to Pizarro's rule over his newly conquered land came from his erstwhile partner Diego de Almagro. He argued with Pizarro over who was to hold what land. King Charles V had granted Pizarro governorship over territory 270 leagues south of the River Santiago. Almagro had been granted land for 200 leagues to the south of that. Just where did Cuzco lie? That was the dispute, and on 6 April 1538 the two men fought for the right to hold the center of Incan society. Pizarro was victorious and imprisoned his former associate, for which he was strongly criticized in Spain. Some of Almagro's followers assassinated Pizarro on 26 June 1541. Soon afterward, a governor was appointed from Spain and an imperial administration was established. Still, no matter which Spaniard ruled, the Inca people were subjected to foreign domination. Just as happened in Mexico, they proceeded to see their culture stripped from them as their wealth was shipped to Spain and their language and religion died in the face of the might of the conquerors.

References: Cieza de Leon, Pedro de. *The Incas.* Translated by Harriet de Onis. Norman: University of Oklahoma Press, 1959 [1553, 1873]; Innes, Hammond. *The Conquistadors.* New York: Alfred A. Knopf, 1969; Means, Philip A. *The Fall of the Inca Empire and the Spanish Rule in Peru, 1530–1780.* New York: Gordian Press, 1971; Prescott, William H. *The History of the Conquest of Peru.* Philadelphia: J. B. Lippincott, 1874 [1847]; Richman, Irving Berdine. *Adventurers of New Spain: The Spanish Conquerors.* New Haven, CT: Yale University Press, 1929.

LEPANTO
7 October 1571

FORCES ENGAGED

Allied: 316 Spanish, Venetian, and papal ships; 30,000 soldiers and 50,000 naval personnel. Commander: Don Juan of Austria.
Turkish: 245 galleys. Commander: Ali Pasha.

IMPORTANCE

Turkish defeat stopped Turkey's expansion into the Mediterranean, thus maintaining western dominance. Confidence grew in the west that Turks, previously unstoppable, could be beaten.

Historical Setting

From the late fifteenth century, Spain was the dominant power in Europe. The wealth garnered from the Spanish colonies in the Americas was the foundation of its military might, and the fact that Charles I of Spain was also ruler of the Holy Roman Empire meant that Spain controlled much of western Europe. This included the Netherlands and Austria, along with claims to lands on the Italian peninsula. Charles saw the Roman Catholic faith as the glue to hold all this together, but he had his share of rivals. Catholic France had no desire to see Charles further empowered as the champion of the Catholic Church, and Pope Clement VII feared anyone with sufficient political power to challenge his authority. Further, France also had claims to Italian possessions that contradicted Spain's. Thus, Pope Clement sought to challenge Charles by organizing his rivals into the Holy League of Cognac, but this was defeated in May 1527 when Charles's forces captured and sacked Rome. After bribing his main naval competitor, Genoa, Charles gained control of the western Mediterranean as well. In 1530, Charles forced Pope Clement to recognize him both as Holy Roman Emperor and king of Italy.

All of this infighting was a blessing for the Turks, who were consolidating their power in the Middle East at this same time. In the first two decades of the sixteenth century, the Ottoman Turks spread their authority from Iran to Egypt, after which they faced west toward the squabbling Europeans. Suleiman I (called "the Magnificent") marched his armies into the Balkans, capturing Belgrade in 1521, defeating the Hungarians at Mohacs in 1526, and attacking Vienna in 1529. Although he failed to capture Vienna, he still put the Turks in control of southeastern Europe. He also oversaw the capture of the island of Rhodes in 1522, after which Turkish forces drove the Knights of St. John out of Crete and on to Malta. Thus, the Ottoman Empire by 1530 threatened Europe on both land and sea.

Charles checked the spreading power of Moslem Turkey by attacking their allies along the southern Mediterranean, the coastal powers Algeria and Tunis in 1535. Scattered naval

warfare through the 1530s and 1540s maintained a balance of power. In 1556, Charles abdicated the thrones of both Spain and the Holy Roman Empire, leaving the former to his son Philip II and the latter to his brother Ferdinand, thus keeping it all in the family. Under Philip, Spain controlled the Netherlands, the French frontier province of Franche Comté, Sardinia and Sicily in the Mediterranean, and most of the Italian peninsula. His driving ambition to unite all of Europe under his rule ran into the nationalistic and religious stubbornness of northern Europe, particularly the Dutch. The Reformation was fully in swing by the middle of the 1500s, and Protestantism was a rallying force against both the Catholic Church and Philip as its champion. To maintain political control as well as crush the hated Protestants, Philip funneled most of the wealth of the Americas into war against his religious and political enemies, which effort proceeded to send money out of Spain and into the rest of Europe.

While focusing his efforts on the Netherlands, however, Philip left the home front unguarded and found himself harassed by Moslems in Spain. Although the Moorish control of the country had ended in 1492, many Moslems remained in Iberia. After 1499, they had been given the option of exile or conversion to Christianity. Most chose the latter, but did so only for show; these came to be called Moriscos. They saw in Philip's religious and political trouble in northern Europe an opportunity to further the cause of Moslem Turkey. They began intriguing with the pirate states of the Barbary Coast of North Africa as well as with Turkish agents. To encourage the Turks even further, the French government began giving clandestine support to Turkish designs on the west. This was done originally solely to hurt Philip, but much of the influence in the Middle East that the French held through the twentieth century began at this time. In 1568, Philip sent his half brother, Don Juan of Austria, to suppress the Moriscos. His success refocused Spanish attention on the Turks.

The Turks were ready for battle, for Suleiman's son Selim (r. 1566–1574) had many aggressive advisors. Although the Turks had an alliance with the Italian state of Venice, Selim coveted the island of Cyprus, which Venice owned. Upon hearing the false report that a massive fire in Venice had destroyed much of the city and most of its fleet, Selim in April 1570 sent a representative to Venice demanding that Cyprus be ceded to the Ottoman Turks. Venice appealed to the rest of Europe for aid, but found few supporters. Because Venice was a republic, the monarchies of Europe had no love for it; all Christians despised the Venetians for making agreements with the Turks; and all naval powers hated Venice for its fleet and its profitable monopoly with the Middle East. Only Pope Pius V responded; he could not allow a Moslem power to dictate to a Christian one, and he hoped that by coordinating an allied effort he might revive the crusading fervor lost to Europe since the thirteenth century. Pius persuaded an initially reluctant Philip not only to supply the fleets from his Mediterranean possessions but to provide soldiers for the Venetian navy as well. Pius called a conference to organize a mutual defense league, which after months of wrangling finally came together in May 1571.

The Battle

Although it was Venice that was in desperate straits, it balked at Spanish control of the forces of the Holy League. Philip demanded that Don Juan of Austria, fresh from a victory over the Moriscos, be placed in charge. He was accepted only after the concession that he would take no action without the agreement of the commanders of each allied fleet. Luckily for the League, however, the 26-year-old commander was able to garner the respect and loyalty of all his subordinates. This was fortunate because the governments of the Holy League all had their own agendas. Venice wanted to use the League forces to defend Cyprus from Turkish attacks,

already under way. Philip wanted to use it to defeat the Barbary pirates so he could control the western Mediterranean. Pope Pius wanted all the Mediterranean under European control, seeing rightly that this would divide the European and African possessions of the Ottoman Empire and weaken any further Turkish offensives into Europe. In the end, the force of personality exercised by both Pius and Don Juan were the keys to victory.

The port of Messina on the island of Sicily was the rendezvous point. There Don Juan took command of more than 300 ships, of which more than half were under Spanish command. The Venetians supplied most of the remainder of the ships, although Philip had been obliged to provide soldiers for the Venetians. That did nothing to endear them to him. The pope supplied 12 galleys and 6 frigates. Altogether the fleet contained 208 galleys, six galleasses, and more than 100 galleons, frigates, and brigantines. The galley of this time was powered by both sail and oars and looked little different than the ships of ancient Greece or Rome; it carried mainly soldiers. The galleons, frigates, and brigantines were sailing ships and carried more cannon than soldiers. The galleasses were a hybrid of both types of ship. The Turkish fleet was comprised almost totally of galleys. The standard method of naval warfare at the time was little different from land warfare. In battle, the ships closed with each other, and the soldiers on board fought for control of their own and enemy shipping. Thus, ships were captured much more often than they were destroyed. It was not surprising that Don Juan, a general, was in command, for the ships were mainly for transport and were maneuvered and commanded in formations similar to those on the battlefield.

While the forces of the Holy League were gathering, the Turks were busy at Cyprus. Since May 1571, the main fortress city of Famagusta had been under siege. It resisted until 1 August, when a lack of gunpowder forced a surrender. The Venetian commander of the city

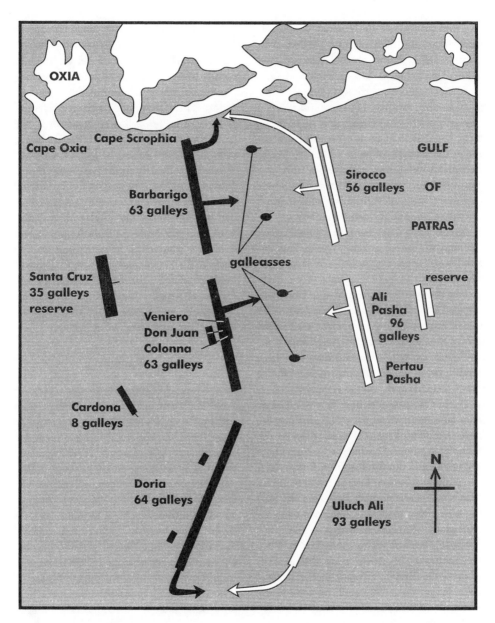

was tortured to death, and his officers were slaughtered. This both freed up the Turkish fleet for action and motivated the men of the Holy League when they learned of it. The Turks spent the next few weeks raiding the Greek islands and then massed at Lepanto, Greece, in the Gulf of Corinth. The Europeans docked for a time at Corfu and then (upon hearing news of the fate of Famagusta) sailed east in search of the Turks. Hearing of their approach, the Turkish fleet under Ali Pasha, reinforced with some Algerian ships under the command of Uluch Ali, sailed west toward the Gulf of Patras. At dawn on 7 October 1571, the two fleets sighted each other.

Don Juan placed the Venetian contingent under Augustino Barbarigo on the left, with orders to sail as close as possible to the shallows along Cape Scrophia. Don Juan commanded the center, and the well-known Genoese admiral Giovanni Andrea Doria commanded a mixed force of Genoese and papal ships on the right flank. Don Juan also formed a reserve under the marquis of Santa Cruz. He placed four of his well-armed galleasses in front as a skirmish line to use their superior firepower against the Turks. Ali Pasha mirrored Don Juan's formation, with Mahomet Sirocco facing the Venetians along Cape Scrophia, himself commanding the center, and the Algerian fleet under Uluch Ali on the Turkish left facing Andrea Doria.

As the two fleets formed up, Don Juan boarded a small, fast ship and sailed down his line of ships, shouting encouragement and receiving the cheers of his crews. At the same time, Ali Pasha was telling his captured Christian slaves rowing his galleys that victory would mean their freedom. As the two fleets neared each other, the galleasses drew first blood, their long-range cannon outdistancing anything the Turks had. This kept Ali Pasha's ships in the center from advancing, while the flanking forces rowed forward, thus breaking the Turkish line.

Mahomet Sirocco knew the waters better than his opposite number Barbarigo. By sailing even closer to shore, Sirocco was able to outflank the Venetians. Barbarigo was killed and his flagship was lost and recaptured twice. Only the capture of Sirocco from his sinking ship stopped the Turkish advance in the shallow water. Meanwhile, Uluch Ali on the left attempted to outflank Andrea Doria on the southern flank. By forcing the Genoese ships to turn to face the maneuver, this opened a gap between them and Don Juan's force in the center. Uluch Ali quickly faced his galleys about and split the gap, but the timely arrival of the reserve forces under Santa Cruz drove them back.

In the center, Don Juan's ships had the advantage over those of Ali Pasha, for he had more

and better cannon for long-range damage. At short range, the superior firepower of the European matchlocks used by his soldiers did bloody work among the Turks, who lost large numbers of men by the time the ships were able to close. Then, the greater numbers and aggressiveness of the Spanish troops prevailed. The main battle took place over Ali Pasha's ship. It took three forays before the Spanish were able to board the Turkish flagship and stay aboard. Cornered, Ali Pasha begged for his life with the promise of a huge ransom, but a Spanish soldier beheaded him. The display of Ali Pasha's head on a pike broke the Turkish morale, and the battle came to a swift conclusion after the death of their commander. Uluch Ali fled with his ships to the protection of the guns of the fortress at Lepanto (modern Navpaktos), but his fighting withdrawal caused the Europeans chasing him some serious damage.

Results

After 4 hours of fighting, the cost was steep for both sides. Sources vary on the numbers of casualties. Oliver Warner (*Great Sea Battles*, p. 23) states that Don Juan's Holy League forces lost approximately 8,000 dead and 16,000 wounded, with the Turks losing probably about 25,000 dead, but some 15,000 of their galley slaves were liberated. J. F. C. Fuller (*A Military History of the Western World*, vol. 1, p. 576) numbers the Holy League losses at 15,000 total, with the Turks losing 30,000 killed in battle, an unknown number drowned, and 8,000 taken prisoner. As for their ships, the Europeans lost 12 galleys sunk and 1 captured, whereas the Turks lost 113 galleys sunk and another 117 captured. In addition, the wealth aboard the captured ships was immense.

Lepanto was a victory that spelled the end of Moslem naval power and ambitions. Although it did not completely break their naval might, the force gathered for this battle was never again equaled. They still exercised some authority in the eastern Mediterranean, and the

Barbary pirates were active through the nineteenth century, but the Moslems were never again able to challenge the Europeans for maritime dominance. Uluch Ali commanded a refurbished Turkish navy, but he twice refused to engage other League fleets. Although the Mediterranean did not immediately become a European lake, the day when that was to happen came much sooner.

More than a military victory, Lepanto was a moral one. For decades, the Ottoman Turks had terrified Europe, and the victories of Suleiman the Magnificent caused Christian Europe serious concern. The defeat at Lepanto further exemplified the rapid deterioration of Ottoman might under Selim, and Christians rejoiced at this setback for the infidels. The mystique of Ottoman power was tarnished significantly by this battle, and Christian Europe was heartened.

However, the political potential that could have resulted never came about. The Holy League was short-lived, and the battle at Lepanto was its sole shining moment. Pope Pius V died shortly thereafter, and the machinations of politicians reasserted themselves. French King Charles IX continued playing the troublemaker, fomenting further Protestant rebellion in the Netherlands and facilitating a peace agreement between Venice and the Ottoman Empire, signed secretly in March 1573. When that was announced, the Holy League collapsed. Political rivalries almost certainly would have remained too strong for a serious long-term unity to have been achieved via the Holy League. No political leader had the personality to take over upon Pope Pius's death, and Philip of Spain, who would certainly have liked to lead such a unified Europe (under his own terms, of course), was once again forced to divert his attention elsewhere. Protestants rather than Moslems again became his adversaries, and they ultimately proved his undoing. They broke away from Spanish and Holy Roman Empire authority thanks to England's victory over the Spanish Armada in 1588 and the bloody Thirty Years' War (1618–1648).

From a naval warfare point of view, Lepanto marks a turning point. Since before the time of Christ, the galley had ruled the seas, but its day was rapidly declining. The sailing ships that appeared in this battle were the wave of the future. They had more speed in the long haul than did galleys (although less for short distances), carried greater capacity for cannon, and were much more seaworthy. As an extension of land warfare, naval warfare fought by soldiers on the high seas saw its last major appearance at Lepanto. As shown by the battle between the English Royal Navy and the Spanish Armada 15 years later, cannon and sail replaced sword and rowers.

References: Beeching, Jack. *The Galleys at Lepanto.* New York: Charles Scribner's Sons, 1983; Fuller, J. F. C. *A Military History of the Western World,* vol. 1. New York: Funk & Wagnalls, 1954; Paulson, Michael. *Lepanto: Fact, Fiction and Fantasy.* Lanham, MD: University Press of America, 1986; Warner, Oliver. *Great Sea Battles.* London: Spring Books, 1963.

SPANISH ARMADA
29 July 1588

FORCES ENGAGED
Spanish: 130 ships.
Commander: Duke of Medina-Sidonia.
English: 197 ships.
Commander: Lord Howard of Effingham.

IMPORTANCE
Spanish defeat marked the beginning of the decline of the Spanish Empire and made England the world's preeminent naval power, allowing the English to begin colonizing North America.

Historical Setting

When Queen Elizabeth I came to the throne of England in 1558, she ruled a disjointed and rather weak nation, having many discontented factions within and few friends without. One of those friends, however, was the most powerful nation in the world at the time: Spain, ruled by Philip II. Philip had lately been tied to the English throne through his marriage to Elizabeth's predecessor, Mary. When she died, Philip proposed marriage to her surviving sister to maintain his influence in a country with a number of Protestants (which he hated) and a burgeoning naval strength (which he coveted). Elizabeth turned down his proposal, but at first the two kept friendly relations, Philip even offering to aid in recovering Calais, England's last possession on the Continent. It was not long before the two countries became bitter enemies.

Elizabeth was ambitious for her country, and she inherited from her father, Henry VIII, a Protestant bent. When she declared the nation's religion to be not Catholicism but the Church of England, this upset the rabidly Catholic Philip. Even more upsetting were England's raids on Spanish wealth. Unable to even consider the idea of challenging Spain's navy in open combat, Elizabeth secretly commissioned privateers to harass Spanish shipping and colonies. This they did to great effect, with the famous pirates Francis Drake, Martin Frobisher, and John Hawkins interfering in Spain's slave trade between Africa and the New World, raiding Spanish ports in the Caribbean and South America, and hijacking treasure ships bound for Spain or traveling from Spain to the Low Countries, where they financed campaigns against Protestant movements. Bad enough that Elizabeth was picking Philip's pocket; she was using much of the money gained from her privateers to support those Protestant uprisings in Europe. Thus, Philip's army in Holland was being opposed by forces supported with his own money.

Philip was not at first of a mind to challenge Elizabeth directly, although some of his advisors suggested he do so. Through the 1570s, the relations between Spain and England waxed and waned, often in relation to changing political fortunes in the various ruling houses on the Continent. At times, the two countries were at each other's throats. In 1571, Philip gave support to the Rodolfi conspiracy, which plotted to assassinate Elizabeth and place her cousin, Mary Queen of Scots, on the throne. Elizabeth gave safe haven to Dutch privateers harassing Spanish shipping. The Spanish and the English severed relations and restored them in an ever-changing set of political circumstances.

In the latter 1570s, Francis Drake circumnavigated the globe, shooting up Spanish colonies and capturing Spanish shipping along the way. As he was doing so, Philip laid claim to the throne of Portugal, which only increased his immense wealth by adding Portugal's eastern empire. Elizabeth granted asylum to Don Antonio, Philip's rival to Portugal, and allowed him to grant letters of marque to English captains, with which they could harass Spanish shipping under his authority. Elizabeth entered into negotiations with Catherine de Medici of France, but the French attempt to challenge Philip's navy off the island of Terceira in 1582 ended in disaster for the French and renewed confidence in the power of Spain's fleet. (This reconfirmed the confidence that the Spanish had carried since their success in the victory over the Turks at Lepanto in 1571.) Owing to England's support of France in this failed endeavor, Philip's advisors again urged an assault on England, but again he hesitated. He changed his mind after two events. In 1584, England and Spain again severed relations in the wake of another assassination attempt against Elizabeth. She also ordered a stepped-up campaign against Spanish shipping and Caribbean holdings, to which Drake and Frobisher gladly obliged. The following year, she ordered 5,000 soldiers under the earl of Leicester to shore up the Dutch military in the wake of the death of their leader, William of Orange. These two direct military actions, on top of the years of intrigue and religious challenge, had to be answered. Then Elizabeth ordered the execution of her Catholic rival, Mary, in February 1587.

In a matter of weeks, Philip ordered the Spanish Armada to be assembled.

The Battle

The original plan for the Armada was proffered by the marquis of Santa Cruz, Spain's most accomplished captain and veteran of the battles of Lepanto and Terceira. He asked for 510 ships and more than 94,000 men to form an invasion fleet. Philip scaled this down considerably to 130 ships, whose primary aim was to secure the English Channel and provide extra forces to assist the duke of Parma. Parma had been waging war against Philip's Protestant enemies in Holland and was regarded as the premier military commander of his day. With the skilled Santa Cruz in command of the fleet and Parma leading the invasion forces, England stood little chance of surviving the onslaught.

Even before the Armada could begin to take serious shape, Drake struck first. In April 1587, he led twenty-three ships toward Spain before the hesitant Elizabeth could stop him. She was leery of war, unsure of her capabilities, and unwilling to spend much money. By the time he arrived off the Spanish port of Cadiz, Drake had destroyed a large amount of Spanish shipping and pillaged enough supplies to push onward to Lisbon. There, on 10 May, he struck terror into the ships lying at nearby Cascaes Bay and caused the loss of twenty-four ships. He sailed on to Cape St. Vincent, where he attacked the Portuguese base there and destroyed the bulk of the Spanish supply of barrel staves, vital for storing the necessary supplies for the upcoming Spanish invasion. Only want of reinforcement kept him from staying and causing even more damage. Before returning to England, he raided toward the Azores and captured the *San Felipe*, which contained a fortune in cargo and (even more valuable in the long run) information on the inner workings of the Spanish/Portuguese trade with India. This proved to be the foundation upon which the future British East India Company was based.

In spite of these setbacks, the Armada was assembled over the succeeding months, while Elizabeth vacillated over the wisdom of fighting Spain. Parma offered peace talks to which she responded, but they were probably just for show as far as both sides were concerned. At this time, England gained an important ally, a small but aggressive Dutch fleet that blockaded Flanders and ultimately stymied Parma's attempts to coordinate action with the Armada.

In early 1588, the two commanders were chosen. Santa Cruz organized the Armada and would have commanded it, but he died suddenly in the spring. Thus, command of the fleet fell to the duke of Medina-Sidonia, a high-ranking nobleman with sufficient authority to issue orders in the king's name. Unfortunately, he had never been to sea and had no military experience, but Philip named as second-in-command the able captain Don Diego de Valdez. When the Armada linked with Parma, the general would become the expedition's commander. Elizabeth also chose a nobleman for command: Lord Howard of Effingham. Unlike Medina-Sidonia, he was a mariner, although not the most talented available. He was assisted, however, by Drake, Frobisher, and Hawkins, and Howard was smart enough to know when to ask for and follow their advice. He supported the pleadings of his subordinates to launch a preemptive strike at the Armada, but Elizabeth would not. Santa Cruz's death and rumors of a storm having scattered the Armada convinced her that the invasion would be postponed, but to her captains that made early action all the more vital. When confirmation of the Armada's departure from Lisbon was received, she did no more than allow Howard's ships to patrol the English coast. She had the best captains available under her command, but she would not take their advice.

The Armada left Lisbon on 20 May, but put into La Coruña after encountering a storm. There the provisions stored in the barrels newly constructed of unseasoned wood proved to have

Hendrik Vroom, "Sea Battle between the Spanish Armada and the English Naval Forces," c. 1600.
Landesmuseum Ferdinandeum, Innsbruck, Austria. (Erich Lessing/Art Resource, New York)

gone bad, and many of the ships and crews were in less than fighting trim. After receiving fresh supplies, they proceeded on 12 July and then rounded Brittany into the English Channel on 19 July. This was the day that the English located the Armada and, according to legend, the captains of the English fleet finished their bowling before boarding their ships and sailing off to battle. In the moonlight of 20–21 July, the two fleets sighted each other and closed. The English had the wind in their favor, plus the advantage of more nimble ships and superior crews. The English ended the first skirmish with a decided advantage. The greater range of their smaller guns allowed them to engage at greater distance than the Spanish would have liked. The Spanish strength lay in shorter range, heavier cannon, but even more in their personnel. The Spanish were following the traditional but obsolescent tactics of closing and boarding, and the faster and more maneuverable English ships would not allow that. Medina-Sidonia wrote that "the enemy's ships were so fast and handy that there was

nothing that could be done with them." The key loss of the day for the Spanish was the *San Salvador*, which carried the fleet's paymaster and his gold.

The English failed to follow up on their early advantage. As the Spanish escaped eastward, Drake, leading the pursuit, was lost in the darkness as he turned to capture and claim a Spanish ship. This caused much confusion in the English fleet and seriously delayed what could have been an early killing blow. The two fleets sailed eastward, with the Spanish aiming toward the Isle of Wight to establish a base of operations. The English chased and harassed the Spanish, causing the Armada to waste its ammunition in long-range duels they could not win. As the English succeeded in catching up and harrying the Armada, Medina-Sidonia decided to bypass the Isle of Wight and sail for Calais, where he expected to find it easier to join with Parma. To the English, the rapidly fragmenting Armada fleeing toward the French coast resembled sheep being driven. Medina-

Sidonia reached Calais on 27 July and anchored his ships in the roads.

Reinforced by ships from the Thames under Seymour and Wynter, Lord Howard knew he was in the best possible position. He held a council of war on Sunday, 28 July, aboard his flagship, the *Ark Royal*. Rather than await small fishing boats, which had been requested to serve as fire ships, the commanders decided to unload eight of their own ships and let the prevailing wind blow them into the Spanish fleet at anchor. Although the Spanish were aware of the possibility of such a move, and had put out picket ships to stop it, the English were able to set the boats alight in the early morning hours of 29 July. Hurrying to cut their anchor cables and avoid the flames, the Spanish fleet began to fall into confusion. Although no ships were directly harmed by the fire ships, collisions occurred and the Armada, at first light, was spread out along the coast in no discernible formation.

This spelled the Armada's doom, as well as that of the entire invasion. Because they had used most of their ammunition during the harassing attacks in the Channel, Medina-Sidonia realized he could not fight the English. Neither could he link up with Parma near his base at Bruges because the blockading Dutch ships had the general bottled up. Medina-Sidonia had no choice but to order a retreat homeward around the north of Scotland.

Results

Medina-Sidonia's only hope of salvaging anything from his expedition would have been to land in Scotland and hope to join with Catholics that may have risen up against Elizabeth. Instead, he ordered his ships home. The provisions that they had brought could not last for such an extended voyage, but the order was given anyway. The lack of food and the heavy weather they suffered in the North Atlantic conspired to whittle away at the Armada's numbers. With the losses in the Channel skirmishes, those collisions off Calais, and the ships sunk by storms off Scotland, Ireland, and Cornwall, the Armada's 130 ships were reduced by half when they dragged back into Cadiz in September. Medina-Sidonia wrote to his king, "The troubles and miseries we have suffered cannot be described to Your Majesty. They have been greater than have ever been seen in any voyage before." The English, on the other hand, lost no ships at all.

Many things changed after this battle. It marked, for one thing, a new era in naval warfare. The tactics of close action, ramming, and boarding, all of which the Spanish had hoped to do in this battle, became a thing of the past. The era of the cannon had arrived. The Spanish Armada actually outnumbered the English in the number of heavy cannon, but they could not be brought to bear with any real effect because of their short range. The smaller culverins that the English employed fired smaller and lighter shot, not as destructive but with greater range. Within a few decades, better guns and the improvement of designs being implemented in shipbuilding made the man-of-war the master of the oceans. The earlier formations, of ships massing line abreast for ramming, was changing as the Armada was being fought. The concept of line astern formations, whereby broadsides could be employed, was seen in the Channel engagements, although there is some dispute whether it was accidentally or intentionally used.

More important were the political effects of the Armada's defeat. The Spanish Empire, which had been on the rise since 1492, had reached its zenith. From this point onward, it began a long, slow decline. The Dutch gained their independence, and the Protestant movement grew as Spanish military power in Europe weakened. Although the Thirty Years' War (1618–1648) finally established the Protestant denominations in Europe, the dedication and financial ability that Spain and Philip II possessed to crush them faltered after 1588. Spain's empire in the Western Hemisphere, growing unabated since Columbus started it almost a century before, ceased to expand northward. Although Spain maintained a stranglehold on most of Latin America for more than another two centuries, its expansion toward North America ended as they went over to the defensive. England, whose navy now had the ability to venture in greater strength into the world, began its rise to greatness. Some English explorers who had plans to try to plant colonies now had greater freedom to do just that, and North America became their goal. Thus, the political, religious, and social fabric of North America became dominated by English foundations, whereas Central and South America were forever Latinized. Further, the ability to access India and its trade followed in the wake of this battle, and the basis of the British Empire lay there. The year 1588 marked the beginning of a changing of the guard, from Spanish and Mediterranean power to English and northern European ascendancy.

Had the Armada accomplished its mission of linking up with Parma and invading, it would certainly have altered the future. Even if they had failed to conquer England, which certainly did not have the military power or ability of the Spanish army, the development of England as a world power would have been seriously postponed. Had the Spanish conquered, their power could have stretched over all of Europe, and Catholicism could have maintained the preeminence it had enjoyed since Constantine in the fourth century. A further expansion into North America would certainly have occurred, and the effects of that on Spanish power and its future may have proved almost limitless.

References: Fuller, J. F. C. *A Military History of the Western World,* vol. 2. New York: Funk & Wagnalls, 1955; Lewis, Michael. *The Spanish Armada.* New York: Thomas Y. Crowell, 1968; Martin, Colin. *The Spanish Armada.* New York: W. W. Norton, 1988; Mattingly, Garrett. *The Armada.* Boston: Houghton Mifflin, 1959; Warner, Oliver. *Great Sea Battles.* London: Spring Books, 1963.

SEKIGAHARA
21 October 1600

FORCES ENGAGED
Eastern Army: 75,000 men.
Commander: Tokugawa Ieyasu.
Western Army: 120,000 men.
Commander: Ishida Mitsunari.

IMPORTANCE
Tokugawa's victory established him as the shogun, military leader, and virtual dictator of Japan. His dynasty ruled Japan until the Meiji Restoration in 1867.

Historical Setting

During the Heian Era (794–1192) of Japanese history, the emperor ruled from the newly established capital at the city of Kyoto. In the late twelfth century, the power of the emperor was challenged by the rise of the samurai, a class of warriors. For more than a century, the emperors had depended on the samurai to fight their wars and maintain regional order, but a struggle between two strong samurai clans resulted in war in the 1180s. The battle of Dannoura in 1185 ended in a victory for the Minamoto clan, whose leader saw an opportunity to challenge the emperor for supreme authority. To forestall such a move, the emperor appointed Minamoto-no-Yoritomi to be commander of all the imperial armies, with the authority to call them out at his own discretion. Thus was created the position of shogun. Although the shogun was officially subservient to the emperor, control of the armies made the shogun the real power behind the throne.

Minamoto established an alternate administration at the town of Kamakura, that town giving its name to the shogunate for the next century and a half. Through the middle of the sixteenth century, the respective powers of the emperor and the shogun waxed and waned. Beneath the shogun and emperor, an aristocracy developed of feudal lords called daimyo. Like the European knights, these were military lords of domains that (in theory at least) served at the will of the emperor. In 1467, the War of Onin, between two daimyo, led to a century-long period of civil war in Japan that ended only with the rise of one of Japan's premier military leaders, Oda Nobunaga. In 1568, he backed Ashikaga Yoshiaki for the shogunate. He was one of the last scions of the Ashikaga family that had held the position through the civil war era. The family had become weak during that time, and Oda seized the opportunity to be the power behind the shogunate, for as a commoner he could not hold the position. With Ashikaga Yoshiaki in position, Oda spent the next 15 years strengthening his hold over his puppet and amassing land and wealth. That resulted in such a stranglehold on the shogunate that Ashikaga staged a revolt; he lost and was exiled in 1573. Oda died in 1582, killing himself during an assassin's attack in that year.

Oda was succeeded by his chief subordinate, Toyatomi Hideyoshi, an even more talented military leader than Oda. Toyatomi's ambition went beyond the shogunate; he wanted to lead an expanding Japan past the home islands on to the mainland. He first had to unify Japan, which he succeeded in doing with his victory in 1590 over the rival Hojo clan. That victory gave him control over the powerful Odawara Castle, near the isolated town of Edo. He established Edo as the new capital of Japan, and the city that grew there later was renamed Tokyo. In 1592, he sent 160,000 soldiers to conquer Korea, but a Korean naval victory denied him the ability to maintain communications, and the invasion was recalled. A second attempt in 1596 gained some successes, but stalled when Toyatomi died in 1598. His death provoked yet another succession struggle.

Tokugawa Ieyasu was Toyatomi's main general and most likely successor. However, Toyatomi left behind a 5-year-old son who had received the oaths of loyalty of all his father's subordinates before Toyatomi died. Tokugawa was named his regent, but he too aimed at the shogunate, being a descendant of the Minamoto clan that had established the office. Within the government council, Tokugawa had his rivals, the main one being a low-born but exceedingly ambitious bureaucrat, Ishida Mitsunari. Ishida plotted with two of the most powerful daimyo, Shimazu and Mori. Tokugawa seemed to have little regard for Ishida, especially after the upstart attempted to assassinate him in 1599. Tokugawa released him, perhaps because he felt he knew his enemy so well that he could predict the actions of those who would rally around him. "Better the devil you know...."

Ishida's allies had managed to get control of Toyatomi Hideyori, the heir to the shogunate, but Tokugawa held his mother captive. The nation's daimyo began to rally around one faction or the other, supporting either Toyatomi's son or the more powerful Tokugawa. In 1600, Tokugawa marched north to suppress a rebellion, and Ishida saw his chance. If he could gain control of the impregnable Osaka Castle and the traditional capital city of Kyoto, he could challenge Tokugawa's power. Knowing that Tokugawa would march against him, Ishida planned a forward defense. To get from Edo to Kyoto, one could take either of only two roads, one along the coast and the other inland. Near the junction of those two, north of Kyoto, lay two castles. Ishida's ally Oda Hidenobu (grandson of Oda Nobunaga) controlled Gifu on the inland road. Tokugawa's allies controlled Kiyosu on the coast road. Luckily for Tokugawa, he was able to march on Gifu before Ishida could place the bulk of his forces there, for an ally controlled Fushimi fortress, halfway between Osaka and Kyoto; Ishida could not leave an enemy force in his rear, so the castle had to be captured before he could place his army forward. Fushimi held out for 10 days, allowing Tokugawa to reach and capture Gifu before Ishida could arrive. Ishida's force marched on Gifu, only to find out it had fallen. They then retreated southward.

The Battle

Tokugawa, based in Edo, commanded what came to be referred to as the Eastern Army; Ishida, the Western Army. Although Ishida was able to muster a larger number of daimyo to the cause of the heir, some of them were of questionable loyalty because they distrusted Ishida's commoner background. Tokugawa had spent the previous months secretly cultivating those daimyo, and he was depending on some of them to change sides when battle came. Under his direct command, Tokugawa led 30,000 men, with another 40,000 commanded by his subordinates and another 35,000 under his son in Edo, with orders to follow the main body to Sekigahara, a town at the junction of the coast and inland roads. He also had secretly received a supply of harquebuses (matchlock weapons). Although the samurai traditionally believed in face-to-face single combat with swords, with pikemen and archers in support, Oda had successfully introduced firearms a quarter-century earlier when he acted as shogun.

On 20 October 1600, Tokugawa learned that Ishida planned to deploy his army in a defensive position at Sekigahara. Their withdrawal from Gifu was made in a driving rain, but Tokugawa's force that followed benefited from somewhat calmer weather. Ishida deployed his troops in a strong defensive position, flanked by two streams with high ground on the opposite banks. On his right flank, an allied daimyo, Kobayakawa Hideaki, held a position on a third rise, Matsuo Hill, on the far side of the Fuji River. Although well positioned, the troops were tired from the day's march, and their own gunpowder was wet.

Tokugawa's advanced guard, marching through a dense fog, stumbled into Ishida's army at dawn on 21 October. Both sides were so surprised that they withdrew rather than fight, but now both armies were alerted to the other's presence. Ishida stood his ground, while Tokugawa deployed his allies' forces in a line to the front,

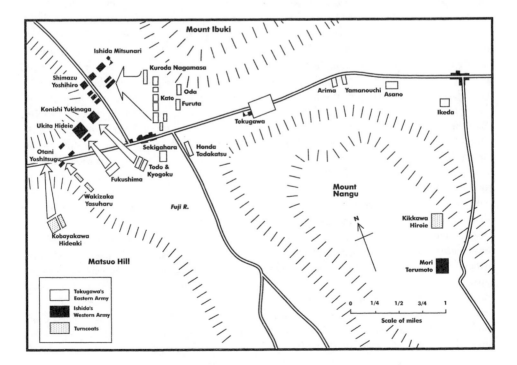

while his forces stood in reserve. About 0800, the wind picked up and blew away the fog. Revelation of the enemy positions caused quick consultations and last-minute orders for both armies. Tokugawa's force opened the battle. Fukushima Masanori led the advanced guard, holding Tokugawa's left flank, and charged north along the Fuji River against the Western Army's right center. The ground was sodden with the previous day's rain, so the battle there soon degenerated into a slugging match. With the battle thus opened, Tokugawa ordered attacks from his right against the Western left, and his center to support Fukushima's attack. This left Ishida's center untouched, and Ishida quickly called on this unit, commanded by Shimazu Yoshihiro, to come to the aid of his buckling right flank. Shimazu refused to move. In the society of the day, the daimyo were stubborn and independent-minded, responding in battle only to a respected commander, which Ishida was not.

On Ishida's right, Fukushima's attack with its supporting troops was gaining ground, but at the same time exposing their own flank to a force across the Fuji River commanded by Otani Yoshitsugu. Just past Otani's force was that of Kobayakawa on Matsuo Hill. Both of these forces were in a position to smash into Tokugawa's exposed left flank, and Otani acted. His men stabilized the line and repulsed a second attack by Fukushima's men. With momentum shifting, Ishida ordered Kobayakawa to charge down from his hilltop and begin to roll up the Eastern Army. Instead, he sat still. Seeing this, Tokugawa sensed a possible ally in the making. He ordered a few shots fired at Kobayakawa's force to see what they would do. Kobayakawa, realizing the time had come to make a decision, threw in his lot with Tokugawa. His men did charge down the hill, but into Otani's force. Unfortunately, Otani's harquebusiers had enough dry gunpowder to deal the attackers a severe blow, and the turncoat's 16,000 men made little impression in their charge. Indeed, they were now exposed

to yet another small force on that flank commanded by Wakizaka Yasuharu. A determined attack could have supported Otani and turned the flank, but they too decided to defect to Tokugawa's army.

Finally outnumbered, Otani had little choice but to retreat. That opened Ishida's right flank, which Fukushima and the turncoat Kobayakawa began to roll up. With his right flank destroyed and his center being pushed back, Ishida decided to make a run for it. As the Eastern forces renewed their effort, the stubborn Shimazu in the center finally decided the time was ripe to order his men into action. Perhaps he had been waiting for Ishida to flee so he could take credit for the victory, but it was too late. By the time he acted, he was too badly outnumbered to have any real effect on the outcome of the battle.

Ishida's only hope for aid in his flight was from two forces placed to the south on Mount Nangu. Mori Terumoto, who had resisted Tokugawa from the beginning, was positioned near a second force of troops of the Western Army commanded by Kikkawa Hiroie. They were on the back side of the mountain from the battle, so unaware it was even being fought until Ishida, who had fled southward through the lines, approached. Joining with them on the mountaintop could have placed a good-sized force in a very strong defensive position, but Kikkawa decided to change sides at this point as well, and he kept Mori at bay. Ishida had no more support, while his army collapsed behind him.

Results

Ishida's Western Army suffered some 40,000 dead, leaving Tokugawa with the largest force in all of Japan. While that was key to his ultimate victory, such victory did not come at Sekigahara. It was merely the turning point in the struggle to establish Toyotomi Hideyori in the shogunate. He still had daimyo that believed in the cause of linear succession, and Tokugawa

Hagakure

About the time of the battle at Sekigahara, a set of aphorisms for warriors was collected under the title *Hagakure*, or *Hidden Leaves*. The short entries describe characteristics of samurai and give suggestions on how they should live. At its most basic, samurai philosophy is called *bushi-do*, the Way of the Warrior. The basic concept of bushi-do is summed up in the phrase, "the way of the warrior is death." This encompasses the nature of the samurai class because not only is fighting the life one chooses, but dying is often the result of that choice. Hence, one should always be ready to die. This is not as fatalistic as it sounds. In fact, it has a strong parallel in Christianity: because one never knows when the last moment will arrive, one should always live a positive and acceptable lifestyle. Thus, the aim of good living is to live each moment as if it is your last.

"There is surely nothing other than the single purpose of the present moment. A man's whole life is a succession of moment after moment. If one fully understands the present moment, there will be nothing else to do, and nothing to pursue. Live being true to the single purpose of the moment. Everyone lets the present moment slip by, then looks for it as though he thought it were somewhere else. No one seems to have noticed this fact. But grasping this firmly, one must pile experience upon experience. And once one has come to this understanding he will be a different person from that point on."

Hagakure also has what seem to be odd bits of knowledge, as well as instruction on manners. "If you cut a face lengthwise, urinate on it, and trample on it with straw sandals, it is said the skin will come off. This was heard by the priest Gyojaku when he was in Kyoto. It is information to be treasured." "Matsudaira Izu no kami said to Master Mizuno Kenmotsu, 'You're such a useful person, it's a shame that you're so short.' Kenmotsu replied, 'That's true. Now if I were to cut off your head and attach it to the bottom of my feet, I would be taller.'"

---

spent another 15 years eliminating them. He was named shogun in 1603, and the emperor moved the capital from Kyoto to Edo. Not until 1615, however, with the capture of Osaka Castle from the now-teenaged Toyatomi Hideyori, was Tokugawa able to exercise unquestioned rule. The Tokugawa shogunate that his heirs controlled lasted until 1867.

Over the following two and a half centuries, Japan remained intentionally isolated. No more expeditions to Korea were mounted, and any attempt by outsiders to enter Japan was resisted. Only the port city of Nagasaki was open to trade from China, while a single annual trade mission from Holland was allowed at the port of Hirado. Except for a Christian peasant uprising during 1637–1638, Japan remained relatively peaceful. The daimyo remained in their position as feudal lords employing samurai retainers. The long peace, however, meant that the skills of a warrior were no longer needed, and the samurai as a class declined into a group reminiscent of Europe's penniless nobility, having social status but no income. The samurai were forced over time to turn away from weaponry to trade or farming or die off after wasting away their lives as *ronin*, soldiers without leaders that often turned to outlawry.

When Matthew Perry led a group of U.S. ships into Tokyo Bay in 1854, Japan was opened to the west. Seeing that their splendid isolation had cost them untold progress, the shogunate was overthrown in what came to be called the Meiji Restoration. The emperor, however, retained his status, and a massive campaign to bring Japan into the modern world succeeded magnificently. Still, the tradition of the samurai never died. It was revived as Japan began to extend its power beyond its borders in the 1890s into China, then Korea, and then into Manchuria during 1904–1905. The new samurai drew on their heritage to create a new warrior class that finally seized power in 1931 and took Japan on a quest for international standing that provoked its ultimate defeat in World War II. The miraculous industrial recovery that Japan achieved after 1854 was duplicated after 1945, taking Japan once again to international prominence. The samurai, as they did in the years of the Tokugawa shogunate, turned to trade. The texts written and studied by the ancient samurai inspired modern business leaders to once again win in the arena of industry rather than on the more traditional battlefields.

References: Sadler, A. L. *The Maker of Modern Japan: The Life of Tokugawa Ieyasu.* London: George Allen & Unwin, 1937; Sansom, George. *A History of Japan, 1334–1615.* Stanford, CA: Stanford University Press, 1961; Tsunetomo, Yamamoto. *Hagakure.* Translated by William Scott Wilson. New York: Avon Books, 1981; Turnbull, Stephen. *The Samurai: A Military History.* New York: Macmillan, 1977.

BREITENFELD
17 September 1631

FORCES ENGAGED
Swedish/Saxon: 45,000. Commander: Gustavus Adolphus, king of Sweden.
Holy Roman Empire: 36,000. Commander: Johann Tserclaes, count of Tilly.

IMPORTANCE
Breitenfeld marked the arrival of Sweden as a major power on the European scene. Gustavus's military innovations became standard in European armies after this time.

Historical Setting

In 1555, the Peace of Augsburg became the law of the Holy Roman Empire, territory that included modern-day Germany, Holland, Belgium, Austria, Switzerland, and the Czech Republic. The ruling Hapsburg dynasty was divided into two branches, one in Austria and the other in Spain, each with its own responsibilities and territories. The Augsburg declaration was an attempt to defuse the rampant religious and political feuding in central Europe, especially in the Germanic principalities. It stated that each prince had the power to decide for his province what its official religion would be. Thus, Catholic and Lutheran provinces were officially recognized; the growing Calvinist denomination, however, was not. The Peace of Augsburg worked for several decades, but by the early 1600s religious alliances became more and more political. A clash between Protestant and Catholic states was inevitable.

In the northern states of the Holy Roman Empire, Frederick V, the Calvinist ruler of the Palatine, a province along the Rhine River, organized the Protestant Union. In the south, Duke Maximilian of Bavaria countered this move with the formation of the Catholic League. Their first conflict occurred in Bohemia in 1618. When Ferdinand of Styria (south of Bohemia) became the Bohemian king in 1617, he was determined to impose his strict Catholicism on the province. The Bohemians tolerated a variety of religious views in their country and had little desire to have Ferdinand impose his will on them, so they threw the imperial governors literally out of the windows of the castle in Prague. They raised an army and offered the throne to Frederick V, who accepted the crown, bringing the Protestant Union and the Catholic League into conflict.

The war was brief. The Catholics, under the brilliant general Baron von Tilly, defeated Frederick's forces in 1620. Ferdinand proceeded to impose Catholicism on Bohemia, and widespread killing and destruction ensued, ruining the nation's economy. The ruling aristocracy was replaced by Ferdinand's supporters, who received large estates. Protestant religious practices disappeared in Bohemia over the next 10 years of persecution, while the Catholic Hapsburgs reasserted their authority.

The Protestant Lutherans and Calvinists were so suspicious of each other that the Lutherans actually assisted the Hapsburgs in Bohemia. Though the power of Catholic Spain frightened the north German Protestant states, those states could not agree among themselves to present a united opposition. The king of Denmark offered his assistance to the Protestants, but he was motivated more by a desire for north German lands than religious unity; the Spanish under Czech adventurer Baron Albrecht von Wallenstein defeated Danish forces in 1625. Wallenstein led a well-trained force that numbered as many as 125,000, but he had personal ambitions above serving the Hapsburgs. He planned to use his army to defeat the Hapsburg's enemies and then carve out a kingdom in central Europe for himself. The Hapsburgs came to suspect this, and by the late 1620s Catholic forces were beginning to quarrel almost as much as were the Protestants; this resulted in Wallenstein's being removed from command in 1630. Still, with the Holy Roman Empire's army supreme and momentum on their side, the Catholic League urged Ferdinand to restore all lost Catholic lands in northern Germany. This decision meant the resumption of war. The loss of their lands as well as their faith finally motivated the Lutherans to action.

At this point, a Protestant champion stepped forward: Gustavus Adolphus, king of Sweden. Gustavus had wisely exploited his country's natural resources of copper and timber to build a strong economy, and he organized the world's first modern professional army based on universal conscription. His army was equipped with the first artillery light enough to maneuver on the battlefield, improved muskets, regular pay, uniforms, and discipline. From 1611 through 1629, Gustavus's army had won victories over Poland, Denmark, and Russia, making Sweden the dominant force in the Baltic. It was this dominance that he wanted to protect from Catholic encroachment.

On 20 May 1631, the city of Magdeburg, on the Elbe River some 60 miles northeast of Leipzig, fell after a 7-month siege. The empire's forces, now commanded by the count of Tilly, were made up primarily of mercenaries, and they quickly set about looting the city. It caught fire and burned to the ground; 25,000 of the city's 30,000 inhabitants died in the blaze.

The Battle

The citizens of Magdeburg had waited for the arrival of Gustavus's army, but in vain, thanks to the interference of Johann Georg, elector of Saxony. He feared both Tilly's Catholic forces and Gustavus's Swedes and could not make up his mind whom to support. Thus, he did not allow Gustavus access through Saxony to relieve Magdeburg. Upon hearing of that city's fate, however, and that Tilly's force was now marching in his direction, the elector allied himself with Gustavus on 11 September 1631. Gustavus wasted no time combining their armies and marching toward Leipzig, which Tilly's forces had just forced to surrender. Gustavus's combined Swedish/Saxon force numbered some 45,000 men, but his more dependable Swedish troops numbered about 13,000.

Upon hearing of Gustavus's advance, in order to face the threat from the north Tilly's men had to halt the looting that they were just beginning to enjoy in Leipzig. Tilly thought that staying inside the city would be wiser, as winter was coming on and Gustavus would have to suffer through the winter outside the city walls while the imperial forces stayed safe within. However, Tilly's cavalry commander, Count Pappenheim, was too much the aggressor to play defense, so to he took his cavalry out of the city to scout the Swedes' approach. On the evening of 16 September, he sent a courier to Tilly in Leipzig informing him that the cavalry was engaged with the Swedes and needed assistance. This may or may not have been true, for Gustavus did not mention any action in his records, but Tilly marched his men to the rescue. By 0900 on 17 September, Gustavus advanced down the Düben-Leipzig road, just south of the town of Breitenfeld, and found Tilly's force of 36,000 arrayed before him: artillery on a hillside, infantry formed into squares of 2,000 pikemen each, cavalry on either flank, the entire forcing stretching across a front more than 2 miles long.

Gustavus formed his army into a different formation. Rather than using the standard Spanish-designed *tercio,* a square of massed pikemen with harquebusiers or musketeers on the corners for cover, the Swedish army operated in smaller, more mobile units in which the pikemen protected the musketeers. Gustavus placed Johann Georg and his Saxons on the left flank and then formed his own men into parallel lines: two lines of cavalry on the flanks and two lines of infantry with cavalry support in the center. His intent was to use his more

mobile formations to maneuver around and through the bulky imperial squares, while his lighter and more mobile artillery took advantage of the packed mass of men in the tercios.

Gustavus did not have to wait for battle. The imperial artillery began blasting at his army as it was deploying. Because of his smaller formations, however, much of the artillery fire passed through the spaces between his brigades, causing little damage. In reply, the Swedish artillery, although smaller, was able to inflict massive damage on the imperial pikemen. In ranks ten to twelve men deep and carrying 30-foot pikes, they were unable to do anything to avoid the cannon fire. This artillery fire went on until midday, when the headstrong Pappenheim, without orders, charged his cavalry forward from the imperial left in an attempt to turn the Swedish right flank. Although Tilly despaired of his subordinate's rashness, he proceeded to move his tercios forward and toward

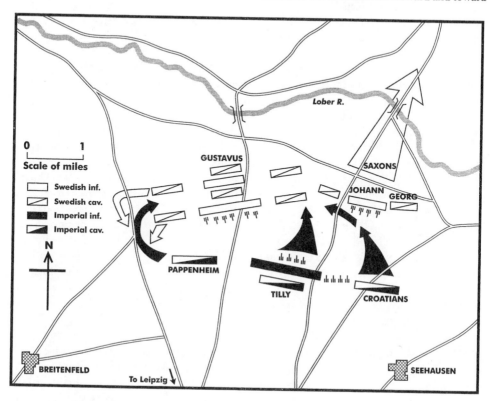

the Saxons, which he correctly assumed were the weakest part of Gustavus's force.

Johann Georg's force put up little resistance, many turning to run with barely a shot fired. The elector himself did not stop his horse for 15 miles, and some of his cavalry stopped only to loot their allies' supply train. By mid-afternoon, Tilly's force seemed about to turn the Swedish left flank and envelop them, but Gustavus was not beaten yet. He had been able to deal with Pappenheim's cavalry thanks to Pappenheim himself, who did not use the heaviness of his cavalry to smash the Swedish formations. Instead, he ordered the use of the caracole, whereby a line of cavalry rode near the enemy, fired their wheel-lock pistols, and then turned to the rear to allow the next line to fire while the first reloaded. As the pistols' range was too short to be effective, Gustavus's musketeers were able to use the greater range of their weapons to kill many of the imperial cavalry, who were easy targets. To further compound the slaughter, the light Swedish cannon turned about to fire grapeshot into the cavalry. The shotgun effect of that fire destroyed any unit cohesiveness, and the Swedish cavalry then counterattacked with sabers to finish the job. Thus, as Tilly's infantry were turning Gustavus's left, Pappenheim's attack on the right was collapsing.

With no cavalry threat now, Gustavus turned his smaller brigades and lighter artillery on the tercios, which, now at close range, were even easier targets than before. Pinning his enemy down with this fire, Gustavus led his cavalry in a sweep around the imperial left flank. The artillery that Tilly had with his force were massive guns, emplaced at the start of battle and not moved until it was over. The guns that Tilly had on the hillside and that had fired at the Saxon units that morning were now pointed directly at where Tilly's army was standing after the Saxons fled. Thus, the Swedes captured the heavy guns and began firing them on the tercios. With artillery fire coming from two directions, the massed squares of pikemen were demolished.

Results

Hard-pressed at 1600, by 1800 Gustavus was victorious. He had lost approximately 3,000 casualties, mostly during the morning cannonade. The Saxons lost few, mainly because they broke and ran so early in the battle. Tilly, badly wounded, fled for Leipzig, leaving behind 7,000 dead and 6,000 prisoners, as well as all his artillery. He stayed the night in Leipzig and then abandoned the city. The prisoners that Gustavus took were primarily mercenaries, and they gladly changed sides to join the winning army. His victory also attracted the support of additional Protestant princes, which aided in the creation of a much-needed unified political front. Breitenfeld, along with Gustavus's victory at Lützen on 16 November 1632, broke the back of Catholic power as exercised by the army of the Holy Roman Empire. The Hapsburgs never recovered the initiative, and the later entry of France as a major player in the war shifted the fighting westward. By then, however, the German states were already so devastated that decades if not centuries were necessary to fully recover physically, materially, and psychologically.

Breitenfeld confirmed Gustavus as the "Lion of the North," but more importantly signaled the introduction of his style of both fighting and organization, both of which he had adapted from the recent theories of the Dutch general Maurice of Nassau. The *tercio* with which most of the European armies fought was a latter-day version of the Greek and Macedonian phalanx: a hedgehog square that pushed its enemies before it. The musketeers that deployed at its corners were there simply to drive off skirmishers. By introducing smaller brigades (a term here introduced to history) and depending more on firepower, Gustavus turned the *tercios* into little more than large targets. His development of not only lighter but mass-produced artillery made that branch of the military more important in battles, whereas before this it had been used mainly in sieges. Thus, mobile firepower destroyed and, after the Thirty Years' War, replaced mass formations.

Gustavus also introduced professionalism to warfare. Although generals were full-time soldiers, up to this time in history the mass of the soldiery was either mercenaries paid by loot and therefore without loyalty or men off the streets and fields pressed into service or joining out of desperation. They too fought for loot. The Swedes were motivated instead by nationalism, a united nation formed around a competent monarch. Gustavus introduced regular pay, uniforms, standing units, discipline, rules, regular training, the stuff of modern armies. Indeed, Breitenfeld and the Thirty Years' War marked the beginning of the modern age, not only in military affairs but in religious and political arenas as well.

As equipping large numbers of men with firearms and procuring the newly perfected artillery were both expensive propositions, only national governments could afford the cost. Hence, nations began to arm, and war became an extension of political will, rather than a moral or religious crusade. From this time forward, one sees the rise of standing armies and professional soldiers.

References: Fuller, J. F. C. *A Military History of the Western World,* vol. 2. New York: Funk & Wagnalls, 1955; Jones, Archer. *The Art of War in the Western World.* Champaign: University of Illinois Press, 1987; Livesey, Anthony. *Battles of Great Commanders.* New York: Macmillan, 1987; Parker, Geoffrey, ed. *The Thirty Years War.* London: Routledge & Kegan Paul, 1984; Rabb, Theodore, ed. *The Thirty Years War.* Lexington, MA: D.C. Heath, 1972.

SHANHAIKUAN

28 May 1644

Forces Engaged

Sino-Manchu: Probably 50,000 Manchu and 40,000 Chinese, with perhaps 70,000 to 80,000 militia. Commanders: Dorgon (Manchu) and Wu San-kuei (Chinese).

Rebel: 50,000 minimum, possibly reaching 100,000. Commander: Li Tzu-ch'eng.

Importance

Rebel defeat allowed the Manchus to occupy Peking and begin exercising authority as the new Ch'ing dynasty, replacing the Ming.

Historical Setting

The Manchus were a Mongol population living in northern Manchuria and were descended from the Jurchen Mongols that had invaded China and established the Ch'in dynasty in the twelfth century. After the fall of the Yüan dynasty begun by Kubilai Khan, the Manchus were tributaries to the subsequent Ming dynasty (established in 1368). The Mings oversaw a period of great culture as well as military success in Chinese history, but, as is the nature of empires, later rulers spent more time enjoying their wealth and power than seeing to the business of ruling the country. By the early 1600s, the Mings were subjected to a fairly regular series of rebellions. The Manchus had remained loyal until 1582, when two Manchu officials serving the Ming government, Giocangga and his son Taksi, died in a civil disturbance. Taksi's son was Nurhachi, and he was determined to avenge his father and grandfather's death while establishing his people as the next rulers of China.

Nurhachi realized that at the time the power disparity between the Manchus and Ming was too great to overcome, so he remained the loyal servant while slowly increasing his influence through marriage and military exploits. Starting in 1599, Nurhachi began campaigning against rival Manchu chieftains and succeeded in gathering almost all of the factions into his camp through conquest or diplomacy. By 1609, he was sufficiently powerful that the Ming government dealt with him as ruler of Manchuria, allowing him local autonomy. Nurhachi organized a system of districts that provided military organization as well as the beginnings of a governmental structure.

In 1616, Nurhachi proclaimed a new Ch'in dynasty, taking the name of the Jurchen Mongol dynasty that had existed in the twelfth century. In 1618, he began launching attacks on Ming territory. By 1621, he had conquered what is today southern Manchuria and in 1625 set up his new capital at Mukden. He finally met defeat at the hands of the Ming General Yuan Ch'ung-huan, who possessed cannon provided by Jesuits in the Ming court. A few months later, in 1626, Nurhachi died, leaving as his successor his eighth son, Abahai. Abahai continued his father's dream of conquest with success in Korea, followed by a wide flanking operation that took him to Peking (modern Beijing) from the west. In 1631, he occupied the Ming capital and returned to Mukden with immense loot. He renamed the dynasty Ch'ing, meaning pure, to avoid comparisons with the harassing, pillaging Ch'in dynasty of four centuries earlier. In spite of that, his armies continued to raid into northeastern China, enriching his dynasty while weakening the Mings. Although Abahai captured a strategic pass through the eastern end of the Great Wall at Shanhaikuan in 1642, he did not want to fight the large Ming forces on the other side quite yet. Instead he turned his attention to securing his northern flank by consolidating his rule as far as the Amur River.

MANCHU AND CH'ING

Although the two terms are somewhat interchangeable, Manchu refers to the population, whereas Ch'ing refers to the dynastic name they assumed. The term "Manchu" was adopted in 1635, replacing the traditional Jurchen name. The dynastic name "Ch'ing" was chosen to replace the Ch'in dynastic title that the Jurchen Mongols had used before Genghis and Kubilai Khan. The reasons behind the title changes are speculative. Done during the reign of Abahai, he probably wanted to remove negative connotations from both. As the Jurchens had long been under Chinese suzerainty, replacing that title would conceivably be a declaration of independence from the Mings.

Describing the convolutions of the titles involves Chinese characters, the English translations of which seem on first glance to be virtually indistinguishable. The original Jurchen Mongols had been called by the Chinese the Man-chu. It was probably an honorable title with little in the way of negative connotation. It could possibly have been taken from the Buddhist term "Man-chu," which meant "wonderful luck," a term discovered in Buddhist writings sent to the Jurchens. The two ideograms that make up the term Manchu also could be seen as coming from the first character of Man-chu and the second character of Chien-chou, to which a stroke was added to signify water. The character for Ch'ing also contains that "water" stroke, probably deliberately. "The character for the Ming dynasty means 'bright', and that for the surname of the imperial family, Chu, means 'red'. The combined image of 'bright' and 'red' is 'fire', which can melt gold, the character of the Chin dynasty. An inauspicious name such as Chin, then, must be changed" (Hsu, *The Rise of Modern China*, p. 25). By adopting a title that included a references to water, that could show the power of water extinguishing the Ming fire.

A more prosaic explanation is merely one of political perceptions. Nurhachi, when striving to unify the Jurchen, readopted the Ch'in title as a rallying point for tribal focus. By Abahai's time, however, the Jurchen were unified, and increasingly more Chinese were joining the anti-Ming cause. To make themselves less regional, they adopted the more Chinese-sounding Ch'ing and less Mongol-sounding Ch'in title, although the two ideograms are pronounced almost identically. It is also possible that a new dynastic name was necessary to cut from the past in a different way because the twelfth century Ch'in had conquered only the northern section of China, being unable to defeat the southern Sung dynasty. A new title would thus distance itself from the failures of the old.

Whatever the reason for the changes, some new dynastic title was important as a marker of change after Nurhachi and his successors decided to defeat and supplant the Ming dynasty.

As if dealing with the Manchus was not bad enough, the Mings had to contend with a number of effective peasant uprisings. The most successful of these was led by Li Tzu-ch'eng. He dislodged Ming armies and took control of Honan and Shensi provinces, just south and southwest of Peking, in 1640. By 1644, he felt himself strong enough to march on the capital city. As Li's forces approached Peking, the Ming Emperor Chuang-lieh-ti recalled two frontier armies to defend the city. The largest of these was at Shanhaikuan, commanded by Wu San-kuei. Some sources say that General Wu would not march to his emperor's defense; others say that he marched but could not arrive in time. Either way, Li and his rebels captured Peking easily on 25 April 1644. Just before the city fell, the emperor committed suicide. General Wu learned of the emperor's fate while on his way to the capital and considered surrendering in response to Li's demands and the fact that the rebel general held Wu's father hostage. Instead, Wu returned to Shanhaikuan. Li, after pillaging the capital, followed.

The Manchus had lost their own leader in 1643 when Abahai died at the age of 51. His 5-year-old son was next in line to succeed him, and did, but actual power was in the hands of the regent, Abahai's brother Dorgon. Dorgon had considered contacting some of the rebel groups to have some inside assistance, but General Wu contacted him first. Caught between two enemies, Wu decided he would rather deal with the Manchus than Li, so requested their assistance to defeat Li's rebels and regain the capital. Dorgon was glad to help.

The Battle

Li spent his first days in Peking gathering up as much treasure as he could find and melting it down into ingots for easier transport. He preferred his home city of Sian to Peking and planned to retire there, but first he had to deal with General Wu's army. On 18 May, Li led his army of at least 50,000 men out of Peking

toward the east, arriving at the town of Yung-p'ing on 22 May. At this point, descriptions of the encounter begin to differ. Boulger's *The History of China* (1898) states that Li deployed his army of 60,000 men just outside Yung-p'ing in a large crescent formation, with the points in a position to outflank Wu's force of perhaps 20,000. Wu had sent for Dorgon's aid, but the Manchus were slow in arriving. Li's army surrounded Wu's and began devastating it, only to be surprised by a sudden charge of Manchu cavalry. This completely disrupted the rebel army and they fled, leaving behind some 30,000 dead.

Probably a more trustworthy account appears in Parsons's *Peasant Rebellions of the Late Ming Dynasty* (1970). In this account, Li passed through Yung-p'ing almost to Shanhaikuan. (The two towns are near each other, so perhaps either town could legitimately give its name to the battle.) Wu sent for aid on 25 May, and Dorgun arrived the next day, camping about 3 miles north of Shanhaikuan. There they skirmished with a detachment of rebel troops and won the day. The next day, Dorgun's army marched into Shanhaikuan, and he and Wu began planning for the battle. Apparently not until 26 May did Li learn that the Manchus were in the area and allied with Wu, although he might not really have known until the battle itself opened. The bulk of Li's army was drawn up in a line stretching from the town southwestward to the coast. Li posted himself on a small hill overlooking the army. The morning of 28 May opened with a dust storm, which covered the deployment of the allied force. Dorgon had brought perhaps 50,000 men and joined them to Wu's 40,000, so, when the battle commenced, they had a numerical superiority as well as more disciplined and experienced troops. Further, Wu may have been able to raise another 70,000 to 80,000 men locally and press them into service, but what, if any, role they played in the battle is not mentioned.

Wu's Ming force was placed on the right flank of Dorgon's Manchus, and probably were the key element in the attack on the rebel flank. Although Li was a talented general and he took direct command of his army, the combined Ming-Manchu force was too much for his army. The battle lasted a few hours, but no other details are available. Li's army fell back in some disorder, and a more determined pursuit may have completely shattered them, but the chase ended after 12 miles. Li was able to rally some of his men at Yung-p'ing and then retreated into the defenses of Peking. He was not prepared for a siege, from the standpoint of either defending forces or supplies. Instead, he hurried through the necessary ceremonies to proclaim himself emperor on 3 June and then executed Wu's father. When the Ming army approached Peking, General Wu saw his father's head hanging from the city walls. Li marched his men westward out of the city early on 4 June, leaving behind a number of burning buildings in a city stripped of its wealth and any transport animals that Li could lay his hands on.

Results

General Wu San-kuei attempted futilely to establish his authority as representative of the Ming dynasty. Dorgon's force was too large and strong to challenge, however, and Wu soon found himself in Manchu service. He gladly accepted the assignment to chase down the rebels and, although it took him more than a year, in the summer of 1645 he caught and executed Li. Although Dorgon was merely regent, he began establishing the power of the Manchus. He first did all he could to allay any Chinese fears by giving the dead emperor and empress a full state funeral. He announced that he and his army had entered China and occupied Peking merely to rescue the city and the country from the rebels. Within a matter of months, however, the Manchu court of the Ch'ing dynasty had moved from Mukden to Peking. The first emperor of this newly established Chinese dynasty was Abahai's son Shuh-chih,

although Dorgon continued to direct military and governmental affairs.

The occupation of Peking in 1644 marked the official end of the Ming dynasty and the beginning of the Ch'ing, but it was not quite that quick. Ming Emperor Chuang-lieh-ti, who had committed suicide, left behind successors. One of his sons proclaimed himself the next Ming emperor in Nanking, but he was no leader. In the spring of 1645, the Manchus defeated at Yangchow the last large army that the Mings could field and then occupied Nanking immediately afterward. That was the last opportunity that the Mings had to retain power because, after Yangchow, a series of pretenders to the throne announced their claims, but none could collect a sufficient following to challenge Manchu power. Between 1648 and 1651, Prince Kuei Wang looked like he might be the one to restore Ming fortunes, but he could only slow the Manchu onslaught. A 10-year war against the pirate Koxinga, who claimed to fight for the Ming cause, proved to be effective in harassing the coastline from a base on Taiwan, but he could not challenge Manchu power inland, and any influence that the pirate faction may have had died with Koxinga in 1662.

The Manchus were smart enough, from Nurhachi to Abahai to Dorgon, to realize that the Ming bureaucracy was quite efficient and should not be tampered with. Indeed, the Chinese possessed many things of which the Manchus were envious. So, like Kubilai Khan when he took over China in the fourteenth century, the Manchus adapted themselves to their new country. Manchu officials were appointed not to replace the Mings but to work with them, providing oversight without interference. Like Kubilai Khan's Mongols, the Manchus were content to set themselves up as a ruling class, in China but not of China.

The emperors of the Ch'ing dynasty were no worse or better than emperors of any other ruling family in Chinese history; they had their share of good and bad rulers. The primary characteristic of the dynasty is that it was ruling and forced to deal with the arrival of large numbers of westerners. Portuguese and Dutch merchants had already begun trading with the Mings, but were still on the periphery of Chinese markets and society. By the early nineteenth century, however, about the time that almost two centuries of rule would begin to mark the high point and decline of any dynasty, the Chinese were obliged to deal with the British, the only ones who could match the Chinese in superiority attitude. The traditional Chinese xenophobia saw a resurgence in response to the aggressive manner of British merchants and diplomats and provoked a military response to which the Chinese could not respond in kind. Through the second half of the nineteenth century, Britain, France, Germany, Russia, and Japan all imposed their economic, military, and diplomatic will on China, to which the Ch'ing dynasty could do little more than grow more conservative and reactionary. The influx of foreign culture, backed by military power, brought the Ch'ings into disrepute with their population, who ultimately engaged in a rebellion that led to the dynasty's demise in 1911.

References: Boulger, Demetrius Charles. *The History of China,* vol. 1. Freeport, NY: Books for Libraries Press, 1972 [1898]; Grousset, René. *The Rise and Splendour of the Chinese Empire.* Translated by Anthony Watson-Gandy and Terence Gordon. Berkeley: University of California Press, 1953; Hsu, Immanuel C. Y. *The Rise of Modern China.* New York: Oxford University Press, 1970; Parsons, James Bunyan. *Peasant Rebellions of the Late Ming Dynasty.* Tucson: University of Arizona Press, 1970.

NASEBY
14 June 1645

FORCES ENGAGED
Parliamentary: 6,500 cavalry and 7,000 infantry.
Commander: Lord Fairfax.

Monarchic: 4,000 cavalry and 3,500 infantry.
Commander: Prince Rupert.

IMPORTANCE
Rivalry between the power of the king and of Parliament in England finally settled provisionally in favor of Parliament, establishing democracy as the basis of government in England, with effects on English colonies, especially in America.

Historical Setting

Ever since the War of the Roses (1455–1485), the government of England had remained remarkably stable. The king ruled, if not absolutely, then certainly with little restriction on his power. This was possible because he was granted a comfortable income via tariffs and the produce of royally held property. With such an income, taxes were minimal, and the successive monarchs had no need to summon Parliament. As long as they ruled with a minimum of wisdom and did not exceed their incomes, the population was happy. For almost two centuries this was the case, but royal ambitions in the early seventeenth century began to stretch the royal bank accounts, and Parliament needed to be summoned to provide extra monies.

The English Parliament as an institution began at this time to feel the need for a more active role in government because the king and his advisors were becoming more internationally active and the bills for Continental forays began to climb. Those expenses, added to the fact that the wealth that Europe was reaping from the Americas had caused inflation, meant that it was increasingly difficult for kings to maintain themselves with the incomes granted them in earlier days. Unfortunately for English Kings James I and his son Charles I, they were badly advised by their most trusted subordinate, the duke of Buckingham. Between 1624 and 1628, Buckingham led failed attacks on Spain and Holland. To pay for these fiascoes, James and then Charles were forced to summon Parliament into session. Each time, Parliament became less cooperative and more ambitious for its own power.

Finally, in January 1629, Parliament assembled under the leadership of John Pym, who challenged King Charles on virtually every governmental matter. Placing the governing body in direct opposition to Charles's two primary subordinates, the earl of Strafford and Archbishop Laud, legal as well as economic struggles ensued. Strafford had assembled a standing army in Ireland that needed maintenance; Laud launched a zealous campaign, attempting to impose much stricter Anglican orthodoxy, which provoked the strongly Calvinist Scots. The need to pay for an army and fight the Scots that rose up against Charles gave Parliament leverage over the king. In 1640, Parliament impeached Laud. In 1641, it forced the king to execute Strafford. Parliament then proceeded to pass a series of laws expanding its authority. John Pym, a leader in the House of Commons, brought charges of treason against the queen, and Charles responded with similar charges against Pym. Failing to take Pym prisoner and with Parliament gaining political and economic support in London, Charles fled northward, established himself in Nottingham, and appealed for public support against an increasingly revolutionary Parliament.

The result of this royal-legislative confrontation was the English civil war. King Charles was able to rally much of the aristocracy, much of the northland, and Wales to his cause, whereas southeastern England (especially London) supported Parliament. Charles was able to assemble a fairly well trained army via his aristocrats, who drew on mercenaries who had been fighting in the contemporary Thirty Years' War on the Continent. Since Strafford's death, there had been no standing army. Charles was hampered most of all by Parliament's control over the navy, which denied him communication and supplies from the Continent. Parliament, although better funded, was not at first able to gain much success because of its own internal squabbling.

Early in the conflict, the Royalist cause had the services of the talented and flamboyant Prince Rupert from Holland, Charles's nephew. Although only 23 years old, he had been a soldier since age 14 and was able to command, if not totally control, the aristocratic Cavaliers, as the Royalists were called. They were adequate for raiding but undisciplined in battle. The commander that came to prominence in opposition was Oliver Cromwell, who organized and trained a cavalry force for the Roundheads (as the Parliamentarians were called) known as the Ironsides. These two men were the greatest talents to emerge from this war.

The Battle

In late summer 1643, Pym renewed a longstanding alliance with the Scots. For their support, the Scots demanded and received freedom for the Presbyterian Church; this abolished the power of the Church of England in Scotland. Learning of this, one of Charles's Scottish supporters, the marquis of Montrose, rode to alert Charles and to offer to rally pro-royalist forces. Rather than provoke a civil war in Scotland as well, Charles refused, only to find himself between two enemies when Scottish troops marched south in January 1644. This led to the Roundhead victory at Marston Moor in early July, which placed the parliamentary faction in solid control of the north while Charles retreated southward. He established himself in Oxford, while his forces gained key victories in Cornwall through the summer. A short truce at the end of the year collapsed when Charles rejected Parliament's proposals for peace and a new government. Parliament was never able to capitalize on its victories because of the excessive dissension in its ranks. Finally, in April 1645, Parliament barred any of its members (except Cromwell) from commanding troops. This separation of power greatly benefited the Roundheads, who could focus on raising a standing army of their own. It came to be called the New Model Army, and the red coats they wore began a tradition in the British military that lasted until the late nineteenth century.

Although made up mainly of men forced into uniform, Cromwell and his superior, Lord Fairfax, worked wonders in instilling discipline. By spring 1645, they were ready to use this army against the Royalists in Oxford.

Charles had his own squabbling subordinates to worry about. He separated Prince Rupert from Lord George Goring by sending them in opposite directions: the former north to try to recover the county of York, the latter west. This division of his forces, already smaller than those of Parliament, was a mistake. Nevertheless, Rupert quickly captured Leicester, a major loss for the Roundhead cause. Soon afterward, however, Charles learned of the Roundhead siege of Oxford, so he overrode Rupert's objections and ordered his army back to the south. Hearing of its approach, Lord Fairfax lifted his siege of the city and marched north to meet the oncoming Cavaliers. The two armies stumbled into each other near the town of Naseby, almost 50 miles north of Oxford and 20 miles south-southeast of Leicester. In the morning of 14 June, Rupert's force was lined up on a hill north of the town. When he rode south to scout the Roundheads, he found them withdrawing toward Naseby. Perceiving this as a retreat, Rupert called his army southward, off its hill, in pursuit. In reality, the Roundheads were not retreating but merely redeploying to a hillside of their own where they formed up on the reverse side of the hill.

Through the morning, both armies marched and positioned themselves. To the north, Charles deployed his men in three successive lines of infantry in the center and cavalry on the flanks. The infantry were mixed units of musketeers and pikemen. Rupert, officially in command of the Royalist force, abandoned that post just before the battle, apparently after an argument with Lord Digby, a sycophant who always played to Charles's

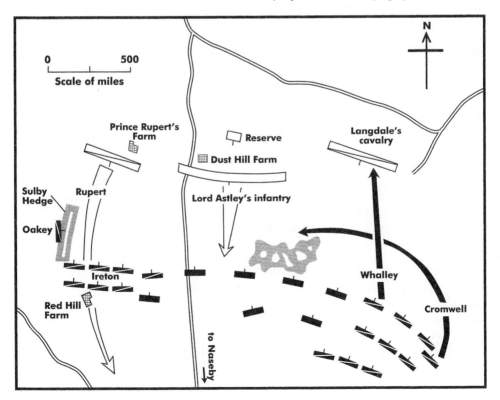

vanity at Rupert's expense. Thus, Rupert took himself out of position to oversee the battle and placed himself in command of the Royalist right wing. This severely hampered the coordination late in the battle.

Fairfax's deployment mirrored the Royalists atop Mill Hill, but outnumbered the Cavaliers 13,500 to 7,500. Fairfax placed his least-disciplined men in the front of his three lines, with the veterans and officers in the second line. This would perhaps hearten the men in the front and provide a stable line if the front rank broke. Cromwell's Ironsides were stationed on the right flank, while a second force of cavalry under Henry Ireton was on the left. A long, dense hedgerow bordered the western edge of the battlefield, and Fairfax placed a force of 1,000 dragoons behind it.

The battle opened at 1000, with the Royalist cannon firing a fusillade. The Cavalier infantry began marching toward their opponents, but tall grass made it difficult to maintain their straight lines. Ireton's cavalry on the Roundhead left began their approach toward Rupert's unit, but the Roundhead infantry remained in place on the reverse of Mill Hill until the Cavalier infantry approached to within firing range. They then moved forward to confront their foe. Rupert ordered his cavalry to charge, leaving the escorting musketeers behind. They closed with Ireton's force, and after a melee the first line of Cavalier cavalry withdrew. Thinking them out of the fight, Ireton turned away from the cavalry and aimed to strike the infantry's flank. Rupert brought up his second line of cavalry and crashed into Ireton's now exposed flank, and the Roundhead cavalry fled the field.

As this was happening, the Royalist infantry was pushing back the front rank of the New Model Army. Unphased by Ireton's abortive attack on their flank, the infantry continued to push ahead while the leading units of Roundhead infantry retreated. Fairfax's decision to place his steadier troops in the second line here

paid off because, under his urging, they advanced and blunted the Royalist surge. Rupert at this point should have struck their flank, just as Ireton had attempted, but the nature of the Cavalier cavalry showed itself: they pushed past the battle in pursuit of Ireton's force and then attacked the baggage camp to acquire what loot they could. A spirited defense of the camp foiled their attempt, but Rupert's inability to maintain discipline cost his side the battle.

On the right flank of the parliamentary line, Cromwell's forces engaged the oncoming cavalry under the command of Sir Marmaduke Langdale. After an intense melee, Langdale's cavalry withdrew. Cromwell detailed his front rank to stand fast and keep the Royalists from interfering, while he led his second rank into the Royalist infantry's flank and rear. Quick action by King Charles could have saved the day had he committed his reserves; he was ordering them to do just that and lead them himself into battle, when an overcautious subordinate warned him off, asking, "Will you go upon your death?" That gave Charles pause, and deflated any momentum the reserves may have had. Instead of striking Cromwell's exposed flank, they stood around in disorganized fashion and watched the infantry being surrounded. Fairfax led a final charge with his third rank, which pinned the Royalist infantry in front and encircled them from the west while Cromwell's cavalry was pounding them from the east. Even the return of Rupert to his king's side could not rally the reserves, and Charles fled the field.

Results

The battle was over by midday. Charles's army was shattered, with at least 1,000 killed and 5,000 captured, along with all his artillery and baggage. When the New Model Army destroyed their opposing infantry and turned to face the king and his reserve cavalry, their discipline so shocked the Cavaliers that they fled, chased by the Ironsides for 14 miles, almost to the gates of Leicester. The Roundheads had lost less than 1,000 casualties.

Charles fled for Wales to try to raise another army, but to little avail. The New Model Army had all the initiative and proceeded over the next few months to reduce Royalist strongholds around the country. By the time the final one surrendered (Harlech Castle, in Wales, in March 1647), Charles had been 2 months in Parliament's hands. As the population believed in the necessity of a king as head of government, Parliament spared Charles and attempted to make him a virtual puppet. When he continued to plot against them and began a new civil war in 1649, Parliament had had enough. They executed him in January of that year. That, however, did not ensure Parliament's control of the country, for the New Model Army became so politicized that it became the real power in England. When Parliament proved ineffective in ruling the country alone, Cromwell used the army to disband Parliament in 1653 and place himself in power as lord protector. He exercised a virtual dictatorship until his death in 1658. A power struggle afterward was won by the army's new commander, George Monck. He oversaw the restoration of the monarchy under Charles II in 1660.

Cromwell's victory at Naseby and his subsequent rise to power at once proved and disproved the need for a king. An out-of-control Parliament needed curbing, and Cromwell curbed it when he disbanded it, showing the need for a strong executive. That parliamentary forces had removed an unpopular king, however, showed that a body more responsive to the needs of the population was vital. Cromwell refused to accept the title of king, a decision that to an extent proved that a monarch was not necessarily the only form of executive that could be employed. Naseby and Cromwell limited the future power of the king. Another battle, near Dunkirk in 1660, would establish the final superiority of Parliament in the English governmental system.

America benefited in another way from the struggle between Parliament and king in England. When Charles I's Archbishop Laud began persecuting the northern church in the late 1630s, a number of Scots fled for North America, swelling its population in the northern colonies. A similar exodus by the upper classes during Cromwell's reign expanded the central colonies, Virginia in particular. Thus, America's population, reflecting attitudes against both king and Parliament, provided some of the ideological basis for the American Revolution; both the English civil war and the American Revolution led the way to the ultimate collapse of the concept of absolute monarchy in the world.

BATTLE OF THE DUNES
14 June 1658

FORCES ENGAGED
Anglo-French: 6,000 infantry and 9,000 cavalry. Commander: Henri de la Tour d'Auvergne, Vicomte de Turenne.

Spanish: 6,000 to 7,000 infantry and 8,000 cavalry. Commanders: Don Juan of Austria and Louis de Bourbon Condé.

IMPORTANCE
Anglo-French victory forced a Spanish peace offer by the end of the year and ended Charles II's last hopes of returning to the English throne on his own terms, thus confirming the ultimate ascendancy of Parliament.

Historical Setting

In January 1649, the Catholic House of Stuart lost its hold on the monarchy of Great Britain. In that month, King Charles I was executed by Parliamentary forces commanded by Oliver Cromwell who, since the battle of Naseby in 1645, had been expanding his military and political power. Charles II, next in line to the throne, attempted to continue the Royalist, or Cavalier, war against the Parliamentarians, or Roundheads, after his father's death. Unfortunately for him, his forces lost to Cromwell on 3 September 1651 at the battle of Worcester; Charles was forced to flee for France. As Cromwell proceeded to act like a king (although he never took the title) in England, on the Continent Charles looked for supporters to aid his return to the throne. He finally threw his lot in with the Spanish, who controlled the Spanish Netherlands (modern Belgium and Flanders) at the time. The Spanish had long had hostile relations with England, ever since Protestant Queen Elizabeth I's navy had defeated the Spanish Armada in 1588.

While the Spanish provided safe haven for Charles, he did what he could to gather loyal troops around him while encouraging Royalists in England to lay the groundwork for his return. Cromwell always maintained a firm grip on power, and his intelligence sources kept him informed of Charles's activities. By cracking down on Royalist groups in England, Cromwell was able to keep Charles on the Continent, for Charles was convinced that, to execute a successful invasion, he needed a strong base of supporters in England to seize a harbor so he could bring his troops in-country. Thus, periodic plans for sneaking across the English Channel and reclaiming the throne had to be continually postponed.

While Charles was plotting, relations between France and Spain were growing increasingly hostile. The two countries had been on opposite sides of the Thirty Years' War (1618–1648), and conflict continued after that war ended. King Louis XIV was ambitious for his country and was always looking for ways to expand his borders at the expense of his neighbors, which included the Spanish Netherlands. In the months immediately after the Peace of Westphalia had ended the Thirty Years' War, a short civil war in France between parliament and king threatened to bring Spanish troops into France. After the two sides agreed to terms,

two of the major figures in the conflict argued: Prime Minister Mazarin and General Louis de Bourbon Condé. When a second civil war erupted in the spring of 1650, Condé left France and entered the service of Spain.

With the second civil war settled in the summer of 1652, the Franco-Spanish war continued. Condé, an outstanding general, was matched against the equally talented Vicomte de Turenne. Through 1657, they sparred along the frontier between France and the Netherlands, neither gaining the upper hand. That same year, the French entered into an alliance with their longtime rival England—which was at the time also engaged in hostilities with Spain—on the supposition that the enemy of my enemy is my friend. Louis XIV and Mazarin were looking for extra troops, and Cromwell was looking for an entry onto the Continent, so he could possibly begin an anti-Catholic crusade.

In the fall of 1657, the Anglo-French forces captured the Flemish town of Mardyck and then aimed toward Dunkirk. This was under Spanish control, and the terms of Cromwell's alliance with France stated that Dunkirk (on the English Channel coast) would become England's property. Turenne led his army to Dunkirk and began a siege in May 1658. He was soon joined by 3,000 English troops under the command of William Lockhart. The English fleet arrived soon afterward, bringing the besieging force up to 21,000 (against the 3,000 defenders behind the city walls). The governor of the Spanish Netherlands, Don Juan of Austria, gathered together an army with Condé to lift the siege. The Spanish force of 5,000 cavalry and 8,000 infantry was supplemented by another 2,000 troops supplied by Charles and commanded by his son James, duke of York.

The Battle

During the second week of June 1658, the Spanish army marched from Ypres toward Dunkirk. On 13 June, Don Juan and Condé camped on the beach northeast of Dunkirk. Learning of their presence, Turenne decided to strike first, so he left a holding force at Dunkirk and marched 6,000 infantry and 9,000 cavalry toward the Spanish position. The Spanish army was deployed perpendicular to the shoreline, with the bulk of their troops among the sand dunes just off the beach. Their left flank (to the south) rested along a road running toward Dunkirk and a canal just south of it, both parallel to the shoreline. A line of Spanish regiments was on the right, English Royalists were in the center right, and a mixed force of Germans, Walloons, and French under Condé was on the left, with two lines of cavalry stretched behind the entire line. A further concentration of thirty cavalry divisions was on the road. They had marched quickly enough to outpace their artillery, so none was available.

Turenne placed his 6,000 infantry parallel to the Spanish, stretching them from the shoreline to the canal, but he divided his superior cavalry into two forces of forty divisions each on the flanks. The cavalry on the left was actually on the strand along the water's edge. At first, the Spanish had a cavalry force there as well, but the arrival of English ships offshore, and the resulting threat of bombardment, convinced Don Juan to concentrate all his horse on the southern flank. Turenne also brought with him some artillery from the siege lines.

The strength of the Spanish position was a large dune, some 150 feet high, on the far right. A contingent of Spanish veterans was deployed there, with some of Charles's infantry in support. The lay of the land was such that Don Juan considered himself to be in a sufficiently strong position that it was better to defend than attack. His entire line was positioned on higher ground than that of the attackers, with much more level ground behind it for the Spanish cavalry to deploy.

The Anglo-French force arrived opposite the Spanish about 0800. Turenne's plan was to pause about 600 yards away from the Spanish lines and take stock of their position before making any final adjustments to his battle plan. He had not counted on the enthusiasm of the British redcoats on his left. Seeing that they were opposite the strong position held by the Spanish, Cromwell's Protestant troops refused to stop short, but continued to march forward to within musket range of the Spanish. When a few Spanish rounds fell among them and caused some casualties, the redcoats decided not to await orders but charged on their own volition. Some French musketeers were sent forward to provide some fire support against the large dune, but the English were not about to wait on others to begin the fight. The front of the hill was steep, so much that the attackers had to crawl up it, but they pressed on in spite of taking heavy fire. The Spanish troops on top were formed into a defensive square, or *tercio*, of pikemen supported by musketeers on the corners. The English closed with them, and with their own musket fire and pikes, and then swinging muskets as clubs, they broke the Spanish square and sent the survivors back down the back side of the hill. The duke of York led a cavalry assault against the redcoats, but their position on the dune now gave them the high ground, and the charge was beaten back. A second charge, made up of cavalry and rallied Spanish infantry, flanked the redcoats, and for a time a melee ensued. The arrival of the French cavalry along the beach, however, turned the tide in favor of the English.

As the battle for the Spanish right flank was being fought, the rest of the army had closed on the Spanish and the fighting was now general. Condé's command on the Spanish left held its own, but the Germans and Walloons in the center began to give way. As the right flank was collapsing, though, it is not surprising that the center buckled; soon Condé's flank was forced to retreat as well.

The Royalists put up a good fight, as did the Spanish on the right, but the aggressiveness of the English in seizing that flank gave the Anglo-French force an advantage that could not be overcome. "In his dispatch Turenne did

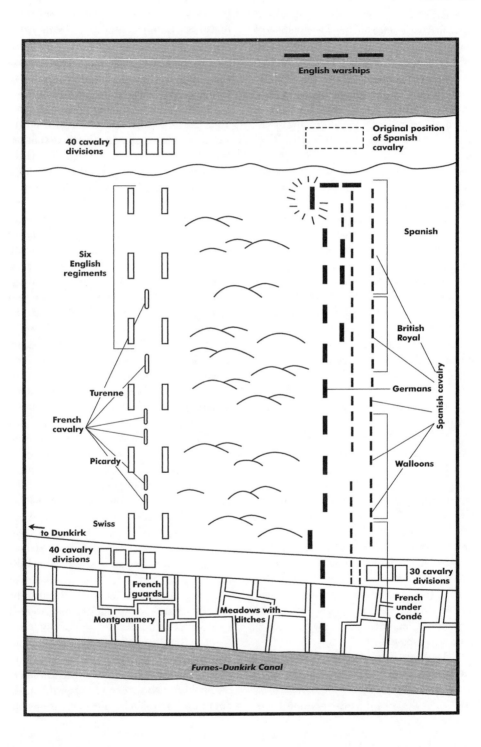

English warships

40 cavalry divisions

Original position of Spanish cavalry

Six English regiments

Spanish

British Royal

Turenne

French cavalry

Germans

Spanish cavalry

Picardy

Walloons

Swiss

to Dunkirk

40 cavalry divisions

30 cavalry divisions

French guards

Montgommery

Meadows with ditches

French under Condé

Furnes–Dunkirk Canal

justice to the vigour with which the English stormed the sand-hill: 'They came on like wild beasts,' said a Spanish officer. 'The English have such a reputation in this army as nothing can be more,' wrote Colonel Drummond.... 'The English are generally cried up for their unparalleled courage,' reported Lord Fauconberg when he returned from the French court" (Firth, *The Last Years of the Protectorate, 1656–1658*, p. 199). By noon the battle was over, which had been Turenne's intention. He wanted to fight the battle in the morning to take advantage of the low tide that would allow his cavalry to operate on the beach. That cavalry, unopposed, was able to sweep the flank in support of the redcoats and roll up the Spanish line. It was such a large force that the drawn-out Spanish cavalry lines could not concentrate and resist. After the close pursuit was completed, the casualty count was impressive. Don Juan and Condé lost 1,000 dead and 5,000 taken prisoner. The Anglo-French force lost about 400 men, mainly redcoats.

Results

Within a matter of days after the Battle of the Dunes, the Spanish garrison surrendered the city of Dunkirk. According to the agreement between Cromwell and the French, Dunkirk became an English possession. For a time, Spain and France remained at war, but Spain finally pled for negotiations, which resulted in the Peace of the Pyrenees in November 1659. This treaty ceded Spanish control over much of Flanders to Louis XIV, hampering Spain's long-established role as a power in Europe. When Louis married the daughter of Spanish King Philip IV, Maria Theresa, Spain from that point forward was, if not a vassal of France, certainly a poor relative.

To this point, Charles II had been banking on Spanish aid to assist him in his return to power in England; after the Battle of the Dunes, it was impossible to return to the throne by force. Charles, however, did get his chance when

Oliver Cromwell died in 1658, just weeks after the battle. Cromwell's son Richard tried to fill his father's shoes and failed. The following May, Parliament reconvened, after having been suspended by Oliver Cromwell in 1653 in a dispute over the size of the English army. When Richard Cromwell found he could control neither army nor Parliament, he resigned. A struggle for power between the Parliament and the English army (commanded by Generals Charles Fleetwood and John Lambert) ensued over the suppression of Royalist uprisings. This resulted in the army in October 1659 ending Parliament's brief session.

Members of Parliament appealed to General George Monck, commanding English forces in Scotland, to save them. Monck had been a supporter of Charles I and spent time in prison for it during Cromwell's time in power, but became a Roundhead and served Cromwell's cause well. At heart, though, he seems to have remained a monarchist; his wife certainly was. Feeling that the only way to restore order to English politics and society was with a king, Monck led his army out of Scotland in January 1660 and occupied London 5 weeks later. Lambert tried to stop him, but his troops were so badly supplied and paid that they deserted him wholesale; that resulted in Parliament reconvening.

Although some members of Parliament distrusted Monck, others supported the idea of reestablishing the monarchy. Monck contacted Charles II, who was beginning to feel some threat from his former Spanish allies. Ultimately, at the urging of some royal advisors and General Monck, Charles released the Declaration of Breda. This pronouncement dealt with three major topics: what to do about those who had been instrumental in the execution of Charles I, what to do about the army (especially its pay), and what to do about the English people's religious views vis-à-vis those of Charles. The Declaration stated that there should be a general amnesty for regicides (with a few exceptions), that the army should be awarded all its back pay, and that in England there should be "liberty of conscience." All of that, however, should be subject to the wishes of Parliament. That was the key. The only way Charles could again sit on the English throne was if Parliament was to be a permanent and respected part of the government. Until the removal of Charles I, and even during Cromwell's rule, Parliament served at the pleasure of the chief executive. From 1660 forward, Parliament became the senior partner in the constitutional monarchy. Never again would any English monarch pretend to absolute rule, and the supremacy of parliamentary rule had a major effect on the development of government in the British colonies in North America, and through them the United States. The Stuart line continued in England for less than 30 years afterward, for Charles's brother James II was too aggressive with his Catholicism and was deposed in 1688 in favor of William and Mary of the House of Orange in Holland. The power of the people to remove an unjust king in 1688 also had aftereffects in the North American colonies.

References: Ashley, Maurice. *Charles II: The Man and the Statesman.* New York: Praeger, 1971; Firth, Charles Harding. *The Last Years of the Protectorate, 1656–1658.* London: Russell & Russell, 1964 [1909]; Gaunt, Peter. *Oliver Cromwell.* Oxford, UK: Blackwell, 1996; Harris, R. W. *Clarendon and the English Revolution.* Stanford, CA: Stanford University Press, 1983; Venning, Timothy. *Cromwellian Foreign Policy.* New York: St. Martin's Press, 1995.

BLENHEIM
13 August 1704

FORCES ENGAGED
Allied: 52,000 men (10,000 of them British). Commanders: Duke of Marlborough and Prince Eugene of Savoy.
French/Bavarian: 56,000 men. Commander: Marshal Count Camille de Tallard.

IMPORTANCE
Marlborough's victory broke the myth of French invincibility, beginning the decline of France and King Louis XIV.

Historical Setting

Through the latter decades of the seventeenth century, King Louis XIV of France was the dominant figure in European political and military affairs. He created the best-organized and -equipped army of its day and wielded it with brilliant insight, expanding France's borders, slowly but surely, at the expense of Italy, the Holy Roman Empire (Austria), the United Provinces (Netherlands), and various German principalities. Blessed with vision, daring, and good generals, Louis's France was the envy and bane of western Europe.

Ambitious to a fault for himself and his country, Louis constantly was on the alert for anything that could expand his power. In 1700, such an event occurred. Charles II of Spain, of the House of Hapsburg, died childless. With no direct heir, there was a scramble for his throne. Before his death, Charles had named Philip of Anjou, a relative but a rather distant one, as his successor. What made the selection unacceptable to most of Europe was that Philip was grandson to Louis XIV, of the House of Bourbon. A Bourbon sitting on the throne of Spain was a portent of entirely too much French power; further, a seemingly closer claimant arose. Leopold I, Holy Roman Emperor in Vienna, put forth his second son Charles as a nominee for the throne. The Holy Roman Empire had for more than a century been ruled by a Hapsburg, and the Austrian and Spanish branches of the family could be reunited in Charles. Leopold was eager to press his son's claim, and he did not have to wait long for other European countries to volunteer their assistance.

Chief among the allies was William III of England. He ascended the English throne in 1688 as a result of the Glorious Revolution, which overthrew the Catholic King Charles II in favor of a Protestant monarch. William of Orange, king of the United Provinces of the Netherlands, was closely enough related to be invited to replace Charles II, so he did. William, as king of the Netherlands, had long resisted French aggression. When Philip of Anjou was crowned king of Spain in 1701, William gladly served as the organizer of the Grand Alliance, the coalition to oppose Louis. Unfortunately, William died in March 1702, but his daughter Anne quickly took up her father's cause. As she was married to Prince George of Denmark, that country soon joined in the coalition, as did Prussia, Portugal, and Savoy (in northern Italy).

Louis knew that by allowing his grandson to accede to the throne, war would certainly follow; rather than wait, he jumped right in. As Spain controlled portions of the Netherlands along the French frontier, Louis sent in troops to occupy those lands on the pretense of transferring them and their garrisons to Philip's authority. As those same lands were previously Hapsburg-owned, Leopold responded (even before the Grand Alliance was complete) by sending Holy Roman Empire troops into the

Italian peninsula, much of which was under Spanish authority. Leopold's commander in this operation was the extremely talented Eugene of Savoy, who quickly pushed Spanish troops back into Mantua.

In the meantime, Louis was provoking England. Catholic himself and a supporter of England's King Charles II before William supplanted him, Louis announced his support of Scotland's Catholic King James III as rightful king of England. As James's House of Stuart had indeed ruled England for most of the seventeenth century, this was not a surprising move for either Scotland or France. Louis also launched economic warfare on England, attacking English shipping and raiding English colonies. England's response was to commit troops to the Continent, but even more importantly to send its finest military leader, John Churchill, the earl (later duke) of Marlborough. Marlborough was not only a master of the military art, he was a first-rate diplomat. He needed both talents because he struggled to hold together a coalition army with squabbling participants as well as smooth the waters for turbulent relations between monarchs.

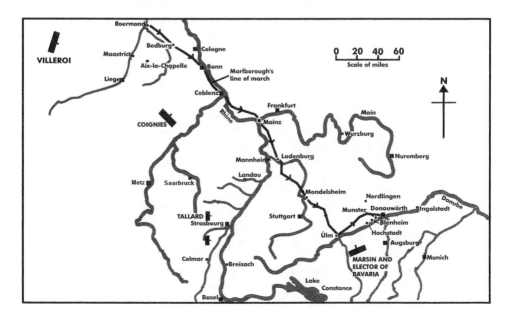

Louis XIV (Gift of J. Paul Getty)

In June 1702, Marlborough arrived with 12,000 British soldiers; combining them with allied forces to a strength of 50,000, he invaded the Netherlands. Although the bulk of his force was Dutch, he struggled to actually use them in combat because Dutch political leaders continually objected to their army being risked. Through 1702 and 1703, Marlborough struggled against French forces and his own allies' intransigence in campaigns along the Rhine River, although Austrian and other leaders sometimes insisted on fighting in other places rather than concentrate their forces in one place under one man. When not checked by his Dutch allies, Marlborough often found himself stymied in the Netherlands by the talented French commander Marshal Villeroi. Marlborough in the summer of 1704 left 60,000 men in the Netherlands and marched for Bavaria, there to join forces with Eugene of Savoy. Together they planned on fighting a combined Franco-Bavarian force under Mar-

shal Count Camille de Tallard. Bavaria had recently joined with France, hoping at the least to gain some territory at the expense of the empire; at the most, the Elector of Bavaria, Maximillian, hoped to make himself Holy Roman Emperor.

The Battle

Marlborough's march from the Netherlands to the Danube was a masterpiece of movement. By enforcing strict march discipline, he kept his troops and horses fresh while covering 250 miles in 5 weeks, an unheard-of feat in its day. He also made occasional feints at potential targets on the French frontier, keeping French forces paralleling his march without closing on them. The French general Villeroi followed for a time and then turned the shadowing of Marlborough's force over to Marshal Tallard, based along the upper reaches of the Rhine River. He was positioned to intercept Marlborough's expected attack toward the province of Alsace. In the meantime, Maximillian held position near Vienna. The original French plans had been for his forces to combine with Tallard's to capture Vienna and install Maximillian on the throne; he positioned himself in Austria just in case Marlborough went there instead.

Marlborough picked up reinforcements from various German principalities along the way and then surprised Tallard by marching his enlarged army overland toward the Danube, placing himself between the Frenchman and the elector. Upon learning this, Tallard hastened through the Black Forest in pursuit. On 2 July, Marlborough reached the Danube at Donauwörth, driving back Maximillian's army to the fortifications of Augsburg. Marlborough proceeded to ravage the countryside, hoping to draw Maximillian out. Instead, the elector avoided confrontation and marched his men south of the Danube to link up with Tallard at Ülm in early August. Marlborough met Eugene

on 12 August, and the two armies were at fighting strength.

With a force of approximately 52,000 men and sixty cannon, Marlborough marched westward up the left bank of the Danube toward his enemy. Tallard and Maximillian had crossed to the northern, left bank of the Danube on 10 August and camped at Blenheim, a small town on the river. Possessing 56,000 men and ninety cannon, Tallard was sure that Marlborough would not be foolish enough to attack. He therefore was quite surprised on 13 August 1704 when the morning fog lifted and multiple allied columns were marching toward him. Because of difficulty traversing rough terrain, Eugene was late in arriving at the battlefield, and that gave Tallard time to deploy his men. He placed the bulk of his infantry on his flanks, the right flank anchored by the town of Blenheim and the Danube, the left flank holding the town of Oberglau. To make this defensive line even more imposing, the French held

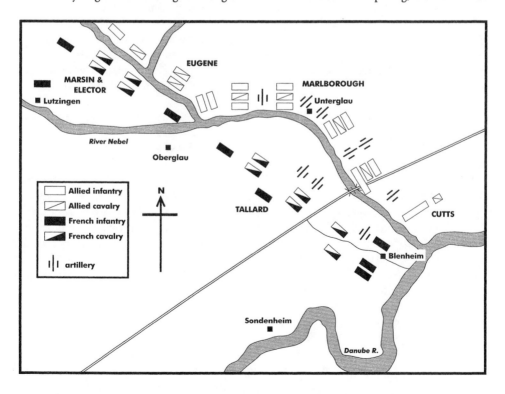

a ridgeline paralleling and overlooking the Nebel, a stream that joins the Danube at Blenheim. Tallard concentrated his cavalry in the center, hoping to crush the advancing allied troops as they attempted to ford the marshy ground along the Nebel.

The battle began shortly after noon, with Marlborough launching an infantry attack on Blenheim and sending Eugene against Oberglau. By these two attacks, he hoped to pin the French flanks and take advantage of their inability to communicate with each other. This he did, and the commander in Blenheim called up substantial reserves to assist in the town's defense. Neither attack made much headway, but they did polarize the defenders on the flanks. Busy beating back these attacks, Tallard did not respond to Marlborough's pushing forces across the Nebel. There he placed alternating units of infantry and cavalry for mutual support and also brought up much of his artillery. With his center forward and exposed, he laid himself open to an attack. Tallard launched his cavalry, but timely assistance dispatched by Eugene in the form of a cavalry assault eased the pressure and drove the French attack back. By 1500, Marlborough's army had the French flanks locked up in their respective towns and a combined force in the center already across the river and well placed against Tallard's cavalry.

The battle went into a lull for an hour and then resumed at 1600. The allied advance was inexorable, and French cavalry charges could not break the infantry supported by artillery. Tallard's call for reserves went unheeded because they had been committed to the flanks earlier. The French cavalry could do little more than cause temporary halts in the allied advance, and, when Marlborough committed his cavalry, the French horses were already spent and unable to effectively respond. An infantry assault with bayonets finished off the French center; Tallard was captured as his soldiers broke. Seeing the disaster in the center, the elector withdrew as best he could from Oberglau, but the French

units in Blenheim were abandoned. After some negotiation, they surrendered.

Results

As the sun set on 13 August, Marlborough enjoyed one of England's most decisive victories. For a loss of some 12,000 men, he had broken Tallard's force: there were 20,000 French and Bavarian dead and wounded, 14,000 taken prisoners, and sixty cannon captured. It was the first major defeat that France had suffered in Louis XIV's lifetime. The Bourbon king who had called the tune in European politics for decades finally began to receive the piper's bill. Marlborough's audacity on the battlefield was the perfect ending to a masterful campaign that stymied both French and Bavarian ambitions.

After this battle, Maximillian was no longer in a position to aim for the Holy Roman Empire's throne. Indeed, before year's end, Marlborough's forces had captured Ülm, Landau, and Ingolstadt, forcing Maximillian to swear fealty to the emperor. Hungarian nationalists, who had hoped a Franco-Bavarian victory would topple the empire and allow them their freedom, also found themselves without hope. Austria thus reasserted its authority as ruler of the Holy Roman Empire. Later victories in this same war placed Austria in a dominant position in the Italian peninsula, a position it enjoyed for almost a century.

Marlborough rose in status from good to great in the wake of Blenheim and further enhanced his reputation over the next 5 years. He proceeded to defeat the best commanders that Louis could put against him in the field: victory over Villeroi at Ramillies in May 1706 delivered the Netherlands from French rule; in 1708, victory over Marshal Louis Joseph Vendôme at Oudenarde evicted the French from Flanders; and a draw at Malplaquet in 1709 did little more than consolidate allied strength along the Franco-Belgian frontier, but further harmed the already dwindling reputation of French arms.

Negotiations finally opened in 1711 and continued for 2 years before the signing of the Treaty of Utrecht on 11 April 1713. By this, Louis XIV recognized the Protestant monarchy in England and ceded some French territory in North America. The reason for the war in the first place, however, remained only partially settled. Philip of Anjou remained King Philip V of Spain, but Louis swore that France and Spain would not join even if the Bourbon family held both thrones; no one king would hold both. Louis also gave up land in Italy as well as abandoning claim to the Spanish Netherlands. Charles VI, Holy Roman Emperor, did not want to cede that point, but with the breakup of the Grand Alliance he could not defeat France alone, although he tried. Spain in the big picture was the big loser, while England proved to be the big winner. After this war, England dominated international trade as well as sea power via her merchant and military navies. Fuller also notes that, from this point forward, the key to England's military future lay in its banking system, which international trade made the strongest anywhere (Fuller, *A Military History of the Western World*, vol. 2, p. 155). Louis's reign as instigator of European adventures came to an end. When he died in 1715, his successors could not match his talents or even competently defend his acquisitions. Not until Napoleon rose to power at the end of the eighteenth century did French fortunes revive. Blenheim broke Louis; every victory after that was merely confirmation of that fact. Absolute monarchy would never be the same.

References: Chandler, David. *The Art of Warfare in the Age of Marlborough.* New York: Hippocrene Books, 1976; Fuller, J. F. C. *A Military History of the Western World,* vol. 2. New York: Funk & Wagnalls, 1955; Hassel, Arthur. *Louis XIV and the Zenith of French Monarchy.* Freeport, NY: Books for Libraries Press, 1972; Jones, J. R. *Marlborough.* New York: Cambridge University Press, 1993; Kamen, Henry. *The War of Succession in Spain, 1700–15.* Bloomington: University of Indiana Press, 1969.

POLTAVA
28 June 1709

FORCES ENGAGED
Russian: 44,000 men and 100 cannon. Commander: Czar Peter the Great.
Swedish: 17,000 men and 4 cannon. Commander: King Charles XII.

IMPORTANCE
Sweden's defeat marked their decline and the arrival of Russia as a serious European power.

Historical Setting

Sweden had expanded from a Scandinavian power to a major force in European politics because of the statecraft and military genius of Gustavus Adolphus. He died in 1632 at the battle of Leutzen in the Thirty Years' War and was succeeded by Charles X. Charles expanded on Gustavus's strong performance by taking Sweden to its greatest limits and power by 1655. During the First Northern War, Charles defeated Poland and Denmark, but the war ended with his death in 1660. Peace lasted for four decades, until the reign of Charles XII, when Poland began showing its traditional restlessness under foreign dominance. In 1700, Polish King Augustus II organized the Northern Union, made up of Poland, Denmark, and Russia. Russia was the most enthusiastic supporter of the Union, not because it desired Polish liberation but because Czar Peter I wanted his country to supplant Sweden as the dominant Baltic power.

Charles XII was but 18 years of age when he rose to the throne of Sweden in 1700, but he did not lack for military talent. He made the first move of what came to be called the Second, or Great, Northern War by invading Denmark, which he viewed as the weak link in the enemy chain. With Copenhagen threatened, the Danes concluded a quick peace, signing the Treaty of Travedal on 28 August 1700. Although the

Danes promised to remain passive and not aid their erstwhile allies, the fact that they possessed a strong fleet worried Charles because it was a potential threat to his lines of communication when he faced Poland and Russia.

Charles quickly turned eastward and landed 8,000 men at Livonia with the intent of relieving the besieged city of Riga, but instead marched on Narva when he learned that the attacking Russian force outnumbered the defenders by a four-to-one margin. The Russians remained unaware of Charles's approach until he attacked them in a driving snowstorm on 20 November. The Russians were badly beaten, losing 10,000 dead, wounded, or taken prisoner, while another 30,000 fled, abandoning all their artillery and supplies. Charles next marched on Poland, where a 4-year campaign against King Augustus finally ended in Swedish victory with the signing of the Treaty of Altranstadt on 24 September 1706. Poland pledged to remain quiet, accepting Swedish puppet Stanislas Leszczynski in place of King Augustus. Charles spent the winter reorganizing and resupplying for the campaign against Russia the following year.

While Charles was defeating Denmark and Poland, Czar Peter had spent his time reorganizing his own army after the embarrassment at Narva. He also built up his fleet in the Baltic at the same time that he was building his capital at St. Petersburg, at the mouth of the Neva River. By not marching to the aid of his allies, Peter had had the time to significantly upgrade his military strength. He needed it; Charles invaded out of Poland on 1 January 1708 with Moscow as his goal. As is so often the case, the Russians were able to slow the invading army by gradual withdrawals and a scorched-earth policy. Accomplishing the desired goal of depriving Charles and his army of supplies, the Swedish king marched his forces southward to join with his new ally, Ivan Mazepa, hetman of the Cossacks. That move meant that the supply line that Charles wanted to maintain became badly strained, and Peter took advantage

of that. He attacked a force under Swedish General Carl Lewenhaupt at Lesnaia on 9 October 1708. Lewenhaupt commanded a force of 11,000 marching to reinforce Charles, but after the defeat at Lesnaia only 6,000 got through, and without artillery or supplies.

The Battle

The winter of 1708–1709 was spent in skirmishes between Peter's army and the combined Swedish-Cossack force, during which time Charles's force of 40,000 was cut almost in half because of combat and the severe cold. In the spring of 1709, Charles decided to press on to Moscow, rather than reinforce his army. Along the line of march lay the town of Poltava on the Vorskla River. Charles laid siege to Poltava on 2 May. Peter sent his cavalry commander Menshikov to distract and observe the Swedes, while he both put down a Cossack rising along the Dnieper River and convinced the Turkish government to stay aloof from this struggle. The Turks not only stayed out of it, temporarily at least, but also forbade Crimean Cossacks from aiding the Swedes. With his rear covered, Peter marched on Poltava, arriving in early June. He established a camp on the west bank of the Vorskla, a few miles north of Poltava.

The Russians defending Poltava had held out much longer than Charles had anticipated, and the Swedish king was running low on both food and gunpowder. To make bad matters worse, on 17 June Charles was wounded in the foot, making it impossible for him to lead his troops in battle with his normal energy. With 40,000 Russians now in the neighborhood, he should have lifted the siege and withdrawn to Poland, but instead he decided to fight Peter. When Peter learned of Charles's wound, he too thought that the time for battle had come. Much closer to Poltava he built a new camp, a fortified square with the east flank on the Vorskla and the south flank along a marshy wood with a stream running through it. That wood and stream separated the Russian camp

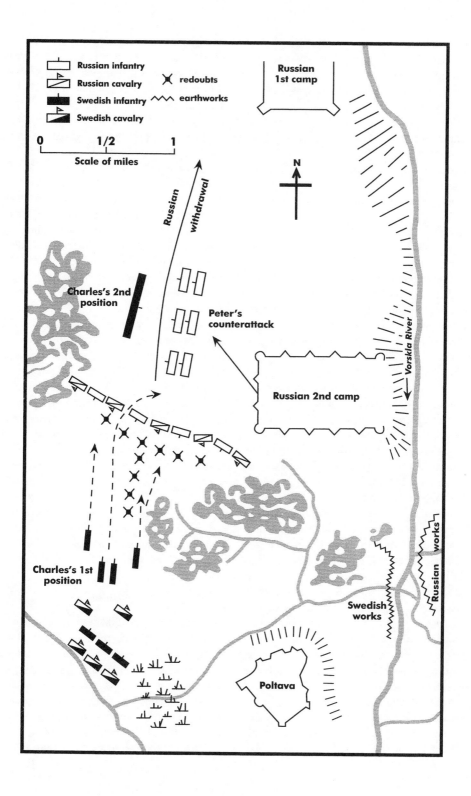

from Poltava. Peter was sure this new camp would provoke Charles to attack, and he was correct.

Charles's army began its march to battle at 0300 on 28 June 1709. They had to move west from Poltava and then turn north to enter a gap between the aforementioned woods and a marsh farther west. Between the woods and marsh, Peter had built six redoubts to slow any advance and then began building four more perpendicular to the six. The result was a T formation with the crossbar between the woods and marsh and the upright pointing at the oncoming Swedes, who had to divide their forces to either side. Charles left 5,600 men behind to cover Poltava and guard the base camp, leaving him with but 12,500 men for his attack. Although Charles moved his men in the dark of night, Peter learned of the operation and quickly established a line of mixed infantry and cavalry behind the line of six redoubts.

Charles was forced by the redoubts to split his force, half to the east and half to the west; he was carried on a litter with the left, western force. His plan was to rush past the fire of the redoubts to engage the Russians behind, who he was sure would not stand and fight; he remembered their shoddy performance at Narva and assumed nothing had changed. The problem with this plan was that he refused to share it with his subordinates for, like Alexander of Macedon, he was a hands-on, lead-from-the-front commander who liked to be in the midst of battle to act and react as circumstances dictated. Because he was on a litter, though, he could not do that, and his primary subordinate, General Rehnskjöld, was not allowed to act on his own initiative. Overcentralized command doomed the Swedes.

On the left flank, the attacking Swedes soon swept past the redoubts and drove back the Russians on the far side. On the right, however, General Roos proceeded to attack the redoubts to reduce or capture them. That meant that he not only made slow progress, but he suffered lots of casualties. When, late in the morning, Charles was ready to press his attack on Peter's camp, he had but half his army with him because Roos was bogged down and soon surrounded and captured. The troops in the center of the attack also managed to break through the line of redoubts and, driving Russian troops before them, were in a position to wheel right and storm the Russian camp. This force, under Lewenhaupt, received orders to retreat and join with Charles, however, thus losing their momentum and giving Peter time to prepare his army. Who sent the order to Lewenhaupt was hotly debated at the time, for both Charles and Rehnskjöld denied sending it, but, with the shifting fortunes of battle and the conflicting reports of success and failure, it could have been sent almost at any time in the previous few hours.

While Charles redeployed his forces on the plain behind the redoubts, Peter brought 40,000 men out of his camp, along with 100 cannon. Charles certainly should not have attacked this greatly superior force, at least until the artillery he had back at Poltava was brought up, but his disdain for the Russian troops overrode good sense. Four thousand infantry and cavalry advanced across the open plain into the teeth of the Russian guns, and they were mowed down by the hundreds. Peter rode constantly through his own lines shouting encouragement and giving orders. Charles was unable to do so, and thus his uninspired men had no chance of breaking the Russian line. By noon, Charles was obliged to leave the field.

Results

Charles left behind 3,000 dead and 2,800 prisoners, including General Rehnskjöld and four other generals. Charles gathered up the troops that he had left at Poltava and they made their way east and south. At the junction of the Vorskla and Dnieper Rivers, he found all boats destroyed, but he built enough rafts to escape with 1,000 men. The remainder were captured on 30 June. Charles fled to seek refuge with the Turks, Russia's traditional enemy, who granted him sanctuary.

Peter scored a major triumph at Poltava, but almost threw it all away. Rather than consolidating his victory, he pressed a campaign against Poland while demanding that the Turks surrender Charles to him. Instead of Charles, the Turks sent 200,000 troops to the Russian frontier. In the spring of 1711, Peter declared war on Turkey and soon found himself in command of 38,000 starving men along the River Pruth, with the region devastated by the Turks, who outnumbered him five to one. On 11 August, the Turks attacked and were beaten back. Their commander, Grand Vizier Baltaji Mehmet, entered into negotiations with Peter and soon granted him and his army parole. A few days' siege would have brought Peter's army to its knees, but instead he lived to fight another day.

War continued between Russia and Turkey on one front and Russia and Sweden on another, while Charles remained in Turkey arguing with his allies. Russia and Turkey signed the Treaty of Adrianople in 1713, but not until 1721 did Russia and Sweden sign the Treaty of Nysted; Charles XII had been killed in battle 3 years earlier. Thus ended the Great Northern War after 21 years, and Sweden, which entered the war as such an important power, exited it a broken country.

Russia, on the other hand, replaced Sweden as the major power in the Baltic region. In the Treaty of Nysted, Russia received Livonia, Estonia, and Ingermanland on the Baltic as well as the Finnish Karelia territory. Peter, who had long envied European progress, had access now to what the west could provide. He imported experts on almost everything to drag Russia into the modern world, and technical advisors as well as intellectuals stayed in St. Petersburg to fulfill his dreams. This brought a facade of western civilization to Russia, which the aristocrats were able to appreciate, but the mass of Russian peasantry remained poor, ignorant, and exploited. Peter's wars and building projects killed tens of thousands; as much as 20 percent of the Rus-

sian population died during his reign. Many of them died in the military, which Peter was determined to make the equal of any European army or navy. When he died, the Russian navy possessed fory-eight ships of the line, and the army had more than 200,000 regulars and 100,000 reserves.

Although Russians began to act like Europeans, their Asian heritage lingered on. Peter had to remedy that to build the empire he wanted. The only way to do that was to adopt European government administrative techniques and philosophies to provide the necessary regular taxation power he needed. The western administration, however, employed eastern ruthlessness in execution, and more dead Russians were the result as Peter suppressed any objections to his actions. Although he did introduce a number of western social reforms, they rarely applied to the masses, who continued to work and produce the labor and taxes, just as they had done for centuries. That resource, coupled with the land and mineral resources that Peter developed, brought Russia overnight into Europe as a country to be reckoned with. Although its power waxed and waned over the following centuries, Russia was here to stay on the world scene. "A new threat to Europe had arisen; again Asia was on the move, but this time her Mongoloid hordes were girt in the panoply of the West" (Fuller, *A Military History of the Western World*, vol. 2, p. 186).

Had Peter lost at Poltava, it is certainly questionable if Sweden would have bent Russia to its will. If the Turks had not let Peter go from the River Pruth, Turkey may well have emerged as the major eastern power that Russia became because the struggle between those two countries never ebbed, and Russian military power certainly acted as a curb to Ottoman desires in eastern Europe.

References: Creasy, Edward S. *Fifteen Decisive Battles of the World.* New York: Harper, 1851; Fuller, J. F. C. *A Military History of the Western World,* vol. 2. New York: Funk & Wagnalls, 1955; Hatton, R. M. *Charles XII of Sweden.*

London: Weidenfeld & Nicolson, 1968; Massie, Robert. *Peter the Great, His Life and World.* New York: Alfred A. Knopf, 1980; Robert, Michael. *Sweden's Age of Greatness, 1632–1718.* New York: St. Martin's Press, 1973.

CULLODEN
16 April 1746

FORCES ENGAGED

English: Approximately 9,000 men. Commander: William Augustus, the duke of Cumberland.

Scottish: Approximately 5,000 men. Commander: Prince Charles Edward Stuart.

IMPORTANCE

Scottish defeat ended attempts by the Scottish Catholic royal line to assume the throne of Great Britain and reconfirmed British-French antagonism that was further exacerbated by the Seven Years' War a decade later.

Historical Setting

The story of Culloden stretches back two centuries before the battle to the time of England's King Henry VIII. Because of a dispute with the pope over Henry's desire for an annulment, the English king announced that he himself was to be the head of the Catholic Church in England. That lasted until his death, when he was succeeded by his young son, Edward VI. Edward was succeeded by his strongly Catholic older half sister, Mary. Mary reasserted the pope's authority in England and married Spain's Catholic King Philip II to show her support for the faith. When she died childless 5 years later, her sister Elizabeth assumed the throne. Her father's daughter, Elizabeth not only reinstituted her father's antipapal policy but she completely banned the Catholic Church and named herself head of the Church of England. This set her at odds with Catholic monarchs on the Continent, but she was their equal if not their superior in the game of power politics.

Elizabeth also died childless, however, and the closest living heir to the English throne was her cousin, James VI of Scotland, of the House of Stuart, who ascended the English throne in 1603. While not a Catholic, he instituted more ritual and established an episcopacy in the Anglican Church. His son Charles I was so aggressive with Parliament and the growing Puritan movement that England was plunged into civil war in 1642. Oliver Cromwell's forces fighting for Parliament ultimately deposed and then executed Charles, and for a time England had no king. After the fall of the Protectorate, Charles II came out of exile in France to assume the throne on terms that made the monarch much weaker vis-à-vis Parliament. When his son James asserted his strongly Catholic ways, he provoked a rebellion as well, which in 1688 resulted in the English government offering the throne to William and Mary, Protestants from Holland.

When their heir Queen Anne died without issue, the English government turned to the House of Hanover and gave the throne to George I, also Protestant. By rejecting the Catholic Stuart line after ejecting James, foreign royalty ruled in Great Britain, which after 1707 officially consisted of England, Scotland, Wales, and Ireland. The Stuarts, with a much stronger legal claim to the throne, lived in France as guests of the Catholic monarchs there. In the 1740s, the latest of the Stuart line, Prince Charles Edward, with the support of France, decided to try his luck at reestablishing his family on the throne that they considered rightly theirs. As can be seen in this summary, religion and politics were totally intertwined. France supported Prince Charles Edward, better known as "Bonnie Prince Charlie," superficially because he was Catholic but in the main because he would politically support France if he came to power.

In 1745, Britain was at war on the Continent. The War of the Austrian Succession began in 1740, and the major powers of Europe chose sides; England and France opposed each other, as they have since at least the Hundred Years' War of the fourteenth and fifteenth centuries. In May 1745, the British and their allies lost a large battle at Fontenoy, in Flanders. That setback, coupled with bickering in the British cabinet, seemed to signal Charles that the time was ripe for asserting his claim. The French government, and some of Charles's own advisors, warned against an invasion of Scotland, but he ignored them. The result was a lack of overt French support.

Prince Charles landed almost alone in the Hebrides Islands off the Scottish coast on 3 August 1745. Scotland at the time was also divided along political and religious lines; the anti-English Catholic clans of the Scottish highlands rose up to support Charles (called Jacobites, after "Jacob," or James Stuart, the first Scottish/English king), but the Presbyterian Protestants and those less hostile to England remained passive. That passivity was sufficient for Charles to raise an army of about 2,000, with which he captured Edinburgh in mid-September. An English army of 3,000 under Sir John Cope marched to put the rebellion down, but were defeated at Preston Pans. Rather than spend the winter in Scotland and consolidate his support, Charles decided to follow up this victory with an invasion of England. He picked up the support of more clans as he moved south against virtually no English resistance. His force, now about 5,000, captured Carlisle and Manchester in November and on 4 December occupied Derby, about 120 miles from London.

The English government was slow to react, and, when they did put some troops in the field, they made a strategic error. They assumed that instead of marching directly on London, Charles would march to Wales and draw on anti-English support there. Thus, not until Charles was in Derby did they realize their mistake. Had Charles marched immediately for London, the capital could have been his. Instead, he mistakenly believed some misinformation sent him by William Augustus, the duke of Cumberland, that 30,000 English troops were marching to oppose him. Unable to meet such a force with his 5,000, Charles decided to return home. Although many Catholics in England also gave him some tacit support, there was insufficient aid to keep his army supplied. A winter in Scotland seemed a good idea.

The Battle

As the Scots approached their frontier, Charles decided to lay siege to the city of Stirling. For 2 months, his forces surrounded the city, beating back relief efforts by two English forces at Penrith (18 December 1745) and Falkirk (17 January 1746). The Scots retreated into their homeland in February, though short of supplies and ammunition. For a time, they campaigned against English supporters, and in early April they camped near Inverness, where word came that Cumberland was 15 miles away at Nairn. Although some of his troops were drifting away to head for home, Prince Charles decided to attack Cumberland, either hoping for a surprise or simply to move before he lost any more men. The two forces met near the moor at Culloden on 16 April 1746.

Charles had some 5,000 Highlanders in his army, which formed up in two lines. On the right was the Clan Atholl, the Macdonalds on the left, and a number of others stretched in between, altogether about 3,800 men. A hundred yards to their rear, the second line consisted of some Lowland clans and a few French troops, numbering almost 1,200. A few cavalry also were there. The Scots possessed thirteen light cannon, but powder and shot was almost nonexistent. Cumberland commanded about 9,000 men of various backgrounds: English, loyal Scots (about 4,000), and some German mercenaries. The English army consisted of fifteen regular infantry regiments, some Scottish militia, 850 dragoons, and thirteen artillery pieces. The fact that Scots faced each other on that day is indicative of clan rivalry and in some cases intraclan rivalry because some men

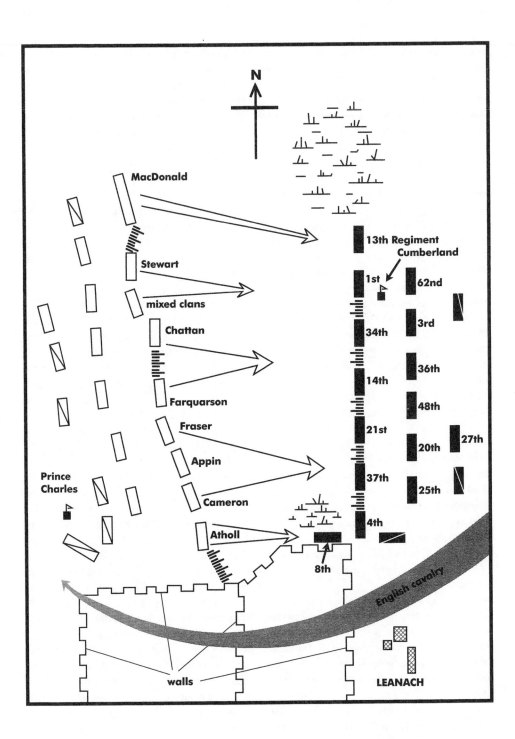

stood with Prince Charlie against the wishes of their chiefs.

The two armies deployed late in the morning and faced each other for a time. Just after 1230, the rebel cannon fired what shot they had to little effect. The English response was much more deadly, and for a time (some sources say an hour) it took its toll on the Scots. Lacking powder and shot, few of the Scots could do more than charge with their swords. After standing and taking the cannonade, that is just what they did. The center and right wing dashed forward without orders. They charged into a heavy fire, which did great damage and disorganized the units, but the assault forced back the first line on the English left flank. The second line stood firm, however, and firing in volleys they withered the Scottish ranks. "The Highlanders ... continued to advance with fury, and although much disordered by their own success, and partly disarmed by having thrown away their guns on the very first charge, they rushed on Sempill's regiment in the second line with unabated fury. That steady corps was drawn up three deep, the first rank kneeling, and the third standing upright. They reserved their fire until the [first line] had escaped around the flanks, and through the intervals of the second line. By this time the highlanders were within a yard of their bayonet points, when Sempill's battalion poured in their fire with so much accuracy, that it brought down a great many of the assailants, and forced the rest to turn back" (Scott, *A History of Scotland,* vol. 3, p. 194).

With so many of his men killed, Charles hesitated. Urged on by one of his subordinates to lead the remaining men and die like a king, he did not respond. Other advisors urged him to save himself, and to those he listened. Of the remaining troops, many withdrew in good order and retreated to Inverness; others withdrew in less good order and fled for their highland homes. Charles's army left behind 1,000 men killed in action and another 1,000 prisoners. They were executed quickly, for Cumberland had given the order for no quarter.

Results

After 10 months of uninterrupted success, the attempted usurpation of the throne, called simply "The '45," collapsed. For the next several days, Cumberland's men killed any survivor they could run down and, according to many reports, anyone who looked suspicious or was suspected of aiding a fugitive. For 5 months afterward, Cumberland hunted down all trace of rebellion, creating a long-lasting hostility in Scotland. Bonnie Prince Charlie had sufficient support to keep himself alive through that time, and, when the English finally marched home, he fled back to France.

The results of Charles's attempt on the throne was extremely harsh in the Scottish highlands. The English government, which had long viewed them with distaste, decided that it was time to depopulate Scotland of such potential troublemakers. The result came to be called the "clearances." The land was awarded to English nobility, who set about clearing the region of population in order to raise sheep. The Highlanders that remained were turned into virtual slaves, while tens of thousands were deported. Most went to America, where they served their new country in a revolution 30 years later. For those that survived at home, their culture was almost destroyed. The symbols of Highland independence and military prowess were outlawed. It became a capital offense to speak Gaelic, wear tartans, or play the bagpipes. English schools were established, and English became the official language.

The clans that had supported the English, however, fared somewhat better. Some of them were taken into the British army, where they served with distinction through the Napoleonic Wars. Although raised officially as temporary units, after Napoleon's defeat in 1815 some of them were made permanent and fought England's wars around the world. Over time, the ban on kilts and pipes was lifted and these items became an integral part of units that served in the British army until World War II, when their use in battle was finally brought to an end.

On a larger scale, the battle at Culloden is significant in removing the final threat to the Hanoverian kings of England, whose descendants still rule today as the House of Windsor. Had the Stuarts been able to reclaim the throne, much would have been different. When the Seven Years' War broke out in 1755 in America between British and French colonists, it was the traditional British-French rivalry that played itself out there and on the Continent. Had Charles Edward been king instead, that war would almost certainly have ended differently. Not only would an arrangement probably have been agreed to over French and British claims in America but Prussia would have had to fight without the English financial support that kept Frederick the Great's army in the field. A different balance of power in Europe, favoring France, would almost certainly have been the result. Although the American Revolution would probably have occurred anyway, the economic factors that forced English taxation on their colonists would have been significantly delayed. A delayed American Revolution would certainly have had an effect on the potential for a French Revolution and all the political and philosophical ramifications that brought about, which of course brings into question Napoleon's ability to rise to power. The English victory at Culloden is therefore much more important for what might have been had the battle gone the other way.

References: Daiches, David. *Charles Edward Stuart: The Life and Times of Bonnie Prince Charlie.* London: Thames & Hudson, 1973; Gibson, John S. *Lochiel of the '45: The Jacobite Chief and the Prince.* Edinburgh: Edinburgh University Press, 1994; Hartman, Cyril. *The Quest Forlorn: The Story of the Forty-five.* London: Heineman, 1952; Preston, Diana. *The Road to Culloden Moor.* London: Constable, 1995; Scott, Sir Walter. *A History of Scotland,* vol. 3. Philadelphia: Porter & Coates, n.d. [1829].

PLASSEY
23 June 1757

FORCES ENGAGED
English: 1,000 Europeans, 2,100 Indians, and 100 gunners with 8 cannon. Commander: Robert Clive.
Indian/French: 15,000 cavalry, 35,000 infantry, 10,000 militia, and 53 cannon. Commander: Suraj-ud-Daula.

IMPORTANCE
Clive's victory secured English dominance in Bengal, leading to England's dominance over all of India.

Historical Setting

The eighteenth century was an active time in India. Domestically, the Mughal Empire was disintegrating because of a succession of weak kings and stronger nobles. Although the capital at Delhi was the putative capital, local princes (nawabs) ruled their own lands and ignored or cooperated with the Delhi government as they saw fit. Arriving in this time of uncertain local rule were both the French and British. The Honorable East India Company represented British trading interests with trading centers, called factories, at Calcutta on the northeastern coast, Madras on the southeastern coast, and Bombay on the northwestern coast. The French operated the French East India Company out of Pondicherry, just down the coast from Madras. Both European powers entered into agreements with local nawabs, primarily for trade contacts, but also hoping to gain influence with whatever government may arise from the Mughal ashes. Not surprisingly, as England and France were rivals in Europe, they supported rival nawabs in India.

The Indian rulers were somewhat ambivalent toward the Europeans. They appreciated the income from trade, but more importantly they appreciated the military power the Europeans could provide to the local balance of power in India. At the same time, many of the nawabs looked down on the Europeans as inferiors and were shocked to learn that the Europeans viewed them the same way. This disgust with Europeans showed itself particularly in the attitude of Suraj-ud-Daula, nawab of Bengal, Bihar, and Orissa in the northeastern corner of India. He despised the British and wanted them out of the Bengali port city of Calcutta, not only because he feared their ambitions toward Bengal but because he was sure that they stored a fortune in Fort William, which guarded the city. In 1756, Suraj-ud-Daula's force of 50,000 attacked Calcutta, defended by just over 515 soldiers, half of them European. After a brief defense, the British government officials fled, leaving behind 170 soldiers. One hundred forty-six of them were imprisoned in a room approximately 18 feet square with but one window for ventilation. The next day, twenty-three survivors of what came to be known as the "Black Hole of Calcutta" emerged.

When news of this outrage reached the British factory at Madras, Robert Clive was dispatched to Calcutta. Clive had gone to India in 1744 at the age of 18 as a clerk with the East India Company. During a conflict with the French near Pondicherry in 1851, Clive had convinced his superiors to launch an attack on the regional capital city of Arcot. Clive was given command of the operation in spite of the fact that he had no military training or experience. With a few hundred men, he captured the city and then held it through a 50-day siege by French-led Indian troops. This along with other acts of bravery earned him rewards and promotions in England. When he returned to India in 1756, he was a lieutenant-colonel in the regular army, units of which were detailed to India to cooperate with the private army that the East India Company operated. Because of the plaudits he won at Arcot, Clive seemed a natural choice to recover Bengal for the Company.

Calcutta lies on the Hooghli River, which diverts due south from the Ganges about 200 miles before it reaches the Indian Ocean. At the mouth of the Hooghli lay Fulta, where the fleeing British officials from Calcutta were isolated. Clive's force of 900 Europeans and 1,500 Indian troops (sepoys) rescued them. Then he recaptured Calcutta on 2 January 1757. After an inconclusive battle in February, Clive and Suraj-ud-Daula concluded a peace treaty in which the Company was allowed to reoccupy Calcutta and be paid damages for their losses over the previous year. It was not a treaty that Clive thought would last very long.

Clive learned of intrigues within Suraj-ud-Daula's court and decided to investigate. He proposed working with Mir Jaffar, Suraj-ud-Daula's uncle, to unseat the nawab. Suraj-ud-Daula kept contact with French personnel in India and demanded that the British and French not fight each other, in spite of the fact that the Seven Years' War had just begun in Europe and once again the two nations were at odds. Clive therefore wanted to subvert possible French influence as well as remove the man regarded as responsible for the Black Hole. While Clive was negotiating secretly with Mir Jaffar, the British attacked and captured a French settlement a few miles from Suraj-ud-Daula's capital city of Murshidabad. That attack, coupled with a demand from the British for concessions that Clive knew could not be granted, provoked Suraj-ud-Daula to raise another army and march once again toward Calcutta.

The Battle

The force bearing down on Calcutta was 60,000 strong, including fifty-three artillery pieces operated by French gunnery crews. Although Fort William was an acceptable defensive position, Clive preferred the offensive. The problem was that he could muster only 3,000 infantry, one-third of them European, and only eight light cannon and two howitzers. Facing twenty-to-one odds seems foolhardy, and even Clive's well-known confidence wavered, but he was assured in secret messages from Mir Jaffar that when the battle started, Jaffar would keep

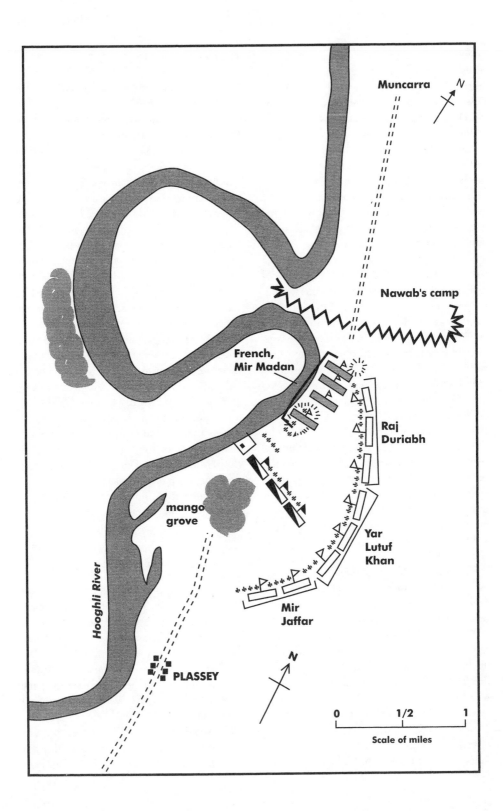

his contingent out of the fighting at first and then join the British side. Banking on that aid, Clive prepared for battle. On the night of 22 June, he camped in a mango grove alongside the Hooghli just north of the town of Pelasi, better known in its English form Plassey.

The next morning, the French opened the battle with a massive barrage against the British. It had little effect, however, because Clive had his men positioned on the reverse side of a hill on the edge of the grove. The Indian force was lined up in a huge semicircle almost surrounding the British, with the center of their force commanded by Suraj-ud-Daula's most talented general, Mir Mudin Khan. Clive's artillery was able to inflict more damage on the exposed Indian troops, and most of the morning was spent in an artillery duel. At noon, a monsoon rain began and the French gunpowder was immediately soaked. Assuming that the same thing had happened to the British, Mir Mudin Khan ordered an attack. Clive, however, remembered the words of an earlier British commander, Oliver Cromwell: "Trust in God but keep your powder dry." Clive had spread covers over his powder supplies and he was ready for the attack. Charging across open ground, the waves of attacking infantry, including Mir Mudin Khan, were mowed down by the British artillery. The Indian force drew back in confusion.

Luckily for the British, Mir Jaffar kept his word and withheld 45,000 men from the battle. Seeing the treachery and then learning of Mir Mudin Khan's death, Suraj-ud-Daula fled to his capital with a bodyguard of 2,000. He ordered his force to withdraw, but many did not receive the command and continued to fight. Clive fired at the remaining troops one last time with his artillery and then ordered his men forward. They swept the field of the Indian force and overran the French artillerists. By 1700, the battle was over and the victory was Clive's.

Results

For a loss of twenty-three killed and forty-nine wounded, Robert Clive achieved one of the great victories of all time. Suraj-ud-Daula lost 1,000 casualties of his massive force, but, considering that Mir Jaffar kept three-fourths of it out of the battle, the percentage was much higher: approximately one in fifteen killed or wounded. More than anything, it was Suraj-ud-Daula's losing his nerve and running that turned the tide of the battle, but, had Mir Jaffar not kept his bargain with Clive, the British may well have been wiped out by sheer weight of numbers. Suraj-ud-Daula was captured and executed a few days later, and Mir Jaffar replaced him as nawab.

Not that Clive trusted Jaffar, but he knew that Jaffar realized that the only reason he was in power was because of British aid; further, that would be the only way to stay in power. Jaffar for a time feared that Clive would not give him the throne, as Jaffar had not fought with the British, as he had promised, but merely held aloof. When Clive kept his word, however, Jaffar responded by giving him a gift of £160,000; other officers serving with Clive received large sums as well. Although this was an outrageous sum of money, such gifts were not unusual in similar circumstances, and many East India Company officials returned to England fabulously wealthy. Clive returned the favor. As governor of Bengal (appointed by the government in London), Clive put down a number of insurrections against Mir Jaffar's rule as well as defended him from attack by neighboring princes. When Clive finally left India in 1760, he was just 35 years old.

More importantly, of course, was the result of the battle on the East India Company and, by extension, Great Britain. First, it confirmed their position in Bengal and guaranteed their control of the port of Calcutta for the lucrative trade that the East India Company carried on in India. Mir Jaffar granted the company the rights of zamindar in the land around Calcutta. This meant that the East India Company became landlords, able to collect rents and (more importantly) taxes from the locals. Thus, the East India Company, already the dominant economic power in Bengal, began to exercise political power as well, and exercise it directly on the inhabitants. What made this remarkable was not that the British collected taxes but that they did so fairly, an act unheard of in India. Thus, with a different attitude, the Bengalis began to look on the British as fair overlords and ready protectors. The stability that was created in Bengal laid the groundwork for similar British administrations around their factories and ultimately throughout India. Although it was often with a high-handed and cavalier attitude, it was still better treatment than many Indians ever received from their own princes.

Britain's victory also made it the predominant European power in India. Although Britain continued to struggle with French forces for another few years, the French defeat in the Seven Years' War coupled with their inability to defeat the British in India meant their complete withdrawal over the next 20 years from colonization attempts. This, coupled with the declining economic and military power of the Dutch, removed any competition that the East India Company faced. They spread British power, money, and society into much of India. When the East India Company was forced by the government to disband in 1857 after the Sepoy Rebellion, the British established a formal colonial administration. By that time, Britain already viewed India as the crown jewel of its empire, and it remained so until independence in 1948. The wealth that flowed out of India after 1757 made England the richest nation on earth, much as the wealth of the Americas had done for Spain in the sixteenth century. For 200 years after Plassey, England drew on India for wealth through trade, strategic positioning in world affairs, and personnel in times of war; in all those roles, India responded and the British Empire benefited.

References: Bence-Jones, Mark. *Clive of India.* New York: St. Martin's Press, 1975; Fuller, J. F. C. *A Military History of the Western World,* vol. 2. New York: Funk & Wagnalls, 1955; Keay, John. *The Honourable Company.* New York: Macmillan, 1994; Mason, Philip. *A Matter of Honour.* London: Jonathan Cape, 1974; Robert, P. E. *History of British India.* London: Oxford University Press, 1952 [1921].

QUEBEC
13 September 1759

FORCES ENGAGED
British: 4,441 troops. Commander: Major General James Wolfe.
French: 4,500 troops. Commander: Major General Marquis Louis-Joseph de Montcalm.

IMPORTANCE
British victory secured their preeminence in North America by forcing France's withdrawal from Canada.

Historical Setting

After the defeat of the Spanish Armada in 1588, England began to seriously pursue a policy of colonization in North America. Unlike the Spanish who went to the New World mainly for conquest and riches, the English primarily went to North America to escape a variety of problems at home, mostly poverty and religious persecution. The English colonies along the eastern coast of North America were slow in growing, but were strong enough to divert most potential rivals elsewhere. The French, slightly behind the English in their pursuit of colonies, went to the remaining open region of North America, Canada. There the only resource that the French could exploit were furs. Unlike the Spanish or the English, whose attitudes toward the American Indian population were cavalier at best, the French saw the Indians as a source of supply. After all, who knew more about trapping animals and preparing furs? The French, therefore, came to Canada in much smaller numbers than did the Spanish or English and, by seeking friendship rather than land and by adapting to the Indian way of life rather than forcing Indians to adapt to European mores, built a solid relationship with the Indians.

The French worked their way gradually into Canada, establishing trading posts and forts rather than colonies. Certainly they claimed the land for their king, but they did not let that get in the way of amicable relations with the Indians. In the middle 1500s, the French explorer Sieur de La Salle floated down the Mississippi River to the Gulf of Mexico. Reaching the delta, he claimed not only the river he had just traveled but all the land drained by it. He had no idea just how much land that was, but it was everything from the Appalachian Mountains to the Rockies. This conflicted with the grandiose claims of both Spain and England, but as the three powers had no inhabitants in this overlapping region it did not really matter. Not until 1752.

By the mid–eighteenth century, the English colonists had begun to fill up the land between the Appalachians and the Atlantic and began to tentatively probe west of the mountains. They soon ran into evidence of a French presence in the form of forts in key places. In 1752, Virginia lieutenant governor Dinwiddie sent a force to build a fort where the Allegheny and Monongahela Rivers join to form the Ohio. This was the upper northeastern limit of La Salle's claim. They were soon surprised by a mixed force of French and Indians who compelled their withdrawal. The French then proceeded to finish the fort, improving it in the process. Colonial attempts to recapture the fort, now named Fort Duquesne, proved fruitless. Responding to an appeal by prominent colonist Benjamin Franklin (who had proposed a Plan of Union to form a governing body to oversee colonial defense and other common concerns), the government in London sent troops. The Plan of Union was never implemented, but the threat to England's colonies spurred the military response.

The first expedition under General Edward Braddock was a colossal failure and encouraged the French and their Indian allies to greater activity along the frontier. This coincided with increasing French and English tensions in Europe. European conflicts spilling over into North America were not new, but this one proved fatal to French ambitions. Braddock's defeat in July 1755 signaled the beginning of what came to be called the French and Indian War in North America; the European counterpart, the Seven Years' War, started the following year.

For a time, the French maintained the upper hand in North America, but that began to change with William Pitt's accession to power in London. Pitt was unlike many officials who viewed the American colonies as little more than a handy dumping ground for undesirables from England. Pitt realized the financial value of colonies for both imports and exports, plus he was not about to lose any possession to archrival France without a struggle. Pitt sent more troops to North America while doing the bulk of the fighting on the Continent via subsidies to Prussia. The Royal Navy was able to curtail French reinforcements, but to securely lock up Canada the key point was the town of Quebec.

The Battle

Pitt planned a four-pronged attack into Canada, via Lake Erie, Lake Ontario, Lake Champlain, and up the St. Lawrence River. Although the French had won a strong victory at Fort Ticonderoga at the bottom of Lake Champlain, they had lost the key harbor of Louisbourg on Cape Breton Island, which guarded the Gulf of St. Lawrence. It was from there that the attack up the St. Lawrence was to commence. Leading some 9,000 British soldiers (and a handful of American rangers) was Major General James Wolfe. He was a young man, but had served with some distinction in the War of the Spanish Succession and had led a few successful raids along the French coast. Opposing him inside Quebec were two men: military commander Major General Louis-Joseph, the marquis de

Montcalm, and governor and commander-in-chief, the marquis de Vaudreuil. Montcalm commanded the French troops, whereas Vaudreuil oversaw the Canadian militia and colonial regulars. Together they commanded about 12,000 men. Vaudreuil was in overall command, but had no military experience. Montcalm was recognized as an outstanding general in France and Canada; the two men openly despised each other. This meant that there would be little or no cooperation within the French command as the British approached.

The city of Quebec is located on the north shore of the St. Lawrence River and sits on a promontory created by that river and its tributary, the much smaller St. Charles. The city sits high on a bluff overlooking the river junction, and defended bluffs ran along the shore downstream (in an east-northeasterly direction). Further, just where the two rivers converge, the long estuary to the Atlantic begins, but immediately upstream the river becomes almost unnavigable. Thus, the only practicable approach to the city is from the west along the north shore across the Plains of Abraham, but it seemed impossible for the British to position themselves to launch an attack from that quarter. Artillery placed on the southern bank can bombard the city, but both Montcalm and Vaudreuil regarded their forces as too few in number to spare any to hold that position. Besides, winter was approaching, and the freezing river would force the British fleet and army away. Everything seemed positive, but for one mistaken assumption: that the river upstream from Quebec was unpassable for British shipping.

The earliest British contingents arrived in the middle of June 1759, with Wolfe making his appearance at the end of the month. He quickly occupied the southern bank as well as the Isle of Orleans just downstream to use as his main base. British artillery began lobbing shells into the city, but it was more demoralizing to the defenders than it was damaging. On the night of 28 June, the French set a number of boats afire to float with the current into the

British fleet, but they proved of little use. Wolfe considered and discarded a variety of plans after getting a good look at the strength of the French defenses atop the bluffs. At the end of July, he ordered a lower redoubt seized, hoping that this would bring the French out of their defenses to recapture it, but poor coordination and weather conspired against the operation. Throughout August, Wolfe sent American ranger forces to destroy area farmhouses and crops, hoping to harm French morale, but this too had little effect other than to give the Americans some satisfaction for years of similar treatment that they had received from French-allied Indian tribes.

The one positive aspect of British operations in August was the discovery by the Royal Navy that it was possible to slip ships past Quebec's weak shore batteries and through the supposedly unpassable narrows. When Wolfe polled his officers for operational suggestions, a crossing above Quebec onto the Plains of Abraham was the consensus, to which he agreed on 1 September. If nothing else, this would place British forces astride Quebec's line of communications to Montreal. Bluffs along the river, even above the city, still challenged an invader; that fact, plus the harassing attacks downstream, kept Montcalm's attention focused in that direction.

For a week before the assault, the British stood idle, and this lulled the French defenders. On the night of 12–13 September, the French pickets along the endangered shore were told of an approaching supply convoy coming upriver from Montreal. They did not, however, learn of its cancellation, so when British boats began plying the river, the French were not unduly alarmed. A French-speaking British officer kept the defending pickets off guard until the last moment, by which time the British were streaming up a narrow path to the top of the bluffs. A diversionary bombardment downstream continued to keep French attentions facing that direction. By early morning, when Montcalm learned of the successful landing, the

A 1792 engraving of General Wolfe killed at the battle of Quebec. (Library of Congress)

British forces were already forming up and facing Quebec's poorly maintained defensive walls.

Had Montcalm waited for troops to come up from the downriver defenses to supplement the garrison in the city, he would have stood a better chance of facing the 4,400 British regulars marching on Quebec. Instead, he marched out of the city with a roughly equal force, although only about half were regular troops. The rest were militia. The first French fighters on the scene were Canadian militia and some Indians, who proceeded to act as skirmishers and lay down a harassing fire. Wolfe ordered his men to lie down to avoid this. When Montcalm had his men formed up in midmorning, he ordered them to advance. The militia fired at too great a range to do any harm, while the British continued to lie prone and hold their fire. As the French line moved forward, it began to lose cohesion. The militia fired and then knelt to present a lower target as they reloaded. The regulars fired in volleys, reloaded, and then marched forward. By fighting in two different styles, the mixed forces found themselves falling apart even before they got into range of the British muskets. The British stood and fired by volleys when the French reached 60 yards. The platooning ranks kept up a steady fire. When the French reached 40 yards, the British line took ten steps forward and fired a volley that shredded the French lines. They broke. The entire fight had taken no more than half an hour.

Tragedy struck both sides during the battle. Wolfe was hit by sniper fire, first in the wrist, then in the abdomen, and then in the chest. He died on the field. Not long afterward, Montcalm was hit, probably by grapeshot from the two cannon that the British had pulled up the bluffs. He was taken into the city and survived until the early hours of the following morning. Although the troops that had been at the defenses along the downstream bluffs soon began to arrive in the city, they did not stay. Governor Vaudreuil abandoned the city soon after Montcalm's death on

15 September. The British, now commanded by George Townshend, entered the city and accepted its surrender on 18 September.

Results

The capture of Quebec gave Canada to the British. Because Quebec controlled the St. Lawrence, it controlled the only access into the country. The French, who had not been able to reinforce seriously since the beginning of the war because of the presence of the Royal Navy, now had no way to support the few remaining troops in Canada. Although the French commander of the garrison at Montreal marched on Quebec the following spring and beat Townshend's force that marched out to face him, the British had in the meantime improved the defensive walls, and these proved strong enough to allow them to hold on to the city until reinforced. Montreal fell to British forces in 1760, and fighting in North America ceased.

War continued in Europe for another 3 years until finally ended by the Treaty of Paris of 1763. The treaty forced the French surrender of all their lands east of the Mississippi River and north of the Great Lakes, although they were allowed fishing rights off Newfoundland, which they retain to this day. The remainder of their claims west of the Mississippi they ceded to Spain in return for a future alliance against Britain, one that went into effect during the American Revolution. Thus, the loss of Canada ended France's chance for a Western Hemisphere empire. They returned for a short time during 1863–1866 with an ill-fated attempt to establish such an empire in Mexico, but, other than possession of a number of Caribbean islands, the major French presence in the hemisphere ended in 1763.

The British hold on the eastern half of North America was secure after 1763, although they kept the American colonies distinct from Canada. Although few American troops fought at Quebec, in much of the rest of the war American militia and British regulars did fight to-gether. This mutual endeavor, plus the expense to which the British government went to defend the American colonies, set up a decade-and-a-half relationship that started in a most amicable way and yet ended in 1775 in revolt. The Americans thought their effort in the French and Indian War to be significant, and the victory as much theirs as anyone's. "So there was the irony: A heightened sense on the part of the colonists of the glory of being Englishmen was coupled with greater determination to stand on their own feet and to defend their rights." One hundred fifty years of being mostly ignored by London gave the colonists too much of a sense of freedom to buckle under to the demands that Parliament began to make as soon as the war was over. Without a common enemy, and with serious disputes over taxation and government procedures coming into play, the American colonies were seemingly destined to rebel. The battle at Quebec gained Canada for Britain, but it set in motion a series of events that ultimately lost America.

References: Gipson, Lawrence H. *The Great War for Empire,* vol. 7. New York: Alfred A. Knopf, 1936; Parkman, Francis. *Montcalm and Wolfe.* Toronto: Ryerson Press, 1964; Smith, Page. *A New Age Now Begins,* vol. 1. New York: McGraw-Hill, 1976; Stacey, C. P. *Quebec, 1759.* Toronto: Macmillan, 1959.

TRENTON
26 December 1776

FORCES ENGAGED
American: Approximately 2,500 infantry. Commander: George Washington.
Hessian: Approximately 1,500 infantry. Commander: Johann Rall.

IMPORTANCE
Washington's victory sparked renewed fervor in the colonial population, without which the American Revolution could not have continued.

Historical Setting

The colonial military forces of the American Revolution got off to a fairly successful start. A surprise attack on the isolated Fort Ticonderoga at Lake Champlain on 10 May 1775 netted about a hundred heavy guns for an army that had none. Using those weapons, American commander General George Washington was able to force the British to evacuate their primary base at Boston in March 1776. With that withdrawal, the vast majority of British forces in the American colonies was removed, eliminating the immediate threat of British action against the Revolution and depriving the British of a port of entry for men and materiel. If they were to continue the struggle to suppress the rebellion and reestablish control, the British had to have a harbor. The next best facility was New York City; in some ways, it was superior to Boston, in that it was more centrally located along the colonial coastline. Further, it threatened the Hudson River, an artery vital to the revolutionary cause for the free flow of American men and materiel between Philadelphia (the site of the Continental Congress) and the primary center of revolutionary ferment in Massachusetts. Washington realized that New York was the most likely location for the British to return, so he shifted forces there as soon as Boston was secured.

In the meantime, political events proceeded rapidly. Washington's success on the battlefield encouraged pro-revolutionary factions in the country. The war had started as an attempt by the colonists to force a repeal of the Coercive Acts, passed by the British Parliament in the spring of 1774 in response to the infamous Boston Tea Party. By the spring of 1776, it was clear that the British government had no intention of repealing those acts, so they became moot as a motivating factor for fighting. In January 1776, Thomas Paine published *Common Sense,* a tract critical of the concept of a monarchy and in favor of establishing a republican government. *Common Sense* was phenom-enally popular, and its straightforward style and message convinced many colonists of the need for a radical change. So, if a monarchy made no sense, if the Coercive Acts were no longer a reason to fight, and if the war was going well, why not make a move for independence? Although this had long been the goal of many in the revolutionary movement, it became in the late spring of 1776 a more popular end. Thus, the Continental Congress voted on 2 July to declare independence from Great Britain. Two days later, Thomas Jefferson's Declaration of Independence was adopted.

On that same day, 4 July 1776, the British returned in force. Washington had spread his forces out in the New York City area, placing some on the mainland and others on Staten Island and Long Island, hoping to deprive the British of an easily acquired base of operations. When the British arrived with 10,000 men (soon reinforced to 30,000), Washington found himself badly outnumbered. He withdrew the garrison from Staten Island to Long Island, abandoning the position to British General Sir William Howe. Washington constructed defenses on Long Island through July and August as Howe established his base. In late August, Howe crossed to Long Island and defeated Washington's force, but his hesitation at a key juncture allowed the Americans to escape a flanking movement. Washington managed to transport his men across Long Island Sound to the mainland, but Howe followed and defeated the Americans again in Harlem Heights in mid-September. A late October defeat at White Plains, north of New York City, was Washington's third consecutive setback, but he fled out of New York across New Jersey to Pennsylvania. Howe did not pursue, but settled his army into winter quarters in a vast semicircle around New York City, stretching from Connecticut to southern New Jersey.

Washington's reputation, so high after the capture of Boston, was in tatters. After each defeat, his army was smaller through casualties, prisoners, and deserters. Few in his force were professionals, as the American military had always been based on militia. Lacking formal training and adequate supply, it is not surprising so few remained with Washington in November. Those that had not deserted had ended their short-term militia commitment with the onset of cold weather, and most of those remaining were committed only until the first of the year. Given the lack of American success and the dominant position now held by the British, how could it be expected that the necessary thousands would reenlist in the spring of 1777? The bleak winter weather foreshadowed the Revolution's prospects for the upcoming year.

Howe's force was primarily British, but, as was normal at the time, it contained a large number of German mercenary troops, about a third of the force. These mercenaries, called by the generic appellation Hessians (from the German state of Hesse), were commonly hired by the British to fill out their ranks. As British so-

ciety recoiled at the concept of conscription and conditions in the ranks were harsh, raising sufficient forces from the British Isles proved impossible during most wars. Hence, the widespread use of hired foreigners. Although not as cutthroat as modern mercenaries, they still had a low reputation. British regular officers looked down on the hirelings, but what was a government to do?

Howe assigned individual units to occupy towns for the winter. In 1774, Parliament had enacted the Quartering Act, which gave the military the authority to requisition housing from almost anyone. Therefore, getting space for the troops was as easy as dislodging tenants from their homes or requiring them to board soldiers. Quartering troops in private homes was unthinkable in England; that it was allowed and encouraged in the colonies was one of the reasons the Coercive Acts, which included the Quartering Act, came to be called by the colonists the Intolerable Acts. Having one's rights thus violated was

The surrender of Hessian Commander Col. Rall at the battle of Trenton, 26 December 1776. (Archive Photos)

bad enough, but to be forced to board mercenaries (considering their reputation for plundering) was insulting. Trenton, New Jersey, was one of the towns that hosted a Hessian garrison during the winter of 1776–1777.

The Battle

Washington realized that, unless he scored a quick and dramatic success with the few remaining forces on hand, the chance of garnering sufficient recruits in the spring was minimal. At this point, he began to show that, although he may not have been practicing great generalship since August, he was both adaptable and imaginative. Contemporary military practice stated that, when the weather got cold, fighting ended until the return of decent weather in the spring. Therefore, an attack in the dead of winter would be completely unexpected. He chose as the day for his attack the day after Christmas. He knew that the Germans would seriously celebrate the holiday and by 26 December could well be suffering the effects of a 2-day party. A dawn attack on a sleeping and possibly hungover garrison stood the best chance of gaining surprise and success.

Washington called for reinforcements, which arrived after some delay from Albany. Israel Putnam, commanding the garrison in Philadelphia, raised some militia, as did other recruiters around Morristown, New Jersey. Washington was able to muster about 6,000 men. He decided to send John Cadwalader with 1,800 men to feint at Bordentown, south of Trenton, to distract a Hessian unit garrisoned there. Cadwalader was unable to coordinate his attack with Washington's, but soon drove the Hessians away and captured the town.

So, on Christmas night, in bitter cold and sleet, Washington drew together about 2,400 men. They rowed across the ice-filled Delaware River and gathered on the New Jersey side. Although the famous painting of this incident shows the commander-in-chief unbelievably standing up in the boat gazing at the opposite shore, the weather and river conditions portrayed in the painting are certainly credible. As the force formed up, however, they were seen by a local farmer who remained loyal to the king. This farmer sped to Trenton to warn the garrison of the impending assault. The guard at the house serving as the headquarters of Colonel Johann Rall stopped the American. His commander was engaged early that morning in (depending on one's source) a poker game or a chess match. He could not be disturbed. A written message warning Rall of Washington's approach went unheeded, either because Rall was too absorbed in his gaming or because he could not bother to have an English message translated into German. The American attack remained unexpected.

When Washington's men attacked just after dawn, the battle was short, lasting no more than about 15 minutes. The minimal defenses erected by the Hessians were not fully staffed and were easily overcome. The surprise was too complete and the Germans too unready for a serious battle to take place. For the loss of four soldiers wounded, the revolutionary force killed 22 Hessians, wounded another 94, captured 950, and scattered 400. The town was liberated of its unwanted guests, and Washington's force returned across the Delaware. He was joined by Cadwalader's force, newly arrived from Bordentown, and reoccupied Trenton, but withdrew again in the face of advancing British forces under Lord Charles Cornwallis. He caught the Americans in Trenton on 2 January. Rather than launch an attack late in the day, Cornwallis set up camp to prepare for a battle the next morning. Through the night, the British kept watch on Washington's campfires in the distance, but were disconcerted on the morning of 3 January to find the American camp empty. Washington had marched his men in the night around the British and attacked another force near Princeton at dawn. They quickly scattered after Washington personally led a charge to rally some disheartened militia, and the Americans scored another fairly easy

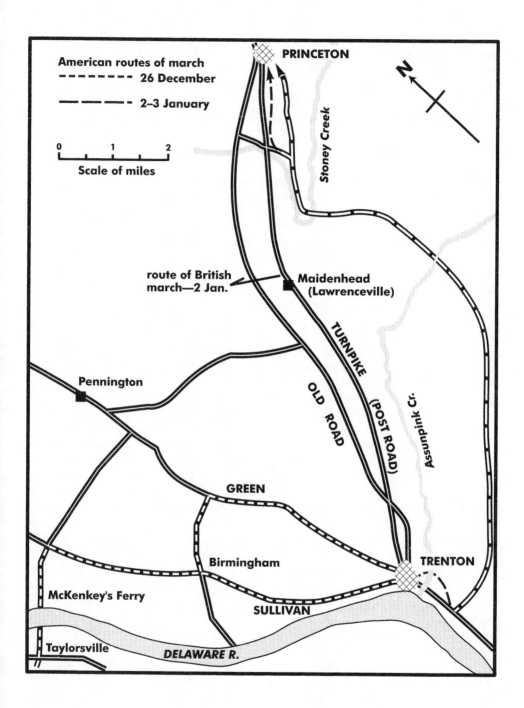

PRINCETON

American routes of march
- - - - - - - 26 December
— — — · 2–3 January

0   1   2
Scale of miles

N

Stoney Creek

route of British
march—2 Jan.

Maidenhead
(Lawrenceville)

TURNPIKE

OLD   ROAD

(POST ROAD)

Assunpink Cr.

Pennington

GREEN

Birmingham

TRENTON

McKenkey's Ferry

SULLIVAN

Taylorsville

DELAWARE R.

victory. Washington marched off to winter quarters at Morristown with two victories under his belt, while Cornwallis withdrew his garrisons back to New Brunswick, New Jersey, to guard his war chest of £70,000.

Results

Although certainly not as high profile a victory as Saratoga or Yorktown, Trenton was a necessary precursor to those battles. In the late fall of 1776, the revolutionary army was in desperate straits, which meant that the revolutionary cause was as well. The entire American military experience to that time was bound up with the nature of the militia, the citizen soldiers. Although some Americans had experience with European-style warfare while fighting alongside British troops in the French and Indian War (and a few other earlier wars in which European conflicts spilled over into the Western Hemisphere), for 150 years Americans had primarily fought Indians. The wars against Native American tribes were generally short, as the numbers involved were rarely great. Although military service was required as a public duty, this did not mean conscription. It was, instead, a short-term and occasional job that men had to do as part of citizenship. The temporary nature of the service meant that no regular army existed; consequently, there were virtually no professional soldiers.

This duty became even more tenuous with the outbreak of the Revolution. The Continental Congress was not an elected body (at the start of the war) and could do little more than act like a government and hope that people would cooperate. Thus, when the immediate passions cooled after early action, no way to compel service was available. Washington and the other revolutionary generals had to win to maintain morale and troop strength when revolutionary ardor flagged. Certainly there were men who were dedicated to the cause and would stick to it until the end, but many colonists were farmers who had families to consider, and often those families came first. Some men would have joined in the spring of 1777 no matter what happened during the winter, but to bring in sufficiently large numbers, most recruits needed the lure of success to justify the temporary abandonment of their homes and possible loss of their lives.

That was why Washington not only needed a victory but why he chose Trenton as his target. The Hessians were sufficiently despicable that to defeat them would prove that the Revolution was dedicated to protecting the welfare of the citizenry. A British officer, John Bowater, in a letter to a friend the following spring, denigrated the Hessians and described how they were painted as icons of evil. "Government has been cheated by their sending one half Militia, and the greatest part of the others Recruits, very few Viterons amongst them, they are Voted British pay, which their Prince Cheats them out of one half, they are Exceedingly dissatisfied at this, so that to make it up they turn their whole thoughts upon plunder. It was their attention to this Plunder, that made them fall a sacrifice to the Rebels at Trenton.... Many Orations was spoke at Philadelphia & other places to explain to the people, what a Contemptible Enemy they had to cope with. By these & other artful methods, they prevailed on their people to Reinlist [sic], and they have now got a considerable army together...."

Further, as the Hessians were professionals, men who made their living by war, a victory over them would go far to restore Washington's flagging reputation for generalship after three straight losses since August. Washington had to have a victory for his status, which was one of the necessary ingredients for gaining recruits. Thus, the Hessians served as a doubly good target. A second victory over the British force at Princeton was icing on the cake.

What if the New Jersey farmer had been able to get through to Colonel Rall the message about Washington's approach? Even if slowed by hangovers, an aroused Hessian garrison almost certainly would have beaten back the American force. A fourth defeat probably would have spelled the end of the American Revolution. Although Howe proved himself to be no great general, with only a minimal American army to fight could he possibly have failed to restore British control? It probably would not have been permanent, for hostility between America and Britain had festered for years, but a military solution in 1777 would have set back the cause of American liberty for a long time. Had the British government wised up and dealt with the American colonies as they ultimately dealt with Canada, the course of the British Empire and hence the world would have been totally altered.

References: Burgoyne, Bruce. *Enemy Views.* Bowie, MD: Heritage Books, 1996; Dwyer, William. *The Day Is Ours!* New York: Viking, 1983; Hibbert, Christopher. *Redcoats and Rebels.* New York: W. W. Norton, 1990; Lancaster, Bruce. *The American Revolution.* New York: American Heritage Press, 1971; Peckham, Howard. *The War for Independence: A Military History.* Chicago: University of Chicago Press, 1958.

SARATOGA

September–17 October 1777

FORCES ENGAGED

British: Approximately 7,200 troops plus artillery. Commander: General John Burgoyne.

American: Approximately 5,000 regulars and 12,000 militia. Commander: General Horatio Gates.

IMPORTANCE

American victory maintained control of the vital Hudson River valley and convinced France to recognize the United States and sign a mutual defense treaty. The flow of French supplies virtually guaranteed American independence.

Historical Setting

After George Washington's stunning victories at Trenton and Princeton the previous winter,

the revolutionary army was rebuilding in the spring of 1777. As was necessary with a force primarily comprised of militia, each spring the ranks had to be refilled because many had ended their short-term enlistments and spent the winter at home with their families. Washington remained in the neighborhood of Philadelphia, awaiting General Sir William Howe's moves out of New York City.

Howe had developed a plan while in winter quarters: he would move some two-thirds of his 30,000 men on Philadelphia. He believed that, by capturing the city that served as the site of the Continental Congress and therefore the capital of the rebellion, the Revolution would collapse. Rather than advancing directly on the city, however, Howe decided to transport his men by sea up the Chesapeake Bay to the region of Baltimore and then march overland on Philadelphia from the west. This was unnecessarily circuitous, but even worse it was time-consuming because gathering the necessary shipping to handle this operation was daunting. The Royal Navy had little love for the army and little inclination to cooperate, and the British possessed no theater commander to coordinate operations. Howe spent all spring and most of the summer attempting to convince some passing admiral to aid him, but not until his brother Admiral Richard Howe arrived did he have any luck.

In the meantime, another plan was being developed in Canada. General John Burgoyne possessed in this instance a greater grasp of the strategic situation in the American colonies. He realized that the northeast contained the firebrands of the Revolution; they had been the most troublesome citizens during the years before the outbreak of hostilities. To physically separate them from the men, supplies, and political leadership east and south of New York would effectively divide and conquer. Thus, Burgoyne's plan was to effect this division by gaining control of New York by controlling the Hudson River. He proposed leading a force southward out of Canada along Lake Champlain to Albany, New York's capital situated roughly halfway between Canada and New York City. His invasion would give Britain control of upstate New York. Simultaneously, he would send a small force down the St. Lawrence River to Lake Ontario and would then proceed eastward down the Mohawk River. This force of approximately 1,000 men under Barry St. Leger would link up with Burgoyne in Albany, thus gaining control of central New York. The third prong of the operation was to come from the south. Burgoyne's plan called for Howe to send much of his force up the Hudson to Albany, thereby gaining control of lower New York. British control would then stretch from Canada southward to the Atlantic, and the colonies would be split.

Burgoyne and Howe both submitted their plans to London and both were approved. Howe, when informed in the spring of 1777 that he needed to support Burgoyne's operation, replied that he would be happy to assist as soon as Philadelphia was in his hands. He was sure it would not take him long to accomplish that feat, and there would be plenty of time to send men north.

Burgoyne's force consisted of almost 8,000 men, including his artillery, of which about half the total were German mercenaries. He also recruited heavily among the Indian tribes of New York, knowing that 150 years of conflict between them and the colonists meant little love lost between the two populations. This recruiting decision proved a mistake because the Indians were not trustworthy allies; they could not be depended upon in a fight and had long experience in attacking civilians. The longstanding enmity between colonists and Indians ensured that New Yorkers, which in the northern areas were often loyal to Britain, would be much less likely to aid Burgoyne's army.

Burgoyne moved south in late June, meeting with his Indian recruits on the western shore of Lake Champlain. They easily captured the northernmost rebel post at Crown Point and had only slightly more trouble with Fort Ticonderoga at the southern tip of the lake. So far, Burgoyne had been able to accomplish much of his movement by water, but from here

he had to march overland to Albany. There were few roads in the region, and the rebels had felled trees along them to slow the British advance. By early September, however, Burgoyne was approaching the small town of Saratoga, about 12 miles north of Albany.

The Battle

Burgoyne and his men were lulled into a false sense of security by the easy time they had had thus far, but soon almost everything began to fall apart. St. Leger's column had entered New York, and near the source of the Mohawk River they laid siege to Fort Stanwyx in mid-August. The Indians serving with St. Leger inflicted heavy casualties on a relieving force at Oriskany, but news of a larger force on the way broke their spirit and they deserted St. Leger's column. With the approach of a thousand men under Benedict Arnold, one of the Revolution's better commanders, St. Leger abandoned his supplies (and the campaign) and withdrew to Canada.

Burgoyne's second problem occurred just east of his position, near Bennington, Vermont. Hearing of a large cache of supplies there, he sent a force of Germans to capture it. They ran into a spirited defense and were defeated. They retreated into a reinforcing column and in the ensuing confusion were attacked by the rebels following up their victory at Bennington. The defeat of the Germans not only disheartened Burgoyne's force, it rallied local support, and thousands of militia swarmed to Saratoga to join with Horatio Gates, whom Washington had just sent from Virginia to take command. Gates had some 5,000 soldiers of the Continental army, and welcomed the flood of volunteers.

As the Germans had been scouring the countryside for supplies, their high-handed methods outraged many citizens. Just as important in motivating local support were the activities of the Indians. Against Burgoyne's orders, they had harassed civilians. The incident that became the best known involved Jane McRae. Although she was engaged to a loyalist in Burgoyne's force, when she was scalped the

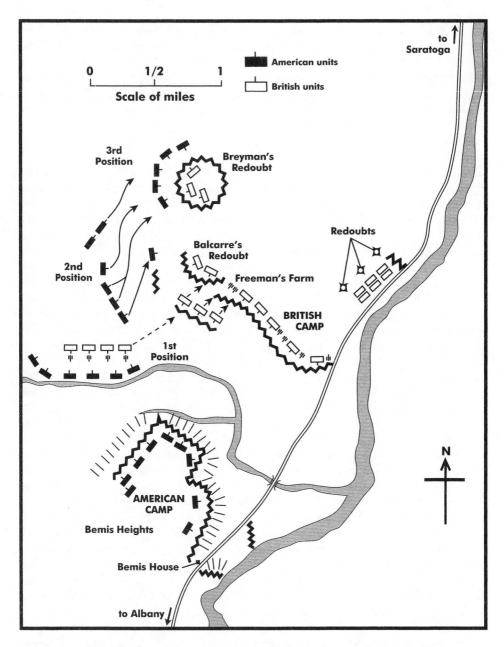

fury of the New Yorkers grew. Making bad matters worse, Burgoyne did not punish the murderers. A staff member argued that if he did hang them, the remaining Indians would desert and possibly bring their tribes against the British. Did he want to fight rebels and

Indians as the same time? His decision became the source of wild propaganda that brought in even more volunteers.

Burgoyne's main body was met by a force of sharpshooters at Freeman's Farm, near Saratoga. Gates had fortified the nearby Bemis

Heights and stood astride the British path to Albany. Burgoyne decided to dig in and await the arrival of troops from New York City, which Howe had finally ordered north under General Henry Clinton. Through the rest of September and into October, Burgoyne waited, while Arnold arrived from Fort Stanwyx and more militia joined Gates's force. On 7 October, with winter weather approaching and no relief in sight, Burgoyne decided to try again to force his way through the Americans and on to Albany. The rebels held better positions on high ground, but much of their success was the result of the inspired leadership of Arnold. He and Gates had feuded, and Gates had ordered him to remain out of the fight, but Arnold disobeyed orders and was the heart and soul of the rebel effort. At the height of the battle, Burgoyne lost one of his best subordinates, Simon Fraser, to a sniper, but the superior rebel numbers were the key. Burgoyne retreated to a fortified position, but he was doomed.

Results

Burgoyne's master plan had collapsed. He was unable to maintain a supply line to Canada because his path of retreat was blocked by hostile civilians and by a force under Benjamin Lincoln that had circled around the British and attacked Ticonderoga. St. Leger had turned back, but even his force would probably have been too small to matter had they arrived. Clinton, approaching from the south, was overly cautious and turned back when he met stiff resistance around West Point. Although a British detachment reached Kingston, less than 50 miles from Albany, it was October by that time and the security of New York City looked much better than the prospect of fighting their way to Albany. On 17 October, short of supplies, Burgoyne surrendered his force to Gates.

The battles near Saratoga proved to be the turning point of the war. First, those encounters removed a significant British force from combat. Second, they thwarted the British plan to divide the colonies. That was the best plan the British had during the war, but after Burgoyne's failure it was rarely pursued. Washington's greatest fear was loss of the Hudson River, but there were no more serious threats to the waterway, except for the attempted theft of the fort at West Point in Clinton's conspiracy with Benedict Arnold in 1781. Most of New York State remained secure, while Clinton seemed content to remain behind his defenses at New York City.

Most important of the results was the response from Europe. For some time, American representative Benjamin Franklin had been lobbying the French government to recognize the United States and sign an alliance. France had resisted because the previous few wars that France had fought against Britain in the eighteenth century had not been successful. France did not want to try it again without some surety of victory. To this point, the American rebels had merely survived, but the victory at Saratoga changed that. Here they had not only beaten a sizable force but had defeated John Burgoyne. The French had experience against him themselves, and they knew that he was the best general the British had in North America. If these rebels had beaten him, and done so in a European-style battle, then they certainly had a chance. The government in Paris agreed to take the chance. In February 1778, France and the new United States signed a treaty of alliance. The following month, the treaty was made public when France declared war on England. Spain declared war in 1779, as did the Netherlands a year after. This was the one thing that the United States needed above all else: a source of supplies for war materiel. The thirteen states of the new country possessed virtually no industry, so acquiring heavy weapons had to be done via trade or capture. Loans from Europe also meant that the Continental Congress could begin to pay soldiers and suppliers. The arrival of French troops fleshed out Washington's army in preparation for the final campaign of the war at Yorktown. More importantly for that battle, the French navy aided the fledgling country; the Americans had no navy of their own. Everything America needed Europe provided. The Revolution had succeeded thus far primarily on valor and luck, and now it had the material means to gain the upper hand. Just as importantly, the declarations of war by the European powers forced England to look in two directions. No longer could it focus on suppressing the rebellion; now England had to look over its shoulder. This meant holding troops and commanders in reserve in case fighting started nearer home. Reinforcements to North America had to be severely curtailed, while the Continental army grew in numbers and quality.

In the United States, Saratoga had much the same effect on recruiting as Washington's victory at Trenton had the previous year. Once again, the Continental Congress could expect to field an army. This morale boost was vital, for Washington failed to provide it in the winter of 1777 as he had in 1776. When Howe's force finally reached Philadelphia in late September 1777, Washington could not stop them from occupying the city. The Continental Congress had already fled to Maryland, so Howe's dream of capturing them and the "capital city" proved ephemeral. Washington's remaining men withdrew a few miles outside Philadelphia and wintered at Valley Forge. In the worst weather of the war, his men starved, froze, and deserted. Gates, not Washington, provided the inspiration for continued recruiting in the spring.

More men, more materiel, powerful friends—these proved to be the factors that would give the Americans their victory and their independence. A British victory in New York, splitting the colonies, would probably have broken the Revolution like a British victory at Trenton would have done. Although it may not have meant a permanent victory (because Anglo-American hostilities ran deep), the British hold on North America would have lasted much longer. An arrangement whereby the Americans had some input into London's handling of co-lonial affairs could have stolen the thunder of the leading revolutionaries. An America remaining in the British Empire for years, if not decades, to come would have had unimaginable consequences.

References: Hibbert, Christopher. *Redcoats and Rebels.* New York: W. W. Norton, 1990; Ketchum, Richard M. *Saratoga: Turning Point of America's Revolutionary War.* New York: Henry Holt, 1997; Lancaster, Bruce. *The American Revolution.* New York: American Heritage Press, 1971; Pancake, John S. *1777: The Year of the Hangman.* Tuscaloosa: University of Alabama Press, 1977; Peckham, Howard. *The War of Independence: A Military History.* Chicago: University of Chicago Press, 1958.

YORKTOWN
September–17 October 1781

FORCES ENGAGED
British: Approximately 6,000 British troops and Hessian mercenaries. Commander: General Lord Cornwallis.
American and French: Approximately 8,800 Americans and 7,000 French troops. Commander: General George Washington.

IMPORTANCE
American victory convinced English public to replace their government, resulting in peace talks that brought independence for the United States.

Historical Setting

After the American victory at Saratoga in the autumn of 1777, the fledgling United States was finally recognized by France, followed soon thereafter by Spain and the Netherlands. This recognition, and the alliance that came with it, gave the American rebels the material resources necessary to match the moral resources displayed by such leaders as George Washington. In the summer of 1778, Washington's forces reoccupied Philadelphia after British forces under General William Howe were ordered back to New York City. Howe's removal from command soon thereafter brought his subordinate, General Henry Clinton, into power.

Clinton had to this point shown no indication that he would aggressively pursue the war against the Americans. Instead, he spent most of his time fortifying New York City against the attack he was convinced Washington was going to launch. Thus, for the 2 years after the rebels' reoccupation of Philadelphia, the war remained rather low key. In the summer of 1780, Clinton attempted to conspire with disaffected American General Benedict Arnold to acquire the major American fort at West Point on the Hudson River. That effort failed, and Clinton spent his time improving his defenses. In the meantime, Washington spent his time trying to improve the caliber of the Continental army, equip it with the supplies arriving from Europe, and begin planning with the French forces arriving under the command of the Comte de Rochambeau.

As Washington was focusing on organizational concerns in the northern states (Rhode Island and Connecticut), Clinton decided to refocus the British effort. To this point, the British had been singularly unsuccessful in any strategy to defeat the Revolution. They had been unable to split the colonies by controlling the Hudson River during Burgoyne's 1777 Saratoga campaign, and they were unable to accomplish the same purpose by dealing with Arnold. Howe's attempt to crush the uprising by capturing Philadelphia had proven likewise unproductive. Since British capture of New York City in the late summer of 1776, the British war effort had for the most part gone nowhere. Therefore, Clinton decided to shift arenas. Instead of fighting in the north, where revolutionary fervor was the greatest, he sent forces to the southern states, where the percentage of loyalists was much higher. By occupying these states, he could roll the Revolution up from the south, isolating the Continental army in the north.

To implement this new strategy, Clinton sent Lord Charles Cornwallis to South Carolina in the summer of 1780. His orders were to take advantage of the loyalist population and occupy the Carolinas and Virginia. It was thought that the loyalists should be able to provide personnel and supplies to make this job relatively simple. Further, the revolutionaries had few troops in the southern states, so fighting was expected to be minimal. From the start, this plan went wrong. The landing near Charleston was not too difficult, and Cornwallis was able to force the rebels under General Benjamin Lincoln to give up Charleston. However, as the occupation took place, fires broke out in the city, although who was responsible has never been determined. Still, it was an inauspicious beginning.

Next, Cornwallis refused to follow Clinton's directives to make maximum use of local support. Instead, he often rebuffed attempts by South Carolinians to join or assist his army. Cornwallis began making enemies of friends, just as Burgoyne had done in upstate New York when he employed Indians and Hessians against the population there. As Cornwallis was settling in, area revolutionary forces began operations. Small groups of militia under commanders such as Francis Marion harassed British outposts and supply trains. They provoked harsh responses from Cornwallis and his subordinates; these actions also served to alienate local support.

Cornwallis marched out of Charleston convinced that he could easily occupy the Carolinas. The Continental Congress dispatched Horatio Gates to command the revolutionary forces, but he immediately lost a key battle at Camden, South Carolina. Washington replaced Gates with Nathaniel Greene, whose ingenuity was well suited to the guerrilla warfare that he needed to conduct against Cornwallis.

Occasional firefights and skirmishes broke out through the winter of 1780–1781, but nothing decisive happened for either army. Cut off from his base of operations, Cornwallis had to live off the countryside, and his arrogant attitude and use of Hessians in requisitioning supplies did nothing to endear him to the people. When he did call for loyalists to join his army, they responded in smaller numbers than he had expected. Greene, on the other hand, tried to pay for supplies, although all he had were IOUs of dubious value from the Continental Congress. Still, it was better treatment than the British were displaying. The British army grew ragged and frustrated as supplies became more difficult to acquire; Cornwallis marched to Wilmington, North Carolina, to resupply and pick up reinforcements.

From Wilmington, Cornwallis marched into Virginia in the spring of 1781. British forces under turncoat Benedict Arnold had been operating there for a few months, but with little positive effect. After a few more months of circuitous marching and little concrete results, Cornwallis marched to the coast. He had been ordered by Clinton to establish a base for the Royal Navy to bring in more men and supplies, and Cornwallis began building facilities at Yorktown, on a peninsula flanked by the York and James Rivers.

In the meantime, Washington had convinced the reluctant Rochambeau to aid him in an assault on New York City. Washington's plan called for the French fleet in the Caribbean to bottle up the Royal Navy in New York harbor while the Franco-American army forced their way through Clinton's defenses. Rochambeau warned Admiral de Grasse that he disliked this plan and preferred operating in the south. Admiral de Grasse complied with Rochambeau's wishes, telling Washington that the French fleet would go no farther north than the Chesapeake Bay. That information, plus his own intelligence concerning the strength of the British defensive positions, convinced Washington to accede to Rochambeau's suggestion for a campaign in Virginia.

Washington was aided at this point by what, under other circumstances, would seem to be a severe misfortune. He had sent details

of his plans for an attack on New York City to his friend the Marquis de Lafayette, commanding troops in Virginia. That letter had been captured by the British, however, and Clinton was preparing for the assault that he now knew was coming. Washington, who began disseminating disinformation, further convinced Clinton that an attack was imminent. When French forces demonstrated near New York, covering Washington's passage into New Jersey, Clinton braced for an assault that never came. By the time Clinton realized there would be no attack, both Washington and Rochambeau were well on their way to Virginia.

The Battle

While American forces under Greene and Lafayette kept an eye on Cornwallis, a French fleet under the Comte de Grasse was sailing north from the Caribbean. It arrived in late August at the mouth of the Chesapeake. Clinton in New York had heard reports of this, but dismissed them as rumors. Once the report was confirmed, a British fleet under Admiral Thomas Graves sailed for the Chesapeake. There he found twenty-four French ships of the line, outnumbering his own nineteen. On 5 September, the two fleets engaged, with de Grasse positioning himself in such a way as to deny the British access into the bay. After a few hours of cannonade, the British received the worst of the damage. Although they remained in the neighborhood for another 3 days, when Graves sailed for New York to repair his damaged ships he signed the death warrant of Cornwallis's force.

When Washington and Rochambeau arrived and joined forces with Lafayette, their combined force numbered almost 16,000, more than twice that of Cornwallis. They began digging trenches that slowly but surely inched their way toward the redoubts around which the British were basing the defense of their position. With superior numbers and artillery, the Americans were able to severely punish the

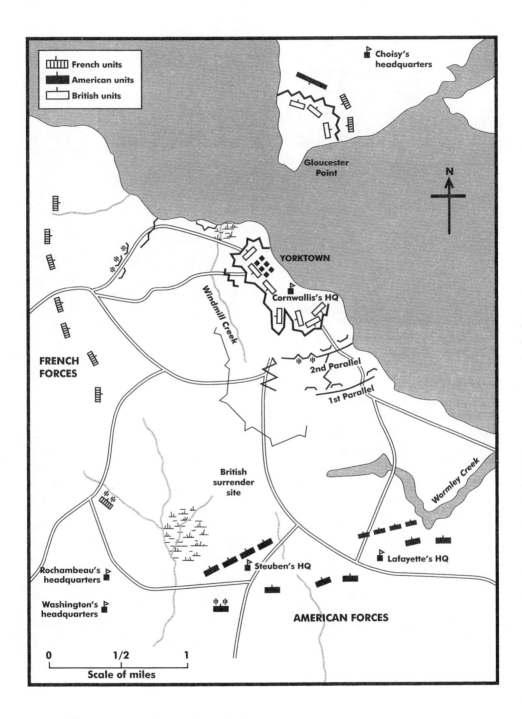

French units
American units
British units

Choisy's
headquarters

Gloucester
Point

N

YORKTOWN

Windmill Creek

Cornwallis's HQ

FRENCH
FORCES

2nd Parallel

1st Parallel

Wormley Creek

British
surrender
site

Lafayette's HQ

Steuben's HQ

Rochambeau's
headquarters

AMERICAN FORCES

Washington's
headquarters

0   1/2   1
Scale of miles

General George Washington fires the first cannon shot to begin the siege of Yorktown, Virginia, in October 1781. (Archive Photos)

defenders, who could do little to respond. The constant pressure proved too much for the British to withstand. Cornwallis attempted an escape across the York River, but was undone by bad weather. On the night of 15 October, the two British redoubts were attacked. The French took the larger one after a short but intense fight; the Americans took the smaller one in 10 minutes with few casualties.

Although Cornwallis ordered a raid on the new rebel positions, it was too little and too late. On 17 October, he asked for surrender terms. He had held his position on the assumption that Clinton was sending reinforcements from New York. How they would break through the French fleet is a matter of conjecture, but Graves was prepared to give battle a second time. When he finally set sail from New York harbor it was 17 October.

Results

Cut off from any serious hope of relief, unable to withstand the bombardment, unable to maintain his troops with the winter approaching, Cornwallis had no choice but to surrender. He proposed that he and his men be paroled, on condition of not taking up arms in America again, but Washington demanded surrender as prisoners of war. On 19 October, Cornwallis's second-in-command, Brigadier General Charles O'Hara, rode out at the head of 6,000 men to surrender. The march from Yorktown to Washington's headquarters was certainly the longest the surrendering soldiers ever took, for it was gross humiliation to be defeated by colonials. O'Hara tried at first to surrender to Rochambeau, but that attempt at avoiding the Americans in favor of a fellow-European failed. When he offered his sword to Washington, he was again rebuffed. As second-in-command, he had to surrender to Washington's second-in-command, Benjamin Lincoln.

Cornwallis and Clinton spent the next months and years blaming each other for the disaster. Clinton got the worst of it, and his career was ruined. Cornwallis was received in

England as a hero and went on to redeem himself with an outstanding performance in India soon afterward. The English public was tired of the war by this time. When the news of Yorktown reached London, the government was unable to survive. In the spring of 1782, the newly elected leadership offered to negotiate a peace, and talks began in Paris in September. They went on for a year before the Treaty of Paris of 1783 was signed. In this, the London government recognized American independence and the borders of the United States were established as the Atlantic Ocean to the Mississippi River and the Great Lakes to the northern border of Florida. In return for assistance rendered the Revolution by the Spanish (particularly their governor in New Orleans Bernardo Galvez), the Spanish received Florida, which they had surrendered to the English in the Treaty of Paris in 1763 at the end of the French and Indian/Seven Years' War.

The defeat at Yorktown ended the British experience in America, although they maintained the colony of Canada. They tried in Paris to claim all the territory west of the Appalachian Mountains, which would have limited the U.S. expansion severely for decades. Hostilities between the two nations did not end, however, for the British were slow to abandon some of their forts in the Great Lakes region and even slower to give the fledgling country any respect on the high seas. Restrictive trade practices between 1805 and 1812 led to a second war between the Americans and the British, after which relations eased considerably. Had Cornwallis escaped the Yorktown peninsula before Washington's arrival in late September, he would have delayed the end of the war for a time, but the length of the war and its interminable drain on the British economy and psyche almost certainly would have brought about a similar end to the war before long. Without Cornwallis's defeat, however, the American bargaining position in London would have been considerably weaker, and the conditions gained in the treaty may well have

restricted American growth for a long time to come.

The French effort in the Yorktown campaign can not be overemphasized, and the results of the war were felt there as well. The huge expenditures that King Louis XVI had spent on behalf of the United States sapped the French treasury. The increasingly bad economy that resulted, in addition to the philosophy of liberty that many of the French soldiers embraced in America, led to their own revolution in 1789. Louis succeeded in harming his old enemy England, but ultimately paid for that success with his throne and his life.

References: Chidsey, Donald Barr. Victory at Yorktown. New York: Crown, 1962; Davis, Burke. The Campaign That Won America. New York: Dial Press, 1970; Hibbert, Christopher. Redcoats and Rebels. New York: W. W. Norton, 1990; Peckham, Howard. The War of Independence: A Military History. Chicago: University of Chicago Press, 1958; Smith, Page. A New Age Now Begins, vol. 1. New York: McGraw-Hill, 1976.

VALMY
20 September 1792

FORCES ENGAGED
French: 36,000 men and 36 cannon. Commander: General Charles-François Dumouriez.
Austro-Prussian: 30,000 to 34,000 men and 54 cannon. Commander: Karl Wilhelm Ferdinand, duke of Brunswick.

IMPORTANCE
Prussian withdrawal from the battle saved France from invasion and confirmed the power of the French revolutionary government. This was the first major success of levee en masse.

Historical Setting

On 14 July 1789, Parisian citizens stormed the prison at the Bastille, freeing only a few prisoners, but marking the beginning of the French Revolution. Not long afterward came the publication of the Declaration of the Rights of Man and the Citizen and the call for a constitutional, rather than absolute, monarchy. In June 1791, King Louis XVI attempted but failed to escape France to rally monarchical forces around Europe to his cause. This failure convinced many aristocrats to either withdraw from public life or to flee the country, and among the emigrants were some 6,000 army officers. Louis for a time was reinstated as a constitutional monarch and reluctantly worked with a new legislative assembly.

The other monarchs of Europe looked with some dread at the situation in France, fearing that the revolution that had removed British power from the American colonies and spread its ideas to France could spread farther still to their countries. In August 1791, in response to the pleas of French emigrants, William II of Prussia joined with Leopold II of Austria with the intent of crushing the revolution. They received the financial and moral support of Russia, Sweden, and Spain. In February 1792, a military alliance was proclaimed, which brought in the support of the north Italian kingdom of Savoy whose troops, like the Austrians and Prussians, began to marshal on their respective frontiers with France. In response, the French legislature declared war on Austria in April.

Because of the defection of so many aristocratic officers, the long-serving noncommissioned officers of the French army rose in rank. That promotion of commoners, as well as the open recruiting practices that attracted many revolutionaries to the colors, resulted in a much larger army than France had fielded before 1789. The recruits of 1791, called into uniform by the legislature, received some training under the new officer corps, but the later volunteers that joined up after the declaration of war were more enthusiastic than able. Through the summer of 1792, French forces launched attacks into the Austrian Netherlands (modern Belgium) with little, if any, success. The most

minor of resistance usually sent them fleeing, and the Austro-Prussian coalition assumed that an invasion of France would prove remarkably easy. The man chosen to command that invasion was Prussian Field Marshal Karl Wilhelm Ferdinand, duke of Brunswick. He had commanded a Prussian invasion of Holland in 1787 and accomplished an almost bloodless victory, primarily because the rules of war were so formalized that he could second-guess and outmaneuver his opponent.

What the duke and every other military officer in Europe failed to realize was that the French had changed the rules. From 1791 onward, soldiers were not conscripted pawns but volunteers motivated by ideals. Any leader who could harness that enthusiasm would lead an aroused army that would stand and fight for a cause or close with an enemy more aggressively than the linear tactics of the day allowed. As shown in the Netherlands campaign, enthusiasm often failed under pressure, but when the Austrians and Prussians actually crossed the frontier into France to challenge the ideals of the revolution, the army responded.

The invasion was planned to take place along three parallel lines. With his king looking over his shoulder, Brunswick commanded the center, marching from Coblenz into the province of Lorraine; his army numbered 42,000 Prussians, 5,000 Hessians, and 8,000 French emigrants. To the north, an Austrian army of 15,000 would march out of the Austrian Netherlands, while to the south, a second Austrian force of 14,000 would advance from the city of Speyer. Although marching along a fairly wide front, the three forces were to enter France between their two primary armies, the *Armée du Nord,* commanded by General Charles-François Dumouriez, and the *Armée du Centre,* commanded by General François-Christophe Kellerman. The primary problem with the invaders' plan was the extremely slow progress they made. The nature of logistics at the time was that everything had to travel with the army, and the baggage train

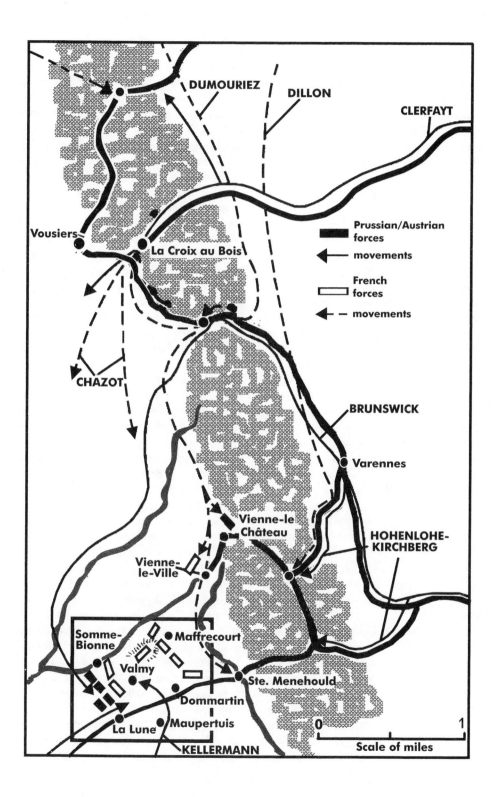

DUMOURIEZ

DILLON

CLERFAYT

Vousiers

La Croix au Bois

Prussian/Austrian
forces

movements

French
forces

movements

CHAZOT

BRUNSWICK

Varennes

Vienne-le
Château

HOHENLOHE-
KIRCHBERG

Vienne-
le-Ville

Somme-
Bionne

Maffrecourt

Valmy

Ste. Menehould

Dommartin

Maupertuis

La Lune

KELLERMANN

0   1

Scale of miles

as well as the cooks and clerks and camp followers all served to hinder movement. In August 1792, the Prussian army marched only 6 miles a day. Still, they reached the French fortress at Longwy on 23 August and forced its surrender in a matter of hours. The major fortress at Verdun surrendered a week later, and the road to Paris seemed open.

The Battle

Both the weather and the nature of the Prussian military aided the French. Able to survive on fewer supplies than the invaders, as well as able to draw on local sources for food, the French were quick to react. Although Dumouriez at first preferred an offensive into the Austrian Netherlands to draw the Austro-Prussian force in that direction, the fall of two major fortresses convinced him to seek a confrontation in France. He marched south to the Argonne Forest, through which the oncoming armies would have to pass. He was able to place himself between the forest and the Prussians and then withdraw into the woods to defend the five routes through them. The Argonne, running north-south, is a hilly and marshy forest, and the few paths through it benefited a defender. Unfortunately, one of the routes was too lightly held: the road through La Croix aux Bois, the second road through the northern end of the forest. When the Prussians advanced by that road, Dumouriez was forced to abandon his stronger position at Grandpré, the central road, and fall back southward to the town of Ste. Menehoud, at the junction of the Aisne and Auve Rivers.

Leaving troops to block the two southern paths through the Argonne, Dumouriez called for reinforcements. The marquis de Beurnonville arrived from Châlons on 19 September, as did General Kellerman leading 18,000 men of the *Armée du Centre*. This brought the French force up to 58,000. The ground they occupied was an open square with the Aisne to the east, the Auve to the south, and the Bionne River to the north. In the middle of this square was the town of Valmy, with hills to the west, south, and north of the town. On the evening of 19 September, Kellerman and Dumouriez argued about their respective deployments, Kellerman stating that he intended to reposition his men the next morning on the south side of the Auve in the villages of Dampièrre and Voilement. At dawn, however, Brunswick's forces marched south out of the town of Somme-Bionne to encircle the French and cut off the road to Châlons. That forced Kellerman to place his troops facing west on the hills just outside Valmy. A forward position at a tavern called La Lune held out long enough to slow Brunswick's move, giving Kellerman time to deploy his men. That extra time, and a dense fog, screened his movements from Brunswick; it also hid the fact that he had ordered infantry, cavalry, and artillery into place through the same location, causing considerable though temporary confusion. The fight at La Lune caused Brunswick to realize just where the French were and to take up a position parallel to them on hills just to the west.

By noon, the fog had blown away and the two armies faced each other. Because of the rainy weather, Brunswick's force was much smaller than the one with which he had entered France; dysentery was rampant in the Prussian ranks. Brunswick also had been unable to combine the three wings of his total army, so he fielded a force of between 30,000 and 34,000 men. The French faced him with 36,000 on the front line with Kellerman and another 18,000 deployed across a marsh to the rear under Dumouriez. Although the French army deployed well, the Prussians were sure that would change after the opening shots were fired. King Frederick William ordered an artillery barrage to soften them up, and his fifty-four guns opened fire. Kellerman's thirty-six guns answered.

The battle at Valmy was for the most part an artillery duel, and that was the one branch of the service in which the French still excelled.

In the 1770s, they had adopted a new and improved type of gun that was more accurate and
had greater range than most of the field pieces
of the day, and the gun crews for the most part
had not defected with the coming of the revolution. Thus, they were the best-trained part of
the French army and fired the best guns in
Europe. Unfortunately for both sides, the two
armies faced each other at approximately 2,500
yards, the maximum range of the cannon. That
meant that the cannonballs were losing momentum by the time they arrived, which, coupled
with the sodden ground that absorbed most of
the impact, meant that little damage was done
by either side.

Brunswick and his officers were amazed to
see that the French troops did not break and
run. Having a few more months in uniform
and a few skirmishes under their belts, the
French soldiers were not the panicked recruits
of early summer. As the French stood their
ground, the Prussians came to the realization
that to win this battle they would have to cross
a mile and a half of open ground under constant artillery fire and then face real soldiers. It
was not a pleasant prospect. Still, King Frederick
William ordered an advance. As a line of Prussian soldiers began to march forward, General
Kellerman rode among his men shouting encouragement. The men responded with cheers
of "Vive la nation!" After a mere 200 paces,
Brunswick ordered a halt. The cannonade continued, and at 1400 a chance Prussian ball
struck a French powder caisson. The explosion

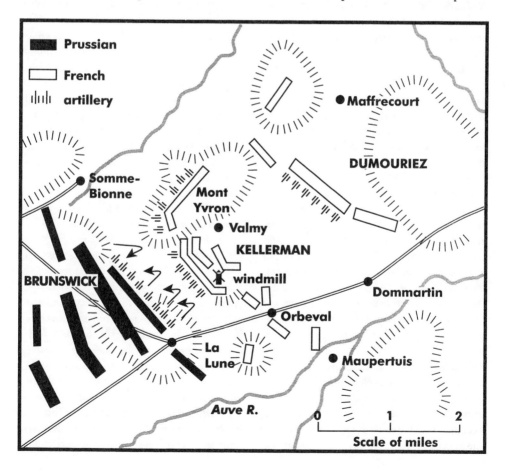

would have rattled the troops a few months earlier and Brunswick sensed an opportunity. He sent his men forward again, but, as the French continued to stand their ground, he knew he could not break them; again he pulled his men back. By 1600, he knew that to mount a serious assault would prove suicidal, so he withdrew from the field.

Results

For the next 10 days, Brunswick and Dumouriez negotiated fruitlessly; then the Prussian commander led his troops home. They were sick and dispirited from the weather and the defeat; even had they won, they almost certainly could not have marched on Paris. That was King Frederick William's desire, but Brunswick all along had resisted the final moves that culminated at Valmy. He had preferred to establish Prussian control over the line of towns that paralleled the Argonne Forest on the eastern side, wintered there, and resumed the offensive the following spring. Had he been in sole command, that would have happened, but the Prussian king was adamant about advancing to save his fellow monarch, and Brunswick had little choice but to obey.

The battle at Valmy was relatively minor in terms of length and casualties; a few hours were spent and a few hundred men were lost on either side. That outcome alone made it virtually the last battle of its kind. Since the end of the Thirty Years' War in 1648, European warfare had depended mainly on maneuver, with battle accepted or pressed only when everything seemed to indicate victory. That was the reason that Brunswick's earlier almost bloodless victory in Holland had been so widely hailed.

In military, political, and social terms, however, Valmy marked a sea change in the way warfare was conducted. When the French volunteers stood their ground in the face of an army of professionals, the day of the truly national army had arrived. Kellerman's force did include a number of veterans, more so than did

Dumouriez's force behind him, but that no one fled meant that France could and would put armies in the field made up of soldiers in numbers never before dreamed of. Gustavus Adolphus in the Thirty Years' War (1618–1648) had introduced the concept of a regular standing army that fought for its monarch, as opposed to the concept of armies of mercenaries, an approach that had been prevalent over the previous two centuries. Since his day, small groups of professional, long-term soldiers fought among themselves. After Valmy, not just armies but entire nations went to war. Soldiers fought not for pay or their king but for their nation, which from this point forward were nations of individual patriots. Nationalism arrived in Europe, and nothing would ever be the same.

Militarily, that meant that the government could call upon the entire nation for personnel, and armies would no longer be small groups but massive hosts. Forces numbering 100,000 and more would soon be common as France introduced nationalism through its conquests and found that same nationalism rising up against them via conquered peoples. Fighting itself began to change, with more mobile artillery arriving on the battlefield and the standard attack in line giving way in many cases to attacks in column, whose striking power could punch holes in enemy lines. All of this meant more deaths, and sacrifice for one's nation became a common theme in public media.

Politically, the battle of Valmy confirmed the power of the new revolutionary government. On the day that Valmy was fought, the Legislative Assembly was replaced by the National Convention, which declared France a republic the following day and executed Louis XVI a few months later. This formally ended the monarchy, which had been losing power for some time, but it led to a nation in arms that fought for more than two more decades almost nonstop. That fighting brought to the fore Napoleon Bonaparte, who took France to its greatest glory before the other European nations banded together successfully against him in 1814 and 1815. Wolfgang von Goethe, the German writer, was at Valmy as an observer. After the battle, he commented to his associates, "From this place and from this day forth commences a new era in the world's history, and you can all say you were present at its birth" (Lynn, "Valmy," p. 97).

References: Doyle, William. *The Oxford History of the French Revolution.* Oxford, UK: Clarendon Press, 1989; Fuller, J. F. C. *A Military History of the Western World,* vol. 2. New York: Funk & Wagnalls, 1955; Lefebvre, Georges. *The French Revolution from Its Origins to 1793.* London: Routledge & Kegan Paul, 1962; Lynn, John. "Valmy," *Military History Quarterly* 5(1), Autumn 1992; Rothenberg, Gunther. *The Art of Warfare in the Age of Napoleon.* Bloomington: University of Indiana Press, 1978.

RIVOLI
14 January 1797

FORCES ENGAGED
French: 23,000 men. Commander: General Napoleon Bonaparte.
Austrian: 28,000 men. Commander: General Baron Josef Alvintzy.

IMPORTANCE
A key battle in the first French campaign in Italy against Austria, Rivoli demonstrated Napoleon's brilliance in his first campaign, established his genius for war, and led to French occupation of northern Italy.

Historical Setting

In the wake of the execution of Louis XVI, his wife, and several thousand of their supporters, the monarchs of Europe felt distinctly uneasy after January 1793. Having seen the Americans successfully throw off royal rule in 1783, most European kings were afraid that the French Revolution was too close to home. Fearing that their own populations might be encouraged by American and French actions, a coalition of European kings decided to invade France, restore the monarchy, and crush the notion of revolution before it spread any farther. They failed. Thanks to a massive conscription policy and new tactics on the battlefield, France remained whole in the face of invasion. By 1796, only Great Britain and Austria remained officially at war with France. With France having spent most of the previous few years on the defensive, the Directory, the French governing body, decided to change tactics and operate on the offensive. They sent Napoleon Bonaparte, a rising star in the new French army, to take command against Austrian forces fighting in northern Italy.

Although this was his first major command, Napoleon showed no hesitation. He joined the French army of Italy at Nice, impressed his older subordinates with his vision and energy, and revitalized morale. He proceeded to take advantage of the fact that his enemies, although more numerous, were scattered across the Piedmont, the westernmost region of northern Italy. Preparing for action on 15 April 1796, he was forced to march early because of an Austrian attack on 10 April led by General Baron Johann Beaulieu against French troops in Allesandria, northwest of Genoa. A second Austrian force was approaching from the west, while a force from the Kingdom of Piedmont encamped at Ceva, farther west. Napoleon attacked the second column first and drove back 20,000 men under General de Argenteau from the town of Montenotte on 12 April. Napoleon then turned west and attacked the Piedmontese at Ceva, driving them out of their position through the town of Mondavi all the way to Turin. This forced the king of Piedmont to sue for peace, while giving Napoleon's troops experience, confidence, and captured weaponry. The provinces of Savoy and Nice were also ceded to France.

With his rear secured, Napoleon could deal with the Austrians alone. They had withdrawn to positions north of the Po River. General

Beaulieu had abandoned Allesandria and placed his men in a strong position covering the main river crossing at Valenza. Napoleon feinted there, but crossed his forces 50 miles eastward at Piacenza, thereby threatening the Austrian lines of supply. Beaulieu retreated northeastward, but was unable to establish another defensive stand at Lodi because of Napoleon's rapid pursuit. Suffering another defeat at Napoleon's hands there on 10 May, Beaulieu withdrew another hundred miles to the Adige River. Napoleon delayed his pursuit of the Austrians in order to occupy Milan on 15 May. While there, he learned that the Directory was threatening to assign him a co-commander, but his increasing popularity with the French public and the steady stream of loot he sent back to Paris changed its inclination.

Beaulieu established himself at the fortress city of Mantua, and Napoleon quickly marched there and laid siege. Through the summer and fall of 1796, Napoleon managed to beat back a number of Austrian countermoves because his central position allowed him to take advantage of interior lines and beat back uncoordinated Austrian attacks. In one of those battles, at Bassano on 8 September, Austrian Field Marshal Dagobert von Würmser was defeated, and the remnants of his force fought their way into Mantua, expanding the city's garrison to 23,000, but straining their already dangerously low supplies. By the end of the year, Napoleon owned the Adige River valley, but had his army stretched thin along the river from Rivoli, near the center of the eastern shore of Lake Garda, through Verona and Ronco to Legnano. He had captured most of northern Italy for France, but the Austrians refused to concede defeat. They were determined to push a force through the French to relieve Mantua and then combine with forces sent from the Papal States, which had just repudiated their concord with France. If the troops from Austria, Mantua, and the Papal States could join together, Napoleon would be badly outnumbered. Once again, he

had to use his central position to keep that junction from occurring.

The Battle

Austrian forces marched out of the Tyrol under the command of General of Infantry Josef Alvintzy. His plan was to divide his force into two columns: one would swing across the Venetian plain toward the southern French flank at Legnano, while the second would proceed down the Adige to attempt to roll up the French from the north. If Napoleon responded to the first by committing his reserves, then the northern attack would have it that much easier. If he did not, then the southern attack could push past Legnano to either raise the siege of Mantua or join the papal army marching north. General Alvintzy commanded the northern attack, while Major General Johann Provera commanded the southern.

Provera divided his force into two columns as well and launched attacks on Verona and Legnano on 9–10 January 1797. Napoleon was unsure whether Provera's attack was the primary offensive, but, considering that this was January, an offensive across the Venetian plains made more sense than one from the mountainous Tyrol. On 12 January, Napoleon was informed that his northern flank at La Corona, under the command of Major General Barthelémy Joubert, was under attack. Napoleon waited for word from either flank as to which seemed to be the main thrust, and on 13 January Joubert warned him that he was falling back before large Austrian forces. He stopped at the small town of Rivoli, about 15 miles northwest of Verona, in the early morning hours of 13 January, and Napoleon marshaled his forces to go to Joubert's aid.

Napoleon left four divisions totaling some 24,000 men to cover the southern end of his line, while he marched north up the Adige toward Rivoli. He arrived in the middle of the night of 13–14 January, meeting the 10,000 men under Joubert withdrawing, as he had received no orders. Napoleon sent the men back

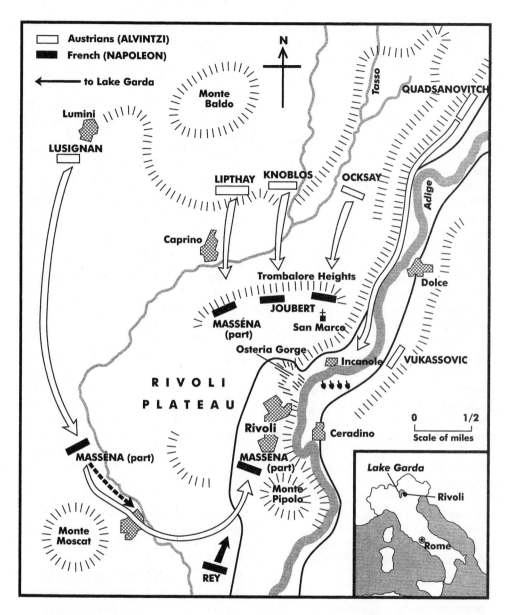

through Rivoli onto the heights on the north-west side of town; the Austrian campfires were glowing across a plateau on the Trombalore Heights. He ordered that his men occupy the church of San Marco, providing a vista of the battlefield, as well as the Osteria Gorge, a deep canyon alongside the Adige that debouched at Rivoli. An Austrian column there could out-flank the French position on the heights. Napoleon presumed the Austrian intention to be a double envelopment, with the bulk of the Austrians attacking across the plateau, while columns moved down the gorge and swung wide around his western left flank. To prevent this, he ordered his men to attack first, which they did at dawn on 14 January.

The attack spoiled the Austrian plans temporarily, but superior Austrian numbers drove the French back, forcing them to abandon San Marco. Before the Austrians could occupy it, however, the French seized the hilltop church and prepared for multiple assaults. The main Austrian force attacked both San Marco and pressured Joubert's line along the heights. Austrian cannon on the opposite bank of the Adige forced French troops to abandon the Osteria Gorge as well, but the Austrians needed San Marco to hold their left center and support an attack out of the gorge. To make bad matters worse for the French, the Austrian flanking move to the west was succeeding brilliantly, with General François-Joseph, marquis de Lusignan, driving back Napoleon's blocking force and threatening the French rear. Such a move would cut the French off from any reinforcements coming up from the south.

Napoleon committed his reserves, a portion of Major General André Masséna's cavalry brigade, to engage Lusignan. Next, he thinned out Joubert's line holding the heights above Rivoli, moving men and artillery to face the opening of the Osteria Gorge. When Austrian troops appeared at its mouth, they met a barrage of grapeshot. A sudden bold charge by a mere twenty-six French cavalry threw the Austrians into a panic, and the threat to the French right flank collapsed. Sensing that the momentum had shifted, Napoleon ordered Joubert's men out of their position and down onto the plain, where the Austrian attacks had been fruitless and tiring. The Austrian army broke and were sent fleeing by a French cavalry charge.

At the same time, Masséna had not only met the Austrian flanking attack under Lusignan but had stopped it cold. While the Austrians were facing northward toward Rivoli and Masséna's men, French reinforcements under Brigadier General Baron Louis Rey arrived on the scene and attacked the Austrian rear; almost half of Lusignan's 4,000 men were taken prisoner.

Results

At 1100 on the morning of 14 January, Napoleon was on the verge of being surrounded by a much larger army. By 1600 that afternoon, the Austrians were in full flight. News of Provera crossing the Adige at Legnano kept Napoleon from following up the pursuit because he had to now deal with the second threat to the extended French line. Napoleon left Joubert in charge at Rivoli and ordered him to pursue the Austrians while he marched south with Masséna to support Brigadier General Charles Pierre Augereau at Legnano. Joubert's pursuit was ultimately successful; when he called it off in midafternoon of 15 January, half of Alvintzy's 28,000 men were dead, captured, or scattered.

Near Legnano, Austrian General Provera broke through the French lines after a night crossing of the Adige, but he was unable to storm the city on 14 January. He did, however, contact Field Marshal Würmser in Mantua, calling for a breakout from the besieged city in conjunction with Provera's relief attack. Unknown to either, Napoleon's swift return from Rivoli allowed him to place himself between the two forces, so the linkup failed. Würmser's force had to retreat back into the city, while Provera found himself between Napoleon's force and that of Augereau, who had followed Provera from Legnano. Provera surrendered his 7,000 men. Learning of this disaster, as well as that at Rivoli, Würmser surrendered his besieged garrison. They were on half-rations already and down to a few days worth of food, with no new Austrian offensive possible for at least 2 months. Würmser opened the gates of the city to Napoleon on 2 February 1797.

After a string of defeats in northern Italy, the Austrian army was in bad shape. Napoleon gave them no rest and was preparing an offensive toward Vienna for the spring. Striking before the Austrians did, French forces drove Austrian troops out of the Tyrolean mountains in March and captured the important arsenal at Trieste on 18 April. The Austrian government finally realized their predicament and opened negotiations with France, leading to the signing of the Peace of Campo Formio on 17 October 1797. Napoleon's campaign not only won for France a victory over one of Europe's premier nations, it gave France control of northern Italy. Napoleon, when not fighting the Austrians, was reorganizing the political structure of the north Italian provinces, and his combination of Milan, Bolgna, and Modena into the new Cisalpine Republic was confirmed by the peace treaty. This brought to Italy for the first time the principles of the French Revolution, marking the first spread of ideology out of France and into other parts of Europe. This look at democracy brought the first semblance of national feeling to Italian provinces since the days of the Roman Empire. The Italian population, however, less literate than that of France, was slower to adopt the concepts that Napoleon introduced. They also were upset that the French did not pay proper respect to the pope, but they soon began to accept French administration and, by learning from it and working in it, were ultimately able to benefit from it.

More importantly for Europe, Rivoli marked the high point of the first campaign of Napoleon, who came from obscurity to international prominence in less than a year. At the battle at Rivoli, he was only 28 years old, but showed a talent almost no one in Europe possessed—or had possessed since Frederick the Great 50 years earlier. Napoleon's masterful use of the central position, the ability to get between separated enemy forces and defeat them individually, became his hallmark. In the next few years, he introduced other innovations, but his ability to see the big picture and react to it with unexpected speed baffled his opponents for the next two decades. Using an ever-increasing and more experienced army, he took France out of its revolutionary phase into empire. At the same time, he introduced the principles of the revolution in every nation he conquered, and therein lay the seeds of his own destruc-

tion. By fomenting nationalism, he created populations dedicated to freedom, not to occupation.

Napoleon remarked in the midst of this campaign, after his victory at Lodi, "that I believed myself a superior man, and that the ambition came to me of executing the great things which so far had been occupying my thoughts only as a fantastic dream" (Green, "Napoleon's Masterful Italian Campaign"). He proved that superiority in Italy and then again throughout western Europe. An observer from the French War Ministry agreed, writing to the Directory after this campaign, "There is nobody here who does not look upon him as a man of genius, and he is effectively that.... It is with calm that I write, and no interest guides me except that of making you know the truth. Bonaparte will be put by posterity in the rank of the greatest men" (Green, "Napoleon's Masterful Italian Campaign"). By breaking the Austrians at Rivoli, Napoleon entered those ranks.

References: Britt, Albert. *The Wars of Napoleon.* West Point, NY: United States Military Academy, 1973; Chandler, David. *The Campaigns of Napoleon.* New York: Macmillan, 1966; Gibbs, M. B. *Napoleon's Military Career.* Chicago: Werner Co., 1895; Green, Jeremy. "Napoleon's Masterful Italian Campaign," *Military History* 14(1), April 1997; Shosenberg, James. "Napoleon's Masterstroke at Rivoli," *Military History,* December 1996.

ABOUKIR BAY (BATTLE OF THE NILE)
1 August 1798

FORCES ENGAGED

British: Fourteen ships of the line. Commander: Admiral Horatio Nelson.

French: Thirteen ships of the line and four frigates. Commander: Admiral François-Paul Brueys.

IMPORTANCE

British destruction of Napoleon's fleet stranded
Napoleon's army in Egypt, severely curtailing
Napoleon's intent to establish French dominance
over the Red Sea. The British also secured control
of Malta, a strategic port and supply base in
British control until after World War II.

Historical Setting

By 1798, Napoleon Bonaparte was the most
successful French general of his day, having recently gained much of Italy for his country. It
was therefore not surprising that he was the one
chosen by the French governing body, the Directory, to lead a daring mission to the east.
Since the British East India Company's victory
over a French-supported prince of India at
Plassey in 1757, French fortunes in the subcontinent had rapidly ebbed. The French were
evicted from their last remaining trading post
at Pondicherry in 1796, and it seemed as if
Britain would remain supreme in India. If, however, Napoleon could seize Egypt, the French
could control the eastern Mediterranean and
the Red Sea, giving them a starting point for a
possible return to India and a base from which
to harass British shipping in the Indian Ocean.
This was Napoleon's secret mission in 1798.

Only the highest people in the government
were aware of the plans, and Napoleon oversaw the collection of ships in the ports of southern France from which the expedition would
be launched. The British learned that something
was afoot, but could not discern what Napoleon's target might be: Malta, the Kingdom of
the Two Sicilies, Turkey, or Egypt? Or would
he sail west and threaten English possessions in
the Caribbean, Ireland, or England itself? The
London government ordered that ships standing watch for French naval activities off the
Spanish coast at Cadiz should sail for Toulon
and Marseilles to shadow the French fleet when
it left harbor. Earl St. Vincent was commanding the fleet off Cadiz, and he detailed his most
promising young commander, Rear Admiral
Horatio Nelson, to undertake this mission.

Nelson had already distinguished himself as one
who would take seemingly foolish risks, but
make them pay off handsomely. St. Vincent
appreciated that, and he sent Nelson with four
ships through the Straits of Gibraltar to Toulon.

Nelson, in his flagship *Vanguard,* ran into
a storm as he was approaching the southern
French coast, and his ship was badly damaged.
Worse, the French had managed to slip past
him. He spent valuable days having his ship
repaired and then was joined by a squadron of
ships that St. Vincent had promised him that
were newly arrived from the Atlantic. That the
newly arrived English ships had not seen any
French fleet on the way meant that the French
ships must have sailed east, and Nelson was soon
in pursuit. He sailed first for Naples, hoping to
gather some information in Italy's busiest port,
but too late learned that Napoleon had landed
forces on Malta and seized the island from the
Order of the Hospital of St. John, the military
order of knights well past their prime. Napoleon installed a garrison of his own after looting the sizable treasure trove of the knights and
then sailed on. Nelson consulted with his captains, and the consensus was to sail for Egypt.
They arrived off Alexandria on 28 June to find
no evidence of any French activity. Little did
they know that just three nights previously they
had sailed past the French fleet in the darkness.

Nelson immediately turned north for Turkey, and the French sailed into Alexandria almost as soon as he had disappeared over the
horizon. Napoleon quickly debarked 30,000
troops off 400 transports and then ordered his
escorting warships to either sail for the French-
controlled island of Corfu or stay in Egyptian
waters and prepare for Nelson's return. Admiral François-Paul Brueys chose the latter course
and parked his thirteen ships of the line and
four frigates in Aboukir Bay, about 15 miles
from Alexandria. The bay is wide and shallow,
and Brueys placed his ships in an almost perfect defensive position. He anchored them as
close to the shore as he dared, in 5 fathoms (30
feet) of water, placed in a line ranging from

shallow water along the coast in the southeast to the waters off Aboukir Island in the northwest. Facing the ships bow to stern, Brueys presented any approaching fleet with a line of fourteen broadsides (the frigates were anchored between the ships of the line and the shore) in a position that could not be outflanked. Sure of the strength of his position, he sent men ashore to dig wells in order to restock dwindling water supplies.

The Battle

Nelson sailed along the south coast of Turkey with no results until the chance capture of a French merchant ship alerted him to the location of his enemy. He turned and sailed south, reaching Alexandria the morning of 1 August. The harbor seemed empty, but he sent in two ships to investigate while he sailed eastward looking for the French. This lessened by two his fourteen warships, but he was eager to find and engage the enemy. He had been briefing his captains for weeks on what he thought would be every potential formation in which he might find the French, so all contingency plans were in place and each captain knew Nelson's views and held his complete confidence. Nelson, never one to shy away from combat, sailed in on a northwesterly wind, with his ships in a line-astern formation. When Nelson sighted the French fleet anchored in a line along the shore, he decided to take advantage of the static position of the French by attacking them piecemeal. This way, he could maneuver his ships into positions where they would outnumber the enemy while leaving other French ships both out of range and facing away from the action. He ordered his ships to attack the vessels in the front and in the center of the French line, leaving the ships on the far southeastern end for later. The English went into action at 1828, with barely half an hour's daylight left.

As each successive British ship rounded the shoals and sailed directly toward the enemy line,

they were to come as close as possible, anchor themselves, and then engage the French at close range. This took advantage of the superior talents of the English gunners, who could load and fire twice as quickly as their French counterparts, and do so with greater accuracy. The first two English ships, *Goliath* and *Zealous,* were quick to show Brueys that he had miscalculated. His ships were anchored approximately 150 yards apart, and the leading ship was not as near the shoals as Brueys had thought. Thus, the English ships were able to sail around the bow of the leading French ship, *Guerrier,* and come up on its landward side. Here a second weakness in Brueys's force was revealed. Because the expedition had been mounted in such secrecy and with such speed, he had been forced to sail with too few men. In addition, many of his sailors were ashore with the digging party and had not been able to return, so quick was Nelson's arrival and attack. Therefore, only the guns pointing seaward had crew to operate them, so the *Goliath* and *Zealous* could blast the *Guerrier* and the second ship in line, *Conquerant,* without having to receive any return fire.

The seaward French gunners fired at the oncoming English ships, but only one ship at a time was visible because they were sailing in column. Once each ran the gauntlet of fire, it was close enough to anchor and begin to use its superior gunnery at ranges of as little as 100 yards. By focusing on only the ships in the front half of the line, Nelson was able to place his thirteen ships alongside six French ships. By the time darkness fell, there was sufficient light coming from burning French ships to see almost as clearly as daylight. Only the dense smoke concealed targets.

Within an hour, the first six French ships were sinking or surrendering, and the British ships proceeded along the line to engage the ships in the center. The last ship in the English line, *Bellerophon,* was just coming into play, and it made for the French flagship, the 120-gun *L'Orient.* Brueys's crew now got into action. *Bellerophon* was badly damaged almost

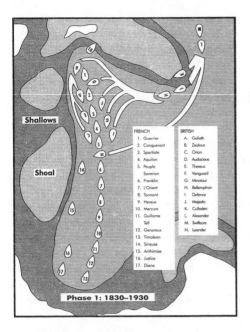

Phase 1: 1830–1930

FRENCH		BRITISH	
1.	Guerrier	A.	Goliath
2.	Conquerant	B.	Zealous
3.	Spartiate	C.	Orion
4.	Aquilon	D.	Audacious
5.	Peuple	E.	Theseus
	Severian	F.	Vanguard
6.	Franklin	G.	Minotaur
7.	L'Orient	H.	Bellerophon
8.	Tonnant	I.	Defence
9.	Hereux	J.	Majestic
10.	Mercure	K.	Culloden
11.	Guillame	L.	Alexander
	Tell	M.	Swiftsure
12.	Genereux	N.	Leander
13.	Timoleon		
14.	Sirieuse		
15.	Arithimise		
16.	Justice		
17.	Diane		

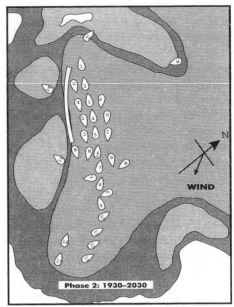

Phase 2: 1930–2030

immediately, and it was soon forced to withdraw minus some masts. It had, however, landed a number of significant shots on *L'Orient,* and Brueys's luck continued to be bad. While sitting in Aboukir Bay over the previous few weeks, Brueys ordered his ship repainted, and cans of paint and thinner were carelessly stacked about the upper deck. English artillery fire set these alight, and the French flagship was soon burning. As *Bellerophon* limped away, Brueys detailed men to deal with the fire, and they were just beginning to contain it when the rest of the English fleet sailed into range.

The two ships that Nelson had sent to scout Alexandria harbor had just arrived, and the *Alexander* and *Swiftsure* made for the burning *L'Orient. Alexander* sailed through the gap between *L'Orient* and *Tonnant* and began pounding the flagship from the unstaffed landward side while *Swiftsure* anchored on the seaward side and did the same. Two more English ships were soon on station and adding their fire. The *L'Orient'*s guns did significant damage to *Swiftsure,* but the flames were spreading and the flagship was doomed. Brueys was killed when his left leg was severed by a cannonball, and at 2115 the crew of *L'Orient* began abandoning ship. At 2130, flames reached the powder magazine and the ship blew up with a roar heard 50 miles away. Flying flaming debris set fire to nearby ships, and the explosion was so deafening and sudden that the guns on all ships fell silent.

Results

Before the English could make their way to the end of the French line, the commander of the rear guard, Rear Admiral Pierre Villeneuve, ordered the remaining four ships to make a run for their lives. Two ships of the line and two frigates escaped. They left behind one of the greatest disasters in naval history, for two of the frigates and eleven ships of the line were sunk or captured. The French lost more than 5,000 men killed, wounded, drowned, or taken prisoner. The English losses were relatively light: no ships sunk, 218 killed, 678 wounded, including Nelson, who suffered a severe cut in his forehead. Many of the surviving ships were converted into Royal Navy ships, and two of

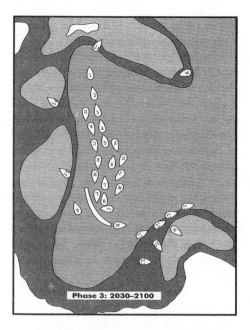

Phase 3: 2030–2100

them served under Nelson at the greatest and last of his battles, Trafalgar in 1805.

The loss of the French fleet doomed France's Egyptian expedition and their dreams of reestablishing themselves in India. Although Napoleon's army had, at first, little trouble defeating Egyptian forces and establishing themselves in Cairo, there were too few troops to last long. Napoleon had mandated that his men respect Islam and all local customs, and he began reforming the administration of Egypt, providing modern ideas in agriculture, science, etc. He also brought with him French archaeologists that studied Egyptian history and discovered the Rosetta stone, the key to translating ancient hieroglyphics. Enlightened as his new administration tried to be, it was too alien for the Egyptians and too threatening for the Ottoman government (which exercised suzerainty in the eastern Mediterranean) to accept. Napoleon was finally forced to abandon his men and sneak back to France.

Aboukir Bay established Nelson as the premiere naval commander of his day, a maritime Napoleon. He was awarded a peerage by the London government, but was offended that it was less important and lucrative than he expected. The award of £10,000 by the East India Company, for "saving" India, eased the disappointment somewhat.

Although the French defeat removed the threat to India, more important to English naval strategy was the acquisition of Malta. Unfettered by serious threats to their Mediterranean operations, the English landed a force on the island and captured it from the French in 1800. This gave them virtual domination of the entire Mediterranean Sea, in spite of the fact that Great Britain itself did not bound that body of water. However, by controlling both Malta in the central part of the Mediterranean and Gibraltar at the western end, they could grant or deny access to almost anyone. Eastern Mediterranean and Adriatic countries that wished access to international markets via the Straits of Gibraltar, or even to western Europe's ports, had to have England's permission. This domination the English exercised until after World War II: "it was the Rock of Gibraltar and the man-hewn stones of the Malta fortress that made Britain [the Mediterranean's] overlord" (Keegan, *The Price of Admiralty,* p. 13).

References: Bennett, Geoffrey. *Nelson the Commander.* New York: Charles Scribner's Sons, 1972; Howarth, David, and Stephen Howarth. *Lord Nelson, the Immortal Memory.* New York: Viking, 1989; Keegan, John. *The Price of Admiralty.* New York: Viking Penguin, 1989; Lloyd, Christopher. *The Nile Campaign: Nelson and Napoleon in Egypt.* New York: Barnes & Noble, 1973; Warner, Oliver. *Great Sea Battles.* London: Spring Books, 1963.

TRAFALGAR
21 October 1805

FORCES ENGAGED

English: Twenty-seven ships of the line.
Commander: Admiral Lord Horatio Nelson.

French: Thirty-three ships of the line.
Commander: Admiral P. C. J. B. S. Villeneuve.

IMPORTANCE

British victory established Britain as the dominant
naval power well into the next century and ended
any possibility of Napoleon invading Britain.

Historical Background

After his failed venture in Egypt in 1798, Napoleon managed to land squarely on his feet.
He overthrew the ruling body of the French
government, the Directory, and established a
three-member Consulate, with himself as First
Consul. He broke up the alliance of countries
arrayed against him, the 2nd Coalition (England, Austria, and Russia), by defeating the
Austrians at Marengo in June 1800. Then he
faced his greatest enemy, England. Napoleon
knew that to make successful war against England he would need both allies and ships. To
this end, he attempted forming a coalition of
his own, but the Royal Navy's victory in the
Battle of Copenhagen in April 1802 scuttled
it. Still, he hoped that by negotiation or conquest he could control the ports of Europe. That
would give him, he reasoned, the bases to amass
a multinational fleet and at the same time deny
the English trade access into the Continent. In
the meantime, a naval demonstration toward
Egypt should draw the bulk of the English Royal
Navy there, giving Napoleon the opportunity
to rush an invasion fleet of small craft across
the English Channel. He began assembling an
army.

The Treaty of Amiens, signed with the
English in 1802, gave him time to organize his
army. It was a cease-fire more than a peace, with
neither side closely observing its terms. The
planned feint toward Egypt never came about,
but Napoleon's control of the European coastal
ports did. France occupied the Netherlands,
acquiring the Dutch fleet, and entered into an
alliance with Spain. This gave Napoleon control of every port from the Dutch North Sea
coast to the Franco-Italian border. He thus acquired a large number of ships, but gathering
them together was the problem.

England's response to Napoleon's acquisition of European ports was to blockade them.
France's Mediterranean ports were blocked by
a squadron under the command of Lord
Nelson, victor of Copenhagen. He had recently
commanded a squadron near the French port
of Boulougne, where Napoleon was building
his invasion fleet. A raid to disrupt that project
was a miserable failure for the English, and
Nelson was eager to come to grips with the
French fleet in order to exact some revenge.
Four other admirals commanded squadrons
blockading the remaining ports, but Nelson
was regarded as the premier naval commander
of his day.

For a time little happened. Although the
Peace of Amiens ended in May 1803, no fighting of any consequence took place through the
spring of 1804. Napoleon continued to mass
troops on the coast for the invasion, and England responded by enlarging its army to more
than half a million men, almost one-twentieth
of the country's population. Napoleon finally
set things into motion in May 1805, when he
ordered Admiral P. C. J. B. S. Villeneuve to
break out of the southern French port of Toulon
and race for French islands in the West Indies.
There he was to join forces with Commodore
Honoré Ganteaume, who was to escape the
blockade at Brest. Together they would harass
English possessions in the Caribbean for 2
months and then sail back to Europe. They
would be strong enough to break through any
blockading squadron, thus freeing French ships
to make a huge and possibly unstoppable fleet.
This would then safeguard the proposed cross–
English Channel invasion and hopefully defeat
the Royal Navy in battle as well.

Nelson, temporarily away from Toulon,
learned of Villeneuve's escape and assumed that
Egypt was his goal. Nelson sailed for Alexandria, but found no French. He then sailed for
the West Indies, where faulty intelligence reports sent him on a useless foray to Trinidad.

The Battle of Trafalgar (National Maritime Museum, Greenich)

Nelson and Villeneuve spent much of the summer sailing back and forth across the Atlantic, neither sure exactly where the other was located or was going. Nelson returned to England in August and then was back at sea aboard his flagship *Victory* on 14 September. Word had come that Villeneuve had picked up reinforcements and sailed for the Spanish port of Cadiz. There, on 28 September, Nelson joined the bulk of the English fleet that he was to command at the upcoming battle. He placed a few ships within site of Cadiz to spy on the Franco-Spanish fleet, while he kept the main body of ships over the horizon.

The Battle

Nelson spent the next few weeks waiting for Villeneuve to move and instructing his captains on his tactics. Nelson here introduced a new

method of naval engagement, abandoning the traditional maneuver of lining up parallel to the enemy and blasting away. Instead, he proposed breaking his ships into three columns that would approach the enemy from the perpendicular. These columns were supposed to break through the Franco-Spanish line of ships, breaking them into smaller groups that could not support each other. Then, each English ship was to close with the nearest enemy and fight in single combat. Nelson depended on the superior maneuverability of his ships, quality of his captains, and discipline and accuracy of his gunners. With the Franco-Spanish fleet out of its own formation, he was sure that the individual enemy captains would not be able to adapt to the concept of single-ship actions.

Villeneuve really was not looking for a battle when he tried to slip out of Cadiz on 19 October, but for a chance to run through the

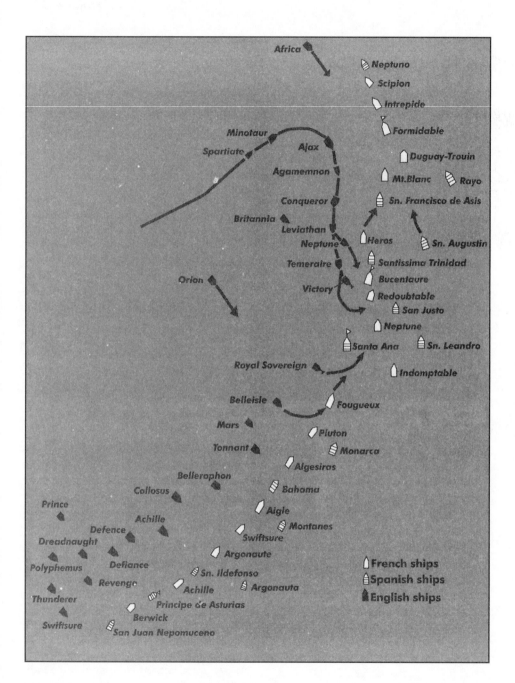

Africa

Neptuno
Scipion
Intrepide
Formidable
Duguay-Trouin
Mt.Blanc   Rayo
Sn. Francisco de Asis
Sn. Augustin
Heros
Santissima Trinidad
Bucentaure
Redoubtable
San Justo
Neptune
Santa Ana   Sn. Leandro
Indomptable

Minotaur
Spartiate   Ajax
Agamemnon
Conqueror
Britannia
Leviathan
Neptune
Temeraire
Orion
Victory

Royal Sovereign

Belleisle   Fougueux
Mars
Tonnant   Pluton
Monarca
Bellerophon   Algesiras
Collosus   Bahama
Prince   Aigle
Achille   Montanes
Defence   Swiftsure
Dreadnaught
Polyphemus   Argonaute
Defiance   Sn. Ildefonso
Revenge   Achille   Argonauta
Thunderer   Principe de Asturias
Swiftsure   Berwick
San Juan Nepomuceno

French ships
Spanish ships
English ships

Straits of Gibraltar and return to Toulon. He headed south with Nelson in pursuit through 19 and 20 October, but had a difficult time keeping his fleet in line astern battle order. On the morning of 21 October, Nelson's fleet had successfully outrun Villeneuve's and came into sight well before Gibraltar appeared. The wind was storming out of the northwest, at Nelson's back, when he saw Villeneuve reverse course and try to run back to Cadiz rather than go to Gibraltar.

Off Trafalgar Point, Nelson ordered his ships into two columns rather than three. He retired to his cabin where he was observed recording a prayer in his journal. When he returned to the upper deck, he ordered a message spelled out in signal flags: "England expects that every man will do his duty." Not all the English ships saw this, or if they did they paid no heed, thinking it was probably a reiteration of the orders they all knew by heart. Nelson led the left column in the *Victory* while Vice Admiral Cuthbert Collingwood commanded the right column.

The engagement began about noon on 21 October. Collingwood's ship, the *Royal Sovereign,* was first to engage, and soon his column had cut the line of Franco-Spanish ships in half. By 0100, the *Victory* was engaged. Nelson's plan was a success; the leading French ships could not come about and aid the trailing ships, and the aggressive English captains pressed their attacks on the confused and now outnumbered enemy captains. The Franco-Spanish fleet soon fell into utter confusion. The French ship *Redoubtable* engaged the *Victory* and scored the one significant French accomplishment that day: a sniper from the *Redoubtable* shot Nelson. The bullet entered his shoulder and struck his spine. He was carried below with his face covered by a cloth so the crew could not see who was injured. He was in agony for the next 3 hours, but there was nothing the surgeons could do. He waited for news of the English victory, which came in midafternoon. The ship's log recorded: "Partial firing continued until 4.30, when a victory having been reported to the

Right Honourable Lord Viscount Nelson KB and Commander-in-Chief, he then died of his wound" (Warner, *Great Sea Battles,* p. 182).

Results

Although eighteen French and Spanish ships struck their colors in surrender, the storm whose winds had favored the English then scattered the victors and vanquished. Only four ships were taken as prizes. In contrast, the English lost no ships, 24 men killed, and about 100 wounded. The *Victory* sailed first to Gibraltar, with Nelson's body embalmed in a cask filled with brandy. The story is told during tours at St. Paul's Cathedral in London that the sailors drank from the cask, and that since then grog in the Royal Navy has been nicknamed "Nelson's Blood."

At first the battle seemed to have no serious positive results because Napoleon's forces soon afterward scored brilliant successes over the Austrians at Ülm and over the Austrians and Russians at Austerlitz. The battle off Trafalgar Point had numerous long-term effects, however. First, of course, was Nelson's death. He dominated not only the Royal Navy but all of naval warfare in his day. He died a hero, but even had he lived he would never again have matched the accomplishment on 21 October 1805. England engaged in no more serious naval warfare, indeed, until more than a century later at Jutland in 1916.

The second effect was that because no more significant naval battles occurred during the wars against Napoleon, the English blockade continued and succeeded in keeping Napoleon's ships bottled up in various harbors. Only a minor skirmish against a Franco-Venetian fleet at Lissa in the Adriatic in 1811 marred the dullness of blockade duty. Without a functioning navy, Napoleon could not seriously threaten an invasion of England nor even harass their possessions around the world. The best he could do was try to maintain his Continental System, which attempted to deny

England its lucrative European trade. The continuing English blockade did have a side effect in North America. Needing sailors to crew the ships, the English began the practice of impressment, forcing foreign (usually American) sailors into the Royal Navy. This practice, virtually piracy, violated international law. That, coupled with the restrictions on neutral trade invoked by England's Orders in Council (1806), so provoked the Americans that they ultimately went to war in 1812.

More importantly for the war in Europe, England's mastery of the sea after Trafalgar allowed England to transport troops onto the Continent. This began in Portugal and Spain in 1809, starting what came to be called the "Spanish ulcer" that so drained French military power and gave valuable experience to the English army. This helped lead to Napoleon's final defeat at Waterloo in Belgium in 1815. After every Continental power had been defeated by Napoleon at least once, England emerged as the spiritual leader of the coalition that finally brought him down. It can be said that the victory at Waterloo was begun at Trafalgar 10 years earlier.

England enjoyed naval superiority until World War II after having struggled against French and Dutch maritime rivalry for the previous century. This allowed the expansion of the British Empire throughout the nineteenth century, but also aroused the jealousy of Germany, whose naval arms race at the end of the nineteenth and start of the twentieth century contributed to the outbreak of World War I. That naval superiority, confirmed at Trafalgar, saved England from any chance of a French invasion in the early nineteenth century, just as it saved them from any chance of a German invasion in 1940.

References: Fuller, J. F. C. *A Military History of the Western World*, vol. 2. New York: Funk & Wagnalls, 1955; Gardiner, Robert. *The Campaign of Trafalgar, 1803–1805*. London: Chatham, in association with the National Maritime Museum, 1997; Howarth, David.

Trafalgar: The Nelson Touch. London: Collins, 1969; Warner, Oliver. *Great Sea Battles*. London: Spring Books, 1963; Warner, Oliver. *Trafalgar*. London: B. T. Batsford, 1959.

JENA/AUERSTÄDT
14 October 1806

FORCES ENGAGED
French: At Jena: 46,000 to 54,000 men. Commander: Napoleon Bonaparte. At Auerstädt: 26,000 men. Commander: Marshal Louis Davout.
Prussian: At Jena: 55,000 men. Commander: Prince Frederick Hohenlohe. At Auerstädt: 50,000 men. Commander: Karl Wilhelm, duke of Brunswick.

IMPORTANCE
Disastrous Prussian defeat led to complete reform of the Prussian military, most importantly the establishment of the General Staff system, leading to the dominance of Prussian military in Europe.

Historical Setting

In 1805, Napoleon was at the height of his power and talent. Although unable to launch his proposed invasion of Great Britain that year, he employed the army set aside for that purpose in the two battles that best showed his genius: Ülm and Austerlitz. Austrian General Mack was so swiftly surrounded at Ülm (20 October 1805) that he had no choice but to surrender before giving battle; at Austerlitz (2 December 1805), Napoleon's army crushed a combined Austro-Russian force. The alliance between Russia and Austria was dissolved at that point, but the fact that Prussia had been urged to join it and had hesitated certainly contributed to the outcome at Austerlitz. Prussian King Frederick William III vacillated in the months preceding the battle, unsure if Austria would conclude a separate peace after he joined Austria and Russia. Napoleon had offered him an alliance and possession of the state of

Hanover if he joined with France, but the war party in Prussia argued strongly against subordinating Prussia to Napoleon. Frederick William's hesitance doomed the Austrians and Russians at Austerlitz.

Soon after the battle, Prussia did accept Napoleon's offer, for Frederick William lusted after Hanover. Unfortunately, so did Great Britain, which had previously dominated that German state through the ruling House of Hanover, which occupied the British throne. In the early months of 1806, Britain negotiated with Napoleon over territories in Italy and Germany, and Napoleon made overtures of returning Hanover to Britain. Further, Napoleon forced on Prussia an agreement ceding the Duchy of Cleves and forcing cooperation with the Continental System, the French emperor's economic warfare against Britain wherein all the Continent would cease trade with it. The potential loss of Hanover and the definite loss of income from British trade aroused Frederick William, and he finally swung his support to the war party in the Prussian court. With the inclusion of 20,000 soldiers from the allied state of Saxony, the Prussians could field an army of just over 200,000 men.

That swing affected Russia, which was also in the midst of talks with Napoleon concerning the recognition of territorial adjustments in Italy. The proposed agreement would establish Napoleon's power in Italy through states that he established, give Russia a free hand in the Balkans, and also withdraw French troops from German territory. Seeing Prussia grow hostile encouraged Czar Alexander to reject the proposed French treaty and instead begin to treat with Frederick William, but any potential assistance from Russia was too far away.

The Prussian army had long held a position of highest respect in Europe, thanks to the organization and reputation of Frederick the Great. In the middle of the eighteenth century, he had made Prussia a power to be respected because of his own genius and the organization of the army, which he inherited

from his father, Frederick I. In the War of the Austrian Succession (1747–1750) and the Seven Years' War (1757–1763), Frederick the Great had consistently shown more skill and daring than any of his opponents, and the iron discipline that he forced on his men made them virtual automatons doing his will. The only problem with such a system was that it depended on an extremely talented leader, but, after Frederick's death, no later monarch had his vision or competence. The army was the same, but its command was not. Still, the reputation endured, and Napoleon had not yet fought such an established military force. Napoleon knew, however, that the men in charge of the Prussian army, from the king through the upper ranks, were still thinking in terms of Frederick the Great's time, and Napoleon's army had changed all the rules. Depending on that ultraconservatism in his enemy, Napoleon on 7 October rejected an ultimatum from Frederick William to leave German lands. It took him only a week to prove to Prussia that their army was not what it used to be.

The Battle

Napoleon had been preparing for this operation for some time. When he learned on 18 September 1806 that the Prussians had marched into Saxony 5 days earlier, he launched his own plans into motion. Concentrating around Bamberg and Bayreuth on the Main River, on 8 October he marched northward in three columns through the Thuringian Forest. He aimed toward the town of Gera, where he assumed that the Prussians would join together the three portions of their army. Along the line of march from Bamberg to Gera lies the town of Jena, some 20 miles east of Weimar. It was there that Prussian Prince Frederick Hohenlohe brought his force, and two other parts of the army under the command of the duke of Brunswick and the king himself met with Hohenlohe just north of Jena on 13 October. They decided to withdraw toward the Elbe River, the western border of Prussia; Hohenlohe was to deploy between Jena and Capellendorf as a rear guard to cover the army's withdrawal through the town of Auerstädt, 12 miles to the north.

Napoleon, on learning of his enemy's position from prisoners, decided to divide his force in two. He would lead one force up the Saale River toward Jena, while the second, under Marshal Louis Davout, would march along a northerly line west of Jena toward the Elbe River. Thus, Napoleon could establish a blocking force under Davout if the Prussians continued to withdraw or use it as a flanking force if they stood to fight. Napoleon approached Jena from the south on the afternoon of 13 October, learning that the bulk of the Prussian army was encamped on a plateau just west of the town. He planned to spend 14 October positioning his men for battle the next day.

Early in the morning of 14 October, Napoleon visited various units to give them encouragement. It was a very foggy morning, but the Saxons in the Prussian army heard the cries of "Vive l'Empereur!" This cry worried not only the Saxons but also the Prussian commander, Hohenlohe, who had assumed that the French force near him was little more than an advance guard or reconnaissance in force. Thus, both commanders misread the enemy's strength. Napoleon thought he faced the bulk of the Prussian army rather than the rear guard; Hohenlohe found out too late that he faced most of the French army.

In the morning fog, the French troops received their orders to march at 0600. Within 3 hours, they had captured the villages that were their objectives, and Napoleon ordered his forces to stop and reassemble their units. The Prussian advanced force, under General Tauenzien, lost a large number of its men in the fighting, but regrouped to the rear of Hohenlohe's force to act as a reserve. As Hohenlohe brought up more men to meet the French, both commanders were positioning their troops for the battle to come. It began much sooner than expected, however, because of the impetuousness of one of Napoleon's marshals, Ney.

Fearing that the battle might be over too quickly for him and his men to gain their share of glory, Ney pressed his attack on the Prussians at the village of Vierzehnheiligen. Napoleon was forced to send in men to support this premature attack, but the supplemental French troops captured the village and immediately met the front of the Prussian army lined up in the open outside town. Retreating back into the protection of the village, the French began shooting at the exposed Prussians. The discipline imposed on the Prussians since the days of Frederick I did not fail; indeed, it was the major cause of the Prussian defeat that day. Under intense musket and artillery fire, the Prussian troops stood their ground for 2 hours and died in huge numbers. As that was taking place, Napoleon ordered attacks on both Prussian flanks. Shortly after noon, he ordered a general advance, and the decimated Prussians were pressed back all along the line.

Hohenlohe ordered a withdrawal northwestward, but the retreat soon degenerated. The only hope to save the Prussians from total rout was the arrival and defensive stand of reinforcements marching from Weimar. They, however, arrived too late and found themselves facing a victorious and exuberant French army that in a matter of minutes tore the reinforcements to shreds. By 1600, the French pursuit was in full swing, with the only serious resistance coming from the Saxon troops, which stood their ground and died.

Napoleon soon learned that his defeated enemy was not the main Prussian force, which was instead engaged to the north with Marshal Davout at Auerstädt. Davout, who was supposed to act as the flanking assault on Hohenlohe's position, found himself with 26,000 men facing more than 50,000 Prussians. The battle there also started about 0600 in the fog, when the two armies stumbled into each other at the village of Hassenhausen. Davout had time to deploy his leading division before the fog cleared, and they soon beat back four Prussian cavalry charges. As more Prussians came up to engage, their commander, the duke of Brunswick, was killed. For a time, the army had no commander because Frederick William had no military knowledge or experience, and he was too paralyzed by events to appoint a replacement. Later Prussian cavalry charges also failed to break the French infantry squares, and the Prussian army withdrew toward Auerstädt, about 3 miles to the southwest of Hassenhausen. The French flanks had advanced far enough forward to bring flanking artillery fire on the retreat. Rather than commit his reserve cavalry to beat back the pressing French, the king shortly after noon ordered a withdrawal toward Hohenlohe, whom he did not know was at the same time watching his men run as fast as they could. As the two retreating armies met and learned of each others' fate, the rout became even worse. Frederick William and his queen fled for Berlin.

Results

The vaunted Prussian army almost vanished in a matter of hours. The French inflicted almost 25,000 casualties on the Prussians and captured as many prisoners. Most of the remainder of the army simply disappeared. The French also captured all the Prussian artillery, some 200 pieces. For this immense victory, the French lost about 4,000 casualties at Jena and another 7,000 at Auerstädt. French forces scoured the countryside for Prussian survivors, while Napoleon led about half the army to Berlin, which he entered without a fight on 27 October. Napoleon offered terms to Frederick William, who turned them down upon receiving a note from Czar Alexander that 140,000 men were to be sent if the Prussian monarch would but stand firm. Any Russian promise was useless because French soldiers occupied every fortress in Prussia in less than a month, taking the prisoner count up to 100,000. Still, Frederick William (based in East Prussia) organized what

troops he could to join with the Russians. Together they fought to a draw against Napoleon's forces at Eylau in February 1807, gaining some hope of a successful future, but that was crushed by Napoleon's decisive victory at Friedland in mid-June 1807. After that, in the Treaty of Tilsit, Russia pledged an alliance and Prussia was truly punished.

In the wake of the battle at Freidland, Napoleon humiliated the Prussians by not only seizing all their military supplies but taking away significant territorial possessions. All land east of the Elbe River was ceded; before the Prussian campaign, Napoleon had organized most German principalities into the Confederation of the Rhine, and western Prussian lands were awarded to them. Large tracts in the east went into the newly created Duchy of Warsaw. The Poles appreciated the territorial acquisition and recognition, but being vassals to the French grated on them.

Jena/Auerstädt was one of the most complete victories Napoleon ever scored; it wiped out an entire army in one blow. It was not, however, the political triumph he hoped for. He assumed that, with Prussia defeated, the British would see the hopelessness of their position and come to terms with him. When they did not, Napoleon announced the Berlin Decree, which shut European trade up even tighter than did the Continental System. It mandated the seizure of any and all British property in Europe and forbade neutral trade with Britain. London responded with the Orders in Council, forbidding neutral trade with France or any of its possessions. Thus, full-scale economic warfare was launched, and the major neutral country engaged in trade with the two combatants was the United States. The strains brought on by the trade restrictions and the British blockade of Europe led eventually to the War of 1812.

The humiliation that Prussia felt had a long-term positive effect. Before the war, a few senior officers warned of the problems inherent in the outdated Prussian military, but theirs were voices crying in the wilderness. The chief voice was that of Major-General Gerhard von Scharnhorst. After the Treaty of Tilsit, Frederick William appointed him head of the Military Reorganization Commission. With the aid of four other forward-looking officers, Scharnhorst began overhauling the Prussian military. Realizing that future kings and commanding officers may not be blessed with sufficient military talent, Scharnhorst and his compatriots developed the concept of the General Staff. Rather than have officers appointed by superiors on the basis of birth or social standing, officers in the future would rise via talent and education. That would keep the best officers in command and advisory positions, able to give the best advice to their superiors, including the king, or to lessen the effect of bad orders given by those same superiors.

Scharnhorst died in 1813, but was replaced by the more aggressive August von Gneisenau. He oversaw the implementation of Scharnhorst's staff concept in the wake of Napoleon's ultimate defeat at Waterloo in 1815. The General Staff was to engage in planning, coordinate the various branches of the military, and oversee operational readiness. The development of institutions of higher military education also promised to locate and promote talented officers. The creation of the concept of war games took the Prussian army to the heights of preparedness, whereas the institution of a staff military history section meant that past mistakes were to be avoided and observers were to visit past and contemporary battlefields to see how battles were won in the past and how other armies fought in the present. The Prussian General Staff created the finest military organization of the nineteenth century, with the goal of institutionalizing excellence. Quick and decisive Prussian victories over Denmark in 1864, Austria in 1866, and France in 1870 showed the rest of the world the value of such an organization, and by the early twentieth century every nation with any pretensions to military power developed their own General Staffs.

Thus, Jena was the fire that destroyed Frederick the Great's army, from whose ashes the phoenix of the nineteenth-century Prussian/German army arose.

References: Britt, Albert. *The Wars of Napoleon.* West Point, NY: United States Military Academy, 1973; Chandler, David. *The Campaigns of Napoleon.* New York: Macmillan, 1966; Dupuy, Trevor N. *A Genius for War.* London: Macdonald's & Jane's, 1977; Fuller, J. F. C. *A Military History of the Western World,* vol. 2. New York: Funk & Wagnalls, 1955; Maude, F. N. *The Jena Campaign, 1806.* New York: Macmillan, 1909.

PROPHETSTOWN (TIPPECANOE)

7 November 1811

FORCES ENGAGED

U.S. Indiana militia: 910 officers and men.
Commander: William Henry Harrison.
American Indian: Approximately 450.
Commander: Laulewasika (the Prophet).

IMPORTANCE

Prophetstown was the scene of the last major attempt to unify American Indian tribes to resist white expansion.

Historical Setting

The first English settlement that survived on North American soil was at Jamestown, founded in 1607, on the coast of what is now the state of Virginia. Several earlier attempts to found colonies failed, mainly because of the colonists' lack of foresight in bringing sufficient supplies to last through the harsh American winters. Raised on stories of the fabulous wealth that the Spanish had been looting from Central America since the end of the fifteenth century, the English expected to find the same gold available in North America. Apparently, gaining quick wealth for the return to England blinded them to the need for adequate food supplies. Jamestown survived primarily because the local Indian tribes took pity on the settlers and aided them in adapting to their new home. This kindness was rarely repaid in kind, however; within 15 years of Jamestown's founding, the English and Indians were fighting. Instances of similar colonist-Indian relations occurred all along the Atlantic coast.

The English colonists came to North America with different intentions than those the Spanish took to Central and South America. Certainly the English were in search of wealth, but the majority of the settlers were as eager to leave England as to go to the New World. They came not to conquer or convert the locals, as did the Spanish, but to start new lives away from poor economic conditions in England. In North America, just about the only thing a colonist could do to make a living was farm. Farming, of course, needs land, and the land was the domain of the established Indian tribes. As long as the colonists were few, the Indians seemed glad to assist, but, as more colonists arrived from England and the need for land intensified, conflict was inevitable.

Unwilling at first to see the Indians as potential converts to Christianity, the settlers instead dealt with them in as callous a manner as possible. Warfare between the two populations quickly degenerated into genocide. Battles ended with the slaughter of the defeated with few prisoners taken. For example, at the end of King Philip's War in western Massachusetts (1675–1676), Metacomet (called King Philip by the English) was beheaded and his head displayed on a pole at Plymouth for 25 years. Which side introduced scalping is a matter of dispute, but both sides ultimately practiced it. Because the Indian tribes had their own rivalries, they rarely combined to resist the English, so better colonial organization proved the difference as more Indians were killed or forced west as the colonists took over their land. This was the story of the first two

centuries of English colonization: the whites, through superior numbers and coordination, pushed the Indians west. White attitudes and actions did nothing to endear the two populations to each other.

Indian tribes occasionally put up serious resistance, such as in the cooperative effort with French Canadian settlers in the French and Indian War (1755–1760) and Pontiac's Rebellion right after that war. These, however, were short-lived, and the English colonists maintained a steady westward movement. Slowed somewhat by the decrees imposed by the English government in the 1760s and 1770s and then by the American Revolution, the pressure started again after American independence was won in 1783.

It was at this time that Tecumseh, a Shawnee from Ohio, was growing up; it was he who would organize the most serious threat to white expansion. Born in 1768 in central Ohio of Muskogee parents from Alabama, Tecumseh was 7 years old when his father was killed by whites. Tecumseh was raised by a subchief named Blackfish and grew close to two white captives who were his foster brothers, Stephen Ruddell and Richard Sparks. Having learned oratory from the British-educated Mohawk chief Joseph Brant, Tecumseh came to be regarded as one of the finest speakers of his day. He also learned from his sister Tecumapease to be forgiving and practice moderation in his behavior. In spite of witnessing a number of Indian deaths at the hands of whites, and fighting whites himself on a number of occasions, he became known for his merciful treatment of captives.

From his foster brothers and a half-white girl that he married in the 1790s, Tecumseh learned some English. When he fell in love with a white girl, he learned even more, reading Shakespeare and the Bible. When she rejected his proposal of marriage unless he would abandon his Indian heritage, he refused to abandon his race. By the turn of the century, his learning and oratory had made him a well-known and well-respected figure among both Indians and whites. He developed a reputation for wisdom and was often called upon to settle disputes between Indians and white settlers.

In 1804, Tecumseh's brother, Laulewasika, fell into a trance (which may have been a drunken stupor). He had a vision of Hell that convinced him to give up his alcoholism and preach to the Indians of the Northwest Territory (between the Ohio River and the Great Lakes). He spoke of a return to an earlier lifestyle before the whites had come, when Indians were more cooperative, and a rejection of white products (especially liquor). When the greatest Shawnee prophet of the day, Penagashega, died, Laulewasika took his place and became known as the Prophet. He set up a religious center, which became known as Prophetstown, at the junction of the Tippecanoe and Wabash Rivers in Indiana, and this attracted Indians from hundreds of miles away to hear his message.

In the meantime, Tecumseh was traveling the countryside in an attempt to organize Indian tribes from the Great Lakes to the Gulf of Mexico into a confederation that would resist white expansion. His oratorical skills, coupled with his phenomenal memory, were put to good use as he spoke at length from treaties that had been broken by the whites. Between 1802 and 1811, he traveled with a group of thirty-four warriors whose bearing and abilities at ceremonial dancing impressed the tribes he visited. Because they all carried war clubs painted red, the organization came to be called the Red Stick Confederacy. Although he had little success in recruiting tribes in Tennessee, which had established economic ties with the whites, he was successful in convincing the Creek Confederation of Mississippi and Alabama to join. As he spoke to the tribes, he told them that they should prepare for war with the whites, and when the time was ripe he would stamp his foot. This would cause the earth to shake and that would be the signal for the tribes to unite and go to war.

The Battle

The fact that Tecumseh had traveled so widely, from the lower Mississippi River valley all the way to Vermont, meant that whites everywhere could be in danger. His well-known refusal to enter into treaties with whites also made him dangerous. Tecumseh's recruiting combined with his brother's religious activities made the whites living along the frontier nervous. If these two could unite the tribes politically, militarily, and socially, then Indians could for the first time field an army that whites would have a difficult time matching in numbers. The white settlers in the Indiana Territory finally appealed to territorial Governor William Henry Harrison to do something about Prophetstown. Harrison had met three times with Tecumseh, in 1808, 1810, and 1811. In all of these meetings, Tecumseh demanded that the whites make no more treaties that took away Indian lands.

Harrison responded to the settlers' pleas by gathering together a force of militia in late September 1811, while Tecumseh was in Alabama talking with tribes there. Harrison received the permission of the secretary of war, William Eustis, to launch an attack, but President James Madison (who was away from Washington at the time) was not informed. The militia marched up the Wabash River, building Fort Harrison at the site of modern Terre Haute. Harrison's militia arrived opposite Prophetstown on the evening of 6 November. Laulewasika, who had been instructed by Tecumseh not to engage in any hostilities during his absence, sent a delegation to Harrison to propose talks. The two men were to meet the following morning, but instead the Prophet ordered an attack on Harrison's camp at 0415. Laulewasika told his warriors that he had performed certain rituals that had made them impervious to the musket fire of the whites, so they attacked with vigor.

The Indians caught the militia camp by surprise, but Harrison quickly mounted an effective defense. The quick response, coupled with the fact that the muskets were indeed killing the attackers, caused the Indian attack to waver. When told of the situation, the Prophet urged them to continue the attack, but he himself fled. All of this broke the morale of the Indian force, which retreated. At daybreak, Harrison ordered his men to attack Prophetstown, which they burned. Harrison sent reports of a major victory back to Washington, but he withdrew within hours of the battle.

Results

When Tecumseh arrived back at the smoking ruins of Prophetstown 4 days later, he was looking at his dreams of a united Indian nation going up in smoke instead. That the Indians had not won a great victory broke his mystique, and the Red Stick Confederacy collapsed. Tecumseh contacted Harrison to arrange a meeting with President Madison, but differences of opinion on how the meeting should take place kept it from happening. Tecumseh disavowed his brother and then took what warriors would still follow him and went to Canada. There he fought alongside the British and Canadian forces against the American invasion that started the War of 1812. After some successes, he was killed at the battle of the Thames in 1813. That battle was against American forces commanded by William Henry Harrison.

It was the connection with the English that was one of the key results of this encounter. The government in London did not want to openly support the Indians against the whites, fearing that it would lead to a conflict between the United States and England. As the Napoleonic Wars were in full swing at the time, London was not interested in fighting two wars at once. On the other hand, local Englishmen were supplying the Red Stick Confederacy with arms, and, when the weapons were discovered in Prophetstown by Harrison's men, it was the final contribution to the already deteriorating Anglo-American relations. Restrictions on freedom of the seas had for years inflamed American passions against England. When it was discovered that the English were arming the Indians, the Americans took it as an affront to all that white Americans had stood for since their opening shots against the Indians two centuries earlier. War against England was declared in June 1812.

Most importantly, however, was the effect on the American Indian population. Two hundred years of defeat and loss of territory had finally brought them to the point of unification, and it all fell apart overnight. The superior numbers and organization that the whites had brought to bear against them for two centuries was by this time a juggernaut. No large-scale Indian tribal alliance was ever again formed; only the Sioux-Cheyenne effort that defeated George Custer's small force in 1876 at the Little Bighorn River showed any major attempt at combining Indian populations to resist the whites, and by then it was far too late. Had Tecumseh been able to hold the Red Stick Confederacy together, major warfare between the Appalachians and the Mississippi River would certainly have occurred. It was probably too late even for him—or perhaps not. In mid-December 1811, an earthquake rocked southern Canada around the Great Lakes and was felt as far away as New Madrid, Missouri, where the Mississippi River temporarily flowed backwards. Another earthquake struck on 23 January 1812, another on 27 January, and a fourth on 13 February. Considering Tecumseh's claim that he would stamp his foot to signal a general tribal uprising, perhaps he did have the power to create a successful resistance movement.

References: Edmunds, David R. *Tecumseh and the Quest for Indian Leadership.* Boston: Little, Brown, 1984; Locke, Raymond F. "Tecumseh: The First Advocate of Red Power," in John R. M. Wilson, ed. *Forging the American Character,* vol. 1. Englewood Cliffs, NJ: Prentice-Hall, 1991; Sugden, John. *Tecumseh: A Life.* New York: Henry Holt, 1998; Tucker, Glenn. "Tecumseh," *American History Illustrated,* vol. 6(10), February 1972.

BORODINO

7 September 1812

FORCES ENGAGED

Russian: 120,000 men. Commander: General
Prince Mikhail Golinishcev-Kutusov.
French: 120,000 men.
Commander: Napoleon Bonaparte.

IMPORTANCE

Napoleon's string of victories, dating back to 1798,
came to an end in the wake of Borodino. By failing
to crush the Russian army, he failed to defeat Russia,
beginning the decline of his fortunes.

Historical Setting

By 1807, Emperor Napoleon had defeated every major power on the Continent at least once. His authority stretched from Spain to Poland, and only Great Britain remained untouchable. Russia was as yet unconquered, but Czar Alexander signed the Treaty of Tilsit in 1807 and that made him an ally, albeit unwilling, of Napoleon's France. Under the terms of the treaty, the Russian monarch was to have his country join Napoleon's Continental System, which was designed to hurt Britain the only way France could, that is, economically. By denying European markets to British merchants, Napoleon hoped to put economic pressure on the British government, much as the American colonists had done to Britain before the American Revolution. In place of British manufactured goods, Russians were to buy products from France, even though they were rather more expensive.

Economic pressure on the populace was not the only problem that Russia had with Napoleon. Napoleon's control of the Duchy of Warsaw bothered the Russian government immensely. Russians and Poles were enemies of long standing, and a French force based in Poland could easily be launched at Russia. To further upset Russian goals, Napoleon was making

threatening gestures toward the Dardanelles, the straits between the Black Sea and the Mediterranean that had long been a target of Russian desires. Thus, the combined economic and political strains wore on Russia, and by 1812 the czar's advisors were urging him to break free of the French constraints. Napoleon knew of these troubling views, and so sent a warning to Alexander. A convoy of British merchant ships were on their way to St. Petersburg; intern them or else. When Alexander did not, that was the excuse Napoleon needed to launch his invasion. Knowing that other European countries might follow Russia's lead, Napoleon needed to punish the czar *pour le encouragement de l'autres,* to encourage the others.

Napoleon's invasion force was massive, 460,000 men in the invasion with another 200,000 covering his lines of communication back to Poland; however, about half of them were not French and therefore were potentially unreliable. The Russians were not without assistance. Alexander had been engaging in talks with Sweden (whose Crown Prince Bernadotte was an ex-Napoleonic marshal), Poland (whose population has historically danced with any devil that would rid them of a current occupier), Prussia, Turkey, and Britain, from which came military advisors to the Russian army. In spite of the fact that this force was the largest that Napoleon had ever assembled, Napoleon's closest advisors counseled against the invasion. Fourteen years of victories overrode their advice. Napoleon was convinced that the invasion would be relatively simple because he was sure that the Russian peasants would embrace the principles of the French Revolution and reject the autocratic rule of the czar. He was also convinced that he could easily live off the land, as he had done in every previous campaign, and the establishment of regularly placed supply depots would make up any lack that may occur.

French forces crossed the Nieman River out of Poland on 24 June 1812. Napoleon's traditionally excellent intelligence corps served him well, and he marched between two widely separated Russian armies. From the beginning, however, weather was a problem. Unusual heat sapped the strength of the men and horses, and the cavalry was also plagued by an epidemic of cholic. When Napoleon's brother Jerome failed to cut off one of the opposing forces, he was relieved of his command and replaced by the much more reliable Marshal Louis Davout. Davout quickly defeated one of the Russian armies, under General Bagration, keeping him separated from the second force under General Barclay de Tolly. Bagration retreated eastward across the Dnieper River, destroying everything behind him. This scorched-earth policy, retreat and burn, was successfully implemented not only by the Russian army but by the populace as well, who apparently did not embrace French revolutionary principles. This meant the establishment of more depots than planned, and the resulting garrisons reduced the invasion force.

Tolly did as he was told in employing the scorched-earth tactics, but was soon criticized for retreating too quickly and not inflicting enough damage on the invaders. Tolly had in actuality done wonders in effectively slowing the French, losing at Smolensk on 17 August but extricating his army before it was surrounded and destroyed. He was replaced, however, by General Prince Golinishcev-Kutusov, who had been on the losing side of Napoleon's masterpiece victory at Austerlitz in 1805. He was not about to take Napoleon lightly, but pressure from the government and the public demanded a battle, and he grudgingly obliged near the small Russian town of Borodino, about 70 miles west of Moscow.

The Battle

The site that Kutusov chose was well suited to defense; about 8 square miles, it was smaller than traditional battlefields of that day. The plain leading up to Borodino lay between two roads, old and new, leading to Moscow from Smolensk, and was somewhat undulating and crossed by numerous small streams with steep banks. The occasional village and forest further impeded an advancing army. Kutusov placed his right flank on the Kalatsha River at the town of Borodino, built the Great Redoubt just southeast of town, and strung the remainder of his forces southward to the town of Utitsa, on the southern road facing a large forest. The center of the line was anchored by the town of Semenovskoi, with smaller redoubts built in front. Thus, it was a good place to make a stand, yet positioned astride the road to Moscow for quick withdrawal if necessary. Kutusov commanded a force of about 120,000 men, which included 17,000 regular cavalry and another 7,000 Cossacks. From end to end, the Russian line ranged 5 miles.

Napoleon arrived on the morning of 5 September 1812, when a stiff fight took place at the advanced Russian position in the town of Schivardino. The Russian force there fell back to the main line at sunset, giving the main force plenty of warning of the French approach. Napoleon's force at this point numbered about 135,000, but his men and horses were tired, and many were sick. Napoleon himself was suffering from a recurrent bladder problem, which may account for the fact that he did not show himself near the front in this battle as he was wont to do. He spent 6 September reconnoitering the field and then decided on a frontal assault against the Great Redoubt after first seizing the town of Borodino. His trusted cavalry commander Davout suggested taking 40,000 cavalry in a great sweep around the Russian left flank, but Napoleon demurred: it would take away too many men and the horses were really in no condition for such a move. Having made this decision, Napoleon spent an uneasy night, worrying about the possibility of yet another Russian withdrawal, the news of a major defeat of his forces at Salamanca in Spain, and his own physical problems.

The battle opened with a French artillery barrage at 0600. Napoleon hoped that this would loosen up the defense sufficiently for his

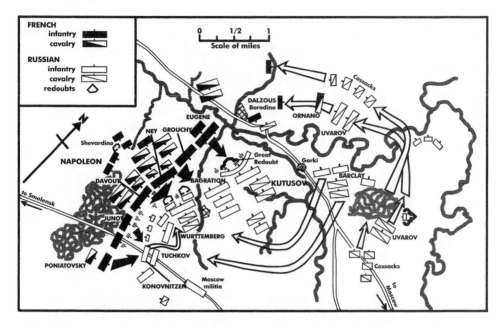

cavalry to charge. That would force the Russian infantry into defensive squares, which would make them easier targets for the light artillery that advanced with the cavalry. After pulverizing the squares, the infantry should take the ground, and the cavalry reserves should provoke a rout. That was the plan, but the Russians proved remarkably uncooperative. Although within an hour the French forces captured the towns anchoring both flanks, the Russians refused to be dismayed. The Great Redoubt proved unassailable, and the French moved their men from Borodino, on the north bank of the Kalatsha, across the river to support the attack. That move convinced Kutusov that his right flank would not be turned, so he rapidly transferred troops from that flank to the fighting around Utitsa on his left flank.

All along the front, the French made progress, but it was slow and costly. The Russians stubbornly defended their smaller redoubts in the center, and the arrival of Russians from the right to the left flank forced the French to withdraw temporarily from Utitsa. At several points during the day, a commitment of reserves at a particular point would have carried the day, but oddly Napoleon refused to commit the Old Guard, the core of veterans upon whom he had always depended for the killing blow in the past. That refusal probably cost him the major victory he desired. By midday the Russians were slowly being pushed back, but Kutusov threw his Cossacks and 5,000 other cavalry at Borodino, now only lightly held. That move stopped a French offensive, but, after the town was regained, the storming of the Great Redoubt recommenced. The pressure of the infantry assault on the front so occupied the Russians that they failed to see until too late the flanking cavalry attack that entered the rear of the Redoubt and killed all the defenders.

Napoleon committed his cavalry reserves, hoping the loss of the Redoubt would break Russian morale, but a well-timed Russian spoiling attack with their own cavalry covered the measured Russian withdrawal. Napoleon now held the lines that the Russians had defended all day, and the enemy was retreating from before him, but he was amazed when they stopped at a ridgeline immediately to the rear and prepared themselves for more fighting. The sun was setting, so Napoleon decided to stand pat. He later wrote in his memoirs, "The most terrible of all my battles was the one before Moscow. The French showed themselves worthy of victory, but the Russians showed themselves worthy of being invincible" (Markham, *Napoleon*, p. 194).

Results

Kutusov decided against testing that invincibility, and withdrew his army in the darkness. The battle at Borodino cost both sides unusually high numbers of casualties: the French lost 30,000 dead and wounded, the Russians 44,000. Only a few hundred Russians were taken prisoner. It was the most expensive day, in terms of human life, of any battle in the nineteenth century. Among the French casualties were forty-seven generals and thirty-two staff officers; the Russian losses were much the same.

Kutusov, before that withdrawal, held a council in the town of Gorky and informed his subordinates that he would not fight for Moscow, but withdraw past the city. This he did, as did almost all the inhabitants. When French forces entered Moscow on 14 September, the city was empty but for a few prisoners escaping from jails. Those prisoners almost certainly included some disguised Russian soldiers, whose duty it was to deny the religious center of Russia to the French, just as supplies had been denied them ever since they crossed out of Poland. Within a matter of hours, much of the city was ablaze, including the Kremlin. Within 4 days, little of the city remained. The French emperor sent messages demanding surrender of the country, but Czar Alexander in St. Petersburg did not respond. Soon, the Russian winter approached.

Unable to stay in the smoking ruins of Moscow, Napoleon ordered his men back to Poland. He has been criticized for pressing his conquest past Smolensk and for not wintering there, but his supply lines were too long even at that point, and the scorched earth meant that he could not live off the land. No sooner had he turned around from Moscow than the Russians did likewise, and the harassment started immediately. Not a day went by that Russian cavalry and Cossacks did not pick off stragglers or entire units separated from the main body. The winter hit early and then teasingly warmed sufficiently for the Beresina River to uncharacteristically remain unfrozen. That meant that the French had to cross the frigid river across two hastily constructed bridges, but possibly 10,000 soldiers and camp followers died at Cossack hands when the bridges collapsed and left them stranded.

Napoleon marched for the French-held city of Vilna, capital of Lithuania, but again the winter bore down on his men. Some accounts place the temperature as low as –32 degrees centigrade. Reports reached Napoleon that a coup against his regime had just been suppressed, the plotters claiming that he had died in Russia. To reestablish his authority and quell such rumors, he abandoned his army and made haste for Paris, arriving there 18 December. The final remnants of his army crossed the Nieman River back into Poland 4 days earlier; they numbered between 5,000 and 13,000 men of the original huge force that had crossed the river eastward 6 months earlier.

Borodino marked the beginning of the end for Napoleon. His trademark aggressiveness and surprise were not apparent on 7 September and would show themselves only on rare occasion afterward. His arrival in Paris quashed any nascent plots against him, and he had another army in the works by the time word of the disaster in Russia reached France. His army was now young and untrained, with only a few veterans transferred from the Spanish theater to stiffen the ranks. The blow to his prestige inspired the nations that he had so long dominated to rise up and join forces against him, and the following October at Leipzig he would be defeated by that newly formed coalition. Too many enemies and too few troops spelled his doom.

The Russians rightly venerate the battle at Borodino, but even more so feel secure in the complicity of Nature in defending Russia. Napoleon failed to learn the lesson winter had taught to King Charles XII of Sweden, just as Adolph Hitler failed to learn the same lesson 130 years later. However, 1812 seems the anniversary that the Russians recall most, perhaps because the world can appreciate the victory as well via Leo Tolstoy's *War and Peace* and Pyotr Tchaikovsky's *1812 Overture*. Thus, "It is quite possible that the French retreat from Moscow is the best-known military disaster in recorded human history. The scale is epic, the suffering incalculable, the outcome catastrophic" (Chandler, *On the Napoleonic Wars*, p. 205).

References: Cate, Curtis. *The War of Two Emperors*. New York: Random House, 1984; Chandler, David. *The Campaigns of Napoleon*. New York: Macmillan, 1966; Chandler, David. *On the Napoleonic Wars*. London: Greenhill Books, 1994; Palmer, Alan. *Napoleon in Russia*. New York: Simon & Schuster, 1967; Tarle, Eugene. *Napoleon's Invasion of Russia in 1812*. New York: Farrar, Straus & Giroux, 1971.

LEIPZIG (BATTLE OF THE NATIONS)
16–18 October 1813

FORCES ENGAGED

Allied: 57,000 Prussians (Army of Silesia). Commander: Field Marshal Gebhard von Blücher. 160,000 Austrians and Russians (Army of Bohemia). Commander: Prince Karl von Schwarzenberg. 65,000 Swedes and Russians (Army of the North). Commander: Crown Prince Jean-Baptiste Bernadotte.

French: 160,000 men. Commander: Emperor Napoleon Bonaparte.

IMPORTANCE

The battle at Leipzig marked the beginning of true European cooperation against Napoleon.

Allied victory broke his power, leading to the invasion of France and Napoleon's abdication the following year.

Historical Setting

After Napoleon's disastrous retreat from Russia at the end of 1812, during which he lost the bulk of the half-million-soldier army with which he invaded, no one in Europe expected him to recover so quickly. He reached Paris well before the news of the Russian fiasco and was able to immediately build another army by robbing future conscription rolls. That meant that most of the enrollees in the new *Grande Armée* were barely of military age, but they were nonetheless enthusiastic. Napoleon transferred some veterans out of Spain to stiffen the ranks with experienced fighters and then marched east toward the countries that he had long dominated and who were now organizing against him.

As Napoleon previously had conquered one European country after another, he had forced them into alliance with him. In the wake of the Russian campaign, many of those countries withdrew from their compacts. Although that weakened Napoleon's hold on northern and eastern Europe, he needed to fear his former allies only if they combined. In early 1813, that seemed somewhat doubtful, as Russia, Prussia, Austria, and a few German principalities such as Saxony eyed each other with suspicion. They looked past the immediate danger of Napoleon's new army to which power might try to fill the vacuum left by the French emperor's demise, and that fear of the future almost stopped any short-term cooperation. The primary figure attempting to coordinate an anti-French alliance was Austrian Foreign Minister Karl von Metternich. He had held his post since 1807 and had brokered a marriage between Napoleon and Marie-Louise, daughter of Austria's Emperor Francis I. In 1813, however, to bring Napoleon down, Metternich was eager to subvert the alliance that he had arranged. Convincing Russia, Prussia, and the other European powers to agree was a slow process. Still, in

March, he organized the Sixth Coalition: Austria, Prussia, Russia, Sweden, and Great Britain. Soon 100,000 men were in position between Dresden and Magdeburg.

Napoleon planned to reconquer these enemies in the same way he had conquered them in the first place, by attacking each separately before they could join and present him with overwhelming numbers. He had two major problems to overcome, however. The first was the inexperience of most of his army; the second was the lack of cavalry, most of which had perished in Russia. Without the cavalry, the gathering of intelligence was severely curtailed, and thus his ability to locate enemy forces and defeat them in detail was hampered. Still, he was active in late spring and summer 1813.

On 2 May, Napoleon defeated a Prussian force outside Leipzig at Lützen, but the lack of cavalry meant that he was unaware of an enemy force on his flank until they attacked. He beat them back and occupied Leipzig, but failed to win decisively. The French quickly marched on Dresden and captured that city and then fought the Russians nearby at Bautzen on 20–21 May. Again Napoleon drove his enemy from the field, but again was unable to destroy them. In the two battles combined, both sides lost about 38,000 men each. Soon Napoleon learned of large armies marching on his position from north, south, and east, so he negotiated a truce on 4 June that lasted just over 2 months.

In that time, he continued to mass and resupply his forces, as did his enemies. Metternich met with Napoleon for 9 hours on 26 June in Dresden, but no negotiated peace settlement could be reached. Metternich offered a lasting peace on the basis of Napoleon ceding almost all the territory he had captured outside France's natural borders. That would mean giving up the desired French border of the Rhine River, as well as French conquests in Italy and Spain. Napoleon, not surprisingly, refused. Metternich later claimed that, to brand Napoleon as the aggressor, he made a reasonable offer that he knew would not be accepted. Napoleon knew he could not accept such an offer and remain emperor of France because his people would not allow their European empire to be taken away from them without a fight. By the time the truce ended on 16 August, both sides had amassed immense forces.

The Battle

Napoleon had 300,000 men in Germany, but he placed a corps in a defensive position at the port city of Hamburg to threaten the Prussian rear and a corps at Dresden (southeast of Leipzig) near the Bohemian (Czech) border. In standard Napoleonic fashion, he had his remaining units spread out to live off the land as much as possible, but near enough together to support one another in case of attack. The allies decided that the best strategy would be to harry Napoleon's subordinates, defeating them as often as possible while avoiding a major battle until overwhelming forces could be arrayed against him.

This they proceeded to do: Swedish Crown Prince Bernadotte (a former marshal of Napoleon) defeated Napoleon's Marshal Oudinot at Grossbeeren, south of Berlin, on 23 August; Prussia's Marshall Gebhard von Blücher beat Marshal Macdonald at Katzbach on 26 August. The enemy being in too many places at once, Napoleon exhausted himself and his men marching and countermarching to aid his subordinates. When he heard of an Austrian attack on Dresden, he forced his young army on yet another rapid move. He beat back the assault, but his worn out troops could not follow up the victory. More such battles took place in September and early October, and then the French withdrew back to Leipzig before allied pressure on all fronts.

On 15 October, Napoleon turned to face Blücher's advancing Prussians from the north, but soon had to face about and deal with the larger Austrian Army of Bohemia approaching from the south. The Army of Bohemia numbered

160,000 Austrians and Russians commanded by Prince Karl von Schwarzenberg. When day broke on 16 October 1813, the field upon which Napoleon had chosen to deploy his men was covered with mist. Both sides had massed artillery, and that weapon did the most damage. The village of Wachau was the scene of most of the fighting, and it changed hands three times during the course of the day. By noon, Prince Karl's troops held the town, and then Napoleon launched his own attack. The land across which the armies fought was crossed by a number of streams, marshes, and woods and was perfect for defense. Napoleon, however, wanted to break the Austro-Russian line with massed artillery and then turn left and roll up the allied armies arrayed in a semicircle to the east of Leipzig. Early in the afternoon, he began pummeling the Austro-Russian force with his artillery. After an hour, he ordered his cavalry under Marshal Murat to attack. Murat's 10,000 men easily pushed back the first enemy troops they encountered, but Russian Czar Alexander quickly ordered his reserves to shift to the southern flank. When they arrived, the French cavalry was exhausted, and the Russian cavalry drove them off the field, restoring the Army of Bohemia's lines.

As Napoleon attempted to break through in the south, he held the northern flank with minimal force. Marshal Marmont defended the town of Mockern against Blücher's Prussians in a bitterly fought struggle. Neither Prussian nor French soldiers showed any mercy, and few prisoners were taken by either side. Marmont held the town most of the day, but in the afternoon a chance Prussian cannonball found a French ammunition wagon and the explosion not only demoralized the French troops but wounded Marmont so badly that he had to be evacuated. By day's end, the Prussians were in possession of the ruins of Mockern.

When the sun set on 16 October, Napoleon had failed to break through the Army of Bohemia and found himself in danger of losing Leipzig to the Prussians. On the next day,

however, little fighting took place. Both sides received reinforcement, however, so the battle was merely delayed. For the allies, the Swedes of Crown Prince Jean-Baptiste Bernadotte finally arrived. Had he made haste and been available on 16 October, the numbers may well have been sufficient for the northern French flank to have been overwhelmed and Napoleon trapped. His arrival, however, boosted the allied armies to 300,000 men and almost 1,500 cannon. After a halfhearted attempt at opening negotiations, Napoleon prepared to stage a fighting withdrawal. On 18 October, fighting was once again intense, and he pulled his forces back into Leipzig after a unit of Saxons under French command defected to the Prussians. That night, he ordered his men to retreat westward down the only road available, through the town of Lindenau, where the only available stone bridge across the Elster River was located. It was very narrow, however, and a bottleneck quickly formed. Napoleon ordered a force of 30,000 to remain as a rear guard, but they were unable to retreat across the Elster because of the premature destruction of the bridge. Many French troops died on the bridge or in attempts to swim across the river, and the rear guard was annihilated.

Results

Napoleon's star, already sinking after the Russian campaign of 1812, finally set at Leipzig. Going into battle with an army less than adequately trained hurt him badly, and the loss of more than 60,000 dead, wounded, and prisoners reduced his force to 100,000 as he retreated toward France. Harassment and desertion whittled that number down to 60,000 by the time he had reached Paris. He still held the throne, but it was only a matter of time before he was forced to step down. The allies, although they also lost about 60,000 men, could better afford such casualties. They also picked up more allies. Bavaria abandoned Napoleon on 18 October, and the Netherlands as well as the collection of principalities that Napoleon had organized into the Confederation of the Rhine both rebelled against his rule in November. On 8 November, the allies once again offered a peace settlement returning France to borders behind the Alps and well back from the Rhine, and foolishly Napoleon rejected the offer. Therefore, on 21 December 1813, the allied armies crossed the Rhine and invaded France. During the first 3 months of 1814, a string of battles was fought across northern France, climaxing in the battle for Paris on 30 March. Napoleon abdicated unconditionally on 11 April and was exiled to the small island of Elba in the Mediterranean.

Napoleon had shown in those battles of early 1814 his traditional abilities to maneuver and win, but each battle depleted his already small forces. After Leipzig, it was a numbers game he could not win. Had he played his cards differently at Leipzig, however, the battle's outcome could have been altered. Instead of leaving thousands of men defending Hamburg and Dresden, a concentration of forces could have given him the strength he needed to win. Marmont's force holding the northern flank against the Prussians was woefully small, and with a greater attacking force against the Army of Bohemia in the south he might have broken through and won the battle. As stated earlier, the allies were cooperating but mutually suspicious; a defeat at Leipzig may have crumbled the united front and given Napoleon much more bargaining power.

The allied victory, however, strengthened Metternich's hand and the result, in 1815, was the Concert of Europe, dedicated to maintaining a balance of power in Europe. That cooperative effort kept European countries from gaining too much individual power and kept them from fighting each other until the Crimean War in 1854. Not until the 1880s did that balance of power begin to fall apart with the ambitions of Kaiser Wilhelm in Germany. The victory at Leipzig not only proved that Napoleon could and would be beaten, but that

European nations could and would profitably cooperate.

References: Barnett, Correlli. *Bonaparte.* New York: Hill & Wang, 1978; Chandler, David. *The Campaigns of Napoleon.* New York: Macmillan, 1966; Lachouque, Henry. *Napoleon's Battles.* Translated by Roy Monkcom. New York: E. P. Dutton, 1967; Lawford, James. *Napoleon: The Last Campaigns, 1813–15.* New York: Crown, 1977; Markham, Felix. *Napoleon.* New York: New American Library, 1963.

WATERLOO
18 June 1815

FORCES ENGAGED

Anglo-Dutch: 50,000 infantry, 12,500 cavalry, and 156 guns. Commander: Field Marshal Arthur Wellesley, the duke of Wellington.

Prussian: 61,000 men. Commander: Field Marshal Prince Gebhard von Blücher.

French: 49,000 infantry, 15,570 cavalry, and 246 guns. Commander: Napoleon Bonaparte.

IMPORTANCE

Napoleon's defeat ended his remarkable career and began four decades of European peace.

Historical Setting

Although Napoleon fought brilliantly in defense of France after his defeat at Leipzig in 1814, he was too badly outnumbered to stay in power. The victorious allied powers of Austria, Britain, Prussia, and Russia restored the French monarchy by placing Louis XVIII on the throne and removed Napoleon from the scene by exiling him to the small island of Elba in the Mediterranean. Louis immediately began to undo many of the reforms instituted by the French Revolution and Napoleon, and that made him immediately unpopular with the French population. Not surprisingly, Napoleon was encouraged to hear this and, taking advantage of the temporary absence of his keeper, stole a boat and sailed to France, arriving 1 March 1815.

The next few weeks were remarkable, as thousands of men flocked to his banner. Louis sent out armies to stop him, and they all defected to their emperor. Napoleon had not fired a shot, but by his sheer force of personality was re-creating another army. Louis soon realized the danger and on 18 March fled for England. Napoleon reassumed the throne the next day.

In Vienna, the allied nations that had exiled the French leader had been squabbling over how to run Europe, but news of Napoleon's return galvanized them into unity and action. Burying their differences, at least temporarily, they refused Napoleon's offer of peace and collectively swore to bring him down once again. This they could do because among them the four countries could field 500,000 men, but in March the troops were scattered across the Continent, and it would take time to gather them together. A separation of enemy forces had been Napoleon's favorite situation, for he was a master at gaining the central position and then dividing and conquering. He quickly moved to defeat the two closest armies, a Prussian army under Field Marshal Prince Gebhard von Blücher and an Anglo-Dutch army under Field Marshal Arthur Wellesley, the duke of Wellington. Napoleon believed that he could beat them separately. After having done so, he would be able to negotiate with Austria and Russia.

Most of the men that marched with Napoleon in the early summer of 1815 were veterans of his *Grande Armée,* but many of the veterans of his final campaigns the previous year had been youths. Still, the old enthusiasm was there and Napoleon did not hesitate. Although he gathered together some 400,000 soldiers, he was forced to divide them across France to guard against early movements by his enemies as well as to suppress the occasional royalist uprising, garrison forts, and provide protection for his supply lines. Thus, when he marched with the Army of the North toward Belgium he had less than 100,000 men.

Napoleon's objective was the frontier city of Charleroi. It lay at a junction of roads running toward Brussels, where Wellington had his headquarters, and toward Namur, where Blücher had his. From Charleroi, Napoleon could then attack either force and, by doing so, drive each back upon its lines of communication, which would take them farther from each other. Napoleon was also a master of deception, and he once again managed to keep his whereabouts a secret from his enemies until it was too late. He arrived at Charleroi and seized the town on 15 June. The English and Prussians were unaware he had even left Paris. The Prussians who held the town indeed fell back eastward toward Namur, but Blücher marched to make a stand at Sombreffe. Napoleon, upon capturing Charleroi, immediately sent a division up both roads to establish contact with his opponents and give him the necessary intelligence as to which to attack first.

The Battle

To truly separate his enemies, Napoleon had to drive Blücher past Sombreffe toward Namur and not allow Wellington, to the north, closer than Quatre-Bras, for the final road linking the two armies passed through those towns. Napoleon sent Marshal Ney to Quatre-Bras on 16 June, but apparently with such vague orders that Ney did not feel compelled to seize the crossroad town in any hurry. Thus, his 25,000 men were held at bay most of the day by a British brigade as Wellington quickly brought men up in support.

At the same time, Napoleon led about 77,000 men up the Charleroi-Sombreffe road. On the way, he encountered 88,000 Prussians at Ligny. He drove them back, but at this point committed his first error. Assuming that Ney had quickly fulfilled his mission, Napoleon sent orders for him to come down the road from Quatre-Bras and fall on the Prussian flank. Such a west-to-east movement would have either crushed Blücher's army or at least driven it east-

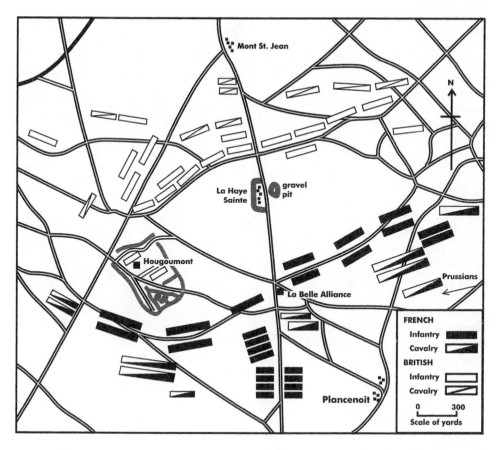

ward according to plan. Assuming that would be done, Napoleon did not launch a serious pursuit himself. Thus, he did not realize that, instead of falling back to the east, Blücher withdrew northward, along a smaller road parallel to Wellington's line of march. Not until the following morning did Napoleon send a force in pursuit, and they went in the wrong direction for some time before learning of the Prussians' real whereabouts at the town of Wavre. The pursuit force under Marshal Emmanuel de Grouchy wheeled left and marched for the Prussians, attacking their rear guard halfheartedly on 18 June, while Napoleon was fighting for his life several miles to the west.

Napoleon spent 17 June marching toward Quatre-Bras, linking his force with Ney's and then moving north up the road toward Brus-

sels. Wellington had abandoned Quatre-Bras the night before and established a position 2 to 3 miles south of the village of Waterloo. Napoleon's advance was hampered by a downpour, which also negated most of his intelligence gathering. Thus, when he approached Wellington's position, he did not launch an immediate attack, but waited until 18 June to get a better view of the field and to allow it to dry out so his cavalry and artillery could better operate. It did not dry sufficiently for either to act as he hoped, so around noon he opened the battle by launching a division under his brother Jerome toward a British position on the French left, the farm of Hougoumont. This was intended to draw in Wellington's reserves, after which Napoleon would launch his major assault at the British center.

Adolf Northen, "Prussian Troops Storm the Village of Plancenoit during the Battle of Waterloo." Oil on canvas. Kunsthalle, Hamburg, Germany. (Erich Lessing/Art Resource, New York)

Wellington deployed his army well. It consisted of about 66,000 men, of whom 31,000 were British and the remainder made up of allied troops contributed by the Dutch or some of the German principalities. Centered just in front of the village of Mont St. Jean, he anchored the British right at Hougoumont and stretched his forces along a west-to-east line behind the villages of La Haye Sainte, Papelotte, and Smohain. Only a screen of men were visible to the French because Wellington, as was his wont, placed the bulk of his force on the reverse of a long ridge. Having seen Wellington do that before in Spain was one reason that Ney hesitated before assaulting Quatre-Bras.

Jerome's assault on Hougoumont was stymied by an impressive British defense mounted by the Scots Guards and Coldstream Guards, aided by some allied troops from Nassau and Hanover. Jerome's attack was intended to be a diversion, but he pressed it too hard and engaged the left wing of the French army rather than drawing out the British reserves. Still unaware of the strength of Wellington's force, Napoleon decided to launch his main assault following a half-hour artillery barrage that opened at 1330. It had little effect because of Wellington's placement of his troops behind the ridgeline, not only out of the line of sight but also the line of fire. As this bombardment was taking place, observers in the French headquarters noticed movement far to the east. Identifying it as an advancing army, Napoleon assumed it was Grouchy returning from his pursuit. Instead, it was the advance guard of Blücher's Prussians. Napoleon immediately sent off a message for Grouchy to strike Blücher's force from the rear, but that message could not possibly reach him in time to affect the outcome at Waterloo.

Convinced that he could drive Wellington away before the Prussians arrived, Napoleon sent in his infantry at 1400. Slowed by the muddy ground, they were thrown back by spirited British counterattacks. A follow-up cavalry assault failed to break the British, whose infantry formed into squares and beat back repeated attacks. Across the open ground before the ridgeline, the battle raged for 3 hours with neither side gaining the upper hand. At 1630, the Prussians struck the French right flank, and Napoleon was forced to weaken his attack in the center to deal with the new threat. Marshal Ney led a massive cavalry charge between Hougoumont and the central village of La Haye Sainte, but, unsupported (until too late) by infantry, the cavalry were slaughtered.

The French finally managed to secure La Haye Saint at high cost, and for a moment the battle hung in the balance. Ney called for reinforcements to press his hard-won success, but the only reserves available were the Imperial Guard. Napoleon had in the past committed them last in order to allow them the killing blow in numerous battles, but here he refused to send them into battle. Unable to press on with his shattered cavalry force, Ney could not keep up the pressure on Wellington's center, which was being reinforced. Wellington, seeing Ney's predicament, finally played his trump card. Calling up the infantry and cavalry that had hidden themselves all day long on the reverse of the ridge, he ordered them to sweep down onto the field. That charge, coupled with the increasing pressure brought by Blücher's army, broke the French line. When the Imperial Guard was finally committed at 1900 to save the day rather than finish off a broken foe, they were too little and too late. When they too broke, the sight of the heretofore unbeaten Guard in flight was too much for the rest of the French army. Only a handful of men stood fast to cover Napoleon's escape. Called upon to give themselves up, the reply was, "The Guard dies, but never surrenders."

Results

The French army collapsed at the end of the day, as did Napoleon's chance of retaining power. Wellington's British and allied forces had lost approximately 15,000 casualties; the Prussians suffered another 7,000. The French army, however, lost at least 30,000, of whom about 7,000 were prisoners of war.

Napoleon made a feeble attempt to keep his throne, but abdicated on 21 June 1815. Less than a month later, he was placed aboard a British warship and taken to the tiny Atlantic island of St. Helena, roughly halfway between Africa and South America. From there he would be unable to sail back to France as he had done from Elba. The new French government, under the restored monarch Louis XVIII, signed the Treaty of Paris in November, by which France ceded more land and returned to the borders that France had originally held when the French Revolution began in 1789. The Quadruple Alliance, or Concert of Europe, made up of Britain, Austria, Russia, and Prussia, agreed that they would enforce the treaty. This made them, for all practical purposes, the police of Europe for the next half century.

Had Napoleon succeeded at Waterloo, had Blücher retreated east instead of north, had the rain not fallen so hard on 17 June, what may have happened? True, with Prussian and British armies out of the way, the Austrians and Russians may well have negotiated a peace settlement. Whether that would have ended the Napoleonic Wars is doubtful, however, because Napoleon never seemed to be able to remain passive. Obsessed as he was, another coalition certainly would have formed against him and ground down his army as they had done at Leipzig and afterward in 1814. Had he been content to rule peacefully, however, the reforms he instituted as emperor would have had a much longer life, and the revolutions that France suffered in 1830 and 1834 would probably not have happened. Then again, with the taste of democracy that the French enjoyed before the wars, perhaps they would not have suffered another ruling family to govern them, to exchange the Bourbons for the Bonapartes. With Napoleon peacefully in power, would the

Concert of Europe have managed the balance of power and kept Europe out of war for four decades? It is probably best that Napoleon ended his career when he did, leaving France a legacy of greatness it has not enjoyed since.

References: Brett-James, Antony. *The Hundred Days.* New York: St. Martin's Press, 1964; Brooke, Archibald. *Napoleon and Waterloo,* 2 vols. Freeport, NY: Books for Libraries Press, 1971; Chandler, David. *Waterloo: The Hundred Days.* New York: Macmillan, 1980; Creasy, Edward S. *Fifteen Decisive Battles of the World.* New York: Harper, 1851; Fuller, J. F. C. *A Military History of the Western World,* vol. 2. New York: Funk & Wagnalls, 1955.

AYACUCHO
9 December 1824

FORCES ENGAGED
South American: 5,780 men. Commander: Antonio José de Sucre.
Spanish: 9,310 men. Commander: José de La Serna.

IMPORTANCE
This last major battle of the revolution in South America marked the end of Spanish colonial rule on the continent.

Historical Setting

Since the voyage of Christopher Columbus in 1492, Spain had enjoyed dominance over Central and South America. Other than the Portuguese colony of Brazil, all of Latin America was exploited by Spain for its natural wealth. Until the defeat of the Spanish Armada in 1588, the Spanish kings had grown amazingly wealthy on the riches of the Americas with no competition at all; after that time, they still maintained a stranglehold on the trade with the colonies. Not until the rise of British and French maritime power in the seventeenth century, dis-

played in the Caribbean and Gulf of Mexico via piracy, did any outside nation have the chance to enter Latin American markets. Although Spanish economic dominance remained, it dwindled through the eighteenth century, reflecting the relative shifts in international power displayed by Spain and Britain.

In the Americas, a power struggle was going on within the Spanish sphere. The conflict was between the creoles (those of pure Spanish blood, but born in the colonies) and the gachupines (officials sent over from Spain to watch out for royal interests). As the creoles engaged in increasingly profitable trade with other European nations, they also wanted to exercise greater local political control and they chafed at the meddling of the gachupines. That sense of independence was enhanced by the introduction into Latin America of the writings of Enlightenment philosophers, just as those works influenced the revolutionaries in the British colonies in North America. The growing discontent with official Spanish interference reached a head during the Napoleonic Wars.

Napoleon established his influence over Spain in the first years of the nineteenth century, but in 1808 that turned into complete control when King Ferdinand VII was removed from the throne and replaced by Joseph Bonaparte, Napoleon's brother. Although the Latin American colonies swore loyalty to Ferdinand, they reveled in their grater freedom of action, although attempts by some colonies to declare independence were suppressed by royalist garrisons. When Ferdinand was restored to the throne in 1814, he wanted to completely restore his power in the Western Hemisphere as well. Unknowing or uncaring of the attitudes of the creoles, he attempted to reestablish his authority and was prepared to use force.

The center of the independence movement in South America was the northwestern section, the Viceroyalty of Rio de la Plata, making up the modern countries of Peru, Venezuela, Ecuador, and Colombia. The leading revolutionary was Simón Bolívar, a native of Caracas, Venezuela. He fought under the command of Francisco de Miranda in an abortive revolt in 1810 and then led a successful invasion that captured Caracas in 1812. Bolívar established a short-lived dictatorship, but was forced to flee by royalist forces in 1814. He returned at the head of a force of European mercenaries in 1817, setting up a revolutionary government in Angostura (modern Ciudad Bolívar). In 1819, he led troops across the Andes into New Granada (Colombia) and fought Spanish royal forces at Boyacá. This victory, on 7 August 1819, marked the beginning of the end of Spanish colonial rule in South America. In the wake of this victory, the Republic of Colombia (which included modern Venezuela) was proclaimed, with Bolívar as president.

Bolívar went from strength to strength. Another victory over the royalists at Carabobo in the summer of 1821 confirmed the new republic's independence, and the following year Bolívar led troops into the district of Quito (Equador). Fighting alongside Bolívar was Antonio José de Sucre, also from Caracas, who became the primary military leader of the revolution when Bolívar began exercising more political power. In 1822, Bolívar met with José de San Martín, whose campaigns in the south had liberated Argentina and Chile. The two tried to cooperate on a plan to expel the final Spanish forces from Peru, but their personalities and visions of the future were incompatible. San Martín withdrew from the scene to leave Bolívar in control. In 1824, the revolutionaries launched the final offensive into the interior of Peru.

The Battle

On 6 August 1824, a cavalry battle was fought at Junín. No shots were fired in the 45-minute struggle; it was strictly the cold steel of sabers that was employed, and the revolutionaries emerged victorious. The commander of royalist forces, José de La Serna, withdrew his troops

farther into the interior of the country and began gathering as many men as he could, for he knew that the fate of his monarch's authority in South America rested on the outcome of the next battle. Sucre's forces came out of the battle with high morale, which translated into greater recruitment for his army as well as the ability to obtain much-needed supplies and equipment from local sources. The two armies parried for several months until the royalists ambushed Sucre's rear guard near the village of Corpahuayco on 3 December 1824. Alerted to the presence of the enemy, Sucre prepared for battle.

On the afternoon of 8 December, the two forces deployed on the pampa of Ayacucho, a small plain measuring some 1,300 yards in an east-west direction and 650 to 850 yards north-south. Along the eastern flank, the plateau ended in a series of gorges, whereas on the west it was bordered by hills. At the northern end of the plateau stood Condorqanquí Mountain. The battlefield was also bisected by a dry riverbed running north-south through the center of both armies. The name Ayacucho is from the native Quechua language meaning "dead corner," referring to a slaughter there during the early Spanish conquest. The royalist army actually contained very few Spaniards, only about 500, primarily the officers and noncommissioned officers. The bulk of the force was comprised of locals pressed into service or prisoners of war given their freedom in exchange for changing sides. Field commander Lieutenant General José Canterac deployed this force on the slopes of Condorqanquí. He positioned five infantry battalions in the center, flanked by another five on the left, across the riverbed, supported by three cavalry squadrons. On the right was more infantry with cavalry on the outer flank, with an elite halberdier unit just behind, commanded by Viceroy La Serna. The seven cannon available to the Spanish were held in reserve along with ten cavalry squadrons. The plan was to pin down the enemy forces with the flanks and then finish them off with the center.

Sucre deployed his army, the United Army for the Liberation of Peru, with three battalions of partisans (the Montoneros) on the left and four infantry battalions on the right. There really was no center, but five cavalry squadrons, which were soldiers from San Martín's southern army and commanded by an English mercenary, William Miller, were held back in reserve along with some infantry. The revolutionaries possessed but one cannon. The night before the battle, Sucre sent his band and a number of soldiers forward. The band played for the Spanish while the soldiers kept up a fairly regular fire into their camp; both kept the Spanish army awake all night and kept them from deploying early onto the plain.

After an exchange of greetings with comrades in each others' force, the battle commenced at 1000 on 9 December. The royalist left wing, on the far side of the riverbed, advanced first. Little cannon fire was evident, and the two forces on the east side of the battlefield closed with each other. The royalists suffered the most. On the western flank, however, more artillery support assisted the royalists in pushing the revolutionaries back, but Sucre committed some of his reserves and stabilized the line. Rather than press his early advantage on his left flank, Spanish General Canterac ordered his center forward, hoping that would encourage his faltering right flank. The advancing troops, coming down off the hillside, were unable to maintain their formation. As their line became extended, Sucre ordered Miller's cavalry to strike them before they could re-form on level ground. At the same time, he ordered his right flank to charge the unsuccessful Spanish left. The commander on the right, General Cordoba, "placed himself about fifteen yards in front of his division.... Having dismounted, he plunged his sword into the heart of his charger, and turning to the troops, exclaimed, 'There lies my last horse; I have now no means of escape, and we must fight it out together!' Then waving his hat above his head, he continued, 'Adelante, con paso de vencedores (on-

wards with the step of conquerors)'" (Miller, in *Famous Battles,* p. 88). Canterac led his reserves to that flank to bolster his wavering troops, but it was too late. The onslaught of rebel cavalry in the center and inspired infantry on the right was too much for the poorly trained and motivated royalist conscripts to stand. By 1300, the king's forces were in flight.

Results

The pursuit lasted until dark. Viceroy La Serna and 60 of his officers surrendered, and another 1,000 of his men were captured. All of his artillery fell into revolutionary hands, and about 1,800 of his men had been killed. Sucre's force had suffered the loss of 309 killed and 670 wounded. For his victory, Sucre was named "Grand Marshal of Ayacucho" by Bolívar. General Canterac signed the surrender documents on 10 December, ceding all the garrisons under his command. Commanders of two of his forts refused the order. General Olañeta in southern Peru established a terrorist force loyal to Spain, but Sucre defeated his troops at the battle of Tumusla the following April. That victory officially freed southern Peru, which was renamed Bolivia in honor of "The Liberator," Simón Bolívar. Sucre became the country's first president. The other recalcitrant force holed up in the port city of Callao under the command of Brigadier General José Ramón Rodil. His force of 400 did not surrender until the end of a siege that lasted just over a year.

The Spanish defeat at Ayacucho destroyed the last seriously organized Spanish force in South America. They had been losing control gradually since 1819, but Ayacucho was the coup de grâce. The tide of change had been swelling for too long for the Spanish to recover their former power and glory. Had King Ferdinand been willing to offer some serious concessions to local autonomy, he may have been able to maintain his colonies, perhaps in the form that Britain maintained its Commonwealth. Apparently his nature argued against

MONROE DOCTRINE

Although few in Spain missed Napoleon's rule in their country, the return of Ferdinand VII to the throne was also a matter of some concern. He was no benevolent despot, and his views on exercising his authority upset many in Spain just as they did in Latin America. In 1820, a revolution deposed him.

Other European monarchs had had their fill of revolutions, fearing that the principles of the American and French Revolutions could spread through Spain into their own countries. Thus, the collective powers of Europe under the auspices of Russia (via the Holy Alliance, which Czar Alexander I had established in 1815) moved to crush not only the Spanish revolt but also popular uprisings in Italy, Portugal, Naples, and Greece. The restored monarch of France, King Louis XVIII, sent his armies into Spain to restore Ferdinand's power, which they did by October 1823.

The Latin American independence movements were by this point in full swing, and the United States decided to recognize the sovereignty of the new governments and enter into relations with them. When the Holy Alliance offered to send troops to the Western Hemisphere to regain Spain's colonies, the United States had to decide what it would do should those foreign armies appear. President James Monroe, assisted by Secretary of State John Quincy Adams, developed a policy statement that has come to be called the Monroe Doctrine. In short, it warned the Europeans away from the Americas. In his annual message to Congress in December 1823, Monroe stated that any attempt by Spain or any other European country to establish or reestablish colonies in the Western Hemisphere would be considered by the United States "as dangerous to our peace and safety" and "the manifestation of an unfriendly disposition toward the United States" (Bailey, *A Diplomatic History of the American People,* p. 184). This statement applied not only to Latin America but also to possible Russian encroachment out of Alaska into the Oregon country.

Although this policy was viewed with either contempt or hilarity in the courts of European kings, the monarchies did not send troops. Ferdinand decided against asking for assistance, and the Russians, because of domestic problems, withdrew back into Alaska. The U.S. population viewed this as a victory for its diplomacy. In reality, it was Great Britain's power, not that of the United States, that kept the Europeans at bay. Even though Monroe had rejected a joint policy with the British, Britain feared losing its growing trade with the new Latin American countries, and so its navy stood solidly in the way of any attempt to restore Spanish colonies.

However, because the United States believed that its stand had cowed the Europeans, the Monroe Doctrine came to be the overriding policy governing relations with Latin America. From that time, the United States has considered itself the police of the hemisphere, to the consternation of practically every Latin American nation at one time or another since the 1820s.

---

such an option, but the occasion of his temporary removal from power because of a revolution in Spain (1820–1823) certainly gave the South Americans further incentive to break away from the homeland. Bolívar and San Martín became the founders of South American independence, but, unlike their counterparts in North America, they were unable to forge a unified country. Too many factions within South American politics, as well as the poor infrastructure that made communication and trade extremely slow, militated against any sort of single national government. Thus, most of the nations of both Central and South America date their existence from this time period.

Spain, once the mightiest nation in the world because of American riches, slid into mediocrity. Even a victory at Ayacucho probably would not have stopped that decline, but only postponed it. Of its far-flung empire, Spain retained only Cuba and Puerto Rico in the Western Hemisphere and the Philippines in the east. Spain remained a minor player in European politics, but after its defeat in 1898, Spain's last remaining colonies fell to the United States, who replaced it in the small club of world powers.

References: Adams, Jerome. *Latin American Heroes.* New York: Ballantine, 1991; Beals, Carleton. *Eagles of the Andes.* Philadelphia: Chilton Books, 1963; Johnson, John J. *Simón Bolívar and Spanish American Independence, 1783–1830.* Princeton, NJ: Van Nostrand, 1968; Markov, Walter. *Battles of World History.* New York: Hippocrene Books, 1979; Miller, William. "Ayacucho," in John Bettenbender and George Fleming, eds. *Famous Battles.* New York: Dell, 1970.

SAN JACINTO
21 April 1836

FORCES ENGAGED

Texan: 783 men. Commander: General Sam Houston.
Mexican: Approximately 1,500 men. Commander: President Antonio López de Santa Anna.

IMPORTANCE

Mexican defeat led directly to Texas' independence from Mexico, the dispute over which led to the U.S.-Mexican War 10 years later. The annexation of Texas by the United States was the first official acquisition of land in western North America, land over which the controversy concerning slavery led to the American Civil War.

Historical Setting

Mexico won its independence from Spain in the early 1820s and, desiring to have sufficient population in case of a return of Spanish armies, advertised in the United States for immigrants who could occupy the lightly populated north-eastern province of Texas. Spanish and then Mexican immigration to the area had been unsuccessful because of the aggressive Comanches, so American settlers could not only hold the ground against a potential Spanish invasion but could act as a buffer against the Comanches for the 4,000 Mexican settlers. American settlers led by Stephen F. Austin began arriving in 1823; by 1830, some 20,000 had moved to Texas. At that point, the Mexican government closed the borders, but over the next 3 years another 10,000 Americans entered Texas illegally, establishing a practice followed to this day (although from a different direction).

In 1833, General Antonio López de Santa Anna was elected president of Mexico, but a year later he rejected the constitution adopted in 1824 and declared himself dictator. Any Mexican province that complained of that action found its population slaughtered; the president believed that was the best example for the others. It worked. In Texas, however, the American immigrants were a different breed. They had been raised as followers of a constitution, the same one upon which the Mexican constitution of 1824 had been based. They had become Mexican citizens as a condition of receiving land grants in Texas and had sworn to uphold the constitution. Knowing that, Santa Anna sent word to the Texians, as they called themselves, that because they had failed to convert to Catholicism (as the terms of their land grants also had provided), they had forfeited their land and now must leave. When the Texians rejected the dictator's orders that violated the constitution that they had sworn to uphold, Santa Anna declared them in rebellion and began operations to slaughter them as he had any other rebels that opposed him.

Mexican forces entering Texas in late 1835 could not impose Santa Anna's will on the Texians. Mexican troops withdrew in the face of serious opposition at the town of Gonzales in October and then in December lost the main town of San Antonio a hundred miles to the west. A force of about 150 men remained in San Antonio through the winter of 1835–1836. In the meantime, a provisional government had been elected and Sam Houston had been appointed army commander. Houston was newly arrived from the United States and a close friend of U.S. President Andrew Jackson. Houston sent 26-year-old William Travis to San Antonio to remove the garrison so he could incorporate them into the army that he was trying to build. Once in San Antonio, Travis and local commander Jim Bowie decided not to withdraw, but to defend a ramshackle mission called the Alamo. It was in reality impossible to defend a position with such a large perimeter with as few men as they had. When Santa Anna arrived in late February 1836 with 4,000 to 6,000 men, the resulting 13-day siege and ensuing massacre was a forgone conclusion.

After the fall of the Alamo on 6 March, Santa Anna marched west looking for Houston's Army of Texas and terrorizing the countryside in the process. A second column of troops southeast of Santa Anna's force surrounded and slaughtered almost the entire 400-man command of James Fannin outside another mission at the town of Goliad. A handful of survivors escaped to Houston's force with the news. Houston's plan was to withdraw eastward, trading land for time, building and training a force as best he could. Throughout March and early April, Santa Anna followed along, unable to corner the Texians. Finally, in mid-April, things began to change. Houston learned that Santa Anna had detached himself from his main body of troops with a contingent of just over a thousand men in order to range ahead, looking for opportunities. When Houston learned of that action, and then discovered the actual location of Santa Anna's detachment, he placed himself in a position to fight.

The Battle

On 19 April, Houston established a camp for his baggage and for his sick and ailing and then set out with just under 800 men. They crossed swollen Vince's Bayou and marched east along the southern bank of a flooded tributary of the San Jacinto River called Buffalo Bayou. The next day, Houston and Santa Anna found each other and fought a light skirmish on a spot of open prairie in a bend of the fast-flowing San Jacinto. The sparring was inconclusive, and neither side tried to press the matter. Because Houston seemed to be trapped between two raging rivers and the Mexican force, Santa Anna was content to retire about three-quarters of a mile, hastily construct a semifortified camp of brush, packs, and saddlebags, and sit down to await reinforcements.

There was no possible escape for the Texians, so there was no hurry. The coup de grâce could be administered when the rest of the Mexican army came up. Meanwhile, Santa Anna was careful to place his camp just over a slight rise in the prairie so that it was protected from Houston's two six-pounder cannon, "the Twin Sisters." He ordered that his men should sleep on their weapons in battle formation and that a keen watch be kept. Then, satisfied with his dispositions, the supremely confident "Napoleon of the West" retired for the evening.

The next morning, 21 April, 500 reinforcements arrived, bringing the total Mexican strength to more than 1,500. The Mexican president's optimism soared. He outnumbered Houston's rabble nearly two to one and was in an easily defensible position. Today he would rest his men, and tomorrow he would successfully conclude his most satisfying campaign ever. Santa Anna sent orders to his men to stand down, and he retired to his tent for an afternoon siesta. His officers lounged under the trees sipping champagne and dozing. By four in the afternoon, the Mexican camp was silent.

By contrast, the Texian encampment was alive with furious, but relatively quiet, activity. The army readied itself to fight, and their commander at last was ready to let them. Houston then made the final preparations. Unknown to his men, he had dispatched Deaf Smith and six other scouts to destroy Vince's bridge, the only span over Vince's Bayou and the only practical access to their present location. This was done to prevent any further reinforcements from reaching Santa Anna, but it also cut off any realistic avenue of retreat for the Texians. Many times the soldiers had used the brave words "victory or death" and had even embroidered the sentiment on their only battle flag; but, when Vince's bridge collapsed into the bayou's swirling waters, the phrase literally became their destiny.

At 1500, the dirty, cold, hungry soldiers of the Army of Texas, all 783 of them, began to form up on the prairie in a line two ranks deep and more than 900 yards long. In the center floated their white and blue battle flag, and beside it rode General Houston. At 1600, he slowly trotted out so that all in the line could see him. Houston made no speech; instead, for a long moment, he was still, gazing intently at the rise that hid the Mexican camp from view. Then he drew his sword, pointed the way, and the army followed. In deadly silence the long line advanced, rifles leveled, while "the Twin Sisters" were forced up the slope with quiet curses. The crest neared: 800 yards, then 500, then the army was almost to it, and still there were no sounds of alarm from the Mexican camp. Incredibly, in what would prove to be one of the most fateful mistakes in military history, Santa Anna had neglected to throw out pickets or scouts. Not until the Texians reached the crest and stood a scant 200 yards away were they noticed by the sentries, and by then it was far too late.

The Mexican artillery boomed, but the shots sailed harmlessly high. The Texian band, three fifers and a drummer, screeched into life, and the long line descended at a trot upon the enemy, "the Twin Sisters" careening along in front. From out of nowhere, Deaf Smith appeared, galloping along the battle line shouting: "Vince's bridge is down! Fight for your lives! Vince's bridge is down!" Those who heard him realized that little hope of retreat now remained, and they drove grimly on. Then, at 80 yards or

so, it was first heard: what has become perhaps the most famous battle cry in history. From the left of the line, Colonel Sidney Sherman bellowed at the top of his lungs, "Remember the Alamo!" How could any Texan ever forget it? Among the attackers were seven survivors of the Goliad massacre and they added, "Remember Goliad!" The Spanish-speaking soldiers took up the cry, "*Recuerden el Alamo!*" and then all semblance of order dissolved. The Texians fired a great volley that swept clear the brush and saddlebag wall, and "the Twin Sisters," at point-blank range, blew it apart. Then the Texians threw themselves upon their disorganized enemies—literally with a vengeance.

The Mexican soldiers had desperately tried to form ranks to fight, but the Texians were too close and it all happened too fast. Mexican officers shouted frantic, conflicting orders at them. Santa Anna was seen "running about in the utmost excitement, wringing his hands and unable to give an order." And then came the terrible, accusing cry again: "Remember the Alamo!" This was not merely shouted to motivate the attackers but to remind the Mexicans what the result of defeat had been 6 weeks earlier in San Antonio.

It broke Mexican morale like a dry twig. As the Texians tore into them, many of the Mexican soldiers threw down their weapons and begged for mercy. They died. Most of the rest fled. Colonel Pedro Delgado, a staff officer, wrote: "I saw our men flying in small groups, terrified, and sheltering themselves behind large trees. I endeavored to force some of them to fight, but all efforts were in vain" (Delgado, *Mexican Account of the Battle of San Jacinto,* p. 10). The actual battle was over in less than 18 minutes. The shooting, clubbing, and stabbing went on for at least an hour, or until the Texians' thirst for vengeance and blood was sated. Though most of the Mexicans ran, there was no escape. The Texian cavalry cut down those who fled across the open prairie, while the vast majority of fugitives found themselves driven back against the San Jacinto. Many drowned trying to swim the muddy river, but most were

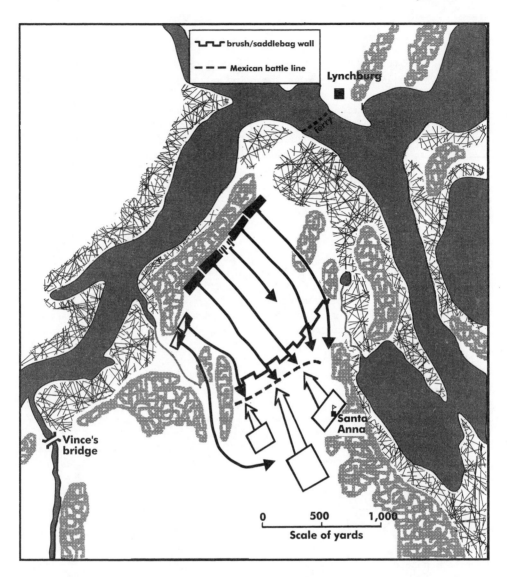

brush/saddlebag wall
Mexican battle line

Lynchburg

ferry

Santa Anna

Vince's bridge

0   500   1,000
Scale of yards

methodically slaughtered by riflemen who poured a relentless fire into the milling helpless mob. Not until late in the day were surrenders accepted.

Results

By the next morning, the extent of the Texian victory had become apparent. They had lost two killed, and another seven would soon die. There were 23 wounded, including Sam Houston. He

had had two horses killed under him and had taken a musket ball in his ankle. Mexican losses were staggering—630 lay dead on the field, including one general, four colonels, two lieutenant colonels, five captains, and twelve lieutenants. Another 208 were wounded, and 730 were prisoners. The Mexican force had literally been erased. But the one man Houston wanted most had eluded death or capture. Santa Anna had fled just before his camp was overrun, and since nightfall Houston's scouts had been scouring

THE ANTAGONISTS

Born in Virginia in 1793, Sam Houston moved with his family to Tennessee. At the age of 15, he ran away from home to spend 3 years with the Cherokees, who made him a member of their tribe and named him "the Raven." During the War of 1812, Houston marched to Florida as a young lieutenant with Andrew Jackson's Creek campaign and was severely wounded at the battle of Horseshoe Bend. General Jackson, impressed with Houston's reckless gallantry, had him transported to his plantation, the Hermitage, and nursed back to health. From that time, Jackson and Houston were fast friends. With the general's patronage, Houston rose rapidly in politics, first becoming a member of Congress from Tennessee and then governor of the state. Most onlookers agreed that one day Houston would also be president.

But in 1829 disaster struck. Houston married young Eliza Allen, daughter of one of the richest families in Tennessee. For reasons still unknown, what should have been an advantageous match for both parties turned sour within months. Eliza went home to her parents, and Houston, after resigning as governor (because of the scandal involved), went to live with the Cherokees in Oklahoma, where he quickly earned an unwelcome new tribal name, "Big Drunk."

In 1832, Houston moved to Texas, became a Mexican citizen, and promptly fell in with the "War Party," those Texans who desired independence. Houston was immensely popular, and after San Jacinto he became the political colossus of the state. He was twice elected president of the Republic of Texas and became governor of the state, and he later served a long term as a U.S. senator from Texas. Along the way, he married again, raised a large family, and at the insistence of his new wife gave up drinking. She even talked him into joining a church. After he had been baptized in a creek, the minister told him: "Your sins are now all washed away." Supposedly, Houston looked into the creek and said: "God help the fish!"

Santa Anna, on the other hand, was by trade a career soldier. He had first gone to war as a 17-year-old lieutenant in the Spanish Royalist Army during the Mexican Revolution. Afterward, he changed sides and political alliances as frequently as he did medal-laden uniforms. He has been described by unsympathetic historians as a vain, egotistical, corrupt, opportunistic lover and opium addict. Others have described him as a charismatic speaker, personally charming and handsome, and frequently brave to the point of recklessness. Whatever his faults and strengths, there can be no denying that he was immensely popular with both the Mexican people and with the military and aristocracy who controlled the country. In 1829, he repelled a Spanish invasion, was hailed as his country's savior, used the publicity to springboard to the presidency in 1833, and the next year placed Mexico under his own style of military dictatorship.

After his humiliating defeat at San Jacinto, Santa Anna was released by the Texans in return for his promise to work for ratification of the peace treaty that he had signed (once back in Mexico he reneged on his agreement, and the Mexican Senate never approved the treaty), but he was deposed. In 1838, he helped blunt a French invasion of Mexico and in the fighting lost a leg. (The limb was given a full state funeral, and a monument was raised over the burial place.) Santa Anna promptly became acting president and, in 1841, led a conservative coup and seized the office full-time, only to be exiled in 1845 by a liberal. The outbreak of the Mexican-American War in 1846 saw Santa Anna return to power long enough to lead his country to ignominious defeat against Zachary Taylor and Winfield Scott.

ing the countryside for him. Unless he could be caught, the great victory would mean little because the Mexican army in Texas still outnumbered Houston's force by four to one. On 22 April, a Texian patrol brought in what they thought was just another dusty Mexican private, but when he was put with the other prisoners, some of the soldiers imprudently cried, *"Est el Presidente!"* It was indeed General Santa Anna, president of Mexico. Houston was at that moment lying under an oak tree, cursing his wounded ankle. But when he looked up and saw a prisoner being herded into his presence by what seemed to be half the camp, his mood brightened considerably.

Although most of the Texian army looked for the nearest hanging tree, Houston realized that Santa Anna's death would be counterproductive. A dead man's signature on a treaty recognizing Texas' independence would be useless. Houston sent Santa Anna under escort to the provisional government to negotiate such a treaty. Within a month, Santa Anna signed a treaty with the Republic of Texas; the treaty ended hostilities and withdrew the Mexican army south of the Rio Grande. Texas had its independence, and the men of the Alamo and Goliad were avenged. In the space of 18 minutes, Mexico had lost an area of land larger than either of the nations of Germany or France, and events were put into motion that within 12 years would cost Mexico one-third of its sovereign territory and push the United States "from sea to shining sea." Seldom in all of military history has more been accomplished in less time.

Although the Texans immediately applied for statehood, the U.S. Congress rejected the application. Northern members of Congress knew that Texas would enter the union as a state that allowed slavery, and in 1836 that was an extremely sensitive political subject. Texas therefore spent 9 years as an independent nation, recognized by and establishing diplomatic relations with the United States, Britain, France, and other European countries. As Texas seemed to be growing closer to Britain in the early

1840s, attitudes toward annexing Texas into the union began to soften. When James K. Polk was elected president in November 1844 on a campaign promise of annexing Texas, the northern Whig members of Congress (soon to be in the minority) negotiated a deal whereby Texas joined the union in 1845. The question of where Texas' border lay led to trouble, however. Santa Anna's treaty had awarded Texas the Rio Grande, from mouth to source, as its border. The Mexican government rejected the treaty, however, and claimed Texas' border to be the Nueces River, well to the north. That dispute ultimately led to war between the United States and Mexico in 1846.

The acquisition of Texas by the United States, and the war that followed, inflamed already hot passions about the nature of slavery in the United States. The viewpoint of the South, that slavery was, like almost all political issues, a matter of states' rights further drove a wedge between the southern and northern United States that led to civil war in 1861.

—*Allen Lee Hamilton*

References: Connor, Seymour, et al. *Battles of Texas.* Waco, TX: Texian Press, 1967; Delgado, Pedro. *Mexican Account of the Battle of San Jacinto.* Deepwater, TX: W. C. Day, 1919; Hardin, Steve. *Texian Iliad.* Austin: University of Texas Press, 1994; James, Marquis. *The Raven.* New York: Blue Ribbon Books, 1929; Pohl, James. *The Battle of San Jacinto.* Austin: Texas State Historical Association, 1989.

MEXICO CITY
19 August–14 September 1847

FORCES ENGAGED

United States: 7,200 troops. Commander: Lieutenant General Winfield Scott.

Mexican: Mexico City garrison of 16,000. Commander: General Antonio López de Santa Anna.

IMPORTANCE

American victory caused the collapse of the
Mexican government and the end of the war. In
the peace treaty, the United States acquired
northern Mexico and the dominant political
position in the Western Hemisphere.

Historical Setting

When Texans defeated the Mexican army of
President Antonio López de Santa Anna at San
Jacinto on 21 April 1836, the surrender document that Santa Anna signed designated the
border of the newly independent country, the
Republic of Texas, to be the Rio Grande. Although the Mexican government never ratified
the agreement that Santa Anna signed, the Texans continued to regard the Rio Grande from
mouth to source as the southern and western
borders of their country. For the following 9
years, Mexico never seriously tried to regain the
lost province, launching only the occasional raid
that accomplished nothing.

The country between the major settlement
of San Antonio and the Mexican town of Santa
Fe in modern New Mexico was a vast plain
populated by the Comanche tribe of American
Indians, one of the most warlike in all North
America. They had kept Spanish and Mexican
settlement out of their territory for a hundred
years. During the time of the Republic of Texas,
an expedition was dispatched through Comanche lands to capture Santa Fe and incorporate
it into Texas. It failed when its members were
defeated and captured just short of their goal,
but the Texans could lay a slim claim to the
intervening territory because they had crossed
it, whereas the Mexicans had not. The Mexican government claimed that the true border
between Mexico and Texas was the Nueces
River, which flowed about 200 miles through
south Texas into Matagorda Bay near modern
Corpus Christi. This was a fairly legitimate
claim, as there was virtually no Anglo Texan
settlement south of that river. However, there
was also virtually no Mexican settlement. It was
indeed a hostile country claimed by both, but
populated by neither.

When the United States agreed to annex
Texas into the union in 1845, the Texans made
it clear that the Rio Grande was the border they
claimed. Thus, that was the border accepted by
the United States when the annexation was
approved. This border dispute was the primary
incident that set off the war between the United
States and Mexico. Mexico at this point was
reluctantly willing to relinquish its claim to
Texas, but only if the Nueces was the recognized border. Any attempt by the Texans and
Americans to acquire the land between there
and the Rio Grande would be cause for war.

U.S. President James K. Polk was in the
process of settling a dispute with Great Britain
over the border between U.S. and British claims
in the Oregon country. Although Polk had
campaigned for the presidency in 1844 on the
slogan "54–40 or fight," he was willing to give
up that latitude as the northern border of U.S.
claims and settle on the 49th parallel. Certainly,
he assumed, if he could reach a diplomatic conclusion with Great Britain and avoid a war, he
should be able to do the same with Mexico.
Hence, Polk sent John Slidell to Mexico City with
an offer to buy the disputed area of Texas and, if
the Mexican government were in a selling mood,
buy all the land west to California on the Pacific. Slidell was never allowed to present the
$15 million offer; the Mexican authorities re-
fused even to accept his credentials.

To reinforce U.S. claims to the land south
of the Nueces, Polk dispatched Major General
Zachary Taylor with some 4,000 men to the
mouth of the Rio Grande. There Taylor began
to construct Fort Brown during the winter of
1845–1846. This action was viewed by the
Mexican government as an invasion, so they
sent orders to expel Taylor's force. Meanwhile,
Polk had been searching for justification to go
to war to claim all of Texas, but he had little to
go on. Slidell's rejection, while undiplomatic,
was hardly a cause for war. Neither were the
unpaid claims to Texan citizens for damages
suffered by the Mexican raids during the time
of the Republic. In April 1846, the Mexicans
gave him his justification. On 22 April, Mexi-

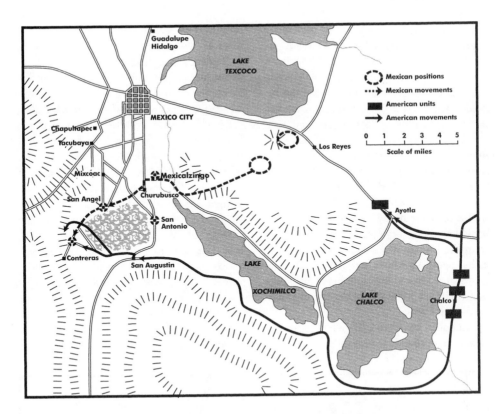

can cavalry had engaged, killed, and captured a force of sixty-four U.S. dragoons. Armed with this news, Polk sent a war message to Congress, telling them "American blood has been shed on American soil." Because of the dispute over the land, this was questionable, but Congress agreed and declared war.

Zachary Taylor spent the summer of 1846 gathering men and material and in September defeated Mexican forces north of the Rio Grande in battles at Palo Alto and Resaca de la Palma. He then crossed the river and marched on Monterrey, which he captured on 25 September. He wintered there and then in February 1847 defeated a larger Mexican army commanded by Santa Anna at Buena Vista. Santa Anna, disgraced after losing Texas, was back in power again. After his loss at Buena Vista, however, he retreated to Mexico City. Taylor was doing well, but in Polk's view he was doing too well. Knowing the U.S. propensity for elevating war heroes to the presidency,

Polk did not want to make Taylor, an avowed member of the rival Whig Party, into a candidate. So he sent senior army general Winfield Scott to take command in Mexico. Scott arrived in Tampico with an army of his own and joined most of Taylor's force to it. He proceeded to Vera Cruz, from whence he would march on the Mexican capital.

The Battle

Scott's force of 10,000 landed unopposed just south of Vera Cruz on 9 March 1847 and then marched to surround the city. With U.S. warships able to bombard offshore, and little hope of relief from inland, the Mexican garrison surrendered on 29 March. With a harbor in his hands with which to maintain a supply source, Scott turned inland. He wanted to get away from the coastal plain as soon as possible to avoid the yellow fever and malaria season, so his force marched into the interior highlands as soon as possible. On 18 April, they met a large and well-situated Mexican force under Santa Anna at Cerro Gordo. A flanking move through rugged terrain surprised the Mexican camp, and Santa Anna withdrew, leaving behind half of his 12,000 soldiers dead, wounded, or missing. Scott lost 63 at this battle, but sickness and harassment by guerrillas began lowering his numerical strength. To make matters worse, 3,000 volunteers had ended their enlistments and marched away to Vera Cruz.

Scott halted at Puebla in mid-May, ordering the garrisons that he had left behind to come up and receiving more reinforcements arriving from the United States. He stayed here until early August, by which time his army had regained strength and now numbered just under 11,000; he left 3,000 sick in the care of a small garrison at Puebla.

Supplied by foodstuffs that he acquired locally, Scott abandoned his line of communi-

cations. This was widely criticized; even the duke of Wellington, following the campaign in England, thought this move spelled Scott's doom. Scott's army entered the Valley of Mexico through an undefended pass and then descended on Mexico City. When he reached Lake Chalco, Scott sent a diversionary force up the main road toward the city and then marched the bulk of his force around the southern end of the lake and past the adjoining Lake Xochimilco. This put him on 18 August about 7 miles due south of the capital city and just south of a large volcanic wasteland called the *pedregal*. Scott's chief engineer, Captain Robert E. Lee, discovered a track across the pedregal, which the Mexicans assumed could not be traversed. This allowed the Mexican position at Contreras (on the southwest corner of the pedregal), held by 1,500 men, to be outflanked and virtually destroyed in a dawn attack on 20 August. This opened the roads leading north-

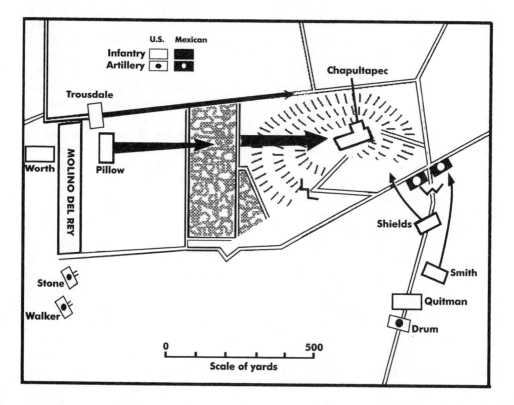

ward into Mexico City. Only a strong Mexican position before the Churubusco River stood in the way. Scott, however, did not hesitate. He quickly moved up the road from Contreras to Churubusco. The strongest point in the Mexican position was a convent defended by not only Mexican troops but the San Patricio force. These were Irish Americans who had deserted the U.S. army to fight for a Catholic country and receive land grants and citizenship in return. They put up a stout defense, for they well knew what their fate would be if they were captured. Captured they were, however, when overwhelmed by U.S. attackers and superior artillery. The remainder of the Mexican army stood their ground until a U.S. detachment forded the Churubusco River and began rolling up their flank, leading to a general withdrawal. Some critics say that, had the Americans followed hard on this retreat, Mexico City wound have fallen, but Scott's troops were exhausted by two battles in 2 days.

At this point, Nicholas Trist arrived. Trist, the second highest official in the U.S. State Department, was sent to negotiate a settlement. The Democratic U.S. Congress, which had declared war for Polk, had turned Whig in the elections of 1846, and they were not supportive of the war. Further, Scott was now the national hero and Polk realized that he too was a Whig. Polk sent Trist to end the fighting quickly by offering the same terms that Slidell had tried to offer 2 years earlier. Polk assumed that the continual defeats that the Mexican army had suffered had made the government more open to negotiations. Trist managed to negotiate an armistice on 23 August calling for a cessation of the fighting and for neither side to improve its position. Santa Anna signed but did not obey the agreement, so on the night of 7 September, Scott gathered his staff to plan the next action. Spies had informed Scott that a foundry at Molino del Rey was casting cannon, so this seemed a good target. It proved not only better defended than Scott had expected but also *not* producing cannon. In the most difficult fight

of the campaign, the Americans lost more than 700 killed and wounded. Occupation of Molino del Rey, however, gave Scott a strong base from which to launch an attack eastward on Chapultepec Castle, the strength of Mexico City's defenses and site of the military academy. Early on 13 September, the U.S. forces burst from the cover of a cypress grove and rushed up the hill to the base of Chapultepec's walls. After a delay in receiving scaling ladders, the soldiers finally forced their way over the walls. The fighting inside the castle was hand to hand, with military cadets as young as 13 years old defending their school and country. Their stubborn defense has enshrined them in Mexican folklore as *Los Niños Heroicos,* but they were too few to repel the assault.

U.S. flanking units kept any attempt at reinforcement at bay, and by late morning the U.S. soldiers were inside the city. By this time, Scott's force had lost more than 850 casualties compared with almost 3,000 lost by the Mexican army, but Santa Anna still commanded another 5,000 at Ciudadela fort and another 7,000 soldiers in various parts of the city. Although the Mexican forces still outnumbered Scott's two to one, Mexico City officials pleaded with Santa Anna to surrender rather than have the U.S. artillery destroy the city. Santa Anna took the rest of his army with him in the night to Guadalupe Hidalgo, a village just north of the city. Mexico City surrendered to Scott just before dawn on 14 September.

Results

With the capital in hand, Scott's first goal was to reopen his line of communications. Soon supplies and reinforcements were flowing inland from Vera Cruz. Scott's garrison at Puebla, now reinforced, beat back Santa Anna's last attempt at salvaging a victory. After Santa Anna's resignation, a new government was created that met with Nicholas Trist in Guadalupe Hidalgo. At this point, the face of the Western Hemisphere could have been radically altered if Trist

The storming of Chapultepec, 13 September 1847. (Archive Photos)

had been able to communicate quickly with Polk. Instead, communications between Mexico City and Washington took 6 to 8 weeks each way. Look at the timing of the messages. Trist reported the first Mexican rebuff of his offer on 23 July 1847; this reached Polk on 15 September. Polk wrote back on 6 October, ordering Trist to return. Polk had by this time decided to demand even more territory from Mexico when they saw fit to negotiate, but he merely told Trist to return to Washington and did not mention his desire for more land. This message reached Trist on 16 November, as the new Mexican government was asking to resume talks. Trist had been operating on Polk's original orders, which were the same as those for Slidell: acquire the disputed area of Texas, get everything as far as California if possible, and do not spend more than $15 million. Should he continue these negotiations, or follow the new order to go home? After days of agonized

reflection, Trist decided to ignore the recall and negotiate. The Treaty of Guadalupe Hidalgo was signed 2 February 1848. Mexico recognized Texas's claim to the Rio Grande; they surrendered lands west of there to California (which had been occupied by other U.S. forces); and they received in return $15 million plus forgiveness for the debts that Texans claimed from the Mexican government totaling $3.25 million, which the U.S. government would pay.

Polk was furious over Trist's refusal to return and his letter of sixty-one pages explaining his motivation. He was equally upset when he learned the details of the treaty. It was a treaty that, to him, was only half a loaf. The Whig Congress, however, would not allow him to continue the war, so he had no choice but to accept it. The Senate did not like the treaty either. The Whigs thought it took too much, and the Democrats thought it took too little, so it was ratified as a compromise. The Mexican government did not like it because they did not want to give up any land at any price, but had no choice.

The Treaty of Guadalupe Hidalgo was one no one liked but all had to live with. Had Trist not been sent to Mexico or had he followed his president's intentions more than his own, the southern border of the United States could have been the Yucatán peninsula. If that remained the case to this day, all of Mexico's resources would be the United States'. Illegal immigration would be a moot point, as would the debate over the North American Free Trade Agreement. In the shorter term, however, what would have happened with Mexico in 1861? When the South seceded from the Union, certainly the Mexicans would have followed suit. If they joined the Confederacy, the Civil War would certainly have had a radically different outcome. Even if they had not, a friendlier Mexico unoccupied by France could greatly have changed the supply situation for the Confederacy. In the final analysis, Trist negotiated from what he considered his own moral base, that Mexico should be a neighbor and not a possession. It cost him his job and much of his future; Polk fired him. Trist, a friend and disciple of Thomas Jefferson and Andrew Jackson, could not bear Polk's aggressive dreams of empire.

As it was, the war was enough to fulfill Polk's dread of producing presidential candidates. Both Taylor and Scott ran as Whigs, with Taylor winning in 1848 and Scott losing in 1852. Scott remained in the army and was still senior commander when the Civil War broke out. His Anaconda Plan proved a successful grand strategy for the Union.

References: Bauer, Jack. *The Mexican War, 1846–1848.* New York: Macmillan, 1974; Connor, Seymour. *North America Divided.* New York: Oxford University Press, 1971; Eisenhower, John. *So Far from God: The U.S. War with Mexico, 1846–1848.* New York: Random House, 1989; Frazier, Donald, ed. *The United States and Mexico at War.* New York: Macmillan, 1998; Singletary, Otis. *The Mexican War.* Chicago: University of Chicago Press, 1960.

ANTIETAM (SHARPSBURG)
17 September 1862

FORCES ENGAGED
Union: Approximately 75,000 men in six corps. Commander: Major General George McClellan.
Confederate: Approximately 45,000 men in two corps. Commander: Lieutenant General Robert E. Lee.

IMPORTANCE
The inability of the Confederate army to gain a major victory in the North doomed their chances to gain foreign aid, vital for their war effort. The Union strategic victory gave President Lincoln the opportunity to introduce the Emancipation Proclamation.

Historical Setting

After the election of 1860, the prospect of living under Republican President Abraham Lincoln held no appeal for Americans in the Southern states. They viewed him as an abolitionist who would work to end slavery, upon which the economy of the South was largely based. The Southern states had long held views of states' rights, wherein the federal government in Washington should have little influence over the decisions made at the state level. Starting in mid-December, Southern states followed South Carolina's lead in seceding from the Union, the ultimate states' rights action. By early February 1861, seven states had formed the Confederate States of America and elected Jefferson Davis of Mississippi as their president. This may have proven a viable attempt at independence, but on 12 April 1961 the newly formed Confederate army opened fire on Fort Sumter in the harbor of Charleston, South Carolina. The fort was garrisoned by Union troops, who surrendered after some 38 hours of artillery fire. Until this point, the actions of the Southern states was one of political theory. Once that first shot was fired, however, Lincoln's decisions were made for him. This was rebellion, and he had no choice but to call for volunteers.

When he asked for volunteers, other Southern states had to make the difficult decision of remaining loyal to the Union and fighting their fellow Southerners or joining them in the Confederacy. Four more states seceded. From Virginia to Texas, army units began organizing, while the short-term Union enlistees were thrown into early action and defeated in the war's first major battle, that along Bull Run Creek near Manassas Junction, Virginia. Union commander Irwin McDowell was removed from command after this loss, and command of a newly expanded Union army made up of long-term volunteers fell to Major General George McClellan. McClellan's forte was organization, and he transformed the civilians into soldiers. He was not so skilled at the offensive, however, and only direct orders from Lincoln sent him into action in May 1862. After early successes against Confederate forces under Joseph Johnston, McClellan was badly outmaneuvered by Robert E. Lee after Lee took command when Johnston was wounded. Lincoln disgustedly ordered McClellan back to Washington. In early August, John Pope tried to force his way toward the Confederate capital at Richmond, Virginia, at Bull Run, but he failed as well.

After a year and a half of independence, the Confederacy lacked foreign recognition. As they were severely deficient in industrial output, it was vital for them to establish foreign ties. Although Confederate diplomats were active in European capitals, they found only reluctant foreign governments. Although they recognized the Confederacy's victories, they were unsure that their defensive strategy was of their own choosing and not forced on them. If the South could prove that it could take the war to the North, then the European governments may reconsider. This demand pointed up the serious dilemma of Confederate war policy. The ultimate goal of the Confederacy was independence, to have the Union leave them alone to go their own way. Further, there was nothing in the North that they wanted that would warrant an invasion. However, if they attacked to prove to the Europeans that they were taking a defensive stand by choice, how could they then tell the Union that all they wanted was to be left in peace? Militarily they needed to attack, to use their superior morale and leadership to force a quick end to the war; diplomatically they needed to stay on the defensive to prove to the Union their intent. Staying on the defensive, however, would lengthen the war and allow the superior industrial power of the Union to overwhelm the agricultural South.

After the second battle at Bull Run, Lee and Davis decided to launch a major raid into Union territory. Lee's intent was to cover as much ground as possible in order to wreak as much havoc as possible. This would allow the Confederate army to feed off Union supplies for a time, while forcing the Union army to chase them, rather than continue offensives

against Virginia. Any damage Lee could do to rail lines and bridges would seriously harm the Union supply lines into the Washington, D.C., area. A major Confederate victory on Union soil would be a bonus, but simply acting at will and returning safely should assure London, Paris, and Moscow that the Confederacy could be a powerful ally. Lee's plan called for his force to divide, march northward through the narrowest part of Maryland, and spread over much of southern Pennsylvania. Capturing the key rail junction at Harper's Ferry, Virginia, on the Potomac River would keep his supply lines open and deny the Union a base in the Confederate rear.

The Battle

Lee's Army of Northern Virginia crossed into Maryland on 6 September. Although originally numbering more than 50,000 men, stragglers and those lost to sickness lowered that number rapidly and dramatically. Lincoln, fearful that Lee's intent was to swing wide around Washington and cut the city off, reluctantly put McClellan back in charge of the Union Army of the Potomac. McClellan's job was to shadow Lee, staying constantly between the Confederates and the capital city. As the two armies paralleled each other, McClellan was the beneficiary of perhaps the greatest piece of luck in all military history. Two of his soldiers found a copy of Lee's orders wrapped around a bundle of cigars inadvertently dropped by a Confederate officer. With this in hand, McClellan knew exactly the size of Lee's force, that it was divided, and just where the parts were located. McClellan told his staff, "Here is a paper with which if I cannot whip 'Bobbie Lee', I will be willing to go home." That was prophetic.

Union forces moved toward South Mountain, where Confederate General D. H. Hill was screening Thomas "Stonewall" Jackson's investment of Harper's Ferry. Hill's men held Turner's Gap for an entire day, one division against 60,000 men. This gave Lee an extra day to try

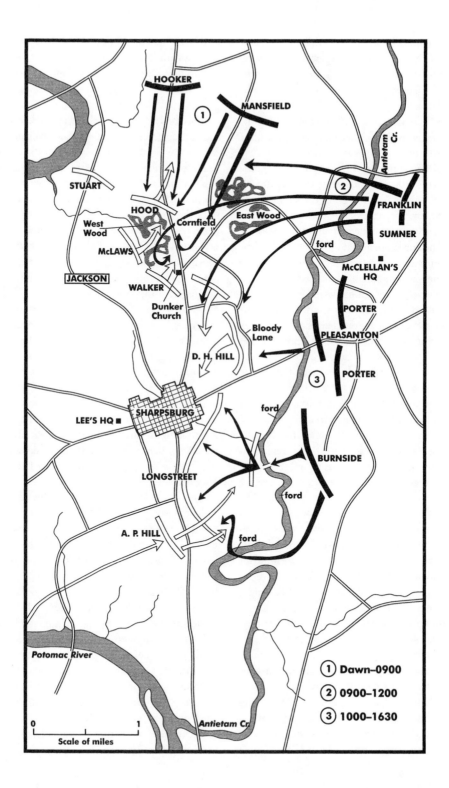

HOOKER

MANSFIELD

1

STUART

HOOD

West
Wood

Cornfield

East Wood

Antietam Cr.

2

FRANKLIN

SUMNER

McLAWS

JACKSON

WALKER

Dunker
Church

ford

McCLELLAN'S
HQ

PORTER

Bloody
Lane

PLEASANTON

D. H. HILL

3

PORTER

LEE'S HQ

SHARPSBURG

ford

LONGSTREET

BURNSIDE

ford

A. P. HILL

ford

Potomac River

Antietam Cr.

0   1

Scale of miles

1 Dawn–0900

2 0900–1200

3 1000–1630

to consolidate his forces, now that his plan was undone. He chose a position near the town of Sharpsburg, Maryland, along Antietam Creek, with the Potomac River to his left and rear. McClellan's advanced forces found him there on 15 September, but did not close. Incredibly, McClellan believed Lee's force to number 110,000, in spite of the fact that he held Lee's orders. Actually, Union forces outnumbered Confederate 87,000 to 35,000 when the battle finally opened on 17 September. McClellan's caution robbed him of certain victory because Lee's separated forces were rapidly marching to his aid.

The battle opened at daybreak on 17 September with a Union attack through a cornfield on the Confederate left. Although badly outnumbered, the Confederates were able to draw on flanking artillery fire from a neighboring hill and the aggressiveness of one of Lee's premier units, John Bell Hood's Texas Brigade. The Union attack was beaten back late in the morning. The second phase of the battle opened in the center, where Union forces marched across open ground into murderous fire from Confederates dug in along a sunken road. After suffering badly, Union forces managed to outflank the road and deal severe damage to the Confederates with enfilading fire that forced the Confederates to withdraw, leaving hundreds of bodies stacked in the lane. The Confederates took up a position a few hundred yards to the rear, but the Union forces did not pursue their advantage. The third phase took place during the afternoon on the Confederate right flank. Here Ambrose Burnside's IX Corps was kept at bay by rifle fire from a small Confederate force that defended a narrow bridge across Antietam Creek. By the time Union soldiers were able to force the bridge and push the Confederates back, reinforcements under D. H. Hill arrived just in time after a forced march from Harper's Ferry. Their stiffening of the right flank saved Lee from being cut off, for Sharpsburg lay open otherwise. At the end of the day, neither side had the upper hand. The two armies faced each

other passively on 18 September. Lee then ordered a withdrawal; McClellan did not follow.

Results

Because he had left the field of his own accord rather than being forced away, Lee claimed victory. It was a hollow boast, for the battle was at best a tactical draw. Both sides lost a roughly equal number of men, but the losses were catastrophic. That day, 17 September 1862, proved to be the bloodiest in U.S. history. Sources disagree widely as to the numbers of men killed and wounded, from 22,700 to just over 26,000 (both sides combined). Still, even the lower count outnumbers by two to one the U.S. deaths resulting from the War of 1812, the Mexican-American War, and the Spanish-American War combined. Although equal in numbers, the percentages favored the Union.

McClellan lost the battle. He had too many opportunities to smash Lee and failed to use them. Waiting too long to launch his attack, pushing his men into the battle piecemeal and completely without coordination, and then failing to commit any reserves whenever any advantage presented itself; all these mistakes cost him the battle. His failure to pursue Lee into Virginia cost him his job. Lincoln could no longer abide McClellan's caution or his excuses, so he relieved him of his command.

More than anything, the battle at Antietam had political significance. Primarily, the Confederacy failed in its attempt to impress Europe, so they failed to gain recognition and an alliance. Without an infusion of European arms, money, supplies, and shipping, the Confederacy could not win. The original plan of the Confederate government, to use its position as the world's major cotton supplier in order to leverage foreign support, never came about. No European government had sufficient cause to challenge the Union, especially if the South could not prove its military power.

Secondly, the nature of the war changed for the Union. Since the outbreak, the goal of

Bloody Lane, still filled with the bodies of the Confederate dead 2 days after the battle. (Library of Congress)

the Union government was to reunite the country and not change anyone's institutions. In spite of that stated intention, Lincoln himself despised slavery and wanted to see its destruction. Although he maintained the Republican Party line that slavery merely needed to be restricted, he personally felt it should be abolished. During the summer of 1862, he decided to issue an executive order abolishing it in the states in rebellion. This would alter the government's war aims, however, and, although abolition was almost universally supported in theory in the Northern states, few were prepared to fight and die to bring it about. Lincoln proposed an end to slavery in order to harm the Confederate war effort. After all, as long as slaves continued to work the plantations, whites were free to serve in the rebellion. Ending slavery would force men to chose between their

families' welfare and the war. If men had to follow the traditional practice of planting in the spring, fighting in the summer, returning home to harvest in the fall, this would severely hurt the Confederate cause. Thus, by presenting abolition as a military necessity, Union soldiers would be much less likely to oppose it.

When Lincoln presented his plan to his cabinet in mid-August, the plan met a warm response. Secretary of State William Seward, however, interjected a note of caution. Even as a military necessity, it was a risky proposal to the Northern public. He suggested waiting for a positive moment to release the statement, as Pope's force had just been beaten at Bull Run. Lincoln saw the wisdom of this and held back the release. Antietam was victory enough to put the public in a good mood. Five days after the battle, he issued the Emancipation

Proclamation. It had no immediate effect at all, for it did not free slaves in the five states remaining in the Union that allowed slavery, and the Confederate states were not about to recognize it. The Proclamation did, however, have long-term effects. Slaves coming into the possession of Union troops were no longer treated as contraband of war. Although Lincoln was certainly no advocate of equal rights for the newly freed slaves, he did allow the creation of regiments of freed blacks, although with white officers. By war's end, some 10 percent of the Union army consisted of black troops.

Although there is some debate over the effect in Europe of emancipation, most agree that it effectively killed any chance of European recognition of the South. European governments had engaged in the polite fiction that slavery was not legal in the Confederacy, but, by the Union's making it an overt war aim, Europe could no longer do that. Public opinion, in England particularly, would never allow the governments to support a country that openly practiced slavery. Whether in response to the slavery question or because of a lack of confidence in Confederate prospects, European support never materialized. A Confederate victory on Union soil in September 1862 could well have changed that, indefinitely postponed the Emancipation Proclamation and its effects, encouraged the growing peace party in the Union, and badly demoralized an already suffering Union army spirit. A Confederate victory could have spelled the independence of the Confederate States of America, and how would a divided America fare both at home and abroad in ensuing decades?

References: Cannan, John. *The Antietam Campaign.* New York: Wieser & Wieser, 1990; Luvaas, Jay, and Harold W. Nelson, eds. *The U.S. Army War College Guide to the Battle of Antietam.* New York: HarperCollins, 1988; McPherson, James M. *Battle Cry of Freedom.* New York: Oxford University Press, 1988; Murfin, James. *The Gleam of Bayonets.* New York: T. Yoseloff, 1965; Sears, Stephen. *Landscape Turned Red.* New Haven, CT: Ticknor & Fields, 1983.

GETTYSBURG
1–3 July 1863

FORCES ENGAGED
Union: Approximately 115,000 men. Commander: Major General George Gordon Meade.
Confederate: Approximately 76,000 men. Commander: General Robert E. Lee.

IMPORTANCE
Although the site was a significant Confederate penetration into Union territory, Lee's defeat kept Union morale and political unity sufficiently strong to continue the war effort.

Historical Setting

Since Robert E. Lee took command of Confederate forces in June 1862, he had engineered an unbroken string of defensive victories. He had failed to obtain vitally needed foreign aid by being turned back (at Antietam Creek near Sharpsburg, Maryland) from a major incursion into Union territory in September 1862, but still his mystique grew with each successive Union general's failure to defeat him on his home ground. Although Lee was successfully defending Confederate territory from Union invasion, his army was suffering severe supply shortages.

Therefore, in June 1863, Lee was determined to try again to attack Union territory. He hoped primarily to live off the production of Northern farms and factories for a time, giving his Virginia base time to recover some of its agricultural output. Strategically, he hoped that by creating havoc in Pennsylvania by pillaging the countryside and disrupting rail traffic he could aid the nascent peace movement in the North, thereby weakening President Abraham Lincoln's government. Finally, Lee had faint hopes of once again interesting European countries in the Confederate cause. Diplomats in European capitals had intimated that a Confederate victory in the North would prove the viability of their military, a necessary condition of European recognition. After Antietam, that viability seemed doubtful, but Lee certainly hoped that a major success in the summer of 1863 could yet bring foreign recognition and military aid.

President Lincoln was increasingly worried about the performance of his army in Virginia. He had hired and fired a series of generals who had failed to win a significant victory in the Union's drive to capture the Confederate capital city of Richmond, Virginia. None of the men he had placed in command had shown sufficient tenacity; after each defeat, they would not hold as forward a position as possible, but instead would return to Washington, D.C., cowed. In the west, Union Major General Ulysses Grant was scoring a string of victories in western Tennessee and along the Mississippi River and had recently invested the city of Vicksburg, Mississippi, the last link between the deep South and the western Confederate states of Arkansas, Louisiana, and Texas. Un-

fortunately, the public was more focused on operations in Virginia, and the failures there had encouraged a peace movement in the Northern states that was gaining momentum with each successive victory Lee's Army of Northern Virginia won. Lincoln's political base was never strong, and a severe setback in Union territory could potentially cause a very strong political backlash.

After soundly defeating Major General Joseph Hooker's army at Chancellorsville, Virginia, in early May 1863, Lee felt his army to be at the peak of its fighting prowess. In late June, he left Virginia with some 76,000 men, marched through a surly population in Maryland, and entered southern Pennsylvania. His main target was the east-west railroad line that passed through Harrisburg, a key supply artery of the Union army. He dispersed his army somewhat in order for them to scour the countryside for supplies, and it was one of those scavenging units that initiated the battle.

Confederate soldiers captured at Gettysburg. (Library of Congress)

The Battle

Learning of the Union army's proximity, Lee decided to concentrate his scattered forces at the town of Gettysburg, Pennsylvania. As a shoe factory was located there, a Confederate infantry brigade was sent forward to seize the town, for much of Lee's army was in rags. Lincoln's latest appointee as commander of the Army of the Potomac was Major General George Gordon Meade, who replaced Hooker on 28 June. Meade had units probing the countryside to locate and monitor Lee's army, and a cavalry brigade had recently arrived at Gettysburg. Thus, on the morning of 1 July 1863, these two units almost stumbled into each other and engaged. Union troops under John Buford deployed just west of Gettysburg astride the road from Chambersburg and met the Confederates under A. P. Hill. The opening skirmish lasted for 2 hours, with Buford's outnumbered force holding its own, but finally being forced to retreat into and through the town because of the arrival of more Confederate troops from the north under Richard Ewell.

The retreating Union troops paused just south of town on Cemetery Ridge. Lee realized that Meade must certainly be marching the bulk of his army forward, so that high ground was vital. Unfortunately, his order to Ewell was to take the ridge "if practicable." Ewell had just replaced Thomas "Stonewall" Jackson, one of the most able generals of the entire war. Jackson, unfortunately for the Confederacy, had been killed at Chancellorsville, and Ewell was nowhere near the commander his predecessor had been. Many later commentators remarked that had Jackson been alive, the battle would have been over the first day as a Confederate victory. Ewell, however, hesitated and lost his opportunity. As the sun set on 1 July, Union reinforcements were streaming onto the hill and establishing a strong position.

After occupying Seminary Ridge, parallel and about a mile away from the Union position, Lee pondered his next move. Seeing that Cemetery Ridge and Culp's Hill on its northern end were strongly held, Lee decided to strike the Union left. A corresponding demonstration against Culp's Hill could be strengthened when Meade weakened that flank to deal with the Southern attack. The task of attacking the Union left flank fell to Major General James Longstreet, one of Lee's most trusted subordinates.

Longstreet had argued for a move of the entire army southward, which would threaten Washington and force Meade to come down from his high ground. By this point in the war, he had learned that victory normally went to the army that stood on the defensive and obliged the enemy to attack. Thus, such a move as he envisioned would put on Meade's shoulders the onus of crossing open ground against a prepared position. Rebuffed in that suggestion, Longstreet moved his men to the Union left flank. What happened in this move has been debated since 2 July 1863. Lee wanted the attack to start as early as possible, but it did not begin until 1600. The left of the Union line was being held by Daniel Sickles, who had left Cemetery Ridge and deployed his men about a half mile forward, completely unsupported. When Longstreet moved into position to attack, the Union army was thus not where it was supposed to be. Behind Sickles stood Little Round Top, an unoccupied promontory from which artillery could easily enfilade the main Union position. A quick seizure of Little Round Top would completely turn the Union flank, but Longstreet's orders were to engage the Union army. Already having failed to convince Lee of his own views, Longstreet apparently decided that he would follow his orders to the letter. While Longstreet's troops engaged Sickles's men, quick-thinking Union officers pushed Joshua Chamberlain's 20th Maine Infantry Regiment on top of the hill. By the time Longstreet's men had defeated Sickles, the opportunity for an easy occupation of Little Round Top no longer existed. Had Longstreet moved more quickly, or seized the opportunity to grab Little Round Top, again the Con-

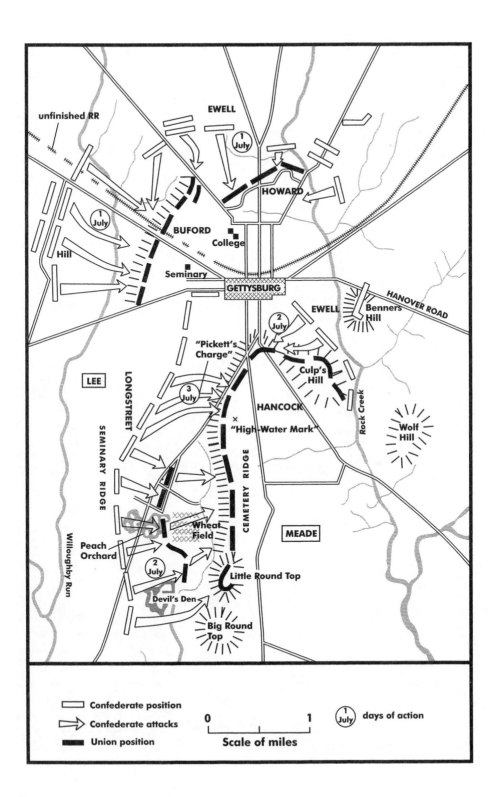

unfinished RR

EWELL

1 July

HOWARD

Hill

1 July

BUFORD

College

Seminary

GETTYSBURG

HANOVER ROAD

EWELL

Benners Hill

2 July

"Pickett's Charge"

Culp's Hill

LEE

LONGSTREET

3 July

HANCOCK

"High-Water Mark"

Rock Creek

Wolf Hill

SEMINARY RIDGE

CEMETERY RIDGE

MEADE

Willoughby Run

Wheat Field

Peach Orchard

2 July

Little Round Top

Devil's Den

Big Round Top

Confederate position

Confederate attacks

Union position

0   1
Scale of miles

1 July   days of action

federate army would almost certainly have won the battle.

On the evening of 2 July, having failed to turn either Union flank, Lee met with his staff. Deciding to stay and fight, Lee proposed a plan that in retrospect was foolhardy. Hoping that the Union army would be weakened in the center by the flanking attacks that day, Lee decided to commit 10,000 men that had just arrived to an assault on the Union center on Cemetery Ridge. This assault, which came to be known to history as Pickett's Charge, should be able to punch a hole in the Union lines that follow-up attacks would exploit. As mentioned earlier, the defense owned the advantage in the American Civil War. Meade had received reinforcements on the night of 2 July, and Lee's assumptions were false. "Longstreet once more urged Lee to maneuver around Meade's left. Again Lee refused, and ordered Longstreet to attack the Union center with Pickett's division and two of Hill's—fewer than 15,000 men to advance three-quarters of a mile across open fields and assault dug-in infantry supported by ample artillery. 'General Lee,' Longstreet later reported himself to have said, 'there never was a body of fifteen thousand men who could make that attack successfully'" (McPherson, *Battle Cry of Freedom,* p. 661).

Lee's decision here has also been the subject of intense debate. Certainly he had complete confidence in his men, for as stated earlier they were at the height of their morale and experience. Some modern historians argue that Lee was suffering from heart problems and possibly had had a mild heart attack within the

The lone soldier monument, Gettysburg National Battlefield, Pennsylvania. (Corbis/David Muench)

previous few days, so he was not thinking as clearly as he might have. Perhaps it was a simple case of overconfidence.

Just after 1300 on 3 July, Confederate artillery began bombarding Union positions to cover the attack. For 2 hours, the opposing artillery batteries fired at each other, with minimal effect. The mile-wide line of Confederate troops began their advance about 1500, marching steadily for 20 minutes across the open ground. Once in range, the Union artillery, which had ceased firing to lure the Confederates on, opened up and began tearing massive holes in the advancing line. At 200 yards, Union infantry began adding to the carnage. In spite of all that, the Confederates crossed the field, went over or through a fence, and closed. For a time, the fighting was hand to hand; a second wave at this point might possibly have made the difference. Instead, the Confederates were too few in number by the time they reached the top of the ridge, and after intense fighting they had to recross that same ground under the same fire. Some 7,500 men in the assault were killed, wounded, or captured.

Results

The following day, the two armies looked at each other without fighting. On the night of 4 July, in a driving rainstorm, Lee withdrew from Seminary Ridge and returned across the Potomac River to Virginia. Meade did not follow. Had he done so, the swollen Potomac would have been an anvil upon which to pound the shattered Confederate army, and the war could have been over in a few days. In the end, the Union army failed to exploit its opportunities as had the Confederates. By sheer coincidence, on the day Lee returned to Virginia for the last time, Grant was accepting the surrender of Vicksburg. That victory gave the Union total control of the Mississippi River, cutting the Confederacy into two parts. If Meade had pursued Lee and crushed him at the Potomac River, the Confederate government would almost cer-

tainly have been forced to sue for peace. Thus, for the Union the victory at Gettysburg was not as decisive as it should have been.

The true importance of Gettysburg is the Confederate failure. Lee's mystique could only have been enhanced by a rebel victory, and Meade would certainly have joined the ranks of dismissed commanders of the Army of the Potomac. Lee's goal of living off the land and terrorizing the Union countryside would both have strengthened his army and weakened Lincoln's administration. Whether European governments would have recognized the Confederate States of America on the strength of a Confederate victory is difficult to say because Lincoln's Emancipation Proclamation—issued 1 January 1863—had taken the issue of slavery to the forefront. Public opinion in European populations may have kept their governments from recognizing and giving military aid to a country that openly practiced slavery after the Union government had officially announced its destruction as a war aim.

In spite of that, the public opinion in the North would have been the most important factor to be considered, and the peace movement, in spite of Vicksburg, may have forced some major changes in the government's actions. Given a Confederate victory, Lee could potentially have marched on Washington, D.C. Although the city was surrounded by strong defenses, the mere sight of an army in gray on the heels of the defeat of the Army of the Potomac could have forced the city's evacuation. With Washington in rebel hands, Maryland, which was a slave state and had many advocates of secession, could have joined the Confederacy. Such a move could also have been the nudge that Missouri and Kentucky needed to secede as well. The possibilities inherent in a rebel victory at Gettysburg, which never came about, indicate the battle's decisiveness.

References: Coddington, Edwin B. Gettysburg: A Study in Command. New York: Charles Scribner's Sons, 1968; Foote, Shelby. The Civil War: A Narrative. New York: Vintage Books,

1986 [1958–1974]; Luvaas, Jay, and Harold W. Nelson, eds. *The U.S. Army War College Guide to the Battle of Gettysburg*. New York: HarperCollins, 1986; McPherson, James M. *Battle Cry of Freedom*. New York: Oxford University Press, 1988; Stackpole, Edward J. *They Met at Gettysburg*. Harrisburg, PA: Stackpole Books, 1954.

ATLANTA/MARCH TO THE SEA

22 July–22 December 1864

FORCES ENGAGED

Union: 98,000 men of the Army of the Tennessee. Commander: General William T. Sherman.

Confederate: 53,000 men of the Army of Tennessee. Commanders: Generals Joseph E. Johnston and John Bell Hood.

IMPORTANCE

The Union capture of Atlanta guaranteed Lincoln's reelection in 1864 over peace candidate George McClellan. The March to the Sea introduced total war to the modern world.

Historical Setting

After the city of Vicksburg surrendered to Union General Ulysses Grant on 4 July 1863, the same day that Confederate General Robert E. Lee was retreating from his defeat at Gettysburg, any chance that the Confederacy had to win the Civil War was fading. Vicksburg's fall meant that the Union controlled the Mississippi River, severing Texas, Louisiana, and Arkansas from the remainder of the Confederate States of America. In the eastern theater, although Lee had repeatedly beaten back Union invasions of Virginia, his lack of supplies meant that his army could not fight in top form. When Grant was transferred from the west to Virginia, Lincoln directed him to do what a half dozen previous commanders had failed to do: defeat Lee and capture Richmond. In early May 1864,

Grant led about 100,000 men into northern Virginia to attempt just that.

At the same time, Grant's successor in the western theater, General William T. Sherman, was beginning his own offensive. His Union forces were implementing the Anaconda Plan, designed by senior army General Winfield Scott early in the war. It was designed to squeeze off portions of the Confederacy until it was so hopelessly divided that no section could support another. The capture of Vicksburg had accomplished a phase of that plan, and now Sherman was to enter into the next phase: by marching southeast from Tennessee, he was to reach the Atlantic and sever the Deep South from the upper South. With almost 100,000 men, he marched out of western Tennessee (which he had secured in January 1864) with Atlanta his first objective.

Facing Sherman's army was General Joseph E. Johnston. He had commanded the Confederate army in Virginia early in the war, until his wounding in June 1862 brought about his replacement by Lee. Like Lee, he was a general well versed in defensive tactics, and he needed all his skill to face a Union army that outnumbered his Army of Tennessee almost two to one.

Johnston was the right man in the right place, and he proceeded to give Sherman problems. Their first meeting was at Resaca (13–16 May 1864), where Johnston's placement of his army forced Sherman to attack frontally. The war had proven the effectiveness of the defensive because armies still went into battle in lines even though technology had brought forth rifles and artillery that made those antiquated tactics futile. In earlier days when armies fought with muskets, whose short range obliged armies to mass their forces to mass their fire, going into battle in lines was necessary. The introduction of rifles, however, meant that soldiers could now kill an enemy at up to 300 yards, more than five times the effective range of muskets. That meant that advancing armies were exposed to fire longer than ever before, so an entrenched army could decimate an attacking one before ever taking casualties themselves. Thus, Johnston's fewer men could deal Sherman's greater numbers severe damage, and they did.

Sherman's response, logically, was to attempt to hold the Confederates in place while marching men around the flanks, but Johnston had almost a sixth sense about Sherman's moves, and he was consistently able to withdraw before a flanking maneuver was effective. The problem was that Johnston had to withdraw, which meant saving the lives of his men, but also meant giving up territory to the enemy. Johnston bought time with this ceded territory, but it was not the kind of war Confederate President Jefferson Davis wanted. Davis wanted Sherman pushed out of Georgia, which Johnston's strategy would not accomplish. Further, Johnston's aloof manner and reluctance to share his plans with his superiors infuriated Davis. Although Johnston repeatedly dealt Sherman serious setbacks, at Resaca, New Hope Church (25–28 May), and Kennesaw Mountain (27 June), Sherman continued to try to outflank Johnston, with limited success. When Johnston pulled his army into the prepared defenses of Atlanta in early July, Davis had had enough.

The Battle

President Davis and the Confederate government lost confidence in Johnston and decided that a more aggressive commander was needed. Thus, they relieved Johnston of his command on 17 July and replaced him with John Bell Hood. Hood had made a name for himself as a divisional commander under Robert E. Lee, where his forces (including the famous Texas Brigade) were Lee's most dependable troops, detailed to achieve the most difficult objectives. Hood proved his ability on the offensive during the Peninsular Campaign of July 1862 and at the second battle at Bull Run in August 1862, Antietam in September 1862, and Gettysburg in July 1863. Transferred to the Army of Tennessee in the western theater, Hood led troops

at the battle of Chickamauga. He was a commander who fought alongside his men, and he had the wounds to prove it. If anyone could be trusted to take the offensive, Hood was the one. His problem was that his aggressiveness was not tempered by wisdom. When told of the decision to place Hood in command, Lee sent a telegram to Davis counseling against it: "Hood is a bold fighter. I am doubtful as to other qualities necessary" (Dowdey and Manarin, *The Wartime Papers of Robert E. Lee,* p. 821). The men of the Army of Tennessee did not want to see Johnston go either, but the will of the politicians prevailed.

Hood quickly went to work. He attacked the Union army at Peachtree Creek, on the outskirts of Atlanta, on 20 July but was driven back. Forced into the defensive lines, Hood could only send sorties out to harass Sherman's attempts to surround the city. In this, Hood was moderately successful, for a time keeping open the final railroad into Atlanta and stopping a Union cavalry raid intended to liberate prisoners from the camp at Andersonville. These efforts were costly for the Confederacy. In a matter of days, they suffered 15,000 casualties, more than twice what Johnston had suffered in 10 weeks, while inflicting 6,000 killed and wounded on the enemy. Still, Union forces slowly worked their way around both flanks in what forebode a total encirclement.

Hood developed a plan that would have made sense a year earlier, when Confederate and Union forces were more nearly equal in number. Hood decided that, rather than stay in Atlanta and endure a siege, he would instead abandon the city and outflank Sherman. By marching around toward the rear of the Union army, Hood hoped that the threat to the Union supply lines would force Sherman to turn away from Atlanta and follow Hood back toward Tennessee. Sherman forced Hood into action when he marched the bulk of his Union forces around the city on 22 August to destroy Atlanta's last rail link. Therefore, at the beginning of September, Hood led his army out of

Fortifications in front of Atlanta, Georgia, 1864. (National Archives)

the city in a wide march around the Union right flank. A smaller army would have been forced to follow him, but Sherman merely divided his forces into two parts. One part, under George Thomas, he sent to follow Hood; the other part, he led into Atlanta on 2 September.

News of Atlanta's fall was celebrated throughout the North, and President Abraham Lincoln breathed a sigh of relief. This slowed the momentum of the peace party in the North and practically guaranteed Lincoln's reelection in November. Although Sherman had little love for Lincoln and disagreed with most of his policies, he kept his army in Atlanta until after the election was over. In the meantime, he ordered all civilians in the city to be evicted. This raised a storm of protest in the Confederacy, but Sherman was determined to turn the city into a supply depot for his men and he would not have civilians impeding his actions. For 10 weeks Sherman stayed in Atlanta, while Hood marched his men into disaster. A frontal assault

against well-prepared Union positions at Franklin, Tennessee, virtually destroyed his army, and the remainder failed to successfully besiege Nashville.

On 16 November, Sherman led 68,000 men out of Atlanta, marching southeast for Savannah. With virtually no Confederate forces to oppose him, he stretched his men out in a line some 50 miles wide and they proceeded to destroy everything they found. Although Atlanta was fairly secure, Sherman cut himself off from that city and lived off the land. His forces took what they needed and destroyed the rest: plantations, farms, railroads, anything that could produce or aid in providing supplies for the Confederacy. He did not make war against the citizens themselves; deaths among the civilian population was low. Instead, he made war against their productivity. This not only deprived the Confederate army of whatever supplies it may have received, but it proved to the South that they were thoroughly beaten. It took just over a month to reach his goal. On 22 December, Sherman sent a telegram to Lincoln: "I beg to present you as a Christmas gift, the city of Savannah, with 150 heavy guns and plenty of ammunition, and also about 250,000 bales of cotton" (Fellman, "Lincoln and Sherman," in Boritt, *Lincoln's Generals*, p. 156).

Results

The autumn of 1864 sounded the death knell of the Confederacy. Although written off as a lost cause by many after the July 1863 defeats at Vicksburg and Gettysburg, in reality the Confederacy had one last chance after that time. When Grant took his army into Virginia in May 1864, he fought a series of bloody battles: Wilderness, Spotsylvania Courthouse, North Anna, and Cold Harbor. Between 5 May and 3 June, Grant lost 50,000 men dead and wounded. That caused an immense outcry in the Union for his removal, but Lincoln refused. He had a general who would not turn and run after a defeat as all those previous to Grant had done, so Lincoln supported him in spite of the terrible losses. Then, in early June, Grant was forced into besieging Petersburg, south of the Confederate capital city of Richmond, Virginia. On the road to Richmond, he had lost men, but at least he was going forward; at Petersburg, he lost men and went nowhere.

Lincoln's continued support of Grant resulted in a peace movement gaining momentum in the North. In the summer of 1864, the Democratic Party nominated former General George McClellan as their candidate and adopted a plank in the platform calling for an immediate truce and negotiations for peace. Lincoln decided in August that if he lost the November election, he would not wait the customary 5 months for the inaugural; he would instead resign immediately and let McClellan take over, for the people would have spoken. Therefore, had Johnston remained in command

of the Confederate army in Georgia, he could possibly have held Atlanta as Lee was holding Petersburg. That could have spelled defeat for Lincoln, which could have given the Confederacy one last chance at independence. Instead, Atlanta's fall convinced the North that victory was imminent, so a peace candidate was unelectable.

In his March to the Sea, Sherman for the first time in modern history made the civilian sector of an enemy nation a legitimate target. This type of warfare had occurred regularly in Europe as late as the Thirty Years' War (1618–1648), but had for the most part become a thing of the past. From 1864 onward, civilians were again fair game. Although this has made Sherman's name an object of hatred in the South ever since, it accomplished a positive purpose. "This was war as politics stripped bare.... For the Confederates had to be defeated in devastating fashion, lest they sustain a longer term armed insurrection of the type which has characterized the histories of such peoples as the Irish and the tribes of the Balkans. In his ruthless marches through the Confederate heartland, at least as much ideologically as militarily, Sherman provided essential elements of the Confederate defeat" (Fellman, "Lincoln and Sherman," in Boritt, *Lincoln's Generals*, pp. 155–156). This certainly must have had an effect on Lee's decision in April 1865 to surrender completely, rather than encourage an ongoing guerrilla war. Sherman's victory at Atlanta, and his subsequent path of destruction, at once ended a war and ushered in a return to an old style of warfare.

References: Boritt, Gabor. *Lincoln's Generals.* New York: Oxford University Press, 1994; Dowdey, Clifford, and Louis H. Manarin. *The Wartime Papers of Robert E. Lee.* Boston: Little, Brown, 1961; Fellman, Michael. *Citizen Sherman.* New York: Random House, 1995; McPherson, James M. *Battle Cry of Freedom.* New York: Oxford University Press, 1988; Royster, Charles. *The Destructive War.* New York: Alfred A. Knopf, 1991.

SEDAN

1 September 1870

FORCES ENGAGED

Prussian: 200,000 men. Commander: Field
Marshal Helmuth von Moltke, the elder.
French: 120,000 men. Commander: Emperor
Napoleon III.

IMPORTANCE

Prussian victory spelled doom for the French
army in the Franco-Prussian War, leading to
consolidation of Germanic states into one country,
as well as long-standing hostility between France
and Germany to serve as one causal factor in the
outbreak of World War I.

Historical Setting

Prussia was the dominant state of Germany in
the middle 1800s. It rose to prominence mainly
through the quality of its military. Ever since
its defeat at the hands of Napoleon Bonaparte
at Jena and Auerstädt in 1806, the Prussian
military had dedicated itself to becoming the
best in the world, both to return to the glory
days of Frederick the Great and to ensure that
no such embarrassment as that at the hands of
the French was ever repeated. They developed
the world's first General Staff, promoting excellence in all phases of military activity. The
system proved itself in 1866 when Prussia easily defeated their former ally Austria in a dispute over the provinces of Schleswig and
Holstein; that war seemed almost a tune-up
for a return match with France. Under the leadership of Chancellor Otto von Bismarck,
Prussia gathered the lesser German states
around itself in a North German Confederation and aimed toward the unification of all
Germanic principalities into one nation. A war
with France would serve as a focus for that
German nationalism.

In France, Napoleon III had reigned as
head of state since the revolution of 1848. The
Second Empire was a shadow of the First Empire established by Napoleon Bonaparte, but
France hoped to maintain a major role in world
affairs, even if it could not return to the earlier
heights of grandeur. During the Austro-Prussian
War, Napoleon III had given Prussia tacit support in return for generalized promises of reward. France had hoped to gain borderlands
along the western Rhine after that war, but Bismarck refused to cede any such territory to non-
Germans. He then stood in the way of a
proposed French purchase of Luxembourg from
Holland. When Napoleon hoped to expand into
Belgium via heavy French investment in that
country's rail system, Bismarck reminded England of possible French control of the English
Channel coast, and English opposition halted
French aims. In the face of these French ven-
tures, Bismarck convinced the southern German state of Bavaria to join in a defense pact.

The question of a new heir to the Spanish
throne brought Franco-Prussian difficulties to
a head. After Queen Isabella was deposed in
1868, the Spanish government reorganized itself as a constitutional monarchy, but they were
in need of a monarch. They secretly appealed
to Prince Leopold of the House of Hohenzollern, a distant cousin of Prussian King Wilhelm. Negotiations for offering the crown to
Leopold were conducted between the Spanish
government and the Prussian court. Although
Wilhelm had little interest in the matter and
occasionally spoke against the scheme, Bismarck
pushed Leopold's cause. When the French
learned of the negotiations, they feared being
surrounded by Hohenzollerns. The French
ambassador to Prussia met with Wilhelm in
Holland and secured the withdrawal of Prussian support for Leopold, but then pressed his
luck by demanding that no future claimant
would ever come from the Hohenzollern dynasty. When Bismarck received word of this
demand in a telegram, he doctored the communication in such a way as to make it appear
that the French were rude to Wilhelm and the
Kaiser had dismissed the ambassador. This provoked French public opinion to the point of

war and Napoleon, frustrated by Prussia at every turn, complied.

The Prussian military was ready, with the states of Bavaria, Baden, and Württemberg mobilizing their armies in support. In less than 3 weeks, Prussia and its allies had almost half a million troops on the frontier, more than the French would muster in the entire war. The French mobilization was totally disorganized, with men arriving at their rendezvous points and at the front badly underequipped. The Prussian General Staff showed its competence by employing the rails for transport, a lesson that they had learned from observing the American Civil War. Their contingency planning for the campaign was ready for employment, whereas Napoleon III hastily threw together a strategy just before riding out to join his troops. He hoped to gain an early victory in southern Germany and bring Austria and Italy into the war on his side. Oddly, for all the chaos, it got off to a good start.

The Battle

On 30 July 1870, four French corps advanced out of the fortress city of Metz against Prussian forces just across the border at Saarbrücken. On 2 August, they easily scattered the small force defending the city, but then, through want of organization and decision, failed to occupy it. It would be one of their few bright spots in the entire conflict.

The Prussians launched a counteroffensive just to the south, driving French forces back toward Strasbourg. In an attempt to slow their advance, French General Maurice MacMahon on 6 August threw a cavalry charge at them near the town of Wörth; the French force was slaughtered. A second Prussian offensive to the north was also victorious at Spicheren. With two rapid defeats, the demoralized Napoleon ordered Metz abandoned and the French army to retreat. Somewhat reluctant to start the war, the emperor now became completely demoralized, and that spirit spread through the ranks. Knowing he could command neither the army's movements nor its respect, he conceded command to Marshal François Bazaine, only slightly more aggressive in his nature than Napoleon. Napoleon left for Châlons to raise another army.

The French retreat toward Verdun found itself cut off by rapidly advancing Prussian troops. Prussian commander Field Marshal Helmuth von Moltke ordered the French destroyed while on the march, but, in the ensuing battle at Vionville, the French soldiers gave a good account of themselves in a bloody encounter. It bolstered their confidence somewhat, but Bazaine ordered the army to face

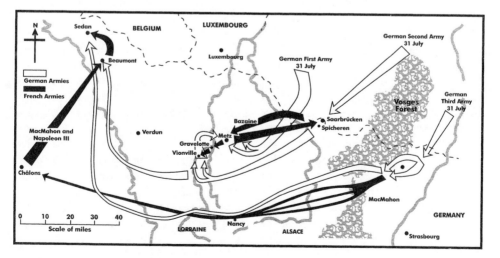

about and return to Metz. On the way, the Prussians attacked again at Gravelotte and suffered a terrible defeat, but this did nothing to encourage Bazaine. His return to Metz ended in a siege.

Marshal MacMahon was ordered to lead the newly formed Army of Châlons to relieve Metz, and he marched his 130,000 men out of that city on 21 August. His army, made up primarily of refugees from Parisian jails, was even less disciplined than Bazaine's force. The dispirited Napoleon rode with them. Learning of the movement, Moltke ordered a holding force to stay at Metz while the bulk of his army turned to face MacMahon. When the two forces ran into each other on 30 August at Beaumont, just west of the Meuse River, MacMahon ordered a retreat into the town of Sedan. It seemed a good defensive position to reorganize and launch a new attack. He deployed his men in a triangle around the town, digging them in on high ground. Moltke's men quickly marched to surround the town, cutting it off from any possible reinforcement. Unfortunately for the French, the Germans occupied even higher ground and by evening on 31 August were lobbing artillery shells into the city.

Early on 1 September, Napoleon decided that his time had come for glory or infamy. Apparently accepting his fate, he became eerily calm. Although he was suffering immensely from kidney stones, he mounted his horse and rode out to battle. The morning started with a Prussian cannonade, followed by an attack on the outlying village of Bazeilles. The fighting there was intense throughout the morning and early afternoon. MacMahon was wounded and turned command over to General Auguste Ducrot. Ducrot immediately ordered an attempt to break out of the encirclement to the west. As the troops were responding to that decision, he was faced by General Emmanuel de Wimpffen, who had just arrived from a command in Morocco. Waving orders from the War Minister, he took charge, countermanding the retreat order and directing the troops to recapture Bazeilles.

Napoleon had spent the day riding near the heaviest action, courting danger and possible death, his new demeanor imparting some confidence to the French soldiers. He returned to Sedan to confer with MacMahon. While there he was informed of a Prussian success at Floing, about a mile north of Sedan. A French cavalry charge there had proved fatally futile and, coupled with the constant pounding of Prussian artillery and the chaos within Sedan, convinced Napoleon to call it quits. Watching soldiers and civilians desperately trying to enter the city, at 1630 he ordered a white flag to be raised. Wimpffen at first refused to allow his emperor to surrender, but when Moltke sent forward two officers under a flag of truce, Napoleon ordered that they be received. The Prussians had no hint, until that moment, that the French emperor was actually in the city.

Results

Negotiations lasted through the night, and on 2 September Napoleon ordered that Wimpffen sign the surrender document. The entire remnants of the Army of Châlons, including more than 100,000 men, 6,000 horses, and 419 artillery pieces, fell into Prussian hands. Emperor Napoleon III turned himself over to Prussian Kaiser Wilhelm, who had been on the scene to watch Moltke's victory. Napoleon spent a few months in Germany and then went into exile in England.

The Prussian victory at Sedan did not end the war, but it broke the French army. Bazaine held out in Metz until 27 October, but with no hope of relief. With the bulk of the French army captured in two battles, the Prussians and their allies faced little opposition as they marched on Paris. The citizens of the French capital put up a valiant defense, but they could not possibly succeed. On 19 January, they also capitulated.

The Prussians, who had dominated the lesser Germanic states throughout the century, now seized the opportunity to unite them. On 18 January, at the French palace of Versailles,

Wilhelm oversaw the creation of the state of Germany. He became its king, and his Chancellor Bismarck led the new German government. They imposed a harsh peace on France: cession of the valuable border provinces of Alsace and Lorraine and an indemnity of five billion francs (roughly $3 billion).

France's defeat ended Napoleon's Second Empire, ushering in the Second Republic. France was at one of the lowest points in its entire history. After the Prussians withdrew, a revolutionary government in Paris was bloodily suppressed by the remains of the French army. Whatever dreams of glory there may have been in the revival of empire in 1854 were long since forgotten. There was only the future to look forward to, and the French army set about making sure that the next time that they faced the Germans the outcome would be different. They created their own General Staff, which oversaw the creation of Plan XVII, the strategy for Germany's defeat in the next war.

Remaining hostile to Germany, the French challenged its eastern neighbor in international affairs, primarily in the acquisition of colonies around the world, mainly in Africa. Allying itself with Great Britain, which feared the increasing size of the German navy, France rebuilt itself into a colonial power, a strategy that aided in restoring the nation's morale at the end of the century.

Prussia, now Germany, emerged from the war the most powerful nation on the Continent. Its military was unchallengeable, and its industry soon rivaled that of Great Britain. That growing rivalry proved another of the many reasons for the First World War. The German military learned that artillery once again proved the upper hand in battle. That was confirmed by observers of the Russo-Japanese War of 1904–1905, so, when World War I broke out, no nation could match Germany in firepower. The military use of railroads, already proven in the United States, gained priority in Europe. The German General Staff proved itself the true instrument of victory, and not only France but every major power soon copied the format. Al-

though Moltke and his subordinates made some glaring mistakes, as at Gravelotte, victory overshadowed them. The wars of the future would be fought not just by soldiers, but by planners and managers.

References: Aronson, Theo. *The Fall of the Third Napoleon.* Indianapolis: Bobbs-Merrill, 1970; Carr, William. *The Origin of the Wars of German Unification.* London: Longman, 1991; Forster, Stig, and Jorg Nagler. *On the Road to Total War: The American Civil War and the Franco-German War.* New York: Cambridge University Press, 1997; Fuller, J. F. C. *A Military History of the Western World,* vol. 3. New York: Funk & Wagnalls, 1956; Howard, Michael. *The Franco-Prussian War.* New York: Collier, 1961.

TEL EL KEBIR
13 September 1882

FORCES ENGAGED
British: 17,401 men. Commander: Lieutenant General Sir Garnet Wolseley. Egyptian: 22,000 to 25,000 men. Commander: Colonel Ahmed Arabi.

IMPORTANCE
British victory placed the British in de facto control of both Egypt and the Suez Canal, and its control led to British influence throughout the Middle East until 1956.

Historical Setting

Egypt was a key part of the Ottoman Empire in the nineteenth century. It gave Turkey, the base of that empire, control over the Middle East and the eastern Mediterranean Sea. Turkey needed all the help it could get, for it was, and had been, a fading power since its naval defeat at the battle of Lepanto in 1571. By the middle of the 1800s, Turkey was regarded throughout the western world as "the sick man of Europe," grimly hanging on to possessions in the Balkans and beating back periodic Russian attempts to gain control over the Bosporus.

Fearing just that eventuality, other European countries usually sprang to Turkey's aid in times of crisis, as they had done in the Crimean War of the 1850s. For that assistance, western European powers demanded and received preferential treatment in Ottoman lands, as well as a fairly free hand in protecting the rights of their citizens in Ottoman possessions.

Britain went to Egypt because of the Suez Canal. Built by a French company and completed in 1869, the canal became the most popular sailing route to the Far East, and British shipping made up 80 percent of the canal's traffic. The khedive (Ottoman viceroy) of Egypt, Ismail Pasha, originally controlled 44 percent of the canal company's shares. Ismail wanted to improve and modernize Egypt and he spent lavishly doing so. He spent on himself as much as his country, all with money borrowed from foreign investors, mainly British

and French. Between 1862 and 1875, Egypt's debt rose from £3 million to £100 million. When the Egyptian government could not pay, Ismail bought some time by selling the British government his shares in the canal company for a mere £4 million. This staved off his creditors for no more than a few months, and the Egyptian government was declared bankrupt in May 1876.

To recover lost investments, a debt commission appointed by the French government took over Egypt's finances, administering revenues and collecting taxes fairly. Rather than allow the mostly French commission to have too much authority, Britain decided to play a more active role. However, Ismail chafed at the loss of personal power, so he removed the foreigners from their governmental duties and replaced them with his son Tewfik, who had little success in restoring Egypt's fortunes. In 1879,

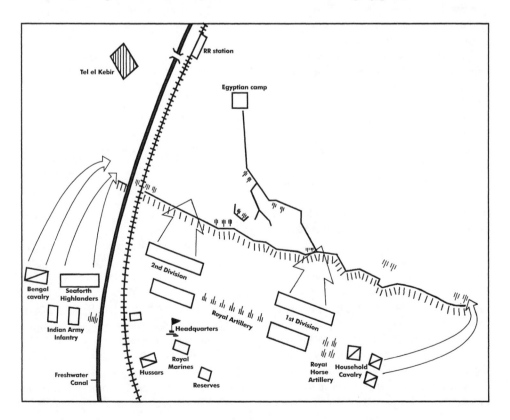

the Ottoman sultan, under heavy British and French pressure, removed Ismail as khedive. He was replaced not with someone responsible but with Tewfik. This soon proved too much for the Egyptian military. Disliking Tewfik and disgruntled with foreigners in the government, Colonel Ahmed Arabi led a revolt that ousted Tewfik in September 1881. This was not merely a coup but a nascent nationalist movement: Egypt (especially the profitable Suez Canal) for the Egyptians.

Although the British government in those days in principle tried not to use its military to bail out troubled businesses in foreign countries, this case was different. After all, as part owner of the canal, the British government could not allow any domestic disturbance that could potentially translate into restrictions on trade. At the urging of the French president, Leon Gambetta, Britain agreed in early 1882 to a Franco-British intervention to maintain both order and income. The arrival of foreign troops provoked an even more violent popular rising. Rather than reinforce, the French parliament voted to withdraw their troops. Britain remained and took action against Arabi. On 11 July 1882, the Royal Navy bombarded defensive positions around the harbor at Alexandria. Arabi had spent weeks shoring up the fortifications around the harbor and placing heavy artillery inside, but nothing he had could match the firepower on British battleships. Although a number of British ships were damaged, Alexandria's fortifications were demolished by the bombardment. When the defending guns fell silent, a British landing party went ashore and seized the forts.

Rather than surrender, Arabi redoubled his efforts at resistance. That meant that if the British were to maintain their control over both the canal and the revenue administration, troops would have to be committed. When alerted to this, the British government assigned the operation to Sir Garnet Wolseley, who had served his country in campaigns all across its empire from India to Africa to Canada. Although disliked in many government quarters for his reformist tendencies, even his harshest critics recognized his command abilities. Wolseley collected a staff of experienced officers with whom he had served in the past, but was also saddled with some political appointees, including Queen Victoria's son Arthur, the duke of Connaught.

The Battle

The resourceful Wolseley was able to turn it all to his advantage. He assigned Sir Edward Hamley, of the War College staff, to prepare plans for an attack at Aboukir Bay, just west of Alexandria. As Wolseley had assumed, the target was common knowledge throughout Egypt in a few days. Now with the enemy, government, press, and most of his own staff focused on Alexandria, Wolseley took about half of his 40,000 men east. On 20 August 1882, he seized the town of Ismailia, at the mouth of the Suez Canal. Arabi had some 60,000 men under his command, but was forced to spread them across three possible lines of attack: Cairo, Alexandria, and Tel el Kebir. At the last, he constructed a defensive position roughly halfway between Cairo and the canal, along the railroad line connecting the two. The 22,000 to 25,000 men he deployed there made up the force that Wolseley's invading army would encounter.

Wolseley sent ahead of the main body a reconnaissance force commanded by General Gerald Graham. Their mission was to march 20 miles into the desert and secure a hold on the Freshwater Canal. With some 2,000 men, he accomplished that mission, entrenching his force at Kassassin. There, on 28 August, they beat back an Egyptian assault and then, with a cavalry charge, forced an Egyptian retreat. When Wolseley's main force arrived, the combined force pushed on toward Tel el Kebir, whence the Egyptians had retreated. The position they prepared there was strong: approximately 4 miles in length along a sloping ridge.

The Egyptians had dug a long trench, 6 feet wide and 4 feet deep, immediately in front of their lines. All of this overlooked a completely level plain with an unobstructed field of fire for Arabi's seventy field pieces.

Wolseley was impressed with the quality of the enemy's work and spent 4 days scouting it out. There seemed to be no real weakness, but the British noted that the Egyptians did not staff their advanced posts during the night. Thus, Wolseley decided to approach them then. British troops are not trained for such operations, and the nature of the ground was such that there would be no landmarks for guidance. The best he could provide for his men were naval navigators to march along and shoot the stars for their direction toward the enemy. On the night of 12–13 September, the force began their march. Wolseley allowed 5 hours to cover the 5.5 miles approaching the Egyptian lines. It was an extremely dark night, but the operation went off with little trouble.

At dawn, the British were in position, less than 200 yards from the defenses. On the right, the 1st Division was composed of English and Irish troops, supported by the Brigade of Guards commanded by the duke of Connaught. On the left, the 2nd Division was made up of various Scottish Highland regiments. Indian army troops and some Highlanders covered the extreme left across the canal, and the Household Cavalry took up position on the extreme right flank. When the sun came up and the Egyptians awoke to find the enemy so near at hand, firing began immediately. The Highlanders were slightly ahead of the rest and hit the Egyptians first, but took the heaviest casualties. Both central divisions managed to break the Egyptian line, but the flanking parties were the key to the rout that followed because they easily were able to envelop the Egyptian line and turn the retreat into mass confusion.

Results

The battle was over in less than 2 hours, not counting the pursuit of the Egyptian force the 50 miles back to Cairo. The violence of the assault broke through the Egyptian lines almost immediately, and Arabi was forced to abandon everything to save himself and as many men as possible. All the Egyptian artillery fell into British hands, and Arabi lost 2,500 men killed and wounded. The British casualties were 58 killed, less than 400 wounded, and about 30 missing. The pursuit was virtually unchallenged and, when Wolseley's men entered Cairo the following day, Arabi surrendered. The revolt collapsed.

Britain was now free to restore the financial administration that had been collecting Egyptian taxes for disbursement to European investors. To oversee that job, the London government appointed Lord Cromer, who became virtually the head of government. He had little desire to function as such, but no one of sufficient ability or trustworthiness could be found to take over the reins of power. Although he went to Cairo to serve only temporarily, Lord Cromer administered Egypt for 23 years. The Egyptian peasant, who had been obliged to bear the burden of the khedive's spending practices, was freed from the forced taxation of previous administrations. Although the taxes were levied and collected fairly (which upset some major landowners), almost three-fourths of Egypt's revenues went to pay the debts, rather than for the direct assistance of the population. In spite of that, the British did oversee a number of progressive endeavors, such as irrigation, school, and railroad projects. The Egyptian army was reorganized, trained, and commanded by British officers. Under the new government, that army aided British campaigns against Islamic fundamentalist rebels in the Sudan in the 1880s and 1890s.

By World War I, Egypt was regarded as a British protectorate, rather than a colony, although the distinction sometimes could hardly be discerned. Although Egypt was still nominally a possession of the Ottoman Empire, when Britain and the Turks went to war with each other in November 1914, Egypt did not join in with its former rulers, but acted as a base for British operations. After the war,

Britain's presence remained and was expanded into Iraq and the Persian Gulf region because of the mandate system inaugurated at the Versailles Conference that ended the war. That system gave Britain oversight authority in the administration of its mandated countries, in which the populations were to be guided toward independence. Although the Middle Eastern mandates did achieve that status (for the most part) before World War II, Egypt remained under British suzerainty. Not until 1956 did that come to an end.

When another Egyptian army colonel, Gamal Adbel Nasser, began a nationalist movement to overthrow royal rule and seize the Suez Canal for Egyptian income, the British once again felt the need to send in troops. However, the days of Wolseley and Queen Victoria were long over, and this time Egypt found a powerful friend in the form of the Soviet Union. Failing to reassert their control, both Britain and France lost a lot of international prestige, as well as control over one of the world's most strategic waterways. The Suez Canal, once regarded by Britain as vital for protection of India, the crown jewel of the British Empire, passed out of its control 8 years after India did the same.

References: Farwell, Byron. *Queen Victoria's Little Wars.* New York: Harper & Row, 1985; Featherstone, Donald. *Colonial Small Wars, 1837–1901.* Newton Abbot, Devon, England: David & Charles, 1973; Marlowe, John. *Cromer in Egypt.* London: Elek, 1970; Pakenham, Thomas. *The Scramble for Africa.* New York: Random House, 1991; Porter, Bernard. *The Lion's Share.* London: Longman, 1975.

MANILA BAY
1 May 1898

Forces Engaged
United States: Asiatic Squadron of five cruisers and two gunboats. Commander: Commodore George Dewey.

Spanish: Nine ships. Commander: Rear Admiral Patricio Montojo y Pasarón.

Importance
The last major sea battle of the nineteenth century, Manila Bay introduced completely steel fleets to naval warfare. U.S. victory established the presence of the United States in the Philippines for the next 50 years and the U.S. role in Asian affairs.

Historical Setting
Little in the events that led to the outbreak of the Spanish-American War in 1898 would have indicated that the first battle of that conflict would take place anywhere else but Cuba. Since 1895, Spanish forces had been struggling with yet another Cuban revolt, but this one was particularly nasty. The Cubans decided on a guerrilla campaign employing a scorched-earth policy. The theory seemed to be that if the island was economically useless, then the Spanish would leave. In response to that guerrilla campaign, Spanish General Victoriano Weyler introduced the policy of *reconcentrado.* Working on the theory that for a guerrilla movement to succeed it must have the support of the population, Weyler decided to make sure that the population could give no support. To accomplish that, he rounded up all the civilians on the island and placed them in a number of barbed-wire enclosures, hence the term, concentration camp. Once the Cubans were rounded up, anyone outside the camps was by definition a guerrilla and could be shot on sight. Although the camps were effective, the lack of clean water, sanitary facilities, medical care, or an adequate food supply guaranteed that the inmates suffered horribly. Some 250,000 Cubans died in the camps. By early 1898, the revolution was failing.

Weyler's tactics and the effects that ensued were front-page news in the United States, where rival newspaper publishers William Randolph Hearst and Joseph Pulitzer competed for the most lurid stories to inflame U.S. sensibilities. Public and government pressure to intervene was great, but President William

McKinley hesitated. A veteran of the American Civil War, he stated that he had no desire to see any more dead bodies. However, when the battle cruiser USS *Maine* blew up in Havana harbor on 15 February, some action had to be taken. When U.S. and Spanish investigations disagreed on the cause of the explosion, Hearst and Pulitzer made sure that the U.S. public was convinced that the Spanish were the culprits. Although McKinley's demands for Spanish concessions seemed to be getting positive response, in mid-April he went to Congress and asked for permission to use force to stop the fighting in Cuba. Given permission to do so, he sent the U.S. Atlantic Fleet to blockade Cuba, which provoked a declaration of war from Spain. The U.S. Congress responded in kind, backdating the declaration so it preceded the one from Spain.

The U.S. army, as usual, was small and needed a major infusion of volunteers to build up the necessary numbers for war. The U.S. navy, on the other hand, was prepared. Over the previous two decades, a number of influential people in and out of the government had been disciples of Alfred Thayer Mahan, whose book, *The Influence of Sea Power on History*, argued that for a nation to be great it must have a powerful navy. Thus, the U.S. navy received generous funding while the U.S. army struggled by. By 1898, the United States had one of the largest and best equipped navies in the world, and it was ready for action. Assistant Secretary of the Navy Theodore Roosevelt received permission to wire Commodore George Dewey in Hong Kong, where the Asiatic Squadron was temporarily stationed. Dewey received orders on 24 April 1898 to proceed to Manila, in the Philippine Islands, and engage the Spanish fleet located there. He steamed at once.

Dewey had been in Hong Kong since the previous summer, sent there by the Navy Department for just such an eventuality. He had spent his time gathering as much intelligence about the Spanish ships and defenses as he could, so, when he left for battle, he was as prepared as possible. Since 16 February, he had been on the alert to be ready for a declaration of war, and he had gone to a war footing. He painted the white ships battle gray and arranged for an emergency base on the southern coast of China. His great fear was for supplies. He was thousands of miles from the United States and he knew that the Spanish had large stocks of munitions at their forts at Cavite and Olangapo near Manila.

The Battle

Dewey's squadron consisted of five cruisers and two gunboats. Dewey sailed on board the flagship USS *Olympia*, 5,870 tons, classed as a protected cruiser, and one of the premiere ships of the fleet. Lighter cruisers *Baltimore, Boston, Concord,* and *Raleigh* were in support, along with the gunboat *Petrel,* cutter *McCulloch,* and a hurriedly purchased collier. In his haste, he ignored the possibility that the waters around the approaches to Subic or Manila Bays might be mined. Upon finding that Subic Bay was empty on the evening of 30 April, he steamed on toward Manila. The squadron sailed into the bay in darkness, past the island fortress of Corregidor. Although intelligence reports spoke of mines at the harbor entrance, the *Olympia* led the way single file through the wider southern channel at 2330. Although fire belched for a few minutes out of the *McCulloch's* smokestacks, the guns on Corregidor for some unknown reason did not fire. The smaller guns in the fort El Fraile loosed a few shots, which the Americans returned, but no other gunfire erupted.

It is 23 miles from the mouth of the harbor to the city of Manila, and at dawn the U.S. ships had arrived. Forts in the city held large guns, which caused Dewey some concern, but he was aided by the Spanish commander, Rear Admiral Patricio Montojo y Pasarón. Not wanting the city damaged in the exchange of gunfire, Pasarón ordered his ships to move to the anchorage at Cavite. Although this move would save Manila, it would not save his ships because there were few protecting guns there. As the U.S. ships sailed past Manila, guns fired at

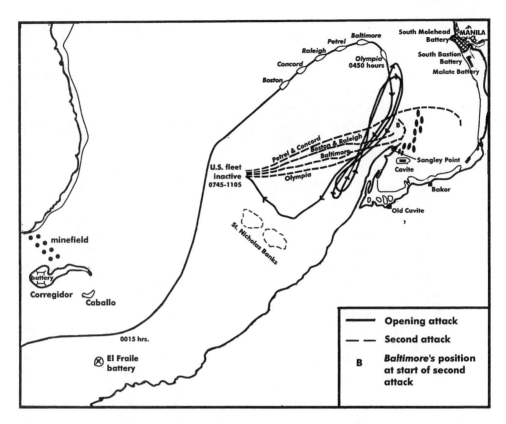

them. A few close shots fell near the *Petrel,* but most were far distant from their targets.

By 0450, the Spanish ships were in sight, and the sun was high enough for them to be singled out. There were seven of them: the flagship was the 3,520-ton cruiser *Reina Christina,* supported by *Don Juan de Austria, Don Antonio de Ulloa, Isla de Luzon, Castilla, Isla de Cuba,* and *Marques del Duero.* Two other ships, *General Lezo* and *Velasco,* were out of sight. The Spanish ships sat at anchor, so that their gunners had a steadier aim. The U.S. ships, by contrast, steamed by in column, shooting as they went. At 0515, the Spanish ships began shooting, but Dewey waited until his ships had closed to 5,500 yards. At this point, he spoke one of the best known phrases in U.S. history. At 0541, he said to the captain of the *Olympia,* "You may fire when ready, Gridley."

As the U.S. ships sailed back and forth, they pounded the Spanish, while receiving little ac-

curate fire in return. They made five passes, using their port side batteries on one 2.5 mile run and their starboard batteries on the return trip. Each succeeding lap drew nearer to the enemy so that on the final pass the gunners had to shoot at only about a mile range. At 0730, Dewey was informed that ammunition was running low, so he ordered the ships to withdraw into the harbor away from any shore batteries and for breakfast to be served to the crew, who had had some coffee and hardtack about 0400. At 1100, the ships returned to the battle, assured that the report of low ammunition had been false. The *Baltimore* reached Sangley Point, the peninsula that guarded Cavite, and proceeded to destroy the fort located there. It surrendered in short order. The *Petrel,* being of shallower draft than the cruisers, then rounded the point and sailed into the cove. It fired a few shots and received no return fire. The Spanish hoisted the white flag at 1220.

Results

The U.S. ships received damage, but all of it minimal. Eight men were wounded and none were killed. It was perhaps the most one-sided naval victory in history. Dewey "sailed boldly into Manila harbor and blew out of the water the collection of antiquated craft that passed for the Spanish fleet" (Bailey, *A Diplomatic History of the American People,* p. 468). The Spanish lost all of their ships and 381 men of a total complement of 1,200. Overwhelming as this victory was, it was of limited immediate effect. Dewey commanded only 2,000 men aboard his ships. That was certainly not sufficient for occupying the city of Manila, so he could do little other than wait for troops to arrive from the United States. He demanded that the Spanish authorities in Manila promise not to shoot at his ships, allow him to use the port facilities, and give him access to the telegraph cable to Hong Kong. They agreed only to the first demand, so Dewey steamed his ships to Cavite and occupied the arsenal there. His threat to bombard Manila if attacked kept the Spaniards in the city sufficiently cowed to hold their fire, but not enough to surrender the city and the islands. Dewey waited until 30 June for U.S. troops to arrive.

In the meantime, however, he worked with an exiled Filipino revolutionary, Emilio Aguinaldo, who had been expelled from his country after an abortive revolution against Spanish rule in 1894. He was in Hong Kong when Dewey sailed. Aquinaldo went with the Americans, and on the voyage to Manila he and Dewey made plans for the Philippines. Since Aguinaldo had contacts in-country, Dewey suggested he be put ashore to raise a force that could control the countryside. With the Americans in control of the waters around the archipelago, the Spanish army would be bottled up in a few cities. That would ensure limited hostilities until the U.S. army arrived. This indeed occurred, but, when the Treaty of Paris was signed ending the war, the Philippines were turned over to the United States in return for $20 million.

Aguinaldo claimed that Dewey had promised him that his homeland would be free. After all, when the U.S. Congress authorized military action, it added the Teller Amendment to that resolution, thereby disavowing any intention of annexing Cuba. Certainly the Philippines should be treated the same, he reasoned. Besides, he claimed, Dewey had promised him that would be the case. Dewey denied it, and no records were kept of their private conversations. Even if Dewey had made such a promise, it was beyond the limits of his authority to do so. Infuriated that the Filipinos seemed to be trading one overlord for another, Aguinaldo withdrew to the hills and jungles and staged a guerrilla war against the Americans. In response, while the United States promised all sorts of progressive improvements for the islands, the U.S. army began a policy of establishing concentration camps. As in the camps in Cuba, conditions were less than healthy, and at the hands of the United States another 250,000 people died. Such are the costs of power.

The Spanish-American War made the United States a world power. Acquisition of the Philippines (along with the additional territories of Puerto Rico, Guam, and the Hawaiian Islands) made it an imperial power. The United States had for the previous decade been enlarging its role in world affairs and had hoped some day to have access to Asian markets. Now, with a naval base in the Philippines, those markets were on the U.S. doorstep. Hawaii and Guam gave the United States fueling stations across the Pacific on the trade route to Manila. In less than a year, U.S. Secretary of State John Hay was proposing to European powers his Open Door Policy in China, so that the United States could gain access to the largest of all markets.

Militarily, the battle at Manila Bay marked a major change in naval warfare. For the first time, fleets that had no ships of wood engaged each other. Steel navies were being constructed after the time of the American Civil War, but this was the first time any such ships (other than ironclads) had seen combat. However, the ships the United States committed to action at

Manila were obsolescent, and the next major development in naval construction, the dreadnought, was about to be launched in Britain. As outclassed as the Spanish were on 1 May 1898, that was how outclassed the U.S. navy soon was. The decade and a half preceding World War I was dominated by the construction of dreadnought-class battleships, whose big guns controlled the seas until they were made obsolescent by the power of aircraft carriers in World War II.

References: Bailey, Thomas. *A Diplomatic History of the American People.* Englewood Cliffs, NJ: Prentice-Hall, 1968; Dewey, George. *Autobiography of George Dewey.* New York: Charles Scribner's Sons, 1916; Friedel, Frank. *The Splendid Little War.* Boston: Little, Brown, 1958; Millis, Walter. *The Martial Spirit.* Boston: Houghton Mifflin, 1931; Wrigley, Herbert W. *The Downfall of Spain: Naval History of the Spanish-American War.* New York: B. Franklin, 1971 [1900].

MUKDEN
19 February–10 March 1905

FORCES ENGAGED

Japanese: Sources vary estimates from 200,000 to 320,000 men, in five armies. Commander: Marshal Iwao Oyama.

Russian: Sources vary estimates from 200,000 to 310,000 men, in three armies. Commander: General Alexei Kuropatkin.

IMPORTANCE

Japanese victory, although at high cost, brought about talks that ended the Russo-Japanese War and established Japan as an internationally recognized military power.

Historical Setting

In the last part of the nineteenth century, China was economically dominated by foreign powers. Britain, France, Russia, Germany, and Japan had claimed economic spheres of influence,

and each held a virtual monopoly in its sphere. In 1899, U.S. Secretary of State John Hay proposed the Open Door Policy, which would have broken up the sectional dominance in favor of free trade. All the powers agreed in principle to this plan, but Russia was the least cooperative. It continued to exclude foreign competition in its economic zone of Manchuria. Japan, a country with great ambition but little in the way of natural resources, looked at Manchuria as the best source of coal, iron, etc., for its burgeoning industry and military. Japan attempted to negotiate with Russia over trade issues in Manchuria, but made little headway. Russia made promises, but took no action and in the meantime built up its armed forces in Manchuria. By 1904, Japan realized that further talks were pointless, so it began preparing for war.

In February, the Imperial Japanese Navy launched a surprise attack on the Russian Pacific fleet based at the Chinese harbor city of Port Arthur. This impaired Russian naval power in the region and allowed Japan to transport troops, which landed on the Liaotung Peninsula in late April and began operations to capture Port Arthur. On 1 May 1904, Japanese troops based in Korea (over which it had exercised suzerainty since the Sino-Japanese War, 1894–1895) beat back minimal Russian resistance along the Yalu River to launch a landward invasion of Manchuria. Few foreign observers gave the Japanese any hope of winning, as they were a small, poor country facing the largest nation in the world. Further, no European observer could conceive of an Asian army defeating a western army.

Japan proceeded to defy conventional wisdom by handing the Russian forces a string of defeats. In late August and early September, Japanese forces captured the city of Liaoyang, effectively isolating the besieged Russian troops fighting for Port Arthur. A Russian attempt to counterattack and break through and lift the siege was beaten back at Sha-ho in October. Port Arthur surrendered on 1 January, and the Japanese army that had been laying siege was freed to march north and join the rest of the

Japanese forces aiming toward the major Russian troop concentration at Mukden.

The Russian commander, General Alexei Kuropatkin, commanded forces far superior in number to the Japanese, but Russian combat doctrine was obsolete. The training that Russian troops received emphasized shock, putting as many men with bayonets as possible in contact with the enemy. They apparently had not learned from the American Civil War that such tactics were futile in an era of improved firepower. Russian artillery was supposed to be used in such a way as to support both offense and defense, but was committed in such small numbers that maximum firepower was rarely achieved. Both infantry and artillery units had to be supported by large reserves, usually equaling the number of troops in the line. The Japanese, commanded by Marshal Iwao Oyama, were trained along the lines of Prussian theory. Firepower was most important, and advancing troops should use all available cover; artillery fire was designed primarily for

infantry support. These two conflicting doctrinal views meant that the Japanese, although the younger army, was better prepared for this war than were the Russians and that the Russians would never commit sufficient troops to a battle until too late.

The Battle

Kuropatkin placed his three armies, numbering some 200,000 to 300,000 men, in a strong position south of the city of Mukden. Across a 90-mile front, his men occupied defenses. The eastern two-thirds of their front were anchored in the Ta-lin Mountains. The western third of the line stretched from the mountains to the Hun River and was anchored along its length by strongly defended villages and towns. Kuropatkin ordered a cavalry reconnaissance on 9 January to locate the Japanese, but the Cossack units that he dispatched were easily kept at bay and misled as to the Japanese intentions. The Russian commander was given the erro-

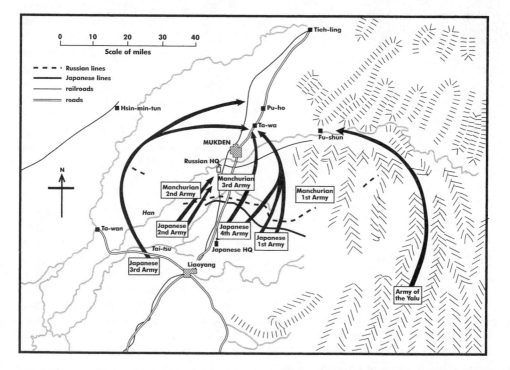

neous report that the Japanese had not yet arrived in any great numbers on the western flank, when in fact Marshal Oyama was almost in position for an attack. This led Kuropatkin to place fewer men on his right flank in the west.

The fighting started on 26 January 1905 when Kuropatkin launched an attack toward the center of the Japanese lines. The town of San-de-pu changed hands three times in 2 days, the battle being fought in the midst of a raging blizzard. After the Russians secured the town on 27 January, a Japanese flanking move convinced Kuropatkin to withdraw to his original lines. That move both ceded the initiative to the Japanese and greatly reduced the morale of the Russian troops.

Reinforced by the arrival of the Third Army from Port Arthur, Oyama launched his own offensive on 19 February. The initial Japanese attacks were launched at the strongest part of the Russian defenses, on the eastern flank in the mountains. The Japanese made slow, costly advances but succeeded in forcing Kuropatkin to commit his reserves to that wing of the battle. When he did so, Oyama launched his Second Army at the Russian lines on the western flank, sending the Third Army in a wide sweep across the Hun River to turn the Russian flank and get behind them and astride the one rail line that kept the Russian army supplied.

After more than a week of close-in fighting in the mountains, that flanking move convinced Kuropatkin to fall back on Mukden. He established a line on the north side of the Ta-lin Mountains on 2 March while wrapping his right flank well back to a north-south position to protect the railroad. Free of the mountains, the Japanese were able to launch larger, more sustained attacks, and within a week the Russians had been forced back to the Ka-ma-lin Mountains on the east flank and the Mukden-Harbin road on the west. Fearing complete encirclement, Kuropatkin ordered a withdrawal on 10 March. That move extricated the bulk of his forces, although Japanese artillery fire inflicted severe casualties.

Results

Casualty counts for the Mukden battle vary wildly, from a low of 20,000 Russians and 53,000 Japanese killed and wounded, to a high of 156,000 Russians and 70,000 Japanese. It is almost certain that Japan lost more men killed and wounded, whereas the Russians lost fewer dead and wounded but significantly more prisoners.

Oyama failed to do what he hoped, to completely destroy the Russian army. Although the Japanese controlled Port Arthur and the Liao-tung Peninsula, as long as a Russian army existed Japan could not be safe. Mukden was already at the limit of its supply capabilities, while the Russians continued to control the vital railway that connected them with reinforcements and supplies from the west. Strategically, therefore, the Japanese victory at Mukden was a failure. The Japanese were not only at the limit of their supply lines, they were also at the limit of which the Japanese government and economy could provide. Russia, on the other hand, retained troop strength and industrial reserves as yet untapped.

In the end that meant nothing. Although in a material position to continue the war, the Russian government and population were not in a psychological position to do so. The lack of victories in the face of what should have been an inconsequential enemy shocked the Russian government and high command; Kuropatkin resigned after the battle. The Russian monarchy, under political pressure from radical groups, felt increasing strain as the successive defeats were reported in the press. Revolution broke out; it was suppressed, but it convinced the Russians that a negotiated settlement with Japan was desirable.

The Japanese government instructed their ambassador in Washington to request (secretly) that President Theodore Roosevelt offer mediation. Roosevelt publicly called on both nations to send representatives to Washington. Russia agreed only if the Japanese publicly agreed first.

Negotiators met in early August 1905 in Washington, D.C., but soon removed to the cooler atmosphere of the U.S. naval base at Portsmouth, New Hampshire. There, on 23 August, the Portsmouth Treaty was signed. Russia ceded the Liaotung Peninsula to Japan, including the harbor at Port Arthur, as well as recognizing Japanese preeminence in Korea and giving up the southern half of Sakhalin Island. Japan tried to bargain for Russian payment for the war but failed; they also wanted to keep Russian ships that were captured during the war, but were obliged to return them. Roosevelt convinced the Japanese that those concessions were outweighed by the fact that they had accomplished what they set out to do: gain access to Manchurian resources.

The fighting that took place in the Russo-Japanese War was a preview of World War I in France, although few countries noticed it at the time. The Industrial Revolution had fully arrived in the military sphere by this time, and huge numbers of artillery pieces were in evidence, as was a new weapon, the machine gun. Armies in trenches with lots of firepower was the norm in Manchuria, as it was 10 years later in France, but only Germany was smart enough to take advantage of the lessons of Manchuria. Observers saw the efficacy of machine guns and made sure that the German army had plenty; only bitter experience in France would teach the British and French armies the same lesson.

The Japanese victory established Japan as a military power of international repute. Victories at Port Arthur, Liaoyang, and Mukden proved that, and they also gained some psychological effects; in particular, the long-held view that the west had a corner on military ability needed rethinking. Japan had been isolated from the rest of the world between 1600 and 1854, when U.S. Admiral Matthew Perry "opened" Japan. Faced with the huge technological lead the rest of the world possessed, the government in Japan moved the country and society ahead 300 years in 50 years. The Russo-Japanese War proved the effectiveness of that advancement.

The war in Manchuria, finished at Mukden, showed two international powers passing each other in different directions. The Russian Revolution of 1905, although crushed, laid the groundwork for the Menshevik and Bolshevik Revolutions in 1917. Japan, however, was on the rise. The Japanese army over the first decades of the twentieth century rose in prominence to the point that by 1931 it dominated the government, directly leading to another invasion of Manchuria in that year and the invasion of the rest of China in 1937. The Japanese navy, also arriving in the Russo-Japanese War as a force to be reckoned with, together with the army completed the force that Japan needed to be the dominant nation in Asia. Public dissatisfaction with the Portsmouth Treaty laid the foundation of U.S.-Japanese rivalry in the Pacific that ultimately produced a showdown in World War II.

The victory also had a psychological effect on all of Asia. The western colonial powers had dominated Asia, directly or indirectly, since the eighteenth century in a long series of international takeovers. No Asian population had successfully resisted any western power until 1904–1905. Japan's victory over Russia signaled a sea change in Asian attitudes toward western powers; similar victories over the British at the start of World War II brought about popular movements that brought most western empires to an end.

References: Asakawa, K. The Russo-Japanese Conflict: Its Causes and Issues. Boston: Houghton Mifflin, 1904; Conaughton, R. M. The War of the Rising Sun and the Tumbling Bear. London: Routledge, 1991; Martin, Christopher. The Russo-Japanese War. London: Hutchison, 1967; Walder, David. The Short Victorious War. New York: Harper & Row, 1973; Warner, Denis. The Tide at Sunrise. New York: Charterhouse, 1974.

TSUSHIMA

27 May 1905

FORCES ENGAGED

Japanese: Four battleships, eight cruisers, twenty-one destroyers, and sixty torpedo boats. Commander: Heihachiro Togo.

Russian: Eight battleships, eight cruisers, and nine destroyers. Commander: Zinovy Rozhdestvensky.

IMPORTANCE

Disastrous Russian defeat spelled Russia's doom as a naval power and marked arrival of the Japanese as a major naval power.

Historical Setting

During 1894–1895, Japan had made the world sit up and take notice when it easily defeated the nation of China in a war over Korea and the Liaotung Peninsula, which juts southward into the Sea of Japan west of Korea. Because of intense European diplomatic pressure, however, Japan was forced to give up almost all the territory it had conquered, including the strategic harbor at Port Arthur on the tip of the Liaotung Peninsula. Immediately after Japan was forced to cede the conquests, Russia leapt in and extorted from the Chinese government the right to build a railroad, the last extension of the Trans-Siberia Railway, through Manchuria to Port Arthur. Russia also gained control of Port Arthur as a naval base for the bulk of its Pacific Squadron, the remainder based farther north at Vladivostok. The Japanese government and population were humiliated by this treatment at European hands and held the greatest grudge against Russia.

In 1899, U.S. Secretary of State John Hay convinced Britain, France, Germany, Russia, and Japan to concur regarding the Open Door Policy, which called for China to be open to free trade with all foreign interests. Japan hoped, through this agreement, to gain access to the raw materials of the northeastern Chinese province of Manchuria. Japan had only since 1854 been open to outside visitation, and the government realized then that serious work had to be done for Japan to catch up technologically with the rest of the world. As Japan is a resource-poor country, the coal, iron ore, and other resources of Manchuria seemed a handy source of supply. Russia, however, balked at fulfilling its Open Door obligations. Japan attempted through negotiation to enter the Manchurian markets, but the Russians failed to bargain in good faith and simultaneously brought in supplemental troops. By early 1904, Japan had had enough.

Just before midnight on 8 February, Japanese destroyers and torpedo boats entered Port Arthur and launched a number of torpedoes at the anchored Russian fleet. Three Russian ships were badly damaged. At first light, Japanese Admiral Heihachiro Togo brought up the remainder of the Japanese navy and began shelling Russian ships and shore batteries. More damage was done to Russian ships and facilities, but, when their return fire began to damage Japanese ships, Togo drew back. The Russians failed to use their superior numbers to sally and engage the Japanese. The Japanese failed to press their attack and destroy the Russian fleet at anchor. What Togo failed to realize was that the Russian fleet was poorly trained and dispirited, and the gunners operating the artillery defending the harbor were for the most part incompetent. Thus, he decided against risking his smaller fleet.

That same day, 9 February 1904, Japanese ships attacked Russian ships anchored in the harbor of Chemulpo (Inchon), damaging two Russian vessels in the harbor that were soon scuttled by their crews. Japanese troops soon after landed and captured the city, setting up an invasion of Manchuria by Japanese forces at the beginning of May.

In the meantime, the Russian fleet in Port Arthur got a new commander, Admiral Stepan

Makarov. He instilled some discipline and training in the crews and sallied out of the harbor on 13 April. His flagship struck a Russian mine and sank, taking Makarov to the bottom. His successor, believing no action was better than bad action, kept the ships parked in Port Arthur's harbor. When Imperial Japanese Army forces attacked the city, their artillery destroyed the harbor facilities and sank the last of the Russian ships. To avenge the loss of the Pacific Squadron, Czar Nicholas II sent the Russian Baltic Fleet to the Pacific. Under the command of lackluster Admiral Zinovy Rozhdestvensky, the aging ships, with four newer battleships included, began the long voyage around the world, a voyage that was in itself virtually a disaster. Afraid of Japanese torpedo boats in the North Sea, the Russian fleet mistakenly fired on and sank British fishing boats off the Dogger Banks, creating an international incident that came perilously close to war. Rozhdestvenski then divided his fleet, half sailing around the Cape of Good Hope, with the other half sailing through the Suez Canal, both to meet at Madagascar. Their arrival there on 1 January 1905 coincided with the Japanese capture of Port Arthur. The combined fleet resupplied in French Indochina and then on 14 May departed for the last leg of the journey to Vladivostok.

The Battle

The Russian commander was fairly sure that he would encounter the Japanese navy if he steered a course west of Japan, but decided to do so anyway. Since his indecisive actions with the Russian Pacific Squadron, Togo had stepped up training and acquired for his big guns improved shells, many of which had earlier proven defective. His four battleships, eight cruisers, twenty-one destroyers, and sixty torpedo boats, although outnumbered in capital ships by the Russians, were newer and faster. The crews possessed much better morale and training than their Russian counterparts. Togo was looking for a fight, while Rozhdestvensky was looking to get to Vladivostok and join with the remainder of the Russian navy based there. Togo also had the advantage of being close to his home bases and had much greater familiarity with the waters that he sailed.

Admiral Togo anchored his fleet in Masampo Bay in southern Korea, hoping for news that the Russians would take the inland sea route. His plans were to set sail as soon as he received word of the Russians being sighted; this was to be accomplished by the newly invented wireless telegraphy. He would then sail for the Russian fleet, using his battleships to cross in front of the Russian fleet while his cruisers flanked the Russian line and attacked their rear. His smaller ships would then enter the fray, using torpedoes to create havoc and finish off damaged enemy ships. He received word of the Russian arrival from the *Siano Maru,* which almost ran into a Russian hospital vessel trailing the fleet in the fog at dawn on 27 May 1905.

Admiral Rozhdestvensky aimed his ships for the straits between the Japanese home island of Honshu and the small island of Tsushima. The Russian fleet, at sea in two parallel columns, was ordered into a single line after the encounter with the Japanese ship. Rozhdestvensky was on a heading almost due north when lookouts at 1000 hours spotted the Japanese fleet approaching from the northwest, and Japanese cruisers took up a parallel course about 6 miles to the west. At 1200, the course was shifted to east by north, while Russian officers in their wardroom drank a toast to the anniversary of Czar Nicholas's coronation. Just before 1400, Togo, aboard his flagship *Mikasa,* arrived with the battleships and made for the head of the Russian line, attempting the classic naval maneuver of "crossing the T." He succeeded, and Japanese ships were able to fire broadsides at the oncoming Russian line, which could bring only their forward guns to bear.

Rozhdestvensky turned to parallel the Japanese in order to bring his guns to bear, but superior Japanese speed and gunnery meant that Togo controlled the battle. The Russian flag-

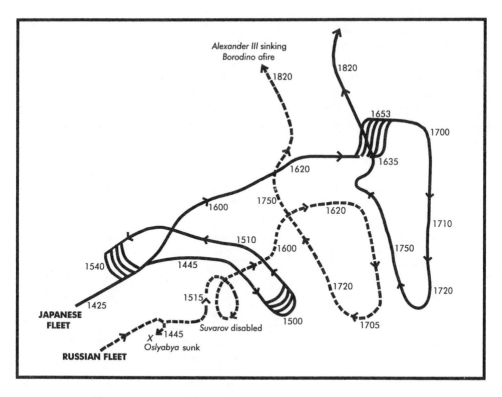

ship *Suvarov* was hit early in the battle, losing its steering capability at about 1500 hours. That seemed to take the fight out of the rest of the Russian fleet. A Japanese officer observed, "After the first twenty minutes the Russians seemed suddenly to go all to pieces, and their shooting became wild and almost harmless" (Warner, *Great Sea Battles*, p. 248). Rozhdestvensky had been twice wounded, and late in the day he ordered his second-in-command, Rear Admiral Nikolai Nebogatov aboard the *Nikolai I,* to get as many ships as possible through the straits to Vladivostok.

Such was not to be. Three battleships were sunk on 27 May, and then Japanese torpedo boats unmercifully harassed the Russian ships all night long. The next day, any Russian ships that had been unable to flee were sunk or captured. Only a single cruiser supported by two destroyers slipped north to Vladivostok, while three destroyers turned around and fled for the Philippines, where they were interned in Manila.

Results

For the loss of three torpedo boats sunk and approximately 1,000 men lost, plus several capital ships damaged, the Japanese scored one of the most impressive naval victories of all time. Not since Trafalgar had such a one-sided victory occurred between two fairly evenly matched fleets. The U.S. victory at Manila Bay, although more decisive in terms of numbers, was a total mismatch in quality of vessels engaged. At Tsushima, the Japanese sunk six Russian battleships and captured two more; four Russian cruisers were sunk, and four others survived the battle by escaping in the darkness. Of the nine Russian destroyers, seven were sunk and two captured. Total Russian personnel losses are estimated at nearly 10,000.

The crushing defeat at Tsushima, on the heels of the military defeat at Mukden a few weeks earlier, sent shock waves through the government in Moscow. The 1905 revolution was one of the side effects, but the one-two punch of Tsushima and Mukden convinced the Russians to accept an offer by U.S. President Theodore Roosevelt to meet in the United States in August 1905. There Russian and Japanese delegates agreed to the Treaty of Portsmouth. One of the most bitterly contested points of that treaty was the disposition of the surviving Russian ships. The *Nikolai I* and *Orel* had been repaired by the Japanese and incorporated into their fleet. They wanted to keep them, but the Russians demanded their return, presumably as the core around which a new Russian navy could be constructed. Only pressure by Roosevelt on the Japanese delegates convinced them to return the Russian vessels.

That action had repercussions on U.S.-Japanese relations. Although the Japanese government accepted the terms of the Portsmouth Treaty, the Japanese public was not happy. The surrender of fairly won prizes smacked of the surrender of Japanese conquests after its victory over China; that, coupled with the inability of the Japanese negotiators to gain monetary compensation from Russia, left a bad feeling among many Japanese toward the United States. When, several months later, the California legislature passed laws discriminating against Japanese immigrants, racial tension flared in both countries. Japanese newspapers began calling for action against the United States.

Fearful of what effects such public opinion may have on the Japanese government, Roosevelt decided to send the U.S. battleship fleet on an around-the-world cruise. Painted white as a symbol of peace, the Great White Fleet called at Tokyo Bay in the summer of 1907. Although the Americans were treated in an extremely hospitable fashion, the experience of the U.S. ships verged on disaster. Several breakdowns along the way showed the age of the U.S. ships in comparison with the later-model Japanese battleships. With no escort ships along and foreign colliers hired to fuel the ships, had the Japanese navy decided to start trouble, the result could have been equal to the outcome of Tsushima. Instead, the two navies got on famously, and the resulting Root-Takahira Agreement spelled out spheres of interest for the United States and Japan in the Pacific region.

Roosevelt realized that Japan had arrived as a naval power, and one that needed to be taken very seriously. Although the Root-Takahira Agreement limited the construction of defenses on U.S.-held islands, it did maintain amicable relations between the two countries in the Pacific for almost 30 years. Theodore Roosevelt did not live to see his vision of a powerful Japanese navy come true in the late 1930s, but it happened after shipbuilding limitation agreements of the 1920s fell apart. The long-standing Japanese resentment at being treated by the West as second-class exploded in 1941, and the war that Roosevelt feared did indeed take place. Only the newer, more modern, and more expanded U.S. navy of World War II put to rest the struggle for naval supremacy in the Pacific.

References: Conaughton, R. M. *The War of the Rising Sun and the Tumbling Bear.* London: Routledge, 1991; Unger, Frederick William. *Russia and Japan and the War in the Far East.* Philadelphia: H. W. B. Conrad, 1905; Walder, David. *The Short Victorious War.* London: Hutchinson, 1973; Warner, Denis. *The Tide at Sunrise.* New York: Charterhouse, 1974; Warner, Oliver. *Great Sea Battles.* London: Spring Books, 1963.

MARNE, FIRST BATTLE (1914)
5–10 September 1914

FORCES ENGAGED

French and British: Sixth, Fifth, and Ninth French Armies and British Expeditionary Force. Commander: General Joseph Joffre.

German: First, Second, and Third Armies. Commander: Count Helmuth von Moltke.

IMPORTANCE
French victory robbed Germany of its planned
rapid defeat of France, resulting in 4 years of
trench warfare in France.

Historical Setting

To ask what caused World War I is almost like
asking, "Who killed John Kennedy?" The answers are numerous and varied: France's desire
for revenge after its humiliating loss in the
Franco-Prussian War of 1870–1871; the alliance system, which created an antagonistic balance of power resulting from France's desire to
gain allies for the inevitable next war with Germany; rampant nationalism, which begat mili-
tarism and imperialism; a lack of government
leaders after the removal of the chancellor of
Germany, Otto von Bismarck, who had been
somewhat able to control the erratic and aggressive nature of Kaiser Wilhelm; German
desire for a navy that rivaled Britain's; Germany's
desire to create *Mitteleuropa,* a central European customs union stretching from the North
Sea to the Persian Gulf; the struggles of ethnic
groups in the Balkans that involved their
respective major-power champions, Austria-
Hungary and Russia; and Britain's need for allies in an increasingly hostile world. Any or all
of these answers apply.

Whatever the social, political, economic,
and military reasons for the war starting, in retrospect war seemed inevitable. It seems even
more so when one looks at the German plan
for winning it, although contingency plans for
future wars are part of the nature of a general
staff, an organization invented and perfected
by the Germans. Germany's General Staff, under the leadership of General Alfred von
Schlieffen, developed an invasion plan for operations against France as early as 1894. Between that date and the outbreak of war in
1914, the Schlieffen Plan underwent occasional
modification, but the attack launched by Germany in August 1914 was a variant on the 20-
year-old set of instructions.

France's alliance with Russia virtually guaranteed a two-front war, which Germany very
much wanted to avoid. Working on the assumption that Russia's mobilization process would
take weeks if not months to implement,
Schlieffen proposed a massive attack against
France to knock it out of the war before Russia
could have its armies ready. Then, German
forces could be transported east to deal with
the inferior Russian army. The Schlieffen Plan
called for minimal forces to be kept on the eastern frontier, as well as minimal forces stationed
along the Franco-German frontier. France's Plan
XVII, even older than the Schlieffen Plan, called
for a massive invasion of Germany in the event
of war, but through an area known for its rugged terrain. German planners were sure that a
small force could defend such ground while the
bulk of the German army swung around the
French left flank and raced for Paris. Bogged
down on the frontier, the French army could
not face about in time to return to defend the
capital. Once Paris fell, as in 1871, France
would surrender.

Schlieffen's plan, however, contained one
major political problem. To bypass not only the
French army but the French fortresses defending the frontier, the German sweep would have
to pass through neutral Belgium, whose very
existence was guaranteed by multilateral agreements to which Germany was a signatory. Violating anyone's neutrality was rarely done, and
that would certainly provoke Great Britain, as
another of the guarantors. If, however, the attack went as planned, France would be defeated
before Britain could effectively respond.

With the Schlieffen Plan in place and the
multiple international factors at play, one
needed only wait for an incident to set events
in motion. Such an incident took place at
Sarajevo, Bosnia, on 28 June 1914, when Austrian Archduke Franz Ferdinand was assassinated by a Serbian terrorist. Austria's demand
for retribution brought in Russia to stand up
for Serbia, and Germany's alliance with Austria
meant a Russo-German war, which therefore

meant a Franco-German war. The interlocking set of alliances developed over the previous three decades guaranteed that if any two nations started fighting, it would almost immediately become a conflict involving all of Europe. When Austria announced that Serbia had failed to meet Vienna's ultimatum (whether Serbia actually did so or not has been debated ever since), the declarations of war began on 28 July. By 4 August, Austria-Hungary, Russia, Germany, France, and Great Britain had all declared war, with smaller countries such as Serbia and Belgium involved as well.

The Battle

On 4 August 1914, German armies violated Belgian neutrality as Germany's First, Second, and Third Armies marched through on the way to Paris. The Schlieffen Plan had called for almost 90 percent of Germany's army to be involved in that attack, but Schlieffen's successor Helmuth von Moltke, who became chief of the German General Staff in 1906, did not have his predecessor's vision or boldness. He had continually altered the plan to have more men in the east and on the French frontier, so the force that went through Belgium was significantly reduced from the original intention. Still, it was initially effective. The French invasion did indeed bog down in the woods and hills of Alsace, but the Germans were slowed by a stubborn Belgian defense around a series of obsolescent but huge forts. Moltke ordered divisions drawn from the sweeping attack to deal with these fortresses, and they were not finally reduced until late August. Another factor that harmed the German plan was the action taking place on the Franco-German frontier. Moltke's shifting of troops had strengthened the German defense but at the same time not strengthened it sufficiently to launch an offensive of its own if the opportunity presented itself, which it did. The Germans attacked the surprised French armies and forced their withdrawal to a series of fortified positions, but the

Germans lacked the numbers necessary to push past those forts. Thus, the French were able to reduce their force, thanks to the strength of their forts, and those personnel were moved west to aid Paris.

The French soon realized that Plan XVII was useless and, unless an immediate defense of their capital could be mounted, then it would be a repeat of their 1870 embarrassment. The person in charge of this defense was General Joseph Joffre. He ordered the creation of a new army, the Sixth, and Parisian military governor General Joseph Galliéni rounded up almost anyone of military age in the Paris region and threw them in front of the city to make a stand at the Marne River. This is one of France's proudest moments. Using the only available transport, Parisian taxis, thousands of men were carried to the Marne and placed in the way of the German onslaught. The "Taxis of the Marne" thus became enshrined in French legend. Meanwhile, British forces were landing much sooner than Germany expected, and the bulk of the French army was ponderously turning itself around and trying to get back to Paris in time.

The Germans still had the momentum, but it was gradually fading. In spite of the Belgian resistance, the German timetable was still a few days ahead of schedule. The ineffective defensive stands made by the four-division-strong British Expeditionary Force (BEF) and the French Fifth Army allowed the German army to move faster than planned. That turned out to be a negative factor, however, because their supply trains could not keep up and the soldiers began feeling the effects of too little food. Then, Moltke again abandoned the tenets of the Schlieffen Plan and gave the French and British an opportunity to strike back. Instead of the "swinging door" effect of a wide sweeping front that would turn the flank of the entire French army and arc north then west of Paris with its far right flank, Moltke ordered a shortening of the line and an encirclement not of Paris but of the French fortress city of

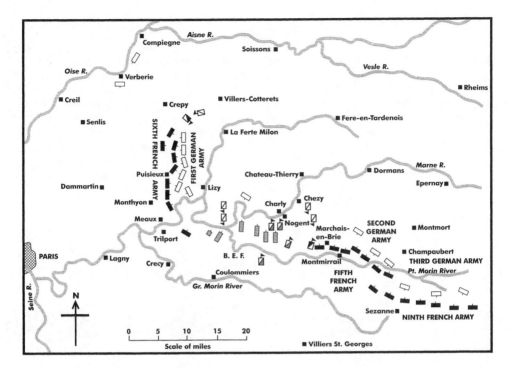

Map labels: Aisne R., Compiegne, Soissons, Vesle R., Oise R., Verberie, Rheims, Creil, Crepy, Villers-Cotterets, Senlis, SIXTH FRENCH ARMY, FIRST GERMAN ARMY, Fere-en-Tardenois, La Ferte Milon, La Ferte Milon, Marne R., Puisieux, Chateau-Thierry, Dormans, Dammartin, Lizy, Epernay, Monthyon, Charly, Chezy, Meaux, Nogent, SECOND GERMAN ARMY, Montmort, Trilport, Marchais-en-Brie, Champaubert, THIRD GERMAN ARMY, PARIS, Lagny, B. E. F., Montmirrail, Pt. Morin River, Crecy, Coulommiers, FIFTH FRENCH ARMY, Gr. Morin River, Sezanne, NINTH FRENCH ARMY, N, 0 5 10 15 20, Scale of miles, Villiers St. Georges, Seine R.

Verdun. That meant that, instead of descending on Paris from the north and west, the German right flank would instead descend east of Paris, offering its own flank as a potential target. That right flank was aimed at the Marne River, where the newly formed Sixth Army was deploying.

The Allies now had the chance to severely harm the German effort. The Sixth Army stood at the Marne, while the French Fifth Army and the BEF stopped their retreats and counterattacked at the now exposed German right flank. Between 5–10 September, the German army ground to a halt and, with its flank and rear open to attack, had to retreat. Both the Germans on their side and the British and French on their side began to dig in, and the next 4 years were fought in the trenches.

Results

German Chief of Staff Moltke proved the adage that fortune favors the bold because his lack of boldness doomed the Schlieffen Plan. Certainly the inability to maintain adequate supplies to the front line troops, as well as the decreasing direct contact between headquarters and the leading elements of the German advance, would have hampered the German effort no matter the effectiveness of the Allied response. However, Moltke continually weakened a plan that should have been wildly successful, and he did because of his own hesitation, thus proving a second adage, "never take counsel of your fears." Legend has it that, on his deathbed in 1913, Schlieffen's final words were "Keep the right flank strong." He did not live to see Moltke subvert that dictum. In critiquing the Schlieffen Plan, military historian Trevor Dupuy wrote, "It was, in fact, the kind of strategic gamble of which Napoleon was so fond, in which even the worst outcome was not likely to be disastrous, and in which the possibility of a good outcome was extremely attractive"(Dupuy, *A Genius for War*, p. 143).

TANNENBERG

Just as important to the outcome of the opening campaign of World War I was the battle of Tannenberg, fought in East Prussia between German and Russian forces. The Schlieffen Plan had called for Russia to be held in check in the east while France was quickly crushed in the west. Russia should have been easy to neutralize; the Germans expected it would take weeks if not months for Russian armies to mobilize and march. Answering urgent appeals from France, however, Czar Nicholas threw his unprepared army into action on 17 August. The Germans, however, were just as unprepared for him to do that.

The Russian attack took place along two parallel lines divided by a large marshy region around the Masurian Lakes. The northern thrust was commanded by General Paul Rennenkampf and the southern was controlled by General Alexander Samsonov, both veterans of the Russo-Japanese War and neither fond of the other. Rennenkampf's opening attack caught the German commander, General Max von Prittwitz, off guard and he quickly began pulling his troops back. He warned the German high command that he would have to retreat to the Vistula River to make a stand and could do so only with reinforcements. Subordinates on his staff, however, convinced him the next day to stand fast and take advantage of the Russian armies being separated and unable to support each other.

Unfortunately for Prittwitz, he did not tell his subordinates that he had contacted the high command, nor did he send word up the chain of command that he had changed his mind. At the German headquarters in Coblenz, Moltke did two things: one positive and one negative. First, he decided to relieve Prittwitz and replace him with someone less anxious and more aggressive. His choices were retired but respected Paul von Hindenburg as overall commander and Erich von Ludendorff (recently a hero for actions at the battle for the Belgian city of Liege) as chief of staff. These two implemented the plans of Prittwitz's subordinates and smashed Samsonov in the south with a massive double envelopment at Tannenberg and then drove back Rennenkampf in the north.

The second, and negative, action that Moltke took was to heed Prittwitz's original warnings and detach troops from France to shore up the German line in the east. That withdrawal, on top of the steady weakening of the Schlieffen Plan that he had implemented before the war, almost guaranteed failure in France. Ironically, the troops that were shifted eastward arrived too late to take part in the German victories.

The German victory at Tannenberg was as crucial as their defeat on the Marne. Had German troops lost to the Russians as well as the French, Germany's government would almost certainly have stopped the war rather than continue in the face of two failures on opposite fronts. On the other hand, had the Germans defeated the French and Russians both, then the Allies would almost certainly have given up. The mixture of victory and defeat meant that the war would not be the quick and successful conflict that the Germans had envisioned but the long slogging war in the trenches of France and the give-and-take war of maneuver across the vastness of the eastern European plains.

Certainly the French turnabout from the frontier was rapid enough to meet the attacks of the shortened German sweep, and the French and British counterattacks finished off the Schlieffen Plan, but in the final analysis Moltke beat himself, and for that he was removed from command on 14 September. A more aggressive commander would almost certainly have made it work, as the quick German defeat of France in 1940 later showed. Surely the tank warfare introduced in the blitzkrieg sped France's demise that year, but the ability to focus on the front and not the rear was the primary difference between 1914 and 1940.

The knockout blow did not land, and the rest of the war proved to be what only a few visionaries had predicted it would look like: firepower ruled the battlefield, and the defense dominated the offense. Millions died in futile efforts to acquire small bits of land, and the effect that had on the European psyche influenced almost everything that happened on the Continent for two decades to follow. Had the Schlieffen Plan been properly implemented, Germany could well have won a short war over France, convinced the British that further conflict was pointless, and forced a peace on Russia much sooner than actually happened. Would that have hastened the downfall of the czar, or aided the Menshevik Revolution or the Bolshevik Revolution that followed? No mater the effect in Russia, surely a victorious Germany would not have listened to Adolph Hitler's vision of the future.

References: Blond, Georges. *The Marne.* Translated by H. Eaton Hart. Harrisburg, PA: Stackpole Books, 1966; Dupuy, Trevor N. *A Genius for War.* London: Macdonald's and Jane's, 1977; Kluck, Alexander von. *The March on Paris and the Battle of the Marne, 1914.* London: Edward Arnold, 1923; Liddell Hart, Basil. *The Real War, 1914 to 1918.* Boston: Little, Brown, 1931; Tuchman, Barbara. *The Guns of August.* New York: Macmillan, 1962.

VERDUN
21 February–18 December 1916

FORCES ENGAGED
French: Second Army. Commander: Henri Philippe Petain (General Joseph Joffre in overall command).
German: Fifth Army. Commander: Crown Prince Wilhelm (General Erich von Falkenhayn in overall command, replaced in late August by Generals Paul von Hindenburg and Erich von Ludendorff).

IMPORTANCE
The massive loss of life typified the nature of World War I warfare on the western front and affected French military and political decision making for years to come.

Historical Setting

After the opening weeks of rapid movement, World War I in France settled into trench warfare. Both the Germans on one side and the allied British and French on the other dug into parallel lines of trench works that stretched from the Swiss border to the English Channel. With neither side able to execute a successful flanking movement before this entrenchment, the goal of both armies was to punch a hole in the enemy's lines through which they could pour sufficient forces to wreak havoc in the enemy rear. Although both Germans and Allies used massive amounts of artillery fire to break their enemy's lines, the only result was an ever-increasing number of dead. The Germans had entered the war convinced that they could easily overcome the French army. They found it impossible to defeat both French and British armies together, so in late 1915, after a year in which each combatant power had lost approximately a million men dead, wounded, and missing, the German high command decided on a strategy that was frightening in both conception and execution.

Still believing that the French fielded the most beatable army, German headquarters developed a plan to attack the fortress city of Verdun, on the Meuse River. Since the beginning of trench warfare, Verdun had been the central point of a salient of land creating a bulge in the German lines. This made it possible to attack from three sides against the city and its twenty major and forty smaller fortresses. The Germans planned to use the character of the French soldier and army for its own devices. Since the French defeat in the Franco-Prussian War in 1870, the French army had concluded that their army lost because of a lack of offensive spirit. If only the soldiers would close with the enemy and engage with the bayonet, then victory would surely follow. That philosophy of offensive warfare had been drilled into the French soldiers and officers to such an extent that they started the war with virtually no heavy weapons because large artillery pieces were good only for defensive warfare. Verdun itself was fitted for large numbers of artillery pieces, but many had been stripped away to fill the needs of armies across the western front.

Thus, Verdun was not as heavily defended (in terms of firepower) as it could have been, so an attack there should create one of two results. Either the German forces would be able to break through the French defensive lines and capture the city (and create in the lines the hole that would allow for exploitation) or the French would throw so many soldiers into the city that they would weaken themselves elsewhere (allowing for a breakthrough in another part of the lines) or simply use up hundreds of thousands of soldiers defending Verdun, thereby weakening their entire military effort. Either way, the Germans felt they would benefit.

To wreak as much destruction as possible on Verdun, and to save as many German lives as possible, the German high command assembled what was possibly the largest amount of artillery ever seen in one location. From long distance they planned on pulverizing the forts and the trenches with guns ranging from 420-mm mortars to 77-mm field guns. Also introduced at Verdun was the newly invented flamethrower. With an opening stockpile of two and a half million rounds, the barrage was expected to reduce any French defending forces to atoms. Operation *Gericht* ("judgment") was the code name given this incredible assault.

The Battle

The opening bombardment of Verdun was scheduled for 12 February, but the weather refused to cooperate. For 10 days, the German troops waited under specially designed camouflage covers, freezing and getting increasingly ill and frustrated. The French also prepared daily for the assault, like the Germans holding their collective breath for the attack and then stepping down from the trenches in the evening. Not until 21 February did the weather clear

sufficiently for the artillery spotters on high ground and in the air to see the effects of the bombardment, and when it started they reported on its efficacy. Starting at 0700, the massive shells pounded the fortifications and trenches, and the spotters reported just before the end of the bombardment at 1600 that nothing could possibly have survived.

When the German troops rushed forward along an 8-mile front, not in a wave but in small groups dashing from cover to cover, they met little resistance. The opening was designed to be little more than a reconnaissance in force, picking out the weakest part to exploit with massive infantry assaults the following day. One German corps, however, disobeyed orders and established a foothold in the center of the French line, creating a seam for future attacks to widen.

The French defenses were laid out by the French commander at Verdun, Lieutenant Colonel Emile Diant. He had used the terrain around Verdun to its maximum advantage, placing his units in fortified positions with overlapping fields of fire. The area around Verdun was dotted with patches of forest that Diant hoped to use as strongpoints. Although these woods were virtually leveled in the opening bombardment, the French had dug themselves deep bunkers, and enough of them emerged to slow the attackers. The withdrawal of French artillery, however, had made those fields of fire much less deadly than they could have been, and the Germans on the first and second days were able to outflank and surround many of the forward redoubts. On the second day of the battle, Diant was killed defending one of those redoubts. His replacement, Henri Petain, became a national hero over the next several months.

In the opening phase, the Germans captured the key defensive position of Fort Douaumont, but stiffer than expected French resistance convinced them to slow their advance and consolidate their gains. Petain, meanwhile, brought in reinforcements and guns. The German assault was renewed on 6 March. Crown Prince Wilhelm, commanding the German forces, threw his men toward Verdun from the northwest this time and again gained early successes, but Petain was determined that any lost ground should be regained as soon as possible. For a month, the two sides rolled back and forth across the countryside, gaining only temporary control of any ground, but spending thousands of lives in doing so. At this point, the rallying cry of Verdun was adopted: They shall not pass *(Ils ne passeront pas)*.

The German artillery barrages were so effective that almost every attempt to resupply or reinforce Verdun came under fire. Finally, only one road was left open. It came to be called *La Voie Sacrée,* the Sacred Way. Petain organized a masterful resupply system that kept a constant stream of trucks moving into and out of Verdun. To make sure that the road remained open in spite of the German shelling, road crews were stationed all along the road to repair immediately any holes that German artillery fire created. During the system's most efficient time, a vehicle passed any given point every 14 seconds.

Petain's ability to maintain La Voie Sacrée meant that he was able to finally match the numbers of men that the Germans had committed. That, plus the addition of artillery, further strengthened the French defense. Beaten back on the northwestern front, German Chief of Staff Erich von Falkenhayn proposed calling off the battle, but Crown Prince Wilhelm believed that his men had sacrificed too much for too little thus far, so the Germans in early April attacked the eastern flank of the Verdun salient and after bitter fighting captured another major defensive position, Fort Vaux, on 7 June. Encouraged, the Germans pressed on, committing more men to capture Verdun itself. Petain begged his superior, Chief of Staff Joseph Joffre, for diversionary attacks to relieve the pressure on Verdun. Both the Russians and Italians obliged, and on 1 July the British launched their own disastrous offensive farther north on the

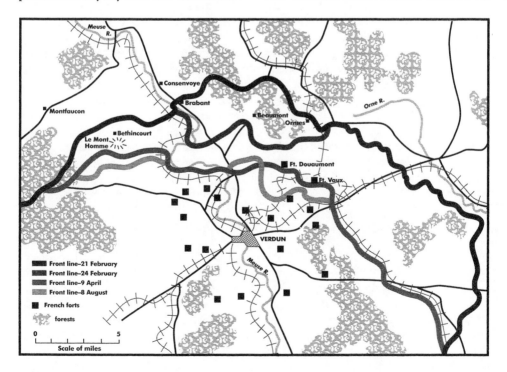

Somme River. Those attacks did indeed draw off German troops. Fifteen divisions were pulled from Verdun to beat back the Russian Brusilov offensive in June 1916, and the British effort against German positions on the Somme became the major battle for the second half of 1916 for both the Allies and Germans, but the killing at Verdun went on. Although at one point in June Petain asked permission to abandon Verdun when the Germans reached Belleville Ridge overlooking the town, Joffre refused to allow any retreat and Petain's forces held on. On 11 July, the Germans almost reached Verdun, but were forced back. After that day, even the crown prince realized that he would never occupy this particular French city.

The Germans found that ending a battle is often more difficult than starting one. Crown Prince Wilhelm was content to hold the substantial gains that his army had made around Verdun even if he could not take the town itself. Petain had different ideas. Although he was promoted and transferred, his successors Generals Robert Nivelle and Charles Mangin took advantage of the soldiers and supplies that Petain had amassed in order to launch their own attacks. After a few months' lull, the French began their own killing barrage on 19 October. It lasted 4 days. Through November and December, the French slowly recaptured almost all the ground that they had lost. Fort Douaumont was retaken on 24 October; Fort Vaux, in early November. By 18 December, their last offensive took them 2 miles past the line of fortresses, almost to their starting point the previous February.

Results

Falkenhayn's plan to sap the strength of the French army almost succeeded, but in the process he almost did the same with his own army. Petain developed a system of rotating fresh troops out of other parts of the western front, giving Verdun a constant stream of relatively well-rested defenders. Almost two-thirds of the French army fought, at one time or another, at

Verdun. The Germans rotated troops through as well, but after 1 July the battle on the Somme River, coupled with the Russian attacks on the eastern front, made that impossible. Indeed, cooperative Russian operations in the summer of 1916 forced Falkenhayn to remove troops from Verdun to reinforce the Austro-German forces in the east. Because of the rotation system, it is difficult to state exactly how many men actually fought at Verdun on either side. The dead are somewhat easier to count. Between February and December 1916, the French lost 542,000 killed and wounded and the Germans lost 434,000.

Verdun was at once a typical World War I battle and the worst of them all. It was typical in that the weaponry of World War I showed itself here in all its destructiveness: not only the standard huge artillery bombardments but flamethrowers and the poison gas phosgene were used here for the first time. The Industrial Revolution brought to World War I a number of new weapons that created death and destruction on a scale of which generals never conceived before the war and often failed to grasp during the war. Verdun also was typical in the attitude that seemed to come from the generals on both sides. Soldiers were commodities to be used rather than lives to be lost. Indeed, the term "death" was rarely used in the corridors of power; instead, it was "wastage." The generals on both sides too often looked at men and battles as little more than the movement of counters on a map; the goal was to "drain enemy resources" rather than kill men. The dehumanization of the war at the higher ranks went far to explain the attitudes of the surviving generation of the lower ranks over the following decades.

Verdun was also the worst of the battles in that the plan that Falkenhayn developed and Crown Prince Wilhelm implemented was devised from the first as nothing more than a meat grinder with few material objectives. The entire point to the battle was death, rather than acquisition of territory or physical objectives. As Falkenhayn predicted, the French sent men

THE DEAD MAN

The opening days of the battle of Verdun were fought on the east side of the Meuse River, which flows north-south through the town of Verdun and the battlefield. The east side, or right bank, is marked by its very rugged terrain, with steep ridges and ravines adding a natural defensive aspect to the forts. On the left bank, however, the land is more open and rolling, with fewer high hills. The dominant rise on the left bank, about 6 miles northwest of the town of Verdun, is called *Le Mort Homme,* the Dead Man. It is a name that had been given centuries earlier for a reason no one can now say, but it earned its title again during the battle for Verdun.

The Germans shifted the focus of their offensive from the right to the left bank on 6 March 1916, and the Dead Man was their objective. Possession of it would give them the highest observation point in the neighborhood, allowing them to direct their own artillery fire on French batteries just to the east. The French were better prepared for the attack on the left bank than they had been for the start of the battle a few weeks earlier, and they were as determined to retain possession of the hill as the Germans were to seize it. Although holding the high ground gives one an excellent view, it also exposes one to enemy fire, and such was the situation on the Dead Man. As possession of the hill came and went, both German and French forces had to try to withstand intense shelling, and the results on that exposed piece of ground were among the most horrible of the entire battle, if not the entire war.

Attackers, once in possession of all or part of the hill, had to try to dig in under fire. If they raised up to use their shovels, enemy marksmen killed them. If they lay still throughout the day to avoid rifle fire, they were exposed to the snow and rain that fell throughout most of March. If they survived the day to dig in the darkness, the ground was unforgivingly hard, allowing a hollow of only a few inches or perhaps a couple of feet within which to hide. Artillery fire was therefore impossible to escape, and the constant fire onto the hill slaughtered thousands. From those who survived, the descriptions are sickening: they watched comrades and enemy bodies alike pounded day after day, over and over again, until bodies became a collection of parts, then smaller parts, and then finally pulp indistinguishable from the mud.

The Germans finally captured the Dead Man at the end of May, after almost 3 months of fighting. It had proven so costly, however, that, although the observation post was in their hands, the German high command decided to shift the focus of the attacks back to the right bank, where key French forts stood. As in so much of the fighting in World War I, massive numbers of men were sacrificed for ground either useless or unused once occupied.

---

flooding into Verdun. What happened from the French point of view is more important, however. Verdun became a symbol for French national pride, more so than any other single place or event in the war. Although the victory made Petain a national icon and gave the French an everlasting point of honor, the cost always overshadowed any memory of the battle. Thus, the symbol of pride became a symbol of the cost of the war.

The French lost approximately 5.5 million men dead and wounded in the war, of a total of almost 8.5 million men mobilized. The cost to society of such numbers is incalculable, and, to make it even worse, almost the entire western front was located and fought for in France. Four years of physical destruction merely compounded the human cost. Because so many soldiers fought at Verdun (and became the future generals and politicians of France), the legacy of Verdun can be seen in French military and political actions through the 1920s and 1930s. The concept of defense, denigrated before World War I, found itself enshrined in the Maginot line, that impregnable series of fortifications that became another symbol of French doom. Although the French possessed (on paper) the largest army in the world in

1940, the Maginot line and the concept of trench warfare was an insidious factor in French military doctrine that made France fall victim to Adolph Hitler's blitzkrieg warfare. Before the invasion, the activities of the French in resisting Hitler (or more correctly in not resisting him), from the occupation of the Rhineland in 1936 through the Munich Conference that abandoned Czechoslovakia in 1938, can be traced to the losses of World War I. The population of France, as well as that of Britain, would not allow their governments to even consider the prospect of going to war again until Hitler's tanks started rolling. The French memory of the First World War, symbolized by the heroism and sacrifice of Verdun, paralyzed a nation.

References: Dutourd, Jean. *The Taxis of the Marne.* Translated by Harold King. New York: Simon & Schuster, 1957; Horne, Alistair. *The Price of Glory: Verdun 1916.* New York: St. Martin's Press, 1962; Liddell Hart, Basil. *The Real War, 1914–1918.* Boston: Little, Brown, 1931; Romains, Jules. *Verdun: The Prelude, the Battle.* Translated by Gerard Hopkins. New York: Alfred A. Knopf, 1939; Stokesbury, James. *A Short History of World War I.* New York: William Morrow, 1981.

BRUSILOV OFFENSIVE

4 June–20 September 1916

FORCES ENGAGED

Russian: 1 million men in the Southwest Front (Army Group), with another 1 million in reserve. Commander: General Alexei Brusilov.

Austro-German: Four Austrian and one German army. Commander: Field Marshal Count Conrad von Hotzendorf.

IMPORTANCE

The last major Russian offensive of World War I, the Brusilov offensive led to the major weakening and ultimate downfall of both the Russian and Austrian monarchies.

Historical Setting

When World War I began on 4 August 1914, German military leaders assumed that the extremely slow Russian mobilization process would keep it out of the war for weeks, if not months. Surprisingly, Russia launched its first offensive against East Prussia within 2 weeks. Poor Russian leadership kept the offensive from succeeding completely, but it made enough progress to frighten the German commander in the area, General Max von Prittwitz. He was replaced by General Paul von Hindenburg and General Erich von Ludendorff, who planned an immediate counterattack. The result was a double envelopment at Tannenberg (26–31 August) that cost the Russians 125,000 men killed, wounded, and captured. Two weeks later, the Russians lost a similar number of men at the battle of Masurian Lakes.

Russia also had to contend with Germany's ally, Austria, which in late August launched an attack from Galicia into Russian Poland (all in the western part of modern Ukraine). The Austrians had some success at first, but soon were pushed out of Galicia and had to be saved by timely German reinforcement. This set a pattern for most of the eastern front in World War I. Hindenburg, although at first operating with minimal support in troops and materiel from Germany, conducted a powerful campaign against superior Russian numbers, skillfully moving his troops by rail to meet successive Russian threats. He managed to gain much of Poland for Germany by the end of 1914. He began launching more attacks in the bitter winter weather of early 1915 and gained modest success, but the Russians fought hard and continued to enjoy victories over the Austrians. When the good weather of summer 1915 arrived, however, the Germans launched an offensive that the Russians could not resist, and the czar's forces surrendered Poland and territory in the Baltic states before the autumn rains saved them. Grand Duke Nicholas, although losing lots of territory, had performed a virtual miracle to keep his armies from being totally annihilated. That was not appreciated in the corridors of power, however, and he was transferred to the Caucasus front to fight the Turks while Czar Nicholas II himself took direct command of Russian forces in late August. The campaigning season of 1915 ended with Austro-German forces holding a line from Riga on the Baltic Sea to the Carpathian Mountains at the Russo-Rumanian frontier.

In late February 1916, German Chief of Staff Erich von Falkenhayn began his assault on the fortress city of Verdun in eastern France with the intent of slowly destroying the entire French army. France begged Russia to launch an offensive to draw off German troops, and in mid-March Russia attacked the Germans at Lake Naroch, but only gained 100,000 casualties for their trouble. In May, the Austrians launched a massive offensive against Italian positions near Trentino. Italy also appealed to Russia to go on the attack to relieve pressure on their front. At first, the Russian generals resisted the request because much of the fighting that they had done during the war had been at the behest of their allies. The generals told the czar that it was not possible, given the troop and material situation, to launch an immediate attack to assist the Italians. Instead, they would continue to build up their forces for a major offensive later in the summer. Only one commander, General Alexei Brusilov, commanding the Southwest Front (Army Group), responded positively. He had recently come to his position and possibly was hoping to make a good impression. Whatever the reason, Czar Nicholas ordered him to launch an attack against the Austrians on a wide front stretching from the Pripet Marshes on the Polish frontier to the end of the Austrian position 300 miles to the south.

The Battle

Other Russian generals resented Brusilov's action and refused to give up any supplies or weapons to help his cause. Thus, without much in the way of artillery, Brusilov was forced to rethink his method of attack. As in France, the standard way of assaulting the enemy was to try to soften them up for a few days or weeks with artillery and then hope that the cannon fire had destroyed their defensive capabilities. This usually did not work, for the barrage usually resulted in two major negative effects. First, it alerted the enemy as to where the assault would be launched, giving them time to shift reserves to the area. Second, it usually destroyed the target area so completely that the attacking force was unable to move across ground that was nothing but craters and soft dirt, while the enemy reserves were coming up on undamaged roads. This meant that, even if the defenders in their trenches were neutralized, it was impossible to exploit the advantage. Brusilov's lack of artillery proved to be a blessing in disguise. General Brusilov began training soldiers in tactics that later became widely used by the Germans in France. Instead of throwing in waves of infantry, he created specialized units to attack and seize particular targets. This would neutralize the strongest defensive positions and allow the larger infantry units following to advance against less intense fire.

On 4 June, Brusilov sent his troops forward after an artillery barrage that was brief, though intense. As the Austrians had not been alerted by the movement of large numbers of troops or the presence of thousands of artillery shells raining down on them, they were completely unprepared for the Russian attack. Launching his assaults at weak points between Austrian armies, the offensive was an unprecedented success. The Austrian Fourth and Seventh Armies collapsed. In the northern sector, Russian forces broke through on a 60-mile-wide front just south of the Pripet Marshes and advanced 25 miles the first week. In the southern sector, they drove the Austrians back across the Dniester River and threatened Czernowitz, the capital of the Polish province of Bukovina.

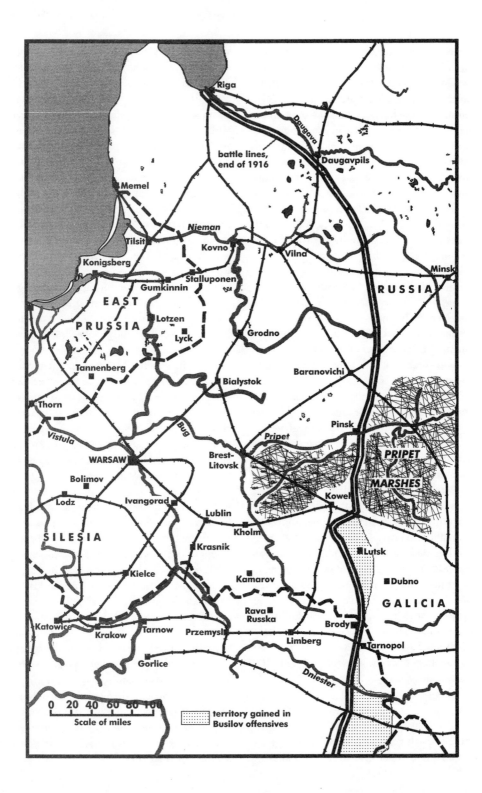

Brusilov was soon the victim of his own success. The other front commanders, jealous of his success, refused to launch their own attacks, as ordered, against the German positions north of the marshes. This allowed the Germans to transfer an entire army south to help shore up the collapsing Austrian lines. The Russians advanced so far that they had to slow down simply to allow supplies to catch up to them. That slowing coincided with the arrival of large numbers of Germans. The czar finally ordered the other generals to cooperate and send reserves from their forces to Brusilov, but the road system was poor and the Germans were able to move more troops more quickly by rail. General Brusilov showed at this point that he probably really did not understand the radically successful nature of his tactics. Had he done so, he would have stopped to consolidate his gains and wait for another opportune moment to do it all again. Instead, now that the czar had assured him of sufficient ammunition, he returned to the old method of blasting his enemy and the ground with artillery fire. Returning to the tactic of massed infantry attacks, he soon began losing as many men to German fire as the attacker traditionally lost in such assaults. Brusilov reached the foothills of the Carpathian Mountains in early September, and that natural defense stopped him as much as did the enemy troops. The arrival of German troops not only from the northern sector of the German lines but also from the battle at Verdun in France served to stop the Austrian retreat and inflict massive casualties on Russian troops.

Results

By 20 September, Brusilov's men could go no farther. Exhaustion as well as enemy action brought the Russian offensive to a halt. It had temporarily been wildly successful, but eventually the effects were more harmful than helpful. Although accurate figures are not available, it is presumed that the Russians lost at least a million (perhaps one and a quarter million) men

dead, wounded, and prisoner. Losses for the Austro-German forces were similar. Although it was the most successful Russian offensive of the entire war and gained more territory than any other, the cost was simply too high. By the time the Brusilov offensive began, the Russian armies had already suffered as many as 5 million casualties since 1914. The long-suffering Russian infantry could take it no longer. Criticism of the czar and army officers from the highest to the lowest levels became common talk in the trenches. The monarchy had been under severe political pressure since at least 1905, and rebellion began brewing in the army as well. The first Russian Revolution took place in the spring of 1917. The Brusilov offensive did not cause the revolution, but the losses suffered in the offensive (on top of those already incurred) meant that the cost of the greatest Russian success was actually the final contribution.

Similar effects were felt on the enemy side. The Austrian military had slowly been submerged into the German army, and after the Brusilov offensive it had virtually no independence at all. German reinforcement saved the Austrian army from total collapse in 1916, but Austrian weakness from that point spelled the doom of the Hapsburg monarchy in Vienna. The last of the continental European empires, Austria-Hungary was comprised of a polyglot population held together by nothing but force. Without a strong military to keep the population quiet, ethnic tensions that had seethed for decades boiled more fiercely, foreshadowing the dismantling of the Hapsburg Empire in 1919 at Versailles and the creation of a number of southeastern European nations.

In the shorter term, the initial Russian success convinced Rumania, which had held aloof from the war, to join the Allied cause. Rather than cooperate with the overall Allied strategy, however, Rumania wasted its troops in foolish operations that had little chance of success. That so weakened the country that Bulgarian forces were able to invade from the south and overrun Rumania by the beginning of 1917.

On the western front, the Brusilov offensive had effects as well. Forced to withdraw soldiers to aid his allies in the east, Chief of Staff Falkenhayn failed in his attempt to destroy the French at Verdun. That failure, coupled with the Rumanian entry into the war, resulted in his dismissal from his post and his transfer to the east. Falkenhayn was replaced by Hindenburg and Ludendorff as chief of staff and first quartermaster-general, respectively. They became the brains that operated the German military for the rest of the war, running virtually the entire German government by war's end. Their assumption of control, away from Kaiser Wilhelm, meant that the Brusilov offensive actually ended three monarchies.

References: Brusilov, Alexei A. *A Soldier's Notebook, 1914–1918.* Westport, CT: Greenwood Press, 1971; Clark, Alan. *Suicide of the Empires.* New York: American Heritage Press, 1971; Liddell Hart, Basil. *The Real War, 1914 to 1918.* Boston: Little, Brown, 1931; Rutherford, Ward. *The Tsar's War, 1914–1917.* Cambridge, UK: I. Faulkner, 1992 [1975]; Stokesbury, James. *A Short History of World War I.* New York: William Morrow, 1981.

MARNE, SECOND BATTLE (1918)

15–17 July 1918

FORCES ENGAGED

Allied: French Sixth and Tenth Armies (with significant U.S., British, and Italian forces included). Commander: General Ferdinand Foch.

German: First, Third, and Seventh Armies. Commander: Field Marshal Erich von Ludendorff.

IMPORTANCE

This final German offensive marked the last turning point in World War I, leading to Allied victory.

Historical Setting

"How apt, if how strange, the historical coincidence by which, as the Marne had been the first high-water mark and witnessed the first ebb of the tide of invasion in 1914, so four years later it was destined to be the final high-water mark from which the decisive ebb began" (Liddell Hart, *The Real War,* p. 419). Also like the events of 1914, the battle that took place at the Marne River in July 1918 had results that were more accidental than planned. Indeed, it began as merely a diversion for a larger offensive elsewhere, but through circumstance it took on a life of its own.

After 3 years of trench warfare in France, German Field Marshal Erich von Ludendorff was ready for a killing blow that would end the war in Germany's favor. After the Bolshevik Revolution of November 1917 began, Communist leader Vladimir Lenin announced Russia's withdrawal from the war. He planned an immediate cessation of hostilities, but, when presented with territorial demands that would have ceded much of European Russia to Germany, he balked. That led to a continuation of German attacks until, in March 1918, Lenin signed the Treaty of Brest-Litovsk, acceding to German demands. That freed hundreds of thousands of German troops for transfer to France.

Ludendorff's position was that of first quartermaster general of the German military, but actually he was commander-in-chief. Thus, he planned and directed the operations of spring and summer 1918 that were supposed to bring the war to a positive end. He planned to do this by decisively defeating the British forces on the northern end of the Allied front. To sufficiently prepare the way for the battle that would do so, however, Ludendorff planned a series of diversionary offensives to hold French troops in place and draw off reserves from the British sector. In March 1918, he began the first of five planned feints.

Ludendorff also planned a tactical change in the nature of warfare on the western front. The concept of smaller units, trained to break through weak points and threaten rear areas, developed almost by accident by Russian General Alexei Brusilov in 1916, had been perfected by German General Oscar von Hutier. The concept of sending in specially trained storm troopers, following an artillery barrage that continually advanced ahead of the troops, would allow German soldiers to disrupt enemy supply and reinforcement lines and ease the path for larger units to follow in behind for consolidation purposes. The British and French forces were unprepared for this type of attack, and it proved extremely successful.

When the first German offensive began on 21 March 1918 along the Somme River, the Germans enjoyed more success than they had since the opening days of the war. The British Fifth Army was virtually destroyed as three German armies advanced along a front more than 40 miles wide and drove the British 40 miles backward before finally being stopped by Allied reinforcements; the Germans had outrun their ability to keep their own men supplied. Both sides lost nearly a quarter-million men killed, wounded, and prisoner. The Ger-

man success allowed the Germans to bring up huge artillery pieces, the "Paris Guns." These cannons had barrels 117 feet long and fired shells up to 80 miles. They did not inflict significant damage on Paris, but did do great psychological harm. British General Douglas Haig's complaint that the French under General Henri Petain were more worried about defending Paris than stopping the breakthrough led to the promotion on 3 April of French General Ferdinand Foch to the position of supreme commander of Allied forces, a position nonexistent before this time.

Ludendorff's second offensive was launched against the region that he was planning ultimately to attack as his last major target. On 9 April, German troops attacked British positions along the Lys River and again made major gains, although not as impressive as those the previous month. Both sides lost about 100,000 casualties. At the end of May, the third German offensive again acquired a major piece of

French troopers under General Gouraud, with their machine guns in the ruins of a cathedral near the Marne, driven back by the Germans, 1918. (National Archives)

territory, establishing a salient 30 miles wide, crossing the Aisne and Vesle Rivers and approaching the Marne 20 miles from where they started. U.S. troops, seeing their first major action of the war, performed admirably at Château-Thierry and Belleau Wood. There they stopped the German offensive and regained some lost ground with a number of counterattacks. The German success, however, altered Ludendorff's plans somewhat. Postponing the killing stroke against the British in the north, he decided to see if he could exploit this localized success and threaten Paris.

The Battle

Ludendorff's plans here ran into serious trouble. Each German offensive thus far, although successful, had seriously depleted the number of men trained as storm troopers. That meant that the more traditional massed attacks would have to be employed, and the German soldiers, after 3 years of such tactics, were not thrilled with the prospect. The result was a large number of German deserters who gave the Allied intelligence officers all the information they needed about the times and places of the upcoming German attack. Thus, the Allies were ready when, on 9 June, Ludendorff readied his fourth attack along a line from Noyon to Mondidier, southward from the territory gained in his first offensive back in March. The French artillery struck first this time and disrupted the German attack. That counterpreparation slowed the German assault considerably, and the new French method of defense also saved many lives and much territory. Now the French were placing only a screen of men in forward positions and digging in more strongly to the rear, out of the range of German artillery. Thus, as the German troops slowly broke through the ground devastated by gunfire, they then met the strength of the resistance. German gains were slight in 4 days of fighting.

Ludendorff at this point probably should have started his grand offensive against the British, but he thought to launch one more diversion to convince the French to stay put. This

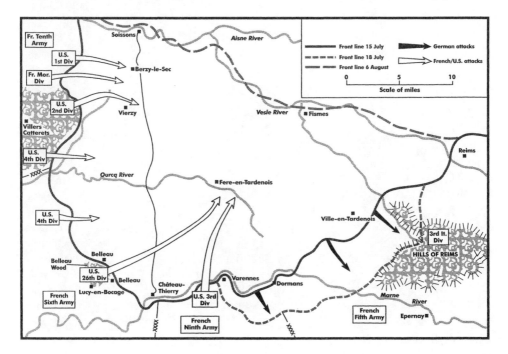

was to be directed against the city of Reims on the Vesle River, bypassed in the third offensive in May and June. The German Third Army was to attack southward east of the city, while the First and Seventh Armies would parallel the Third on the west side. Again, however, the large number of deserters alerted the Allies to the exact time and place of the attack, and the Allies were able to forestall that attack as well. To the east, the Third Army made almost no progress, while to the west of Reims the First and Seventh crossed the Marne.

It did them no good because Allied artillery and aircraft knocked out the Marne bridges once the Germans were across, cutting the attackers off from any supply or reinforcement. Again the U.S. forces, the 3rd Infantry Division in particular, barred the German advance. After only 2 days of fighting, Ludendorff ordered his troops to withdraw to a defense position along the Vesle.

The Allies were quick to exploit the German retreat. General Foch, always an advocate of the offense, on 18 July sent the French Tenth and Fifth Armies after the withdrawing Germans. The U.S. 1st and 2nd Divisions spearheaded the Tenth Army assault, with six other divisions formed into two corps in other sectors. The counteroffensive was so successful that on 20 July Ludendorff canceled the great offensive in the north for which all the previous attacks had been the prelude. By 5 August, the Allied attack had completely regained all the territory lost to the Germans in their third offensive in May and June, and the German army from that point onward was completely on the defensive.

Results

In five major assaults, the Germans suffered about a half-million men dead, wounded, and prisoner. Ludendorff had announced in advance that this was the big push, the great leap forward that would win the war. When it failed, the morale of the German army plummeted.

The second battle of the Marne, although not an overwhelming tactical success for the Allies, was the morale boost they sorely needed. The arrival of the Americans not only brought the Allied numbers up but their competence in battle did wonders for Allied spirits. Both Foch and Haig tried desperately to have arriving U.S. troops serve as replacements for their tattered units, but U.S. commander General John Pershing, supported by President Woodrow Wilson, would not cooperate. Pershing demanded, and ultimately received, the right to commit U.S. troops to combat in independent units. They would serve alongside French and British units and under overall Allied command, but they would not serve as replacements in Allied units. The Americans paid dearly for their trial by fire in Belleau Wood and at Château-Thierry, losing almost half of their troops in casualties in the fighting from 18 July through 5 August.

Because of the creation of the position of commander of Allied forces, the second battle of the Marne was the first true cooperative venture of the war for the Allies, and its success further enhanced their morale. Only a year earlier, large parts of the French army had mutinied in protest at the slaughter, but in the summer of 1918 it was the German troops who gave up the fight. After the reduction of the German salient between the Vesle and the Marne, the Allies continued to push the Germans, and, after almost 4 years of stalemate, the front shifted radically. After the failure at the Marne, the German high command and government realized that they could not win the war. The German populace was on extremely short rations because of the costs of the war and the effective Allied blockade. That, coupled with the outbreak of the worst influenza epidemic of modern times, virtually broke the German ability to manufacture the tools of war. Although Ludendorff realized on 8 August that the war was lost, not until 6 October did the German government request talks. President Wilson demanded the resignation of

Germany's military leadership, and, after Ludendorff resigned on 27 October, the German situation deteriorated rapidly. The High Seas Fleet at Kiel mutinied and Communist-inspired strikes broke out across the country. A socialist government took power on 9 November and proclaimed a republic, and on 11 November an armistice was signed. The peace treaty that followed punished Germany so severely that its desire for redemption led directly to the Second World War.

References: Gies, Joseph. *Crisis, 1918.* New York: W. W. Norton, 1974; Liddell Hart, Basil. *The Real War, 1914 to 1918.* Boston: Little, Brown, 1931; Stallings, Laurence. *The Doughboys.* New York: Harper & Row, 1963; Stokesbury, James L. *A Short History of World War I.* New York: William Morrow, 1981; Terraine, John. *To Win a War: 1918, the Year of Victory.* Garden City, NY: Doubleday, 1981.

WARSAW

16–25 August 1920

FORCES ENGAGED

Polish: 180,000 men. Commander: Marshal Józef Klemens Pilsudski.
Russian: 200,000 men. Commander: Marshal Mikhail Nikolayevich Tukhachevsky.

IMPORTANCE

Defeat of Red Army in Poland established Poland's post–World War I borders and stopped westward expansion of communism.

Historical Setting

Through its history Poland has been both a region and a nation, often occupied by more powerful neighbors, even more often overrun by one enemy or another bent either on conquering the Poles or passing through on the way to meet another enemy. Like Palestine, Alsace/Lorraine, or a number of other fortu- itously placed pieces of land located near too many rivals, Poland has known more than its fair share of war. In the late eighteenth century, the nation of Poland was divided three times (1772, 1793, 1795) between Russia, Germany, and Austria-Hungary. Overbearing policies imposed by the occupying powers fruitlessly attempted to break Polish spirit, and in the wake of World War I, circumstances seemed right for the Poles to reassert their nationalism. Germany and Russia had fought across Polish territory for almost 4 years, but Russia's withdrawal from the war after the Treaty of Brest-Litovsk in March 1918, followed by Germany's defeat in November of that year, gave the Poles a stellar opportunity to not only reestablish a nation but to possibly expand their traditional borders and exact a little revenge for more than a century of brutal occupation.

The man destined to shape Poland's nationhood was Józef Pilsudski. A victim of "Czarist Justice" in his youth, Pilsudski harbored not only a burning passion for his country but a bitter hatred for Russia. While Woodrow Wilson, David Lloyd George, Georges Clemenceau, and Vittorio Orlando met in Versailles to hammer out a peace treaty, Pilsudski took matters into his own hands. He laid out a plan for a return to Poland's 1772 borders and the reestablishment of a federation of nations under Poland's leadership, a federation that once included Ukraine, Belorussia, and Lithuania. Although the population of those regions had no love for the Russians, they saw little reason to trade that overlord for a Polish one. No matter, he thought; seize land now while Russia is busy with a civil war between communist Red and conservative White armies.

In November 1918, Pilsudski sent troops into Galicia in western Ukraine; in February 1919, he sent his armies north into Lithuania. By April they had captured the city of Wilno (Vilna) from occupying Communist forces. Wilno was historically Polish but had recently been named capital of an independent Lithuania. By October, Polish troops were in control of most of Belorussia and Galicia. In December 1919, Allied governments announced that the Poles should accept as their eastern border what came to be called the Curzon Line. To accept this border, Polish forces would have to retreat out of Lithuania, Belorussia, and Ukraine, a demand Pilsudski was not about to accept.

By the beginning of 1920, the Soviet Red Army finally gained the upper hand over the Whites, and Soviet leader Vladimir Lenin turned his attention to the conflict with Poland. He ordered his army commander, Leon Trotsky, to prepare for operations in the west to regain land lost to Poland through the previous year. Pilsudski, meanwhile, allied himself with Ukrainian General Semyon Petlyura, who ceded Galicia to Pilsudski in return for Polish aid in setting up a Ukrainian government in Kiev. After Polish troops drove Communist troops out of the Latvian fortress of Dvinsk on 3 January 1920, Lenin offered to negotiate a settlement, but the talks that ensued were little more than window dressing for both sides. On 25 April, Pilsusdski launched a massive offensive toward Kiev, which he captured on 7 May. Pilsudski was praised throughout Poland as a savior, but the tide soon turned against him. Trotsky's Red forces launched a number of cavalry attacks that cut the Polish lines of communication, forcing a withdrawal from Kiev. Under the field command of Mikhail Tukhachevsky, 160,000 Red Army soldiers harassed the Poles out of Ukraine and well past their own borders, taking from Pilsudski all the territory he had acquired thus far.

The Soviet army was advancing rapidly, and the Polish army seemed to be collapsing, so Lenin decided not to stop pushing west. Against the advice of several of his subordinates, Lenin in July 1920 ordered that Warsaw be captured in preparation for an assault on Germany. Trotsky warned that merely taking Warsaw would stretch Soviet supply lines to the limit, but Lenin's revolutionary fervor was not to be denied. Poland seemed doomed, but at this point the western governments intervened. In return for Pilsudski accepting imposed borders with Czechoslovakia, Germany, and Lithuania, British and French supplies and weapons would be made available. The Polish leader had no choice, and his government agreed to the Protocol of Spa on 10 July 1920. Immediately, materiel and military advisors were on their way to Poland.

The Battle

While the Polish government pressed as many men into service as they could find, Tukhachevsky's forces neared the capital city of Warsaw. He advanced across a wide front, threatening the Poles in so many places that Pilsudski, who was convinced the only way out of his predicament was with a counteroffensive, did not know where to launch one. Finally convinced by French advisors to weaken the southern sector, he transferred troops away from their position opposing one of the Red Army's elite units, the First Red Cavalry Army. This transfer of men, coupled with a massive conscription campaign, gave Pilsudski a numeric superiority around Warsaw.

Tukhachevsky decided to hold his main force in place to the northeast of Warsaw, then send his Sixteenth Army in a sweep north of the city to the Vistula River. From there, the Soviet forces would attack Warsaw from the northwest. The Fourth Red Army was already in place at Ciechanow, between Warsaw and the border with East Prussia, so the Sixteenth would have its right flank covered on the approach and then a larger reserve once the turning movement toward Warsaw was complete. Tukhachevsky had no idea that the Poles had managed to build their forces back up to 370,000 men (although most were only minimally trained and equipped). All he had seen thus far were retreating Polish forces, so he was sure Warsaw would fall easily. Tukhachevsky ordered the Sixteenth Army forward on 13 August, leaving a mere 8,000 men to guard its left flank.

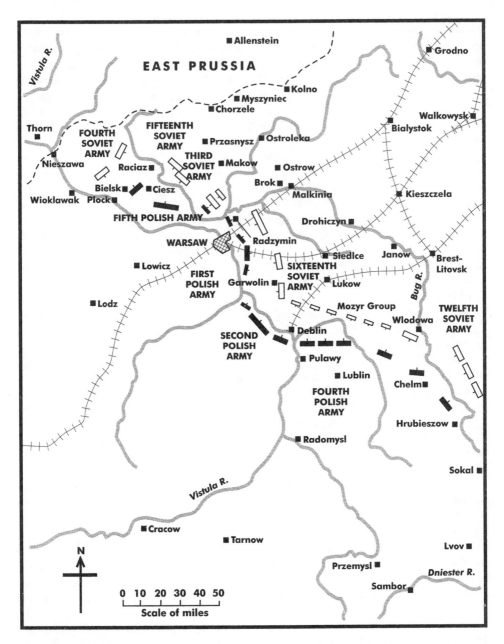

Although the Reds quickly captured their first objective, the city of Radzymin, a Polish counterattack recaptured it. At the same time, the Polish Fifth Army attacked the Soviet Fourth at Ciechanow and drove it back in disorder. The Polish Fifth Army commander, General Wladyslaw Sikorski pushed the Soviets hard with tanks, cavalry, armored cars, and motorized infantry. At this point Sikorski was pushing his luck by driving so far so fast, but squabbles between Soviet commanders ensured that a Soviet cavalry force that could easily have attacked Sikorski's rear and severed his lines of communication, did not do so. Instead, they withdrew into East Prussia, where they were interned by German authorities.

As Sikorski drove the broken Red Fourth Army back along the Sixteenth Army's northern flank, Pilsudski was attacking Tukhachevsky's lines of communication from the south. With the Sixteenth Army stalled at Radzymin, these two drives threatened to encircle Tukhachevsky. On 18 August, realizing how dangerous his position was, Tukhachevsky ordered the Sixteenth Army to withdraw. It soon turned into a rout. Troops ran as quickly as they could to escape the closing ring; those that were too slow found themselves overpowered by numerically superior Polish forces. The entire Fourth Army had to surrender, and Tukhachevsky with the Sixteenth did little better. In their rapid retreat the Soviets abandoned more than 200 cannon, 1,000 machine guns, 10,000 vehicles, and 66,000 prisoners. They also lost approximately 100,000 dead and wounded. The Polish casualties numbered about 50,000.

Results

The mutual dislike and distrust exhibited by the Communist generals was exhibited once more in the wake of the battle outside Warsaw. General Semyon Budyonny's First Red Cavalry Army had remained passive throughout the entire battle, comfortable in their position to the southeast at Lvov. With Tukhachevsky's forces disposed of, Pilsudski ordered troops south to deal with Budyonny. On 31 August, a massive cavalry battle took place, the likes of which history will probably never again witness. Budyonny's forces were routed and almost annihilated.

Pilsudski was not about to lose his momentum. He drove his army after the retreating Tukhachevsky, destroying the Red Third Army on 26 September at the Nieman River in Belorussia. Not content, Pilsudski continued to chase the Communists, pounding Tukha-

chevsky again at the Szcara River a few days later. The Reds lost a further 50,000 prisoners and 160 artillery pieces. An armistice was announced on 12 October, and the resulting Treaty of Riga (signed 21 March 1921) granted Poland much of what Pilsudski had originally envisioned for his nation. Territory in Lithuania, Ukraine, and Belorussia all went to Poland, putting about 12 million people of other nationalities under Polish dominion. This treaty, coupled with lands ceded to Poland by the Versailles Treaty in mid-1919, gave Poland expanded borders at the expense of not only her eastern neighbors but also Germany, which was obliged to cede a corridor of land between Germany proper and the state of East Prussia that included the port city of Danzig (Gdansk).

The battle of Warsaw thus led to the creation of an independent Polish nation for the first time in 150 years. Sadly, it was a relatively brief life. In 1939, Nazi German forces overran Poland in just over a month, establishing yet another foreign occupation. The Soviet Union picked up where Nazi Germany left off in 1945, dominating if not occupying Poland until the late 1980s.

More importantly for the rest of Europe, Tukhachevsky's defeat in August 1920 turned back the tide of communism, which did not return for 25 years. If Lenin had been able to establish a Communist government in Poland, the effects could well have been felt in Germany. In the wake of World War I Germany was filled with rival political factions vying for power, and there was a fairly large and influential Communist movement. Indeed, the western powers had difficulty transporting materiel to Poland owing to dock strikes by Communist longshoremen in Germany. With Britain, France, and the United States fearful of rising communism, a successful Communist coup in Germany could have provoked an invasion by the Allies. Either such an occupation by the west or a successful coup by the Communists would have altered the nature of Germany in the early 1920s. A stronger Weimar government with Allied troops on hand could have crushed the nascent Nazi Party; a Communist government certainly would not have allowed such a movement to exist. Germany's fate over the next decades, under either of these two scenarios, is impossible to suppose.

From a military standpoint, the war in Poland foreshadowed the next war in Europe. After 4 years of stalemated trench warfare, the combat in Poland was once again free-wheeling. Mechanized infantry used by the Poles certainly was a precursor to similar tactics in the Nazi blitzkrieg. Cavalry, of course, could not survive in World War II, but fast-moving tank columns supplanted the cavalry arm and acted in much the same fashion: driving defeated and demoralized troops into rout and destruction. How much the war in Poland affected German military thinkers in the interwar years is difficult to surmise, but the Poles were on the receiving end of the same type of warfare they practiced in 1920.

References: Dupuy, R. Ernest, and Trevor Dupuy. *Encyclopedia of Military History.* New York: Harper & Row, 1970; Fiddick, Thomas C. *Russia's Retreat from Poland.* New York: St. Martin's Press, 1990; Jedrzejewicz, Waclaw. *Pilsudski: A Life for Poland.* New York: Hippocrene Books, 1982; Szymczak, Robert. "Bolshevik Wave Breaks at Warsaw," *Military History* 11(6), February 1995.

POLAND

1 September–5 October 1939

FORCES ENGAGED

German: 1.25 million men in Army Group North (Third and Fourth Armies; Commander: General Fedor von Bock) and Army Group South (Eighth, Tenth, and Fourteenth Armies; Commander: General Gerd von Rundstedt).

Polish: 800,000 men in six armies. Commander: Marshal Edward Smigly-Rydz.

IMPORTANCE

Nazi invasion of Poland started World War II with the introduction of the blitzkrieg, heralding a new era of warfare after the defensive struggle of World War I.

Historical Setting

In the spring of 1933, German Chancellor Adolph Hitler began dismantling the Versailles Treaty, the peace agreement that ended World War I, and imposed impossible financial burdens on Germany. After he refused to continue payment of reparations for damages caused during the First World War, and the western Allies failed to force compliance, the treaty had become another in a long line of history's scraps of paper. In violation of the Versailles Treaty, he rebuilt the armed forces and embarked on a mission to return Germany to greatness by acquiring territory where German-speaking people lived and lands that Germany needed for *lebensraum,* living space. Hitler proceeded to implement his plans by reoccupying the Rhineland in 1936, acquiring Austria in March 1938 and the Czech province of the Sudetenland in September 1938, and then occupying the remainder of Czechoslovakia in March 1939. The western Allies, Britain and France, stood back and watched, refusing to honor their defense agreements with the Czechs.

Hitler had promised British Prime Minister Neville Chamberlain and French President Edouard Daladier that after reincorporating German-speaking people from Czechoslovakia in a "Greater Reich," he had no more territorial demands in Europe. Other than the reacquisition of the city of Memel from Lithuania, regaining for Germany a Baltic port, Hitler seemed to grow more passive. Still, some German-speaking people in Poland had not yet been reunited with their homeland, and few doubted that Hitler would soon want them as well. In April 1939, Britain and France reconfirmed their commitment to defend Poland. To really protect that country, assistance from the Soviet Union was vital, but the Poles and Russians have a long history of antagonism.

Chamberlain approached Soviet Premier Josef Stalin, asking for a public guarantee that the Soviets would support Polish sovereignty. Stalin wanted more, including a treaty of alliance and mutual defense with Britain and France. The government in London thought that would merely serve to provoke Hitler, but, when they hesitated, the Soviets believed that Britain and France did not take them seriously. Further, western requests for a guarantee of Rumanian sovereignty seemed like a ploy to es-

tablish their influence in eastern Europe at Soviet expense. Unable to get the agreement he wanted from London or Paris, Stalin secretly turned to Berlin. In the early 1920s, when both Germany and the Soviet Union were pariahs in Europe, the two countries had engaged in some military exchanges. That cooperation ended with Hitler's accession to power in 1933, for *Der Führer* was virulently anti-Communist. Because Hitler's military and diplomatic actions thus far had been directed primarily against western Europe, perhaps he would be willing to grant Stalin the influence he desired in eastern Europe.

German troops parade through Warsaw, Poland, in September 1939. (National Archives)

Hitler remembered the devastating effects on Germany of a two-front conflict in World War I, so an agreement with the USSR seemed possible. He sent Foreign Minister Joachim von Ribbentrop to discuss the possibility with Soviet Foreign Minister Vyacheslav Molotov, and talks proceeded through the summer of 1939. As the secret negotiations continued, Hitler began laying the groundwork for his Polish demands. He wanted the return of Danzig (Gdansk) as an outlet to the Baltic for international trade and that had been awarded to Poland in the Versailles Treaty. In August, Hitler demanded the return of the German-speaking people of the city and the corridor of land that separated Germany from the state of East Prussia, on the other side of Danzig. After that, he assured anyone who would listen, he had no more territorial demands in Europe. That brought renewed commitments to Poland from Britain and France, but their appeals to Stalin still fell short of his desires. Thus, Stalin rejected the British and French in the Molotov-Ribbentrop Non-Aggression Treaty signed on 23 August. This surprised the world and shocked the Poles, who never conceived that Stalin would allow a potential Nazi invasion that would put an enemy at the Soviet gates.

The Battle

German Army Commander-in-Chief Walther von Brauchitsch oversaw the deployment of two army groups for the Polish invasion. In the north, he placed the Fourth Army in Pomerania with orders to drive east to occupy Danzig and link up with the Third Army stationed in East Prussia. This would place about one-third of the Polish army, stationed in the Danzig corridor, in a pincer. In the south, troops were stationed in Silesia and Slovakia. The Fourteenth Army would drive due east along Poland's southern border, occupying Cracow and crossing the San River at Przemysl. The Tenth Army on the Fourteenth's left flank was also to drive due east, destroying the Polish forces directly

in their path. On the Tenth's left flank, driving into the central part of Poland, the Eighth Army was to drive directly for Warsaw, the capital city on the Vistula River.

The German forces were mainly traditional infantry divisions, but most of the Eighth Army was made up of Germany's new mechanized and armored forces, designed to strike hard and deep. These units made up only about 10 percent of Germany's forces; the rest still moved on foot supplied by horse-drawn transport.

The Polish army, though large, was completely unmechanized. They eschewed the defensive in favor of a strategy that would employ numerous counterattacks. A third of the army, however, was based in the Danzig corridor where there was little room for maneuver. Another third of the army was held in reserve for the counterattacks. That meant that the final third was spread too thinly across Poland's open, flat frontier with Germany. Lacking tanks or antitank weapons, as well as trucks for rapid reaction, the Polish defense plan was impracticable. By placing most of their units right on the German frontier, they occupied the economically important coalfields, but placed themselves on ground that had few natural obstacles. A defense established farther east, behind the Warta and Vistula Rivers, would have given the Poles natural terrain assistance at the cost of abandoning large portions of western Poland without a fight.

On the night of 31 August–1 September, Hitler had an incident staged along the border that gave him a "legitimate reason" for launching his invasion. The Polish army was completely unprepared for the blitzkrieg, the "lightning war," that German forces launched against them. The armored and mechanized columns quickly drove between Polish troop concentrations while close air support blasted strong points. At the same time, the German air force, the Luftwaffe, caught much of the Polish air force on the ground; within 3 days, Polish air power ceased to exist. Free of any opposition, Luftwaffe bombers proceeded to

pound cities as well as military targets and troops concentrations. The German land forces moved so quickly that Polish armies were soon surrounded and cut off, not only from other forces but from any communications with Polish headquarters.

The thin Polish defense offered almost no serious resistance, and by 8 September the first German units were at the outskirts of Warsaw. The Eighth Army, attacking through the center of the country, arced northward to establish a blocking position on the Vistula River upon which the retreating northern Polish forces were hammered. Other Polish forces were sur-

rounded and eliminated as all five German armies picked up speed as resistance crumbled. By 17 September, the Fourteenth Army in the far south had hooked northward to link up at Brest-Litovsk, a hundred miles east of Warsaw, with the Third Army moving southward out of East Prussia. Almost all the remaining Polish forces were withdrawn to defend Warsaw, which was under round-the-clock aerial bombardment. Then things got worse.

On 17 September, Soviet forces invaded from the east. Unknown to the world until that day was a provision in the Molotov-Ribbentrop Pact that called for Poland to be divided between Germany and the USSR. The Soviets met almost no resistance, and they occupied the southeastern portion of the country, which was the final proposed fallback position if Warsaw fell. There was now no such possibility.

Pockets of resistance held out as long as food, water, and ammunition allowed, but Poland was doomed almost from the first day. Facing an outbreak of typhoid and a rapidly dwindling food supply, Warsaw surrendered on 27 September. The naval base at Hel on the Baltic lasted until 1 October, and the final surrender of Polish forces involved 17,000 men defending Kock, southeast of Warsaw, on 5 October.

Results

The Polish army was wiped out: 66,000 killed, some 200,000 wounded, and almost 700,000 made prisoner. Poland itself was also wiped out as an independent country for the next 50 years. Nazi/Soviet occupation in 1939 was replaced in 1941 by complete Nazi occupation, that to be replaced by Soviet domination in 1945. Modern Poland, born in 1919, was struck down and held passive after age 20. Not until the 1980s did Poland's labor movement, Solidarity, open the first cracks in the Communist wall.

Poland received no help from Britain or France, both of whom swore to uphold their defense treaties. True, they did declare war on Germany, but not a single British or French soldier, plane, tank, or gun arrived in Poland. As the only access from where such support could have arrived was through the Skagerak straits between Denmark and Sweden, German aircraft could easily have stopped any attempt at aid. Any threat to Germany's western border, which may have given the Nazis some pause, never materialized because of France's slow mobilization process. By the time the French reserves had been called up, Poland was already doomed.

Germany's invasion of Poland showed the world the face of warfare for the coming era.

The trench warfare for which most of Europe was prepared was made obsolete in 5 weeks; offensive warfare was once again back in preeminence, and both armor and mechanized infantry had arrived as the instruments of blitzkrieg. Also introduced in Poland was the perfection of close air support with which the Germans had been experimenting during their assistance to General Francisco Franco in Spain's civil war between 1936 and 1939. Although ground support by aircraft had been used in World War I, the development of the dive bomber brought that tactic to its highest level. The Germans proved in the first days of the Polish campaign that air superiority was vital to modern warfare, marking the true arrival of the air forces as an equal partner in the military establishments of the world. All of this was clear to the astute observer during the Spanish civil war, but such eyes were few and far between in the corridors of power in the 1930s. To a great extent, the lesson was not learned until the late spring and early summer of 1940, for many Europeans viewed Poland's collapse as a reflection on that country's state of readiness rather than an indicator of German power; Nazi victories in Scandinavia and France provided the necessary example of Germany's land and air might.

War of maneuver implemented by armor has remained the doctrine of warfare in the developed world ever since. The first year of the Korean War was remarkable for the ebb and flow of the armies engaged; although the war settled into a replay of World War I in the trenches, the need for air superiority was once again demonstrated. In the Arab-Israeli wars of 1956, 1967, and 1973, tanks and aircraft were the primary weapons. In 1991, the forces implementing Desert Storm showed the Iraqis the true ability of mobile forces to overcome static defenses. Although the theory for this type of warfare actually was developed in Great Britain during the years between World Wars I and II, only a few Germans with vision and influence, such as Heinz Guderian, were able to convince their commanders of the possibilities of the tactics that came to be called blitzkrieg.

References: Guderian, Heinz. *Panzer Leader.* Translated by Constantine Fitzgibbon. New York: E. P. Dutton, 1952; Liddell Hart, Basil. *History of the Second World War.* London: Cassell & Coompany, 1970; Mason, Herbert Molloy. *The Rise of the Luftwaffe, 1918–1940.* New York: Dial Press, 1973; Pitt, Barrie. "Blitzkrieg," in *History of the Second World War,* no. 1. London: BBC Publishing, 1966; Zaloga, Steve. *The Polish Campaign, 1939.* New York: Hippocrene Books, 1985.

DUNKIRK
24 May–4 June 1940

FORCES ENGAGED

German: Fourth and Eighteenth Armies, employing nine divisions in the assault, numbering approximately 200,000 men. Commanders: Generals Gerd von Rundstedt and Fedor von Bock.

British: Nine British and five French divisions, plus fragments of the Belgian army, totaling approximately 400,000 men. Commander: Field Marshall Lord Gort.

IMPORTANCE

German hesitation allowed British forces to escape from France, saving the British army for defense of Great Britain and for later combat on the Continent.

Historical Setting

Starting with the Nazi invasion of Poland on 1 September 1939, German armies had had everything their own way. Poland fell in less than a month, and then, after waiting out the winter, German forces swept over Denmark and occupied Norway in April and May 1940. Starting on 10 May, German forces attacked Holland and Belgium on their way toward France. As in the Franco-Prussian War of 1870 and World War I in 1914, the Germans had plans to paralyze the French and defeat them quickly. The French, however, believed that this time they had the answer to German aggression in a series of fortifications called the Maginot line. This line of interlocking fortresses and strongpoints stretched from the Swiss border along the Franco-German frontier to Belgium. Therein lay the problem: the defenses stopped at Belgium. The Belgian government between the wars had not wanted to spend the money to cooperate with the French in this venture and were sure that after the German fiasco of World War I that they would never violate Belgian neutrality a second time. France could not extend the Maginot line to the coast, for to do so would point guns at its Belgian ally. Thus, the route that Germany used in 1914 to outflank the massed French armies in the Ardennes lay open once again in 1940.

As in 1870, the German attack was aimed at the frontier fortress city of Sedan. Pinning down the French armies here meant that German armor could drive toward the coast, thus isolating the British Expeditionary Force (BEF) positioned along the Belgian border. Neither the British nor the French had done much since 1918 to update their tactics, so their readiness to refight World War I was completely undone by the German blitzkrieg.

The plan worked perfectly and German armored units, with their left flank covered by strong infantry units, drove back all Allied forces. Still, the British and Belgians managed to withdraw in a fairly orderly fashion and maintain (at least for a time) a unified front. The lack of coordination between French, British, and Belgian units made a strong defense difficult. This was made worse by the ever-changing command structure of the French army, which was supposed to exercise overall command. The supreme commander at the start of the Battle of France was General Maurice Gamelin. He was replaced after a week by General Maxime Weygand. Their direct subordinates also varied, as did the chain of command, which stretched to the British. To make

The evacuation of Dunkirk, showing British troops on a beach forming into winding lines ready to take their turn in boarding small boats to take them to larger vessels, June 1940. (Archive Photos/ Popperfoto)

matters worse, the generals rarely communicated by radio or telephone, but sent messages by motorcycle or drove to meet face-to-face. None of this could possibly be effective against the rapid warfare that Germany was waging. On top of all this confusion, BEF commander General Lord Gort had permission to appeal to the government in London any order that could endanger his forces.

German armor, commanded by Heinz Guderian, stunned the Allies with its speed. More stunning was the discovery by the Allies that the German goal was not Paris but the English Channel. When they finally realized this, and that German armor was outracing its infantry support, the logical countermove was to have British and French forces attack toward each other and link up, severing the panzer divisions' contact with the remainder of the army.

As shown earlier, the inability to communicate directly (Gamelin's headquarters did not even have a radio) doomed any such maneuver. Therefore, by 20 May, Guderian's tanks had reached the coast against little resistance.

The BEF had very few tanks, but they threw them at the German flank at Arras on 21 May. The seventy-four newly arrived tanks from England struck just behind the German armored columns and for 2 days caused the Germans serious concern. German airpower and the introduction of German 88-mm antiaircraft guns as antitank weapons turned the tide, and, when the British withdrew on 23 May, they had but two tanks left. Meanwhile, German tanks continued up the coast from Abbeville, isolating Boulogne on 21 May and Calais the next day. German tanks stood at this point at Gravelines, 10 miles from Dunkirk, the final remaining port in British hands. Had the drive continued, Guderian's armor would have pushed the BEF into the oncoming forces of General von Bock pushing in from Belgium. Thanks to Adolph Hitler, it did not happen.

Hitler visited the headquarters of Field Marshal Gerd von Rundstedt at Charleville near Sedan. Rundstedt had just overridden orders from Berlin ordering a continuation of the armored assault. The British attack at Arras, as well as the massing French armies to the south, made him stop his armored divisions for a rest and to have the infantry catch up to them. Hitler confirmed this decision, although his exact reasoning is a matter of conjecture. His advisors in Berlin had warned against the use of tanks in the usually muddy areas of Flanders, an area in which Hitler had served in World War I. He also worried about the French armies because, up to this point, the invasion had gone more smoothly than anyone had expected and he was therefore wary. Finally, the head of the Luftwaffe, Reichsmarschall Hermann Göring, assured him that the air force could easily finish off any resistance in the Low Countries as well as the isolated British and Belgian forces. It has been suggested that Hitler also refrained for political reasons, thinking that a complete rout of the British would embarrass the British and therefore stiffen their resolve. Whatever his reasoning may have been, the pressure on the BEF was delayed for 3 days, and in that time a more secure line of defense around Dunkirk was prepared. It was not so much the defense of Dunkirk, however, as the escape that makes the battle significant.

The Battle

Since 19 May, Lord Gort had been planning an evacuation through Dunkirk. Most of his actions at this time were to achieve that end, no matter what orders he may have gotten from Weygand. Although his force had a reprieve from fighting Guderian's tanks for a time, the Belgian army was still hard-pressed from the east. Lord Gort sent some reinforcements to aid their defense, and that move, coupled with the tank attack at Arras, gave him the time he needed to draw his men into a salient around Dunkirk. It did little to aid the Belgians in the long run, however, for King Leopold surrendered his country on 28 May. The British government urged Lord Gort to fight on, but having seen his right flank exposed by the French retreat early in the campaign and now knowing that the British were taking troops away through Dunkirk, there seemed no particular reason to press his already beaten forces any further.

Lord Gort had convinced the government in London to agree to the evacuation, and they instituted what came to be called Operation

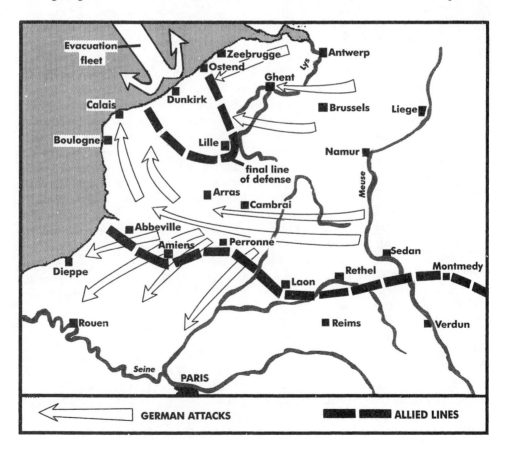

Dynamo. This called for every seaworthy craft along the southeastern English coast to mobilize for action to aid in bringing men out of France. Starting on 26 May, noncombat personnel were evacuated. This move was kept secret from the French, whose forces, which had been cut off along with the Belgians and British, were retreating to Dunkirk to stage a defense, not an evacuation. The port city had been heavily bombed, and most electrical power was out, making the cranes in the harbor unusable. The harbor was littered with sunken ships, and Dunkirk had been struck also by an attack of incendiary bombs. Still, most of the troops that left did so via the harbor, with less than a third being taken off the beaches.

Naval command of the operation was in the hands of Admiral Sir B. H. Ramsay, who had been gathering whatever craft he could since 20 May. He was ordered on 26 May to attempt the removal of 45,000 men in 2 days. The government at the start did not think any more men could feasibly be evacuated. More than 800 boats and ships participated in the evacuation, with most men being taken offshore by smaller boats and ferried to ships in deeper water. Throughout the entire evacuation, Göring attempted to make good on his promise, but the Royal Air Force (RAF) contested the skies daily. Dunkirk's location made this difficult for both air forces because German aircraft operated out of western Germany and British fighters had to cross the Channel; this left planes of both forces with little fuel for combat over Dunkirk. As the weather was usually cloudy, most of the fighting went on out of sight of the men on the ground, and this had a negative effect on morale there and in Britain. What the soldiers at Dunkirk tended to remember (and report when they got to Britain) was the attacks by German bombers and strafing fighters. The RAF appealed to the government for a clarification of its role, and the public was assured by Prime Minister Winston Churchill that the RAF was indeed doing its part. Still, much of the evacuation had to take place at night to avoid air attacks. The men on the beaches, while exposed, were lucky that the sand absorbed much of the effect of the bombs.

When the German tanks returned to action after a 3-day hiatus, they ran into prepared British positions and stiff resistance. Ultimately there were too many German tanks and too few British and French antitank weapons, but the easy victory that could have been accomplished a few days earlier now had to be fought hard. The encirclement of the French 1st Army at Lille diverted a number of German divisions, but the remainder pounded the British perimeter as men were leaving by sea.

Although the opening of Operation Dynamo had not gone as planned (28,000 rather than the planned 45,000 had been rescued), by 30 May it was in full swing. By that date, 125,000 men had been evacuated. The harbor at Dunkirk was by this point virtually unusable, so many of the remaining men waited on the beaches for the next available boat. For the most part, the troops maintained extraordinary discipline, waiting in line for their turn. At first, the boats had orders to remove only British soldiers; the French had their orders to stand and fight, so at first this created few problems. As the situation worsened, however, the French troops wanted evacuation as well. Churchill ordered on 30 May that all soldiers should be treated equally, no matter their nationality. That order was rather slow in reaching the stranded troops and some difficult moments ensued. On the nights of 2 and 3 June, the last sorties to Dunkirk dedicated themselves to rescuing French soldiers, but on 4 June the operation was terminated.

Results

By the time Operation Dynamo concluded, 338,226 men had been evacuated, including 123,095 French troops. In the final 2 days, 60,000 French soldiers had been evacuated, but, with German troops closing in on Dunkirk, the end of the operation at 0330 on 4 June left some 40,000 in the city. The remainder of the French army struggled against the German invasion for several more weeks, but a cease-fire went into effect on 17 June, and surrender documents were signed on 22 June. Hitler was at this point ruler of the Continent.

In his jubilation, he did not seem to fret much about the escaped British Expeditionary Force. He had always hoped that if the British would not cooperate with him, they certainly would at least allow him domination of mainland Europe. Hitler said that "his aim was to make peace with Britain on a basis that she would regard as compatible with her national honor to accept." Churchill's response was a masterpiece of oratory: "We shall fight in France, we shall fight on the seas and oceans, we shall fight with growing confidence and growing strength in the air, we shall defend our island, whatever the cost may be. We shall fight on the beaches, we shall fight on the landing grounds, we shall fight in the fields and in the streets, we shall fight in the hills; we shall never surrender."

Dunkirk made that vow possible. If the BEF had not escaped from France, there would have been little left in Britain to call an army. The retreating soldiers had been forced to abandon a massive amount of equipment, which would take time to replace, but more importantly what arrived in Britain were *veterans*. Around this core of men who had seen combat, an enlarged army could be formed. Without them, any army would have been made of men with little or no experience to match their little or no equipment. Hitler's plan to invade Britain may have been launched as nothing more than the civilian Home Guard defended the beaches. Not only did the presence of veteran troops mean an immediate force to resist an invasion, it meant men to take the war to the Germans in North Africa, the Mediterranean, and ultimately back to France.

The fighting around Dunkirk had a sobering effect on the German military. The Luftwaffe in particular met a formidable foe for the first time in the war. They lost 240 aircraft in the 9 days of the evacuation; 30 percent of their aircraft were forced out of action between the opening of the invasion in early May and the armistice in late July. The Royal Air Force showed that its Hurricane and Spitfire fighters could more than hold their own against the German Messerschmitts, which had met little effective opposition in previous campaigns. The decision by the British government not to reinforce the Royal Air Force in France, once it was clear that the Germans would succeed, kept a solid core of planes and pilots ready to defeat German attempts at gaining air superiority in the summer of 1940 during the Battle of Britain.

References: Bryant, Arthur. *The Turn of the Tide.* Garden City, NY: Doubleday, 1957; Churchill, Winston. *Their Finest Hour.* New York: Houghton Mifflin, 1949; Guderian, Heinz. *Panzer Leader.* Translated by Constantine Fitzgibbon. New York: E. P. Dutton, 1957; Liddell Hart, Basil. *History of the Second World War.* London: Cassell & Company, 1970; Murray, Williamson. *Strategy for Defeat: The Luftwaffe, 1933–1945.* Maxwell AFB, AL: Air University Press, 1983.

BATTLE OF BRITAIN
Summer 1940

FORCES ENGAGED
German: Luftflotte 2 (commanded by Albert Kesselring) and Luftflotte 3 (commanded by Hugo Sperrle); 1,260 bombers, 316 dive bombers, and 1,089 fighters. Overall commander: Hermann Göring.

British: Royal Air Force Fighter Command, approximately 700 Spitfire and Hurricane fighters. Commander: Air Marshal Sir Hugh Dowding.

IMPORTANCE
British victory kept Germany from launching an invasion of Great Britain, which could have guaranteed domination of Europe.

Historical Setting

Having easily overrun Poland in September 1939, German forces remained quiet through the winter. In April 1940, however, they roared back into action with surprise offensives into Denmark and Norway. Denmark surrendered in a matter of hours; Norway lasted several weeks. In early May, German forces violated Belgian and Dutch neutrality on their way into France. This maneuver bypassed the strong French defenses of the Maginot line, and rapidly moving armored columns drove deep into France heading for Paris. The British army, stunned by the speed of the offensive, found themselves separated from French forces and driven back to the coastline. There at Dunkirk, they stood isolated as German panzers bore down on them. Only the shift from a ground to an air attack saved the British, as a massive flotilla arrived to spirit the British away from under the noses of the German tanks.

France fell in a matter of weeks, leaving Adolph Hitler in control of most of Europe. He now focused on Britain, ordering the development of an invasion plan that came to be called Operation *Seelöwe*, or Sea Lion. This called for an amphibious invasion of the British Isles, but such an operation required a number of preconditions to be met. First, the German navy was in no way able to face the Royal Navy in a head-to-head confrontation; there was simply too much of a numerical difference. Still, control of the English Channel was vital for an amphibious invasion to occur. Thus, a way to keep the Royal Navy at bay was needed.

Germany's strength at this point lay in airpower. Between the world wars, U.S. General Billy Mitchell had proven the ability of aircraft to destroy shipping. In the Spanish civil war, the Luftwaffe had developed the ability to attack surface targets with their extremely accurate dive bombers, the Stukas. These had performed well against British shipping in April and May during fighting off the coast of Nor-

way. Surely, that was the way to keep the Royal Navy safely out of the Channel. To accomplish this feat, however, it would be necessary to achieve air superiority over the Channel and southern England. This the Royal Air Force would certainly contest.

Churchill and Air Chief Marshal Sir Hugh Dowding made the difficult decision late in the battle of France not to reinforce the dwindling Royal Air Force presence across the Channel. The planes saved by this move meant that Dowding in July could draw on roughly 800 aircraft in Fighter Command, but about 100 of those were twin-engine Bristol Blenheims unsuited to dogfighting. The remaining 700 aircraft were Hawker Hurricanes and Supermarine Spitfires. Both were modern designs that could compete with the German Messerschmitt Bf-109, although the Spitfire was the superior machine in air-to-air combat. The Hurricane squadrons were chosen to engage the German bombers as often as possible, leaving the Spitfire squadrons to be the primary aircraft for fighter engagements. Most important, however, was not the aircraft but the newly invented radar. This British development proved the key to defending the islands. Without it, aircraft would have had to have been flying constantly, patrolling for German raids and using valuable fuel. With radar, pilots could maintain a state of readiness on the ground and respond to radar reports that would vector them to meet German air fleets. This gave the British a distinct advantage in fuel supply during aerial combat because the German Messerschmitts had little more than 15 minutes' worth of fuel at combat consumption rates while over Britain. As they had to escort the bombers (owing to the poor self-defense capabilities of the bombers), the limited combat time of the Messerschmitts left the bombers exposed to attack by the Hurricanes. The German hope that Messerschmitt Bf-110s, twin-engine fighters, could adequately defend the bombers proved ephemeral.

The Campaign

The battle is regarded to have officially begun on 10 July 1940, during which time German bombers attacked convoys in the English Channel and British harbor facilities from Plymouth to Dover. Their success was limited because the radar's ability to locate the Germans while forming up over France allowed the British to mass their planes over the ports. Still, the loss to the Royal Air Force (although it was roughly half of the losses it inflicted on the Germans) was significant enough to give Dowding pause. As the weeks passed, he grew increasingly hesitant to maintain aerial escort for the convoys, fearing that significant losses, coupled with new German attacks on other targets on land, would stretch his forces too thin and make it impossible for sufficient replacement aircraft to be built.

Dowding's fears came true in mid-August, when the Germans changed their targets. Hitler

deemed 13 August *Adlertag* (Eagle Day), marking the beginning of direct assaults on ground targets preparatory to invasion. The radar had proved sufficiently troublesome that German Luftwaffe commander Hermann Göring ordered attacks on the radar facilities. The construction of the masts (tall, thin, and made of girders typical of radio broadcast antennae) was such that destroying them was difficult. The Stukas were sufficiently accurate to hit these small targets, but they were so slow that they proved easy prey for British fighters. Several days of this type of attack proved relatively fruitless. The concurrent attacks on coastal airfields, however, was a bit more successful and more worrisome. Luckily, most of Britain's airfields were dirt strips rather than paved, making repairs much easier. Hangar and repair facilities, however, were much more difficult to put back into operation after damage.

Most importantly, however, the British aircraft factories, under the direction of Lord

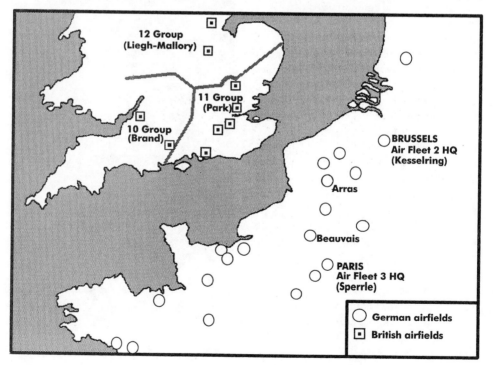

Beaverbrook, maintained high production. Through the middle of August, they were able to replace lost aircraft almost at a one-to-one ratio, building almost 100 aircraft per week. The training of replacements for killed and wounded pilots, however, could not be dangerously rushed, although most final training was reduced from 6 to 3 weeks. Unbelievably, however, the training schools did not aggressively recruit new pilots, and transfers of pilots from Bomber Command or Coastal Command was minimal. Also, trained pilots in administrative positions were not transferred to combat, further increasing the strain on those pilots that survived. Also, Dowding kept a large percentage of his aircraft well back from the coastal airfields, in reserve for the day when the German invasion took place. Thus, the men at the front were pushed to their limits, as they had to fly and fight day in and day out, with little respite. In the midst of this trying time, Prime Minister Winston Churchill spoke to the nation and in his words immortalized these "airmen who, undaunted by odds, unwearied in their constant challenge and mortal danger, are turning the tide of the world war by their prowess and by their devotion. Never in the field of human conflict was so much owed by so many to so few. All our hearts go out to the fighter pilots, whose brilliant actions we see with our own eyes every day."

Although intense bombing and fighting went on through the end of August and into early September, it was not the fighter pilots but British bombers crews that turned the tide in the Battle of Britain. On the night of 24–25 August, an off-course German bomber missed its target of oil storage facilities on the outskirts of London and instead dropped its bombs unknowingly on a civilian area. Churchill responded by ordering British bombers to strike at Berlin, which they did the following night. Although the attack infuriated Hitler and embarrassed Göring, the German dictator waited almost 2 weeks to seriously retaliate. He gave his fighter aircraft through 6 September to

establish air superiority for the invasion; if they could not achieve it by then, targeting would again shift. On 6 September, he ordered that the primary goal of German bombing be the destruction of British cities, London in particular. Additionally, he hoped that this would bring all the British reserve aircraft into play where they could be destroyed (or so the Germans thought).

Results

The decision to stop the attacks on airfields, radar sites, and factories proved to be one of Hitler's greatest mistakes. Hanson Baldwin wrote, "It was one of the great miscalculations of history. The bombing of London gave the great Fighter Command a chance to recuperate, and it forced the Luftwaffe to a deeper penetration and thus exposed the bombers and

Children taking shelter watch a dogfight between planes over Kent, 1940. (Archive Photos/Popperfoto)

short-legged fighters to greater loss. It antagonized world public opinion, mobilized global sentiment in support of Britain, stiffened English resolution and helped lead to Germany's loss of the war" (Baldwin, *Battles Lost and Won*, p. 85). City buildings and civilians could not stop a German invasion; aircraft could. Air superiority was vital to a German invasion, and bombing of civilian areas would not achieve it. This decision guaranteed British independence.

Had the Luftwaffe accomplished its goal of air superiority, could Hitler have invaded the British Isles? The British Royal Army was badly shaken by the ordeal in France and almost without equipment with which to fight, and coastal defenses were rudimentary at best. Once in Britain, the Germans may have had a good chance, but they had to cross the Channel first, and with what? The Germans possessed no amphibious landing craft, only barges that were in need of major conversion if they were to carry sufficient troops and materiel and survive the choppy waves of the Channel. Through the summer of 1940, as the Battle of Britain raged, the Germans began to scour Europe for anything that could be used for troop and equipment transport. They massed the varied collection of craft in French ports, where they were regularly bombed by the British. Never did they collect enough transport to succeed.

Secondly, the choice of invasion sites was flawed. The German army wanted a wide-front invasion stretching from Ramsgate on the east to Lyme Regis in the southwest, with landings at Ramsgate, Folkstone, Bexhill, Brighton, and the Isle of Wight. The Royal Navy repeatedly stated that it could not possibly protect such a wide front, even with air superiority. Had the landings actually taken place, the terrain did not favor the invader. Much better would have been an invasion through East Anglia. Such an invasion could have driven westward to and above London. The beaches there are much flatter and give directly onto flat ground, the type of terrain vital for the German blitzkrieg. The rocky south coast with its numerous cliffs would

have slowed any German attempt at implementing tank warfare.

Finally, the Germans lacked the one thing vital to success, and that was the dedication of Hitler to the idea. Although he ordered the concentration of shipping and troops through the summer of 1940 (and continued to delay the possible invasion through 17 September while hoping for the Luftwaffe's success), he had a deeper desire to fight the Communists to the east than the Anglo-Saxons to the west. As soon as France had fallen, Hitler had proposed a peaceful solution, since Germans and Britons were of similar racial background. Better, he thought, that the two ally against the Slavic Bolsheviks than fight each other. It was that inner need to exercise his racial and political prejudices that sent Hitler's armies eastward. Although officially putting Operation *Seelöwe* on hold on 17 September, it was never seriously reconsidered after the autumn of 1940.

British freedom meant that Hitler would have to fight on two fronts, a situation he should have known from World War I was never to be sought. Indeed, he argued against such a venture in 1924, when he published *Mein Kampf*. The British Isles became, as one U.S. leader put it, the world's largest stationary aircraft carrier, from which constant bombing of continental targets followed for the remainder of the war; it served also as the base from which the landings in northern France took place in June 1944. Without that base of operations, could the United States have conducted a war against Germany? A German-controlled Britain could have virtually guaranteed a Nazi-dominated Europe.

References: Baldwin, Hanson. *Battles Lost and Won.* New York: Harper & Row, 1966; Bishop, Edward. *Their Finest Hour.* New York: Ballantine, 1968; Deighton, Len. *Blood, Tears, and Folly.* London: Jonathan Cape, 1994; Galland, Adolph. *The First and the Last.* London: Methuen, 1955; Hough, Richard, and Denis Richards. *The Battle of Britain.* London: Hodder & Stoughton, 1989; Shears, David. "Hitler's D-Day," *Military History Quarterly* 6(4), Summer 1994.

MOSCOW
30 September–5 December 1941

Forces Engaged
Soviet: Approximately 1 million men.
Commander: Marshal Semyon Timoshenko.
German: Approximately 750,000 men.
Commander: Field Marshal Fedor von Bock.

Importance
German failure to capture Moscow doomed the Nazi attempt to conquer the Soviet Union.

Historical Setting

After Adolf Hitler failed to bend Great Britain to his will in the summer and fall of 1940, he postponed the invasion of that country and turned his attention toward the east. Hitler had long despised communism. In spite of the convenient nonaggression pact that Germany had signed with the Soviet Union before the invasion of Poland in 1939, Hitler was determined not only to wipe out the hated political system, but to acquire for Germany much-needed *lebensraum,* or living space, as he had outlined in his 1925 book *Mein Kampf.* To that end, Hitler in December 1940 issued Directive 21, which laid out his operational goals. He stated that capturing Moscow, the Soviet capital, was a secondary objective. Instead, the more important targets were Leningrad and Stalingrad. The capture of these two cities, named for the leading lights of the Soviet state, would surely bring communism tumbling down.

The German generals argued instead for a more direct attack, with Moscow as the primary goal. Moscow offered everything necessary to accomplish both military and political ends. Strategically, it was the Soviet Union's primary rail nexus and a major industrial center. Capture of the city would not only hinder Soviet productivity, it would also deny access to the west of any reinforcements brought in from the Far East. Politically, it was too impor-

tant for the Soviets to abandon, so, in fighting to save their capital city, the Soviets would feed immense numbers into a killing ground that would annihilate their armies. At the same time, the German invasion would destroy communism by bringing down the headquarters of a highly centralized form of government. Although other targets in the Soviet Union offered advantages, none would so completely end the Communist menace. Hitler's obsession with Stalingrad and Leningrad as powerful symbols, described as "mystical bunkum" (Fuller, *A Military History of the Western World,* vol. 3, p. 421), was too powerful for his military advisors to overcome. Thus, the invasion of the Soviet Union was planned.

Hitler ordered the creation of three army groups. Army Group North would drive on the northern port city of Leningrad; Army Group South would aim toward Kiev and the Ukraine; and Army Group Center would pierce the center of Soviet defenses and then arc northward to link up with Army Group North in a huge pincer movement that would engulf masses of Soviet troops. This plan did offer concrete advantages because conquest of the Ukraine (followed by a further drive to the Caucasus) would give Germany control of the center of Soviet food production as well as (with the occupation of Belorussia in the north) allow it to occupy the majority of industrial cities. Both would aid the German invasion as well as seriously harm the Soviet defense.

On 22 June 1941, the invasion started and was as hugely successful as Hitler had envisioned. Hundreds of thousands of Soviet troops were captured along with immense amounts of guns and tanks. Much of Soviet airpower was destroyed on the ground, and long-range bombers sent in from farther east were easy targets for the superior German fighter aircraft. In less than a month, German armies were approaching Leningrad in the north and fighting for Smolensk, barely 200 miles from Moscow. On 19 July 1941, Hitler issued Directive 33, which ordered large elements of Army Group Center to detach and move north and south to assist the respective army groups there.

This diversion of troops immediately after the Nazi victory at Smolensk was viewed by the Soviet high command as nothing short of a miracle. They expected the Nazis to drive down the one major highway that existed in the Soviet Union, between Smolensk and Moscow, and there was little they could do about it. Instead, Soviet commander Marshal Timoshenko was granted time to concentrate forces to protect his capital and to establish defensive lines that virtually did not exist before this time. He had almost 2 months to accomplish this task while German forces concentrated on Leningrad and Kiev. Leningrad resisted German assaults, but Army Group South captured Kiev in a massive encircling operation that netted almost two-thirds of a million prisoners, almost 900 tanks, and more than 7,000 other motor vehicles. When that operation was complete, on 26 September, those elements of Army Group Center that had assisted in the victory returned to their original command. At this point, Hitler became interested in Moscow.

The Battle

The German generals had been begging Hitler to focus on Moscow, to strike immediately after Smolensk while the Soviet army was reeling. The Leningrad battle was developing into a siege, and Stalingrad was still far to the east, so Moscow now became the tempting target for Hitler that it had always been for his commanders. Hitler decided that Moscow should not be captured, but leveled. Its complete destruction would be the symbol of the destruction of communism, but he would allow as many refugees as possible to escape east in order to spread terror through the population. None would be allowed to escape west because that would force Germany to feed them and to Hitler they were not worth the effort or expense. The primary problem with Hitler's decision was not that he made it, but that he did so too late.

His generals pushed for an attack, if not immediately upon the heels of the Smolensk victory, then at least by 1 September. That would provide sufficient good weather for taking Moscow, as well as denying the Soviets the time to improve their defenses. Instead, Hitler waited until the Kiev encirclement was complete before transferring the necessary troops back to Army Group Center. This was not done until the beginning of October. Under renowned armor theorist and field commander Heinz Guderian, II Panzergruppe had to pull out of the Kiev region, move north almost 200 miles, and go directly into combat, leading off the attack on the southern end of a broad front. Facing the Germans were nine armies, deployed at least a hundred miles west of the primary defensive position that the Soviets were constructing along a north-south line (the Mozhaysk line) about 50 miles west of Moscow.

The opening German attack took place in sunny weather on 30 September, with two major pincers moving from just north and south of Smolensk. By 10 October, they had met behind six of the Soviet armies. That success, coupled with a similar encirclement of three armies to the south, resulted in the Germans acquiring 673,000 prisoners, 1,242 tanks, and 5,412 guns. It was impressive, but followed by frustration. On 8 October, autumn rains began, and the low-quality Russian roads turned into quagmires. Nothing, not even tracked vehicles, could make headway through the mud. The momentum built in a week and a half of victory ground to a standstill. The Germans had advanced two-thirds of the necessary distance to Moscow from their jumping-off points, but for another month they could move forward only slowly, though move forward they did. Not until cold weather in November began to freeze the mud did the offensive seriously resume, and by 15 November the Germans had broken through the Mozhaysk line. The weather that froze the roads, however, soon froze the soldiers. By 5 December, although the Germans had made serious advances to both the north

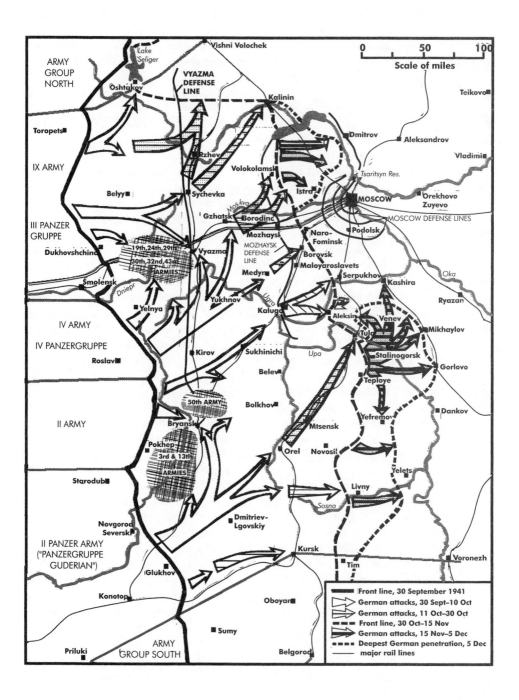

and south of Moscow, the weather was too formidable. On 5 December, Hitler allowed his troops to withdraw slightly to positions better suited to defense.

As soon as the German offensive stalled, the Soviets were prepared to take the offensive themselves. Immediately, counterattacks were launched from the major city of Kalinin northwest of Moscow, northern anchor of the Mozhaysk line, and against Kaluga at the southern end. Stalin had transferred an additional 100,000 troops and 300 tanks from farther east, as well as large numbers of antitank weapons. The Soviets were able to reestablish their defenses in front of Moscow, and the city was saved.

Results

On 6 December 1941, Marshal Timoshenko, who had commanded the Soviet forces in the long defensive withdrawal from Smolensk, was replaced by Marshal Georgi Zhukov. Zhukov's offensives began turning the tide of German fortunes before Moscow, and he was the man who ultimately commanded the Soviet troops that occupied Berlin in 1945. More than Zhukov or the stolidity of the Russian soldier, two factors defeated the Nazis in front of Moscow and ultimately caused their total defeat in the east. First was the weather. Late spring rains had delayed the opening of the invasion of the Soviet Union from late May to late June. If one moves all action on the eastern front up one month, then the opening of the delayed offensive against Moscow would have started at the beginning of September instead of at the end. That could well have placed German troops in the city before the autumn rains halted their advance. A German officer involved in the actions on the eastern front wrote, "A period of good weather similar to that when we started would have enabled us to put our forces, in full strength, at the gates of Moscow. It was the weather, not the Russians, which stopped us" (Philippi, "Battle for Moscow: The German View," p. 739). Just as the rains stopped the

October offensive, so did the cold stop the November/December assault. The German army was unprepared for the bitter cold. Neither the troops in the field nor the transport vital to bringing up the needed supplies were able to function in the Russian winter.

The reason they were unprepared is the second factor that doomed the Germans in Russia, and that reason was Hitler. After a string of easy victories from Poland through France, while the Soviets had struggled mightily to overcome Finnish resistance during the winter of 1939–1940, Hitler was convinced that there was no way his forces could lose a war against the Soviet Union. The rapid advances that characterized the blitzkrieg victories in Poland and western Europe would certainly put his troops in Leningrad, Moscow, and Kiev by the time the winter struck. Thus, little was spent on winter uniforms and accessories. When they were needed and were shipped from Germany, little of the needed clothing arrived because of another of Hitler's mistakes.

When the Germans entered the Soviet Union, one reason they captured such huge numbers of prisoners was that many of the enemy could not wait to turn coat. The Communist regime had never been popular, especially in the western provinces of Ukraine and Belorussia. The population there viewed the Nazis as liberators and begged to be allowed to assist in overthrowing Stalin and his regime. Hitler instead ordered them shot or hauled back to Germany as slave labor. He had an opportunity virtually unique in military history: to expand his army with motivated recruits as it drove deeper into enemy territory. Instead, by abusing the population, the Soviets were able to organize an incredibly effective underground resistance movement, the partisans. They proved so harmful to the Nazi war effort, because of their attacks on lines of supply, that at the height of the war the Germans were obliged to maintain almost half their forces in the rear areas guarding the supply lines. Thus, the German army lost most of its effectiveness at the

OTHER RUSSIAN BATTLES

Choosing Moscow as the turning point of the Russian campaign is not to overlook the potential decisiveness of other battles between the invading Nazis and the defending Soviets. By directing three separate army groups into Russia, the fortunes of each affected that of the others. The shifting of troops among northern, central, and southern fronts weakened or strengthened the invaders and helped determine their ultimate success or failure.

Had Leningrad fallen before the winter of 1941 set in, Army Group North would have secured the Baltic front and been in a position to strike down the Volga toward Moscow. The 900-day siege of Leningrad certainly made sure that such an eventuality never occurred.

Stalingrad is probably the best known of the battles in Russia and is often the choice as the most decisive. When General von Paulus marched his Sixth Army into the city, the result was one of the most bitter fights in all military history, not just that of World War II. Soviet tanks rolled off assembly lines directly into combat. The fighting was street to street, house to house, room to room for months. Only the arrival of troops transferred from Siberia to encircle the city saved it from capture, while at the same time guaranteeing that only about 5,000 of the third of a million Germans who entered the city ever saw their homeland again. Hitler's determination to capture the city named for his nemesis overwhelmed any rationality. As before Moscow, a well-timed tactical withdrawal probably would have saved the situation and possibly meant ultimate German victory. Hitler's dictum "Where the German soldier once sets foot there he remains" spelled the doom of tens of thousands of his soldiers.

The coup de grâce for the Nazis in Russia was probably Kursk, the massive tank battle of July 1943. Each side threw into the fray about 3,000 tanks, so many that no battle before or since could match the amount of armor on the field that day. The Soviet T-34 proved itself equal to or superior over German tanks; the German Panthers proved too easy to burn, and the Tigers, although superior in armor and gun, were easy prey for swarms of Soviet soldiers that dropped explosives or fire into any available air vent. After Kursk, German armored forces were unable to replace their losses to any significant degree, and the German withdrawal out of Soviet territory began in earnest.

front as the Soviets were rebuilding their armies with soldiers transferred from Siberia and new tanks churned out of factories in the cities that remained in Soviet hands.

Had Hitler driven directly for Moscow and captured it, Stalin's government could well have collapsed. Had Hitler played the role of liberator and accepted the hundreds of thousands of volunteers yearning for the opportunity, Stalin's government certainly would have collapsed. With Moscow in German hands, the primary rail nexus of European Russia would have been controlled, and whatever the Soviets may have kept to the east would have been difficult if not impossible to shift to the west. With the center of Communist government in Nazi hands, the cities and regions that Hitler had originally set for his goals in the east would easily have fallen to him. All of these mistakes, and the weather, coincided providentially with the entrance of the United States into World War II. December 1941 almost certainly marks the beginning of the end for Hitler's Germany.

References: Carrell, Paul. *Hitler Moves East, 1941–1943.* Translated by Ewald Osers. New York: Little, Brown, 1965; Dupuy, Trevor N., and Paul Martell. *Great Battles on the Eastern Front.* Indianapolis, IN: Bobbs-Merrill, 1982; Fuller, J. F. C. *A Military History of the Western World,* vol. 3. New York: Funk & Wagnalls, 1956; Guderian, Heinz. *Panzer Leader.* Translated by Constantine Fitzgibbon. New York: E. P. Dutton, 1952; Philippi, Alfred. "Battle for Moscow: The German View," in *History of the Second World War,* no. 27. London: BBC Publications, 1966.

PEARL HARBOR
7 December 1941

Historical Setting

Starting in 1931, Japan began aggressively expanding its domain. Its first acquisition was Manchuria, the resource-rich northeastern province of China. Although the League of Nations condemned the aggression, no international action was taken. As the United States and most of the industrialized world was suffering from a severe depression, any nations that might otherwise have acted were too busy with their own problems. Japan declared Manchuria to be the independent state of Manchukuo, under Japanese suzerainty.

In 1937, the Japanese government, now firmly under the direction of the military, launched an invasion into the rest of China. The Chinese were at the time deep in a civil war between the Kuomintang (called the Nationalists) under the leadership of Chiang Kai-shek and the Communists under the leadership of Mao Tse-tung. This internal conflict allowed the Japanese to make rapid advances into China; this compelled the warring Chinese factions to put aside their differences and face a common enemy. The Nationalists fought primarily in the southern sector of China; the Communists, primarily in the north. Western powers again refrained from intervention, until an incident in 1937 brought U.S. attention. As the Japanese forces were attacking the city of Nanking, a U.S. gunboat, the *Panay*, was struck by bombs from Japanese aircraft and sunk. The Americans demanded payment of damages, which the Japanese were quick to provide. Apology and money in hand, the United States pulled back, but began to pay closer attention to the China situation.

When Japanese forces secured most of the Chinese coastline and then acquired Indochina from the Vichy French in 1940, the United States began to fear for its western Pacific possessions. Late in 1940, U.S. Secretary of State Cordell Hull warned the Japanese that the United States would not allow the Japanese to invade the Netherlands East Indies, a major source of oil. At the same time, the United States began an embargo of oil and scrap iron. This provoked a problem for Japanese expansion. The U.S. supply lines would be reopened only if Japan withdrew from China, which was unacceptable to the Japanese government and population. On the other hand, to secure the necessary raw materials to continue the war in China would make acquisition of the Netherlands East Indies necessary, although that would provoke a war with the United States.

Thus, the Japanese government in early 1941 began a two-pronged strategy. Diplomats in Washington were to enter into negotiations to come to some accommodation with Japanese desires in Asia; at the same time, the Japanese navy was directed to develop plans for an attack on the Americans should the negotiations fail. The more the diplomats talked, the more apart the two sides drifted. By the summer of 1941, Japanese naval planners had an operation mapped out: an attack on the U.S. naval base at Pearl Harbor in Hawaii. This would disable the U.S. fleet while Japanese forces simultaneously launched invasions into Southeast Asia and Pacific islands. The plans were developed under the direction of Admiral Isoroku Yamamoto. He had spent a number of years in the United States, and, along with his plans, he gave the Japanese government a warning: if the United States could not be convinced to grant Japan the dominance it sought in Asia within 6 months of the attack on Pearl Harbor, then U.S. industrial power would begin to overwhelm Japanese military forces. He predicted that only a quick victory would succeed, while a prolonged conflict favored the United States.

By November 1941, talks in Washington were bogging down, and the Japanese government ordered a task force to sail secretly from Tankan Bay in the Kuril Islands north of Japan. It was ordered to remain under strict radio silence, and the forecasts predicted sufficient inclement weather to cover an approach toward Hawaii from the north. Talks proceeded in Washington and the task force was ordered to be prepared to return if last-minute negotiations succeeded. They did not.

U.S. cryptanalysts had recently succeeded in cracking the Japanese diplomatic code, and intercepted communiqués from Tokyo to various embassies indicated that war was imminent. Thus, the United States was prepared for an outbreak of hostilities, but was convinced that an attack would be directed against Siberia (to take advantage of the Soviet conflict against the invading Nazis), Southeast Asia, or possibly the U.S.-owned Philippine Islands. No one expected that the Japanese would or could launch multiple attacks at targets ranging from the central Pacific to Burma.

The Battle

At dawn on 7 December 1941, the Japanese task force was positioned 275 miles north of Hawaii. They had steamed to this point completely undetected, and the attack on Sunday morning was designed to catch the U.S. garrison when it was least alert. The first wave of fifty-one dive bombers, forty torpedo bombers, and forty-three escorting fighters took off without incident. As they approached Hawaii, they were detected on U.S. radar screens, but, because the technology was new and the tech-

nicians poorly trained, the technicians were unable to read the size of the approaching force. They assumed it was a flight of B-17 bombers arriving from the U.S. mainland. Thus, the Japanese were able to launch their attack with no warning given at the target. Just before 0800, when flight leader Mitsuo Fuchida saw the U.S. ships completely open to attack, he signaled the code words for success: "tora [tiger], tora, tora."

Not until the bombs began to fall and the torpedoes run through the harbor did the Americans respond. As "battle stations" sounded on the parked ships, the sailors operated whatever guns they could reach. There was little they could do as the attacking aircraft scored hits immediately. Four of the docked battleships were hit by torpedoes in the first 5 minutes as the dive bombers and fighters attacked from above. Japanese fighter aircraft strafed U.S. aircraft parked at the half-dozen airfields on the island of Oahu, destroying or badly damaging most of them. Only thirty-eight U.S. aircraft were able to get airborne and engage the attackers, and ten of those were shot down.

The first attack went on for 25 minutes and then was followed by a second wave at 0845. The second wave was less successful, suffered more casualties, and did little more than add finishing touches to the already battered U.S. ships. In all, the Japanese lost twenty-nine planes and fifty-five aircrew. It was as complete a surprise attack as possible and well beyond the greatest hopes of those who had planned it. Japanese planners had expected and were prepared to accept the loss of half their task force as a result of U.S. counterattacks. There were none, so no ships were lost in the assault. It was an operation that could not have better met expectations.

Results

The Japanese assault on the U.S. fleet docked at Pearl Harbor was both an unqualified success and a miserable failure. The Japanese in-

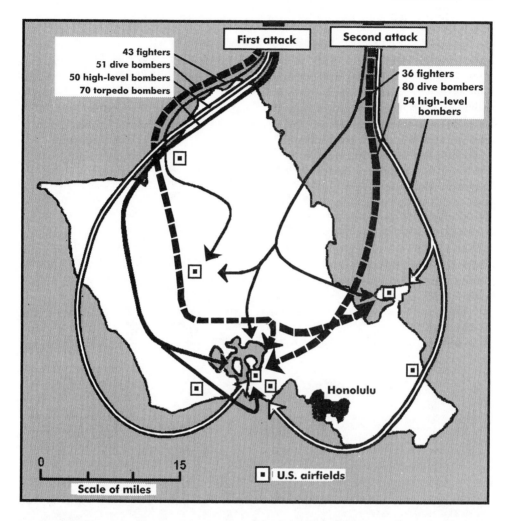

First attack

43 fighters
51 dive bombers
50 high-level bombers
70 torpedo bombers

Second attack

36 fighters
80 dive bombers
54 high-level bombers

Honolulu

0   15
Scale of miles

▣ U.S. airfields

flicted casualties numbering 2,403 dead and 1,178 wounded while sinking six battleships and three destroyers, as well as damaging three battleships and a number of cruisers. They came to knock out the U.S. battleship fleet and they had done so, at almost no cost to themselves. How then could this be considered a failure?

First, the nature of the attack on Pearl Harbor showed that the day of the battleship was past. The future of naval warfare lay in aircraft carriers, as the Japanese had just proven. The U.S. carriers *Enterprise, Yorktown, Hornet, Wasp, Lexington,* and *Saratoga* were out to sea or at other bases on 7 December, so none were lost.

This allowed the U.S. navy to plan operations almost immediately, with the raid by James Doolittle's bombers launched against Tokyo the following April and aircraft carriers in position in May to fight the battle of Coral Sea and in a position to fight and win the battle of Midway in June. Battleships from this point forward were no longer the primary ships of the fleet.

Second, although the Japanese destroyed or badly damaged everything they attacked, they failed to attack key targets. Most importantly, they did not bomb the huge oil storage facilities. Had those been destroyed, and they could have been taken out easily, the U.S. fleet would have been forced to operate from California. By maintaining Hawaii as the forward U.S. base, the entire nature of the Pacific war was affected. The central location made transportation of troops and materiel much simpler and made submarine operations much easier because of the shorter distances necessary to reach combat zones. Without the bases in Hawaii, it would have been virtually impossible to defend the islands from Japanese attack. Admiral Nagumo's reluctance to press his luck with a third attack saved the facilities around Pearl Harbor. Failure to destroy the submarine base also had a long-term effect. The U.S. submarine force (after some initial problems with defective torpedoes) became one of the primary reasons that the Japanese merchant navy became ineffective after 1943.

This point brings up the third failure of the Japanese. Had they brought an invasion force with them, they could not have failed to capture the islands. With Hawaii and Pearl Harbor in Japanese hands, Yamamoto's 6-month deadline might well have been met; the Americans might have had to concede Japanese dominance of the western Pacific and much of Asia. The Greater East Asia Co-Prosperity Sphere that the Japanese desired to establish, designed to give them at least economic if not political power over much of Asia, could indeed have become reality. Only the Japanese overestimation of the costs involved in the attack kept this scenario from taking place. They never dreamed that the islands would be so open to invasion, so they did not try. When, in June 1942, they tried to capture Midway as a possible jumping-off point for Hawaii, they met defeat in another turning point in World War II.

Finally, the fear Yamamoto expressed came true. He knew that the United States was a "sleeping giant" that would ultimately produce

Taken by surprise during the Japanese aerial attack on Pearl Harbor, smoke rises from Hickam Field in the distance. (National Archives)

so much weaponry that Japan would be pounded into submission. The attack on Pearl Harbor galvanized the nation into instant response in a way nothing else could. The concurrent quasiwar in the Atlantic against Hitler's U-boats would probably have taken the United States into World War II eventually, but certainly the isolationist element in the population that had so long counseled against military involvement was almost completely silenced. The attack on Pearl Harbor, by not being a killing blow, served only to anger and motivate the United States into action.

Almost from the day the attack took place, theories have abounded that President Franklin Roosevelt knew of the impending attack and allowed it to happen in order to take the United States into the war. Those involved with breaking the Japanese codes have stated that this was certainly not the case, at least not from the knowledge they had. As they had not yet succeeded in breaking the military code, they knew nothing other than what had been sent to Japanese embassies. As that gave warning of imminent action, certainly Roosevelt did know an attack somewhere was imminent. However, nothing other than a general warning was sent to Hawaii. The Philippines were regarded as the most likely target if U.S. bases were to be attacked. How much British Prime Minister Winston Churchill knew of the impending attack on Pearl Harbor has never been proven. He has been accused, however, of learning of the attack from British intelligence sources and not sharing it with Roosevelt, knowing that the Americans would certainly join the war as a British ally. If, however, he did share it with Roosevelt, then the culpability lay in the White House. It is a question long debated but never completely answered.

References: Clausen, Henry. *Pearl Harbor: Final Judgement.* New York: Crown, 1992; Levite, Ariel. *Intelligence and Strategic Surprise.* New York: Columbia University Press, 1987; Mintz, Frank. *Revisionism and the Origins of Pearl Harbor.* Lanham, MD: University Press of America, 1985; Prange, Gordon. *At Dawn We Slept.* New York: McGraw-Hill, 1981; Slackman, Michael. *Target—Pearl Harbor.* Honolulu: University of Hawaii Press, 1990.

SINGAPORE
31 January–15 February 1942

FORCES ENGAGED

Japanese: 40,000 men. Commander: Lieutenant-General Tomoyuki Yamashita.

British: 107,000 Australian, Indian army, and British troops (including 27,000 administrative troops). Commander: Lieutenant-General Arthur Percival.

IMPORTANCE

Japan's capture of Singapore capped off the successful Japanese invasion of the Malay Peninsula, robbing Britain of its prize defensive position in the Far East. This was the first of the many losses that led to the dissolution of the British Empire.

Historical Setting

Great Britain took control of Singapore in the early 1800s, using it as their primary trading post to compete with the Dutch merchants of Southeast Asia. The island city served as the major British defensive position in the region as well, coming to be called the "Gibraltar of the East." The huge artillery protecting the city from invasion gave those stationed there, as well as those viewing the outpost from London, the impression of impregnability.

Japan, however, was not daunted. Certainly the big guns could inflict heavy damage on any invading fleet, but therein lay their weakness: they were positioned only to defend against a seaborne landing, not an invasion from the Malay Peninsula. The possibility of an assault from the landward side appeared incredibly remote because only two roads existed through otherwise impenetrable jungles and swamps. The bottling up of any invasion force foolish enough to commit itself to those two arteries should have proven easy. The British Empire troops defending the city, however, labored under a false sense of security. On the Japanese-controlled island of Formosa, experts in jungle warfare spent much of 1941 developing tactics to pass soldiers through such terrain, and, by training men in the jungles of Formosa, the Japanese developed the finest jungle fighters of their day.

As the Japanese threat to Asia increased through 1941, British military and civilian officials in Singapore begged London for additional troops. Churchill's commitment to Europe and the campaign in North Africa meant that few troops, ships, or aircraft would be made available from Britain, but some troops were transferred from the Indian army to supplement the existing defensive forces made up primarily of Australian troops. By the time the war in the Pacific broke out on 8 December 1941, approximately 107,000 men of the Australian 8th Division, the Indian Army 9th, 11th, and 17th Divisions, and the British 18th Division stood ready to defend the city. Many of these troops, especially those dispatched from India, were not well equipped and were irregularly trained. Prewar plans for deploying troops at the most likely landing spots in Thailand and the Malay Peninsula were not implemented, the authorities in London fearing that any such action before the outbreak of hostilities could be deemed provocative.

That decision meant that, when the Japanese invasion force launched its amphibious assault on 8 December, they captured the key positions of Kota Bharu, Patani, and Singora with virtually no resistance. They did indeed begin moving south down the two Malay roads, but when the Indian 11th Division attempted to establish a roadblock at Jitra, they were shocked to find themselves being outflanked through the jungle. After those forces abandoned their attempted roadblock on 12 December, it seemed that the shock of the Japanese tactics completely deflated the defenders. Any attempt at making a stand failed, as empire troops began to withdraw before any threat, rather than stand and try to inflict serious damage. The retreat involved little more than holding each river crossing just long enough to destroy the bridge, but the Japanese had anticipated such a strategy and brought a surplus of engineering troops and bridging equipment. Even when the terrain proved too difficult for even the Japanese to penetrate, the empire troops found themselves outflanked by well-handled amphibious landings. By the end of January, the entire peninsula was in Japanese hands, and the British Empire troops fled into Singapore.

The Battle

Japanese Lieutenant-General Tomoyuki Yamashita engineered a brilliant offensive, but he was still less than satisfied. He had made some political enemies in Tokyo and therefore his operation was not as well staffed or equipped as he would have liked, and one of his divisional commanders was consistently insubordinate. He also was operating with a hastily assembled staff, yet in spite of these imperfect conditions he had succeeded admirably. All that was left to him was the city of Singapore itself. For 4 days, he probed the defenses and then decided to attack with a feint against the eastern part of the straits. He hoped this would draw the British reinforcements. The main assault then followed with two divisions across the western part of the straits. The causeway from the mainland to Singapore stretched about 1,100 yards, but at its narrowest point the straits were only 600 yards wide. Thus, an amphibious landing could take place quickly. Once ashore, the invaders would have to fight through the virtually non-existent beach defenses and then across jungle and rubber plantations to reach the city on the southeastern part of the island. It seems that a determined defense should have been able to withstand a landing.

At this point, Singapore's defenses showed their weakness. No trenches or tank traps had been dug anywhere except a small line near the western shore. Although the large coastal artillery pieces could be turned around to face toward the invaders, they were forced to fire across the city at targets out of sight and more than 15 miles away. There was no system of artillery spotting in place, so by the time any corrections could be transmitted to the gunners, the targets had changed position. Units were deployed to defend the beaches, but the invasion came ashore at night and across such a wide front that the defending units were easily infiltrated and outflanked. The next morning, the Japanese landed tanks, which the defenders had no guns of any size to repel.

Churchill ordered that the city be defended to the last defender and destroyed, if need be, to deny its value to the enemy, but the defenders could not hope to make a long fight of it. They were desperately short of water because Japanese aircraft attacking the city had knocked out the pumping facilities. More importantly, the troops seemed to have lost all hope, and the lack of training of many of the Indian units showed itself in their poor defensive showing. The constant Japanese barrage pounded away at morale as effectively as it did the buildings of the city, and the Japanese exercised total command of the air. Little did the defenders know that Yamashita's forces were rapidly running out of ammunition. Yamashita decided that rather than conserve his ammunition he would maintain pressure for as long as possible; if he slackened his fire, the British may have sensed his plight and stiffened their resolve. His plan succeeded and the British surrendered the city on 15 February 1942.

Results

Between 8 December and 15 February, the British Empire's forces suffered approximately 9,000 dead and wounded. The Japanese, although outnumbered in virtually every engagement, lost 3,000 killed and 7,000 wounded. They gained the city of Singapore virtually undamaged, with its excellent harbor facilities intact and a large amount of materiel in the city's warehouses. They also gained some 130,000 prisoners, civilian as well as military. Although the British commanding officer, Lieutenant-General Arthur Percival, extracted a promise from Yamashita that the city's inhabitants would be well treated, such was not the case. Many of the Chinese population suffered, with as many as 70,000 people tortured and/or killed. Some empire troops slipped through Japanese lines during the invasion and faded into the jungle, there to raise a Malay militia kept supplied by airdrops from the Indian army, but they were more of a nuisance to the Japanese than a serious threat. One of the resistance units that was created, however, laid the groundwork for much of Britain's postwar problems in Singapore: the Malayan People's Anti-Japanese Army, a Communist organization.

It was organizations such as the Malayan People's Anti-Japanese Army that agitated most strongly for independence when British rule was reestablished after the war. For a few weeks after the fighting stopped, rival underground units accused each other of collaboration and engaged in retribution executions. The first administration was a British military one that tried to maintain order. The political struggles matched the survival problems of the Malay population, for agriculture during the war had not been productive, and the economic infrastructure was in a shambles. By 1946, Britain was prepared to give the Malay Peninsula, but not Singapore, its independence. London was not willing to part with its key trading post. The constitution that the British attempted to impose on the peninsula created a strong central government, which the independent Malay states were unwilling to follow. An adapted document in 1948 created more of a confederation, more suitable to the population. Singapore remained a British possession for another decade, but in 1958 the island city gained self-rule, the British retaining only defense rights.

To a great extent, Britain's loss of Singapore in 1942 began the dissolution of the British Empire. After World War I, the victorious powers managed to hold on to their colonial possessions, but the wave of popular independence movements after World War II was too great to withstand. One thing that the Japanese did accomplish in their southeast Asia strategy was to show to the Asian population that the Europeans that had dominated them for so long were not a "master race." That Singapore fell was humiliating enough for the British, but that it fell so easily was too much for them psychologically to overcome. In quick succession, the imperial possessions of the eastern Indian Ocean region began to break away after the war. The Dutch were the biggest losers in the area, but Britain's loss of India was a foregone conclusion after World War II, and the fall of Singapore was the first step toward that end. Only Hong Kong remained a British possession, and even that was ceded back to China in 1997. The British Empire, upon which the sun never set, broke apart; the British Commonwealth, made up of most of the imperial possessions, remained, but it was nothing more than a shadow of Britain's former world power.

References: Caffrey, Kate. *Out in the Midday Sun: Singapore, 1941–1945.* New York: Stein & Day, 1973; Ienaga, Saburo. *The Pacific War, 1931–1945.* New York: Random House, 1978; Ryan, N. J. *A History of Malaysia and Singapore.* Oxford, UK: Oxford University Press, 1976; Swinson, Arthur, Tokuji Morimoto, and Mutsuya Nagao. "The Conquest of Malaya," in *History of the Second World War,* no. 26, Barrie Pitt, ed. London: BBC Publications, 1966; Toland, John. *But Not in Shame.* New York: Random House, 1961.

MIDWAY
4–6 June 1942

FORCES ENGAGED

Japanese: Strike force, built around four aircraft carriers, included two battleships and two heavy cruisers and support ships. Commander: Admiral Isoroku Yamamoto.

United States: Task Force 17, built around aircraft carrier *Yorktown.* Overall commander: Rear Admiral Frank Jack Fletcher; Task Force 16, built around aircraft carriers *Enterprise* and *Hornet.* Commander: Rear Admiral Raymond Spruance.

IMPORTANCE

American victory marked the first clear-cut Japanese defeat since the outbreak of the war; from this point on the Japanese were on the defensive, their navy suffering irreplaceable losses.

Historical Setting

After their attack on Pearl Harbor, the Japanese were successful in all their endeavors to control as much of the western Pacific area and Southeast Asia as possible. They met little effective resistance as they acquired U.S. islands from Wake to the Philippines. British forces at Singapore also put up little resistance to the Japanese invasion there, and the British were threatened by Japanese forces approaching India via Burma. For 6 months, the Japanese were unstoppable, but they met their first check in early May 1942 at the Coral Sea, northeast of Australia. There an attempt to bypass Australian forces and land on the southern coast of New Guinea was turned back by a U.S. fleet in the first naval battle in history in which ships never engaged, only aircraft against ships. Although tactically a draw, the battle proved a strategic defeat for Japan. It stopped the juggernaut.

Within a few days of the battle at Coral Sea, U.S. cryptanalysts deciphered the Japanese military code. Their work on the diplomatic code had forewarned the U.S. government about the onset of war in early December, but the ability to read the military code made military reaction much easier. Commander-in-Chief of the Pacific Fleet Chester Nimitz learned that the upcoming attack on U.S. bases in the Aleutian Islands was to be a diversion covering the main Japanese thrust at Midway. Control of Midway would put Japan in a position possibly to strike at Hawaii and accomplish what it had failed to do 6 months earlier:

occupy the key U.S. position in the Pacific Ocean. Without Hawaii, the U.S. fleet would have to operate from the west coast of North America, severely hampering attempts to regain control of the Pacific. Most importantly, from the Japanese view, was the probability of drawing the remainder of the U.S. navy out of Pearl Harbor for a killing blow.

Nimitz was unable to call on his most aggressive commander, William Halsey, because Halsey had contracted chicken pox. Command of the naval forces countering the assault toward Midway thus fell to Rear Admiral Frank Jack Fletcher. Fletcher was given command of two task forces based on the aircraft carriers *Enterprise, Yorktown,* and *Hornet.* No heavy ships were called on to escort the carriers, owing to the destruction wrought by the Japanese at Pearl Harbor and the fact that battleships would slow the progress of the faster carriers. Only a few cruisers aided by destroyers and submarines were all that were mustered for escort.

The Japanese sent the cream of its navy under command of Admiral Isoroku Yamamoto, the planner of the Pearl Harbor attack. He personally commanded the main body of the First Fleet, consisting primarily of three battleships. This force trailed the main carrier force and was to be the chief instrument of destruction when the U.S. fleet arrived. Although the Japanese had just 6 months earlier proven that the battleship had been eclipsed by the aircraft carrier as the prime ship of the fleet, the doctrine of surface battle still dominated Japanese naval strategy. Under Yamamoto, in command of the 1st Carrier Strike Force, was Chuichi Nagumo, who had commanded the

Navy dive bombers during the attack on the Japanese fleet off Midway, 4–6 June 1942. A burning Japanese ship is visible in the center. (National Archives)

attack on Pearl Harbor. He had at his disposal the fleet carriers *Akagi, Kaga, Hiryu,* and *Soryu.* For escorts, he was able to draw on battleships *Mogami* and *Mikuma,* as well as a host of lesser vessels. In addition, the Japanese dispatched an invasion fleet under Admiral Kondo and an advanced force of twelve submarines under Admiral Komatsu.

The Battle

Midway, two small islands, was defended by a small garrison. Its airfield hosted two B-26 Martin "Marauder" medium bombers, six new TBF "Avenger" torpedo bombers, a squadron of B-17 "Flying Fortress" heavy bombers, and a handful of PBY "Catalina" flying boats for long-range reconnaissance. The Catalinas were on patrol from the time that Nimitz determined that the main Japanese thrust was against Midway rather than the Aleutians. On the morning of 3 June, the Catalinas made their first contact, spotting elements of the Japanese fleet through the clouds. It was an impressive sight, eliciting the comment from pilot Ensign Jack Reid, "It must be the whole Jap Navy." It was, however, the transports of Kondo's invasion fleet and not the main Japanese battle force. The B-17s sortied against the transports that afternoon, but scored no hits. The U.S. carriers were near Midway, and Fletcher was eager for news of the position and direction of the Japanese fleet. He was unable, however, to launch any strikes against them on 3 June.

The fourth of June proved to be the primary day of battle. Nagumo sent half of his aircraft to raid Midway early in the morning, and they were followed back to the fleet by U.S. aircraft from Midway. The B-26s were rigged with makeshift torpedo launchers and made a run against the Japanese with no hits scored but immense damage received. The Avenger torpedo bombers had no better luck, as the Japanese combat air patrol of fighters covering the ships was effective in its mission. Although the Japanese assault did some damage, it was not as effective as it needed

to be, so a second attack was prepared with the bombers remaining. As the Japanese bombers returned from their strike against Midway and were reloading bombs, word reached Nagumo that a U.S. aircraft carrier possibly had been located. As the report was somewhat vague, and he was sure that more than one carrier was in the neighborhood, Nagumo hesitated. Should he continue loading bombs for another attack on the island, which was his primary objective, or remove the bombs and load torpedoes for an attack on the U.S. ships? Conflicting reports of size, number, and location of the U.S. ships caused him to deliberate further.

While he was trying to decide his course of action, U.S. aircraft from the carriers attacked. The first dive bombers to attack were the older Vought "Vindicators," and they were easy targets for the far superior Japanese Zerosen fighter aircraft. The opening attack scored no hits. The second wave of U.S. planes were the Douglas TBD "Devastator" torpedo bombers, far slower and less maneuverable than the half-dozen Avengers based on Midway. Again, the Japanese fighters found the attackers easy prey and had no trouble keeping the fleet safe from hits. Coming in from various directions, the Devastators at first accomplished little other than their own destruction. However, their wave-top attacks brought the defending combat air patrol down to low altitude.

The attention that the Japanese fighters paid to the torpedo planes kept them near the surface, leaving the air high above the fleet unprotected. When American Douglas SBD "Dauntless" dive bombers arrived, they met no opposition and were able to launch their attacks without harassment. They were deadly. Able to dive almost vertically, the Dauntlesses launched their bombs at the Japanese carriers, which still had the bombers parked on deck and in the hangers, shifting back and forth between bombs and torpedoes for the attack they hoped to launch. Thus, when the U.S. bombs struck, the devastation was immense. Within minutes, three of the Japanese carriers were

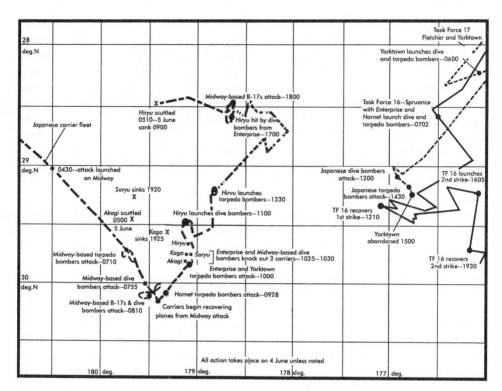

28 deg.N

Task Force 17
Fletcher and Yorktown

Yorktown launches dive
and torpedo bombers--0600

Midway-based B-17s attack--1800

Hiryu scuttled
0510--5 June
sank 0900

Hiryu hit by dive
bombers from
Enterprise--1700

Task Force 16--Spruance
with Enterprise and
Hornet launch dive and
torpedo bombers--0702

Japanese carrier fleet

29 deg.N

0430--attack launched
on Midway

Soryu sinks 1920

Akagi scuttled
0500
5 June

Kaga
sinks 1925

Hiryu

Midway-based torpedo
bombers attack--0710

Midway-based dive
bombers attack--0755

Midway-based B-17s & dive
bombers attack--0810

Hiryu launches
torpedo bombers--1330

Hiryu launches dive bombers--1100

Kaga   Soryu
Akagi

Enterprise and Midway-based dive
bombers knock out 3 carriers--1025--1030

Enterprise and Yorktown
torpedo bombers attack--1000

Hornet torpedo bombers attack--0928

Carriers begin recovering
planes from Midway attack

Japanese dive bombers
attack--1200

Japanese torpedo
bombers attack--1430

TF 16 recovers
1st strike--1210

Yorktown
abandoned 1500

TF 16 launches
2nd strike-1605

TF 16 recovers
2nd strike--1930

All action takes place on 4 June unless noted

30 deg.N

180 deg.   179 deg.   178 deg.   177 deg.

burning, their planes and the bowels of the ships destroyed by their own exploding ordnance. *Akagi, Kaga,* and *Soryu* had no chance of survival. The strength of the Carrier Strike Force was rapidly sinking.

Admiral Yamamoto and his staff were shocked speechless. When he recovered, he ordered Kondo's invasion fleet to postpone its assault and for the strike force targeting the Aleutians to come south. The sole remaining Japanese carrier, *Hiryu,* launched an attack that scored hits on the *Yorktown,* badly damaging it. Meanwhile, Yamamoto brought his battleships up, hoping for an encounter with the U.S. fleet. As they rushed forward, the sighting of a U.S. submarine caused the ships to go into evasive maneuvers. Accidentally, the two heavy cruisers *Mogami* and *Mikuma* collided, damaging both.

On 5 June, the Americans put the finishing touches on the Japanese fleet, yet suffered their own loss as well. Dauntlesses bombed and sank the *Hiryu* the next morning and then sank the heavy cruiser *Mikuma* later in the day. The Japanese exacted a measure of revenge, however. The *Yorktown,* suffering a heavy list, was repaired sufficiently to make way for Pearl Harbor, but it was attacked by a patrolling Japanese submarine. Its sinking was the only serious loss the United States suffered in the battle.

Results

Without air cover and with one of his battleships out of action, Yamamoto was forced to abandon the invasion of Midway and return home. The Japanese navy was unable to recover from the loss of four aircraft carriers, but just as important (perhaps more so) was the loss of so many skilled pilots. Before the outbreak of the war, Japanese pilots were among the best trained in the world; after the war started, the Japanese were never able to expend the same amount of time and dedication to training their replacements. The cream of the naval flying corps was lost, once they had no more ships upon which to land. In later battles, the superiority of U.S. aircraft design and production, coupled with the increasing skill of U.S. pilots, doomed the Japanese navy pilots in almost every encounter. Although the Japanese still had a number of aircraft carriers left, the four lost at Midway were veterans of Pearl Harbor and the best in the fleet.

Japan's inability to capture Midway ended its ability to expand. Six months of running amok now came to an end, and the remainder of the war was spent almost completely on the defensive. Never again did the Japanese Imperial Navy launch a major invasion effort, and only rarely was it able to interfere with U.S. offensive movement. After a surface action victory off Guadalcanal later in 1942, the Japanese could no longer stand before the increasing numbers and quality of U.S. warships.

Although the Americans lost the *Yorktown* (on the heels of the sinking of the *Lexington* at Coral Sea and before the soon-to-be-lost *Wasp* in the Solomons), the core aircraft carriers were soon surrounded by more flattops as well as support ships. Multiple task forces virtually guaranteed the U.S. ability to move at will through the Pacific as the war progressed. This mobility put U.S. naval firepower and airpower in control of every invasion.

Retention of Midway was important, but, more importantly, the Japanese were unable to accomplish any of their desired goals: to gain a necessary bastion to protect their Far Eastern frontier or to destroy the remaining U.S. fleet in a massive surface engagement. The U.S. loss of Midway could have spelled the loss of Pearl Harbor and the Hawaiian Islands. If Japan had taken them, the United States may well have been forced to sue for peace. Even without a Japanese invasion, the key position that Midway represented could well have slowed or stopped U.S. offensive moves for some time to come. It is for this reason that Midway, and not Guadalcanal (launched 7 August 1942, the first offensive of

the United States against the Japanese), is included in this work. A U.S. loss at Guadalcanal in late 1942 to early 1943 would have forced a longer war and attacks at other locations. A U.S. loss at Midway, however, may have precluded any U.S. offensive into the Pacific.

Japan in control of the majority of the Pacific Ocean would, of course, seriously affect the nature of today's world. How the Japanese would have fared in their continuing war in China, Southeast Asia, and the East Indies is problematic. China, if not conquered, would almost certainly have ended up in some way being subservient to Japan. Australia may or may not have been invaded or conquered, but Japanese control of the East Indies, Philippines, and Samoa would certainly have isolated the Australians and New Zealanders. The Greater East Asia Co-Prosperity Sphere, the projected Japanese economic domination of the Far East, would have been a strong possibility had the United States withdrawn from the war after a loss at Midway.

References: Barker, A. J. *Midway: The Turning Point.* New York: Ballantine, 1971; Layton, Edwin. *"And I Was There."* New York: William Morrow, 1985; Lord, Walter. *Incredible Victory.* New York: Harper & Row, 1967; Prange, Gordon. *Miracle at Midway.* New York: McGraw-Hill, 1982.

NORMANDY
6 June 1944

FORCES ENGAGED

German: Army Group B, approximately 80,000 men. Overall commander: Field Marshal Gerd von Rundstedt; field commander: Field Marshal Erwin Rommel.

Allied: Five armies (two U.S., two British, one Canadian); approximately 175,000 men. Overall commander: General Dwight Eisenhower; field commander: General Sir Bernard Montgomery.

IMPORTANCE

Landing of Allied forces in France led to recapture of Nazi-occupied territory in western Europe while allowing Soviet forces to occupy eastern Europe.

Historical Setting

Since the autumn of 1940, when Hitler postponed and ultimately abandoned the invasion of Great Britain, Allied forces had been looking forward to the day when they could take the war to the Germans on the Continent. With the Nazi invasion of the Soviet Union in June 1941 and the Nazi declaration of war on the United States in December 1941, those two powers had been working with Britain on the planned assault on Europe. When Prime Minister Winston Churchill met with President Franklin Roosevelt in August 1941 at the Atlantic Conference, they had decided that, if or when the United States got involved in the war and if or when the Japanese got involved, the primary adversary was to be Hitler. U.S. Army Chief of Staff George Marshall proposed a landing in Europe in 1943, but Churchill wanted to postpone that until stronger forces could be amassed. As an alternative, the Americans landed in Morocco and Algeria in November 1942 and drove eastward toward the British, who began driving the German Afrika Korps backward from Egypt at about the same time. By May 1943, all German and Italian forces in North Africa were captured or forced out. This led to subsequent invasions of Sicily in June and Italy in September.

In November, Churchill and Roosevelt met face-to-face for the first time with Joseph Stalin, head of the Soviet government, in Teheran. Stalin berated the other two for not doing enough to hurt Germany, while the Soviets fought a life-and-death struggle on their own soil. He demanded that they invade the Continent as soon as possible to ease the pressure on his own beleaguered nation and military. Churchill and Roosevelt agreed that needed to be done, but just where the invasion was to take place remained a point of contention. At a meeting in Cairo in October 1943, Churchill and Roosevelt provisionally selected Normandy as the invasion site, although the British leaders preferred a Mediterranean solution.

Churchill proposed an Anglo-American invasion into the Balkans, or at least an increased effort in Italy. As they already possessed the necessary base of operations in North Africa, as well as an ever-strengthening position in Italy, an invasion in the Balkans would prove easy to support. German defenses and troop strength in southeastern Europe were not that impressive, and a landing there would give the most direct assistance to the Soviets by striking toward Hitler's flank. Stalin disagreed. He pressed hard for the landing in northern France that the Americans had been planning because this would oblige the Germans to fight on two fronts and do the most to ease pressure on the Soviet Union by drawing German forces in the completely opposite direction, rather than redirecting them toward a flanking attack. Roosevelt and Churchill had developed a close personal relationship, but Roosevelt was looking at this decision from a perspective of future military action.

Roosevelt hoped that he could draw on Stalin's support for a commitment of Soviet troops to the Pacific theater when Germany was defeated. The United States assumed the lion's share of fighting in the Pacific, although the Chinese kept a large percentage of the Japanese military busy in China and Burma. Roosevelt hoped that by his agreeing with Stalin's proposal, the Soviet leader would return the favor in the future and send his military against the Japanese. He therefore favored Stalin's plan over Churchill's.

Both Churchill and Stalin were looking to the future as well, but to the political future after the war. Stalin hoped to dominate eastern Europe to create a large buffer zone to protect his country from any conceivable resurgence of German power. After invasions in 1914 and

1941, he wanted plenty of land between his country and Germany to protect his frontiers. Churchill saw this also and wanted to deny Stalin control over eastern Europe. An Anglo-American invasion there would give them military control of the region, which would do much to guarantee that those countries would establish democratic governments after the war. Stalin would certainly not allow that. Thus did the decision for an invasion of northern France come about.

U.S. troops and supplies poured into Britain at an increased rate through the first months of 1944 in preparation for the invasion. Such an effort was impossible to keep a secret from German intelligence, so a massive disinformation campaign was launched. An entirely fictitious army was created in southeastern England under the supposed command of George Patton, who had made a name for himself as an aggressive leader in North Africa and Sicily. Constant radio traffic ordered the disposition of fictitious men and equipment into a position to launch an invasion across the English Channel at Calais, the narrowest part of the Channel and the site the Germans considered the most likely landing zone. British and U.S. intelligence efforts succeeded in keeping the Germans convinced of that. Meanwhile, the real concentration of forces took place in southern England for an invasion due south onto the beaches of the French province of Normandy.

Inclement weather kept the invasion from taking place in early May. Moon and tides had to be just right to facilitate the invasion, and the next best window of opportunity was 5–6 June. Again rough weather postponed a decision, while troops sat in landing craft getting seasick and increasingly nervous. Finally, General Dwight Eisenhower, commander of Allied forces in Europe, made the decision to go. The operation was launched in the early hours of 6 June.

The Battle

The first troops committed to battle were paratroopers and glider-borne troops. This was something of a gamble, as the only previous airborne operation the Americans had launched was in Sicily, and it had not gone well. The American 82nd and 101st Airborne Divisions, along with the British 1st Airborne Division, were to land in the darkness and seize bridges and key road junctions. When the Germans realized that the invasion was not to be in the Calais area, they would certainly order a major shift of troops and tanks to the less developed Normandy defenses, and the airborne troops had to do everything they could to delay that reinforcement. Although many of the gliders were badly damaged upon landing, and many of the paratroopers were scattered over a wide area, their insertion behind the lines accomplished its purpose and also succeeded in baffling the Germans as to the strength and concentration of the airborne effort.

At dawn, the invasion fleet of 5,000 ships and landing craft stood off the Normandy coast. The battleships and cruisers pounded the fortifications while destroyers got closer to shore and attacked particular targets pointed out by the landing forces. The German defenses varied depending on the landing site. On one of the British beaches, troops were building fires and brewing tea shortly after going ashore. On one of the two U.S. beaches, code-named Omaha, the invaders lost one man killed or wounded per square yard.

At Omaha Beach, the Germans had the strongest defenses on Pont du Hoc. These were concrete gun emplacements on top of a cliff. Ranger forces were assigned the task of scaling the cliffs and capturing the fortifications. In one of the most difficult tasks of the invasion, the Rangers succeeded and thus gave relief from the fire raking the soldiers cowering on the open beaches below. Getting off the beaches as soon as possible was the key to success, and footholds inland were gained by all five invading armies by the end of the day.

Luckily for the troops on the beaches and the airborne troops in the countryside, the German reinforcement did not immediately take place. When informed of the landings,

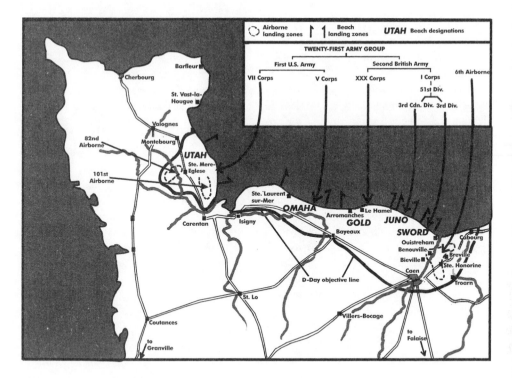

Hitler was convinced they were a diversion, so he refused to allow the reallocation of forces away from the Calais area. When he finally authorized such a move several days later, it was much too late, for the Allies were well off the beaches and into the surrounding countryside. Another positive for the invasion forces was the complete air superiority enjoyed by the Allies. Only two German fighter planes strafed the beaches the morning of the invasion, so Allied aircraft were free to roam over the Normandy area attacking targets of opportunity and maintaining the ability to observe and disrupt German troop movements.

To maintain the beachhead and keep supplies flowing to the soldiers as they advanced inland, it was necessary to have a harbor. None existed at the landing site, and, until facilities in cities such as Cherbourg could be captured, an alternate means of getting supplies ashore was needed. This was accomplished with the development of an artificial harbor, code-named Mulberry. Large blocks of concrete were fer-

ried across the channel and sunk offshore to create a breakwater that would serve as a temporary port. Mulberry was unexpectedly successful, although it was ultimately broken apart by severe weather later on.

Once off the beaches, the invaders found themselves facing even more difficulties. The farmland in Normandy, called the *bocage,* is broken into small fields surrounded by hedgerows. These hedges have been growing for centuries and are extremely dense and thick, making them excellent for defense. The Germans were able to hold the farmland almost field by field, each turned into a small fortress. Only tanks and bulldozers could break through the hedges, and getting through the bocage proved extremely slow. Not until 1 August were the Allies in a position to break out, but, when they did, it became a race for the Rhine. The blitzkrieg, which the Germans had introduced and perfected at the outset of the war, now came back to haunt them as Patton's Third Army, now a reality, led the drive across France.

Results

The Normandy invasion marked the point beyond which Hitler's dream of a German-dominated Europe could not be revived. Although German troops suffered immensely fighting the Soviets, both because of the Soviet military and the harsh winters, the landings in France were the coup de grâce. Any possibility, however remote, of defeating the Soviets died on 6 June 1944.

The remainder of the summer and fall of 1944 saw Allied forces running across France, as well as landing on France's Mediterranean coast and attacking northward. The two drives met along the German frontier, and, as the weather turned cold, the Allies were in a line stretching from Switzerland to Holland. British forces under Bernard Montgomery held the northern sector, while the U.S. Third and Seventh Armies held the central and southern sectors under the overall command of Lieutenant General Omar Bradley. The Allies settled into defensive positions for the winter because their advance across France had been much more rapid than anyone had expected, and the front-line troops had outrun their supply lines. The winter was to be spent consolidating the gains and stockpiling supplies for the advance into Germany itself in the spring of 1945.

This plan for a quiet winter was shattered on 16 December when Hitler launched his last-gasp offensive through the Ardennes Forest. He attempted to drive a wedge between the U.S. and British forces and reach the port of

A makeshift monument to a dead American soldier on the shell blasted shore of Normandy. (National Archives)

Antwerp. This would give him a huge cache of supplies, deny them to the Allies, and so frighten the Allies that they would conclude a separate peace so that the real enemy, the Communists, could be defeated. Although the resulting Battle of the Bulge did put a temporary fright into the Allies, the rapid reduction of the German salient finished off Hitler's dream of ending his two-front war. By mid-January, the line had been restored and Germany had almost nothing left.

The Anglo-American forces driving into Germany in the spring put increasing pressure on the collapsing German war effort, but it also put political pressures on the Allies. While Stalin demanded increased pressure in the west to kill and capture even more Germans, he also demanded that his forces be allowed to capture Berlin. Thus, lines were drawn by the Allied leaders at the Yalta Conference in February 1945 that stopped the British and U.S. forces at the Elbe River. When Hitler committed suicide at the end of April and Germany surrendered a week later, the Soviets controlled the eastern section of Germany. However, German troops and civilians spent the last weeks of the war fleeing westward to avoid capture by the Soviets and domination by their military and their government after the war. Had the British and Americans not been there, where the Soviets would have stopped and what lands they would have controlled can only be a matter of speculation. True, Churchill did not achieve his goal of keeping the Communists out of eastern Europe, but without the Normandy invasion even western Europe may not have been safe.

References: Keegan, John. *Six Armies in Normandy.* New York: Viking, 1982; Kemp, Anthony. *D-Day and the Invasion of Normandy.* New York: Harry N. Abrams, 1994; Marshall, S. L. A. *Night Drop.* Boston: Little, Brown, 1962; War Department Historical Division. *Omaha Beachhead.* Washington, DC: Center of Military History, 1984 [1945].

OKINAWA
1 April–22 June 1945

FORCES ENGAGED
United States: Tenth Army, III Amphibious Corps, XXIV Corps, totaling 180,000 men. Commander: Lieutenant General Simon Bolivar Buckner.

Japanese: Variously reported as 117,000 to 130,000 men. Commander: Lieutenant General Mitsuru Ushijima.

IMPORTANCE
Invasion marked the final offensive of World War II, the cost of which influenced the decision to use atomic weapons.

Historical Setting

After the U.S. landings at Guadalcanal in the Solomon Islands in August 1942, the offensives had not stopped. Douglas MacArthur commanded army forces that drove the Japanese from the western Solomons and New Guinea, and then he took aim at the Philippines in September 1944. The Marines had followed a different path toward Japan, capturing scattered Japanese strongholds in an island-hopping campaign. That strategy of capturing a few key islands to dominate those surrounding them gave the Americans firm bases to maintain a steady advance through the central Pacific. As MacArthur's forces were assaulting the Philippines, Marine forces under the command of Admiral Chester Nimitz were consolidating the Marianas. This meant that long-range Boeing B-29 craft could take the war to the home islands with incendiary attacks that destroyed Japanese war production. In February, Americans landed at Iwo Jima in the Bonin Islands. At that point, army forces and Marines joined together to merge the two paths at Okinawa.

Okinawa, in the Ryukyu Islands chain, was the southernmost prefecture of Japan. Although the islanders were not originally Japanese citizens, they came under Japanese authority around the turn of the twentieth century. This meant that, when Americans went ashore here, it would provide some indication of what landings on the main Japanese islands might be like. If the civilians resisted with the same tenacity that the Japanese soldiers had shown throughout the war, capturing Japan would cost vast numbers of lives.

Foregoing any attempt at surprise, operation commander Lieutenant General Simon Bolivar Buckner pounded the island in preparation for the landings. Although this was hoped to soften up the island's defenses, it also put U.S. shipping in a position to be attacked by land-based aircraft from southern Japan. Thus, large numbers of aircraft carriers were necessary to provide air cover for the fleet as well as to assist in the preinvasion bombardment. The threat of air attack from Japan was significant. During the U.S. invasion of the Philippines, the Japanese had introduced the kamikaze, suicide aerial attacks. Named for the "Divine Wind," or typhoon, that destroyed invading Mongol fleets in the thirteenth century, the suicide pilots were to deliver their homeland from foreign invaders by destroying enemy fleets. Although large numbers of pilots were employed, not enough damage had been inflicted in the Philippines or Iwo Jima to deter planning or operations. Large numbers of medium-sized bombers from Japan, however, could possibly inflict serious harm.

In preparation for the landings they knew were coming, the Japanese military administration on the island organized an unbelievable propaganda campaign. The civilians were encouraged to resist the Americans; they were told that, if captured, they would suffer horrible torture before death. Rape and mutilation would be common, they were told, and the Marines would have no compunction about eating captured children. The demonization of the invaders did succeed in too many cases; many parents killed their children and themselves once the invasion started, rather than suffer the consequences. Thus, the soldiers and Marines often had to fight a psychological war as well as the physical one against the well-entrenched Japanese garrison.

The Battle

The landings started on 1 April 1945, Easter Sunday. They took place on the island's western shore and were almost unopposed. The bulk of the Japanese army was entrenched in the island's southern quarter, where the rugged terrain and commanding position of Shuri Castle provided excellent defensive positions. The northern three-fourths of the island were lightly defended, primarily by the Okinawan civilians. They put up strong resistance in some cases, but died in large numbers by their own hands. Conscripted islanders were also stationed among the Japanese forces, and they too killed themselves or were killed by the Japanese. The northern three-fourths of the island was in U.S. hands, with operational airfields, in less than 3 weeks. The remaining one-fourth was another matter.

In spite of the massive bombardment, the Japanese forces suffered few casualties. The soil of Okinawa made tunneling easy, and most of the Japanese Thirty-second Army was underground. How the survivors were to fight the Americans, however, was a matter of dispute. General Ushijima was advised by subordinates on the best method for resisting the invasion. The aggressive General Isamu Cho thought that an early banzai charge would throw the invaders back into the sea. Alternate advice came from Colonel Hiromichi Yahara, who thought that the human-wave banzai charge was playing into the hands of superior U.S. firepower. Better, he advised, to stay dug into caves and bunkers with overlapping fields of fire, making the Americans pay for each inch of ground. Yahara's plan at first found favor, and the Japanese artillery and machine guns were placed to facilitate maximum crossfire. Within 3 days of the invasion, however, Ushijima gave in to Cho's pleadings for an attack. It was scheduled for 4 April, but a diversionary demonstration near the Japa-

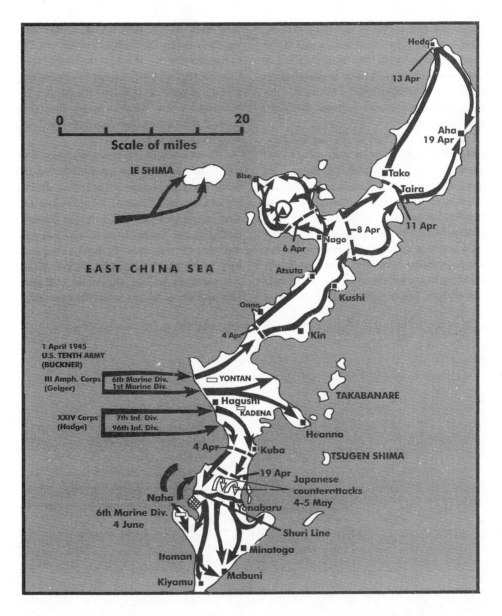

Map legend and labels:

0 20
Scale of miles

IE SHIMA

Bise

EAST CHINA SEA

Hedo
13 Apr

Aha
19 Apr

Tako
Taira
11 Apr

8 Apr
Nago
6 Apr
Atsuta
Kushi

Onna
4 Apr
Kin

1 April 1945
U.S. TENTH ARMY
(BUCKNER)

III Amph. Corps
(Geiger)
6th Marine Div.
1st Marine Div.

YONTAN
Hagushi
KADENA

XXIV Corps
(Hodge)
7th Inf. Div.
96th Inf. Div.

Heanna

TAKABANARE

Kuba
19 Apr
Japanese
counterattacks
4-5 May

Naha
6th Marine Div.
4 June
Yonabaru
Shuri Line

Itoman
Minatoga

Kiyamu
Mabuni

TSUGEN SHIMA

nese positions convinced Ushijima to cancel the plan. Over the course of the month of April, however, occasional banzai charges did take place. Yahara was correct; they sacrificed large numbers of soldiers for no positive result.

Once fully engaged in the southern end of the island, the battle became agonizingly slow. Like some of the massive battles of World War I, huge numbers of soldiers died for gains of mere yards. The Japanese in caves and bunkers ambushed every U.S. force, and well-placed artillery made tanks almost useless. Soldiers and Marines had to operate in units no larger than squad size, covering each other and taking advantage of the terrain features to work their way forward. When a cave was captured, or abandoned by a group of defenders that decided to attack rather than wait, a gap in the Japanese defense could then be exploited. The crossfires were negated, and flanking movements could be employed. Still, action remained slow. Not until 2 July was the island declared secure.

The Americans had to dig out the Japanese position by position, usually using flamethrowers or explosive satchel charges. This served to paralyze the defenders, and often bulldozers came up to close the mouths of caves. In typical Japanese fashion, the defenders fought ferociously and then died by burning or burying. There were those that chose not to die this way. Some killed themselves with guns or grenades; some exposed themselves to fire in headlong charges. For the first time in the war, a fairly large number surrendered, a taboo that was rarely violated in the Japanese military. The conviction that one should suffer death before dishonor was followed innumerable times, but, whereas in previous invasions where often no more than a few dozen survivors were taken prisoner at battle's end, at Okinawa some 7,400 soldiers surrendered.

The conviction of self-sacrifice showed itself in the kamikazes that operated during the battle. The attacks came not only from aircraft but also in small boats or by individual soldiers carrying explosives. The largest Japanese battleship, the *Yamato,* sailed on a suicide mission with the remnants of Japan's once-proud navy, but it was destroyed by torpedo planes before it could get into range of the U.S. fleet. The Japanese aerial attack was the most effec-

Landing crafts of all kinds blacken the sea at a beachhead about 350 miles from the Japanese mainland, Okinawa, 13 April 13 1945. (National Archives)

tive, with the U.S. navy losing 33 ships sunk and more than 350 damaged. It was insufficient to force U.S. redeployment, much less defeat the Americans outright. In the end, the sacrifice was not enough for the Japanese, and the numbers were too great to deny the Americans.

Results

When Okinawa was finally declared secure, the cost had been horrific. Some 150,000 Okinawans died, approximately one-third the island's population. An additional 10,000 Koreans, used by the Japanese military as slave labor, died as well. Of the 119,000 or so Japanese soldiers, as many as 112,000 were killed in the battle or forever sealed inside a collapsed cave or bunker. Aside from the human cost, most of the physical aspects of Okinawan culture were razed. Few buildings survived the 3 months' fighting. Collectively, the defenders lost more dead than the Japanese suffered in the two atomic bombings combined. The United States lost 13,000 dead: almost 8,000 on the island and the remainder at sea; another 32,000 were wounded.

The loss of life on both sides, particularly among the Japanese civilians, caused immense worry in Washington. New President Harry Truman was looking at the plans for a proposed assault on the Japanese main islands, and the casualty projections were unacceptable. Projections numbered the potential casualties from 100,000 in the first 30 days to as many as 1 million attackers, and the death count for the Japanese civilians would be impossible to calculate. If they resisted as strongly as did the citizens of Okinawa—and the inhabitants of the home islands would be even more dedicated to defending their homeland—Japan would become a wasteland. It was already looking like one in many areas. The U.S. bombing campaign, in place since the previous September, was burning out huge areas of Japanese cities. How much longer the Japanese could

have held out in the face of the fire bombing is a matter of much dispute; some project that, had the incendiary raids continued until November, the Japanese would have been thrown back to an almost Stone Age existence. The problem was this: no one in the west knew exactly what was happening in Japan. The devastation could be estimated, but the resistance could not.

Thus, with the casualties of the Okinawa battle fresh in his mind, when Truman learned of the successful testing of an atomic bomb, he ordered its use. This is a decision debated since 6 August 1945, the date of the bombing of Hiroshima, and even before. Just what was known of Japanese decision-making processes before that date is also argued to this day. Was the Japanese government in the process of formulating a peace offer, in spite of the demand for unconditional surrender the Allies had decided upon in February 1943? If they were doing so, did anyone in the west know about it? Who knew what, when they knew it, and what effect that knowledge had or may have had on Truman's decision making is a matter of much dispute. Whatever the political ramifications of the atomic bomb on the immediate and postwar world, Truman's decision was certainly based in no small part on the nature of the fighting on Okinawa. Truman wrote just after his decision, "We'll end the war sooner now. And think of the kids who won't be killed." Horrible as the effects of the two atomic bombs were, the number of casualties in Hiroshima and Nagasaki as compared with the potential number an invasion could have caused is small indeed.

References: Feifer, George. *Tennozan: The Battle of Okinawa and the Atomic Bomb.* New York: Ticknor & Fields, 1994; Leckie, Robert. *Okinawa: The Last Battle of World War II.* New York: Viking, 1995; Sledge, E. B. *With the Old Breed at Peleliu and Okinawa.* Annapolis, MD: U.S. Naval Institute Press, 1996; Yahara, Hiromichi, and Frank Gibney. *The Battle for Okinawa.* New York: John Wiley & Sons, 1995.

ISRAEL'S WAR OF INDEPENDENCE
14 May 1948–7 January 1949

FORCES ENGAGED
Jewish: Hagenah forces numbering approximately 30,000 active and 30,000 reserves, with another 4,000 in Irgun and Stern Gang. Commander: David Ben Gurion.

Arab: 39,000 soldiers made up of the Arab Liberation Army, plus troops from Lebanon, Syria, Iraq, Jordan, and Egypt, plus 50,000 unorganized and untrained Palestinians. Commander: King Abdullah of Jordan.

IMPORTANCE
Israel's War of Independence established the Jewish homeland, but at the expense of the local Arab population, precipitating ongoing conflict between the two populations.

Historical Setting

For almost 2,000 years, the Jews had been without a homeland, the Diaspora beginning in the first century A.D. during Roman occupation. Not until the end of the nineteenth century was the concept of reestablishing a Jewish homeland seriously considered, and organizations dedicated to Zionism (the founding of a Jewish state in the land the Jews had occupied in biblical times) began to blossom in Europe. This was sparked by the publication of *The Jewish State*, by Austrian journalist Theodore Herzl. Acting through European philanthropists such as Baron de Rothschild, agents bought up some 100,000 acres of land from absentee Arab landlords by 1914, by which time some 60,000 Jews had moved to Palestine. They did so not only in response to Herzl's book but to escape pogroms in eastern Europe.

During World War I, Great Britain's major goal in the Middle East was to defeat the Turks, who were allied with the Germans. To do this, the British encouraged the Arabs to revolt against the Turkish Ottoman Empire. In return, they were promised independent status after the war. In 1917, British Colonial Secretary Arthur Balfour, hoping to court Jewish support in the Middle East and in Britain, issued the Balfour Declaration in response to a request by Chaim Wiezman, the leading British Zionist. This promised a Jewish homeland along the lines envisioned by Herzl. Unfortunately for the British, such land was under Arab control. These conflicting promises came to a head in 1920, when the League of Nations gave Britain the task of overseeing territory from the Persian Gulf to the Mediterranean under the mandate system, which theoretically was designed to nurture the mandated population on their way to independence. Thus, Britain was to occupy territory promised to both Arabs and Jews, both of which expected the British to grant them their nationhood.

Through the 1920s and 1930s, Jewish immigration grew as the Jews continued to buy up land. By introducing modern agricultural techniques, they were able to succeed in farming marginal lands that had long been out of production. The economic success that they enjoyed further increased local Arab hostility, and violence between the two populations was not uncommon. In 1921, the official Zionist organization in Palestine was the Jewish Agency, with the Hagenah being their military wing; these were created to pressure the British into honoring the Balfour Declaration. The Jewish Agency was at first dedicated to working closely with the British, a tack that some Jews thought was futile. Thus was formed the more radical Irgun Zvai Leumi (National Military Organization), which spawned the Lohamey Heruth Israel (Fighters for the Freedom of Israel), known as the LHI or the Stern Gang, after its leader Avraham Stern.

Both Arabs and Jews held their fire when World War II began. Neither wanted to alienate the British. But when the tide turned and Allied victory seemed inevitable, the Jewish political and military groups began agitating for their independence. Once the war was over, the British had little desire to keep fighting anywhere, so they very reluctantly sent troops to Palestine in an attempt to maintain order while hoping some arrangement could be worked out. From 1945 through 1947, the British and Jews fought almost constantly, with the terrorist Stern Gang getting increasingly violent. The British finally appealed to the United Nations (UN) in 1947, and the UN proposed that the region be divided into two countries, one Jewish and one Arab. This satisfied no one: the Arabs wanted to give up no land and the Jews thought they got a country both too small and too indefensible. The Arabs, who had stood aside while the British and Jews fought each other, now began to organize their own military forces.

From January to April 1948, both populations jockeyed for position, trying to establish military superiority anywhere possible. The Arab Liberation Army was founded in Syria in January and began raiding Jewish settlements. In April, the Irgun and Stern Gang retaliated, killing more than 250 unarmed Palestinians at Deir Yassin, outside Jerusalem. After this, the Palestinian civilians began fleeing the area, creating the refugee problem that has plagued the region ever since. By late April, the surrounding Arab states (still under British and French mandate) decided to invade Israel as soon as the British mandate in Palestine ended and the UN plan went into effect, on 14 May 1948. The nominal leader of this coalition was King Abdullah of Jordan, but in fact there was little coordination between the Arab forces. The nations of Iraq, Syria, Jordan, and Egypt provided some 39,000 troops, but the best of them all was the 10,000-soldier Arab Legion of Jordan, trained and commanded by a British officer, John Glubb (called Glubb Pasha). The Jews, whose total population by 1948 was 650,000, had a force of about 30,000 trained troops, with another 30,000 semitrained troops in reserve guarding villages. The problem was that only a few hundred of these were full-time soldiers, and there were not enough weapons for all of them. The Arabs were much better armed, but lacked the coordination necessary to put constant pressure on the defenders.

The Campaign

David Ben Gurion, commander of the Hagenah and leader of the Jewish Agency, declared Israel independent at 4:00 A.M. on 14 May, 2 hours before the British were officially withdrawn. Israel was promptly recognized by both the United States and Soviet Union, but neither were willing to get directly involved in the war, which began almost immediately. In the north, a Syrian and Lebanese invasion was stopped at the frontier, while the Iraqi thrust enjoyed some early success. It was soon forced back, however, from territory it had gained in Samaria. In Jerusalem, Glubb's Arab Legion fought house to house for much of the Jewish Quarter, and they finally captured the city on 28 May. Two relief attempts sent from Tel Aviv were beaten back, and the road from Tel Aviv to Jerusalem was the scene of the most bitter fighting of the war. In the south, Egyptian troops made good headway through the Negev Desert, reaching Ashdod and Bethlehem in early June.

At this point, 11 June, a cease-fire was brokered. The UN sent Swedish mediator Count Bernadotte to try and arrange a peace. The truce lasted almost a month, but fighting broke out again on 9 July. The Jews enjoyed some success in the north toward Syria, but made little progress against the Arab Legion or the Egyptians in the south. A second truce was declared on 18 July, which lasted until mid-October. The Jewish forces grew during this time, reaching almost 90,000 by October. Bernadotte continued to try to make peace, trying to formulate an agreement whereby both sides would return to the positions spelled out in the original UN plan. While working on the agreement, Bernadotte was killed, probably by the Stern Gang. He was replaced by Ralph Bunche of the United States.

The cease-fire began to fall apart in the south first in mid-September, and by 15 October it had completely collapsed and the two sides went back to full-scale fighting. The Arabs were shocked at the quality of the training of the Jewish forces, as well as by their determination, and were more ready than the Jews to stop fighting. In the north of Israel, Jewish forces drove Syrian and Lebanese troops back, securing northern Galilee and seizing part of southern Lebanon. A cease-fire went into effect there on 30 November. Fighting in the central part of the country had been fierce, with the Jews making headway against the Arab Legion, but unable to defeat them. A cease-fire also went into effect there on 30 November. In the south, however, the Jews enjoyed the most success, recapturing Beersheba on 21 October and forcing an Egyptian withdrawal to Gaza. An Egyptian counterattack from 19 November through 7 December failed to regain their lost territory. With the cease-fires holding in the other areas, the Jewish forces concentrated their efforts in the south and launched an offensive into the Sinai on 20 December. Through 7 January, they succeeded in a number of encirclements, which forced the Egyptians back almost to the Red Sea, where they asked for a truce on 7 January.

Results

Ralph Bunche was finally able to bring an end to the fighting, and the state of Israel was somewhat expanded from its original borders because of the fighting. The Jews acquired all of Galilee west of the Jordan River and a corridor 5 miles wide leading to Jerusalem. They did not get any of Jerusalem, however, which remained under Jordanian control. A plan to internationalize Jerusalem failed. The final armistice, signed with Jordan, went into effect on 3 April 1949, but it did not guarantee peace, or even (from the Arab point of view) the existence of a Jewish state.

The dream of many Zionists came to fruition during 1948–1949, yet at the same time

their vision of what Israeli society should be did not. The agricultural base that the Jews had established in the first decades of the century was to many Zionists the foundation of a bonding with the land that would revitalize the Jews who had been forced into city ghettos throughout Europe. However, the first prime minister, David Ben Gurion, led a government that embraced western values and built a modern multifaceted economy and society. The willingness of the Israelis to accept aid from western countries gave countries such as the United States a foothold in the Middle East, an area in which they had not traditionally shown much interest. This strengthened Israel economically and militarily, while simultaneously making their Arab neighbors more jealous and angry. In the wake of the War of Independence, the Arab nations continued to plot against their unwanted neighbor, staging guerrilla attacks when not openly fighting. For years, the way to gain popularity and political influence in the Arab Middle East was to champion any cause that threatened Israel. Decades of warfare, overt and covert, has been the legacy of Israel's birth. The circumstance that first appeared during the War of Independence, a greater division among attacking parties than among defending parties, continued to plague Arab political and military leaders in every other war between the two populations.

Another major outcome was the problem of Palestinians. Much of the Arab population that inhabited the region before the arrival of the Zionists was forced out of the country by the fighting. After 1948, they were a people without a country, living as refugees in Jordan, Syria, and Lebanon. Since that time, at least one of the goals of every Arab-Israeli war (1956, 1967, and 1973) has been the return of the Palestinians to what they consider to be their homeland. The hostility between Palestinians and Jews has resulted in a virtual siege mentality for the Israelis, with security being the highest priority for both government and society. Not until the middle 1990s was the conflict somewhat abated, when Shimon Peres of Israel and Yasir Arafat of the Palestine Liberation Organization met and began talks regarding the return of some of the land that Israel has acquired in order to establish a Palestinian homeland. Hard-liners in both camps resist the notion of compromise, but, as of this writing, peace in a country that has never had much of it remains a strong possibility. The shame of the situation is that both Arabs and Jews are right: it is their country. How it will ultimately be settled is impossible to predict.

References: Barker, A. J. *Arab-Israeli Wars.* New York: Hippocrene Books, 1981; Carver, Michael. *War since 1945.* New York: Putnam, 1981; Dupuy, Trevor N. *Elusive Victory: The Arab-Israeli Wars, 1947–1974.* New York: Harper & Row, 1978; Herzog, Chaim. *The Arab-Israeli Wars: War and Peace in the Middle East.* New York: Random House, 1982; Ovendale, Ritchie. *The Origins of the Arab-Israeli Wars.* New York: Longman, 1992.

HUAI HAI (SUCHOW)
7 November 1948–10 January 1949

FORCES ENGAGED
Communist: 500,000 men.
Commander: General Chen Yi.
Nationalist: 500,000 men.
Commander: General Pai Chung-hsi.

IMPORTANCE
A Communist victory sealed the fate of Nationalist leader Chiang Kai-shek, who was forced to resign as president. This led to destruction of the Nationalist army and government in China, establishing Communist rule on the mainland and Nationalist rule on Formosa (Taiwan).

Historical Setting

The Chinese Communist Party (CCP) was formally established in 1921 as the Chinese government was recovering from Japanese domination during World War I. In the mid-1920s, the CCP cooperated with the ruling Kuomintang, or Nationalist Party, but in 1927 started a civil war that raged until 1937. In that year, the Japanese invaded out of Manchuria and drove deep into China down the coast toward Hong Kong. This external threat convinced Communist leader Mao Tse-tung to conclude a wary alliance with Nationalist leader Chiang Kai-shek. Mao's forces operated in the northern part of China, whereas Chiang's armies, aided by the Americans, fought in the southern and western parts. Mao's forces, never well equipped, did their best to harass and pin down Japanese troops while Chiang held the south and cooperated with U.S. and British activities in Burma.

When the Japanese were defeated in August 1945, Communist-Nationalist cooperation evaporated. Both parties proclaimed their desire for peace, but neither did anything to accomplish it. Instead, they both scrambled to grab land and materiel owned by the Japanese during the war. From late August to early October 1945, Mao and Chiang met in Chungking for discussions that were overseen by U.S. ambassador Patrick Hurley and resulted in a statement of mutual peaceful goals. However, both Chinese leaders continued to struggle for control of the resource-rich province of Manchuria. Later that year, U.S. President Harry Truman sent General George Marshall to broker talks between the Communists and Nationalists, resulting in a temporary cease-fire. An agreement on an updated version of the 1936 constitution was also announced after 3 weeks of talks, but both sides soon showed their unwillingness to exhibit any true cooperation. Unsuccessful, Marshall left in January 1947.

Fighting continued in Manchuria, where the cease-fire agreement did not apply, and soon was general throughout the country. Since late 1946, the Nationalists had been seizing key cities and towns from the Communists; in March 1947, they pushed the Communists out of their stronghold in the city of Yenan, some 400 miles southwest of the capital of Peking (Beijing). The Communists did the most to make political capital out of these aggressive actions, both to motivate support in China as well as to lessen U.S. support for Chiang. Communist-inspired demonstrations wore down the morale of the Kuomintang troops and probably hastened the withdrawal of U.S. troops from China in early 1947. U.S. military aid to Chiang dried up as well. With growing mass support, the Communists on 10 October 1947 issued a call for the overthrow of Chiang Kai-shek's administration. They also promised a number of personal freedoms, an easing of land taxes, and a democratic government.

Mao Tse-tung's forces gathered growing support, not only through their propaganda but through their actions. Where Kuomintang troops had looted the cities they occupied, Communist troops were under strict orders to behave themselves. The peaceful nature of the Communist takeover of cities, with very little retribution, had the same effect on the population that similar strategies have done through the ages: Cyrus the Great of Persia, Alexander the Great of Macedon, and Genghis Khan all were magnanimous to cities that did not resist, thus encouraging the others.

On the battlefields, the Communists were enjoying similar successes. In April 1948, they recaptured Yenan, reestablishing Mao's headquarters. By May, Communist forces had isolated much of the Kuomintang army by capturing Hopei and Shansi provinces. This placed their forces in two masses: Manchuria was almost completely under their control, with the second area stretching from the coast to the Yellow River. Only a strip of Nationalist-controlled railway running east-west from Tientsin through Peking to Paotow separated the Communist armies. Meanwhile, in the south, large Communist partisan groups operated inland from Hong Kong, Canton, and Indochina. In east-central China, Chiang's army controlled a cross-shaped area of land along two railroad lines: east-west from Kaifeng through Suchow to the coast, and north-south from Nanking to Tsinan. It was at Kaifeng and Suchow that the Communists would launch their largest offensives in 1948 and where they would find success.

The Battle

Until the summer of 1948, the Communists had depended on guerrilla tactics, using harassment of supply and railroad lines, attacks on isolated outposts, and localized numerical superiority to establish the widespread control they had attained. They now felt strong enough to engage in traditional warfare, and the battle for the city of Kaifeng was their first attempt. They were aided in their effort by Nationalist political actions. During the elections for president in April, Chiang Kai-shek's choice for vice-president was rejected by the National Assembly. This rejection was an indication of Chiang's weakening political power. He was able to fill military positions, however, and Generals Ku Chu-tung and Yu Han-mou became chief of the supreme staff and commander in chief, respectively. They were notable both for their strong loyalty to Chiang and their lack of strong military ability.

Kaifeng, capital of Honan province and situated at a key railroad junction, was defended by 250,000 regular Kuomintang forces and about 50,000 auxiliaries. The Communists attacked with about 200,000 regular troops supported by guerrillas. After 2 weeks of maneuvering beginning in late May 1949, Communist General Chen Yi received intelligence that the garrison defending the city had been weakened in response to the maneuvers. He thus launched an immediate attack on the city on 17 June. Communist forces quickly captured the city's two airfields, and then the city itself fell on 19 June. This was a major defeat that Chiang could not afford, so he took personal command of the operations to respond. Ordering attacks from east and west down the rail-

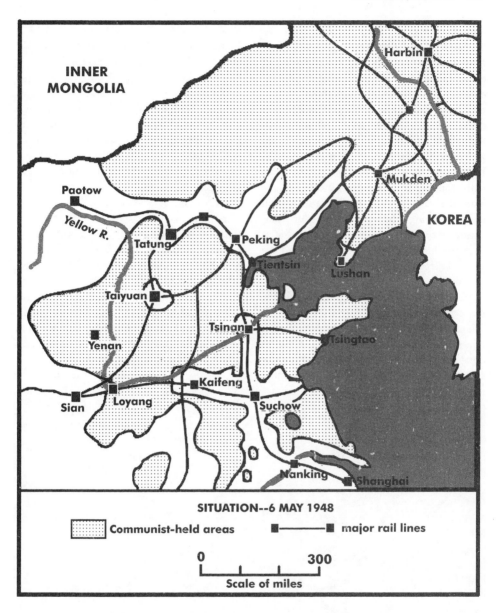

SITUATION--6 MAY 1948

Communist-held areas   ■————————■ major rail lines

0   300

Scale of miles

road lines, he force Chen Yi to abandon Kaifeng, retreating southward, where the Kuomintang pincers inflicted a defeat on the Communists. Chen Yi, after inflicting 90,000 casualties on the Nationalists, ordered his troops to disperse. The Nationalists regained Kaifeng, but their success was primarily the result of superior numbers rather than tactical ability, in which they proved lacking. Again, the behavior of Communist troops during their occupation of Kaifeng was exemplary, and the Communists had time to plant saboteurs and party organizers throughout the city.

Through the summer of 1948, realization of the growing power of Mao's forces became apparent even to the Nationalists. The defense minister openly criticized generals who enriched themselves in the midst of the crisis, and many generals openly criticized the defense ministry for meddling in operations, giving conflicting orders, and disseminating unchecked intelligence reports. It was also reported that the forces of the two enemies were now almost equal, each with about a million soldiers under arms and with almost equal artillery; 2 years earlier, the Kuomintang forces had outnumbered the Communists under arms by almost five to one. Almost half the Communists were in central China, showing a shift in emphasis from Manchuria to the southern region. The battle at Kaifeng illustrated both the strength and the shift in strategy that the Communists now employed.

The autumn of 1948 was disastrous for the Nationalists. They were forced to surrender Tsinan, their final city on the Shantung Peninsula, strengthening the Communist hold on the northeast coast. The few remaining Kuomintang garrisons besieged in Manchurian cities also were defeated. By early November, all of Manchuria was under Communist control, and almost half the Nationalist army was captured or killed. The Nationalists also ceded to the Communists vast amounts of weapons and materiel. With no threat to their rear, the Communists could now face southward and carry on the war against a greatly reduced enemy force. Their next target was the major Kuomintang force in the south based at Suchow, near the Huai Hai (River).

Communist General Chen Yi teamed with General Liu Po-cheng to field a force of almost 600,000 men. Kuomintang command fell to General Liu Chih, who also commanded about 600,000 men in four army groups: 2nd, 7th, 13th, and 16th. The 13th was based in Suchow, the 7th to the east at the junction of the Lunghai railroad and the Grand Canal, the 2nd to the west on the railroad to Kaifeng, and the 16th to the south along the railroad to Peng-pu on the Huai. The battle opened on 5 November when Chen Yi attacked from the east at the

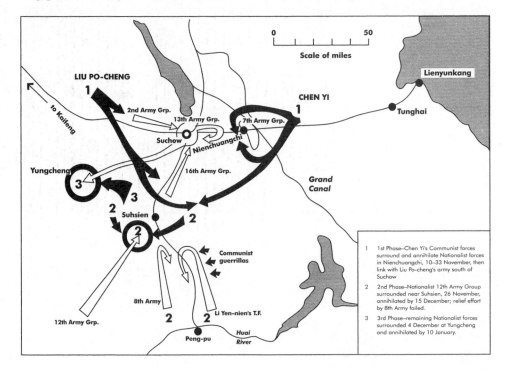

1 1st Phase—Chen Yi's Communist forces surround and annihilate Nationalist forces in Nienchuangchi, 10–33 November, then link with Liu Po-cheng's army south of Suchow

2 2nd Phase—Nationalist 12th Army Group surrounded near Suhsien, 26 November, annihilated by 15 December; relief effort by 8th Army failed.

3 3rd Phase—remaining Nationalist forces surrounded 4 December at Yungcheng and annihilated by 10 January.

7th Army Group while Liu Po-cheng drove the 2nd Army Group in the west back into Suchow and then swung south to drive back the 16th into the city. Chen Yi's attack was facilitated by the defection of two Kuomintang generals and 23,000 men. The 7th Army Group was quickly encircled 30 miles east of Suchow, their retreat hampered by even more defections as well as the rapidity of Chen Yi's attack.

Chiang ordered fifteen divisions from the 2nd and 16th Army Groups to relieve the surrounded 7th, but they moved too slowly and lost too many men, only to learn of the 7th's defeat and surrender on 22 November; only 3,000 of its original 90,000 men escaped. In spite of the fact that the Nationalists had complete air superiority and flew as many as 500 sorties per day, the air forces failed to work cooperatively with the ground forces and were therefore rarely effective. A relief column comprised of the Nationalist Eighth Army and 12th Army Group was also ineffective; poor coordination kept them from linking up before being attacked by Chen Yi's forces from the east and Liu Po-cheng's from the northwest. The 12th Army Group, 125,000 strong, found itself surrounded at Shwangchiaochi on 26 November.

At this point, Chiang decided to abandon Suchow. He hoped that the troops remaining in the city could march to the rescue of the 12th Army Group and then escape southward. The 13th Army Group marched out of the city on 1 December, but, because of poor leadership, poor morale, or both, they found themselves outmaneuvered, pushed westward, and surrounded at Yungcheng on 6 December. Inside that encirclement were the remnants of the 2nd, 13th, and 16th Army Groups, numbering about 200,000 men, with all their artillery and tanks. Although nine infantry divisions remained free to act along the Huai Hai, they were too small and uncoordinated to relieve either of the surrounded forces. The isolated embattled forces were living off what food could be scrounged from local farms or dropped by parachute, but low morale soon hit rock bottom.

Huge numbers of troops, sometimes entire divisions at once, defected to the Communists.

Chiang's last hope was to commit his Sixth Army from Peng-pu, but 15 days of fighting netted them only 17 miles against fierce guerrilla attacks. By 15 December, the Communist noose closed on the 12th Army Group. At Yungcheng, the remains of the three army groups had been reduced by half from combat and defections. Bombarded by propaganda as much as artillery, the Kuomintang troops had almost no fight left in them. After 3 weeks of only light skirmishing, the Communists launched their final assault on 6 January 1949; by 10 January the battle was over.

Results

Virtually the entire Nationalist force of 600,000 men around Suchow ceased to exist. Approximately 327,000 men had either been captured or had voluntarily given themselves up to the Communists. Every Kuomintang general in the battle had been captured or killed. The military disaster merely reflected the condition of the Nationalist government. Inflation was so rampant that the currency was worthless. Black marketeers operated openly and with the support of the population. Attempted currency reform failed. The countryside was filled with bandits and looters while food supplies rapidly diminished. U.S. aid came under close government scrutiny in Washington, with George Marshall (now secretary of state) stating that the only way to save the Chinese administration from Communist takeover was to have Americans completely take over, an option he did not relish: "The present regime has lost the confidence of the people, reflected in the refusal of soldiers to fight and the refusal of the people to cooperate in economic reforms" (Chassin, *The Communist Conquest of China*, p. 202). All aid was suspended on 20 December 1948.

Faced with nothing but disaster all around him, Chiang Kai-shek on 21 January 1949 resigned the presidency. The next day, Peking surrendered to the Communists and Mao transferred his capital to that city. When new Nationalist President Li Tsung-jen sent representatives to Mao on 1 April to discuss peace terms, "unconditional surrender" was the response. Unable to comply, the Nationalists continued to try to wage war, but with decreasing positive results. Communist forces crossed the Yangtze River on 20 April, followed by the rapid capture of most of south China's major cities: Nanking on 22 April, Nanchang on 23 May, and Shanghai on 27 May. The Nationalists kept shifting their capital city, from Nanking to Canton to Chungking to Chengtu, and finally to Formosa, completely off the mainland of China.

The victory at Suchow broke the Nationalists' back, which had long been bending. When Chiang, the heart and soul of the Nationalist cause since the 1920s, gave up power in the wake of the battle, no clearer sign of their demise could have been given. He was able to reorganize a government in exile on the island of Formosa, naming it Taiwan, on 7 December 1949; he also retained control of three small islands between Formosa and the mainland. More importantly, Chiang kept international recognition of his position as leader of the Chinese people. Although Mao Tse-tung established a de facto government that was recognized by Communist regimes around the world, the Nationalists kept western recognition and assistance, as well as a seat on the Security Council in the United Nations. That seat, as well as the question of sovereignty in general, led to Sino-U.S. tensions for the following two decades, not eased until the administration of Richard Nixon. Mao's accession to power gave him control over the largest Communist population in the world, but differences in philosophical and political matters kept him from being solidly in Moscow's camp. The Moscow-Beijing rivalry probably went a long way toward keeping the Cold War relatively cold, for neither China nor the Soviet Union could focus on the United States with a suspicious neighbor at its back.

References: Chassin, Lionel Max. *The Communist Conquest of China.* Cambridge, MA: Harvard University Press, 1965; Fairbank, John K., and Albert Feuerwerker, eds. *The Cambridge History of China,* vol. 13. New York: Cambridge University Press, 1986; Houn, Franklin W. *A Short History of Chinese Communism.* Englewood Cliffs, NJ: Prentice-Hall, 1967; Morwood, William. *Duel for the Middle Kingdom.* New York: Everest House, 1980.

INCHON
15 September 1950

FORCES ENGAGED

United States: X Corps. Overall commander: General Douglas MacArthur; X Corps commander: Major General Edward Almond.

North Korean: 1,000 men in Inchon, another 5,000 nearby in Seoul. Overall commander of North Korean army: Marshal Choe Yong Gun.

IMPORTANCE

This successful operation destroyed the North Korean attempt to dominate South Korea, marking the first effective military action sponsored by the United Nations.

Historical Setting

In January 1950, U.S. Secretary of State Dean Acheson spoke to the National Press Club. In his presentation, Acheson laid out the primary security interests of the United States, that is, those countries that the United States would immediately defend if threatened. In Europe, that included the countries involved in the North Atlantic Treaty Organization (NATO); in the Pacific region, Acheson described the "defense perimeter" of the United States. This stretched from the Aleutians to Japan to the Philippines to Australia. Any place within that line was vital to U.S. security; any place outside that line should appeal to the United Nations (UN) if threatened.

Just outside that line were two nations heavily dependent on U.S. assistance. One was Taiwan. The previous September, the Communists had seized power in mainland China by defeating Chiang Kai-shek's Nationalist forces after years of civil war. Chiang retreated to the island of Formosa (renamed Taiwan), where he established a government in exile and continued to claim his authority as leader of the Chinese people. As he had been consistently supported by U.S. financial and military aid since the 1930s, he needed continued U.S. aid if he was to ever return to the mainland and resume his place at the head of the government. Although the United States continued to recognize Chiang as the legitimate head of government, the placement of Taiwan outside the U.S. defense perimeter seemed to belie U.S. stated support.

The other nation just outside that perimeter was South Korea. The Republic of Korea had been established in 1947 when the Soviet Union sponsored the formation of a Communist government in the northern part of the Korean peninsula. It was a national division without any historical basis. The Soviets had occupied the northern part of Korea at the end of World War II and were directed by decisions made at the Yalta and Potsdam Conferences to accept the surrender of Japanese troops north of latitude 38 degrees. The Soviets announced that the citizens they had liberated begged them to help establish a Communist government, in spite of the fact that U.S. forces occupying the southern end of the peninsula were asked by no one to do this. Rather than confront the Soviet Union over this, the matter was submitted to the UN. In August 1947, the UN mandated internationally supervised elections to determine which government the people wanted. The Soviets refused to allow this to happen and the Democratic People's Republic of Korea was born. The Republic of Korea in the south was established almost by default.

Since that time, a country that had never been divided became two antagonistic halves. The Soviets assisted the North in building a strong and powerfully equipped army, while the United States aided the South in establishing a much more lightly armed defense force. Through the remainder of the 1940s, the two Korean governments accused each other of violating the border as well as agitating within each others' country.

When Acheson made his speech in January 1950, it certainly must have appeared to the North Koreans as if the United States no longer cared to defend the South. This was seemingly confirmed by the start of U.S. troop withdrawals. North Korean dictator Kim Il Sung traveled to Moscow to confer with Soviet leader Joseph Stalin, who promised military aid to Kim for an invasion of the South. This invasion started on 25 June 1950 and got off to a roaring success for the Communist forces.

Quickly South Korean President Syngman Rhee appealed to the UN for assistance in repelling the invasion. U.S. President Harry Truman called a meeting of the Security Council, a meeting that the Soviet delegate did not attend. Since the previous autumn, the Soviets had been boycotting Security Council meetings in protest of U.S. refusal to allow Chinese Communist leader Mao Tse-tung to appoint the Chinese delegate to the Council. The United States, supported by Britain and France, continued to recognize Chiang as the legitimate head of state, so his appointee sat on the Security Council. Without the Soviet delegate in attendance, the Security Council voted to send troops from volunteer nations to aid the South Koreans.

Truman ordered General Douglas MacArthur into action. MacArthur had served as military governor of Japan since the end of World War II and had the only significant U.S. force in the region. He used U.S. aircraft based in Japan to attack North Korean troops and supply lines, and he sent his ground forces across

Brigadier General Courtney Whitney, General Douglas MacArthur, and Major General Edward Almond observe the shelling of Inchon from the USS Mt. McKinley, *15 September 15 1950. (National Archives)*

the straits to the port of Pusan to establish a defensive line. These incoming Americans, bolstered by the arrival of fleeing U.S. and South Korean soldiers, established what came to be called the Pusan Perimeter. By early August, they were hard-pressed all along the line by the bulk of the North Korean army.

As the U.S. military scrambled to put together forces to rush to South Korea, MacArthur planned his strategy. Rather than push more troops into the Pusan Perimeter, MacArthur proposed instead an amphibious landing at the port city of Inchon, located on Korea's west coast near the capital city of Seoul. This landing would place U.S. forces in the rear of the North Korean army and would allow the assault force to drive eastward across the peninsula, isolating the Communists in the south and cutting them off from their bases in the north.

Attempting to get behind the enemy rear is not brilliant strategy; any basic student of military science would not recommend it. What made MacArthur's plan daring was not the concept but the location. The harbor at Inchon presents an almost impossible task for an amphibious invader. The tidal swell is 37 feet, the most extreme in the world. This means that high-tide landings would be relatively simple, but ships at low tide would be stranded in the mud. Thus, an invasion had to be quick. Troops needed to be inserted with sufficient soldiers and equipment to hold on for 12 hours, when the tide came back in. This piecemeal commitment of troops, and the inability to rapidly reinforce or withdraw, meant that a serious defense or counterattack could doom those troops onshore.

It took all of MacArthur's considerable persuasive power to convince the Joint Chiefs of

Staff to agree to this attack. When naval staff officers told the representatives of the Joint Chiefs that the operation was not impossible, they gave their reluctant consent.

The Battle

MacArthur cobbled together what came to be designated X Corps, made up of the 1st Marine Division and the 7th Infantry Division, both of which were understrength. Elements of other units were pulled away from the Pusan Perimeter just before the operation in order to supplement these forces, so the unit was rather a ragtag group. They were to be transported by Joint Task Force 7, the best prepared and equipped unit in the operation.

The invaders had two main problems. In Inchon's outer harbor lies the island of Wolmi-do. If that was not taken first, whatever units the North Koreans had placed there could deliver serious flanking fire. To take the island first, however, meant having to wait 12 hours for the follow-up landings, which meant that the defenders in the city of Inchon would be prepared. The second major problem was landing in Inchon itself. Not only were the tides a problem, but the city was protected by a seawall. This meant landing in early evening, climbing up out of landing craft and over the wall, and then facing immediate exposure to enemy fire. There were not, like the landings of World War II, beaches onto which the boats could run. It was a problem that could not be overcome, and the Marines and soldiers would just have to deal with it.

Marines landed on Wolmi-do at 0630 on 15 September. The island had received 5 days worth of preliminary air strikes and 2 days of naval bombardment. The bombardment had proven to be much more successful than similar softening-up barrages had been against the Japanese in World War II. The Marines had control of the island in 45 minutes, with elimination of the defenders who had dug in the deepest taking a few more hours. For a loss of twenty Marines wounded, the island was cap-

tured along with 200 North Korean prisoners; the defenders lost about 120 men killed. The remainder of the day was spent digging in and waiting for the afternoon landings.

The second landings were launched in two prongs, against the city directly and just to the south of it. The Marines and soldiers climbed up ladders and grappling lines or, if the LST (Landing Ship, Tank) craft they were in were tossed on top of the wall by the current, they were deposited directly into the city. They were also forced to land tanks and heavy equipment under fire, but the armament on the LSTs as well as the aggressiveness of the landing forces made the fighting with the defenders brief. U.S. troops were on the high ground of Cemetery Hill within an hour and a half, and by morning the two prongs had linked. The beachhead and city were in their control within 24 hours.

Losing 20 men killed and about 200 wounded, X Corps had quickly accomplished its objective. The exact number of North Koreans in the Inchon area is unknown, but intelligence estimates, which seem borne out by the resistance met, placed it at about 1,000 in Inchon, with another 5,000 in Seoul, just inland, and another 500 around the major airfield at Kimpo. The invaders outnumbered the defenders by at least ten to one at the point of attack, but similar operations in other wars against smaller numbers of defenders proved costly. The handful of Turks defending the beaches at Gallipoli against the Australians and New Zealanders in 1915 comes to mind, where the Turks pinned down the invaders long enought for reinforcements to arrive. The success at Inchon is almost certainly attributable to MacArthur's determination, for he was correct in his assumption that the North Koreans considered an Inchon landing impossible.

Results

X Corps quickly secured its objectives around Inchon. Within days, it had recaptured the South Korean capital city of Seoul, secured undamaged the improved airfield at Kimpo, and drove across the peninsula and reached the eastern coast within 2 weeks. All of this was timed to coincide with an offensive northward out of the Pusan Perimeter. General Walton Walker's Eighth Army had been sufficiently reinforced to launch attacks all along the North Korean line and within a few days were driving the North Koreans back against X Corps in a classic hammer-and-anvil operation. Cut off from their home base and pressed from two sides, the North Korean army was virtually destroyed. Numbering probably 70,000 by the time the two U.S. attacks started, the Communists were now seriously outnumbered, outgunned, and outequipped. They were soon running away from the advancing Eighth Army, either into the hills or into the waiting arms of X Corps. There was some desperate fighting in places, but by 1 October South Korea was recovered from Communist occupation.

The Inchon landing was the key element in the defeat of the North Koreans, but the entire commitment of UN forces is what makes the Korean War significant. When the UN decided to commit forces to aid South Korea, it did so knowing that, if they did not, the UN might never be an effective organization. The League of Nations, established by the Versailles Treaty after World War I, talked about mutual security, but was proven repeatedly to be a paper tiger. If the UN did nothing more than condemn North Korean aggression, the perception worldwide would be that this organization was no better than the last. Although the UN has been often criticized for inaction in later years, when it rose to its first challenge successfully, the potential for positive action was set.

The battle at Inchon, therefore, was a victory for the UN, although the forces involved in the invasion were completely those of the United States. The actions after the situation was restored have, of course, been open to criticism since 1950. When U.S. President Harry Truman ordered MacArthur to continue up the peninsula to place all of Korea under UN control, a decision confirmed by the UN several

days later, he laid the groundwork for 3 years of war after Communist Chinese forces entered the conflict in November 1950. The war in Korea became for the United States a war unlike any we had ever fought. It became a war not just of U.S. victory but a war with much more limited aims and therefore limited options for action. The fact that it was (in spite of the huge commitment of U.S. troops) a UN operation meant that the UN did, and would continue, to matter in international relations.

That the war ended not in victory but in a stalemated armistice has had long-range effects as well. North Korea remains at the end of the twentieth century one of the few remaining solidly Communist dictatorships. The talks between Communist and UN delegates, begun in late 1951, continue as of this writing. The relationship of the west to both North and South Korea is an ongoing problem: South Korea as a growing economic power, but with a paranoid neighbor to the north; North Korea in an ever-desperate economic condition, but with continuing military prowess and possibly expansionist designs. Korea, a flashpoint in 1950 and site of one of the main events in the Cold War, could erupt into war again.

References: Fehrenbach, T. R. *This Kind of War.* New York: Macmillan, 1963; Hastings, Max. *The Korean War.* New York: Simon & Schuster, 1987; Langley, Michael. *Inchon Landing.* New York: Times Books, 1979; Schnabel, James F. *Policy and Direction: The First Year.* Washington, DC: Center of Military History, 1992; Stokesbury, James L. *A Short History of the Korean War.* New York: William Morrow, 1988.

DIEN BIEN PHU
20 November 1953–7 May 1954

FORCES ENGAGED

Viet Minh: 50,000 men.
Commander: General Vo Nguyen Giap.

French: 16,000.
Commander: Colonel Christian de Castries.

French defeat led to the end of the French colonial
experience in Southeast Asia and formed the
groundwork for U.S. involvement in the region.

Historical Setting

By the 1890s, the French had established their
hegemony over much of the Southeast Asian
peninsula, which was called Indochina. The
area had long resisted any colonial expansion
by China to the north, but the population was
unable to maintain their independence in the
face of superior French firepower. The French
established a colonial administration and introduced to the region the basics of French culture and education. Advancement in the local
administration came via literacy in French, so
the people that came to dominate local society

were educated by the French and often converts to Catholicism. Herein lay the seeds of
France's colonial destruction.

First, by teaching French history, the tenets of the French Revolution—liberty, equality, and fraternity—were disseminated to the
dominated population. Liberty and equality are
hardly compatible with a colonial society, so as
the intelligentsia learned to cooperate with the
French, they also learned the ideas necessary to
overthrow them. Second, by establishing a
Catholic elite in a predominantly Buddhist society, those in power became less religiously
tolerant of the majority of the country. Neither
was this designed to promote a harmonious
colonial relationship. By the time of World War
I, nationalist movements were starting, aimed
at freeing Indochina from French rule.

The figure that rose to prominence in the
liberation movement was Nguyen Ai Quoc,

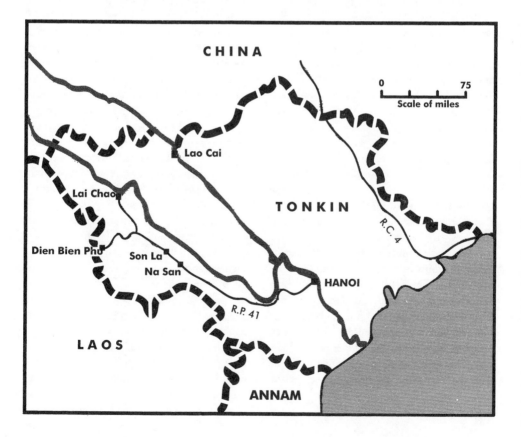

who later took the name Ho Chi Minh. He traveled to France in 1919 to appeal to the participants of the Versailles Conference to bring an end to all empires, not just of those of the vanquished nations, but failed to achieve his goals. Then, with some training in Marxism and revolution from the new Soviet regime, he returned home to lead the struggle for liberation. Through the 1920s and 1930s, Ho moved throughout Indochina and China organizing resistance to the French regime, creating a movement called the Viet Minh, the Vietnam Independence League. When the Japanese took over Indochina in 1940, the Viet Minh began fighting against them. In 1945, U.S. agents from the Office of Strategic Services met with Ho Chi Minh. He asked for U.S. assistance in establishing a free Vietnam, Cambodia, and Laos, but the U.S. alliance with France overrode such considerations. Thus, when France reestablished its colonial administration in 1945, Ho Chi Minh's followers returned to their prewar resistance movement.

The U.S. government did speak to French leader Charles de Gaulle on Vietnam's behalf, but did not seriously attempt to delay or halt reestablishment of the French regime. U.S. President Harry Truman's administration was critical of French military action against the Viet Minh until 1950, when Ho Chi Minh's Communist leanings inflamed the rising anti-Communist movement in the United States. Chinese aid to North Korea in 1950 gave the United States the impression of a potential Asian Communist bloc, so U.S. aid began to flow freely to French troops in Vietnam.

When the Communist regime was established in China in September 1949, military aid to the Viet Minh began to flow into Indochina in large amounts. Primarily, it was U.S. weaponry captured from the Nationalist Chinese forces supplemented with Russian weapons supplied to the Chinese from Moscow. That influx of weaponry for a short time gave the Viet Minh the advantage, especially

in the northern region of Indochina, but it tapered off significantly when the Korean War began. That coincided with the arrival in Vietnam of French General Jean de Lattre de Tassigny. He brought a new sense of duty and intensity to the French troops, and for a time the initiative and victories went to the French, while the forces of Ho Chi Minh and his chief commander, Vo Nguyen Giap, suffered severe losses. De Lattre had success not only with French Foreign Legion paratroopers but with the establishment of *hérissons,* or hedgehogs. These strong points bristling with machine guns and artillery, placed deep in Viet Minh–occupied territory or along supply routes, inflicted heavy losses on Viet Minh troops trying to overcome them.

All of this began to change when de Lattre died of cancer in January 1952 and was replaced by General Raoul Salan, a much more cautious soldier. Salan's strategy was to strike overland with heavy columns of troops and materiel against suspected Viet Minh strong points. This went on for about a year with poor results for the French. Giap allowed the French to drive deep into his countryside and then attacked their lines of communication and ambushed the withdrawing troops in valleys and gorges. In May 1953, Salan was replaced by General Henri Navarre, more in the aggressive, confident mold of de Lattre. Unfortunately for Navarre, public and governmental support for the war against the Viet Minh was waning in France, and he was ordered to win and do it quickly. His response was to reintroduce the hérisson strategy, and the site he chose was Dien Bien Phu, a village near the border between Vietnam and Laos. Laos had remained a strong ally of France and therefore made itself a target for Viet Minh attacks. By placing his strong point there, Navarre was sure it would provoke a strong response from Giap, who would not allow this French post deep in his rear and protecting Laos. Navarre was correct, but starting and winning the fight were two different matters.

The Battle

Command of the operation at Dien Bien Phu fell to French Foreign Legion Colonel Christian de Castries. His 1,827 paratroopers occupied the village on 23 November 1953 and began construction of nine fortified positions, each of which bore a feminine name (reputedly names of Castries's lovers). Four (Eliane, Dominique, Huguette, and Claudine) were built at the four corners of Dien Bien Phu itself. Between Dominique and Huguette on the north side of the village was the main airstrip, from which air operations were to be conducted against the Viet Minh and supplies were to be brought in. At the end of the airstrip, to the northwest, was the position named Anne-Marie; Gabrielle was on a hill about 1,500 yards to the north; Beatrice was located about 1,000 yards northeast of Dominique, also on a hilltop; Françoise lay about 500 yards to the west of Huguette; and Isabelle was located a few miles to the south, covering an emergency airstrip. Each position consisted of a number of mutually supporting strong points surrounded by barbed wire. With aircraft, machine guns, lots of artillery, and large numbers of French troops, Navarre was convinced that Giap would bleed his forces while attempting to capture this position; afterward, the French would easily be able to crush the remainder of the Viet Minh.

More troops and weaponry flowed into the position through the early months of 1954, and the French were confident of victory. Their force reached approximately 13,000 and was built around the French Foreign Legion paratroopers. Some of the auxiliary forces, Algerians and Moroccans, were well trained but irregularly motivated, as anti-French movements were beginning in their home countries as well. The main problem was one of overconfidence. The bunkers were not constructed as strongly, minefields were not as deep or extensive, and barbed wire was not strung in sufficient amounts or directions as should have been done.

General Giap, meanwhile, was determined to reduce the French outpost, but he was in no particular hurry. He had learned the lessons of the earlier French hedgehogs, and this one he was going to attack methodically. For 4 months, he had his men drag artillery to the hills surrounding Dien Bien Phu and then dig them into deep emplacements covered by trees. The fact that the French had not seized the high ground was critical in this battle, and Giap was not slow to capitalize on it.

At 1700 on the afternoon of 13 March 1954, Giap's artillery opened up on position Beatrice. The entire position was pounded, and early rounds destroyed the command bunker, paralyzing the defense. By midnight, the Viet Minh had captured the position, denying the French one of their primary artillery spotting posts. French return fire had little effect because Giap had made sure that his guns were hidden and protected. The following night, 14 March, the Viet Minh launched an attack on position Gabrielle, the furthest north. Its garrison of 500 men were almost all killed or captured by noon on 15 March. Not only were two positions lost almost immediately upon the battle's commencement but the Viet Minh artillery totally dominated the French airfield, making it almost useless from the beginning. A few medical craft were able to land and take off through the end of March. After that, the garrison was supplied completely by airdrops.

More paratroopers dropped into the position within a week of the fall of the two positions, and on 14 March the monsoon began. It severely hampered resupply efforts and made life miserable for the troops in the valley, less so for the Viet Minh on higher ground. The Viet Minh also began digging trenches toward the French outposts, so their assaults would not have to cover so much open ground. On the evening of 30 March, they attacked again, striking Eliane and Dominique on the eastern side of the village. Some strong points within each position were captured, but French counterattacks regained the ground they lost. Artillery fire was at its most intense, and both sides ended that round exhausted. Between 2 and 5 April, fighting raged over Huguette, with strong points lost and won, but the French ended up with all their positions regained.

Both French and Viet Minh losses were high, but French reinforcements were slow in arriving. What did come in had to do so by airdrop, and the staff officers in the French headquarters in Hanoi insisted on doing things according to peacetime procedures. Only direct threats from officers at Dien Bien Phu got

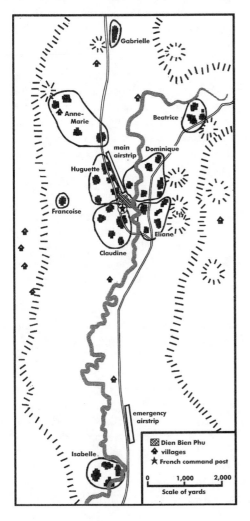

the troops dropped into the French positions. Help was slow in coming because of inertia in the French command and political decisions made in other countries. The United States in early 1954 was considering aid to the French force in Indochina. Air strikes by U.S. planes were discussed, but finally rejected, by the high command in Washington. Southeast Asia was not strategically important enough, they decided, to get involved with airpower, which would certainly lead to the commitment of ground troops. International talks over Indochina were scheduled for mid-May; outside interference might have kept the French going up to that point, providing bargaining chips in the talks. General Giap likewise wanted bargaining chips, so he pressed the attack.

Throughout April, artillery bombardment of French positions remained almost constant, with harassing attacks common. By 21 April, Viet Minh forces captured Huguette, dominating the airstrip and making antiaircraft fire that much more effective. French supplies were running very low and reinforcements were arriving in small numbers, dropped during breaks in the weather and the fighting. Even auxiliary Vietnamese paratroopers dropped in to assist, certainly knowing that to be captured by their compatriots would not be pleasant. In a counterattack to regain Huguette, French forces were caught in the open, and 150 men were killed or wounded. They kept up patrols and skirmishes, but the days of the defense were numbered.

On the night of 6–7 May, Viet Minh forces finally captured Eliane and the defense began to collapse. At 1730, Castries sent a message to Hanoi, alerting them that he was destroying the last of his ammunition and surrendering his command.

Results

The defenders of Dien Bien Phu lost almost 2,300 killed, with more than 5,100 wounded. The wounded, as well as the remaining soldiers that were captured, were not well treated. They

MONEY, DRUGS, AND GUERRILLAS

The French have often been criticized for establishing a base at Dien Bien Phu, too far away from the French bases in the Tonkin River delta for direct support. Although it was chosen as an obstacle to defend Laos from invasion, the reason for both the defense and the invasion has only recently been revealed.

After World War II, as the French reestablished their regime in Indochina, they encouraged volunteers to serve in the military there by offering a higher rate of exchange for the piasters with which they were paid than the standard international rate. This meant that the French government would honor the piasters at twice the rate of any other currency exchange. That resulted in widespread fraud by buying and selling piasters and francs through third currencies. French officials and Viet Minh operatives all did this and made significant fortunes for themselves and their causes, until public exposure in 1953 forced the French government to abandon the policy.

The French administration in Indochina used its profits to finance a resistance movement comprised of the northern Montagnard hill tribes, the Meo and Tai, living along the Vietnamese-Laotian border. As soldiers, they scored only modest successes, but the French were wedded to the idea that they would be a significant thorn in the Viet Minh's side. When the illicit money trade could no longer be employed, the French

turned to opium. Grown in the hills where the Meo and Tai tribes lived, it proved to be a source of financial support for both French and Viet Minh. In 1952, the Viet Minh seized the opium crop from the Meo in Laos and bought arms with the profits. In 1953, the French beat them to it, buying the crop before the Viet Minh could arrive. That was a major reason for the early conclusion of the Viet Minh invasion that year, traditionally ascribed to bad weather and lack of supplies.

If the French wanted to control the 1954 opium crop, they had to keep the Viet Minh out, and Dien Bien Phu lay on the invasion route into Laos. If they wanted to keep the resistance groups organized, equipped, and paid, they needed to keep the Viet Minh out. When Chinese advisors in late 1953 convinced Ho Chi Minh not to attack the French bases in the Red River delta but instead to attack the guerrilla bases, General Navarre was in a dilemma. If he stayed in his coastal defenses, he would keep his main strength secure, but sacrifice his guerrillas; if he went to assist them, he would place his men in an almost untenable position far from direct support. Considering the previous success of the hérisson strong points, he took the gamble to protect his guerrilla troops and the opium crop that financed them. Thus, the choice to fight it out at Dien Bien Phu, and the resulting disaster.

were marched out of the Dien Bien Phu valley to prison camps up to 500 miles away. Perhaps 10,000 men died in the process; only about 3,000 prisoners were repatriated to the French later that summer. Although the defenders at Dien Bien Phu represented only about 5 percent of the total French military in Indochina, they were the cream of the crop. Approximately 8,000 Viet Minh died in the course of the battle, with at least 15,000 wounded. During the battle, General Giap had hurled his men at the French in virtual human waves, with the casualty count (approximately 46 percent) reflecting that tactic. Even for the long-suffering Viet

Minh soldier, it was almost too much, for Giap's forces were at the point of mutiny at times during the siege.

The timing of the victory was all important. Representatives from the Viet Minh and French sat down in Geneva in mid-May to discuss the future of Indochina, and the French entered the talks on the defensive. The war had become increasingly unpopular in France with both the government and the public, and few were desirous of continuing it. France agreed to grant independence to Vietnam, Cambodia, and Laos, and within 2 years to have its personnel removed and elections held. In the meantime, the French-sponsored administration based in Saigon was to oversee the area of Vietnam below latitude 17 degrees, whereas Ho Chi Minh's administration would dominate the area above that line. Each would remove its troops from the other's territory, and free elections in 1956 would determine the nature of the new government.

Just as Britain began losing its empire with the Japanese capture of Singapore in 1942, France's empire, such as it was, also began its collapse in Southeast Asia. After the Napoleonic Wars, France had lost most of its overseas possessions, primarily to the British; the colonies that France acquired in the latter part of the nineteenth century (Indochina, some Pacific islands, and areas of Africa) now began to break away. Algeria was next to try for independence, staging its own guerrilla war, but the military lessons that France learned in fighting the Viet Minh were applied to the Algerians. Unfortunately, for both France and Algeria, political lessons were not learned, and the result was a bloodbath in North Africa and political turmoil in the French government and army before Algeria gained its independence anyway. Decolonization, which the British had managed to do peacefully in India in 1948, was now shown to be a potentially bloody and bitter experience. More colonies fought for their independence in the 1940s through 1960s than were granted it outright.

In Southeast Asia, things did not go smoothly either. The Geneva Accords were honored by the French and Viet Minh, but not by the United States and the Vietnamese administration in the south. Although the United States had not been a signatory to the Geneva Accords, U.S. President Dwight Eisenhower felt the need to get involved. U.S. foreign policy by this time was firmly rooted in containment of communism, and Eisenhower could not allow Communist regimes to survive unopposed. Thus, with U.S. support, the Republic of South Vietnam was created in 1956, before national

elections could be held. Ho Chi Minh's popularity was such that he almost certainly would have won an easy victory as leader of the entire nation. Instead, the 17th parallel became a political boundary that caused continued fighting, now among the Vietnamese themselves. The remnants of the French-trained and -educated elite dominated the southern government, and their mismanagement of the country, along with large amounts of U.S. financial and military aid, ultimately took the United States into a war that Eisenhower's advisors in 1954 had convinced him was not in his country's best interests.

In international affairs, the U.S. failure to support French troops at Dien Bien Phu directly with air strikes so angered French President Charles de Gaulle that he severed relations with the North Atlantic Treaty Organization (NATO) and began charting his own military course, which included nuclear weapons. Not until long after de Gaulle's death did France return as a full member of NATO, but suspicion of the United States and its motives continued to linger.

References: Davidson, Phillip. *Vietnam at War: The History 1946–1975.* New York: Oxford University Press, 1988; Fall, Bernard. *Hell in a Very Small Place.* New York: J. B. Lippincott, 1967; Keegan, John. *Dien Bien Phu.* New York: Random House, 1974; Porch, Douglas. "Dien Bien Phu and the Opium Connection," *Military History Quarterly* 7(4), Summer 1995.

TET OFFENSIVE
31 January–2 February 1968

FORCES ENGAGED

North Vietnamese: Approximately 84,000, mainly Viet Cong. Commander: General Vo Nguyen Giap.
United States/South Vietnamese: Unknown. Commander: General William Westmoreland.

IMPORTANCE

The perception of the effectiveness of Communist forces in Vietnam turned public opinion strongly against U.S. involvement in Vietnam, leading ultimately to U.S. withdrawal and Communist victory.

Historical Setting

After the French withdrew from Southeast Asia in 1956, the United States stepped up its support for an anti-Communist government in South Vietnam. Although the Geneva Accords signed in 1954 called for national elections, U.S. certainty that North Vietnam's Ho Chi Minh would win those elections and usher in a Communist regime brought about a withdrawal from participation in those elections. The South Vietnamese government that was left behind upon France's withdrawal was at first under the direction of Bao Dai. He was soon succeeded by Ngo Dinh Diem, who welcomed the economic and military support the United States supplied. The French-trained and -educated Diem was a Catholic, who appointed other Catholics (as well as family members) to key positions in the government, where they proved to be less than tolerant of the predominantly Buddhist population.

Ho Chi Minh's North Vietnamese government encouraged Communist movements in the south that opposed Diem. These groups came to be called the Viet Cong. Convinced that Buddhist priests in the south were secretly supporting the Viet Cong, the Diem regime began persecuting them. These attacks on religious leaders and facilities alienated much of the population. Even those with little interest in communism began to turn toward the Viet Cong for their anti-Diem stance. That in turn provoked Diem to increase his suppression of suspected Viet Cong sympathizers in the Buddhist community.

Diem's increasingly oppressive tactics bothered U.S. President John Kennedy, who entered office in January 1961. At first, Kennedy seemed uninterested in the southeast Asia foreign policy problem that he had inherited from the Eisenhower administration. After his support for the disastrous Bay of Pigs invasion in April 1961, however, Kennedy realized that he could not afford to appear weak in the face of international communism. He soon focused more attention on South Vietnam and the Diem government. He would occasionally caution Diem, warning him to be less repressive or risk losing U.S. aid. Diem would comply for a while, but then return to his old ways. This finally led, in November 1963, to Diem's assassination, with tacit U.S. approval. It has been argued that Kennedy was on the verge of abandoning Diem to his fate, but did nothing before his own assassination a few weeks later.

Lyndon Johnson, succeeding Kennedy, also appeared at first to want to shy away from Southeast Asia. That changed when, in early August 1964, he told Congress that U.S. warships had been attacked in the Gulf of Tonkin off North Vietnam. Armed with overwhelming congressional approval in the Gulf of Tonkin Resolution, he began planning operations to bring a quick end to the Communist threat to South Vietnam. In February 1985, he ordered the implementation of Operation Rolling Thunder, a strategy designed to force the Communists to the bargaining table through strategic air strikes. Instead, it led to increased Communist military activity, which in turn led to increased U.S. troop deployment. By late 1967, some half million Americans were involved in South Vietnam.

Although there were some isolated antiwar activities across the country, public opinion in the United States, for the most part, favored the U.S. intervention as necessary to implement the policy of containment of communism that had dominated U.S. foreign affairs since the late 1940s. U.S. military representatives gave weekly press briefings on the course of the war, counting up Communist casualties as the indications of success. By early 1968, most Americans were sure that the war was being won. At the end of January, that perception was radically altered.

The Battle

The Communist leadership in North Vietnam spent much of 1967 debating the strategy for attack. The southern government that had replaced Diem was proving fairly stable, and the Americans were attacking at will all across the country. The Communists wanted to make sure that North Vietnam was not invaded, but primarily they were looking to shore up their crumbling military situation. The Communist leaders were convinced that an overwhelming offensive would provoke a general peasant uprising in the south, give them a hold on the major cities, and seriously weaken the government. Commander-in-Chief Vo Nguyen Giap decided that his North Vietnamese Army (NVA) regulars would launch a diversionary attack at the U.S./ARVN (Army of the Republic of Vietnam) base at Khe Sanh just south of

the demilitarized zone along latitude 17 degrees. With the U.S. and ARVN forces drawn northward, the southern countryside and cities would be much more lightly defended. The task of attacking cities, towns, and military bases fell to the Viet Cong, which mustered some 84,000 people for the offensive.

Late in 1967, the North Vietnamese began to lay the groundwork for the offensive. They began hinting at the possibility of peace talks and requested a truce for the Tet festival, celebrating the Asian New Year. Knowing that the South Vietnamese government did not want any negotiations at all, it was hoped that rumors of peace negotiations would create some tension between the allies. For the few months leading up to the offensive, massive amounts of supplies were smuggled into the south, a feat impossible to keep completely hidden from U.S. intelligence services. The U.S. commander in Vietnam, General William Westmoreland, reported to his superiors in Washington that a major enemy action was imminent, and he pre-

M-113 armored personnel carriers stand by as Vietnamese refugees evacuate the village of My Tho during the Tet offensive, 1968. (National Archives)

dicted it would take place at or near the Tet holiday at the end of January. Little heed was paid to his warning, even when the attack on Khe Sanh began on 21 January 1968.

Just as Giap had planned, the U.S. and ARVN command poured reinforcements into the defense of Khe Sanh. On the night of 30–31 January, while half the ARVN forces were on Tet holiday leave, the Viet Cong began the offensive. Attacks were launched against five of the six major cities, thirty-six of forty-four provincial capitals, and virtually every military base in the south, almost a hundred separate targets. In Saigon, the U.S. embassy was assaulted just after midnight, with intense fighting taking place in the compound until just after dawn. The Viet Cong had infiltrated a few thousand guerrillas into Saigon the previous week, and the fighting that ensued was house to house. Four Viet Cong corps were in action from the demilitarized zone southward to the Mekong delta.

As these attacks were taking place, 7,500 NVA troops overcame the U.S. and ARVN troops defending the old imperial capital city of Hue. Within hours, the NVA was in control, raising its flag over the old fortress and killing some 2,800 civilians assumed to be cooperating with the Americans. This was the largest political massacre of the war up to that time and marked a change in Communist political terror tactics. Within hours, Westmoreland had reinforcements on the way, but recapturing the town was a major undertaking. Not wanting to destroy any more of the historic city than necessary, wholesale artillery support and air strikes were ruled out. Thus, the fighting was house to house, street to street, for more than 3 weeks. Not until 24 February was the city declared secure. With the Hue attack defeated, the Tet offensive ground to a halt.

Results

U.S. and ARVN operations to regain control of all Viet Cong targets took some weeks, but it was accomplished. Giap, who had feared that the U.S. forces were too strong to attack directly, was proven correct. Guerrilla warfare doctrine called for "war in the shadows" until numerical superiority could be achieved. Only then would a head-to-head battle be undertaken. Such a shift in strategy had occurred in 1954 just before the French defeat at Dien Bien Phu. The Tet offensive proved that the Communists were not yet at that stage in this war. Exact casualty counts for the Communists are unknown, but the generally accepted figure is approximately 40,000 dead, including 5,000 killed at the battle for Hue. In comparison, the United States lost about 1,100 dead, and the ARVN lost just over twice that many men. More significantly, perhaps 45,000 civilians were killed or wounded in the fighting and another million were homeless.

Everything the Communists had hoped for failed to materialize. The peasant population did not rise up and welcome them as liberators. Indeed, when the U.S. and ARVN troops reentered Communist-held towns, the Viet Cong were usually turned over to them. The government of Nguyen Cao Ky and Nguyen Van Thieu remained as strong as ever. The dream of establishing strongholds in southern cities never happened. It was the greatest tactical defeat that the Communists ever suffered in this war, and afterward the Communist leadership could do little more than wonder how their plans could have gone so far awry. The Viet Cong forces in the south were, of course, the most badly decimated by the offensive, and they never again were able to field complete units. That meant that war in the south would have to be conducted increasingly more by northern troops, meaning more drain on personnel and longer supply lines.

With that type of description, it would seem that the Tet offensive as a decisive battle would have spelled the beginning of the end for the Communists. In reality, exactly the opposite happened, and in a way that Giap and Ho had never conceived. North Vietnamese

General Tran Do later commented, "As for making an impact in the United States, it had not been our intention—but it turned out to be a fortunate result" (Olson and Roberts, *Where the Domino Fell*, p. 187). Having been told for months that the situation was well in hand, that the Communists would soon lose the war because they would have no one left with which to fight, the U.S. public wanted to know just where all those soldiers came from that could attack everywhere at once. If the body counts announced every week were indeed accurate, how could such an offensive take place? Worst of all, it was on the evening news, watched by the entire country. Even the presence of General Westmoreland standing in the embassy compound failed to assure the public. Could it all be lies? The public came to believe the early reports that the Communists had, temporarily, occupied the embassy. Untrue, but later denials were viewed skeptically.

What the U.S. public saw was Viet Cong in the embassy compound. What they did not see, because the news cameras did not follow, was the massive U.S. and ARVN counteroffensive that smashed the Communist forces. The perception of stalemate, if not defeat, settled into the American psyche. The antiwar movement suddenly exploded, and members of Congress who previously had been unheard became commonly interviewed on television. With the primary elections just starting for the 1968 presidential campaign, Lyndon Johnson found himself seriously challenged by Robert Kennedy and Eugene McCarthy, both highly critical of the war.

Ever since Rolling Thunder had marked the beginning of U.S. military action, Johnson had responded to his military advisors' regular calls for more troops. Just a few more, just a little longer, and it would all be won. Now, after the Tet offensive, General Westmoreland reported the severe thrashing the Communists took and said that, with the enemy on the run, just a few more men were all that was necessary. Johnson had had enough. Disillusioned by both the military and political challenges,

Johnson on 31 March addressed the nation. He stated that he would stop bombing targets in North Vietnam as a show of good faith, hoping to convince the Communists to negotiate. As that would take all of his effort, he told U.S. citizens "I will not seek nor will I accept the nomination of my party." The perception seemed to be confirmed; things apparently were not as rosy as the military had implied.

The public response led to Johnson's downfall. His successor, Richard Nixon, campaigned for the presidency on the platform of law and order at home, peace with honor in Vietnam. After the Tet offensive, the American people seemed to want not victory, just an end to the war. Although it took 5 more years for final arrangements to be concluded, the war had long been lost. The struggle in Vietnam, the only serious U.S. setback in the entire Cold War era, was in the end not a struggle of military might, but of national will.

References: Berman, Larry. *Lyndon Johnson's War.* New York: W. W. Norton, 1989; Hammel, Eric. *Fire in the Streets: The Battle for Hue, Tet 1968.* Chicago: Contemporary Books, 1991; Maclear, Michael. *The Ten Thousand Day War.* New York: St. Martin's Press, 1981; Olson, James S., and Randy Roberts. *Where the Domino Fell.* New York: St. Martin's Press, 1996; Spector, Ronald. *After Tet.* New York: Free Press, 1993.

DESERT STORM
24–28 February 1991

FORCES ENGAGED
Allied Coalition: 665,000.
Commander: Major General Norman Schwarzkopf.
Iraqi: 350,000.
Commander: Saddam Hussein.

IMPORTANCE
Desert Storm denied control of a large portion of the Middle East oil reserves to dictator Saddam Hussein and showed the ability of a

multinational coalition to succeed in the post–Cold War world, perhaps setting an example of future international military action.

Historical Setting

By early 1990, Iraq was in a delicate situation. It had recently ended a long war with Iran in which it had received a large amount of military support from both the Soviet Union and the United States, both of which feared Iranian domination of the Middle East. This support, although able to bring about only a draw in the Iran-Iraq war, gave Iraqi dictator Saddam Hussein the fourth largest military force in the world. It also made him deeply in debt, primarily to other Arab states, which had floated large loans to finance his war. The largest creditor was Kuwait, just south of Iraq on the Persian Gulf. Assuming that no nation would seriously contest him, Hussein decided to use his large military to erase his large debt. An invasion of Kuwait would both remove the government to which he owed the money and place him in control of their huge oil reserves. Claiming Kuwait to be in reality a province of Iraq, Hussein massed his army on the border. After several weeks of threats and no significant international counteraction, Iraqi forces invaded Kuwait on 3 August 1990.

International reaction came almost as quickly as did Iraq's victory. Not only the blatant aggression but the cruel nature of the occupation aroused anger around the world. British Prime Minister Margaret Thatcher made the first major speech of condemnation, but U.S. President George Bush was not far behind. He announced that fundamental U.S. interests were involved and Hussein could not be allowed to control Kuwait and its oil wealth. To argue that Hussein just wanted oil is much the same as arguing that Hitler just wanted land. The nature of the dictator in this case was more important than any physical rationale. Hussein had already proven his indifference to human life by his use of poison gas against Iranian troops, as well as against Kurdish rebels living

in the northern region of Iraq. Further, evidence was strong that Iraq was nearing its goal of acquiring nuclear military power. Such weaponry in the hands of an unstable personality had to be curbed, whether in the Persian Gulf or anywhere else.

Acting through the United Nations (UN), the United States began organizing a multinational coalition to restore Kuwait's sovereignty. After convincing Saudi Arabia that they could easily be Iraq's next target, that government allowed the United States to begin amassing forces first to defend Saudi Arabia and then to recover Kuwait; this action began under the code name Desert Shield. The core of the U.S. and coalition force was U.S. Army Central Command, led by Major General Norman Schwarzkopf. CENTCOM, as it was called, was at first little more than a paper force, but it quickly filled out. First on the scene were U.S.

Kuwait oil burning: Iraqi-sabotaged oil well near Kuwait City. (Reuters/Archive Photos)

fighter aircraft, with tactical and reconnaissance aircraft not far behind. Although many U.S. air force planners were convinced that airpower alone could force Hussein out of Kuwait, Schwarzkopf and his immediate superior, Chairman of the Joint Chiefs of Staff Colin Powell, planned for a land campaign as well. To keep Hussein from claiming that his army was unbeaten, as Hitler did in Germany in the 1920s, it was necessary to defeat all parts of the Iraqi military.

The United States, which provided the bulk of the forces, had a well-trained, well-equipped, and technologically sophisticated army with which to fight. Military planners assumed that Iraq did as well. Because Iraq had large amounts of western electronics (primarily Soviet, but some French and U.S.) as well as large numbers of veterans from the Iran-Iraq war, many staff officers proposed that the Iraqi army was more than ready for a long, hard fight. Intelligence analysts failed to learn that the typical Iraqi soldier was a recent recruit and that the veterans were exhausted from the last war. Further, the technology they possessed was neither well understood nor well operated. To a great extent, this resulted in coalition planners putting together a more massive force than was actually necessary. Hussein himself believed in the power of his forces. He was sure that not only would he be able to destroy coalition airpower with his sophisticated radar and air defense systems, but he believed that the Americans did not have the stomach for a long fight. He was more than willing to spend lives; the westerners would not.

When Hussein ignored a deadline for withdrawing from Kuwait, President Bush ordered the beginning of Desert Storm, the transformation from a defensive to an offensive operation. At 0300 on 17 January 1991, U.S. stealth bombers and fighters easily penetrated Iraqi radar and proceeded to destroy their air defense network. With the destruction of the main electrical grid for the country, Hussein's command and control capabilities were severely hampered.

Soon follow-up strikes took out peripheral radar sites as well, giving coalition forces complete air superiority. Iraqi aircraft were destroyed on the ground, in air-to-air combat, and in their bunkers before Hussein ordered the surviving planes to flee to Iran. Within a matter of hours, Hussein's ability to coordinate his military was severely hindered. He responded by attempting to drive a political wedge into the coalition. With intermediate-range ballistic missiles, Russian-designed SCUDs, he launched attacks on Israel, hoping that Israel would respond and bring Arab support to Iraq. Attacks on Saudi targets were intended to demoralize the Saudis and force their withdrawal from the coalition. Neither strategy worked. Although some collateral damage killed some civilians and gave the western politicians pause, for the most part the coalition remained steadfast. Unfortunately for the Iraqi army, so did Saddam Hussein.

The Battle

For 2 weeks, coalition aircraft roamed at will across Iraq and Kuwait, destroying much of Iraq's armor and personnel. Still convinced that his army could not be beaten, Hussein launched an attack on U.S. lines near Kuwait on 29 January. Although it was a surprise, staunch defense by the U.S. Marines being attacked, as well as response by airpower, quickly broke up the attack. The poor Iraqi performance convinced the Marines on the ground that their enemy was overrated, but such an assessment never reached the high command. Instead, more U.S. troops arrived from Germany, fleshing out the force necessary for the planned offensive. Another deadline for Iraqi withdrawal came and went, and on 24 February coalition leaders were convinced that the time had come to launch the land campaign.

The first troops in action were contingents composing the XVIII Airborne Corps: the U.S. 101st and 82nd Airborne Divisions, the 24th Infantry Division, and the French contribution, a light armored division. Their role was to drive through the Iraqi desert to a position on the Euphrates River, there to block any reinforcements coming from the interior of Iraq and threaten an attack on Baghdad, thus pinning down reserves there. This sweep made its way through totally trackless desert through which even the Iraqis would not go, but, thanks to the abilities of global positioning satellites, the column was able to navigate without problems. The flanking force was therefore completely undetected by any Iraqis until it was at the Euphrates. Just to their east, VII Corps was to

drive north into Iraq and then turn east and cut off the mass of Iraqi forces in Kuwait and southeastern Iraq. VII Corps was made up primarily of Germany-based U.S. troops along with a British heavy armored division.

The Iraqis were in a static position behind defenses that they had been digging for more than 6 months. Never conceiving the possibility of a flanking movement, Hussein was sure the frontal attack that the coalition forces would have to make would enter a killing field. The coalition forces demonstrated in front of these

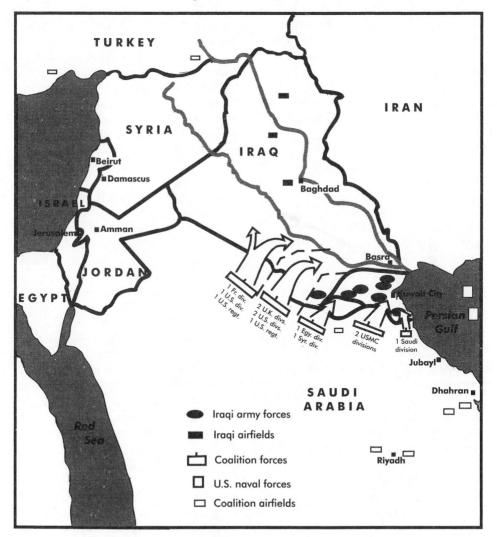

defenses to hold the Iraqis in place. There was also a diversionary attack on the Persian Gulf coast, where Hussein had placed large forces to beat back a Marine amphibious invasion that he was convinced would occur. The demonstration on the Iraqi defenses proved successful, not only in holding them in place but in completely breaking through. The weeks of pounding from the air had taken their toll, and the Iraqi soldiers in many cases could not surrender fast enough. Kuwait City was soon in U.S. hands, and Iraqi forces were streaming north, harassed by air strikes the entire way out of the country. Coalition troops found scenes of widespread devastation, not only in Kuwait City but also in the oil fields, which Hussein had ordered to be torched. Oil spills and black smoke from the oil wells marked one of the first attempts at environmental warfare, but the pollution in the end was much more limited than Hussein had hoped.

The success in the south meant that the VII Corps thrust needed to be launched earlier than planned, and the fact that it failed to completely encircle the Iraqis, especially the elite Republican Guard, has been criticized. In the fog of war, however, troops trained to defend Germany from a Warsaw Pact onslaught had difficulty altering their mission to one of pursuit. VII Corps commander General Frederick Franks pleaded insufficient intelligence on Iraqi positioning and movement as well as the need to maintain supply lines, vital in a desert war. VII Corps was successful, but not as completely as it might have been.

Overwhelming numbers on the ground and in the air proved too much for the Iraqi army to face. Accurate long-range fire from U.S. tanks as well as tank-busting by A-10 tactical aircraft broke any attempt at serious Iraqi armored response. It could have been worse for the Iraqis. A change in air control, shifting the line of targeting to north of the Euphrates for air force planes, in order to allow unrestricted use of helicopters without air force control, allowed many Iraqi tanks and trucks to flee, as the new line of targeting was beyond the range of forward observers to direct air attacks.

Results

With his military in ruins, and with no outside support to aid him, Saddam Hussein early in the morning of 28 February asked for a cease-fire. It went into effect at 0800. Exact numbers of Iraqi casualties are unknown, but have been estimated at 60,000 killed and 175,000 prisoners. In one of the worst military performances since the Italian debacle before the British in Egypt in World War II, Iraqi soldiers surrendered in huge numbers, and their stories are pathetic. One report tells of an Iraqi tank that came upon a U.S. jeep stuck in the sand; the Iraqis pulled the jeep to solid ground and then surrendered to the occupants. Other reports tell of soldiers surrendering to war correspondents or to remotely piloted aircraft flying overhead. Most of the Iraqi tanks, armored personnel carriers, trucks, and artillery were also destroyed or captured. In this 100-hour war, coalition casualties numbered less than 500.

For what seemed to have been a "splendid little war," as U.S. Secretary of State John Hay described the Spanish-American War, the results were not quite as spectacular. By not destroying the Iraqi army, sufficient troops (especially the loyal Republican Guard) remained under Hussein's control, allowing Hussein to maintain power. He quickly employed his troops in crushing uprisings of rebellious Kurds in the northern part of the country as well as Shi'ite Moslems in the south. Like Stalin, Hussein managed to survive a military disaster of his own making, for he (like the Soviet dictator) had killed talented commanders that he believed were politically unreliable. In spite of that, his hold on the reins of power, exercised through key people and positions undestroyed in Baghdad, kept him in control. If President Bush and other coalition leaders planned on Hussein being killed during the war or overthrown afterward, they were sadly disappointed.

HI-TECH VIDEO WAR

To the world outside the Persian Gulf theater of operations, probably the most impressive aspect of the Gulf War was high technology. First, so much of the war was televised live, or shortly after the fact, thanks to Cable News Network (CNN). Saddam Hussein allowed reporters from CNN to remain in Baghdad through the conflict, hoping that they would be on hand to report firsthand on his victory. Indeed, their coverage of the destruction of a headquarters bunker in Baghdad that was filled with civilians (relatives of high-ranking government personnel) caused the U.S. government to halt any more bombings of civilian areas. That decision allowed Hussein to maintain control over key facilities that were instrumental in maintaining his political control in the immediate wake of the war. The first western view of the war was CNN footage of antiaircraft fire streaking through the night over the Iraqi capital.

Second, what the average viewer witnessed on those broadcasts was amazing. Video of laser-guided weapons striking with pinpoint accuracy gave the impression almost of video games. World War II veteran pilots, who were thrilled in their day to land a bomb within 500 feet of a target, stood in awe of the precision with which modern technology was able to place an explosive device within a few feet of its mark. Patriot missiles, based in Israel and Saudi Arabia as defense against SCUD missiles, gave instant televised views of their abilities. These views, however, were misleading. Patriot "kills" were fewer than they seemed to be, although they did cause malfunctions in SCUD targeting and provided a great morale boost for Israeli civilians.

On-site, what the soldiers themselves used and saw could be shown only after the war was over. The success of the flanking movement was solely the result of the introduction of global positioning systems. Iraqi tank crews were convinced that they were being attacked by aircraft, when in actuality U.S. tanks were targeting and hitting them from almost 2 miles away, much farther than in any tank battle before. Depleted uranium shells fired from those tanks, as well as from antitank A-10 support aircraft, easily pierced any armor that the Iraqis owned. Infrared sensors allowed F-111 aircraft to locate Iraqi tanks at night and knock them out in great numbers. Night vision equipment allowed all coalition forces to move in the dark, keeping constant pressure on enemy defenses. The possession of this equipment and ability to use it contributed greatly to the overall performance of the coalition forces and the defeat of Iraq.

From a more positive angle, Kuwait was liberated, as UN resolutions intended. The oilfield fires were brought under control much more quickly than anyone had predicted, saving the Persian Gulf from an ecological disaster that could have been permanent. The ability of disparate nations, east and west, to work together under a single command and achieve their stated goal bodes well for the future of international cooperation. Further, Hussein was stopped before he could finish his nuclear project, and his ability to produce and employ biological and chemical weapons has been the focus of a UN investigation still proceeding as of this writing. The fact that an embargo imposed on Iraq, until their programs to produce weapons of mass destruction are dismantled, has been maintained throughout that investigation period is also a testimony to international cooperation.

The U.S. military, for all its successes in this war, found itself lacking in some areas. It was able to coordinate and conduct a massive logistical operation to make the military operation succeed. It was lucky, however, that Saddam Hussein sat still for months while forces and supplies were gathered for his destruction. Had he waited for his atomic program to come to fruition before provoking the rest of the world, he almost certainly would have used whatever atomic weaponry he had. It is still being debated whether he actually did employ some chemical or biological weapons because U.S. troops suffered postwar illnesses, which some have suggested are linked to such weapons or their antidotes. Had his air force been functional, use of such weapons can almost have been guaranteed. Intelligence gathering proved wholly inadequate in many cases.

Desert Storm has therefore been depicted as a huge military success with mixed or negative political results. Debates are still going on as to the wisdom of stopping the war so soon, of not capturing Baghdad, of not ensuring Saddam Hussein's downfall. Although the Americans temporarily enjoyed some popularity in the Middle East for their efforts in Desert Storm, had they been the primary force responsible for capturing Baghdad and implementing some

king-making, long-standing fears of western imperialism would certainly have been quick to rise again. The future of coalition warfare seems hopeful because similar attempts to field only international forces in the former Yugoslavia owe much of their heritage to Desert Storm.

References: Clancy, Tom, with Fred Franks. *Into the Storm: A Study in Command.* New York: Putnam, 1997; Murray, Williamson. "The Gulf War as History," *Military History Quarterly* 10(1), Autumn 1997; Pimlott, John, and Stephen Badsey. *The Gulf War Assessed.* London: Arms and Armour Press, 1992; Schubert, Frank N., and Theresa L. Kraus. *The Whirlwind War.* Washington, DC: Center of Military History, 1995; Schwarzkopf, Norman. *It Doesn't Take a Hero.* New York: Bantam Books, 1992.

BIBLIOGRAPHY

Adams, Jerome. *Latin American Heroes.* New York: Ballantine, 1991.

Adcock, Frank. *The Roman Art of War under the Republic.* Cambridge, MA: Harvard University Press, 1940.

Allmand, C. T. *The Hundred Years War: England and France at War.* Cambridge, UK: Cambridge University Press, 1988.

Allsen, Thomas. *Mongol Imperialism.* Berkeley: University of California Press, 1987.

Ammianus Marcellinus. *Ammianus Marcellinus.* Translated by John Carew Rolfe. Cambridge, MA: Harvard University Press, 1950 [1935–1939].

Antonucci, Michael. "Siege without Reprieve." *Military History* 9(1), April 1992.

Armstrong, Karen. *Holy War: The Crusades and Their Impact on Today's World.* New York: Doubleday, 1991.

Aronson, Theo. *The Fall of the Third Napoleon.* Indianapolis, IN: Bobbs-Merrill, 1970.

Arrian. *The Campaigns of Alexander.* Translated by Aubrey de Selincourt. Baltimore: Penguin, 1958.

Asakawa, K. *The Russo-Japanese Conflict: Its Causes and Issues.* Boston: Houghton Mifflin, 1904.

Ashley, Maurice. *The Battle of Naseby and the Fall of King Charles I.* New York: St. Martin's Press, 1992.

———. *Charles II: The Man and the Statesman.* New York: Praeger, 1971.

Babur. *The Babur-nama in English: Memoirs of Babur.* Translated by Annette Susannah Beveridge. London: Luzac & Co., 1921.

Bailey, Thomas. *A Diplomatic History of the American People.* Englewood Cliffs, NJ: Prentice-Hall, 1968.

Balász, György, and Károly Szelényi. *The Magyars: The Birth of a European Nation.* Budapest, Hungary: Corvina Press, 1989.

Baldwin, Hanson. *Battles Lost and Won.* New York: Harper & Row, 1966.

Baldwin, John. *The Government of Philip Augustus.* Berkeley: University of California Press, 1986.

Balyuzi, H. M. *Mohammed and the Course of Islam.* Oxford, UK: G. Ronald, 1976.

Bar-Lochva, Bezalel. *The Seleucid Army.* New York: Cambridge University Press, 1976.

Barber, Noel. *The Sultans.* New York: Simon & Schuster, 1973.

Barker, A. J. *Arab-Israeli Wars.* New York: Hippocrene Books, 1981.

———. *Midway: The Turning Point.* New York: Ballantine, 1971.

Barker, John. *Justinian and the Later Roman Empire.* Madison: University of Wisconsin Press, 1966.

Barnett, Correlli. *Bonaparte.* New York: Hill & Wang, 1978.

The Battle of Badr. <www.islaam.com/ilm/battleof.htm>.

Bauer, Jack. *The Mexican War, 1846–1848.* New York: Macmillan, 1974.

Beals, Carleton. *Eagles of the Andes.* Philadelphia: Chilton Books, 1963.

Beeching, Jack. *The Galleys at Lepanto.* New York: Charles Scribner's Sons, 1983.

Bence-Jones, Mark. *Clive of India.* New York: St. Martin's Press, 1975.

Bennett, Geoffrey. *Nelson the Commander.* New York: Charles Scribner's Sons, 1972.

Benson, Douglas. *Ancient Egypt's Warfare.* Ashland, OH: Book Masters, 1995.

Berman, Larry. *Lyndon Johnson's War.* New York: W. W. Norton, 1989.

Billings, Malcolm. *The Cross and the Crescent.* New York: Sterling, 1990 [1987].

Billows, Richard A. *Antigonos the One-Eyed and the Creation of the Hellenistic State.* Berkeley: University of California Press, 1990.

Bishop, Edward. *Their Finest Hour.* New York: Ballantine, 1968.

Blond, Georges. *The Marne.* Translated by H. Eaton Hart. Harrisburg, PA: Stackpole Books, 1966.

Boritt, Gabor. *Lincoln's Generals*. New York: Oxford University Press, 1994.

Borza, Eugene. *In the Shadow of Olympus: The Emergence of Macedon*. Princeton, NJ: Princeton University Press, 1990.

Boulger, Demetrius Charles. *The History of China*, vol. 1. Freeport, NY: Books for Libraries Press, 1972 [1898].

Bradbury, Jim. *Philip Augustus: King of France, 1180–1223*. London: Longman, 1998.

Breasted, James Henry. *A History of Egypt*. London: Hodder & Stoughton, 1905.

Brett-James, Antony. *The Hundred Days*. New York: St. Martin's Press, 1964.

Britt, Albert. *The Wars of Napoleon*. West Point, NY: United States Military Academy, 1973.

Brooke, Archibald. *Napoleon and Waterloo*, 2 vols. Freeport, NY: Books for Libraries Press, 1971.

Browning, Robert. *Justinian and Theodora*. London: Weidenfeld & Nicolson, 1971.

Brusilov, Alexei A. *A Soldier's Notebook, 1914–1918*. Westport, CT: Greenwood Press, 1971.

Bryant, Arthur. *The Turn of the Tide*. Garden City, NY: Doubleday, 1957.

Buckler, John. *The Theban Hegemony, 371–362*. Cambridge, MA: Harvard University Press, 1980.

Burgoyne, Bruce. *Enemy Views*. Bowie, MD: Heritage Books, 1996.

Burn, A. R. *Persia and the Greeks: The Defence of the West, c. 546–478 BC*. Stanford, CA: Stanford University Press, 1984 [1963].

Caesar, Julius. *War Commentaries of Caesar*. Translated by Rex Warner. New York: New American Library, 1960.

Caffrey, Kate. *Out in the Midday Sun: Singapore, 1941–1945*. New York: Stein & Day, 1973.

Canard, M. "Byzantium and the Moslem World to the Middle of the 11th Century," in J. Hussey, ed. *Cambridge Medieval History*, vol. IV. Cambridge, UK: Cambridge University Press, 1966.

Cannan, John, *The Antietam Campaign*. New York: Wieser & Wieser, 1990.

Carr, William. *The Origin of the Wars of German Unification*. London: Longman, 1991.

Carrasco, David. *Montezuma's Mexico*. Niwot, CO: University of Colorado Press, 1992.

Carrell, Paul. *Hitler Moves East, 1941–1943*. Translated by Ewald Osers. New York: Little, Brown, 1965.

Carver, Michael. *War Since 1945*. New York: Putnam, 1981.

Cary, M. *The History of the Greek World, from 323 to 146 B.C.* London: Methuen & Co., 1932.

Cassius Dio. *Dio's Roman History*. Translated by Earnest Cary. New York: Macmillan, 1924.

———. *The Roman History: The Reign of Augustus*. Translated by Ian Scott-Kilvert. New York: Penguin, 1987.

Castlewitz, Donald. "Siege Forces a Kingdom," *Military History* 12(2), June 1995.

Cate, Curtis. *The War of Two Emperors*. New York: Random House, 1984.

Chandler, David. *The Art of Warfare in the Age of Marlborough*. New York: Hippocrene Books, 1976.

———. *The Campaigns of Napoleon*. New York: Macmillan, 1966.

———. *On the Napoleonic Wars*. London: Greenhill Books, 1994.

———. *Waterloo: The Hundred Days*. New York: Macmillan, 1980.

Chassin, Lionel Max. *The Communist Conquest of China*. Cambridge, MA: Harvard University Press, 1965.

Ch'i-ch'ing Hsiao. *The Military Establishment of the Yuan Dynasty*. Cambridge, MA: Harvard University Press, 1978.

Chidsey, Donald Barr. *Victory at Yorktown*. New York: Crown, 1962.

Churchill, Winston. *Their Finest Hour*. New York: Houghton Mifflin, 1949.

Cieza de Leon, Pedro de. *The Incas*. Translated by Harriet de Onis. Norman: University of Oklahoma Press, 1959 [1553, 1873].

Clancy, Tom, with Fred Franks. *Into the Storm: A Study in Command*. New York: Putnam, 1997.

Clark, Alan. *Suicide of the Empires.* New York: American Heritage Press, 1971.

Clausen, Henry. *Pearl Harbor: Final Judgement.* New York: Crown, 1992.

Clot, Andre. *Suleiman the Magnificent: The Man, His Life, His Epoch.* Translated by Matthew J. Reisz. London: Saqui Books, 1989.

Coddington, Edwin B. *Gettysburg: A Study in Command.* New York: Charles Scribner's Sons, 1968.

Conaughton, R. M. *The War of the Rising Sun and the Tumbling Bear.* London: Routledge, 1991.

Connor, Seymour. *North America Divided.* New York: Oxford University Press, 1971.

Connor, Seymour, James Day, Joe Frantz, et al. *Battles of Texas.* Waco, TX: Texian Press, 1967.

Cook, J. M. *The Persian Empire.* New York: Schocken Books, 1983.

Cook, Theodore. "Mongol Invasion," *Military History Quarterly* 11(2), Winter 1998.

Creasy, Edward S. *Fifteen Decisive Battles of the World.* New York: Harper, 1851.

Daiches, David. *Charles Edward Stuart: The Life and Times of Bonnie Prince Charlie.* London: Thames & Hudson, 1973.

Davidson, Phillip. *Vietnam at War: The History 1946–1975.* New York: Oxford University Press, 1988.

Davis, Burke. *The Campaign That Won America.* New York: Dial Press, 1970.

Deighton, Len. *Blood, Tears, and Folly.* London: Jonathan Cape, 1994.

Delgado, Pedro. *Mexican Account of the Battle of San Jacinto.* Deepwater, TX: W. C. Day, 1919.

Dewey, George. *Autobiography of George Dewey.* New York: Charles Scribner's Sons, 1916.

Diaz del Castillo, Bernal. *The Discovery and Conquest of Mexico, 1517–1521.* Translated by A. P. Maudslay. New York: Harper, 1928.

Diodorus. *Diodorus of Sicily.* Translated by C. H. Oldfather. Cambridge, MA: Harvard University Press, 1933–1952.

Dodge, Theodore A. *Caesar: A History of the Art of War among the Romans.* Boston: Houghton Mifflin, 1892.

Dorenberg, John. "Battle of the Teutoburg Forest," *Archaeology Magazine* 45(5), 1992.

Dorey, T. A., and D. R. Dudley. *Rome against Carthage.* Garden City, NY: Doubleday, 1972.

Dowdey, Clifford, and Louis H. Manarin. *The Wartime Papers of Robert E. Lee.* Boston: Little, Brown, 1961.

Doyle, William. *The Oxford History of the French Revolution.* Oxford, UK: Clarendon Press, 1989.

Dudley, Donald. *The Romans.* New York: Alfred A. Knopf, 1970.

Dunbar, Sir George. *A History of India from the Earliest Times to the Present Day,* vol. 1. London: Nicholson & Watson, 1943.

Dupuy, R. Ernest, and Trevor Dupuy. *Encyclopedia of Military History.* New York: Harper & Row, 1970.

Dupuy, Trevor N. *Elusive Victory: The Arab-Israeli Wars, 1947–1974.* New York: Harper & Row, 1978.

———. *A Genius for War.* London: Macdonald's & Jane's, 1977.

Dupuy, Trevor N., and Paul Martell. *Great Battles on the Eastern Front.* Indianapolis, IN: Bobbs-Merrill, 1982.

Durant, Will. *The Age of Faith.* New York: Simon & Schuster, 1950.

———. *Caesar and Christ.* New York: Simon & Schuster, 1944.

———. *The Life of Greece.* New York: Simon & Schuster, 1939.

———. *The Reformation.* New York: Simon & Schuster, 1957.

Dutourd, Jean. *The Taxis of the Marne.* Translated by Harold King. New York: Simon & Schuster, 1957.

Dwyer, William. *The Day Is Ours!* New York: Viking, 1983.

Edmunds, David R. *Tecumseh and the Quest for Indian Leadership.* Boston: Little, Brown, 1984.

Ehrenkreutz, Andrew. *Saladin*. Albany: SUNY Press, 1972.

Einhard, and Notker the Stammerer. *Two Lives of Charlemagne*. Translated by Lewis Thorpe. New York: Penguin, 1969.

Eisenhower, John. *So Far from God: The U.S. War with Mexico, 1846–1848*. New York: Random House, 1989.

Ellis, John. *Philip II and Macedonian Imperialism*. London: Thames & Hudson, 1976.

Eusebius. *The History of the Church from Christ to Constantine*. Translated by G. A. Williamson. New York: Dorset Press, 1984 [1965].

Fairbank, John K., and Albert Feuerwerker, eds. *The Cambridge History of China*, vol. 13. New York: Cambridge University Press, 1986.

Fall, Bernard. *Hell in a Very Small Place*. New York: J. B. Lippincott, 1967.

Farmer, W. R. *Macabees, Zealots, and Josephus*. New York: Columbia University Press, 1956.

Farwell, Byron. *Queen Victoria's Little Wars*. New York: Harper & Row, 1985.

Featherstone, Donald. *Colonial Small Wars, 1837–1901*. Newton Abbot, Devon, England: David & Charles, 1973.

Fehrenbach, T. R. *This Kind of War*. New York: Macmillan, 1963.

Feifer, George. *Tennozan: The Battle of Okinawa and the Atomic Bomb*. New York: Ticknor & Fields, 1994.

Fellman, Michael. *Citizen Sherman*. New York: Random House, 1995.

Fernandez-Armesto, Felipe. *Ferdinand and Isabella*. New York: Taplinger, 1975.

Ferrill, Arther. *The Origins of War*. London: Thames & Hudson, 1985.

Fichtenau, Heinrich. *The Carolingian Empire*. Translated by Peter Munz. Toronto, Canada: University of Toronto Press, 1991 [1978].

Fiddick, Thomas C. *Russia's Retreat from Poland*. New York: St. Martin's Press, 1990.

Firth, Charles Harding. *The Last Years of the Protectorate, 1656–1658*. London: Russell & Russell, 1964 [1909].

Foote, Shelby. *The Civil War: A Narrative*. New York: Vintage Books, 1986 [1958–1974].

Forster, Stig, and Jorg Nagler. *On the Road to Total War: The American Civil War and the Franco-German War*. New York: Cambridge University Press, 1997.

Frasier, Antonia. *Cromwell: The Lord Protector*. New York: Alfred A. Knopf, 1973.

Frazier, Donald, ed. *The United States and Mexico at War*. New York: Macmillan, 1998.

Freeman, Edward. *The History of the Norman Conquest of England*. Chicago: University of Chicago Press, 1974.

Friedel, Frank. *The Splendid Little War*. Boston: Little, Brown, 1958.

Friendly, Alfred. *The Dreadful Day: The Battle of Manzikert, 1071*. London: Hutchinson, 1981.

Fuller, J. F. C. *A Military History of the Western World*, 3 vols. New York: Funk & Wagnalls, 1954–1956.

Furneaux, Rupert. *The Invasion of 1066*. Englewood Cliffs, NJ: Prentice-Hall, 1974.

Gabba, Emilio. *Republican Rome, the Army, and the Allies*. Translated by B. J. Cuff. Berkeley: University of California Press, 1976.

Gabriel, Richard, and Donald Boose. *The Great Battles of Antiquity*. Westport, CT: Greenwood Press, 1994.

Galland, Adolph. *The First and the Last*. London: Methuen, 1955.

Gardiner, Robert. *The Campaign of Trafalgar, 1803–1805*. London: Chatham, in association with the National Maritime Museum, 1997.

Gascoigne, Bamber. *The Great Moghuls*. New York: Harper & Row, 1971.

Gaunt, Peter. *Oliver Cromwell*. Oxford, UK: Blackwell, 1996.

———. *The British Wars, 1637–1651*. London: Routledge, 1997.

Gershevitch, Ilya. *The Cambridge History of Iran*, vol. 2. Cambridge, UK: Cambridge University Press, 1985.

Gibbon, Edward. *The Decline and Fall of the Roman Empire*. Abridged by Frank Bourne. New York: Dell, 1963.

————. *The Decline and Fall of the Roman Empire,* vols. 5 and 6. New York: Gallery Press, 1979 [1737].

Gibbs, M. B. *Napoleon's Military Career.* Chicago: Werner Co., 1895.

Gibson, John S. *Lochiel of the '45: The Jacobite Chief and the Prince.* Edinburgh: Edinburgh University Press, 1994.

Gies, Frances. *Joan of Arc: The Legend and the Reality.* New York: Harper & Row, 1981.

Gies, Joseph. *Crisis, 1918.* New York: W. W. Norton, 1974.

Gipson, Lawrence H. *The Great War for Empire,* vol. 7. New York: Alfred A. Knopf, 1936.

Grant, Michael. *Constantine: The Man and His Times.* New York: Charles Scribner's Sons, 1994.

————. *Julius Caesar.* New York: M. Evans & Co., 1992 [1969].

Green, Jeremy. "Napoleon's Masterful Italian Campaign," *Military History* 14(1), April 1997.

Gregory of Tours. *History of the Franks.* Translated by Ernest Brehaut. New York: Columbia University Press, 1916.

Grousset, René. *The Rise and Splendour of the Chinese Empire.* Translated by Anthony Watson-Gandy and Terence Gordon. Berkeley: University of California Press, 1953.

Guderian, Heinz. *Panzer Leader.* Translated by Constantine Fitzgibbon. New York: E. P. Dutton, 1952.

Gurval, Robert. *Actium and Augustus: The Politics and Emotion of Civil War.* Ann Arbor: University of Michigan Press, 1995.

Guttman, Jon. "Survival of the Strong," *Military History* 8(2), August 1991.

Haig, Sir Wolseley, ed. *The Cambridge History of India,* vol. 3. Delhi: S. Chand & Co., 1965.

Hammel, Eric. *Fire in the Streets: The Battle for Hue, Tet 1968.* Chicago: Contemporary Books, 1991.

Hammond, N. G. L. *Philip of Macedon.* Baltimore: Johns Hopkins University Press, 1994.

Hansen, Victor, ed. *Hoplites: The Classical Greek Battle Experience.* London: Routledge, 1991.

Hardin, Steve. *Texian Iliad.* Austin: University of Texas Press, 1994.

Harris, R. W. *Clarendon and the English Revolution.* Stanford, CA: Stanford University Press, 1983.

Hartman, Cyril. *The Quest Forlorn: The Story of the Forty-five.* London: Heinemann, 1952.

Harvey, L. P. *Islamic Spain, 1250 to 1500.* Chicago: University of Chicago Press, 1990.

Hassel, Arthur. *Louis XIV and the Zenith of French Monarchy.* Freeport, NY: Books for Libraries Press, 1972.

Hastings, Max. *The Korean War.* New York: Simon & Schuster, 1987.

Hatton, R. M. *Charles XII of Sweden.* London: Weidenfeld & Nicolson, 1968.

Heather, Peter. *Goths and Romans.* Oxford, UK: Clarendon Press, 1991.

Herodotus. *The Histories.* Translated by Aubrey de Selincourt. Baltimore: Penguin, 1954.

Herzog, Chaim. *The Arab-Israeli Wars: War and Peace in the Middle East.* New York: Random House, 1982.

Hibbert, Christopher. *Cavaliers and Roundheads.* New York: Charles Scribner's Sons, 1993.

————. *Redcoats and Rebels.* New York: W. W. Norton, 1990.

Hignet, Charles. *Xerxes' Invasion of Greece.* Oxford, UK: Clarendon Press, 1963.

Hillgarth, J. N. *The Spanish Kingdoms, 1250–1516.* Oxford, UK: Clarendon Press, 1976–1978.

Hodgkin, Thomas. *Charles the Great.* Port Washington, NY: Kennikat Press, 1970 [1897].

Holt, P. M., Ann K. S. Lambton, and Bernard Lewis. *The Cambridge History of Islam,* vol. 1. Cambridge, UK: Cambridge University Press, 1970.

Horne, Alistair. *The Price of Glory: Verdun 1916.* New York: St. Martin's Press, 1962.

Hough, Richard, and Denis Richards. *The Battle of Britain*. London: Hodder & Stoughton, 1989.

Houn, Franklin W. *A Short History of Chinese Communism*. Englewood Cliffs, NJ: Prentice-Hall, 1967.

Howard, Michael. *The Franco-Prussian War*. New York: Collier, 1961.

Howarth, David. *1066: The Year of the Conquest*. New York: Viking Penguin, 1977.

———. *Trafalgar: The Nelson Touch*. London: Collins, 1969.

Howarth, David, and Stephen Howarth. *Lord Nelson, the Immortal Memory*. New York: Viking, 1989.

Hsu, Immanuel C. Y. *The Rise of Modern China*. New York: Oxford University Press, 1970.

Ienaga, Saburo. *The Pacific War, 1931–1945*. New York: Random House, 1978.

Innes, Hammond. *The Conquistadors*. New York: Alfred A. Knopf, 1969.

Irving, Washington. *Mahomet and His Successors*. Madison: University of Wisconsin Press, 1970 [1868].

James, Marquis. *The Raven*. New York: Blue Ribbon Books, 1929.

Jedrzejewicz, Waclaw. *Pilsudski: A Life for Poland*. New York: Hippocrene Books, 1982.

Jenkins, Romilly J. H. *Byzantium: The Imperial Centuries, A.D. 610–1071*. Toronto: University of Toronto Press, 1987.

Johnson, John J. *Simón Bolívar and Spanish American Independence, 1783–1830*. Princeton, NJ: Van Nostrand, 1968.

Jones, A. H. M. *The Herods of Judaea*. Oxford, UK: Clarendon Press, 1967.

Jones, Archer. *The Art of War in the Western World*. Champaign: University of Illinois Press, 1987.

Jones, J. R. *Marlborough*. New York: Cambridge University Press, 1993.

Jordanes. *The Gothic History of Jordanes*. New Haven, CT: Yale University Press, 1915.

Kagan, Donald. *On the Origins of War*. New York: Doubleday, 1995.

Kamen, Henry. *The War of Succession in Spain, 1700–15*. Bloomington: University of Indiana Press, 1969.

Kar, H. C. *Military History of India*. Calcutta: Firma KLM, 1980.

Keay, John. *The Honourable Company*. New York: Macmillan, 1994.

Keegan, John. *Dien Bien Phu*. New York: Random House, 1974.

———. *The Mask of Command*. New York: Little, Brown, 1982.

———. *The Price of Admiralty*. New York: Viking Penguin, 1989.

———. *Six Armies in Normandy*. New York: Viking, 1982.

Kemp, Anthony. *D-Day and the Invasion of Normandy*. New York: Harry N. Abrams, 1994.

Keppie, L. J. F. *The Making of the Roman Army*. London: B. T. Batsford, 1984.

Ketchum, Richard M. *Saratoga: Turning Point of America's Revolutionary War*. New York: Henry Holt, 1997.

Kluck, Alexander von. *The March on Paris and the Battle of the Marne, 1914*. London: Edward Arnold, 1923.

Koprulu, Mehmet. *The Seljuks of Anatolia*. Translated by Gary Leiser. Salt Lake City: University of Utah Press, 1992.

The Koran. Translated by N. J. Dawood. Hammondsworth, NY: Penguin, 1974.

Kwanten, Luc. *Imperial Nomads*. Philadelphia: University of Pennsylvania Press, 1979.

Lachouque, Henry. *Napoleon's Battles*. Translated by Roy Monkcom. New York: E. P. Dutton, 1967.

Lamb, Harold. *Babur the Tiger*. Garden City, NY: Doubleday, 1961.

———. *Charlemagne*. Garden City, NY: Doubleday, 1954.

———. *Cyrus the Great*. Garden City, NY: Doubleday, 1960.

———. *The March of the Barbarians*. New York: Literary Guild, 1940.

Lancaster, Bruce. *The American Revolution*. New York: American Heritage Press, 1971.

Lane-Poole, Stanley. *Medieval India under Mohammedan Rule*. New York: Krause Reprint, 1970 [1903].

Langley, Michael. *Inchon Landing*. New York: Times Books, 1979.

Lawford, James. *Napoleon: The Last Campaigns, 1813–15*. New York: Crown, 1977.

Layton, Edwin. *"And I Was There."* New York: William Morrow, 1985.

Lazenby, J. F. *Hannibal's War: A Military History of the Second Punic War*. Warminster, UK: Aris & Phillips, 1978.

Leckie, Robert. *Okinawa: The Last Battle of World War II*. New York: Viking, 1995.

Lefebvre, Georges. *The French Revolution from Its Origins to 1793*. London: Routledge & Kegan Paul, 1962.

Levite, Ariel. *Intelligence and Strategic Surprise*. New York: Columbia University Press, 1987.

Lewis, Michael. *The Spanish Armada*. New York: Thomas Y. Crowell, 1968.

Liddell Hart, Basil. *A Greater than Napoleon: Scipio Africanus*. New York: Biblo & Tannen, 1971 [1927].

———. *History of the Second World War*. London: Cassell & Company, 1970.

———. *The Real War, 1914 to 1918*. Boston: Little, Brown, 1931.

Livesey, Anthony. *Battles of Great Commanders*. New York: Macmillan, 1987.

Livy. *The War with Hannibal*. Translated by Aubrey de Selincourt. Baltimore: Penguin, 1965.

Lloyd, Christopher. *The Nile Campaign: Nelson and Napoleon in Egypt*. New York: Barnes & Noble, 1973.

Locke, Raymond F. "Tecumseh: The First Advocate of Red Power," in John R. M. Wilson, ed. *Forging the American Character*, vol. 1. Englewood Cliffs, NJ: Prentice-Hall, 1991.

Lord, Walter. *Incredible Victory*. New York: Harper & Row, 1967.

Luvaas, Jay, and Harold W. Nelson, eds. *The U.S. Army War College Guide to the Battle of Antietam*. New York: HarperCollins, 1988.

———. *The U.S. Army War College Guide to the Battle of Gettysburg*. New York: HarperCollins, 1986.

Lynn, John. "Valmy," *Military History Quarterly* 5(1), Autumn 1992.

Maclear, Michael. *The Ten Thousand Day War*. New York: St. Martin's Press, 1981.

Markham, Felix. *Napoleon*. New York: New American Library, 1963.

Markov, Walter. *Battles of World History*. New York: Hippocrene Books, 1979.

Marlowe, John. *Cromer in Egypt*. London: Elek, 1970.

Marshall, S. L. A. *Night Drop*. Boston: Little, Brown, 1962.

Martin, Christopher. *The Russo-Japanese War*. New York: Abelard Schuman, 1967.

Martin, Colin. *The Spanish Armada*. New York: W. W. Norton, 1988.

Mason, Herbert Molloy. *The Rise of the Luftwaffe, 1918–1940*. New York: Dial Press, 1973.

Mason, Philip. *A Matter of Honour*. London: Jonathan Cape, 1974.

Mason, R. H. P., and J. G. Caiger. *History of Japan*. New York: Free Press, 1972.

Massie, Robert. *Peter the Great, His Life and World*. New York: Alfred A. Knopf, 1980.

Masson, Gustave. *Medieval France*. New York: Putnam, 1888.

Mattingly, Garrett. *The Armada*. Boston: Houghton Mifflin, 1959.

Maude, F. N. *The Jena Campaign, 1806*. New York: Macmillan, 1909.

Maurice, Frederick. "The Size of the Army of Xerxes," *Journal of Hellenic Studies* 50, 1930.

McCarthy, Justin. *The Ottoman Turks*. New York: Longman, 1997.

McPherson, James M. *Battle Cry of Freedom*. New York: Oxford University Press, 1988.

Means, Philip A. *The Fall of the Inca Empire and the Spanish Rule in Peru, 1530–1780*. New York: Gordian Press, 1971.

Meier, Christian. *Caesar*. Translated by David McLintock. New York: HarperCollins, 1995 [1982].

Miller, William. "Ayacucho," in John Betten-bender and George Fleming, eds. *Famous Battles*. New York: Dell, 1970.

Millis, Walter. *The Martial Spirit*. Boston: Houghton Mifflin, 1931.

Mintz, Frank. *Revisionism and the Origins of Pearl Harbor*. Lanham, MD: University Press of America, 1985.

Morris, William. *Hannibal: Soldier, Statesman, Patriot*. New York: Knickerbocker Press, 1978.

Morwood, William. *Duel for the Middle Kingdom*. New York: Everest House, 1980.

Muir, William. *The Mameluke, or Slave Dynasty of Egypt*. London: Smith, Elder & Co., 1896.

Muller, Herbert. *The Loom of History*. New York: Harper & Brothers, 1958.

Munro, J. A. R., in *The Cambridge Ancient History*, vol. 4, J. B. Bury, S. A. Cook, and F. E. Adcock, eds. New York: Macmillan, 1928.

Murfin, James. *The Gleam of Bayonets*. New York: T. Yoseloff, 1965.

Murray, Williamson. "The Gulf War as History," *Military History Quarterly* 10(1), Autumn 1997.

———. *Strategy for Defeat: The Luftwaffe, 1933–1945*. Maxwell Air Force Base, AL: Air University Press, 1983.

Narvane, M. S. *Battles of Medieval India*. New Delhi: APH Publishing, 1996.

Norwich, John J. *Byzantium: The Decline and Fall*. London: Viking, 1995.

Olson, James S., and Randy Roberts. *Where the Domino Fell*. New York: St. Martin's Press, 1996.

Oman, Charles. *The Art of War in the Middle Ages*. Ithaca, NY: Cornell University Press, 1953 [1885].

———. *The Byzantine Empire*. London: T. F. Unwin, 1892.

O'Reilly, Donald. "Besiegers Besieged," *Military History* 9(6), February 1993.

Ovendale, Ritchie. *The Origins of the Arab-Israeli Wars*. New York: Longman, 1992.

Pakenham, Thomas. *The Scramble for Africa*. New York: Random House, 1991.

Palmer, Alan. *Napoleon in Russia*. New York: Simon & Schuster, 1967.

Pancake, John S. *1777: The Year of the Hangman*. Tuscaloosa: University of Alabama Press, 1977.

Parker, Geoffrey, ed. *The Thirty Years War*. London: Routledge & Kegan Paul, 1984.

Parkman, Francis. *Montcalm and Wolfe*. Toronto: Ryerson Press, 1964.

Parry, V. J. *A History of the Ottoman Empire to 1730*. Cambridge, UK: Cambridge University Press, 1976.

Parsons, James Bunyan. *Peasant Rebellions of the Late Ming Dynasty*. Tucson: University of Arizona Press, 1970.

Paulson, Michael. *Lepanto: Fact, Fiction and Fantasy*. Lanham, MD: University Press of America, 1986.

Peckham, Howard. *The War of Independence: A Military History*. Chicago: University of Chicago Press, 1958.

Perrett, Bryan. *The Battle Book*. London: Arms and Armour Press, 1992.

Petrie, William. *A History of Egypt*, vol. II. Freeport, NY: Books for Libraries Press, 1972 [1904].

Philippi, Alfred. "Battle for Moscow: The German View," in *History of the Second World War*, no. 27. London: BBC Publications, 1966.

Pickard-Cambridge, A. W. *Demosthenes*. New York: Putnam, 1914.

Pimlott, John, and Stephen Badsey. *The Gulf War Assessed*. London: Arms and Armour Press, 1992.

Pitt, Barrie. "Blitzkrieg," in *History of the Second World War*, no. 1. London: BBC Publications, 1966.

Plutarch. *The Lives of Noble Grecians and Romans*. Translated by John Dryden, revised by Arthur Hugh Clough. New York: Modern Library, 1979.

———. *The Lives of Noble Grecians and Romans*. Translated by Bernadette Perrin. Cambridge, MA: Harvard University Press, 1914–1926.

Pohl, James. *The Battle of San Jacinto.* Austin: Texas State Historical Association, 1989.

Polybius. *The Histories.* Translated by W. R. Paton. New York: Putnam, 1922–1927.

Porch, Douglas. "Dien Bien Phu and the Opium Connection," *Military History Quarterly* 7(4), Summer 1995.

Porter, Barry. "Actium: Rome's Fate in the Balance," *Military History* 14(3), August 1997.

Porter, Bernard. *The Lion's Share.* London: Longman, 1975.

Prange, Gordon. *At Dawn We Slept.* New York: McGraw-Hill, 1981.

———. *Miracle at Midway.* New York: McGraw-Hill, 1982.

Pratt, Fletcher. *The Battles That Changed History.* Garden City, NY: Doubleday, 1956.

Prescott, William H. *Conquest of Mexico.* Garden City, NY: Blue Ribbon Books, 1943.

———. *The History of the Conquest of Peru.* Philadelphia: J. B. Lippincott, 1874 [1847].

Preston, Diana. *The Road to Culloden Moor.* London: Constable, 1995.

Procopius. *Procopius,* vol. IV. Translated by H. B. Dewing. New York: Putnam, 1916.

Rabb, Theodore, ed. *The Thirty Years War.* Lexington, MA: D.C. Heath, 1972.

Rashid al-Din Tabib. *The Successors of Genghis Khan.* Translated by John Andrew Boyle. New York: Columbia University Press, 1971.

Regan, Geoffrey. *Saladin and the Fall of Jerusalem.* New York: Croom Helm, 1987.

Rhoads, David M. *Israel in Revolution: 6–74 C.E.* Philadelphia: Fortress, 1976.

Riché, Pierre. *The Carolingians.* Translated by Michael Idomir Allen. Philadelphia: University of Pennsylvania Press, 1993.

Richman, Irving Berdine. *Adventurers of New Spain: The Spanish Conquerors.* New Haven, CT: Yale University Press, 1929.

Riley-Smith, Jonathan. *The First Crusade and the Idea of Crusading.* Philadelphia: University of Pennsylvania Press, 1986.

Robert, Michael. *Sweden's Age of Greatness, 1632–1718.* New York: St. Martin's Press, 1973.

Robert, P. E. *History of British India.* London: Oxford University Press, 1952 [1921].

Romains, Jules. *Verdun: The Prelude, the Battle.* Translated by Gerard Hopkins. New York: Alfred A. Knopf, 1939.

Rossabi, Morris. *Khubilai Khan: His Life and Times.* Berkeley: University of California Press, 1988.

Rothenberg, Gunther. *The Art of Warfare in the Age of Napoleon.* Bloomington: University of Indiana Press, 1978.

Royster, Charles. *The Destructive War.* New York: Alfred A. Knopf, 1991.

Runciman, Sir Steven. *The Fall of Constantinople—1453.* Cambridge, UK: University of Cambridge Press, 1968 [1903].

———. *The First Crusade.* New York: Cambridge University Press, 1992 [1980].

Rutherford, Ward. *The Tsar's War, 1914–1917.* Cambridge, UK: I. Faulkner, 1992 [1975].

Ryan, N. J. *A History of Malaysia and Singapore.* Oxford, UK: Oxford University Press, 1976.

Sadler, A. L. *The Maker of Modern Japan: The Life of Tokugawa Ieyasu.* London: George Allen & Unwin, 1937.

Sansom, George. *A History of Japan, 1334–1615.* Stanford, CA: Stanford University Press, 1961.

Schnabel, James F. *Policy and Direction: The First Year.* Washington, DC: Center of Military History, 1992.

Schubert, Frank N., and Theresa L. Kraus. *The Whirlwind War.* Washington, DC: Center of Military History, 1995.

Schwarzkopf, Norman. *It Doesn't Take a Hero.* New York: Bantam Books, 1992.

Scott, Sir Walter. *A History of Scotland,* vol. 3. Philadelphia: Porter & Coates, n.d. [1829].

Sears, Stephen. *Landscape Turned Red.* New Haven, CT: Ticknor & Fields, 1983.

Shears, David. "Hitler's D-Day," *Military History Quarterly* 6(4), Summer 1994.

Sheldon, Rose Mary. "The Great Jewish War against Rome: Taking on Goliath," *Military and Naval Forum Proceedings* 3(9): 15–29, March 1996.

Sherwood, Roy Edward. *Oliver Cromwell: King in All but Name, 1653–1658*. New York: St. Martin's Press, 1997.

Shosenberg, James. "Napoleon's Masterstroke at Rivoli," *Military History,* December 1996.

Sima Qian. *Records of the Grand Historian: Han Dynasty I.* Translated by Burton Watson. New York: Columbia University Press, 1993.

Singletary, Otis. *The Mexican War.* Chicago: University of Chicago Press, 1960.

Slackman, Michael. *Target—Pearl Harbor.* Honolulu: University of Hawaii Press, 1990.

Sledge, E. B. *With the Old Breed at Peleliu and Okinawa.* Annapolis, MD: U.S. Naval Institute Press, 1996.

Smallwood, E. Mary. "The Jews under Roman Rule from Pompey to Diocletian: A Study in Political Relations," in *Studies in Judaism in Late Antiquity,* Jacob Neusner, ed. Leiden, Netherlands: Brill, 1981.

Smith, Jonathan Riley. *The Crusades.* New Haven, CT: Yale University Press, 1987.

Smith, Page. *A New Age Now Begins,* vol. 1. New York: McGraw-Hill, 1976.

Spector, Ronald. *After Tet.* New York: Free Press, 1993.

Stacey, C. P. *Quebec, 1759.* Toronto: Macmillan, 1959.

Stackpole, Edward J. *They Met at Gettysburg.* Harrisburg, PA: Stackpole Books, 1954.

Stallings, Laurence. *The Doughboys.* New York: Harper & Row, 1963.

Starr, Chester. *A History of the Ancient World.* New York: Oxford University Press, 1965.

Steindorff, George, and Keith Seele. *When Egypt Ruled the East.* Chicago: University of Chicago Press, 1957.

Stokesbury, James L. *A Short History of the Korean War.* New York: William Morrow, 1988.

———. *A Short History of World War I.* New York: William Morrow, 1981.

Suetonius. *The Twelve Caesars.* Translated by Robert Graves. London: Penguin, 1957.

Sugden, John. *Tecumseh: A Life.* New York: Henry Holt, 1998.

Sumption, Jonathan. *The Hundred Years War: Trial by Battle.* Philadelphia: University of Pennsylvania Press, 1988.

Swinson, Arthur, Tokuji Morimoto, and Mutsuya Nagao. "The Conquest of Malaya," in *History of the Second World War,* no. 26, Barrie Pitt, ed. London: BBC Publications, 1966.

Syme, Ronald. *The Roman Revolution.* Oxford, UK: Clarendon Press, 1939.

Szymczak, Robert. "Bolshevik Wave Breaks at Warsaw," *Military History* 11(6), February 1995.

Tacitus. *The Annals of Imperial Rome.* Translated by Michael Grant. London: Penguin, 1974.

Tarle, Eugene. *Napoleon's Invasion of Russia in 1812.* New York: Farrar, Straus & Giroux, 1971.

Tarn, W. W. *Alexander the Great.* Cambridge, UK: Cambridge University Press, 1948.

Terraine, John. *To Win a War: 1918, the Year of Victory.* Garden City, NY: Doubleday, 1981.

Thompson, E. A. *A History of Attila and the Huns.* Oxford, UK: Clarendon Press, 1948.

———. *Romans and Barbarians.* Madison: University of Wisconsin Press, 1982.

Thucydides. *The Peloponnesian Wars.* Translated by Benjamin Jowett. New York: Twayne Publishers, 1963.

Toland, John. *But Not in Shame.* New York: Random House, 1961.

Treadgold, Warren. *Byzantium and Its Army, 284–1081.* Stanford, CA: Stanford University Press, 1995.

Tsunetomo, Yamamoto. *Hagakure.* Translated by William Scott Wilson. New York: Avon Books, 1981.

Tuchman, Barbara. *The Guns of August.* New York: Macmillan, 1962.

Tucker, Glenn. "Tecumseh," *American History Illustrated* 6(10), February 1972.

Turnbull, Stephen. *The Samurai: A Military History.* New York: Macmillan, 1977.

Twitchett, Denis, and Michael Loewe. *The Cambridge History of China,* vol. 1. New York: Cambridge University Press, 1986.

Unger, Frederick William. *Russia and Japan and the War in the Far East*. Philadelphia: H. W. B. Conrad, 1905.

Vale, Malcolm. *English Gascony, 1399–1453*. London: Oxford University Press, 1970.

Vambery, Arminius. *Hungary in Ancient, Medieval, and Modern Times*. Hallandale, FL: New World Books, 1972.

Venning, Timothy. *Cromwellian Foreign Policy*. New York: St. Martin's Press, 1995.

Wailly, Henri. *Crecy, 1346: Anatomy of a Battle*. Poole, Dorset, UK: Blandford, 1987.

Walder, David. *The Short Victorious War*. London: Hutchinson, 1973.

War Department Historical Division. *Omaha Beachhead*. Washington, DC: Center of Military History, 1984 [1945].

Warner, Denis. *The Tide at Sunrise*. New York: Charterhouse, 1974.

Warner, Oliver. *Great Sea Battles*. London: Spring Books, 1963.

———. *Trafalgar*. London: B. T. Batsford, 1959.

Wheeler, Bonnie, and Charles T. Wood, eds. *Fresh Verdicts on Joan of Arc*. New York: Garland, 1996.

White, Jon Manchip. *Cortés and the Downfall of the Aztec Empire*. London: Hamish Hamilton, 1971.

Williams, L. F. Rushbrook. *An Empire Builder of the Sixteenth Century*. Delhi: S. Chand & Co., 1916.

Winston, Richard. *Charlemagne: From the Hammer to the Cross*. Indianapolis, IN: Bobbs-Merrill, 1954.

Wrigley, Herbert W. *The Downfall of Spain: Naval History of the Spanish-American War*. New York: B. Franklin, 1971 [1900].

Xenophon. *Cyropaedia*. Translated by Walter Miller. Cambridge, MA: Harvard University Press, 1979–1986.

———. *A History of My Times*. Translated by Rex Warner. Baltimore: Penguin, 1966.

Yahara, Hiromichi, and Frank Gibney. *The Battle for Okinawa*. New York: John Wiley & Sons, 1995.

Young, Peter. *Naseby: The Campaign and the Battle*. London: Century Publishing, 1985.

Zaloga, Steve. *The Polish Campaign, 1939*. New York: Hippocrene Books, 1985.

INDEX

Note: Headings formatted in SMALL CAPITALS refer to names of battles covered by this encyclopedia; **boldface** page numbers following these headings refer to the main entry for that battle.